THE LADS IN BLUE

The Complete History of
CARLISLE UNITED F.C.

Paul Harrison

Published by:
Yore Publications
12 The Furrows, Harefield,
Middx. UB9 6AT.

© Paul Harrison 1995

....

British Library Cataloguing-in-Publication Data.
A catalogue record for this book
is available from the British Library.

ISBN 1 874427 51 8

Every effort has been made to trace and acknowledge the source of illustrations, and ensure that copyright has not been infringed. In a number of cases it is recognised that the quality of such reproductions are not to a standard that is desired, however despite detailed searches, in such instances original photographs were not traced and reliance had to be placed on the best copy available. For the interest of readers, and in order to maintain completeness it was felt appropriate to include such illustrations.

YORE PUBLICATIONS specialise in football books, generally of an historical nature, including Club Histories, Who's Who Books, and general interest - both League and non-League (See also page 256) Three free newsletters per year are issued. For your first newsletter please send a S.A.E. to the above address.

Printed and bound by The Bath Press

ACKNOWLEDGEMENTS

It is with great satisfaction that I write these acknowledgements, with twelve published books behind me it seemed that the one which would escape publication would be the Carlisle United work. To be truthful it has sat collecting dust for the last six or seven years, but now, at last it has been released on an unsuspecting world.

For too long the club's history has been ignored, thus inaccurate information has been engineered and has as such become fact. Now at last the Brunton Park ghosts can be laid to rest, everything from the formation to attendances, to player and match statistics is contained in this one volume. It is the complete history of Carlisle United Football Club.

No work of this sort could be accomplished without the assistance of others, thus my sincere thanks and appreciation goes to Mr David Dent, Secretary of the Football League and his kind staff in the archive department of the Football League Headquarters in Lytham St. Annes for assisting me with my hundreds of requests and queries. To David Steele, without whom much of the statistical data would not have been possible. Dave Twydell for supporting the publication of the work, a hard task master indeed. Raymond Willmott, my father-in-law whose recollections of events dating back donkeys years was incredibly accurate, to Ashley Kendall, Cumberland News, Stephen White of Carlisle City library local studies, and Mr. Denis Easterby for their assistance with illustrations. The Final League Tables, Computer databases, were kindly supplied by Tony Brown.

Appreciation also goes to the Football Association for their kind assistance with research data, the staff of the Public Records Office Kew, and the British Newspaper Library, Colindale. To Keith Wild whom all those years ago travelled the length and breadth of the country with me, following the 'Lads in Blue'.

Finally my utmost appreciation goes to the 'Lads In Blue', Carlisle United AFC without whom none of this would be possible.

Each and every statistic contained within this work has been accurately researched from the official Football League Records held at Lytham St. Annes, some seven months work. Attendance records in particular are recorded with 100% accuracy, thus a new official ground record can be found within. This then is the book to settle all the arguments, this is the ultimate book upon Carlisle United Football Club, penned by a genuine supporter.

To anyone whom I may have omitted from these acknowledgements my apologies, please read on and enjoy

Paul Harrison September 1995.

Contents

FOREWORD

It was an honour for me to be asked by Paul Harrison to write a few words of introduction for his history of Carlisle United. It is a subject that both he and I have a soft spot for and I know that he has spent a great deal of time and effort on his researches.

Reading through all the manuscripts brought back many memories of my eighteen years at the club and I congratulate him on collating so much information. I am sure the supporters of Carlisle United will find it absorbing.

My own interest in United started as a schoolboy in Appleby and my association with the club started in January 1960 when I was appointed secretary. I will never forget the first day when I was met on the doorstep by the Manager, Andy Beattie, a gentleman of the highest order. He offered to help me in any way although he did not profess to know much about my side of the business. He reminded me that the players would need to be paid on Friday and that for the away match on Saturday, transport and meal arrangements would need to be made. Other than players, the full time staff at Brunton Park in those days numbered only four! Andy Beattie, Dick Young, Herbert Nicholson and myself.

Much water has gone under the bridge in the intervening years. The club has reached the heights and plunged the depths. Thankfully it is now on the upward path again and the supporters can look to the future with optimism.

I am sure you will enjoy browsing through the following pages.

David Dent
Football League Secretary
September 1995

Introduction

On Saturday the 31st day of August 1968 I made my first ever visit to a Football League fixture. The venue was Brunton Park, Carlisle, the game, a Second Division clash with Huddersfield Town. Nothing sensational about that you may feel, yet something occurred to me that very day which basically directed the course of my life.

As a mere youngster aged just 8 years, my brother introduced me to something which I had never before encountered, an emotion so deep, so strong, as to excite me. I can best describe it like the excitement a child feels on Christmas Eve, yet my brother did nothing special on that day, he simply lifted me over a turnstile as I was too small to force through it, then handed me a blue coloured programme which had a monotone photograph of Carlisle United on it's cover. I had no idea why he took me, but I am dearly grateful to him for doing so, for on that day, at the tender age of 8 years, I fell in love with my local football team, Carlisle United F.C.

Since then it has been a traumatic time, I have witnessed many highs and even more lows. At times I have doubted my sanity, to this day I am still uncertain about it. After all, who would travel all the way down to Twerton Park, Bristol, in freezing conditions and driving snow on a Saturday, to see a Division Three game which held no importance in the promotion or relegation stakes. Three hundred plus miles of hazardous drivng conditions, to find the match off!

There I sat in the Pirates social club, eagerly watching a giant screen television, the Saint and Greavsie show, when those nauseating words were uttered from Ian St.John's lips, *"another postponed fixture today, Bristol Rovers Vs Carlisle United".* My world mementarily stopped turning, I was there, why hadn't anyone told me, how could I have been so stupid as to travel down anyway! Depressed, I took a mouthful of my beer and tried to look unflustered and apathetic about the whole thing, I failed miserably.

Just an ordinary programme - in fact the first home game of the 1968/69 season.... but of particular significance to the Author, since this was the first football match attended.

Football League Division. Two 1968 / 69

Carlisle Utd.

Today's Visitors **HUDDERSFIELD**

SATURDAY. 31st AUGUST. 1968 : K.O. 3 p.m.

In came the Rovers manager, Bobby Gould, he walked straight over to me, sat down and apologised for the inconvenience the posponement had caused me. As a gesture of goodwill he offered me some soup, a cup of sollace, I gratefully accepted. A short time later Bobby gave me a guided tour of the ground and several souvenirs of my day out!

"You are what football is all about" he said, *"Carlisle United deserve success with supporters like you"*. It was a sycophantic remark but I cared little, it made me feel that much better, especially when I contemplated that I was the only idiot in such circumstances in the whole of England. Unless you've been there too, you can never understand what it feels like to be miles away from home, without a match, and with a minimum five hour drive ahead of you. My day was ruined. This was eased only by the thought of further fixtures, more occasions when I could be with my heroes, just me, them and the two thousand average crowd. Once home, there was more suffering, phone calls from friends, *"you didn't go all the way to Bristol did you?"*. Or the infamous statement, *"you must be mad going all the way down there"*. These people didn't understand, these things have to be done. Saturdays or Tuesdays wouldn't be the same without them. I need my fix of Carlisle United.

You see, supporting Carlisle has not been an easy passage, successes have been few, it's been hard, very hard, and there have been times when I promised myself, 'never again'. Sadly though, I am a lost cause, no amount of rehabilitation or counselling will cure my desire for Carlisle United to do well. One consolation is that I am not alone. Over the years I have stood or sat with the same nameless faces, socialising before a match, very few of us know each others identities. We are thrown together by a solid bond, a love for the club, (among these I categorise some family members as being worse than most). A trip to Torquay means nothing, so long as Carlisle United will be there, be it on a Tuesday night or a Saturday afternoon. It's a crusade, something that was meant to be. When the crowd used to sing about Bob Stokoe being the King, I believed them, but then so did several thousand others who used to pay hommage upon the Brunton Park terraces each week. We have had a lot of Kings since then, although granted we have had a few jesters in the pack over the years! To me though, they have all been gods, and yes I really did sponsor Wayne Entwhistle's shirt!

Going back to that first ever visit to Brunton Park 27 years ago, I can still see the old cinder track surrounding the pitch, the rickety wooden fence which acted as a barrier between the supporters and the playing area. I stood at the front of the Waterworks end, (now more commonly known as the Petteril End) right behind the goal. I was overawed, the gaint scoreboard which was supported between two telegraph poles stood behind me like some towering giant watching over the ground. I can still see the bloke, who used to climb onto it just before half time to hang the numbers up beside the respective letters, which represented the half time scores from elsewhere in the country. I wanted his job, it seemed wonderful. Later, much later, I used to laugh at his antics as these scores were frequently wrong, those he couldn't get on his transistor radio (which seemed superglued on top of his right shoulder) he made up! Then, and only then was I glad that I didn't do his job. Then there was the time someone took away the ladder which he used to get up and down from the scoreboard, he was stranded up there. It was in good taste and was wonderfully funny.

Back to the Huddersfield game, it was in fact a nil all draw, I vividly remember the Huddersfield goalkeeper John Oldfield diving full length to save from George McVitie, it was, and still is the greatest save I have ever seen. I swear he was horizontal as he dived from one side of his goal to the other, a full five feet from the ground, colliding with his left hand post in his bid to scramble the ball clear. Forget your Gordon Banks', this was the real world, that save, in my eyes had never been matched. For a few years later I followed the career of John Oldfield in the hope that Carlisle would sign him, they never did, but for a few minutes that Saturday afternoon I thought he was the best goalkeeper in the world. He was my first footballing hero, and he didn't even play for

Carlisle United! Whenever we played football thereafter I was John Oldfield, that is, until I found Alan Ross, then there was only one 'keeper for me. Oddly enough, I still find myself being Alan Ross when playing footy with my kids!

Of course the eyes of a child see things in a different manner from others, however, these eyes still view Carlisle United in the same manner, devoted and biased, yes, very biased. Carlisle United can do no wrong, it's always the other team, the opposition are always lucky to beat us, we are always the better team on the day. Bookings and sendings off are a result of bad refereeing, or the opposition cheating, and our supporters always sing louder, much louder than anyone elses. Yes everything about Carlisle United is perfect, every player who dons the blue and white (or the deckchair) shirt is carefully scrutinised and has to be that little bit special, you see Carlisle United never make bad signings. 27 years has made no difference. I am still passionately in love with this club, they have hurt me on many an occasion and I sometimes wonder if the love affair is a one sided matter. Then they go and produce something which proves it's a two way relationship, a fine 1-0 win, or a good 0-0 draw away from home, all inspire greater devotion and is, I am certain, the club's way of showing me they care.

This then, is the book I alway wanted to write, having had eleven other works published in recent years, this one represents my life, and is the most comprehensive history of the club ever printed. I own a collection of Carlisle United home and away programmes from the 1920's to date, several thousand issues. I know each and every programme, all are special, all hold memories of some kind. The basis of this book is taken from this collection, and all that goes with it, from old playing strips, to photographs of Carlisle F.C. from the early part of the twentieth century. I want everyone to share in those memories, which will hopefully allow you to recollect those moments special to you, courtesy of Carlisle United F.C.

From a personal point of view, everything in my life has been arranged around United, my marriage in 1980 was held during the close season, as too are holidays and other family events. Albeit there was one close shave when my son was christened on a Sunday morning before a home fixture with Portsmouth. The church service was over, I belted home, donned my blue and white top before making my way to the match, we lost 1-0 - a lucky Mike Channon effort! (told you the opposition were always lucky). Upon returning home, the Christening party was finished, family and guests had gone. Alone, I picked up my son, cradled him in my arms and said *"Never mind, there's always next week, Portsmouth were dead lucky, we'll win next week you wait and see"*. But then that's the way it is in my house.

Now, in 1995, I have fulfilled a lifetimes ambition, I have actually seen Carlisle United at Wembley, the memories of that day are recorded elsewhere within this book so I won't dwell upon them too deeply here. However, when I saw that C.U.F.C. flag hanging from the stadium roof I all but cried, everything that had gone before, the hundreds of thousands of miles of travelling all but pailed into insignificance. That one moment sent the adrenalin whizzing through my body, it was sensational, it was a moving moment, that flag it seemed to make a statement, just what I don't know. My father-in-law, himself a Carlisle United addict, summed it up when with tear filled emotional eyes he turned to me and said, *"What the hell are we doing here, this is Wembley"*. The important thing to remember is, we were there, no matter what the competition, Carlisle United have graced a full Wembley statium. Now, we have done the lot, Divisions 1, 2, 3 and 4, Division 3 North, Europe (yes we've played in a European competition), and Wembley.

In 1974 the legendary Bill Shankly said it was a marvellous achievement, Carlisle United gaining promotion to the First Division. Taking everything into context from our formation, I think what we have achieved since then is bloody brilliant!

****

So read on and enjoy it, take a walk in a 'winter wonderland' with me and Carlisle United.

SOCCER'S MOST NORTHERLY OUTPOST!

Like all football supporters I dislike it when the so-called soccer experts and pundits begin to malign my club.

For as long as I can remember, every time the national media visit Brunton Park be it newspaper, television, or radio, they find it necessary to make comment about our ground being 'soccer's most Northerly outpost.' This is generally followed with a shot or descriptive passage upon sheep grazing in fields behind the 'Scratcher', to a backdrop of undulating countryside. That very image is the one held by football fans from all over the world who have never visited our soccer mecca.

This prompts me to quote the words of a popular song which are pertinent to my feeling upon this matter. *"Heaven is a place on earth."* Brunton Park is indeed my heaven, and when I am there I forget all my worries; there the real Paul Harrison emerges from the shell which masquerades as a perfectly average human being. I love the place, it is a very personal experience for me on each occasion I visit. So why then is my heaven made out to be a bleak remote place?

Visit Anfield, Old Trafford, Arsenal, Tottenham, Everton, Chelsea, indeed any of the so called fashionable clubs and you will find yourself lost in a virtual maze of narrow streets and back alleys, lined by red bricked terrace houses. This to me is a truly miserable environment, it is as though these streets are meant to confuse the football fans, and disorientation is a very real prospect. On a cold wet winter's evening these streets seem almost oppressive, mind-blowing by their uniformity and blandness. Walking them is like being in some crazy relentless nightmare. Shoe-horned in the middle of this positively bland urban district you will suddenly find a football stadium,

unattractive and squatting there like some large alien spacecraft which has just landed.

These places are not for those with claustrophobia, nor for anyone who may suffer from vertigo, for in many instances the only way these grounds can evolve is by building upwards. The reality is far removed from what we see on our television screens. I have visited them all on my travels with United, and each time I find myself greatly disappointed. At Carlisle we have no such problems; a golf course, a park, a river, and a panoramic view set spaciously behind two sides of the stadium. A car park which any of the Premier League clubs would be grateful for lies behind the Waterworks (Petteril) End. I know full well where I would prefer to spend my football days and nights, albeit we have no futuristic space age stadium, but what we do have is traditional and very much unique to Carlisle United.

Perhaps two of the most unrealistic quotes ever to be made about United's rural surroundings are in Brian James' *'Journey to Wembley'* (Marshall Cavendish 1977), in which he states; *"Nothing moves out there. It is a football frontier post guarded by sheep; the notion that a ball kicked over the fence would go on bouncing until it dropped off the end of the world is hard to shake off.*

"Carlisle, the Alice Springs of League soccer, is a place that demands gradual acclimatisation if a team is not to suffer from football's equivalent of the bends."

I agree, 'beauty is in the eye of the beholder', yet if that is the case then those who so describe Brunton Park and the surrounding area, in a manner similar to Mr James, are clearly blinkered in their views, and are quite simply exaggerating how remote we actually are.

Incidentally, Newcastle United are geographically more Northerly than Carlisle, so let's bury the idea that Carlisle is the most Northerly soccer outpost.

****

United have played their football at Brunton Park since September 1909, before then the club occupied two separate grounds, actually playing at three different venues within the city - Millholme Bank, Devonshire Park, and the Rugby Ground immediately behind the present main stand.

Millholme Bank was the club's first ever stadium, located off Boundary Road, in Currock. Several

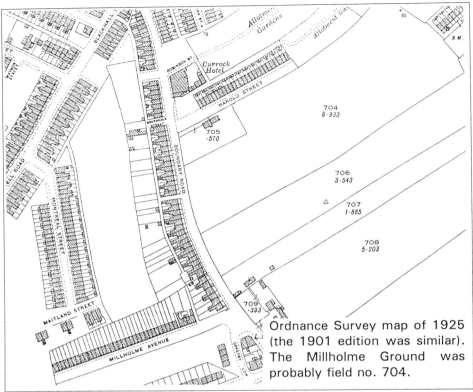

Ordnance Survey map of 1925 (the 1901 edition was similar). The Millholme Ground was probably field no. 704.

newspaper reports of the early part of the 20th century refer to this ground as either 'Millholme' or 'Boundary Park.' The ground itself was situated close to the Currock Inn and has long since disappeared.

Millholme was used by the newly formed Carlisle United for the first time on the 1st of September 1904, when Victoria Wanderers were the visitors, the official attendance was never recorded but was believed to be over the 5,000 mark. United won the friendly fixture 2-1. Millholme Bank was in fact an apt title for the ground, although a wooden grandstand did exist, and this was the most popular part of the ground as it afforded shelter from the occasional downpour. The rest of the ground was literally mounds of earth formed into a basin, albeit parts of it had been installed with old railway sleepers to form a basic form of terrac-

ing. A part wood, part brick perimeter wall tried, without complete success, to ensure that no one could gain access into the ground without paying an admission fee.

Perhaps the biggest attraction ever to come to Carlisle at that time was the mighty Glasgow Rangers, in April 1905, encouraged by the prospect of a high percentage of the gate receipts. The 'Gers' ran out 2-1 winners in front of a crowd estimated to be around 3,000. Due to the dilapidated state of Millholme Bank this game was actually played at the Rugby Ground off Warwick Road. The rugby ground had two stands and was more secure than United's Currock based home, thus all spectators had to pay to see the game, unlike Millholme, where (with some cunning) you could skip over the perimeter wall.

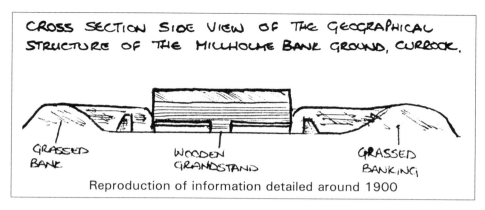

CROSS SECTION SIDE VIEW OF THE GEOGRAPHICAL
STRUCTURE OF THE MILLHOLME BANK GROUND, CURROCK.

GRASSED BANK   WOODEN GRANDSTAND   GRASSED BANKING

Reproduction of information detailed around 1900

The fixture had been arranged by a Carlisle United board desperate for publicity in an effort to prove their ability to play in a higher grade. The plan worked, as United were invited to play in the Lancashire Combination Second Division.

United had in fact offered to pay all the visiting teams' expenses for two seasons should they be granted admission into this league. The club were further instructed that Millholme Road was not a suitable venue and that a new ground had to be found (a typical story we still hear of in the modern game).

Thus the last match United ever played at Millholme Bank took place on the 6th of May 1905. It couldn't have been with more glamorous opposition, that of local City rivals 'Red Rose' in the Hospital Cup Final.

United had already won the Cumberland Senior League Championship and the Cumberland Cup (the first side ever to win both), and having beaten Red Rose in that Cup final, 2-0, they hoped for a clean sweep of all the county's major football silverware. It wasn't to be, for the game was won by Red Rose 1-0.

The hitherto assumption that United was formed by an amalgamation of Shaddongate United and Carlisle Red Rose is thus proved inaccurate, as Red Rose were clearly still in existence after United were born.

As a point of interest, Red Rose continued to use the Millholme Bank ground, but with the ascendency of Carlisle United and support drifting in their favour, the Rose faced an uphill battle. The town simply wasn't big enough to support two good quality sides. In July 1905 Red Rose resigned from the Cumberland League, for financial resources had dwindled as the football public flocked to Devonshire Park to watch United.

The Cumberland League clearly didn't want to lose any side. Yes, Carlisle had absconded to a higher league but they were not about to lose Red Rose. League officials met with the owners of Red Rose and convinced them that things could only improve. The club agreed to stay in the Cumberland League but were forced to concede that Carlisle United were the major club, especially after United defeated them 3-0 in the 1st qualifying round of the 1905/06 F.A. Cup competition. Thus Red Rose all but dissolved. A statement made by a club official at the time depicts the feeling of disappointment held by everyone concerned with Rose. *"Each and every game we have competed in since the other club was formed has placed a further burden upon us. The important matter being that football in this area continues, to this end we wish the other Carlisle club every success, it saddens me to say that as such, Red Rose can no longer continue in this present form."* Goodbye Carlisle Red Rose.

So to a higher league and a better ground, albeit the stadium was still a long way from being satisfactory, however, it served its purpose. The new stadium was at Devonshire Park, now part of the Newman School playing fields. The ground had the benefit of a large, obscene wooden stand, which consisted of eighteen angled rows of bench style seating. It was a bigger and better development than Millholme Bank, although a sum of £1,200 had to be paid to bring it up to an acceptable standard. The other three parts of the ground were not dissimilar in their

CROSS SECTION SIDE VIEW OF DEVONSHIRE PARK GROUND. NOTE SLEEPER STYLE BANKING. THE WOODEN STAND RAN VIRTUALLY THE LENGTH OF THE PITCH. THE DRESSING ROOMS WERE ON THE LEFT SIDE OF THE STAND. SPECTATOR ACCESS WAS VIA THE CENTRAL STAIRWAY ONLY.

(Above) Basic sketch details of the Devonshire Park ground.
(Below), Site of ground, and proposed 1906 Stand extensions.

appearance to Millholme, with natural banking. Again the club utilised the town's main employer, the railway, to supply wooden sleepers which were used to form terracing in certain more popular areas.

It is also worth mentioning at this point that the club had realised the power of the press, and in order to keep visiting journalists content the club built a small press box, similar to a hen house, but better than some of the draughty areas offered by some present-day clubs. The press box was situated next to the main stand, but it could house no more than four seated journalists.

Later, an area of the wooden stand was allocated to those who preferred an enhanced view of proceedings. The capacity of this stand was later increased (in 1906) with further seating for some 1,500 fans.

Devonshire Park was officially opened on the 2nd of September 1905, when St. Helens Town were the visitors in the Lancashire Combination Second Division fixture. It was a disappointing start, a 3-2 defeat. A comfortable mid-table position was achieved. The following season, 1906/07 United were crowned as Lancashire Combination Second Division Champions.

During the next season, on the 11th of January 1908, a new attendance record was set at Devonshire Park when 5,068 saw United draw 2-2 with Southern League side, Brentford; four days later United won the replay 3-1, after extra time. It was the highlight of the season as the team were thrashed in the next round by Grimsby 6-2.

A crushing blow, but one which was in the long term to benefit the club, occurred during the 1908/09 season. The club was faced with some vicious financial blows, for the heavy spending in the transfer market, and the ground improvements, were now weighing a heavy burden. In debt and owing rent to their landlord, the Duke of Devonshire, it was crisis time. Eventually, in April 1909, they were told to vacate the Devonshire Park ground. The club had in fact known of this for several months but had refused to make an official announcement until absolutely necessary. Numerous groups of supporters gathered to raise funds which would assist in the purchase of a new ground. The Duke of Devonshire waived the overdue rent in an attempt to support their survival attempts. No less than £800 was raised by public appeal. Club officials had already pledged £1,000 towards a 5 acre plot of land adjacent to the Rugby club in Warwick Road, Carlisle, but the land was to be sold for £2,000, no less. Eventually shares were offered at £1 each and the outstanding £200 was raised, making a grand total of £2,000. Funds were further enhanced with gate receipts from home

fixtures against Workington - which set a Devonshire Park attendance record of 13,890 - Bolton Wanderers reserves and Atherton, the latter two each attracting crowds of around 3,000.

Eventually, Accrington Stanley visited Devonshire Park. It was the 29th of April 1909, and the last home fixture of the 1908/09 season; United's last ever game at Devonshire. The night before the game the rain began to fall, and it continued to do so incessantly for the next twenty-four hours. Matters were made worse with the introduction of wicked thunderstorms, a day when you wouldn't have put your dog out. United got the go-ahead for the game to be played, when 312 spectators were in attendance. It was a farce, but a pleasant one as United won the game 4-0, a nice end to the Devonshire Park history.

So to the present home at Brunton Park. Much has been penned upon the ground, more than is perhaps necessary, for the majority of views are critical and undeserved. Brunton Park is not a bad ground, it is clean and tidy and of a good presentable standard when compared to many of it's contemporaries. The original stadium was designed by local architect, H.Foxall. Three sides were banked with railway sleepers and cinders. A wooden stand was erected along one side, where today's main stand exists, and this was gradually extended as attendances increased.

In 1929, having now attained Football League status, the pitch was completely relaid, with what is known locally as Cumbrian turf, but more commonly titled Solway Turf. It was for a long time accepted that this turf was the best there was, for bowling greens used it too, as did Wembley Stadium. Carlisle's playing surface, right up until the late 1970's was known to be among the best there was.

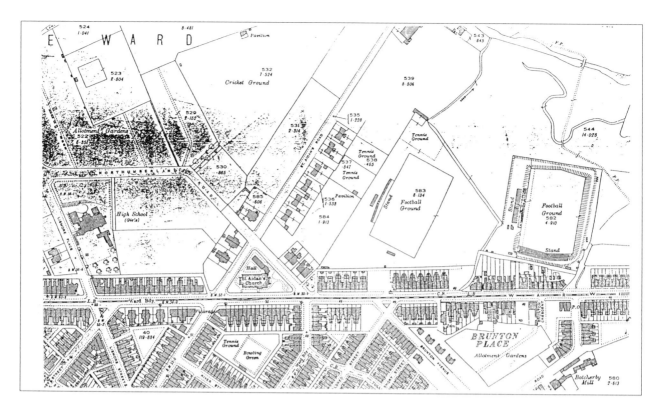

The O.S. map of 1924, showing the three grounds sites: Devonshire Park (plot 523, top left), the Rugby Ground (plot 583. Earlier the only Stand was on the opposite side), and current Brunton Park (plot 582)

In 1930, John (Jackie) Cape, an exciting winger, was sold to Newcastle United for a fee of £1,500, the proceeds of this transfer were used to cover and rebuild what was once the 'Scratching Shed', the side of the ground immediately opposite the main stand.

At one time bars and other amenities were present beneath it's huge frame, and on matchdays it was a popular venue. Later, it housed the groundsman's equipment and cupboard space. It was even used as a ticket office for big games, with the old hatches still evident up to the time of writing.

Brunton Park in 1949, with the 'hencoop' stand which later burnt down.

The 'Scratcher' as it was affectionately termed by United supporters, was at one time used as the area where United fans would base themselves to sing and chant their anthems. This was brought about when it was split in half, the Waterworks end of it's boundary housing away supporters, with the two sets of supporters being divided by metal railings and 'no-mans' land, generally filled in the 1970's by Police officers. Curiously, standing elsewhere in the ground, you could gauge what the attendance was likely to be by how full the Scratcher was. For some reason it was generally the last part of the ground to fill, particularly the uncovered area next to the Warwick Road End.

In 1952 United became the first club outside London to install floodlighting, and they were first used in a friendly fixture against Blackburn Rovers on the 25th of February 1952. To put the record straight, United were also involved in the first ever competitive fixture between two League clubs under floodlights, at Brunton Park, Carlisle, on Tuesday the 22th of November 1955 - an F.A. Cup first round second replay against Darlington which United lost 3-1.

Some 13 months later, in March 1953 after a friendly fixture against Falkirk, an overnight fire burnt down the whole of the main stand, destroying all the club's records and equipment. The cause of the fire was believed to have been a discarded cigarette, which had been kept alight by the strong wind long after the spectators and groundstaff had gone home. The only thing which remained intact was the safe.

Twenty-four hours later, United faced Tranmere Rovers in a League fixture. A strip was borrowed from Newcastle United, and the changing room facilities of the old James Street public baths were used, with the players being transported to the game by bus. United won the fixture 4-0.

A 'stand appeal' was duly launched to finance the rebuilding of a new stand, and it was launched by the Mayor of the City, Mr George Bowman. Without going into the matter too deeply, it failed. Local business seemed apathetic to the club's cause, and matters were further exasperated when it was discovered that the ground (which was to be used as a security for a loan) was already subject of a security on an overdraft!

The aftermath of the 1953 fire

After many meetings, United were given the necessary loan by the Football Association, a sum of £4,000. The insurance money from the stand raised around £2,000 and was used to pay players wages during the summer, thus discrediting any opinion that it was deliberate arson.

The United manager of the time, Fred Emery, called together the heads of a number of independent organisations who had been

The United players examine the remains of the dressing rooms

formed to raise money for the club, these included the Carlisle United Buildings Appeal, and the United Shareholders Association. Emery told those present that everything should be under one roof, and each organisation had to work together under one title, thus the Carlisle United Development Committee was formed. This organisation was later entitled the Development Club, and is now known as the Supporters Club. This group has since raised thousands of pounds for the parent club and financed other ground improvement work. United player, Geoff Twentyman, was sold to Liverpool for £12,000 in December 1953, which helped to raise the new the new stand from the ashes. Work officially began in April 1954 and was all but complete on the 24th of August of the same year, and that same stand remains to this very day.

During the building work a temporary stand had to be erected at the Warwick Road end of the ground, and a similar structure was present when the present ground attendance record was set on the 5th of January 1957, when 27,500 people saw a 3-3 draw with Birmingham City in a classic F.A. Cup encounter. In 1965 the Warwick Road end of the ground was made into a permanent structure, terracing was laid, and then

covered with its near unique triple pointed multi-span roof. The only one similar to this was at Tranmere Rovers', Prenton Park, with that example being a smaller version of Carlisle's. This entire operation was funded by the Development Club, which up to 1965 had raised and donated some £150,000 to Carlisle United F.C.; all in just ten years. The Warwick, as it better known, is United's kop. For the last three decades those who have stood within its huge shell have felt a closeness not familiar anywhere else in the ground, as they bounce, dance, and sing their way through home games.

Once, in a home F.A. Cup tie against Tottenham Hotspur, a number of fans were injured and the game stopped as the rickety wooden fence at the front of the Warwick collapsed due to the pressure placed upon it. Several people were trapped beneath a pile of bodies who tumbled forward. 'Spurs keeper Pat Jennings will be remembered for pulling people out of the pile of bodies which scattered behind his goal. Thankfully the most serious injury sustained was a broken bone and the incident passed off without tragedy. A similar incident occurred in another F.A.Cup fixture (against Everton in 1968), and then also injuries were minimal. The Warwick almost had the rest of the

The old (original) floodlights
are replaced in 1970.

have a dart thrown at him from the War-wick, it missed his head but he did feel the draught from it as it flew past his face. Both incidents occurred in the early part of the 1970's, and thankfully such incidents have never been repeated.

Finally the two wing stands were added to each side of the main stand in 1969, again financed by the Development Club. On 7th of February 1970 the Brunton Park attend-ance record was equalled, with 27,500 sup-porters watching an F.A. Cup 5th round tie against Middlesbrough.

Plans were drawn up for a new modern Brunton Park, an all-seater stadium with ultra modern amenities. It will be a splen-did achievement, and a proud monument suggesting how far the club has travelled since Millholme Bank. Yet, no doubt, for several thousand United supporters, Brunton Park as it was has character. A glance at a certain section brings back memories of great games, or particular instances, some-thing modern day stadiums can never do as their uniform design and all plastic seating look identical from all sides. There are no Scratching Sheds to be found in the modern stadium!

ground cleared, when in 1970, Chelsea goalkeeper Peter Bonetti was knocked un-conscious by a stone thrown by a hooligan within the peripheries of the United kop. Bonetti was not seriously hurt, but the mat-ter was a serious one.

Similarly, 'Spurs goalkeeper Pat Jennings, a well respected player, had the misfortune to

Brunton Park - and the rugby
ground - from the air, in 1980.

Chapter 1
THE BIRTH OF CARLISLE UNITED AFC

The border city of Carlisle was not, in the early part of the twentieth century, what you could class as a hotbed of football. Some thirty odd miles to the South-West, Workington was rather more organised and had it's own football team which was originally formed in 1884 and first featured in the F.A. Cup competition of 1887, albeit they failed to score a solitary goal in the Cup until 1892, that being in a 9-1 home defeat by Bootle.

As such, Workington were at this time the county's top football side; Cumberland Cup winners 1887-1891, and 1896-1899 all inclusive. The competition began in the 1885/86 season and then featured such local sides as Wigton Athletic, Newcastle, Distington, and Cockermouth Rangers. Records show that in it's inaugural season a side known simply as 'Carlisle' reached the final of the competition, facing Workington at Highmoor Park, Wigton, on the 27th of March 1886. The Carlisle side ran out 2-0 winners and were the first ever winners of the competition. Reports state that the winners were victorious by virtue of, *"playing association football as it is played by the likes of Rovers and Darwen"*!

The following season saw a repeat of the final, this time the venue was Workington Cricket Field, on the 19th of March 1887. The Carlisle lads could not match the vigour and stamina of their West Cumberland counterparts and were convincingly thrashed 8-0, still one of the biggest ever winning margins in a final of the competition.

Incredibly one of the first most serious scenes of football hooliganism to occur in the English game occurred after one such game between the two Cumberland rivals. The Carlisle followers, of which there was a reasonable number, were greatly upset by a defeat, and duly stoned the Workington players as they left the field. John Roberts Fisher, a wing half, was struck on the head several times by missiles, hurled by the angry mob, so serious was his injury that he was rushed to hospital where he lay in a coma for some nineteen weeks before finally expiring from injuries sustained during the attack.

When the Cumberland Association League was formed in the 1889/90 season Workington became unofficial champions, as they dominated the local county game. For the city and people of Carlisle there seemed little hope of loosening 'The Reds' stronghold as winners, especially as Carlisle, being the larger populated area, had not yet made up it's mind as to who was it's top local side.

Carlisle itself had two top teams competing in local competitions from the late Victorian era, Carlisle Red Rose, and Shaddongate United. From all accounts Red Rose were the stronger of the two and the one most likely to prosper. Understandably competition between the two was fierce, not only for glory, but for local support. Many claimed that Red Rose had the city's title in their name, whereas Shaddongates was simple a suburb.

Shaddongate United 1902/03 season:
(Back) Graham (Trainer), G.Stubbs, Shepherd, Minns, Spottiswoode, Campbell, Hind (Trainer)
(Middle) Thompson (Asst.Sec.), Hetherington, Routledge, Burgess D., Graham, Burgess W., Kirkbride (Sec.)
(Front) Keddy, F.Stubbs, Shannon.

The two top teams in Carlisle in the early 1900's

● Carlisle Red Rose, 1903-1904 winners of the Cumberland Shield, Carlisle Charity Shield and District League.
Back Row (left to right): G. Knighton, J. Kenyon, J. Morley, T. Sewell, T. Pullen, C. Scaife, R. Groggains,
G. Notman. Middle Row: W. Tinning, match secretary, C. Lomas, W. Oliphant, captain, A. Burns, R. Peat,
E. Tinning, W. Austen, financial secretary. Front Row: J. Morley, W. Hutton, W. Johnston, J. Stalton.

Public disorder would often break out in public houses as the separate factions argued over the top side: *"Several drunken persons were placed in the Carlisle lock-up for destroying the peace in Botchergate, the incident occurred through disharmony over association football, one party making claims as to Shaddongate's superiority, the other to Carlisle Red Rose, no persons were hurt in the incident."*

Carlisle of course was no different to any other city or town, quite simply football fever had gripped many of it's inhabitants. Modern day psychologists attempt to explain that football culture is a recent phenomenon, they are inaccurate in such assumptions, nothing happens in todays game which has not already previously occurred.

So regular was the report of such outrage that Shaddongate United officials actually requested that supports of their club should refrain from becoming involved with public disorder as it, *"brought great shame upon the good name of the club."* Red Rose followed suit, thus maintaining the status quo, however an air of sensibility did prevail but it was somewhat shortlived, as alcohol related football debates continued within the city.

Shaddongate worked hard to build a good reputation within the community. Jimmy Minns, one of the clubs main subsidisers, got out and about among the Carlisle public basically carrying out a public relation exercise, in his spare time he would also do a bit of scouting and coaching to the Shaddongate team as he fancied himself as something of a football entrepreneur.

Slowly but surely Shaddongate United grew in stature and technique, but theirs was no meteoric rise for it was all down to hard work and - dare it be said - professionalism. Not that any of the players were pro-fessionals, but the way in which the football club was administrated dictated that things ran on an even keel, thus allowing the team to concentrate on football alone. In 1901 they lifted the Cumberland Cup and had grown in popularity. It is with Shaddongate United that we should concentrate since Carlisle Red Rose had very little to do with the formation of Carlisle United AFC.

Not too long after this success the club was dealt a crippling blow when several of it's players were, according to the County Football Association regulations, permitted to play in a sponsored five-a-side competition. By sponsored it meant that players were provided some financial remuneration for their efforts. At an emergency meeting it was decided that the football club should be fined £9, a colossal sum for such a misdemeanour. The fine, despite great appeals, was paid as the club got on with the business of playing football.

The Cumberland Cup was retained the following 1902/03 season, and the team had virtually chosen itself during the two successful campaigns with the first eleven generally consisting of; Shepherd, Stubbs, Spottiswoode, Campbell, Hetherington, Routledge, Burgess, Graham, Burgess, Keddy, Stubbs G., with Shannon also playing a big part.

Team captain, George Stubbs was described as a, *"terrier of a player, diminutive, yet as strong as an ox both in physical attribute and commitment."* His number two, vice-captain Bob Keddy, was more of an artistic type player who would amuse himself before the game by practising ball skills, flicking the ball deftly from foot to foot before launching it high into the air and trapping it dead as it returned. Another star of the side was Frankie Burgess who was a great favourite of the ladies, tall and elegant he looked more like a city gentleman with his broad moustache and perfectly groomed hair. Frankie to be fair was more interested in playing football and by all accounts took the game very seriously, with a deep hatred for losing. Other characters included 'Man Mountain Harry Campbell', who was a, *"determined and very rugged footballer."* Officer Spottiswoode, whose stern appearance and erect posture looked as though they had come directly from the drill square. A half back, he possessed a marvellous sliding tackle and passing movement which apparently stunned 'audiences' wherever he played.

The following, 1903/04, season saw the County Championship draw to a fantastic climax. It was a two horse race between Shaddongate and Workington. The West Cumberland outfit had played two more games than United, and held a four point lead at the top of the table. Shaddongate had four matches remaining, Workington two, even more incredible was the fact that the sides had yet to play each other home and away.

On the 21st of April 1904, Shaddongates faced Workington at Millholme Bank, their last home game of the season. Sadly, it ended in defeat as Workington opened up a six point lead at the top of the table. Despite this fact it seemed clear that Shaddongate could still win the championship, with three away games (one at Workington), and three victories would see them equal the Reds' points total.

For some inexplicable reason (and no supporter of Carlisle United should ever complain about it, for this was the one of the main contributory factors in the birth of Carlisle United) the county's governing football body decided that the season was all over, and no further games would be played. Workington were crowned as Champions.

There was uproar, as officials from Shaddongate appealed against the decision, but such appeals fell on deaf ears. Apparently the two outstanding games were postponed fixtures from earlier in the season, the reason for the postponements had been down to Shaddongate United who had failed to fulfil these within a reasonable time! Quite correctly, the club's appeal was based upon the fact that Workington had played more games and therefore had an unfair advantage. If all things were to be equal, Workington should have the four points obtained against the teams that Shaddongate did not play deducted from their final total. The remaining fixture between the two sides could then be played as a Championship decider. The County F.A. would have none of it, *"a more ridiculous proposal has never been heard,'* was their verdict upon the Shaddongate appeal. The decision was, and still remains today ridiculous, it still stands as a unique reminder within the game as to how a football club lost a Championship through an irrational administrational decision.

As such this was the straw which broke the camel's back, and club officials held several meetings discussing the way forward. It had become clear that unless they held greater power, then the larger clubs, as Workington were in county circles, would continue to profit.

An 'unofficial' approach was made to the officials of Carlisle Red Rose to hold a meeting to discuss amalgamation, clearly if both of Carlisle's top sides joined forces then the balance of power had a greater chance of swaying. To put matters into perspective, Carlisle Red Rose declined the invitation electing to remain independent. Red Rose officials believed that United's approach had been made due to their poor financial situation, and that the club was all but ready to collapse.

```
                                                                SHADDON
                                                                Tel Carlis

A/M/m/TG.
4/04




        Dear

        The Annual General Members Meeting of Shaddongate United Association Football
        Club has been arranged for Tuesday the 17th day of May 1904.
        The event is to be held at the Temperance Hall, Caldewgate, Carlisle, with
        all matters commencing at 6.15pm prompt.
        We would like as many members and supporters of the club to be present as is
        possible and would ask you to pass on the time of the engagement to fellow
        members who may not be aware.
        I look forward to seeing you on the night.

        If it is not possible for you to attend, may I take this opportunity of
        thanking you for your continued support.
        An itemised agenda is detailed below for your perusal, it is anticipated
        that this format should be maintained.


        Chairman



        AGENDA.

        1.  Chairman to open meeting/speech.
        2.  Secretary's report.
        3.  Treasurers report.
        4.  Membership Elections.
        5.  Matters arising.
        6.  Other business.
```

The Birth of Carlisle United F.C.

How wrong they were. On Tuesday the 17th of May 1904, the shareholders of Shaddongate United met at the Temperance Hall, Caldergate, Carlisle, for what was to most, a straightforward end of season get together. Some 80 plus supporters were present as the meeting was opened by Mr Atkinson, Chairman of the committee, ably assisted by Harold Kirkbride, Honourable Secretary, and Thomas Graham, Honourable Treasurer.

Those gathered heard how the club had ended the season with a profit of £24 and 4 shillings, compared to £35 from the previous season when the County Cup had been won. Nowhere on the agenda for that meeting can one find any mention of the proposed alteration of the club's identity, which must have come as a great shock to many of those present. It was Mr Atkinson who first raised the subject, and this sparked off deep and agitated discussion.

Many stood by their principles, claiming that it was extraordinary that such a matter should be raised without prior consultation of the members. The majority listened to the reasoning behind the name change. One speaker proclaimed: *"It is desirable that we should have a representative Carlisle team, from both a financial and football standing Carlisle will profit. With just one side we can prosper and progress to a greater standing within the national game."* A rousing speech indeed, and one which seems to have inspired many of those present as it received rapturous applause.

However, there were those who objected to what they saw as a direct show of disloyalty. *"What will become of Shaddongate United? I strongly object to this change, it is foolish to think that matters will be any different by a name change, I strongly object to the change."*

Arguments and heated discussion continued until eventually a vote was demanded, the result of this vote was almost three to one in favour of Shaddongate United changing their name to Carlisle United. The matter was resolved, and Carlisle United was born.

A breakaway group of Shaddongate United supporters, some sixty odd in number, all of whom refused to have anything to do with the new club, held an emergency meeting at the Duke of York public house in the city, on the night of the 20th of July 1904. At this meeting these supporters declared their right to maintain the name of Shaddongate United, thus the original club continued albeit in a different form, but they were never again able to compete at the same level as the newly formed Carlisle United.

Jimmy Hind, trainer of Shaddongate United, and as such in charge of team affairs, was offered terms at Carlisle United, as too was Harold Kirkbride, another local man, who acted as club secretary. Thomas Graham volunteered his services as treasurer. Thus administrationally the set-up remained identical. Modern day records inaccurately dictate that Harold Kirkbride was team manager, this is not so as Jimmy Hind was without doubt in overall control of first team football matters. Harry Kirkbride was simply there to ensure that administration affairs were dealt with promptly and efficiently. Jimmy Hind maintained such a position within the club until 1908 and the arrival of Bert Stansfield. Thus all records depicting Kirkbride, McCumiskey (who was actually the club chairman) and Jack Houston as team manager prior to 1907 should be regarded as being incorrect.

Jimmy Hind   Harry Kirkbride

On the field, few players were signed from Shaddongate - just five to be precise; the Stubbs brothers, along with Routledge, Hetherington, and Spottiswoode, the others were to remain with Shaddongate United or played other local football. From this it can be seen that the 'new' Carlisle United had made efforts to extract themselves from the old Shaddongate club without causing too much disharmony for those who wished to keep the former club alive. Harry Kirkbride explained to some of the Shaddongate people: *"It is not the wish of the newly formed Carlisle United to force Shaddongate United to dissolve, both clubs are separate, if at all possible we want to work with the Shaddongate club, not against it.".*

Despite this apparent plea for peace and tranquillity between the two clubs it was, quite understandably for the Shaddongate supporters, an acrimonious split. The new club had been formed, taking with them Shaddongate's finest, already the balance of power was beginning to sway.

The disgruntled, remaining, Shaddongate officials need not have fretted for too long as within a twelve month spell, not one of the ex-Shaddongate players who registered for Carlisle United during that first season was to feature in the immediate first team plans.

Carlisle United played their first ever fixture at Millholme Bank, a friendly match against Victoria Wanderers, which ended in a 2-1 victory, and this was followed by another friendly match, plus another victory, this time over Hexham. With greater confidence, United entered the national F.A. Cup competition. The first qualifying round draw paired them with a home tie against Workington. The game took place on Tuesday the 14th of October 1904 before 5,000 spectators, and the result was a 2-2 draw, thereby requiring a replay. In that first ever cup-tie the team consisted; Bendle, T.Stubbs, Fisher, Spottiswoode, Hetherington, Routledge, Hunton, G.Stubbs, Martland, Rae, Morton.

The replay was so far as United are concerned, something of a farce, and ended in a 3-1 defeat. Somewhat gallingly, Workington's first team were playing a Lancashire Combination league fixture at Blackpool that same day, thus it was the Reds second eleven which dumped United out of the cup! Despite this, for some 72 minutes it was Carlisle who looked the better side, leading 1-0. But with 18 minutes to go the defence collapsed, allowing the Reds forwards to pillage three goals.

Interestingly, Carlisle Red Rose knocked Workington out of the competition in the next round, 4-0!

Still only competing in the Cumberland Senior League, United were desperate to prove that they had the capability to compete with the bigger clubs and to eventually attract better quality players to the club. With this in mind Glasgow Rangers arrived in the city in the April of 1905. No ground was suitable thus the match was played where the present Carlisle Rugby Club stands, when the Scottish side ran out 2-1 winners.

Less than one month later, in May 1905, Carlisle United created history when they became the first ever club to win the Cumberland Senior League championship and the Cumberland Cup. Had it not been for the old enemy, Carlisle Red Rose, they would have made a clean sweep of all the county's major trophies. However, Red Rose were victorious in the final of the Hospital Cup, defeating United 1-0.

The season over, Carlisle made an application to the Lancashire Combination League in an attempt to move to a higher standard and more testing level of football. The club offered to pay the visiting sides expenses for two years should their application be successful.

There was no way with such an offer that the application could be anything but successful, thus on the 19th of May 1905 Mr R.P. Gregson of the Lancashire F.A. announced: *"We are pleased to welcome Carlisle United who have been accepted as members of the Lancashire Combination League Second Division."* Other clubs joining the league at the same time being, Burnley, Bolton St. Luke, and Lancaster.

Carlisle United 1905/06 season:
(Back) Kirkbride (Sec.), McCumiskey (Chair.), Lorimer, Scott, Hamilton, Dalton (Trainer).
(Middle) Hunton, Smith, Killop, Henderson, Colvin. (Front): Burge, Groggins, Foster.

The club's Millholme Bank ground was visited by Lancashire F.A. officials and was at once declared as 'not suitable' for the standard of the league. Carlisle were instructed to make good necessary repairs or to find an alternative ground offering improved facilities for crowd control. It was from this directive that United moved grounds to Devonshire Park (now Trinity School playing fields).

That first season was hardly filled with highlights, the first Combination fixture at Devonshire Park took place on 2nd September 1905, and saw St. Helens Town run out 3-2 winners, the United team for that game was; Scott, Lorimer, Hamilton, Hunton, Smith, Killop, Henderson, Colvin, Burge, Groggins, Foster.

Although eventual mid-table security was achieved it was a great struggle for the club. In the F.A. Cup Carlisle Red Rose were handed out a thrashing before an estimated crowd of 5,000 who braved torrential rain and screaming winds from the river Eden.

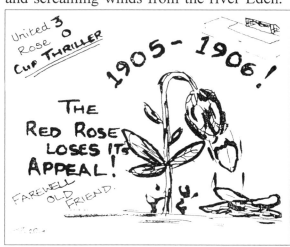

A cartoon depicts the match which saw the effective end of Red Rose.

In the following round it was Barrow who dashed any hopes of a cup run when before some 3,000 spectators they dished out a 4-2 defeat on their own turf.

Team group 1906/07 season: (Back) Clarke, Burns, Cifford, Carter, Burge, Smith, Hind(Trainer)
(Middle) Spottiswoode, Thompson, Maher, Blyth, Collins, Pickering, Raisbeck
(Front) Hunton, Winter, Cowie, Lyon, Sanderson, Jenkins, Johnston, Gunzon.

The following season saw an incredible turn round of club fortunes, as they ran out as Combination Second Division Champions, scoring 115 goals and losing just five games all season. The club had won promotion to the Lancashire Combination First Division, a marvellous achievement in such a short span of time. It is worth mentioning that despite a first eleven, the club also ran two reserve sides. A first team squad photograph of the era depicts some 25 players, of which two were goalkeepers - Messrs. Burns and Scott. Strength of depth must have created some nice selection problems for Jimmy Hind to contend with.

Money was spent improving Devonshire Park as the squad was again strengthened for the challenge of a higher league. Club officials, looking to the future and never afraid of change, looked to build on the back of the team's success. To this end they introduced Ton Paley as right-hand man to Jimmy Hind who was beginning to feel the physical demands of handling such a large squad. Further changes had been made behind the scenes a few months earlier when Jack Houston was brought in as company secretary, replacing Harry Kirkbride. By the end of the 1907-08 season the team finished as runners-up to Champions Everton!

In the F.A. Cup some success did follow. Victories over Windermere 7-1, Workington 3-0, Darlington 7-0, and Southend United 4-0, ensured a place in the first round proper for the first occasion ever. The draw paired United with Southern League side, Brentford.

After a 2-2 draw at Devonshire Park, with both United goals coming from Powell, United travelled to London for the replay. The second game went to extra time with Carlisle eventually easing their way through to the second round, by winning the tie 3-1, with goals from Jimmy McAteer, and Robinson 2.

The second round consisted of 32 teams, and saw United travel to Second Division Grimsby Town who had defeated First Division club Bristol City in the first round. Pre match press speculation in Grimsby identified United centre half

(A cartoon of the time)

Jimmy McAteer as a real danger. *"The Carlisle centre half is called McAteer, a sheep farmer he possesses huge thighs and a ferocious crunching tackle. This man apparently says very little and lets his actions speak louder than words, there are dismembered centre forwards all over the North of England who have faced a McAteer challenge."* Out of interest, this season proved to be Jimmy's sole first team season with United, a team photograph does actually depict him as described, for he is easily twice as broad as many of the United team, without appearing fat; not the sort of player you would want to mess with!

Blundell Park, Grimsby, was at that time little better than a tip, having one stand with half of its roof blown away in a storm, and the pitch was a nightmare. Heavy frost had caused some doubt as to whether the game would be played. Go ahead it did on Monday the 1st of February 1908. All eyes were on Blanthorne the ex-Liverpool and current Grimsby centre forward, and McAteer the Carlisle centre half. For 75 minutes Carlisle held their own, with a goal from McAteer, and a Danny Maher equaliser keeping United in the game at 2-2, although United did miss a penalty to add to the excitement.

With legs tiring and the Cleethorpes gale howling, the defence eventually collapsed, finally losing 6-2. Blanthorne played out his greatest ever fifteen minutes in football, scoring five of Grimsby's goals. The game is still recalled in Grimsby as "Blanthorne's Game".

(Back): Hetherington, Paley (Trainer), McKenzie, Foster, Wishart, Wilson, Harrison, Fletcher, Carter, Perks, McIntyre, Collins, McAteer, Houston.
(Middle): Clark, Smith, Tait, Blyth, White, Black, Spottiswoode.
(Front): Powell, Drain, Dalton, Irving, Spottiswoode, Maher, Sanderson, Robinson, Campbell, Bauchop, Cartey.

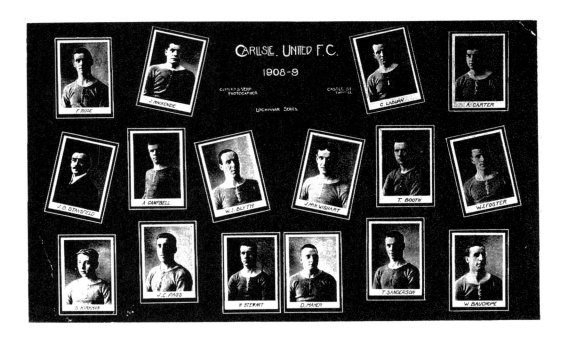

CARLISLE. UNITED F.C.
1908-9

CLIFFORD S VERO
PHOTOGRAPHER

CASTLE ST
CARLISLE

LOCHINVAR SERIES

The following season, 1908/09, was less auspicious, and in came James Brown (Bertie) Stansfield to oversee United's fortunes. Stansfield had been secretary with Rossendale United and was seen as the man to take United forward. Out went Jimmy Hind, although this was expected and was more of a voluntary decision. Ton Paley took over as first team trainer in the hope that continuity would ensure a similar pattern and standard of play. A position of fifth in the league was attained.

The same season saw a titanic F.A. Cup struggle with Coventry City. 1-1 draws on both occasions were played before United eventually ousted them from the competition, 3-1 at Hyde Road, Manchester - the first home of Manchester City. In the first round proper the team was faced with an away tie at Second Division Fulham. The game was a non-starter so far as Carlisle were concerned - a 4-1 defeat - with United's consolation goal being scored by the tall figure of centre forward Sanderson.

Devonshire Park, although a reasonable stadium, was not acceptable for the heights to which United hoped to aspire, for the Football League was the obvious goal. Situated close to the river Eden and with little room for expansion the club was less than happy with the situation, added to which the land was reclaimed by it's owner thus meaning that United had to find alternative accommodation.

It never fails to surprise how when faced with such calamities, football clubs, and in particular Carlisle United, seem to come out of it stronger and in a better position.

This was certainly the case with Devonshire Park. The F.A. Cup runs had proved that the club's following was supportive enough, so much so that a new ground at Brunton Park was purchased for £2,000, with the club officially moving into their new home on the 2nd of September 1909.

(Back): Paley (Trainer, Martin, Noble, Downs, Rose, Wilcox, Young, Law, McKenzie, Carter, Auld (Sec.).

(Middle): Winning, Maher, Blyth, Sanderson, Smith, Makin, Jobling.

(Front); Pigg, Berry, Phillips, Robertson, Foster, Fell.

In the league, it was again mid-table consolidation. It was the glamour and fantasy world of the F.A. Cup which aroused great excitement in the city. Out went club sides Tonge 1-0, and Mexborough 4-0 after a 0-0 away draw. United were again in the first round proper and once again it was London opposition in the shape of Southern League West Ham United. On the 15th of January 1910, an estimated 1,500 Carlisle supporters travelled to the capital and witnessed a memorable 1-1 draw, with a Carter goal earning United a replay. The city went football mad at the thought of the Hammers playing at Brunton Park, Carlisle, especially as there seemed every opportunity of Carlisle beating them and progressing into the second round.

Unfortunately the supporters were denied such an opportunity, unbeknown to anyone outside Brunton Park, the club was struggling to make ends meet. Bertie Stansfield in his infinite wisdom had increased players wages and commanded a reasonable fee for himself.

Expenditure had virtually doubled in the previous two seasons. West Ham meanwhile, uninspired by the thought of travelling 300 odd miles to Carlisle, heard of the club's plight and made an offer the directors could hardly refuse. The Hammers would give Carlisle £160 plus half the gate receipts if the game was staged at their Boleyn ground. Carlisle agreed, and West Ham won the second game 5-0!

March 1910 saw the departure of Bertie Stansfield who took up a managerial role at Norwich City, taking several of United's better players with him. Without being too disrespectful to him. Stansfield was as such the first outsider employed by the club. His reign at Carlisle was hardly memorable, and it is fair to say that he, more than anyone else involved in Carlisle United up to that time, detracted from the commitment and dedication shown by everyone else who had taken the club to such a stage. Stansfield never won a major honour within the game and eventually went into hotel management, an occupation at which he was considerably more effective.

With financial problems still prominent, the club resigned from the Lancashire Combination in May 1910 and joined the North Eastern League, where they remained in one form or another (including reserve team football) until the 1960's. The reason behind the move was purely financial, for travelling expenses would be less extravagant and there was the optimistic view that attendances may increase with more localised derby matches.

In essence Carlisle had come too far too quickly, it was fine when things had been run on a shoestring budget and just about everybody involved in the club was local. However, fame had it's downfalls, as the club had grown, outsiders with little or no dedication to Carlisle United stepped into the fold offering their alleged expertise. It was perhaps a lesson well learned so quickly in the club's history.

Company Secretary, Jack Houston, was put in charge of team affairs and found the going tough, extremely tough. United struggled all season and finished among the bottom few places of the league. They fared little better in the F.A. Cup, a 3-0 victory over Newburn was followed by a 1-1 draw at Crewe, before the Railwaymen visited Brunton Park and won 4-3 in the fifth qualifying round replay. The average attendance had fallen from the 4,000 mark to around 2,500, thus more revenue was lost on a regular basis.

Suddenly everything that could go wrong, went wrong. An official club statement was released: *"The board of Carlisle United are sad to announce that due to matters forced upon them by previous seasons the club's financial situation has been compromised. Without a sudden input of funds we shall have no alternative but to resign from the club's North Eastern League commitments."*

There was public outrage as the blame was laid firmly at the door of Bertie Stansfield who had sorted himself out with a position 350 miles from the city thus well away from the criticism he knew would be levelled at him. Supporters held their own emergency meetings as funds were yet again raised which would be sufficient to keep the club afloat for a short term. Newcastle United, themselves a prosperous and fully self sufficient club and business, bent over backwards to assist United's cause, and made a £300 donation which greatly relieved the situation.

Newcastle was a club which appreciated its footballing roots, and voluntarily came to United's aid during at least one other time of crisis; the Magpies made donations to other local club sides, albeit Carlisle's was of the greatest amount.

The players held their own emergency meeting at a public house in Kingstown, Carlisle, where they unanimously decided that they would play on without payment until the club was once again in a position to reimburse them. Without this marvellous gesture, Carlisle United would almost certainly has folded.

1913   1914

W. Doughty.
C. M. Ellis.   G. Bristowe.
J. Smith.
W. Scott.   W. Blythe.   W. Steel.   E. Nixon.
H. Irving.   R. McGough.   H. Routledge.
E. Patheson   D. Maher.   W. Cockburn.   F. Mills.   J. H. Bowerbank.

CARLISLE UNITED A. F. C.

The 1911/12 season was forgettable as the team struggled in the league, finishing in the lower reaches of the table. Accrington Stanley inflicted a 3-0 F.A. Cup defeat at Peel Park, Accrington.

Poor old Jack Houston managed his resources to the best of his ability but the strain of it all was beginning to tell on his personal health, thus in 1912 he resigned from his post, due to ill health. After the Stansfield affair it was refreshing to see honest endeavour which undoubtedly reflected in the goodwill of the players. Jack Houston deserves a great deal of credit for keeping the spirit of this football club alive. His replacement for one season only was yet another man with a fantastic knowledge of the local game, Davie Graham. Restricted to local talent, Graham was forced to look at anyone and everyone who offered their services. The results from the 1912/13 season are to be fair appalling, and perhaps go to show why Graham was in his role for for just one season.

At Brunton Park, 6-1 defeats by South Shields, and Darlington were suffered, whereas away from home Darlington inflicted a 9-0 massacre, and Spennymoor a 7-0 defeat. Morale dropped to an all-time low, and both on and off the field the future looked bleak, yet somehow the team found some consistency and managed to achieve an almost respectable fourteenth league position. In the F.A. Cup, Barrow humiliated Carlisle 4-1 at Holker Street.

In came George Bristowe, a man with a tremendous knowledge of football, someone who could be described as Carlisle United's first ever manager. Initially Bristowe looked at what he had inherited and was quietly impressed, for the local players gave their everything, no amount of money can buy heart, and this is what this United team were playing on. The league form remained static, fourteenth position, while in the F.A. Cup there was slightly more satisfaction. Lancashire Town were beaten 4-2 after a replay, followed by Frizington 2-1, Lowca 7-1, then Southport Central 2-1, before the team succumbed 4-1 to Glossop at their North End ground. The following season was little better, seventeenth position in the league, with a disappointing 9-0 away defeat in the final league game of the season at Sunderland Rovers. In the F.A. Cup, Barrow St. Mary's were beaten 4-1, Lancashire Town 3-1, before Fizington ended the run with what can only be described as an ignominious 3-1 defeat.

Because of the outbreak of war that same season was the last of organised football in this country, it was to be a full four years before the club could contemplate a competitive fixture again in the North-Eastern League. It was a break which selfishly came at the right time for Carlisle United, albeit the cause was needless, caused by the weakness of the human being in the often relentless search of ultimate power.

Football resumed in 1919/20 season, but for the supporters of Carlisle United things had deteriorated. The club finished bottom of the North-Eastern League but did manage to reach the fifth qualifying round of the F.A. Cup before being dumped out by South Liverpool 3-1. The F.A. Cup offered all the promise that season. Wigton Harriers had been demoralisingly thumped 8-1 at Brunton Park, followed by a 6-1 demolition of Cleator Moor Celtic. Home attendances, presumably because supporters were desperate to see their favourites in action, rose to around the 5,000 mark. More importantly, on the financial side of affairs, Carlisle United were again a viable proposition.

George Bristowe made several signings and did manage to field a more consistent side during the following season as the team achieved sixth place in the league. The side which played much of that season being; Guthrie, Crawford, Snaith, Forbes, Routledge, Henderson, Irwin, Ward, Kirkpatrick, Birrell. Later, the skilful artistry of Willy Henderson saw him transferred to Arsenal. Henderson was sufficiently competent to take on opponents and to beat them two or three times before crossing or finishing himself, a master of 'the nutmeg' he would draw a defender into him before slipping it through his legs dropping his shoulder and ducking round on a run after the ball. There are many who witnessed Hendersons skills and believed him to be as good as anything around in football at that time.

In the F.A. Cup an administrative hiccup caused the club serious problems. Frizington had been beaten 3-1 in the first qualifying round, then followed Barrow, after a 1-1 away draw, United won through with an extra time goal at Brunton Park. Barrow appealed against the result as Carlisle had fielded an unregistered player.

Team group and officials from the 1920/21 season. (Back): G. Ellis (Treasurer), Stoneham. (Middle): Nixon (Vice-chair.), Kirkpatrick, Crawford, Snaith, Whitson, Routledge, Bristow (Sec.) (Front): W.Ellis, Henderson, Keen, Craig, Birrell, Campbell.

It was deemed a reasonable appeal, and the tie was awarded to Barrow! By the end of the 1920/21 season the club was formed into a Limited Company, thus for official business purposes becoming Carlisle United Football Club 1921 Ltd, it was an organisation which still exists to this very day.

It has always been the case at Carlisle United that when things go well they are fantastic, there is no middle of the road in football. The following season it was as though someone had waived a magic wand over Brunton Park, for things began to fall into place. The North Eastern League Championship was won in the 1921/22 season, with a crowd of 7,000 watching the team beat Shildon 2-0 at Brunton Park to clinch the title. United's league record for that season stood at.

P	W	D	L	F	A	Pts
38	24	8	6	85	39	56

Programme for the Championship clinching match (1921/22 season)

Also, typically, when league performances improve the F.A. Cup runs diminish. Having already beaten Vickerstown, Penrith, Arcledon Red Rose, and Cleator Moor Celtic, it was Stalybridge Celtic who earned a 0-0 draw at Brunton Park before knocking United out of the competition by 3 goals to 2 in the Bower Fold replay. Despite everything else, United were Champions, and no amount of F.A. Cup defeats could take that honour away from the club.

Over the following few seasons, form became somewhat erratic as the team were never quite able to emulate the wonders of the 1921/22 season. Sixth position was obtained in 1923, 1924, and 1925, with an improved fifth position in the 1925/26 season.

The F.A. Cup competition offered little more in the way of excitement or success with the exception of two victories over Workington in the 1924/25 and 1925/26 seasons respectively.

The last non-League derby match

The 1926/27 league season was decidedly average, eighth position in the table, with the best form being left for the F.A. Cup competition. Whitehaven Athletic were beaten 7-1, then followed Hartlepool United with goals from Graham 2, Hamilton, A.Pigg, Ward, and Sinclair. Messrs Pigg and Smiles grabbed a brace apiece in the following round against Bedlington United, putting Carlisle United into the third round of the competition proper for the first time since they were founded in 1904.

The third round offered a chance of a crack at one of the country's top clubs. Carlisle were drawn against Wolverhampton Wanderers, then in the Second Division. The match which was played at a frantic pace in dreadful winter conditions before an estimated Brunton Park crowd of some 14,000. United lost 2-0. The team made every effort to match their football opponents, and for long periods off the game they looked worthy contenders, but goals from Lees and Weaver eventually sent the Wolves through to the next round. The United line up that day is probably worth mentioning since it was something of an historical yardstick for the club; Hood, Smiles, Reid, Harrison, Chambers, Pigg(W), Hamilton, Sinclair, Pigg(A), Ward, Graham.

The following season (1927/28) was to be the first team's last ever in the North-Eastern League. Yet it was not until the final run, in when United went on a magnificent eleven game unbeaten sequence, which saw them climb to runners-up position, although still ten points behind the Champions, Sunderland Reserves. The season was also the one when a striker who was arguably the best United have ever had first made his name. Jimmy McConnell was signed from the USA, an ex-Nithsdale Wanderers player he went on to break all kinds of scoring records for the club.

In the F.A. Cup, Doncaster Rovers were beaten 2-1 at Brunton Park with goals from McConnell and Ward. In the next round United fell 1-0 to Wrexham, although they enjoyed the majority of the play but failed to find the net by virtue of the woodwork saving the Welsh side.

On the 24th of June 1928, Carlisle United applied for election to the Football League. It was shortly after midday when the news filtered through that the club had been accepted into the Football League, replacing Durham in the Third Division North. The official voting made by the Football League club representative went as follows; Nelson-37 votes, Carlisle United-33 votes, Durham-11 votes, York-7 votes and finally Chester-2 votes.

Poor old Durham had in fact finished second from bottom of Division Three North, one place and three points above Nelson, with their last remaining fixture in the Football League taking place on the 5th of May 1928 which produced a 5-1 thrashing of Crewe Alexandra. Incredibly, Nelson bottom of the League with just 10 wins and 26 defeats, lived to fight another day.

This was the dawning of a new era for the supporters of Carlisle United, who now had such places as Bradford, Halifax, Rotherham and Tranmere to visit, all a far cry from the days of Shaddongate United and Carlisle Red Rose. One can only imagine what the hard core Shaddongate United supporters must have thought, indeed, Red Rose actually ceased to exist sometime during the 1905/06 season. Thus it is likely that there was an exodus to Carlisle United thereafter, since no self-respecting Red Rose fan would swop allegiance to what was described as, *"the lot from Shaddongate."*

Chapter 2

UP THE FOOTBALL LEAGUE WE GO

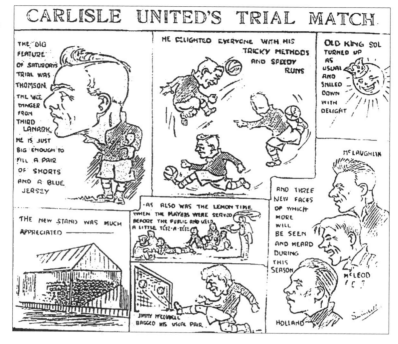

The whole of the city celebrated United's marvellous achievement, for League football had always seemed a million light years away. Prior to 1928 the club had made two attempts to join the football league.

On both occasions insufficient votes were accumulated, and there was many who believed it would never be attained. Bill Nicholson, the club chairman, was anything but a man who failed to speak his mind. After the success of June the 24th 1928, he proudly proclaimed: *"Carlisle United was one of the biggest club sides in the North-Eastern League, we should look to the season ahead of us with great anticipation I am sure United will prosper from this day forth."*

Prosper they certainly did, as funds were raised to subsidise the further development of the wooden main stand, and facilities for the press were further incorporated into the updated Brunton Park. Some ten extra turnstiles were added to various points around the ground, and three of the exit gates were widened and improved upon. Terracing was added in the form of dis-

carded wooden railway sleepers, and these same sleepers were in some areas to remain in use as partial terracing on the ground over the next forty plus years.

Season tickets went on sale at the following prices; ground 25/- (£1-25p), or 1/- (5p) per game; Central Grandstand 65/- or 3/- per game; Grandstand Wings 45/- or 2/- per game. The improved standards of facilities and higher grade of football being a major contributory factory to a price increase which caused some concern to the Brunton Park regulars.

As well as work on the ground there was the little matter of building a side worthy of competing in what was then described as the 'Third League'. The club's general secretary George Bristowe, who also doubled as what we would today officially describe as team manager, scoured the United Kingdom in search of fresh talent. Bristowe found his task a great deal easier with his club now members of the Football League. Players such as Davie Hutchinson (Motherwell) and George Prout (Grimsby) were signed. Hutchinson especially proved a fine piece of business, an inside forward he forged an excellent front line relationship with the now almost legendary figure of Jimmy Mc-Connell.

Pre-season inhouse friendly fixtures were played at the ground - 'Blues v Stripes' encounters - providing an opportunity for trialist or squad members to prove their worth. The two games which took place in August 1928 attracted a combined attendance figure of around 6,500.

Saturday the 25th of August 1928 was indeed a special occasion for Carlisle United and it's excited support. An estimated 500 fans travelled to Accrington Stanley's Peel Park to witness United's first ever game in League football. The previous season, Stanley had finished in 9th position in the Third League, losing just three home games all season and winning 14. Had it not been for their inconsistent away form they would have been title contenders. The home side were clear favourites to dispose of the newcomers, but things are seldom so simple.

The United side which took the field that day was: George Prout, Tom Coulthard, George Cook, Graham (Ginger) Harrison, Robert Ross, Bill Pigg, Alf Agar, Davie Hutchinson, Jimmy McConnell, Billy Ward, Bill Watson.

An official 6,714 spectators witnessed a tough but fairly fought tussle between the two sides, the highlight of the game coming in the first half when United centre forward, McConnell, received a pass and ran towards the Stanley goal. He unleashed a terrific shot which, according to press reports of the day, *"flew into the top corner of the goal causing those gathered behind the Stanley keeper to stoop down in fear of the ball bursting through the net and taking off their heads."*

It was United's first League goal, which was celebrated with apparent relief more than anything else. Alf Agar and Billy Ward netted a further goal apiece as United ran out 3-2 winners.

The atmosphere at Brunton Park for the first home league game was electrifying, it took place on Thursday 30th August against Bradford City, and ended in a 2-2 draw before 11,771 spectators. It was as such a disappointing result, for everyone at the club had hoped for a further victory which would arouse even greater interest in the team. However, when one considers that the previous Saturday had seen City slam 11 goals past a stunned Rotherham side, then a draw was in fact no mean feat.

On Saturday 1st of October 1928, just one week after the club's Football League debut, a further page was to be recorded in the history of the club. On this day Hartlepools were the visitors to Brunton Park. United fielded; Prout, Jimmy Smiles, Cook, Billy Robinson, Ross, Pigg, Agar, Hutchinson, McConnell, Ward and Watson. A crowd of 7,346 turned out in the hope of witnessing United's first home League victory, and they were not to be disappointed. Goals by McConnell (3), Hutchinson(2), Robinson, Agar and Ward - one apiece - ensured what still remains United's record League victory of 8-0. It is incredible to think that this happened in the club's third ever Football League game.

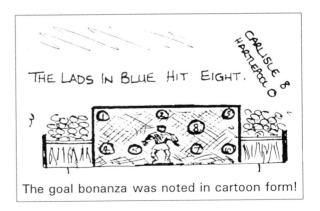

THE LADS IN BLUE HIT EIGHT. CARLISLE 8 HARTLEPOOL 0

The goal bonanza was noted in cartoon form!

Not surprisingly, with two wins and a draw behind them, United soared to the top of the league. Three days later, in the return game with Bradford City, United tasted defeat, losing 4-2 with United's replies coming from Jimmy McConnell.

In the F.A. Cup, revenge was gained over the previous season's opponents, Wrexham, a Billy Ward goal doing the damage (interestingly the official club travel, then by rail, saw just 47 United stalwarts make the journey to North Wales). This victory lined up a home tie with fellow Division Three North side, Lincoln. The game ended in a disappointing 1-0 defeat, a Roberts goal sufficient to see Lincoln through to the third round proper and an attractive money-spinning home tie with Division One side, Leicester City.

In February 1929 the football club purchased number 259 Warwick Road as their headquarters, the premises backed onto the ground and was a sensible business move by the club as it offered extra facilities for the administrational side of things. Slowly but surely United were cementing their roots, ensuring that football would remain in the city and in particular at Brunton Park for many years to come.

By the end of that first season Jimmy McConnell ended as the division's top marksman with some 42 goals, indeed, only two players in the entire Football League beat his total - both by just one goal! Jimmy McConnell's goalscoring record for that season remains a club record, and it will take a goalscorer of some quality to beat it. The club finished in a creditable 8th position. The away form saw just 13 points attained on their travels. No less than 8 teams put 4 or more goals past United, including champions, Stockport County who humiliated them 5-0 before a Brunton Park crowd of 10,779.

The defensive frailties of that first season were hardly improved upon the next year. George Bristowe further strengthened his squad. Another 'Blues v Stripes' encounter took place on Saturday 24th August 1929. In came Jimmy Thomson, a tricky winger from Third Lanark, who was described as being, *"just big enough to fill the pair of shorts and a blue jersey."*

Also featuring in that same game, and all of whom signed for the club, were full back Hubert McLaughlin who came from Celtic, inside forward Jimmy McLeod from Partick, and a further forward in the form of John Holland from Clapton Orient. During the game Jimmy Thomson apparently delighted all those in attendance with his tricky methods and speedy runs; Jimmy McConnell bagged his usual pair. Also playing that day was a youngster signed from Penrith, a skilful winger by the name of John Cape, a player who was to prove more than a worthwhile capture.

The first game of the season opened with a 2-0 home victory over Crewe, it was at this fixture that a spectator sadly collapsed and died during one of United's second half raids. Thankfully the players knew nothing of the tragic event and played on. The death, it should be noted, was of natural causes and not as a result of any physical confrontation.

The season itself was a disappointing one as United's inconsistency infuriated the fans, although some excellent results were achieved at Brunton Park - 7-1 over Barrow, 6-0 versus Chesterfield, 5-0 Wigan Borough, 5-1 Wrexham, and 5-2 Hartlepools. Such positives were cancelled out by some real hammerings, the majority away from home; 7-2 at Accrington, 7-1 at Stockport, 8-0 at Wigan Borough, and 5-2 at South Shields (later Gateshead).

The exciting Jimmy Thomson flattered to deceive, as no less than 32 different players donned United shirts in League outings. Thomson managed just 3 goals in 15 first team appearances as the goalscoring was left to Hutchinson (25) and McConnell (27), with newcomer John Holland bagging 13 in his solitary season at the club.

With the average attendance standing at 6,000 and just one home crowd rising above the 10,000 mark (v Stockport County of 10,204) the euphoria of League football was beginning to dwindle within the club's support. Things had to be changed, thus it came as no real surprise when secretary George Bristowe stood down from his position to be replaced by Billy Hampson, who was, for the first time in the clubs history, officially termed as team manager. Sammy Armes, another exciting forward, was signed from non-League football, and made his United first team debut away to Wigan Borough on the last day of the season. He scored twice giving the club's supporters some encouragement for the following term.

Despite the frustrating League form United did fare slightly better in the F.A. Cup, beating Halifax Town and Crewe Alexandra, to reach the third round proper and a home tie with the mighty Everton; Dixie Dean and all. A 20,000 capacity crowd saw Everton forced to work hard to overcome a defiant Carlisle side of; Little, Coulthard, McLaughlan, Miller, Frew, Parker, Cape, Hutchinson, McConnell, Holland, Watson. Two goals each for the Toffeemen's Critchley and Dean were sufficient to see the First Division side through, although United did net with solitary goals apiece from McConnell and Warson.

The game was also John 'Jackie' Capes last for the club as he was sold to North-East giants, Newcastle United, for what was then a large fee of £1,800.

This money went towards ground improvements and the building of the Scratching Pen.

Hapson, who had introduced Sammy Armes, now signed ex-West Ham striker, Arthur Sharp, and together they netted a total of 22 League goals during the 1930/31 season, which was in fact the best season the club had during the whole of the 1930's. Goalkeeper, John Kelly arrived from 'Spurs, while Joe (Jerry) Kelly - a giant of a centre half, not in nature but in determination and ability - moved from Glasgow Celtic. Once again though Jimmy McConnell proved to be the star striker, netting some 37 League goals and a further 4 in the F.A. Cup. He was once more the Division's leading marksman. On the 28th of March 1931, he was actually presented with a Chesterfield three piece suite in recognition of becoming the first United player to score 100 goals, an unusual gift which had been requested by the striker. Some fans saw this as the club's way of intimating that McConnell would be soon on his way, they were of course wrong.

The McConnell - Hutchinson partnership was, when at it's best, awesome. That same season McConnell's partner in front of goal grabbed 19 League goals and a further 2 in the F.A. Cup. Winger Bill Watson, the only ever-present in the League side, scored 13 times as United hit the goal trail. Accrington were thumped 7-3, Halifax Town 6-2 at home and 5-1 away, Rochdale 7-1, and Wigan Borough 6-1. In all a total of 98 League goals (a club record) were scored with 81 being conceded as the club finished in 8th position. With 20 League victories being the highest the club had achieved up to that time.

The average home attendance dropped yet again, this time to 5,838, with the highest Brunton Park attendance being 9,680 for the League visit of Gateshead.

In the F.A. Cup, New Brighton and Tunbridge Wells were dispatched, before 1,000 United spectators were hit by Cup fever and made the relatively short journey to Burnden Park, home of then First Division Bolton Wanderers, who were also the F.A. Cup holders. Typically, United turned in what was probably their best performance of the season, and were decidedly unlucky not to come away from Lancashire with at least a replay. Sadly a Blackmore goal silenced the Cumberland hordes who thoroughly made the most of their day as they made merry on the cold damp terraces of Wanderers embankment end, as United slipped out of the competition by one goal to nil.

The following season, with attendances dwindling and success seemingly evasive, other - non football - related matters were of real concern. Behind the scenes the club was in a real mess. Somehow the directors managed to subdue the fact that United was virtually bankrupt. Attendances actually dropped to around the 2-3,000 mark as the goals dried up. Again McConnell (20), Watson (17) and Hutchinson (13) were the main men in front of goal. Despite this there were some bright spots, and the signing of centre half Archie Gomm from Millwall was a shrewd piece of business. Gomm progressed to become one of the most consistent players in the squad over the following two seasons.

However, with just 12 victories all season, including the 3-1 F.A. Cup victory over Yorkshire Amateurs (Darlington putting United out in the 2nd round, 2-0 at Brunton Park), it was a miserable period for the football club. Eventually, with half the season gone, the United board announced that the club looked like it was going to have to resign from the Football League due to financial problems. An emergency board meeting was held resulting in all of the clubs directors resigning. After a short

period a brand new board was elected, but there was no simple solution to the club's financial problems.

It was quite clear what the club would have to do to remain a financially viable proposition - sell players. On the 15th March 1932, half back Les Heelbeck was sold to Wolverhampton Wanderers, and Jimmy McConnell was another to bid Brunton Park a fond farewell as he moved to Crewe Alexandra.

The legendary Jimmy McConnell

These fine players were followed at the end of the season by Arthur Sharp, free transfer to Bristol City, Sammy Armes to Chester, and Davie Hutchinson to Luton Town. In essence United's entire forward line had been ripped apart and moved to pastures new.

When manager Billy Hampson resigned to take up the manager's role at Yorkshire giants, Leeds United, things looked far from good for the coming season.

Before moving on, Hampson did endeavour to replace some of the outgoing players, to this end he signed William James Slinger, a busy and bustling centre forward from the army. Slinger's goal per game ratio is was equally as inspiring as that of the man he was brought in to replace, Jimmy McConnell. Willy Clarke took on the temporary role as manager of first team affairs for the remainder of the season.

At the beginning of the 1932/33 season, off the field things could hardly have been worse, yet the only way was up, the sole consolation being that the club was at least financially solvent. Incredibly after three games the team topped the League, albeit their lead was a brief one as no less than 8 out of the following 12 fixtures were then lost and United slipped uncontrollably down the table. Some 22 League defeats were endured during the campaign with a final position of 19th being achieved. Had it not been for the goals of Bill Slinger (15), then United would have undoubtedly struggled even more.

In the F.A. Cup Denaby United were beaten by the narrowest of margins, 1-0 - a Slinger goal. The team were then drawn against Hull City. After a 1-1 draw at Brunton Park, Hull eventually won through 2-1 with an extra time goal being scored by Forward. The average home attendance was now 5,210, incredibly a rise of over 500 on the previous season's average of 4,689. The season also saw the emergence and disappearance of a future star. Bill Shankly had been signed from Glenbuck Cherrypickers, played 16 games, and moved on to Preston North End.

With funds still low the club asked Willy Clarke to continue in his dual role as secretary/team manager. Clarke who was a United man through and through was only too pleased to help and agreed to do so.

The 1933/34 season will be best remembered as one of tragedy and despair. On the field United's form was difficult to find. Although Bill Slinger netted 31 times he was the only real goalscorer, for United's next highest marksmen was ex-Ayr United outside left, Pearson Ferguson, with just 8 goals to his name. New arrivals that season included two half backs, Gardiner Blake, from Airdrie, and Dornam Bell, from Colwyn Bay. Playing between this pair was another new signing, John Clark from Third Lanark. The defensive trio soon got to grips with the task at hand and apart from the occasional heavy defeat there were few forwards who ran them easy opponents.

In the December of that season Birmingham District League side, Cheltenham Town were the visitors to Brunton Park, in an F.A. Cup second round tie. United were expected to thrash the part-timers but crashed out of the competition with a Bob Bradley own goal crowning a poor team performance before 7,437 spectators. The League form continued to stutter, a good performance to gain a 3-3 draw at Chester gave the impression that the club had a last turned the corner, as the team dominated the game but found Chester in equally irresistible form.

The mood during the return journey from Chester was a good one, for three goals away from home had become something of a rarity. The following day, Sunday the 18th of February 1934, Willy Clarke received a telephone call which caused him to sink to his knees. *"United captain Bob Bradley sadly passed away at his home address earlier today."* It was a devastating blow, for Bradley had been one of the side's most consistent players over the previous two seasons. A tremendous motivator of his men and a determined leader, his battling and never-say-die attitude ensured that he never failed to give 100% until the final whistle blew.

The loss of the team captain at such a critical stage of a season could have proved catastrophic for the team, however, many simply rolled up their sleeves and said, *"we will do it for Bob"*!

Results were still inconsistent, typifying this was the 8-1 defeat at Wrexham, the second time in the club's history that the opposition had scored so many. Shortly after the team showed the opposition side to their character as they gave Gateshead a solid Brunton Park hiding, by 6 goals to 1. Eventually a League position of 13th was attained with 38 points, 15 games had been won, 19 lost, 10 of which were by the odd goal.

By the beginning of the 1934/35 season, Willy Clarke was finding the pressures of trying to build a successful football team, with little or no funds available, a great burden indeed. It had been decided in the summer that long-serving player Willie John Miller, who had played in each of United's League seasons thus far, should assist Clarke. Miller signed Len Darnell from Reading as a secondary coach in the belief that the more the workload was shared, the easier the job would be.

Half back Jack Johnson was signed from Barnsley, an uncompromising defender yet almost elegant in the air, Johnson went into every game as though his life defended upon it. The new management team was keen to see the season start, as once again Brunton Park was filled with optimism.

The season started with a 3-1 defeat at Tranmere Rovers and really deteriorated from then on in. A 6-1 home defeat by Walsall in February, during which there was cries of *"rubbish"* from the terraces, did little to instill faith in the Brunton Park faithful, who had witnessed some shocking performances. The most humiliating of which had been in the F.A. Cup.

Having lost at home to a non-League side the previous season, United, who had drawn Cheshire League side Wigan, intended to do a professional job on their non-League counterparts. In their previous League game before the cup-tie, United had drawn 1-1 at home with Doncaster the season's Champions-elect, and as such this was the best result of the entire season. With such a result behind them it was announced that there was little to fear in the Wigan side. Someone had clearly read the wrong script. The Wigan side included ex-United players Eric Felton and Sammy Armes, the latter of whom ran riot in the United defence.

It was a cold November day, and the result was a record 6-1 victory to the non-Leaguers. United's solitary goal was a controversial affair, allegedly scored by Ransom. Some claim that the ball went wide of the post and actually entered the goal via the back door so to speak, squeezing through an undetected tear in the webbing of the net. Whether the decision was a correct one or not was of no consequence. It was the lowest point yet in the club's history, indeed the score is still a record away victory by a non-League club over a Football League side in the F.A. Cup. To make matters worse, Sammy Armes netted twice against his old club and received a fantastic reception from United's supporters.

Not unnaturally, the team was heavily criticised for their lack of passion and commitment, *"there are certain players at the football club who should never again wear the colours of Carlisle United,"* declared one newspaper. *"There are a number of qualities required to the art of football, skill, physical strength and heart, not one Carlisle United footballer displayed the heart the club's support deserve,"* said another.

In March 1935, with the club firmly rooted to the foot of the table with little chance of making any last ditch escape, a manager was brought in, as Willy Clarke stood down. Bob Kelly was simply a figurehead for the remaining weeks of the season, and he suffered the indignity of a 7-0 thrashing at York City and at once declared, *"How some of these players can sleep at night is beyond my comprehension. I dislike defeat, yet some of my players apparently accept it before the game commences, such players have no further part to play for this club."*

The abysmal record for that season saw just 23 points won - 8 victories, 7 draws and 27 defeats. So, for the first time in their relatively short League career, Carlisle United were forced to apply for re-election. The result was of no concern, with a clear margin of 40 votes in front of Shrewsbury Town who received just 6 votes. Rochdale were involved, but they too were re-elected.

The press recorded the event in cartoon form.

The close season saw a hectic amount of transfer activity as Bob Kelly disposed of every player, with the exception of Jack Johnson, and a totally new squad was assembled. The new manager's intention was to create some spirit among his players. His genuine honesty aroused public interest, as once again supporters began to believe in the club. A crowd of 9,911 turned out to see the first home game of the season which was convincingly won 3-0.

Perhaps the season's low point, and one which still haunts the club to this day, occurred on Saturday the 9th of November 1935 during a home League fixture against Chester, when a crowd of 8,778 was in attendance. After 30 minutes Chester scored what appeared to be an offside goal. Referee Mr L.Caswell immediately disallowed the effort. The Chester players were furious and remonstrated with the match official who agreed to consult his linesman. Several seconds later he gave the goal, much to the annoyance of the Carlisle defence and the home supporters.

A few minutes later the match ball was kicked into the crowd and was never returned. The atmosphere became volatile as Mr Caswell lost control of the game, Kerr of Carlisle, and Sergeant, of Chester, were continually niggling each other whenever they could. Eventually, after some time, Mr Caswell decided to have a word with the pair of them, but his words of caution went unheeded. Much later, as though to exasperate the situation, Caswell disallowed a Chester goal which appeared quite legitimate, with the ball entering the goal and exiting through a hole in the side netting.

Chester began to celebrate only to see the Carlisle keeper Hartford positioning it for a goal kick at the referee's instruction. The result mattered little - 3-1 to Chester - and at the final whistle hundreds of spectators surged onto the pitch and surrounded the referee, who was whistled at and booed from the field of play. No physical harm came to him, but as a result of this incident Mr Caswell submitted a full report to the Football Authorities, and the findings of the inquiry led to the club being ordered to close Brunton Park for two weeks.

A further refereeing problem occurred just one month later, this time involving the United reserves who were playing at West Stanley. The referee, Mr J.Bradley of Ashington, clearly lost control of the game and was lucky to escape without physical injury as his decisions did nothing but incense the home crowd. With Carlisle reserves winning 3-1, with goals through Hardon, Dodds and Hamilton, the home side had what appeared to be a clear-cut penalty decision turned down. The crowd went berserk and threats were screamed at Bradley. It reached a stage where the referee stopped the game and called on the club secretary; he then demanded at the end of the first half and at the end of the game a Police escort from the field.

The second half of the game saw little improvement from the home fans point of view, and Carlisle scored again, this time from the penalty spot with a goal from James. Less than one minute later Mr Bradley was whistling for a penalty at the other end, and the West Stanley supporters gave a loud cheer. This cheer turned to an angry roar as once again Mr Bradley, having consulted his linesman, reversed his decision and gave a free kick to Carlisle United.

With 22 minutes remaining Hamilton rounded two defenders to score United's fifth, but his celebrations turned to amazement as the referee adjudged him to have fouled and disallowed the goal! Hamilton did eventually score as too did West Stanley. However, United reserves were the victors

5-2. At the end of the game hundreds of West Stanley supporters ran onto the pitch and attempted to get to the referee only to find the Police forming a protective barrier around him. There can be few reserve fixtures in the modern game which would arouse such emotion. Refereeing is a difficult enough role today, so let alone what horrors confronted the poor officials all those years ago.

Home form was second to none as the club lost just three times at Brunton Park. However, on their travels they managed just one victory, that being a 3-0 win over Southport, who ended the season seeking re-election. Come the end of the campaign United had attained a relatively good standing in the League, that of 13th position. Compared to the previous season this was a success! In the F.A. Cup the club fell at the first hurdle, going out 3-0 at Tranmere.

Bob Kelly was pleasantly surprised by the way his players had responded during the long hard season, *"there is a stigma attached to being the side at the bottom of the League, we have worked hard both on and off the field to rid ourselves of that stigma. The next stigma I want attached to us is that of success!"*

The following season (1936/37) saw very few incoming transfers as Kelly hoped that a regular unchanged side would work better without constant interference and change. He was in for a surprise, for after just a handful of games his team was languishing in second from bottom position. In November 1936 Bob Kelly resigned as team manager and moved to a similar role at Stockport County.

A few days after his move, Kelly's Stockport County faced Carlisle United in the F.A. Cup competition.

His return to Brunton Park was not favourably received as a section of the crowd voiced their opinions regarding his departure. Kelly took it like a man as he was forced to eat humble pie, for United cruised through to the second round with a 2-1 victory, goals coming from Mantle and McArdle. Before they ventured into the next round a new manager had taken up residence at the club, as Fred Westgate more or less swopped roles with Bob Kelly, having left the Stockport County hot-seat in September 1936.

Clapton Orient were the next F.A. Cup opponents to visit Brunton Park, they returned to London, with tails between their legs, having being thrashed 4-1. United next faced Swansea Town at the Vetch Field, Swansea, and lost 1-0.

In the League, apart from two glorious victories over Champions-elect Stockport County, there was little to shout about, and the attendances fluctuated with an average of 6,488 over the season. Off the field there was the sad loss of yet another influential player as Jack Round died on New Year's Eve, having suffered complications after an appendix operation. It is pleasing to report that at the subsequent match a minute's silence was held as a sign of respect, *"not one pin was heard to drop at Brunton Park."* Jack was a giant of a man, thick set and 6'2" tall, he commanded his defensive area and would fight tooth and nail to win the ball. The type of player difficult to replace.

The team sheet for the first matches in 1938.

The fact that United never won a game for almost two months after his death tends to speak for itself. Some players are naturally influential, and their presence on and off the field can be felt by everyone concerned. When Jack Round died his presence, the magical aura he created, was lost forever; it was a sad day indeed. Eventually the team pulled themselves together and rallied, putting together a string of good results and climbing to a final League position of 10th.

The 1937/38 season was inconsistent as were the majority of others in the 1930's, for the club struggled near to the bottom of the League before putting together an unbeaten run of 10 games which saw the team climb to a position from which a real championship bid could be launched. No sooner had everyone began to believe in the strength and quality of the side than they suddenly spiralled downwards.

The F.A. Cup was a cause of further disappointment, knocked out in the first round in an away tie with Tranmere Rovers, 2-1, with United's goal coming from Leach. With very little to cheer about, Fred Westgarth resigned as United supremo. taking up a similar role with Bradford City. In came Dunfermline Athletic boss David Taylor, who could do little else but sit and monitor, and a final position of 12th was achieved.

David Taylor, confidently, and certainly recklessly, announced that the 1938/39 season was going to be Carlisle United's. *"I have seen the standards set in this League and believe Carlisle can aspire to much more."*

One can only feel sorry for Taylor. He brought in a stronger, more physical style of player - John Howshall, a half back, and centre forward Sam Hunt, both from Accrington Stanley; Murphy, a tricky forward from Leith Athletic, and Eddie Ashton a speedy winger from Sheffield United.

After two games United were joint top of the League, then came the type of run every manager and supporter dreads to imagine. Defeats at Rotherham United 4-0, and Southport 7-1 left the side slipping perilously close to the bottom pack. A 3-1 win over table-topping Barnsley, appeared to be the platform for greater things. The team crashed out of the F.A. Cup at the first hurdle losing 4-1 at Walsall. It was hoped that fortunes would change for the good in the New Year, no such thing!

The first game of 1939 saw the team visit Hull City on the 14th of January. The result remains United's record defeat and Hull's record victory, with the score 11-1. Sam Hunt grabbing United's reply. The following Saturday, the 21st of January, United lost 7-1 to Crewe Alexandra in another away fixture. Other vicious results were inflicted upon the team that season, including 5-0 at Barrow, and 6-0 at Oldham Athletic. In all 111 goals were conceded of which 78 were conceded on opponents territory!

Although the 1939/40 season was abandoned through the commencement of hostilities, football in Carlisle did continue. It is reasonably well known that the club entered the Carlisle District League and played much of their football locally. However, in October 1939 they were invited to play in the North-West Regional League which consisted of twelve sides; Accrington Stanley, Bolton Wanderers, Burnley, Bury, Barrow, Blackpool, Blackburn Rovers, Rochdale, Oldham Athletic, Southport and Carlisle United. Thankfully the League was not highly competitive, with United losing 14 games, drawing 3 and winning just 4.

Once again some serious hammerings were endured; 8-0 at Burnley, 5-0 at Preston North End, 4-1 at Bolton Wanderers, 4-0 at Southport and 8-1 at Oldham Athletic. On the plus side a 6-1 win at Accrington Stanley was the highlight, although First Division Blackpool fell 3-1 at Brunton Park along with Southport 3-2, and Barrow 1-0.

United utilised guest players, with servicemen stationed in the area, (the majority at Hadrian's Camp) during the period. Perhaps the most successful player to guest during the 1939/40 season was 17 year-old Andy McLaren, then on the books of Preston North End. An inside forward, McLaren went on to win four full Scottish International caps as well as having a marvellous career at Burnley, Sheffield United, Barrow, Bradford P.A., Southport and Rochdale.

Another star was Sunderland's John Spuhler, a centre forward and an ex-England Schoolboy International who went on to play for Middlesbrough and Darlington. Other guests that season included John Bickerstaffe (Bury), William Blackshaw (Oldham), Lewis Bradford (Preston), John Finlay (Sunderland), Jimmy Moir (Accrington Stanley), goalkeeper Mattie Middleton (Plymouth A.), Cliff Mansley (Preston N.E.), Len Patrick (Southport), Pete Trainer (Brighton & H.A.), Eddie Smith (Crystal Palace), John Smith (Gateshead), Reg Weston (Plymouth A.) and John Wharton (Preston N.E.). These players did not exclude the likes of Jackie Laidler, Tommy Kerr, Sam Hunt and other United regulars who appeared whenever possible.

There were several occasions when servicemen footballers would be given specialised postings and light duties in order that they could turn out for League clubs. In some cases, certainly in United's, club officials made it their business to find out who was posted in Hadrian's Camp and made every effort to introduce Carlisle United to would be guest players. On more than one occasion special invites would be handed out to Senior Officers in charge of the camp, offering seats in the grandstand to watch a United match. The V.I.P. treatment was no bribe, it was simply a thankyou from the club to the services for allowing the footballers the opportunity to turn out in the blue of Carlisle United.

The average fee the club paid guest players varied. Pete Trainor, a Workington born centre half told the writer many years ago that those who guested were lucky to get 'twenty bob' (£1). *"Money was tight for everyone, let alone football clubs, although I made relatively few appearances for Carlisle there was a marvellous spirit amongst the chaps who did play.*

"Wartime football was a great leveller whether you played for Arsenal, Bolton Wanderers, Everton or Wolves, once guesting for a local side you were simply another serviceman playing football."

Pete Trainor went on to make some 37 League appearances for Brighton and Hove Albion immediately after the war, and scored 4 goals, sadly, he passed away in 1979.

After the 1939/40 season no further officially recorded fixtures were played, thus player records were never maintained by the Football League. Hugh Harkness took over first team affairs for the duration of the war, as he looked to his side featuring in Carlisle District League fixtures only.

Activities elsewhere took priority over the interests of Carlisle United, despite this Brunton Park still required tender loving care. The quality of the playing area was maintained, and the occasional spruce up was given to the terracing. It was here that the commitment and dedication required to keep a football club alive was shown by those who volunteered their services. During an extremely depressing period, those people maintained the belief that first class competitive football would one day return to the city.

It goes without saying that those involved at this time were what a club like Carlisle United is all about; nothing magnificent, nothing majestic, not even consistently successful, this is where the real football supporter is to be found. The war not only sorted the men out from the boys, it caused an absence of football, an absence which was eagerly brought to an end with the announcement that League football would re-recommence with the introduction of the 1946/47 seas

The war was over, but many inhibitions remained extant. Football clubs, like everyone else, had suffered greatly during the hostilities. Some grounds, thankfully Carlisle's was not among them, were bombed and sustained serious structural damage. However, typically British, it was decided that normality had to be restored almost immediately, and that included football. Although League football was not to restart for another year, the F.A. Cup competition was restored. That same season was a unique one in the history of the competition, for the first time ever - from the first round to the quarter-finals - all games would be played over two legs. Through petrol rationing, and other associated problems, the early rounds were on a localised basis thus producing economies of resources. Carlisle drew North Shields, then in the North-Eastern League, and nobody's fool.

As it stood the home leg turned into something of a rout, with goals coming from Adamson, Hamilton 2, Clarke and Cape, giving United a 5-1 victory. The return leg one week later provided a further three goals for United, courtesy of Hamilton, Douglas and Clarke as Carlisle eased through to the second round with an 8-3 aggregate score. Barrow were next, and at Holker Street, United lost 4-2 with - the now returned - Jackie Cape scoring both Carlisle goals. At Brunton Park, Barrow slammed a further four past their hosts, with the Carlisle replies coming from Adamson, Clarke and Dellow, and an exit from the competition 8-5 on aggregate.

Full competitive first class League football resumed in August 1946, with United's campaign commencing at Boundary Park, home of Oldham Athletic. It was of course an ideal opportunity for United to put behind them the perils and tortures of the miserable 1930's decade. To instil fresh confidence in the club and it's support a brand new player/manager was installed, his name, Ivan Arthur Broadis, a mere 23 year-old, without any Football League experience, and the youngest ever Football League club manager! Ivor (as he is more commonly known) Broadis was a rare talent, a mature footballer and leader and clearly a player with a bright future ahead of him. Having made several guest appearances for the club in wartime football and serving in the 1383 Transport Command of the RAF he had been stationed at Crosby on Eden, thus he knew the area reasonably well. The season started with an excellent 2-0 away victory over the Latics. This win was followed by a run of inconsistency which included a 6-0 defeat at Rochdale on the 28th of September.

The F.A. Cup did offer a little more success. In the first round Cheshire Counties League side, Runcorn, were beaten 4-0 at Brunton Park with goals from Jimmy Dougal, Lloyd Osborne Iceton (2) and Broadis. The second round saw another decidedly difficult encounter, at South Liverpool. Such ties create 'no win' circumstances, everyone expects the professionals to win at a canter, anything less is arguably seen as a poor result. Absolute nonsense, for all that matters is the winning.

United had to work hard and did manage to scrape through 3-2, Iceton again grabbing a brace with Jimmy Moir also netting.

The following round saw a distinct role reversal, for United became the underdogs as they travelled to Bramall Lane, home of First Division Sheffield United. It was a disappointing encounter with the South Yorkshire side running out comfortable 3-0 winners on a 'bog' of a pitch, with driving snow and a chilling breeze adding to Carlisle's woes. Sheffield's Alec Forbes and Ernie Jackson dominated the midfield, as United, without Broadis and by the end of 90 minutes down to nine men, struggled in the Yorkshire mudbath. The Sheffield side had been installed as favourites to win the Cup that year, although they were to eventually fall to Newcastle United in the sixth round. One final point of interest from this encounter, displayed the promise United showed, and this appeared in the programme for that same fixture where the editor declared, *"someday there may be second division football in Carlisle".*

In the League it was another South Yorkshire side who were dominating affairs, Doncaster Rovers, who were the eventual Third Division North Champions. They taught United a lesson in the art of goalscoring as they romped to a 9-2 victory at their Belle Vue stadium. Rovers actually scored a total of 123 goals that same season compared to Carlisle's still impressive 70!

For Carlisle it was a long hard learning process, although the club's support remained devoutly loyal throughout the entire campaign as the average overall home attendance rose to 10,263. The club finished in 16th position, suffering a 4-0 defeat at Wrexham in the final League fixture of the season. In August 1947, Broadis signed 25 year-old Bury centre forward, John (Jackie) Lindsay, who had previous League experi-

ence with Morton, Sheffield Wednesday and Bury. His partnership up front alongside Ivor Broadis was at times breathtaking, as both men would instinctively read each others game, and this resulted in 46 League goals between them.

John (Jack) Lindsay

Lindsay actually scored 27 goals in 38 games that season, one of which was scored in the F.A. Cup.

The next League season opened with a determined 4-2 home victory over Darlington, and as things continued in a fortuitous vein, talk was of United looking a real hot bet for promotion, although other teams were also playing well. Lincoln City were grinding out victories away from Sincil Bank, Rotherham United were another in-form team - in only the second game of the season they stuck five past Oldham Athletic at Boundary Park.

It was Rotherham who Carlisle encountered on 13 September 1947 at Millmoor. Any thoughts of a serious promotion challenge were laid to rest on that day as the Millers were victorious by a 7-2 margin. United's response to this was to beat Stockport 4-0, and Crewe 5-2 at Brunton Park in the following two fixtures. There was a glimmer of hope early into the New Year when a run of wins left the club three points behind the Division leaders, Lincoln City. The Imps actually beat United 5-2 at Brunton Park and 3-0 at Sincil Bank.

The second half of the season saw a Carlisle collapse with Lincoln eventually being crowned as Champions, finishing 17 points clear of United who finished in ninth position.

A new League attendance record at Brunton Park was set on Saturday 24th January 1948, when 17,339 turned out to see the visit of Hull City. The Tigers were one of the Division's top teams, but inconsistency had cost them dearly. The week prior to the Carlisle fixture they had beaten Rotherham 5-3, they had also been the first team that season to come away from Lincoln with two points. As such the game turned into something of a non-event, ending with a nil-all scoreline.

The average Brunton Park attendance for that season stood at 13,128, a rise of almost 3,000 on the previous campaign. In the F.A. Cup it was Barrow who continued to hold the upper hand as United fell 3-2 at Holker Street, the United goals coming from Broadis and Lindsay. Barrow also achieved the double over the team in the League programme.

In the summer of 1948 Broadis continued his search for more talent. Scouring the local scene he came across a stockily build centre forward by the name of Billy Gordon who was duly signed by the club. Also signed was half back Les Horton from Oldham Athletic; Bobby McCaig a forward hailing from Dumfries, centre half Reg Simpson from Preston, and wing half Dennis Stokoe from Chesterfield.

This squad had later additions of Scott McLaren, a goalkeeper from Chester, and Dick Yates, another striker, this time from Wrexham. The increase in transfer activity saw a rise in season ticket sales, with a fine total of 930 being sold prior to the season's start.

Two new men Simpson (above), and Stokoe (below)

To be fair, the League campaign was a miserable one, for despite the new signings there was very little for supporters to shout about. On the 4th of December, Rotherham came to Brunton Park and won 8-1, still Carlisle's record home defeat in League Football.

Ivor Broadis, now growing in ability, technique, and overall confidence was beginning to attract the attention of some of the country's bigger clubs, for Sunderland, Blackburn Rovers, Preston North End, and Manchester City, had shown an interest and all had made offers to him. In the end it was Sunderland who won the battle, taking him to Roker Park for a fee of £18,000.

Typical of all such moves, a section of the United support declared their annoyance at the move declaring their intention to never return to Brunton Park.

Whether they did or not we shall never know, however, there was no appreciable decrease in attendance figures after the move, albeit the average attendance by the end of the season dropped to 11,129. New Brighton dismissed the team from the F.A. Cup after inflicting a 1-0 defeat. This was the fourth time in succession that the club had been drawn away from home in the competition and the second consecutive season that their exit from the F.A. Cup came at the first hurdle.

It is curious to note that at the end of this campaign the club's support had been asked to name the greatest ever Carlisle United side up to that time. The 'winning' side was detailed in the final League programme of the season against Hull City on the 7th of May 1949. The most popular eleven up to that point was; McLaren, Bradley, Adey, Shankly, Taylor, Weightman, Cape, Broadis, McConnell, Ward and Watson. In March 1949 it was announced that Bill Shankly had taken over as the club's new manager. Although 35 years old, Shankly remained a more than capable footballer. Preston though were not about to let a footballer of such quality loose anywhere else.

Part of the agreement for Shankly to take over the Carlisle managerial position was that he could never play in first class competitive fixtures for the Cumbrians, thus he officially retired upon his return. If one footballer could be chosen to replace Broadis as manager then Bill Shankly was the one every United supporter would have requested. Despite the arrival of Shankly, season ticket sales did drop, this time to 866 which caused the manager to optimistically state, *"this time next year we will top one thousand in advance ticket sales."*

The new manager was busy in the transfer market during the summer recess. Wing half Tom Buchan came from Blackpool, as did Willy Buchanan a full back from Motherwell, John Billingham a centre forward from Burnley was signed in September, but the real jewel in the crown was a right winger signed from Manchester City, again in September 1949, his name was Billy Hogan. Following Hogan into Brunton Park in October 1949 was a full back by the name of Alex McIntosh from Barrow. Both signings were shrewd pieces of business as Shankly rebuilt his inherited team with several other signings; Bill Caton, a defender from Stoke City, local winger John Carruthers, forward George Dick (West Ham), and striker Phil Turner from Chester. Out went Yates, Tagg and Sweeney, whilst Hutton was given a free transfer.

Yates

Tagg

Hutton

The result was less than spectacular, although it has to be said that when they clicked the forwards proved that they could score goals galore; five at Hartlepool, four at Chester, plus a further five against the latter, at Brunton Park. George Dick finished up as the club's top scorer with 19 goals, while the defence conceded just 51 League goals, then a club record.

In the F.A. Cup the club were at last drawn at home. Lincoln City arrived with high hopes but were despatched by a solitary strike by ex-Stockport and West Ham inside forward George Dick. In the next round Swindon Town were the visitors and were also ejected from the competition, courtesy of two John Lindsay goals. Having progressed through to the third round, the club drew yet another home tie, this time against Second Division side Leeds United. The Yorkshire giants were far too strong for United and won the tie 5-2, the Carlisle goals coming from Lindsay and Dick.

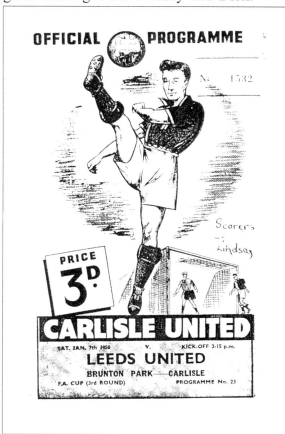

It was also at this fixture that a new Brunton Park record attendance was set at 22,822.

Despite the disappointment of finishing just ninth in the league, the average League attendance at Brunton Park remained virtually static at 11,800.

Always an achiever, Bill Shankly sought promotion and maintained his constant search for new, brighter, talent which would enhance his side. With Billy Hogan, a player who Shankly once described as, *"brilliant,"* operating on the right wing he elected to go for some extra pace on the left side, this brought in 22 year old left winger Alex McCue from Scottish club side Falkirk.

Scunthorpe United and Shrewsbury Town were new additions to the League, thus taking the seasons total of League games to be played up to 46. Shankly's ambitious statement that season tickets sales would increase was well judged as some 1,125 were sold, provoking Shankly to make a generous quote: *"that's a good start, they are good people here, they deserve a footballing side, that is what I will give them, I want us to top that figure again and again."* The season commenced with a 1-0 defeat at Southport, Shankly was incensed, *"Just what the hell this lot thought they were playing at I do not know, not one of them did as I asked, if that's to be the case then they will leave before I do!"* The problem was, the manager seldom said something he did not mean!

Team performances did improve with an incredible run of five months without a League defeat, taking in some 24 games, between the 30th of September 1950 when a 2-1 defeat was suffered at Mansfield Town, until March the 17th when Rochdale duly ended the run winning 4-1 at Spotland. Incredibly this run still never gave the club pole position in the League, which was won by Rotherham United. For much of the time United had held second place but eventually slipped down to third. The average home League attendance had been a satisfactory 11,696.

The big story of this season came in the F.A. Cup. Barrow were beaten 2-1 at Brunton Park in the first round with goals coming from McCue and Turner. In the next round the team travelled to Southport where another victory was recorded, this time 3-1 with Lindsay 2, and Turner easing United through. Before the game the team had stayed at the same Manchester based hotel as the mighty Arsenal, who were in Lancashire for a Division One encounter at Burnley.

Shankly spoke with the Gunners manager Tom Whittaker and wished him well, in return Whittaker bid United a good cup run. Shankly retorted, *"we want you in the next round!"* The draw for the third round was made and sure enough paired Carlisle with the F.A. Cup holders, the mighty Arsenal at Highbury Stadium. An estimated 5,000 United fans made their way to North London in the hope of one of the biggest Cup upsets ever, there was after all reasonable cause for optimism.

The Gunners had hit a run of terrible form prior to the Carlisle cup-tie, a 3-0 home defeat on Christmas Day to Stoke City, followed by a 1-0 defeat in the return encounter the following day. North London rivals Spurs had also notched a 1-0 home victory. Earlier in the month of December, Blackpool had drawn 4-4 at Highbury and Burnley had recorded a 1-0 victory there. The poor results came to an end with a 2-0 victory over struggling Sheffield Wednesday on the 30th of December. Comparitively, Carlisle had notched five League victories and a draw in the month of December, and the scene was set for an epic cup battle.

There is no doubt that Carlisle were fired up for the game, with Arsenal matched up against their unknown opposition players. Some 57,932 packed Highbury and saw the hitherto unheard of minnows from Carlisle fight tooth and nail for every ball.

The generally nonchalant England left full back, Lionel Smith had never before been run so ragged, as United right winger Billy Hogan put on the style and turned the International defender inside out. To his credit Smith remained calm and maintained fair play at all times. The late great Joe Mercer, then an Arsenal wing half, said of Hogan's performance: *"The man was electric, it was as though he danced on air, I could not get near the ball, I am certain it was at times permanently attached to his feet, I feel sorry for poor old Lionel, he will have nightmares about this one... we are not looking forward to the trip to Carlisle."*

Carlisle, fielding; MacLaren, Coupe, McIntosh, Kinloch, Twentyman, Waters, Hogan, Turner, McCue, Billingham, and Jackson. Missing was Jack Lindsay, out through a facial injury sustained a few weeks earlier (a game he greatly regretted missing). Chances for either team were few and far between, yet it was Carlisle who looked the most likely to break the deadlock. Phil Turner racing through the Gunners defence drove a shot from the edge of the area towards the Arsenal net, it looked a goal all the way.

Arsenal supporters gasped in horror, awaiting the rustling of the net as the ball caressed it. Turner, believing it to be a goal all the way, stopped in anticipation of a celebratory dance. It was like slow motion. The ball was going to the right of the Arsenal 'keeper who somehow twisted himself in mid-air, stuck out his hand, and managed to get sufficient touch on it to flick it over the crossbar.

Memories of the Arsenal Cup-ties

(Top left) Billy Hogan, arguably United's best ever winger - in action at Highbury. (Top right) The cameras come to Brunton Park - for the replay. (Above) Ticket madness hits Carlisle for the replay.

It was Arsenal who were pleased to hear the final whistle, not Carlisle, and the Highbury crowd afforded United a rare football standing ovation as they left the field.

The replay took place five days later in front of large Brunton Park crowd. It was a completely different game, and will be particularly recalled for two different reasons. Firstly Billy Hogan sustained an injury fairly early on in the game; that was that, United's flying winger and Arsenal's biggest concern had been dealt a severe blow.

The final score matters little, it was 4-1 to Arsenal, United's goal coming from Alex McCue, what was important to each and every United fan was the fact that the team had held Arsenal on their own territory, and had on the day looked the better team. Few nil-nil scorelines stick in the memory like this one, yet ask any Carlisle supporter old enough to remember, and they will recall it with a glint of satisfaction clearly evident in their eye. The scoreless draw at Arsenal ranks alongside any that United have achieved over the years.

The second reason the replay will be recalled for is rather less auspicious. Tickets for the sell-out 20,900 game went on sale at Carlisle Market Hall at 7p.m. on the Tuesday prior to the game. Men, women and children queued outside the market, along Fisher Street round the market and along towards the Castle, an estimated 25,000 people desperately trying to get their hands on tickets for the big game.

The ticket distribution was best described as 'poor' a first come first served basis, the end result being that several hundred so called 'stalwart' United supporters failed to get tickets. Once sales ceased and the Police secured the Market Hall doors, those remaining in the queue surged towards the

now secure building and held their own demonstration outside, blaming everyone from the Police, to the football club, to market stall holders, no one escaped criticism. The football club afterwards received dozens of letters appealing for tickets for a variety of reasons: *"My father has followed the blues since 1904.... I have not missed a game at Brunton Park since I was ten.... years old.... My father is badly disabled and unable to queue for tickets."* Request refused. *"I am prepared to pay double the price for tickets for the visit of Arsenal."* Request refused. *"I am a true blue and was away when tickets went on sale, can I now purchase two."* Request refused. The list and reasons were endless, everything from disability to theft.

Back at the Market Hall the Police were able to disperse the assembled throng without too much further trouble, but there was a great deal of discontent within the city.

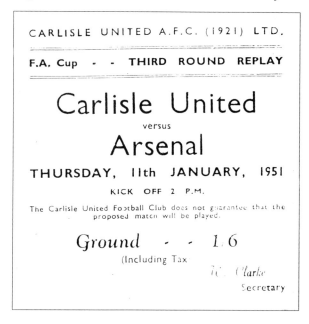

Returning to the football, the 0-0 draw at Highbury unfortunately - for Carlisle - provided evidence of Bill Shankly's ability as a team manager, for once again several clubs came knocking on United's door. Shankly the manager left United in July

1951, moving to Grimsby Town, where he believed there to be more potential at that time, although the Mariners had finished bottom of the Second Division and were actually relegated to the Third Division North. Some years later, a successful Shankly was to say about his departure, *"The problem I had at Carlisle was that the board of directors, all of whom were devoutly loyal to the club, could stand no more financial pressures, the buying of more experienced or better players never came into the equation, if I wanted someone, somebody better than I had, then I would have to sell three maybe four players to raise the cash, it was a never ending circle. Despite this, Carlisle United will always hold a very special place in my heart."*

That same month Fred Emery was instated as United's new manager. The ex-Bradford boss was quick to sign up a youngster from Nottingham Forest, centre forward Allan Ashman, who had made 13 League appearances for Forest and netted 3 goals. Joining him a few months later, was forward Jimmy Whitehouse who arrived from Rochdale.

Season ticket sales hit a record high with some 1,240 being sold before the season commenced. On the pitch, Allan Ashman grabbed a debut hat-trick at Rochdale, as United romped home 4-0. Later, another debutant - Jimmy Whitehouse - scored two goals on his debut, against Bradford City on the 27th of October 1951. Also making his debut that day was local inside forward Ron Thompson who was dropped into a defensive role. Both men made good starts in their respective United careers with Whitehouse's goals providing the team with a valuable 2-1 away win.

Meanwhile out went Turner, Scott, Maxfield, Lindsay, Hayton, and Coupe, to name but a few. The new manager had his own ideas and wanted to implement his style of play on the club as soon as possible without creating disharmony throughout the squad. Like his predecessor, Emery was his own man, *"If players at this club think that I am here for an easy ride then they are mistaken. I want Carlisle United in the Second Division and I will do my utmost to ensure that we get there, even if it means getting rid of some of them!"* The Ashman/Whitehouse partnership up front was an instant success, for together the pair scored 30 League goals between them. The away victory at Rochdale was just one of eight won on opposition soil.

The low point of the League season was Shanks' Grimsby Town doing the double over his ex-club, 4-1 at Blundell Park and 2-1 at Brunton Park. In the latter, the Mariners scored early, after what was - and it is believed still is - an official joint record 6 seconds.

Another ex-player who came back to haunt the club was centre forward John (Jackie) Lindsay who was released to Southport. Lindsay actually scored the Sandgrounders winner in the away League encounter in December 1951.

January 1952 saw the club's first ever football League visit to county neighbours Workington. The West Cumbrians had faced Liverpool at Anfield in the F.A. Cup the week before, when they lost the game but had apparently played out of their skins. It was never going to be an easy encounter, with local pride at stake. The Carlisle Police contacted their West Cumbrian counterparts and warned of an invasion of United supporters. No less than five full size football special trains had been booked, together with around 30 plus motor coaches from the city.

A crowd of 17,185 filled Borough Park as the pre-match atmosphere grew tense.

Thankfully the provocation was all verbal with no physical battles taking place, other than those between both teams on the field. Carlisle won the game 2-1 with both goals coming from Ashman.

In the F.A. Cup, Bradford City ended the run of reasonably good fortune in the competition, beating United 6-1 in the first round. It was a less than auspicious start for Fred Emery; a final League position of seventh and an average home attendance of 10,100.

Two friendly fixtures were inserted into the League season, *"arranged to keep the players mind on football and to maintain a reasonable degree of fitness,"* was the manager's reasons for these games. The first took place on 15th December 1951 against Northampton Town at the County Ground, Northampton. The result was a 1-1 draw with United's goal coming from Ashman before a crowd of 6,951. The second mid-season friendly was a home game against Queen of the South, which resulted in a 4-1 win, with goals from Ashman (2), Hogan and Duffett, before 5,903 spectators.

The following season saw a flurry of transfer activity as ex-Manchester United star, Ernie Bond came to Carlisle and won over the fans. Bond had made 20 League appearances for Manchester United the previous season scoring 4 goals, and was an incredible signing as several clubs had been after his services. Emery though had got in first, convincing Ernie that Carlisle was the place for him, and got his signature. Later, much later, Ernie let himself down, scoring a sensational own goal from the halfway line. It was a senseless back pass made in front of the Scratching Pen to the Carlisle keeper, which flew straight into the top corner of the net. As one supporter later put it, *"Ernie was never quite forgiven after that!"*

Jim Drury, a striker from Rochdale, also signed as did centre forward Archie Smith from Exeter City. Smith in particular was a proven goalscorer, with 44 goals in 115 League appearances for Exeter City. There was another nine scored in the F.A. Cup, including a breathtaking four against Barnet in December 1948.

Also to arrive in October of that year was an outside right with such silky skills as to make him one of the Brunton Park favourites. Bobby Harrison was to score on his United debut in a 1-1 home draw with Chester.

Season ticket sales dropped to just 801, although this still was a great deal more than the majority of clubs in United's League.

The opening fixture was at Accrington Stanley's Peel Park. This ended in a miserable 1-0 defeat, and was quickly followed by a further defeat away from home, this time at Gateshead 2-0.

In November, Scunthorpe and Lindsey United were the club's F.A. Cup opponents, where a solitary strike by Whitfield was enough to see Scunthorpe through in what was a thoroughly forgettable game. It was Scunthorpe who faced United at Brunton Park on Christmas Day 1952, seeking revenge for the miserable F.A. Cup defeat, Carlisle ran riot demolishing their opponents and equalling the club's record League victory of 8-0. In an incredible display, Jimmy Whitehouse bagged five of the goals, with Ashman (2), and Bobby Harrison also netting. The scoring feat achieved by Whitehouse was almost equalled 16 days later when United went on the rampage against Rochdale, winning 5-0, with Whitehouse netting four and actually hitting the woodwork twice!

Jimmy was an incredible footballer, a true goalscorer, he went on to score 100 goals for the club, second only to the legendary Jimmy McConnell, and with just 26 goals fewer.

The month of March 1953 saw a virtual disaster strike the club when after a friendly match with East Fife, a discarded cigarette butt, kept alight by a continuous breeze, burned the 'wooden rabbit hutch' stand to the ground. In this blaze all the club's records were destroyed as too were the playing strips, boots, etc. Incredibly the fire, although creating a serious inconvenience at the time, was to become a stepping stone for greater achievements.

A new more modern stand was erected in it's place, and is still in position to this very day. At the time it was a devastating accident, then Chairman, John Corrieri recalled: *"I believe that it was something from which the club would never recover, the old stand was rather dilapidated but it had character, everyone who visited Brunton Park referred to it as the 'Hencoop' after Billy Shankly had described it as such. Everyone at the club was thrilled by the way the local public and other football clubs supported us after the fire. Our old friends from Newcastle United bent over backwards to supply everything from playing strips to footballs, from that day on, Carlisle United never really looked back."*

By May 1953 United had finished in ninth position in the League with an average attendance of 8,103.

The free-scoring Jimmy Whitehouse

Although the highlight of the season was the thrashing of Scunthorpe United, Bradford City inflicted a serious 7-2 hammering upon the team in April. Striker, Jimmy Whitehouse topped the scoring charts with 29 goals followed by Allan Ashman with 22.

Elsewhere rumours were rife in the county as Workington, in only their second season in the football League, were forced to apply for re-election in consecutive seasons. At the pre-vote in Manchester (the Division Three North's meeting), Workington finished with just 11 votes. The press and football supporters from all over Cumberland discussed the fact that Reds' neighbours Carlisle United, had and would vote, against Workington remaining in the League. Contact was made between the two clubs, the contents of the meeting can only be of a speculative nature, but clearly the meeting was to clear the air. Eventually Workington were successfully re-elected with 18 votes.

Fred Emery stuck with the majority of his first team squad for the following season, although there were some interesting newcomers, such as Willie McHale, an inside forward who hailed from East Fife, and whose sole appearance for the club came in a 1-1 draw at Barrow in September.

Outside right Eddie Bloomfield signed from the local game made just 3 appearances all season. Quick and lively the winger's final ball always seemed to lack that quality which would have made him a real star. Herbert Rawes, another speedy winger, also arrived from local football and again made few appearances during the season - just five - as Emery tried desperately to find an orthodox right winger who could supply Messrs. Ashman and Whitehouse with the service they deserved.

Perhaps, though, two of the most influential players to break into the first team had to be centre half, Bobby Doran, and full back Billy Graham. Although both played relatively few games, these were sufficient for the manager and the clubs support to see, to make them realise that both youngsters had promising futures ahead of them. Billy Graham actually scored on his League debut on the 27th of February 1954 in an away fixture at Darlington. Season ticket sales dropped to just 409, mainly due to a price increase forced on the club by the higher wage bill and club running costs.

The rise in admission prices caused one supporter to state: *"The football clubs are pricing the average working man out of football, soon it will be a sport dominated by money!"*. Goodness only knows what the writer would make of professional football clubs today!

The League season opened with an incredible 7-0 home victory over Rochdale, and other clubs met a similar fate at Brunton Park; Mansfield Town 5-0, Scunthorpe United 5-1, Halifax Town 5-0, and Crewe Alexandra 5-0. Although Chesterfield inflicted a 5-0 defeat away from home and Barnsley won 4-2 at Brunton Park. Perhaps one of the greatest feats to occur during the League season took place on the 16th of January 1954, when Carlisle and ex-Leicester City full back Alex Scott collected a ball deep in his own half in a League game against Mansfield Town at Field Mill. Pushing the ball forward several times he made his way to around the half way line.

With a gusting wind in his favour he unleashed a ferocious left foot shot which flew like an exocet missile directly into the top corner of the Mansfield goal, leaving the helpless Town 'keeper flapping at thin air. When the ball hit the net there was an eerie silence around the terraces as most of the 6,386 crowd in attendance were stunned by the effort.

In the F.A. Cup there was again an away draw and another Cup defeat, 1-0 at Southport, a goal by Hitchen seeing the Sandgrounders through. Fred Emery stood defiant, he wanted to build a team strong, and solid, in all departments, and while some 83 goals were scored (the second highest in the Division) 71 were conceded. It was again the partnership of Ashman and Whitehouse who scored over half the goals, Ashman bagging 30 and Whitehouse 22.

A League position of thirteenth was attained and the inconsistency of the results assured that support dwindled as the average home attendance dropped to 6,955. Once again all the early season promise had disappeared and there was the old murmurings of discontent on the Brunton Park terraces. Fred Emery was equal to it, for he made every effort to personally answer his critics, and this was carried out in a dignified and mature manner which earned him a great deal of respect from the majority of United supporters. The manager was a great believer in sampling different styles and standards of football in 'friendly fixtures'. During the 1953-54 season the team featured in no less than 6 such games, albeit one of these was Billy Hogan's benefit match.

For the record, United beat Airdrie at Brunton Park on the 13th of October 1953, by 6-2 with goals from Whitehouse 2, Jackson 2, Harrison, and Ashman, in front of a crowd of 5,888. Queen of the South were also beaten 3-1 in front of 11,999 spectators; Rawes 2, Jackson being the scorers on the 27th of October 1953. Raith Rovers arrived in the city on the 2nd of November 1953 and trounced United 4-1 before 7,621 spectators, Atkinson netting United's reply.

The team travelled to Bradford City on the 12th of December 1953, and again lost 4-1, this time in front of 3,002 spectators, with Harrison scoring for United. East Fife scored four at Brunton Park on the 16th of February 1954 before a crowd of 3,599, when Atkinson pulled one back for Carlisle. Finally, on the 16th of March 1954, came the Billy Hogan benefit game against Liverpool, when an estimated crowd of 6,500 turned out to see a 3-3 draw. United's team was: McLaren, McIntosh, Scott, Thomspon, Doran, Johnston, Graham, White, Ashman, Atkinson, Bond; United's goals came from White 2, and Ashman.

In the summer Gilbert Mitten, a goalkeeper, was signed from Preston North End, and joining him from Cowdenbeath was flying outside left Tom Moran. Fred Emery optimistically claimed, *"I have strengthened the squad in areas where I feel we require greater cover. Mr. Mitten and Mr. Moran are excellent signings for this club... promotion is well within our reach."*

Of course football managers in the game today never make such rash statements as they generally end up regretting them. Fred Emery certainly did, as United struggled to reach any form whatsoever, when goals were leaked so freely and so often that one wonders if two nets were necessary behind the Carlisle goal as the first one must nearly have been worn out. Despite this, there was some optimism amongst the United support during the summer, for season ticket sales did increase, this time to 686, still well above the average for the Division, and nobody who saw the team play that season could say that they never received value for money!

John (Jackie) Lindsay returned to the club in January 1955 after his spell with Southport, in the hope that he would find a rich scoring vein. He was to make 13 more appearances for United, scoring 2 goals, before retiring from the English professional game.

At Brunton Park, York City scored 5, Workington 4, and Barnsley 4, albeit United did score 7 for the second time in successive seasons against Rochdale - duly assisted by three own goals from Messrs Murphy, Underwood and Boyle. Oldham Athletic were defeated 5-2, Crewe Alexandra and Barrow went down 4-0, whilst on their travels the club's worst defeat came at Tranmere Rovers, who were themselves struggling near the foot of the table. The 6-1 reverse came in April and virtually ensured that United would be fighting off a bottom four League placing. Thankfully victories over Oldham and Bradford City assisted the team's cause, as re-election was staved off by virtue of a superior goal average compared to Bradford City, who finished with the same number of points (36) as United.

One point of conjecture occurred on January 15th 1955 in the home fixture with Gateshead. Some 4,321 supporters had braved fierce winter storms, and many of those present claimed that the game should never have kicked off. However, in virtual blizzard conditions both teams played out what can only be described as a farce. Eventually with the score standing at 0-0 after 29 minutes, and snow and hail falling, the referee was forced by the continuous booing of the crowd and the apparent lack of interest of the players to take action. He consulted his other match officials, then the two managers, before deciding that enough was enough and abandoning the game. The decision was greeted with a rousing cheer and great applause from the crowd as well as the players. One part of the ground was heard to sing *"For he's a jolly good fellow,"*, presumably directed towards the referee.

An average home attendance during the season of 5,619 was registered, the 7th lowest in the entire football League. Interestingly the team with worse attendance averages than United's were all members of the Third Division North; Chester, Tranmere, Gateshead, Crewe, Barrow and Southport. The F.A. Cup brought some respite, but only just, as a 1-0 away victory at Stockport County, courtesy of an Ernie Bond goal, saw the club paired with Watford in the second round. Goals from Ashman and Whitehouse earned United the right to a replay in Hertfordshire. On the day the team flattered to deceive and were well beaten by the disciplined Hornets by four goals to one, United's reply coming from Ashman.

On the friendly front some history was made at Brunton Park during one of the four matches United featured in. The first mid-season game was at home to Lincoln City on 26th October 1954, when United played out a 4-2 victory in front of 3,429 spectators who saw goals from Ashman, Moran, Atkinson and a Kinloch penalty. It was on the 14th of February 1955 when club history was made at Carlisle United, with the visit of Columbia Wien, United's very first overseas visitors. A crowd of 4,189 turned out in typical winter conditions to witness a Carlisle win by three goals to two, with Whitehouse, Ashman and Moran doing the damage. A week later on the 21st of February 1955, Bury, then a Second Division side, visited Brunton Park and strolled out comfortable 3-0 winners in front of 3,225 spectators. Raith Rovers were the final 'friendly' visitors on the 14th of March 1955, as 2,759 saw Carlisle cruise to a 5-2 victory courtesy of strikes by Whitehouse 2, Ashman, Atkinson and yet again a Tommy Kinloch penalty.

JIM MacLAREN BENEFIT MATCH

CARLISLE UNITED

v

GEOFF

TWENTYMAN'S XI.

AT BRUNTON PARK
THURSDAY, 5th MAY, 1955
KICK-OFF 7 p.m.

J. S. MacLAREN — CARLISLE UNITED 1948-1955

Souvenir Programme · Price 3d.

The very last game of the season, a well deserved Testimonial - MacLaren amassed 261 appearances for the United.

The summer of 1955 offered little in the way of optimism for the hardened United supporter, which was reflected in the sale of just 590 season tickets. Although there was one bright spot with the signing of ex-player/manager Ivor Broadis from Newcastle United. The centre forward arrived as player/coach as Emery hoped that his experience and influence would rub off on the team. Ex-Chelsea and Chesterfield keeper John Burn was signed, as was experienced full back Vince Kenny from Sheffield Wednesday.

The season started on a reasonably bright note, five games without defeat, although three of the five were draws. There was some good home results as the team netted four or more goals at Brunton Park on six occasions. There was also a fine 5-3 away victory at Darlington, a club who were to enter the record books by virtue of a particular F.A. Cup encounter with United.

These results, although excellent in their own right, were something of a novelty as the team suffered some awful defeats. County neighbours Workington completed a League double over the team, 4-2 at Carlisle and 4-0 at Borough Park Workington. Stockport County hit the team for eight in April as a bottom four League position was forced upon the club.

An incredible 95 goals were conceded, compared to champions Grimsby Town who conceded just 29. The clubs leading scorers were Ashman and local lad Ian Atkinson, both with 17 each.

Incredibly the average home League attendance at Brunton Park rose to 6,894, a full thousand up on the previous season. It is difficult to appreciate why this should be the case, although it was generally accepted that there was always the opportunity to see plenty of goals in a match featuring Carlisle United!

In the F.A. Cup Darlington were the first round opponents, after 0-0 draw at Feethams, Darlington visited Brunton Park on the night of 22nd November 1955. This game was played under floodlights, the first ever F.A. Cup-tie between two League teams to be played under lights, before a crowd of 19,035, and was a repeat scoreline of 0-0 after extra time. This result necessitated a second replay. The third game was played at Newcastle United's St. James' Park ,on the 28th of November, and ended in a 3-1 defeat, with United's goal coming from Kinloch, in front of 34,256 spectators.

Two friendly matches were played mid-season, both at Brunton Park. Second Division side Lincoln City came on the 4th of October, and ended 2-1 to United with Whitehouse and Broadis scoring for Carlisle. Then on the 8th of November, Doncaster Rovers - also of the Second Division - were the visitors and drew 2-2 before a crowd of 10,117, again Messrs Whitehouse and Broadis scored for Carlisle.

The seasons ended with the announcement that Jimmy Whitehouse, such a prolific scorer for the club, was to retire. Fred Emery had already identified his replacement in Derby County striker Alf Ackerman, who eventually joined United the following November. Also signed was ex-Manchester United and Blackburn Rovers outside right, Frank Mooney. The 1956/57 season saw some improvement in United's League standing when a final position of 15th was attained.

The best performance of the season was prabably the 6-1 drumming of Mansfield Town in December who had beaten United 5-1 in only the second week of the season; four goals were scored away from home at Wrexham yet the team still lost 6-4! Alf Ackerman finished as top scorer with 20 goals, followed by Ivor Broadis with 16, and Frank Mooney with 10.

Another Friendly was played in February.

The average League attendance at Brunton Park again rose, this time to 7,430, but season ticket sales had again dropped, with only 572 having been sold in the summer recess.

It was the F.A. Cup competition next season which offered the most excitement as United again drew a big gun. In the first round Billingham Synthonia disappeared 6-1 at Brunton Park, with centre forward, John Garvie grabbing a hat-trick, plus Alf Ackerman (2), and Ivor Broadis netting. Next came Darlington, again at Brunton Park, when two Ackerman strikes sent the Quakers packing and First Division Birmingham City were the third round opponents.

The tie aroused great enthusiasm in the city of Carlisle as scarves and hats were knitted and created to show off the team's colours. It was, as such, the battle of the blues.

Birmingham, a reliably solid top Division outfit, and the previous season's Cup finalists, came to town.

It was the 5th of January, 1957, and an officially recorded crowd of 27,164 crammed, really crammed, into Brunton Park. Interestingly since then, this gate has always been recorded as United's record attendance - 27,500 - although clearly this was not the case. Attendance figures supplied by the media were, until recently, highly irregular and should rarely be accepted as being accurate. It seems like so much in football history, that one individual makes a claim which becomes an accepted fact for many years, until someone else discovers something to the contrary.

What actually happened on this occasion is that an enthusiastic journalist reported that the ground was filled to capacity, the football club was approached for the capacity figure which was given as 27,500, thus this figure is printed and the incorrect official attendance becomes an acknowledged fact. Bearing this in mind, the stadium was far from the complete article, with temporary stands being the order of the day. Quite simply, the Birmingham City fixture did create a then ground record for Carlisle United, but it is not the official record attendance. There are somewhat spurious claims that some three hundred plus unofficial spectators got into the ground without a ticket, after they had been locked out of the ground. The authorities wishing to keep everyone happy forced then in! Such tales are of course associated with many such games, although possible, it does bring into question the reasoning behind it being all ticket!

Carlisle's profit from the Brunton Park cup-tie stood at £421.9s.6d., this was after the F.A. and other agencies had taken their share of the takings, and this is the sum made by the club via the turnstiles.

65

Ackerman scores one of his three, in the Birmingham Cup-tie

A temporary stand was erected on the Warwick Road end of the ground, and there were queues up and down Warwick Road as rosette wearing United supporters clamoured to get inside the stadium. Some cup-ties are called classics before they even start, but this game really was a hot-blooded affair. Birmingham looked a classy outfit and swept into a 3-1 lead as Carlisle battled away. This was the day Alf Ackerman scored his way into United folklore.

It was his skills and scoring ability, notching a hat-trick, which provided United with a well earned draw and a money spinning replay at St. Andrews. The noise emanating from Brunton Park was incredible, and the roar from United's late equalising goal was actually heard in London Road and Botchergate. The replay at St. Andrews four days later was a different affair as Birmingham ran out 4-0 winners, but Carlisle could at least say that they pushed them to the limits.

Birmingham eventually lost in the semi-finals of the competition, 2-0 to Manchester United.

United played Workington on the 7th of May 1957 in a County Cup match, but it was little more than a friendly end of season game, when just 3,479 turned out to see Workington trounce United 6-3 at Borough Park, Workington. The Carlisle scorers were Ackerman, Ashman and a Vince Kenny penalty. To be fair both clubs were tired after a long season, with little at stake but local pride it was very much an anti-climax.

The 1957/58 season was a comparatively barren one, although season ticket sales increased to 648 as it was announced that instead of regionalised football there was to be a Third and Fourth Division at the beginning of the 1958/59 season. All teams finishing in the top half of the respective regionalised third divisions (North and

South), would take part in a new Third Division, those finishing in the bottom half would form the new Fourth.

United finished in 16th position with 44 points, just two points adrift of the top half and administrational promotion, instead they now faced administrational relegation. Average attendances had again increased, this time to a splendid 8,525. Alf Ackerman continued to find the net, scoring 35 goals and finishing as the Division's leading goalscorer. Meanwhile Ron Tulloch, signed from Southend United in July 1957 and finished the season with 14 goals. A 5-2 home victory over Darlington in March 1958 offered the most frantic moments of the season, when with 39 minutes of play gone the score stood at 1-1, six minutes later (at half time), Carlisle left the field for their slices of orange, leading 5-1.

The low point came during the Boxing Day League encounter at Workington. George Thompson in the United goal, a sensible and effective goalkeeper, was heavily charged by Workington's overweight striker Ted Purdon (Purdon was labelled a 'flop' by Workington officials), who went in with his feet at neck height. It was a disgusting challenge, enough to test the anger of any footballer. George Thompson was caught by Purdon but not to any serious effect, and he vented his anger at the Reds' forward, who retaliated as the pair pushed and shoved each other. The referee, in an attempt to quell the volatile atmosphere which prevailed on and off the terraces, sent both players off. United lost the fixture 2-1. Curiously in the following fixture at Borough Park, Workington, the Rochdale goalkeeper was forced to leave the field!

In the F.A. Cup, Rhyl were beaten 5-1 at Carlisle, with goals from Bond (2), Broadis (2), and an Ackerman penalty. Accrington Stanley knocked the club out in the next round after a 1-1 draw a Brunton Park which meant a replay, and an eventual 3-2

defeat for the Cumbrians. The 1957/58 season was also the last one, as a player, for another great United stalwart, Paddy Waters. Allan Ashman also retired, to become a chicken farmer, working for one of Carlisle United's directors, Mr. Monkhouse.

Fred Emery parted company with the club in April 1958 having achieved very little, but he was, beneath his almost morose exterior, a real character. In his place came Andy Beattie, an ex-Scottish International full back. Beattie was a positive man in everything he did, he wanted promotion at Carlisle and made no secret of the fact.

United fans had of course heard it all before, but Beattie did manage to enthuse a few more into purchasing season tickets as some 685 were bought pre-season. A good League position of tenth was attained in Beattie's first and only full season in charge. A 6-1 home defeat by Coventry City apart, the teams home form improved. Away from home there was still the odd hiccup, 5-0 at Walsall, 4-1 at Shrewsbury Town and Gateshead, and a shocking 4-0 defeat at Aldershot who finished third from bottom of the League.

A League game at Northampton Town's County Ground was abandoned after 82 minutes, with United leading 2-0 through goals from McKenna and Mooney. When the fixture was re-played in April, the result was a 0-0 draw, and hence point dropped. The average Brunton Park attendance dropped to 7,172, as many fans became disillusioned with the club's relegation to the new fourth, gloomily proclaiming it to be, 'the end of the line'! The club's leading scorer was ex-Glasgow Celtic full back, Hugh Fletcher, who had been signed by Fred Emery in the summer of 1956. Beattie reverted Fletcher to a forward, a move which worked well, especially as Alf Ackerman had been sold to Millwall in January, 1959.

Mooney shoots during the September 1959 Brunton Park encounter with Watford.

In the F.A. Cup, Heanor Town were blitzed out of the competition 5-1, a scoreline which still stands as a club record for an away win in the competition. Then came Chesterfield, and after a dismal 0-0 draw at Carlisle, Chesterfield's Frear scored the only goal of the game at Saltergate to put the Spireites through. One highlight of the season came with silverware being won as United achieved a 4-0 home victory over near neighbours, Workington in the Cumberland Cup; Carlisle's goals came from Troops (penalty), Mooney, Ackerman and Tulloch.

New faces were drafted in during the summer break, including Austin McGill a forward from Queen of the South, and left winger Matt Murray from Barrow, as Beattie did his utmost to build a promotion winning squad. There was an air of apathy around the place as supporters were reluctant to pay out for season tickets, the sales of which dropped to 473, but still the Brunton Park faithful refused to stop believing. If anything it was an even greater disappointment than the previous season, as at the midway point of the campaign United were just tucked in nicely among the top three.

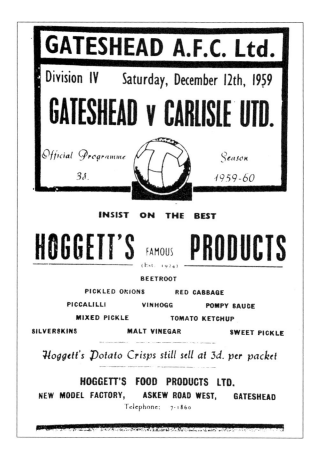

United's last visit to Redheugh Park
The Tynesiders were voted out of
the League a few months later.

With a spare Saturday free in December 1959, Beattie invited Barnsley to Brunton Park for a friendly fixture, and it was a disaster. Both clubs fought tooth and nail, tackles were going in hard, seemingly pointless for such a needless encounter. The result was a 3-2 victory for the Tykes, Carlisle goals coming from Brayton and Ticknell. From that point, Carlisle lost five consecutive fixtures! Holiday period games can be influential in sorting the men out from the boys, and Workington (again) achieved a League double, with 1-0 victories on both occasions.

With the exception of a win at home to Darlington (1-0), on 31st January 1960, played before a paltry attendance of just 1,855, United did not win another game until 18th April, when Hartlepool were beaten 2-1. Indeed just three games were won in the second half of the season!

Carlisle born striker, Barry Brayton was signed in January 1960 in the hope that he could inject some goal power to the forward line. He managed just one goal in eighteen games, through no fault of his own, as even the great Sir Stanley Matthews would have struggled to score in a side which managed just 51 goals all season.

In March 1960, with the club well and truly secured in the lower reaches of the Fourth Division, Andy Beattie walked out on Carlisle United in favour of a position with Nottingham Forest. The average League attendance figure had again dropped, this time to 5,308. Austin McGill finished the season as top scorer with 12 goals, followed by ex-Bristol City forward, George Walker with 11. Even worse, county rivals Workington achieved the League double over the team for the third time since the West Cumbrian outfit had gained League membership in 1951.

In the F.A.Cup, it was another first round exit, Rochdale being the hosts at Spotland, United had several chances to wrap up the game but having to settle for a 2-2 draw, with United goals from McGill and Walker, which led to a Brunton Park replay. At Carlisle, before the season's biggest and only home attendance to get into the five figure mark (13,300), Rochdale proved tougher opposition and outfought and outbattled United in every department, eventually winning through 3-1. Carlisle's consolation effort coming from ex-Bradford Park Avenue right winger, Joe Devlin.

Top scorer McGill

Chapter 4
THE SWINGING SIXTIES

Andy Beattie was replaced as team manager by Ivor Powell in May 1960, in the hope that some improvement could be found in the team's fortunes. Little happened to instill confidence in the Brunton Park faithful, just 601 season tickets were sold. Pre-season, Powell insisted that there was much to offer at Brunton Park, *"I have brought in a number of players, not all of them will be immediately on show, but my intention is to create some competition for places, anyone who doesn't pull their weight will be replaced."*

Powell's honesty was well appreciated, and when the team gained a point from a scoreless draw at Exeter on the opening day of the season, things looked reasonably promising. There followed a serious drop in form, with a 4-1 home defeat by Stockport, which was followed by the visit of the League's new boys, Peterborough United. So bad was the United performance against Stockport that a decrease of almost one thousand attended for the visit of Posh, when 8,334 saw a 3-3 draw, compared to the 9,261 who saw the Stockport debacle.

The return League fixture at Stockport on Monday August 29th was played in a thunder and lightning storm. The loud rumbles and electrifying lightning strikes silhouetted the players on the pitch against the eerie terracing of Edgeley Park. During the second half in particular, the rain fell like stair rods and the increasing likelihood of the game being abandoned looked certain. But the referee refused to stop play, and in that second half County bagged two goals to

see off the Carlisle challenge. It was a dreadful start to the campaign, nine games without a win saw the team at the foot of the League table. There were cries from the terraces for Powell's resignation, and things looked bad. By the time United won their first game, on September 19th, home attendances had fallen by almost fifty per cent. The 3-1 victory at Mansfield was the first of four consecutive wins, which was immediately followed by four defeats!

The introduction of the Football League Cup competition meant another distraction from the League programme. United were drawn away to Stockport County and duly lost 1-0. For the record, the United team for their inaugural game in the competition was: Thompson G, McBain, Terris, Bradley, Doran, McMillan, Brayton, Cavanagh, Smith, Stewart, Morgan. In the F.A. Cup, Chester were beaten 1-0 by a Bevan goal, before Port Vale inflicted a cup exit at Vale Park, 2-1, with Carlisle's goal coming from Walker.

At the end of the season, 19th position had been attained with an average crowd of 4,446 at Brunton Park. A poor season which left the Carlisle manager in a defiant mood. *"Despite a poor season we have some good players here, players who can win prizes for this club."*

How right he was, for the 1961/62 season provided the Carlisle support with a great deal of excitement, and the club's first ever promotion.

A total of only 461 season tickets were sold in anticipation of another struggle. Accrington Stanley were forced to resign from the League in March 1962 with debts of £62,000 thus expunging all records in relation to League results. For the record, Carlisle had actually lost 1-0 at Peel Park, but defeated them 2-0 at Brunton Park, with goals from Stark and Walker.

In the League Cup, two legs were introduced. After a 1-1 draw at home, the team went out 3-0 at Huddersfield in September. The F.A. Cup offered slightly more success, as wins at Darlington (4-0), then Barnsley (2-1) paired the side with Wolverhampton Wanderers in the third round. There was no Cup upset at Molineux as Wolves ran out 3-1 winners before 26,800 spectators. The Cumberland Cup was again won, Workington being thrashed 3-0 at Brunton Park on October 24th, Brayton 2, Taylor, being the Carlisle scorers.

So back to the League, where silly defeats had cost the club dearly as they surged up the Fourth Division table, on the verge of a top four place. Defeats at Exeter (4-0), plus at home and away to Bradford City (4-2 & 3-2 respectively), left a mountain to climb with two games remaining. Two victories would see the fourth promotion place. The first win was achieved at Doncaster Rovers, when Walker grabbed a brace to ease United's worries, in a 2-1 win.

Thus came the finale, a home game with Chester, and 12,660 saw Brayton and Walker score to give Carlisle a 2-0 victory and clinch promotion. The average home League attendance was 6,763, which had been boosted by the big gate on the final day of the season. To be fair, although promotion had been achieved and much celebrating did occur in the city streets, the team had finished a poor fourth. Fortunate to squeeze in, there was no doubting that the following season was going to be a long difficult one, some supporters still believing that the team won promotion two seasons too early.

During the summer, goalkeeper Joe Dean was signed as too was defender Hughie Neil. Season ticket sales increased to 543 as the club looked to get off to a flying start with two home games to kick the season off. In fact, two heavy home defeats dictated that the more pessimistic fans' opinions were accurate. The team struggled to hit any sort of consistent form, and for much of the season they were among the strugglers, before eventually finishing in 23rd position, and relegated. A 1-1 home draw with Reading all but ending the survival hopes. One of the high points of the season was the arrival of centre forward Hughie McIlmoyle whose goalscoring exploits were to become almost legendary at Brunton Park.

Hugh McIlmoyle

In the League Cup, Tranmere were beaten 3-2, and Torquay 2-1, before Norwich City managed a 1-1 draw at Carlisle. In the replay the Canaries smashed five past a lethargic United defence, all without reply.

The F.A. Cup competition was even more miserable, having edged their way past Hartlepool 2-1, plus Blyth Spartans 2-0, United were given a relatively easy home tie with non-League Gravesend and Northfleet. It was dreadful, the weather was bad, the play was poor, and Gravesend won the game 1-0. The result of which was the sacking of Ivor Powell! To be fair to Powell, prior to the Gravesend result, the club had not played a solitary game for one calender month, for the big freeze had decimated the football programme. Thus when the game took place some lethargy and complacency had set in, albeit there can be no excuse for the performance on the day - and some supporters still believe it to be the worst ever performance by a Carlisle United side.

Powell had been a keep fit fanatic, on one occasion he found several players arriving for training in cars. This incensed him, he would expect them to run to the ground. At the end of that day's session he gathered the players around him and told them that they were to run to the ground, for those who lived too far outside Carlisle, they could, *"catch the public conveniences to the town hall, then run to the ground."* Everyone but Powell knew what he had said, yet not one player dared laugh!

In February Allan Ashman was given the manager's job on a temporary basis until the end of the season. A position which was to the credit of the club's directors and in particular to Jim Monkhouse, his employer at the Penrith chicken farm. It was a major gamble by the United director who had monitored Ashmans skills at Penrith. The new manager had lifted team spirits, and

with the arrival of McIlmoyle some pride was restored when bottom position was avoided.

The new manager brought in new players, in particular Alan Ross and Jack Lornie, both of whom arrived from Luton Town in exchange for Allan McBain. Ross was a goalkeeper who had never played in a first team fixture for Luton. As a 17 year-old, he was selected to make his first team debut when regular 'keeper, Roy Baynham failed to arrive. The sides were lined up in the tunnel ready to enter the field. Suddenly a linesman took ill, and the kick off was delayed. During this delay, Roy Baynham arrived at the ground and took his place in the first team, with Alan Ross relegated to watching as a spectator.

What a season. Just 511 season tickets were sold, for there was many who felt that there was little to offer at Brunton Park, and this looked likely with a third game 6-1 defeat at Tranmere. That result was in fact the turning point of the entire season. Hartlepool suffered the wrath of Carlisle, with first a 6-0 Cumbrians victory at the Victoria Ground, followed two weeks later by a 7-1 home win, in which McIlmoyle plundered four goals.

The goals continued to pour in all season, 113 of them, with 39 going to prolific McIlmoyle. Unfortunately, 58 were conceded and as the season closed, Carlisle lost the Championship to Gillingham on goal average which at that time was calculated on a different mathematical equation! Ridiculously, Gillingham had scored just 59 goals and conceded just 30, but won the title. In reality, it mattered little, Carlisle were still promoted, although to go up as Champions would have been even nicer.

In the League Cup, Crewe were beaten 3-2, before Manchester City sent the club packing 2-0 at Maine Road. The F.A. Cup offered the clubs best run up to that point. York City were thrashed 5-2 at Bootham Crescent, then followed Gateshead 4-3, Queens Park Rangers 2-0, and the conquerors of Newcastle United, Bedford Town, 3-0. The fifth round saw a tough battle at Preston North End, where trailing 1-0, Carlisle tore into the North End defence. Sammy Taylor, a real live wire, weaved through three tackles before hitting a sweet shot which looked a goal all the way. Unfortunately for Carlisle, the ball struck a post, rebounded along the goal line, and struck the other post before being hoofed clear by an anxious Preston defender. The Cup run came to an end that day. However, Preston could count themselves fortunate to progress through to the next stage. It was a satisfying season, with an average home attendance of 8,346 bringing in extra revenue to strengthen the team.

The following season proved to be an even better one for the club, although there were some groans from supporters when £30,000 was received for the transfer of Hughie McIlmoyle to Wolves in October. However, a short time later the striker was replaced by Willie Carlin who was signed from Halifax Town for a fee of £10,000.

Carlin was affectionately termed by his new coleagues as 'Wee Willie' or the 'Mighty Midget'. An exciting talent, Carlin was a different style of player to McIlmoyle, quick and skilful he was more of a provider than a finisher, *"the type of player who brings the crowds back,"* said Dick Young.

Early season inconsistencies meant a mid-table position, but curiously enough a rich vein of form arrived with Willie Carlin, as suddenly the team became real contenders for the title. Frank Large, an explosive striker on his day, weighed in with goal after goal. Frank was something of a footballing enigma, when he was good he was brilliant, however, when he was bad he was awful; there were no average performances from the striker.

With the Third Division Championship virtually in the bag the side, hit a nervous patch, a surprise 2-1 home defeat by Reading, then a draw at home to Bristol City in front of 16,069 fans, before going down 2-0 at Mansfield Town. It was down to the last game, with Mansfield the visitors to Brunton Park. A crowd of 18,764 filled the stadium, rattles clicked, scarves were waved, and the Brunton roar spurred the team to a comfortable 3-0 victory with all the goals coming in the first half, from Large (2), and Evans.

Frank Large nets the first goal in the Championship winning Mansfield match.

(Above) Large again to make it 3-0 (Below) The crowd take to the pitch to acknowledge their heroes.

The result ensured that United were crowned as Third Division Champions. Consecutive promotions, it was the most successful era in the club's history.

In the F.A. Cup, a horrible 1-0 away defeat at non-League Crook Town ended all hopes of another Cup run.

In the League Cup Southport were eventually beaten 1-0, followed by title rivals, Bristol City 4-1. It was Chesterfield who finally ended any ambition in the competition, by 3-1 at Saltergate. The average home attendance for the season stood at a very creditable 10,794.

The start of the 1965/66 season saw the arrival of a player who was possibly the best footballer ever to grace a Carlisle United shirt. Chris Balderstone was signed from Huddersfield Town for £7,000, little could anyone realise that for the next decade his influence would dictate that United's team would be built around his undoubted skill and ability. Yes, there can be no doubting, 'Baldy was the king of Brunton Park'.

On the opening day of the season, Norwich City were literally destroyed at Brunton Park, with two goals coming from Simpson, and one each from Balderstone and Large. The season was very much a testing ground, but there were other good victories over Bristol City 5-0, and Bury 4-1, both at Brunton Park. A final League position of 13th was finally attained.

Not too bad for the first season in the higher division. Season ticket sales had soared to 1,357, and there was an average home attendance of 12,066.

In the League Cup, Charlton Athletic dumped the club out in the second round, 4-1 at the Valley, whereas the F.A. Cup offered more excitement. Crystal Palace were beaten 3-0 at Brunton Park before a three game titanic struggle with Shrewsbury Town. A 0-0 draw at Gay Meadow, was followed by a 1-1 draw at Carlisle. The second replay took place at Preston, and this saw the Shrews win through 4-3 after extra time. Dundee United were the visitors to Brunton Park for a mid-season friendly on November 2nd 1965, and in front of 5,404 they defeated a useful Carlisle team 3-2, United's goals coming from Balderstone and Evans.

Another star of that season was a truly fine outside right signed from Exeter City. Eric Welsh arrived in the October making his debut in the 1-1 home draw with Bolton Wanderers.

An unusual training session during the 1965/66 season (Wilson, Welsh, Ross, Caldwell, Evans, McConnell, Harland, Passmoor, Neil & Balderstone.

Eric is in fact the only United player to gain full International recognition whilst at the club, four caps and one goal with Northern Ireland (versus Wales, West Germany and Mexico in 1966, and Wales again in 1967).

In recognition of these achievements, United Chairman George Reed presented the player with a gold watch. Whilst on the subject of International recognition it is worth mentioning that in the 1969/70 season, United keeper Alan Ross was actually called up into the final pool of 16 for Scotland's full International Championship games, but unfortunately he progressed no further.

The 1966/67 season was eagerly awaited for by the clubs supporters, and 1,535 season tickets were sold as four new faces arrived at the club; a tricky winger by the name of Tommy Murray, John Rudge - a centre forward - plus two further wingers in the shape of Frank Sharpe and Barry Hartle.

Tremendous home form enabled the side to achieve a fantastic final League position of third place. Bolton were beaten 6-1 at Carlisle and Portsmouth 5-1. Whilst on their travels, eight games were won and three drawn, meanwhile an incredible fifteen home games ended in victory. It was the most successful season since 1904.

In the League Cup there was equally as much excitement to maintain the fans interest, Tranmere were beaten 2-0 in a replay, followed by Southampton after a 3-3 draw at the Dell, when a 2-1 home victory was achieved at Brunton Park. Next came Blackburn Rovers, themselves challenging for a top spot in the Second Division. The result was a formality, 4-0 to Carlisle, thus to the fifth round and an away tie at Queens Park Rangers which sadly ended in a 2-1 defeat.

In the F.A. Cup, the team was again paired with Blackburn Rovers and won through 2-1 at Ewood Park with goals from Wilson and Carlin. Ipswich terminated all interest in this competition with a 2-0 win at Portman Road.

All in all it was a sensational season, and with an average crowd of 12,200 it was always going to be a hard act to follow.

In the summer Alan Ashman moved to West Bromwich Albion as United brought in Tim Ward. Season ticket sales immediately dropped, this time to 1,249. To be honest it was very much a case of after the Lord Mayor's Parade, for inconsistent form early on ensured that the team was always going to struggle. Hughie McIlmoyle returned, Mike Sutton (the father of five million pound player Chris Sutton) was signed, but neither could prevent the odd defensive lapses which cost goals and results.

In the end a final League position of 10th was attained, with Tommy Murray the top scorer with just 14 goals. Tim Ward was none too happy about matters, *"I feel that I may have made a mistake in coming to this club, the fans seem pre-occupied with the previous incumbent of my seat. All I can do is my best, if the players give theirs then we will do well next season."*

In the F.A. Cup there was a fantastic 1-0 victory over Newcastle United followed by a 2-0 home defeat to Everton. This game was televised by Border Television, the match commentator being Derek Batey who was incredibly biased towards the home side.

Workington inflicted a 2-0 defeat in the League Cup, this ending all interest in that season's competition.

The
BRUNTON ROAR

Official Magazine of
CARLISLE UNITED

Vol. 1 No. 1   September 1967

1/-

United's first official magazine

Several friendly fixtures were played during the season, notably, Queen of the South on the 31st October which ended in a 4-1 Carlisle victory, Sparta Prague on 13th December watched by 9,522 spectators who saw the visitors win 2-1, and finally St. Mirren on 8th March 1968 which ended in a scoreless draw. Brunton Park was also used for a second replay of the Oldham versus Workington League Cup-tie when 3,278 saw the Reds win through 2-1. The average League attendance was 10,746.

The 1968/69 season saw the resignation of Tim Ward, after banners strategically placed around the ground cried for his departure, 'WARD OUT', was the cry. The fans had their wish granted in September when Ward walked out, to be replaced by a man who was to serve the club well, Bob Stokoe. At this stage in the proceedings the team had attained just 3 points from 10 League games! Season ticket sales had been a reasonable 1,436, but there were many who claimed that this would be their last season ticket, that is of course, unless matters improved!

The new manager was very much more of a man-manager. Stokoe cared about the little things, he was meticulous in his pre-match build up and expected nothing less that 100% from his players. Stokoe did manage to get that bit extra from them, as United finished the season in 10th position, with an average crowd of 9,212. Very little was achieved in either Cup competition, Chelsea defeating United in the F.A. Cup, and Leicester in the League Cup after Cardiff City had been seen off at Brunton Park.

It was the Cup competitions which aroused the most interest during the following campaign (1969/70), when season ticket sales had dropped to 1,201, as the club looked to consolidate and prosper. League form was inconsistent, which was reflected by the final position of 12th. John Gorman was signed from Glasgow Celtic, a defender who was strong in the tackle and possessed a sweet left foot. The sight of Gorman accelerating past the opposition up the left wing was something to behold; few United left backs have been as graceful. Dick Young said of him, *"John Gorman could turn defence into attack with the blink of an eye, that left foot is the most educated I have seen on a defender in all my years in the game."*

However, the cup competitions were something else, especially as United had a new weapon in their armoury, namely one Bob Hatton, as lethal a striker since Jimmy Whitehouse or Jimmy McConnell.

In the League Cup, Huddersfield Town, Blackburn Rovers and Chelsea were all despatched at Brunton Park. Then followed a 0-0 draw at Oxford before Chris Balderstone scored from the penalty spot to put United into the semi-finals of the competition for the first time ever. After a tremendous 1-0 home victory over West Bromwich Albion, the team travelled to the West Midlands for the second leg.

A Hatton header struck the inside of the post rolled along the line and struck the other post. From the breakaway Albion scored, and an onslaught on the Carlisle goal followed, led by winger Dennis Martin whose performance that night caused United fans to gasp in awe as he weaved his magic. The final result was 4-1 to Albion, 4-2 on aggregate.

In the F.A. Cup Nottingham Forest were beaten in a replay. Aldershot then managed a 2-2 draw at Carlisle before succumbing 4-1 in front of their own record home attendance of 19,138. United drew Middlesbrough in the fifth round, after Hughie McIlmoyle had signed for 'Boro, who had several Internationals in their line-up. Tyne Tees television covered the fixture. This game officially produced Carlisle United's record attendance of 27,603, some 103 above the previously accepted figure of 27,500. The result went against the lads in blue as Middlesbrough won through 2-1.

M.V.V. Maastricht were mid season friendly visitors, and their side included many Internationals, but it was something of a non-event ending in a tame 1-1 draw.

(Above) an unsusual cover for the League Cup match at the Hawthorns, and (right) a very basic design for the home match against the Dutch team.

Programmes from two contrasting matches played during the 1969/70 season........

..... And two different training methods.

Leap-frogging at Brunton Park, and a hard slog at Skinburness.

During the close season, team manager Bob Stokoe procured the services of Dennis Martin for £20,000, the winger who single handedly destroyed United in the previous season's League Cup Semi-Final, and striker Bobby Owen from Manchester City for £25,000.

One sad departure was all but agreed with the Dennis Martin deal. Winger George McVitie was transferred to West Bromwich Albion for a fee of £30,000. McVitie was a tremendous footballer with a jink of his hips and a drop of the shoulder he could leave the quickest of defenders in his wake.

Two straight League defeats and an away point at Leicester left the team at the foot of the table after three games. Form improved as the club began to climb. Portsmouth were crushed 6-0 at Brunton Park with goals from Hatton (4), and Owen (2), in the reverse fixture at Fratton Park United again hit top scoring form, running out 4-1 victors with Winstanley, Owen, Hatton and Murray all on the score sheet. With five of the last six games won, the other being a 0-0 draw at Swindon, United finished the season in fourth place, having scored 65 goals and conceding 43, then a club record.

The quantity of goals ensure a place in the late summer Watney Cup competition, which had been initiated for the highest scorers in the divisions. The season was somewhat marred by the on-off fiasco of the move of Bob Stokoe to Blackpool. As early as the 1st of December, the United manager had turned down the Seasiders offer, on the 20th of the same month he claimed to have changed his mind and now wished to join Blackpool. The club declined to release him unless some form of compensation was paid, something similar to a transfer fee. There was much negotiating between the two clubs, but eventually on 28th December, Stokoe was released.

Ground improvements were forced upon the club by the Lang Report which covered all aspects of Football Crowd Control and Safety. The ruling that wherever possible adults should be placed in separate areas to juveniles saw the introduction of the 'Kids Pen' on the Paddock side of the Warwick Road End. The Pen still exists to this day.

Ian MacFarlane came in to replace Stokoe, his own man, his thinking and coaching ability were undeniably good. MacFarlane was seen as the ideal replacement and the man to take the club to a higher plain. The new manager was no diplomat, for he spoke his mind and sometimes that hurt, and his free talking was to eventually get him the sack.

In the F.A. Cup, a professional 3-0 victory was attained at Southend, before a home tie with Tottenham Hotspur in the fourth round, in a game which was more of a midfield battle. The First Division side took the honours 3-2, with United's goals coming from Dennis Martin and Bobby Owen.

In the League Cup, Manchester City, complete with Summerbee, Lee and Bell, were dumped out of the competition 2-1 at Brunton Park, courtesy of goals from Martin and Hatton. Oxford United followed suit in the next round, a Bob Hatton hat-trick easing the home side through.

In the fourth round Aston Villa proved too tough an obstacle with a solitary goal scored for Villa by Brian Tiler, who was later to become a United star. The season's average attendance stood at a healthy 10,657, a rise of 1,269 on the previous campaign's figures.

During the summer the Watney Cup competition came and went. United were drawn away to Crewe Alexandria on the 31st of July 1971, and won through 3-1 with goals from Hatton (2), and Martin.

Five personalities of the period:
(Top) 'Tot' Winstanley
and Chris Balderstone.

(Bottom): Dennis Martin
and Tom Clarke
(Inset) Bob Hatton

In the same round Halifax Town knocked out Manchester United 2-1 at the Shay. It may be assumed this this was the Manchester reserves, it wasn't, for it was their complete first team which included Best, Charlton, Law etc.! The Watney Cup was taken very seriously by all the competing teams, including Carlisle United.

In the following round, which was also the semi-final, another away tie was drawn, this time at Fourth Division Colchester United, on August 4th 1971.

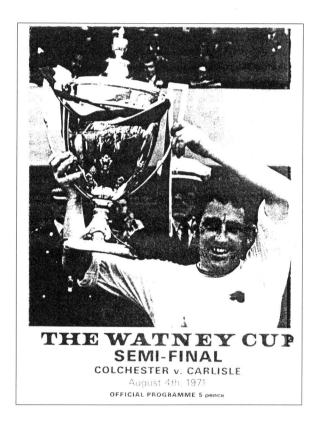

THE WATNEY CUP
SEMI-FINAL
COLCHESTER v. CARLISLE
August 4th, 1971
OFFICIAL PROGRAMME 5 pence

A midweek game and a long journey. Anglia television covered the fixture, which saw a poor United performance as Colchester eased through to the final a 2-0 win. Colchester actually went on to win the trophy, beating West Bromwich Albion in a penalty shoot-out.

The following season was something of an anti-climax, League form dipped as a final League position of 10th was achieved. The average home attendance also dropped, this time to 9,479. MacFarlane was forced to revamp his squad during the season as transfer bids were coming in thick and fast for Tommy Murray, who joined Hearts in September, then on the 28th of October the news every United fan dreaded was released; Hatton had been sold to Birmingham City for £80,000. A number of letters were received by the club from disillusioned fans who were angry at the sale. However, MacFarlane was to put matters straight when he signed the brilliant Stanley Bowles from Crewe Aledandra for a £12,000 fee.

'Our Stanley'

Bowles was on his day amazing and wonderful. He had magical feet and tremendous vision, for this he is still classed as one of the top footballers this country has ever had. It is difficult to describe just how good he was, something of a cross between Glenn Hoddle and Gary Lineker... yes, he really was that good! His rise to the top commenced with his move to Brunton Park.

At Crewe he had a bad reputation for being something of a gambler. MacFarlane literally picked him up by his bootlaces and instilled discipline into his game and lifestyle. During his time with Carlisle 'Our Stanley' as he was affectionately known, was never a problem, for he was far too much in awe of the manager not to do as he was told. There is an interesting story linked to Bowles, who was in Manchester and had missed a training session due to injury. MacFarlane rang him up and told him to get to the ground by a certain time or else he would come and drag him back. Not fancying this, Bowles decided that public transport was too unpredictable and so got a taxi from Manchester to Carlisle!

Further ground improvements were carried out as the Warwick Road End was separated from the Scratching Shed enclosure where it had always been possible to walk through. Now the only entry into 'The Warwick' was via the four turnstiles nearest to Warwick Road, which again, still exist.

The anger and disruption of the Hatton transfer quickly subsided as Bowles displayed his talents. He eventually finished the season as joint top scorer along with Bobby Owen.

The Cup competitions were hardly profitable. Sheffield Wednesday were beaten 5-0 at Brunton Park in the League Cup, but Norwich City inflicted a 4-1 win in the next round, at Carrow Road.

In the F.A. Cup it was Tottenham away. A Stan Bowles strike earned a replay, although there should have been no requirement as Stan Webb missed a sitter in front of the Spurs goal. The replay, on the 18th of January 1972, was a real let down as the Tottenhams power in midfield earned them a 3-1 win in front of 21,560 spectators.

The summer recess provoked some real confusion at Brunton Park as Ian Mac-Farlane was sacked and Alan Ashman returned. It was a bitter pill to swallow for the 'Big Man' who had proved himself to be a capable leader with an eye for real talent. In the end he had been the master of his own destiny, for his honesty when expressing opinions was just too much for the club's directors to take. He had to go.

The pre-season period saw European football come to Carlisle in the form of the Anglo-Italian Tournament. A fine 3-2 win against A.S. Roma and a 1-0 win over Catanzaro, both in Italy, saw the two Italian sides then visit Brunton Park.

The Roma fixture was a real cracker which finished 3-3. It was Stan Bowles who grabbed the headlines, striking one real bender against the post/crossbar from the right hand side of the penalty area. It was a terrific shot worthy of a goal. Our Stanley had been magnificent throughout the tournament and was clearly destined for greater things. Catanzaro were beaten 4-1 at Brunton Park as Carlisle topped the 'English League', only to find themselves losing out to Blackpool who had beaten Lanerossi 10-0. With extra points for goals scored, Blackpool actually finished 8 points clear of Carlisle. Ironically they lost to Roma in the final!

On September the 8th, Stan Bowles was sold to Queens Park Rangers for a fee of £110,000. It looked for some time as though Bowles was in fact heading for Crystal Palace, however, they could not rise to Carlisle's asking price. The following month, another Stan was on his way out of Brunton Park, this time it was Stan Webb who was sold to Brentford for a £15,000 fee.

Coming into the club was striker Joe Laidlaw. Captured from Middlesbrough, Joe proved to be a tremendous acquisition. Also signed was the greatest enigma ever to don a United shirt, Kenny Wilson who was signed in September from Dumbarton for a then record £36,000 fee. By all accounts he was a prolific goalscorer in the Scottish game where he had scored 83 goals.

The League campaign opened with a 2-2 draw at Burnley followed by a 3-0 home win over Swindon. The new tower floodlights were switched on for the first time in a League game against Blackpool, on Tuesday 26th September, 1972. United lost the fixture 3-2 in front of 10,969 spectators. The lights were 130 feet tall, the highest in the League.

Each tower had twelve, 3.5 kilowatt, Mercury Halide Lamps. So bright were the 'lights, that complaints were received from motorists two miles away on the M6 that they were being dazzled by the glare!

Despite such a reasonable start the club slid down the table, despite excellent home wins over Brighton 5-1 and Preston 6-1, the latter of which saw Kenny Wilson bundle in his one and only goal for the club. A final League position of 18th was achieved, and the average attendance figure for the season stood at 7,606.

The League Cup paired football giants Liverpool with United at Brunton Park, and in front of 16,257, a Les O'Neill goal earned a 1-1 draw, after Keegan and given the Merseysiders a 1-0 lead. In the Anfield replay, it was one way traffic as the Reds thrashed Carlisle 5-1, United's goal being scored by Bobby Owen. The highlight of the game was an Alan Ross penalty save from Tommy Smith. Big Tom missed few penalties, indeed it may well be the only one he did, and it was a fantastic save by the United keeper.

In the F.A. Cup, Huddersfield Town were beaten after a replay and Sheffield United followed in the Brunton Park mud. The fifth round saw First Division leaders Arsenal come to Carlisle, where an Alan Ball tap-in was equalised when Dennis Martin struck home before half-time. A defensive lapse allowed McLintock, the Arsenal captain, to steal in with a header in the second half and give the Gunners an undeserved victory. The highlights of the game were on BBC TV's Match of the Day.

The 1973/74 season started with some controversy for Carlisle skipper, Chris Balderstone, decided to play out the cricket season, thus missing the club's opening few matches.

Balderstone the cricketer, meets Balderstone the footballer!

Alan Ashman immediately responded by taking away the captaincy from him. To be fair, Balderstone was an outstanding cricketer, having played for Yorkshire and Leicestershire, however he was contracted to Carlisle United and was perhaps fortunate that no stiffer punishment was afforded him.

On the 17th of August, Frank Clarke, elder brother of Leeds striker, Allan, joined the club for a £35,000 fee from Ipswich Town, he was to end the season as the clubs leading goalscorer.

The season got off to a poor start, from a home draw with Cardiff City followed by a 6-1 defeat at Luton Town. Slowly but surely things improved. BBC TV arrived at Brunton Park to film the home League game with promotion rivals Orient, when millions saw a flying header from Joe Laidlaw and two splendid goals from Frank Clarke give United the points. Indeed until April the 20th a 4-0 away defeat at Blackpool the club were being tipped for the third promotion place introduced for the first time that season.

With just two games remaining it seemed that promotion had been blown, however, a 1-0 away win at Oxford United, followed by a 2-0 home win over Aston Villa put United third. The celebrations after the Villa match will long remain in the memories of the 12,000 odd United fans present. Everyone was on the pitch, and the team came out into the directors box to applaud the celebrations. Things though are never that simple. Orient could still overtake Carlisle if they won their final League game against Aston Villa. Ron Saunders the Villa boss came out to speak to the Carlisle crowd. *"We will stop Orient from going up, mark my words, you are in the First Division, well done all of you."* A Ray Graydon penalty earned Villa a 1-1 home draw with Orient on Friday May 3rd, 1974, and the result meant that Carlisle United had won promotion to the First Division.

The Orient/Villa game had been broadcast live on BBC Radio Carlisle, and was listened to by thousands. The whole of the city of Carlisle went wild. Border television flashed latest score messages for those tuned into their network.

ORIENT 1 ASTON VILLA 1: CARLISLE UNITED PROMOTED TO FIRST DIVISION!

It was a marvellous achievement by everyone concerned with the club.

A party was held in the supporters club bar at the ground that same evening, and all the players, and Alan Ashman, danced the light fandango. Border Television cancelled a programme to broadcast live from the party, although for many it had not sunk in that Carlisle had won promotion to the First Division.

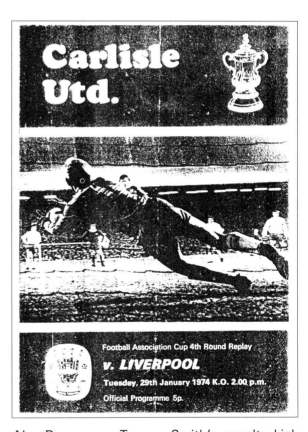

Alan Ross saves Tommy Smith's penalty kick in the F.A.Cup match at Anfield. A scoreless draw (but a home defeat in the replay), almost paled into insignificance compared to the promotion success.

Chapter 5

The promotion party continued throughout the summer. There was a civic reception, with the team proudly travelling through the city in an open top bus, before acknowledging the adulation of the thousand or so fans gathered in Rickergate, beneath a civic centre balcony.

There was mass booing when Malcolm MacDonald's name was mentioned. The overweight Newcastle striker said of Carlisle's promotion: *"It's farcical to think that Carlisle United are in our League, they will go*

Mr.E.G.Sheffield, the Chairman who took the club into the 1st Division.

straight down, goal fodder for the bigger clubs." Meanwhile Jack Charlton, then manager of Middlesbrough commented: *"I am pleased for Carlisle and for football although I doubt whether the ground or the team will be up to this standard."* Another player quick to denounce United's promotion was Kevin Keegan. *"This three up promotion is all good and proper but when the likes of Carlisle get promoted it takes the shine off First Division status. Despite that, I wish them every success, it will be great for their supporters."*

Les O'Neil, Allan Ashman and John Gorman continue to celebrate

There were many denouncers but even more credits, Leeds skipper Billy Bremner....
"Marvellous, I have heard a lot about them, from what I hear they are a good footballing side."
... Bill Shankly... *"It is the greatest achievement in football, a real football miracle."*

The exciting 'first' days:
(Right) The first First Division game.
(Below) Bill Green scores the first goal, at
Stamford Bridge - after only 106 seconds!
(Above) A 'First Day Cover' for the first
home match in the top flight.

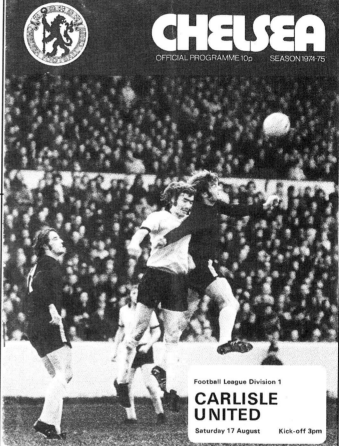

There can be no doubting this was the greatest time in the club's history, nothing before nor since, Wembley included, could reproduce the emotions felt by so many. Carlisle United in the First Division, the World's toughest league.

The party continued as first Chelsea then Middlesbrough lost on their own territory to United. Tottenham followed suit in the first home fixture, when a Chris Balderstone penalty secured the points. On the evening of Saturday 24th August, 1974 Carlisle United sat proudly on top of the First Division, although they had been there since the 20th of August it never really sank home until the League tables were shown on national television on the evening of the 24th. There is little point in attempting to describe how every Carlisle supporters felt at that time, the ultimate compliment of the achievement came when subbuteo revealed their 'New Line' Carlisle United team, priced at 90p! United had arrived.

Middlesbrough inflicted a 1-0 defeat at Brunton Park and the bubble, rather than burst, disintegrated. Too many games were lost in the final few minutes, and there was a definite weakness in front of goal as just 43 goals were scored. United plummeted to the bottom of the Division.

It can hardly be said that the side were outplayed, indeed just one team taught them a footballing lesson, not once, but twice.

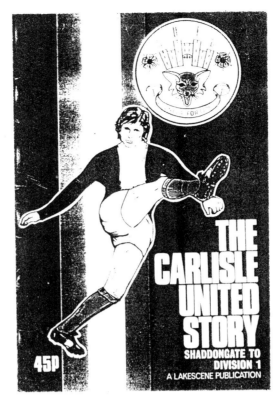

The first book ever published on the Club.

Stoke City won 2-0 in a torrential rainstorm at Brunton Park, then inflicted a 5-2 defeat at the Victoria Ground. The eventual Champions, Derby County, were thrashed 3-0 at Carlisle, as too were then table-topping Everton, a spectacular Dennis Martin strike being the most memorable goal of the season during that win. Everton were also beaten at Goodison Park, 3-2 courtesy of a late Joe Laidlaw goal. Burnley were beaten 4-2 on a cold April night, but it was Liverpool who put the final nail in the coffin, when they relegated United with a 3-0 victory at Anfield.

With little else but pride at stake, Carlisle visited Champions Derby County on the final day of the season, and over 1,500 United stalwarts made the journey, when the celebrations were incredible. Both sets of supporters enjoyed the day and applauded each others team and their respective achievements. *"We'll see you all next year"* was the cry as Rams supporters believed that Carlisle would bounce straight back. The final result of that truly memorable League season was a 0-0 draw. Insufficient to lift the team from bottom place, but the team and it's support could hold their heads high as they had earned the utmost respect from a number of unexpected sources. Don Revie the England manager was one such ally; *"One of the best footballing sides I have seen this season has to be Carlisle United, they can count themselves unfortunate to be relegated."* Praise indeed!

In the F.A. Cup, which it has to be said was destined for Brunton Park that season, the team reached the sixth round for the first and only time in their history. Preston, managed by Bobby Charlton, were beaten 1-0 at Deepdale with a Joe Laidlaw goal. West Bromwich Albion went down 3-2 at Carlisle, and in the fifth round Mansfield Town lost 1-0 at Field Mill in front of BBC TV's Match of the Day cameras, a tremendous turning shot from Bobby Owen doing the damage. The sixth round saw second Division Fulham as the visitors.

```
CARLISLE UNITED AFC
Brunton Park  -  Carlisle
F.A. CUP - SIXTH ROUND
────────────────────────────
FULHAM
SATURDAY, 8th MARCH, 1975    k.o. 3 p.m.
Admission 50p
SPONSORED BY YOUNGER'S TARTAN

POPULAR SIDE

No  6760                           SECRETARY
```

Never in the history of the Cup can any team have put one defence under so much pressure as Carlisle did Fulham that afternoon. Sadly, the blonde haired Peter Mellor in the Fulham goal was in spectacular form, making world class saves from O'Neill twice, Laidlaw twice and Owen on several occasions. The ball quite simply would not go in the Fulham net. Then to add insult to injury a stupid mix up between Peter Carr and Alan Ross allowed Fulham to score, and so ended the F.A. Cup dream. To this day each and every United supporter will state that it was 'Our' F.A. Cup that season, the fates really did conspire against the team in 1974/75.

The League Cup was hardly memorable, a 1-0 win at Bradford City followed by a disappointing 2-0 defeat at Colchester.

The average home League attendance stood at 14,530 the 28th highest of all 92 League clubs, understandably it is the club's highest ever average.

The 1975/76 season was never going to be anything other than a struggle. Chris Balderstone bid the club farewell, maintaining an excellent standard of cricket and representing England. Football-wise he joined Doncaster Rovers where his shuttles between sports were to receive high profile media attention. It was a fond farewell, everyone at the club wished 'Baldy' the very best, including the man who had stripped him of the team captaincy, Allan Ashman.

In October, after a truly horrific start, Allan Ashman turned his back on the club and resigned. In his shoes stepped the devoutly loyal Dick Young, a man who more than anyone deserves the title of 'Mr. Carlisle United'. No other man in the club's history has been of greater influence than Mr. Young. Someone once said of him, *"Dick Young is the most respected man in this city"*, they were right.

Despite everything, Dick could do little to halt the slide he inherited, when performances were at best, poor. Indeed, with an average League attendance of 8,279, it was clear that the footballing public of the city were hardly impressed by the team's demise. The team finished one place above the relegation zone in 19th place.

In the F.A. Cup it was West Bromwich Albion who ended the interest in the third round, 3-1 at the Hawthorns. Earlier in the League Cup, Gillingham were beaten 2-0 at Carlisle before a 2-0 defeat at Everton. The only real highlight of the season was a spectacular 35 yard volley from Mike Barry at Chelsea which won awards from the ITV network as 'Goal of the Month'.

Two stalwarts of the '70s - (Left) Bobby Owen and (Right) Dennis Martin

In the summer, striker Billy Rafferty and central defender Ian McDonald arrived. Rafferty made an immediate impact, scoring twice in the opening day victory at Southampton, a victory which the Saints avenged 6-0 at Brunton Park in a game which was best described as disheartening.

Nottingham Forest put five in the Carlisle net, as did Luton, both on away soil. In contradiction with these poor performances came some exhilarating play; Cardiff City were the visitors at Carlisle on the 18th of December and were leading 3-1 with seven minutes remaining, but in a tremendous fightback, Billy Rafferty bagged a hat-trick to earn Carlisle an incredible 4-3 win. Bolton Wanderers were comfortably beaten 4-3, and Wolves left Brunton Park pointless after a 2-1 defeat. These results apart, United were well and truly in the relegation mire. Everything rested on the final home game of the season, a home game with fellow strugglers Bristol Rovers. By half time it looked all over, 2-0 to the Cum-

brians. Then came an incredible collapse, architected by Rovers' wiry winger Jimmy Hamilton. Rovers netted three times in the second period, and hence relegating United to the Third Division.

Dick Young had resigned from his managerial role to be replaced by the high profile ex-Newcastle United and Scottish International Bobby Moncur. Dick Young reverted to his coaching role in the hope that the move would inspire the team to greater things, but it didn't. Another star to arrive at Brunton Park, albeit on a temporary basis, was Celtic striker 'Dixie Deans', a football enigma Deans produced some quality finishing and neat touches in his four appearances, however other matters outside the game were of a greater influence to the exciting striker, and he left Carlisle just as he was winning everyone over. Departure-wise, John Gorman left for Tottenham Hotspur in early November.

In the F.A. Cup, Matlock were thrashed 5-1 at Brunton Park, but it was Liverpool who ended any hope of a decent Cup run with a 3-0 scoreline at Anfield. In the League Cup, Southport were despatched on the away goal rule, for after a 2-1 away win, Carlisle managed to lose the home tie 1-0. Arsenal were the next opponents, at Highbury, and it was a close fought encounter but the Gunners won through 3-2 with United's goals coming from Phil Bonnyman and Frank Clarke.

The average home League attendance again fell, this time to 7,680.

The 1977/78 season saw the arrival of lanky striker Les Mutrie from non-League Gateshead, as Moncur attempted to maintain the majority of his squad. To be fair to him, Mutrie looked incapable of meeting the standards expected, and he was gone by the end of the season. This was also to be striker Frank Clarke's last season as the experienced front man finally hung up his boots. An improved League position of 13th was achieved.

In the F.A. Cup Manchester United were brilliantly held 1-1 at Brunton Park but won the Old Trafford replay 4-2, and in the League Cup, Huddersfield Town were taken to three games before United finally succumbed. The average home League attendance was falling fast, and now stood at just 5,319, an ominous omen indeed.

The 1978/79 season was a memorable one for a number of reasons, few of which are pleasurable. The most devastating blow came in November with the death of United's loyal servant and chief scout Hugh Neil, in a car crash on the A74, en route to a scouting mission at Motherwell .

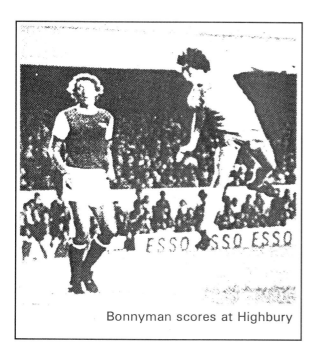
Bonnyman scores at Highbury

Hughie was a kind and generous man, a real football nut. No matter who, where, or when, he would spare a word for anyone who wished to chat football with him.

Ivor Broadis, a great pal of the United man, said: *"It's like losing one of the family."*

In the matchday programme a simple but effective poem was printed in dedication to the great man, it read:

"We'll miss you Hugh, look back with pride,
Oft took the goal in glorious stride.
Safe passage 'cross the Great Divide,
God's welcome on the other side."

Another loss came in the shape of Allan Ross who played his last ever game for the club - against Swindon on the 28th of October, 1978. 'Rossy' played some 465 games, plus one as substitute for United. He was a master craftsman, admittedly prone to the odd blunder, but one of the best reflex 'keepers United have ever had.

On the pitch, a new club record, twenty-two games were drawn. Although the club were up among the promotion pack for much of the season, and it was a heavy 5-1 defeat at Oxford which all but ended any talk of promotion, when an eventual position of 6th was attained. The attendance average again dropped, this time to 5,204, the fans were beginning to vote with their feet.

In the F.A. Cup, Halifax and Hull City were defeated before Cup holders Ipswich squeezed through 3-2 at Portman Road, whereas the League Cup interest was ended by Blackpool 4-3 on aggregate.

All in all it was hardly a good season in the history of the club, although there were some pleasing signs with the progress of local lads, Keith Sawyer, Geoff Fell and Andy Collins, confirming Moncur's belief that local talent was available if one searched deep enough for it. The players were a suitable reminder of the astute eye of the late Hughie Neil.

The next (1979/80) season saw the arrival of a young lad from Wallsend Boys Club, Peter Beardsley, who cost Carlisle United a set of shirts!

The Geordie genius has to be one of the shrewdest signings the football club have ever made, as Beardsley has graced stadiums all over the world, with some of the World's top club sides.

Joining Beardsley in the October was then record signing Gordon Staniforth who cost £120,000 from York City, a quick lively forward, 'Stanny' proved his worth as a goalgetter.

It was, by everyone's standards, a poor season, for inconsistent form saw a persistent struggle, although by early January they had begun to climb out of the bottom few places. In February, Bob Moncur resigned, taking up the manager's job at Heart of Midlothian, and he was replaced by his right hand man Martin Harvey.

To his utmost credit Harvey was now able to put his own managerial ideas into place, preventing the opposition from scoring becoming a priority, it worked as the club eventually climbed to 6th place with 48 points. The League attendance slide continued, this time to an average of 4,460.

The F.A. Cup looked promising as Hull City were beaten after a replay, then came Sheffield Wednesday 3-0, and Bradford City 3-2. There was hope of a big draw in the fourth round, but such hopes were dashed as Wrexham were the visitors to Brunton Park. The Welsh side came for a draw and completely spoiled the game with negative tactics and getting what they came for.

In the replay three days later it was a different Wrexham who devoured Carlisle 3-1, and thus ending the F.A. Cup ambitions for another season. In the League Cup the Welsh side were again the opponents, and after a 1-1 draw at the Racecourse Ground, United lost the second leg 2-1 at Brunton Park. The names of Bobby Moncur and Wrexham were mentioned in the same vein on the Carlisle terraces that season!

Martin Harvey found the managerial hotseat uncomfortable during the early part of the 1980/81 season, when he spent £100,000 for Hull City full back Paul Haigh, a quality defender and a player who was also to prove to be a loyal servant to the club. For the return the directors expected improved team performances, instead they dropped.

The September of 1980 saw the return of Bob Stokoe, who received United's offer whilst on the golf course. He rushed to the club house to accept the manager's job. Harvey was offered the coaching role alongside Dick Young, but declined the invitation and duly left in somewhat acrimonious circumstances. Harvey was a genuine man who one can sympathise with, in different circumstances who knows what he could have achieved.

The fans were pleased with the return of Stokoe, although it was another season of struggle, with a final position of 19th and an average home attendance of 4,064. Peter Beardsley was sold to Vancouver Whitecaps for a club record fee of £275,000 in April 1981, a sad departure but the financial profit raised through the Beardsley deal kept the club on an even keel for some time to come.

In the Cups it was dismal failure. Workington were well beaten 4-1 at Brunton Park after a 0-0 draw at Borough Park, Walsall were then beaten 4-0 and Mansfield 2-1 after a 2-2 draw a Field Mill. However, it was Bristol City in the fourth round, who thrashed in five without return at Ashton Gate in the F.A. Cup, whereas Charlton sent the club packing from the League Cup 4-2 on aggregate.

Few supporters could expect much better from the 1981/82 season, however, the arrival of Bryan 'Pop' Robson and 'Big Bob' Lee along with central defender Jackie Ashurst gave cause for some thought, Tommy Craig was to join this trio as Assistant Manager and Coach. United took the Division by storm, but it was not until November that they topped the table with a hard earned 1-0 away win at Bristol Rovers, on an ice packed pitch. The club remained in pole position until the faltering final few weeks of the season, when Fulham were the major force.

At one point Carlisle had dropped to fifth and looked out of contention, but some grafting performances from Tommy Craig lifted the whole team and results were won over a full ninety minutes.

The penultimate game of the season was a home fixture against a Bristol Rovers side who were

Robson's goal, that clinched promotion.

The adulation was for the team and especially, Stokoe the King, the Messiah, he was everything to all United fans.

In the newly named Milk Cup (formerly League Cup), Bury were beaten 5-4 on aggregate. Bristol City won the next tie 2-1 at Ashton Gate.

In the F.A. Cup there was a 3-2 win over

hardly championship contenders. Carlisle needed just one point to gain promotion, a victory would more or less assure the championship. As is so often the case, nerves got the better of the team as Rovers ran out 2-1 winners, virtually ensuring that Fulham were champions.

As a result, Carlisle had to gain a point at Chester in the final game of the season, it was real pressure. Some fifteen hundred United fans travelled to Sealand Road to witness a 'Pop' Robson goal which provided a 1-0 victory and promotion back into the Second Division. The celebrations on the Chester pitch were pleasant reminders of things past.

Darlington, but not before the Quakers had earned a 2-2 draw at Feethams.

Following Darlington was Bishop Auckland, the original game was abandoned after 69 minutes as torrential rain waterlogged the pitch.

The tie was repeatedly postponed as water, then snow and ice prevented the game taking place. Eventually it was played at Workington's Borough Park, with United sliding through 1-0 from a Bob Lee goal. Huddersfield were the third round opponents and duly knocked United out, 3-2 at Brunton Park.

During the summer Malcolm Poskett arrived from Watford and Alan Shoulder from Newcastle United, the pair were dynamite. Poskett, a lean striker with a real eye for goal, became something of a cult hero, whereas Alan Shoulder reminded some of the more mature United supporters of a 1950's style winger - crafty, skilful, artistic and lethal in front of goal.

An opening day away win at Derby County augured well, however, three straight defeats put matters into perspective, especially as Leicester had slammed six past the United defence in 45 minutes. There followed something of a swan song, Crystal Palace arrived at Carlisle full of enthusiasm and confidence, but Poskett single handedly destroyed them, scoring four delightful goals, one of which was an exquisite back flick which would have received rave reviews had it come from the foot of a Brazilian. Palace were well beaten 4-1. Tommy Craig netted two brilliant goals to pin Sheffield Wednesday back 4-2 as Carlisle surged back into the top places.

Unfortunately form dipped and results were average rather than exceptional, United found themselves among the basement pack, only to fight clear in the final few weeks of the season. A great 5-0 win over Bolton at Brunton Park just about ensuring Second Division football for another season. Eventually the side finished in 14th place, scoring 68 goals into the bargain.

In the Milk Cup there was a 3-3 draw at home to Bolton before a disastrous 4-0 rout at Burnden Park, with Dave Rushbury being sent off for handling the ball on the goal-line. In the F.A. Cup, Burnley drew 2-2 at Brunton Park but won the Turf Moor replay 3-1.

It was in the 1982/83 season that the club attempted to reward loyal and devoted fans by running a 'Top Ten' fans competition. Now, with a hint of embarrassment, the author can confess to being selected as one of these, receiving a plaque and free match tickets for the home fixture with Barnsley. The plaque was presented in front of the players tunnel at half-time by United defender Bobby Parker.

With finances tight, Stokoe looked to strengthen his squad during the summer. Goalkeeper Dave McKellar was virtually taken from the dole queue and went straight into the ranks of Second Division football. The ex-Ipswich, Derby and Brentford 'keeper had been dumped on the soccer scrapheap. Bob Stokoe provided the opportunity for him to prove himself, but McKellar's problem had been a recurring back injury. Also arriving that summer was influential defender Don O'Riordon, signed from Preston North End. He could be as inspirational as Chris Balderstone yet as rugged as Nobby Stiles.

Bobby Parker made 373 appearances for United between 1974 and 1984

League form was good, for there was a 15 match unbeaten run, as Newcastle United, Manchester City, Leeds United and Middlesbrough all came to grief. Bob Stokoe received the Divisionional Manager of the Month award for January 1984.

With ten matches to go the side sat in third place in the table, behind Chelsea and Sheffield Wednesday, and above big spending Newcastle United who were well and truly beaten 3-1 at Brunton Park. Unfortunately the hype failed to last, as five draws and five defeats were suffered in the last ten games, thus producing a final league position of 7th. The average attendance figure stood at a reasonable 5,611.

In the cup competitions, there was an element of real misfortune. The Milk Cup saw the First Division leaders Southampton, embarrassed by two Malcolm Poskett strikes at Brunton Park, earning Carlisle a 2-0 lead for the away second leg. It could have and should have been more as Peter Shilton in the Saints goal was outstanding.

In the second leg an early goal by Saints striker David Armstrong put the Carlisle defence ill at ease, but it was not until late in the game that they forced a deflected equaliser. Up to then Dave McKellar had produced save after save to prevent the home side getting the all important equaliser. In extra time, Saints grabbed the all important winner, going through 3-2 on aggregate.

The F.A. Cup saw Third Division Swindon as the visitors, when Carlisle peppered the Robins' goal with shot after shot, but Swindon 'keeper Scott Endersby was superb, ultimately impressing Bob Stokoe sufficiently as to warrant him being purchased. The result was a 1-1 draw, and in the replay a shock 3-1 defeat meant an early cup exit for United.

A good season was marred in February 1984 by the sudden death of physiotherapist Herbert Nicholson at the age of 64. Herbert had worked with the club since 1953, first in a part time role under Bill Shankly, before turning full time in 1958. As well as his full time role Herbert will be remembered by many for supervising the workmen who terraced the Waterworks End of the ground, when he refused to let them take too many tea breaks and time for inspecting their workmanship. It was of course all in good humour, although Herbert would want the best from everyone connected with the club, be it from the tea lady to the programme sellers.

Over the years he assisted on scouting missions as the search for fresh talent increased. Club Chairman Andrew Jenkins said of the death, *"Herbert's death is a tragic loss, we will all miss him but he will never be forgotten."*

The 1984/85 season was not one of the best, indeed United were installed as favourites for relegation, much the same as they had the previous season. New faces were signed in the form of ex-Middlesboro striker Garry Macdonald, along with midfielder Steve Tupling, ex-Stoke defender Dave McAughtrie, and Mark Hutchinson from Leicester City. The pre-season results were hardly sensational. Berwick Rangers were beaten 4-1 at Shielfield Park, the Isle of Man Tournament saw a 2-1 defeat to Sunderland, a 1-1 draw with Athlone Town and a 1-0 win over St. Mirren. Coventry City visited Brunton Park on a pre-season tour and were beaten 2-1.

The season got off to a poor start with seventh position the highest obtained, in the third week. Generally the team sat in the lower reaches, and with some of the early performances being poor, Stokoe looked to bring in better quality.

Later to join Blues was the influential pairing of Ian Bishop and John Cooke, the latter initially on loan. Ian Bishop was a real gem, a beautiful passer of the ball he was the playmaker of the team. Cooke was more of an old fashioned inside forward who liked nothing better than running for goal. Mick Halsall was brought in as a terrier-like midfielder with an eye for goal. One of the season's best signings was the electrifying winger John Halpin from Celtic. The clever player had everything and was being watched by several clubs. Later, whilst still at Carlisle, it was rumoured that Liverpool were about to come in with a big offer, only for the unfortunate winger to break his leg!

A final League position of 16th was attained, with an average home attendance figure of 4,016. The low spot of the season came with Blackburn Rovers as visitors on December the 23rd. After the game the hooligan element confronted each other in the main car park behind the main stand, and one fan - a Carlisle supporter - was hit on the head and later died as a result of his injuries. A brick had been thrown from the pathetic hand of a mindless Blackburn yob who was later jailed for manslaughter; there is no way this individual could be remotely classed as a supporter. The incident left a black cloud over Brunton Park for the remainder of the season.

In the Cup competitions there was little to cheer about. Dagenham were beaten 1-0 at Carlisle in the F.A. Cup, before Leicester City luckily scraped through with a 1-0 victory at Filbert Street in the following round. Carlisle had a perfectly good penalty decision turned down, and a Don O'Riordon shot struck the inside of the Leicester post in the second half. In the Milk Cup, Fulham dumped the team out 4-1 on aggregate in the second round.

During the summer Bob Stokoe was busy on the transfer front, with Dave MacAughtrie, Alan Shoulder, Malcolm Poskett and Don O'Riordon all moving on to pastures new. New arrivals were winger, Mark Gavin from Leeds United, Paul Baker a utility player from

Malcolm Poskett

Southampton, strikers Wayne Entwistle and Alan Mayes, plus Newcastle goalkeeper Kevin Carr. Dave McKellar who had looked anything but confident in the closing games of the previous season asked for a transfer which was duly granted by the club.

Pre-season friendlies were played at Workington, with a 4-0 victory, followed by three games in the Isle of Man Tournament which saw defeats against Manchester City 3-0, and Stoke City 1-0, whilst an Isle of Man XI were beaten 2-1, with goals from Entwistle and ex-Everton player Ian Bishop. Newcastle visited Brunton Park in early August and played out a 0-0 draw, whereas Workington were again faced and beaten 3-1 in West Cumbria.

The League season started with a defeat at Bradford City. New 'keeper Kevin Carr made a good penalty save and another new boy, Wayne Entwistle, scored as both had memorable debuts. Both would suffer to the wrath of the fans within a very short period at the club as obvious shortfalls in their performances were highlighted.

(Left) Manager Bob Stokoe and (Right) Tommy Craig who made nearly 100 appearances for United.

Carr in particular was considered to be the most inept of 'keepers. He was quickly dropped as Scott Endersby was brought to the club and he soon became a crowd favourite.

After just a few games Bob Stokoe stood down to allow Bryan 'Pop' Robson the opportunity to take over as manager, and time was to prove that it was a mistake. Robson was a player of undoubted quality, but the real influence had come from Tommy Craig who had been allowed to leave the club a short time earlier.

Wes Saunders was signed on loan from Newcastle United as injuries began to hit the squad. Saunders was a good quality centre half who eventually signed for United. Managing Director Colin Hutchinson left the club in August after five years at Brunton Park, and went on to take the role as Chief Executive at Wimbledon F.C. The departure was not unique, as on the 14th of October

1985 it was revealed that: *"At a meeting of the Board of Directors of Carlisle United F.C. the Directors reluctantly accepted the resignation of team manager Bryan Robson."*

To all intents, Robson ran away, providing an inglorious end to a marvellous career for this well respected man. Robson's departure saw the return of Bob Stokoe as team manager. Results were less than inspirational and the team was in the relegation dogfight all season. John Halpin scored one of the greatest goals ever seen at Carlisle against Blackburn Rovers in February when he weaved between four Rovers defenders from the halfway line, cut into the penalty area, then took on two more before calmly nutmegging the Blackburn 'keeper. Few modern day Carlisle players could arouse the enthusiasm of the crowd as Johnny Halpin, he could do things with a football that most other players could only dream of.

Halsall and Halpin look on in apparent admiration as Bishop scores with a long range shot against Sheffield United.

McGarvey scores from the 'spot', as Dave Beasant (Wimbledon) goes the wrong way.

1985/86 season

Another signing was made in the form of peroxide blond Robbie Wakenshaw from Everton. Robbie was heralded as the new Hughie McIlmoyly, and on his Everton first team debut he had scored against Manchester United - he was to be a young star of the future. In reality he struggled to fit in with the team's style of play.

Scott McGarvey, ex-Manchester United and Portsmouth, also became an instant cult hero. He was a big name, and he commanded a high wage, but lacked quality in his initial loan period, scoring just three times in ten games. Other loan signings were made, including the slightly built midfield/winger by the name of Jim Tolmie from Manchester City. In the penultimate game of the season United faced Charlton Athletic at Brunton Park. Carlisle needed to win to have a chance of staying up, while Charlton needed a win to achieve promotion. As half time approached Carlisle were in full command at 2-0 up with the visitors looking a hapless lot.

For some inexplicable reason, Tolmie hit a back pass to Endersby from the half way line, the ball was struck far too hard, it was caught by the gusting wind. Scott Endersby stood on the edge of his penalty area unaware that anyone should conspire to pass the ball to him, while the Warwick Road End inhaled deeply in a vain attempt to suck the ball back as it floated towards the Waterworks End goal. In slow motion it cleared the shocked Endersby and dropped into the Carlisle net! Just the fillip Charlton needed at half time. Tolmie was booed each time he touched the ball thereafter, and, following the game, he was never heard of again; most United fans would agree that it was probably just as well!

In the second half Carlisle panicked, Charlton equalised, then scored a third, relegating the Cumbrians back to the Third Division.

The average League attendance stood at 4,010, just ten lower that season than the once mighty Wolverhampton Wanderers. There had been a brief encounter in the Full Members Cup which ended in tears, with a 2-0 defeat at Middlesbrough. In the Milk Cup it was disaster and embarrassment rolled into one. A 3-3 draw at fourth division Crewe set up the second home leg nicely. It was one of the most humiliating performances ever given by a United side. Crewe filled with passion and very little else ran out 4-3 winners, at least three of the goals can be laid firmly at the foot (or hands) of Kevin Carr; one effort struck a post rebounded and hit the overweight 'keeper full in the face before rolling into the goal. The team was quite rightly booed off the pitch.

In the F.A. Cup some self respect was gained when First Division Queens Park Rangers were beaten 1-0 at Brunton Park, courtesy of a sweet strike from John Cooke, who had signed for the club in the October.

However, in the following round Peterborough unceremoniously dumped the team 1-0 at London Road.

The big news of the 1986/87 season came with the arrival of Harry Gregg as team manager, with Bob Stokoe finally retiring from team management. Gregg secured the services of Scott McGarvey, and ex-Everton and Birmingham City midfielder Billy Wright.

The new manager spoke openly of his ideas for a youth policy and immediately implemented them. He was to utilise local football to bring in young blood and nurture the youngsters until hopefully a few stars were made; there was some successes. Mark Patterson was signed on, and later went on to play for Derby County having been sold for a vast profit. Gregg was a shrewd individual who gave his all to the club. On the pitch it was a constant struggle, and results were poor as the average attendance plummeted to just 2,641. During the season several players were sold on - Mick Halsall to Grimsby Town, Alan Mayes to Blackpool, Rob Wakenshaw to Rochdale, and the lanky striker who had for a couple of seasons been everyone's favourite, Andy Hill, was forced to retire through a back injury.

In Gregg's attempt to fight clear of the relegation zone, he used loan players, including Alan Davies the ex-Manchester United winger who shot to fame when he made his Red Devils debut in the 1983 F.A. Cup Final at Wembley. His career had nosedived after that match, joining Newcastle United and finding himself something of a nomad. At Carlisle he hardly seemed capable of playing on a higher stage. Sadly, some years later he ended his life, perhaps the pressure of early fame was too much for him to live with.

Goalkeeper Eric Nixon came on loan from Manchester City, and Guy Russell a striker from Birmingham City. Without doubt Nixon was the best of the bunch and everyone was disappointed when he returned to his club.

The team was relegated, finishing in 22nd position. To make matters worse there was a breach of the club's discipline code by one of the club's players who was told in no uncertain terms that he would never again play for the Carlisle United. The player, Scott Endersby, moved at the end of the season; a great shame as he could be inspirational when he elected to put effort into his game. Also leaving was Scott McGarvey. Quite simply the club could not afford to keep him, a celebrity, but an expensive one, and Gregg had to let him go.

In the F.A. Cup, after gaining a good 1-1 draw at Notts County, defeat followed in the home replay 3-0. The Littlewoods Cup offered little more with Grimsby Town victorious 3-1, on aggregate.

In the Freight Rover Trophy there were home victories over Stockport County 1-0 (an own goal), and Bury 3-2 - loan player Alan Davies scored twice in this game, and McGarvey grabbed the other. It was Preston who knocked the team out 2-1, in a poor encounter played before a Brunton Park crowd of just 1,400. There was little to look forward to in the Fourth Division.

With no money available Gregg was forced to implement his youth set-up far quicker than he could have anticipated, and players were brought in to replace the majority of the previous season's squad. Included were Steve Crompton, an unspectacular and somewhat inadequate 'keeper, plus local lad Brent Hetherington, who it has to be said under exceptional circumstances was outstanding.

United became one of County's last visitors in the League. Relegation and subsequent folding was to be the lot of the Welsh team.

___

On the field things were bad, very bad, with a highest League position in the season of tenth, that after two games! The goalkeeping situation was miserable. Crompton, a nice enough lad but seriously lacking ability, was released, and in his place came Martin Taylor on loan from Derby County. Taylor was quality, but in reality there was never any hope of signing him on a permanent basis, it was just too big a drop from the First to the Fourth Division. A permanent replacement was found in the form of Mark Prudhoe who signed after a loan spell from Walsall. Injury kept him out for four games and the Sunderland reserve 'keeper, Tim Carter, played four games.

Elsewhere, injury to John Halpin kept him sidelined for 20 games, Ian Bishop was out for 19 games, and the defence just couldn't find a reasonable formation. The first black player to join the club arrived in the shape of Garry Fulbrook, sadly his time was limited at the club as he became homesick and returned to Bath City from whence he came. In a good side Fulbrook would have settled and matured, at Carlisle he struggled, although there were flashes of brilliance with his ball control and distribution.

In November, Harry Gregg was ousted from the managerial role, and replaced by ex-Workington defender Clive Middlemass. With an average home league crowd of 2,236 the future of the club looked bleak indeed. It was no real surprise that the final League position was a lowly 23rd, second bottom of the Fourth Division, with only Newport County lying below. Dismal times indeed.

In the Cup competitions the showings were shameful. The Littlewoods Cup saw good wins over Stockport County 4-0 on aggregate, before Oldham Athletic won through 8-4 over two legs! In the F.A. Cup - Macclesfield Town at Moss Rose - United cruised into a 2-0 half time lead (Garry Fulbrook scoring his solitary goal for the club), and the second half looked a formality. It was, for Macclesfield Town! United crashed out of the competition 4-2 in a display which belittled the non-Leaguers part time status, they looked quicker, sharper and a damn-site fitter than Carlisle.

In the imaginatively titled Sherpa Van Trophy there was a home win against Chester City, followed by a good 1-0 away victory at Blackpool. In what seemed the easiest tie of them all the team was humbled 2-0 by Hartlepool at Brunton Park!

One curiosity factor of this season was the loan signing of one Dean Holdsworth from Watford. The mid-1990's multi-million pound valued star played 13 games for the club, scoring once in the 2-0 home win against Rochdale. At the time he was keen to join the club in an attempt to get first team football, if only he had!

Holdsworth (who also scored in the match), looks on as Wright's shot finds the net - Vs. Rochdale in February 1988.

Central defender Wes Saunders left in February, and signed for Dundee. Defender Billy Wright left at the end of the season, leaving the centre of defence looking somewhat exposed.

In the summer the manager looked to strengthen the defence with the signing of Mark Ogley and Ian Dalziel; Simon Jeffels was the last of the defensive trio to join in November. Defensively, things improved, although Mark Prudhoe suffered a dramatic loss of form which ultimately saw him replaced by Dave McKellar who had been sold to Hibernian in 1986, later appearing for Newcastle United and winning rave reviews. He was again transferred, this time to Dunfermline Athletic, where he was unsettled, and after a brief spell on loan with Hartlepool United it was Carlisle who again provided him with the opportunity to do well. To be fair he did, always a good goalkeeper he gave his all for the club. Other players to emerge during this decided-

ly average season were Tony Fyfe, a lean striker who weighed in with 4 goals, Steven Harkness, a delightful defender who was clearly destined for greater things - indeed Liverpool were to sign him the following July. Paul Proudlock and Paul Fitzpatrick also looked to be good buys.

A League position of twelfth was achieved, something of a success compared to the previous season. In the Littlewoods Cup it was an early exit, with Blackpool going through 4-1 on aggregate. The F.A. Cup did at least earn the club some desperately needed cash.

Telford United were first beaten 4-1 after a 1-1 draw at the Bucks Head ground, the goals of which were featured on BBC TV's 'Match of the Day'. A good 1-0 win at Scarborough in the next round earned a plum home tie with Liverpool. Again, the 'Match of the Day' cameras were present, no doubt expecting lots of goals, and any hopes of a cup shock were dashed with a stunningly professional Liverpool performance. Never in top gear they brushed Carlisle aside with relative ease, winning 3-0 on the day.

In the Sherpa Van Trophy there was a 1-1 home draw with Scarborough and a 3-2 away defeat at Darlington. By this time the supporters hopes of the team rising to the Fourth Division challenge had all but evaporated.

The 1988/89 season was to be remembered for a sad event, for on the 31st of January, United's most loyal servant, the great Dick Young died. Born in April 1918 he played his first serious football with Wardley Colliery. A centre half he was strong and willing, a real workaholic. He scored 18 goals in one season for Wardley, and following this feat several League clubs monitored his performances, among them, Leeds United, Sunderland and Sheffield United. It was the latter for whom he signed in November 1935.

Dick made 71 appearances for the Blades before moving to Lincoln City in March 1949 where he made 100 league appearances and scored goals. In 1949 United manager Fred Emery enticed him to Brunton Park as trainer, a post he desperately wanted, and the rest as they say is history. To put it into perspective Dick Young (affectionately known among United faithful of the 70's as 'Sir Dick Young' for what he had achieved for the club) was a genius, respected by footballers and managers all over England, many of whom asked for his advice on the abilities of certain players.

There will be nobody again in the club's history who will be so revered, and acknowledged as a true professional. He turned down several opportunities to leave Carlisle for 'bigger clubs', but in his own

words, *"I don't want to leave here, this club is my life."* The great man would have enjoyed witnessing his beloved Carlisle at Wembley, but to be fair to him there was very little else which could have impressed him. Incredibly with Carlisle United he had seen football in all the major leagues, Cup Semi-Finals, European sojourns the lot.

The following summer saw the arrival of big Keith Walwyn from Blackpool, an old fashioned style centre forward, who was to finish the season as top scorer with 11 goals. Tony Shepherd, an exciting midfielder arrived from Celtic along with David Miller from Preston North End who joined in the September. John Halpin was allowed to leave for Rochdale in a transfer which angered many United supporters who felt that the player had been unjustly punished for the tragic two leg-breaking tackles he endured in a short period of time. Thankfully Johnny was to later to return to the club after his playing days were over, working as a 'Football in the community' officer.

On the pitch it was inconsistency which caused the team not to capitalise on some good results, indeed for much of January and February they topped the League, but there followed six consecutive defeats and a drop to 8th position.

By May the team was left with nothing more than a hope of a play-off place. At 3 p.m. on the 5th May, they sat in fifth position, then comfortably holding such a place, but in a disastrous performance at Maidstone United on this, the final day of the season, a 5-2 defeat was suffered. Other results went against the club and a final League position of 8th had to suffice, one place outside the play-off positions.

The average home league attendance had improved to 4,736 mainly due to the teams pole position after the New Year.

In the Cups there was limited success, a 3-2 aggregate defeat to Halifax Town ended all interest in the Littlewoods Cup, whilst the F.A. Cup saw a good 3-0 home victory over Wrexham, but Wigan won a dour battle in the second round at Springfield Park 2-0. The newly titled Layland Daf Cup produced a 1-0 away win at Scarborough, a home 1-1 draw with Scunthorpe United with finally a 2-1 reversal at home to Stockport County.

The 1990/91 season was to see the emergence of several quality youngsters, when Darren Edmonson, Jeff Thorpe and Jason Priestley all forced their way into the first team and never looked out of place. Prolific goalscorer Steve Norris was signed, and left within six League games, he was in the starting line up for just two of them. Norris later claimed that he could not see eye to eye with team manager Clive Middlemass who was struggling to keep his job. The manager had signed veteran Eric Gates and hoped that he would be the catalyst to success, but he was wrong.

Eric Gates

To be fair Gates was still able to produce the skills he was recognised for, but he was a player in the last throws of his career, a player who cost the club heavily so far as the wage bill was concerned.

Three wins from eleven games saw the back of Clive Middlemass who left the club in March 1990, a good coach he never seemed to have the persona to make himself popular with the Carlisle public. There was some celebrating when Middlemass departed, for many hoped that a big name player/manager would fill the breach, but no one then knew how heavily the club was in debt.

The signing of 'has been' stars cost the club dearly, although to be fair the board of directors supported the manager to the hilt, trusting that he knew what he was doing. It seemed to the majority that Clive Middlemass had lost the will to win promotion, the desire for success had been drained, therefore both he and the club needed a change. The new manager was revealed as Aiden McAffrey who had been brought in by the ex-manager to assist with the coaching aspects of the club. It was a natural progression for McAffrey, he knew what was expected of him, and knew the limitation and financial restraints from the outset.

A final League position of 20th was achieved with an average attendance figure of 3,006. Even in the Cup competitions there was little to be proud of. In the freshly titled Rumbelows Cup, Scunthorpe United were beaten 2-1 on aggregate in the first round, First Division outfit, Derby County were the next opposition, and in a close encounter the first leg ended all square at 1-1, a Paul Proudlock strike giving Carlisle the lead at Brunton Park. In the second leg Derby scrambled through with a fortunate 1-0 win; Carlisle striker Keith Walwyn struck the County post with a fine header which looked goalbound all the way.

The F.A. Cup was a dead loss, a 5-0 thrashing at Wigan Athletic, and the Leyland Daf Cup was little better. A home 1-1 draw with Preston and a 1-0 away defeat at Rochdale being the outcome.

Halpin scores in the home match versus Peterborough.

The 3-2 victory in January 1991, was a welcome result after a run of four defeats.

The summer transfer madness continued with Keith Walwyn joining non-League Kettering Town, just a few games later Walwyn was to collapse in a game against Altrincham, suffering a mild heart attack which effectively ended his career. Replacing Walwyn was Dean Walling, a signing from Guiseley. Walling looked to be a player with real potential having once been on the books of Leeds United.

Also to arrive was ex-Leeds United striker Gwyn Thomas, as McAffrey looked to a mixture of youth and experience. Goalkeeper Kelham O'Hanlon was signed from Rotherham United in an attempt to instill confidence in the United rearguard. O'Hanlon, who it was claimed once received death threats from the IRA whilst on Middlesbrough's books, was a Republic of Ireland International. Sadly he failed to live up to the long term expectations, and found himself moving on to Preston a couple of seasons later, in 1993/4.

The 1991/92 season can be described as miserable, and the average home attendance

again dropped, this time to 2,554. One cup game attracted just 894, the lowest ever home attendance for a first class fixture in the club's history. This occurred on the 19th of November 1991, in an Autoglass Trophy fixture against Stockport, the stay aways were punished as Carlisle won 4-0!

It was a constant struggle as the club sat in 21st position for much of the season, then a final day 4-0 away defeat at Scunthorpe was the final nail in the coffin, the bottom position in the entire Football League, the worst team in the Football League! Tears, and there were many, especially as Club Chairman Andrew Jenkins had virtually stated that unless some miracle occurred during the summer then Carlisle United would have no alternative but to resign from the Football League. It was devastating news to the Carlisle faithful, those 2,554. In an attempt to keep the club afloat it was also announced that the entire playing staff may have to go part time.

In no way can the Chairman, (as devout and loyal supporter of the club as anyone could have hoped for) be blamed for the circumstances in which the club now found itself. There were several suggestions, and some fans even wrote to Jack Walker, the Chairman of Blackburn Rovers, basically begging for money, pleading for anything which might help save the club. As is generally the case during such periods, the vultures begin to gather. Suddenly all kinds of organisations claimed that Carlisle United owed them money, including the dreaded Taxman!

Just when everything seemed finished, and a deadline had been placed on the repayment of outstanding debts, in walked a man now affectionately known as 'JESUS' - Michael Knighton. The debts were cleared as the new Chairman surveyed his new kingdom. Speculation was rife that the ground would be sold to developers, Knighton ended all such speculation with a sweeping statement which effectively outlined his plans for Carlisle United. A ten year agenda to get the club into the Premier League!

Suddenly the eyes of English football were concentrating upon the team propping up the rest of the Football League. McAffrey was given the opportunity of proving himself, new players were brought to the club, including Ian Arnold. A skilful and inventive player from Middlesbrough, but very much an individual; it is fine having individual talent in a team, but when it comes to the crunch it is all about working together. Arnold's attitude, both on and off the field was most arrogant, and his deliberate snubbing of fans ensured that he would never be a crowd favourite. Other new arrivals included Richardo Gabbiadini from Scarborough, George Oghani from Evagoras, and David McCreery from Hartlepool.

Aiden McAffrey failed to inspire the side or the support, and thus was relieved of first team managerial duties on the 28th of Sep-

tember. The following day David McCreery was installed as manager. League performances were reasonable when compared to the previous season, and the majority of supporters were content to finish anywhere but bottom of the League, but the team finished in 18th place, with an average attendance of 3,209. The hero of the season was without doubt Michael Knighton who had instilled confidence into the support and the team.

In the cup competitions, Burnley were thrashed 4-1 at Brunton Park and held to a 1-1 draw at Turf Moor in the refreshingly sounding, renamed Coca-Cola (League) Cup. Norwich City were held 2-2 at Carlisle before United lost 2-0 at Carrow Road. In the F.A. Cup it was Wigan who were again the nemesis, winning 3-1 at Springfield Park. The Autoglass Trophy saw a 4-0 defeat at Scarborough, but a 2-0 home win over Hartlepool United was insufficient to proceed any further, and it ended any further Cup interest for the season.

Then, for the first time in many years, there was a buzz around Brunton Park, one could almost sense that a new era in the club's history was about to evolve, a very special era.

In June 1993 David McCreery stood down as manager, causing some speculation as to the relationship between Chairman and Managerial responsibilities; press speculation was rife that Knighton was interfering in team affairs, rumours and idle gossip which had no foundation whatsoever. Mick Wadsworth was revealed as the new man in charge of team affairs, his title would not be 'Manager' but that of 'Director of Coaching'. The modern day evolution meant that coaching and management roles had turned the complete circle, for in the early days of Carlisle United it was down to the 'Coach' to dictate team affairs, a simple yet practical job description.

The new manager said of his position, *"All I do is concentrate on coaching and first team matters, I don't know how much anyone gets paid, I'm not interested as long as they play well."* Joining Wadsworth was Leeds United 'keeper Mervyn Day as player coach, and Barnsley's Joe Joyce. David McCreery remained on the playing staff until January.

Knighton silenced his doubters in October 1993, when he signed striker David Reeves from Notts County for a club record fee of £121,000. The entire team was transformed from being perennial strugglers to promotion contenders, and football flowed as United soared up the League, eventually earning a play-off position in 7th place. The play-offs paired United with Wycombe Wanderers, and in a two legged match Wycombe won through 4-1.

They ultimately appeared at Wembley where they clinched promotion. The average home League attendance at Brunton Park had risen to 5,524.

In the Cup competitions, Chesterfield ended Coca-Cola Cup progress 4-2 on aggregate at the first hurdle, the F.A. Cup saw Knowsley defeated 4-1 at Goodison Park, Stalybridge Celtic were beaten 3-1 at Brunton Park, before Sunderland fluked a 1-0 victory, also at Carlisle, after a 1-1 draw at Roker Park. In the Autoglass Trophy Preston were defeated 2-0 in front of 3,909 Brunton Park fans. An incredible 2-1 win at Burnley was followed by another home win, this time 2-1 over Bury. Mansfield came to Carlisle in fine form and took the game into extra time before a Rod Thomas goal earned Carlisle a 2-1 victory.

Now in the Northern Area final they faced Huddersfield Town going down 4-1 at Leeds Road and winning the second leg 2-0, thus losing out, but only just.

In the summer Derek Mountfield and David Currie arrived as the team were made favourites to win the League title.

The champagne flows after a play-off place is achieved in the 1993/94 season.

Derek Mountfield celebrates another goal, in the Third Division promotion season

The bookmakers assumptions were proved correct as United not so much won the league but walked it. An outstanding record which finished:

P	W	D	L	F	A	Pts.
42	27	10	5	77	31	91

On top of this Mick Wadsworth was named Third Division Manager of the Year, and no less than three United players were voted as being the best in their respective positions in the Division - Dean Walling, Tony Gallimore and David Reeves. The highest attendance in the League was for the Carlisle United vs Lincoln City game, at 12,412. There were some outstanding team performances, including the 5-1 demolition of Hartlepool at the Victoria Ground, the 3-1 win at Fulham - which some reporters claim was the most fluent football ever to have graced

the (by now re-numbered) Third division. It was indeed a marvellous season which was further enhanced by a trip to Wembley - at last some success was gained in a cup competition.

The Coca-Cola Cup saw a 3-0 aggregate defeat to Queens Park Rangers, disappointing yes, but at no point was the team outplayed by their First Division opponents. The F.A. Cup ended in a third round defeat to Sunderland, but only after the team had been struck down by a flu epidemic. After a 1-1 draw at Roker Park, Sunderland won through 3-1 at Brunton Park, causing some embarrassment to the BBC who had believed that Carlisle would have beaten Sunderland and duly purchased the rights to televise live the next round tie with Tottenham Hotspur. Ultimately Sunderland vs Tottenham Hotspur just didn't quite have that romance about it, everyone wanted to see the lower division side taking on Jurgen Klinnsman and Co.

The Autoglass Trophy was something else. First, Darlington were beaten 3-2 at Feethams, then came Hartlepool 2-0, Chesterfield 1-0, and Wrexham 2-1 at Brunton Park. Crewe Alexandria were beaten 1-0 at Gresty Road, lining up a Northern Area Final against Rochdale. A tremendous 4-1 home win in the first leg ensured that Rochdale had it all to do at Spotland. Panic set in when the Dale went 2-0 up, but Derek Mountfield calmed nerves with a headed goal and just about killing the tie stone dead.

It was incredible, Carlisle United were about to be crowned Champions and going to Wembley all in the same season. The other Autoglass finalists were Birmingham City. Wembley's second biggest crowd of the season, 76,633, saw a rather dour game which did not detract from the Cumbrian hordes enjoyment.

This was Wembley, this was Carlisle United. It was wonderful, everywhere smiling faces, everywhere deckchairs.

The Carlisle side for that historic occasion consisted: Caig, Edmonson, Walling, Mountfield, Gallimore, Hayward, Prokas (Thorpe 90), Conway, Thomas, Reeves, Currie.

Three influential players of the season:
David Reeves (ever-present), Rod Thomas (37 games) and Tony Caig (only missed one League match)

After ninety minutes it ended all square at 0-0, and extra time was played, with a new Golden Goal rule, which basically decreed the first team to score win the game. United had the perfect opportunity to win the trophy when Paul Conway struck wide when given time and space from 18 yards. Perhaps it was nerves, perhaps it just wasn't to be, we can never be certain. In the 103rd minute disaster struck, when Birmingham's Otto, who had been a constant threat, clipped a ball forward into the penalty area and Tait glanced a header wide of Caig. Birmingham had scored, the game was over.

The Carlisle players fell to their knees exhausted both mentally and physically. In the stands, grown men and women cried, it was all over, a cruel way to end a Wembley final which had seen the team give their all. Once the disappointment had been addressed the Carlisle thousands burst into song, *"We're proud of you, We're proud of you"* followed by *"Michael Knighton's blue and white army."* No matter what anyone says, not even the England national side could attract as big an attendance at Wembley that season.

So what does the future hold? To put it into the words of club Chairman and Chief Executive Michael Knighton, *"I don't say what I don't mean, together we are going to the top."* With such a positive character as the driving force, who would dare doubt Knighton's claims, one thing that is for certain, for the supporters of Carlisle United it is the dawning of a new era....

The LADS IN BLUE have done good.

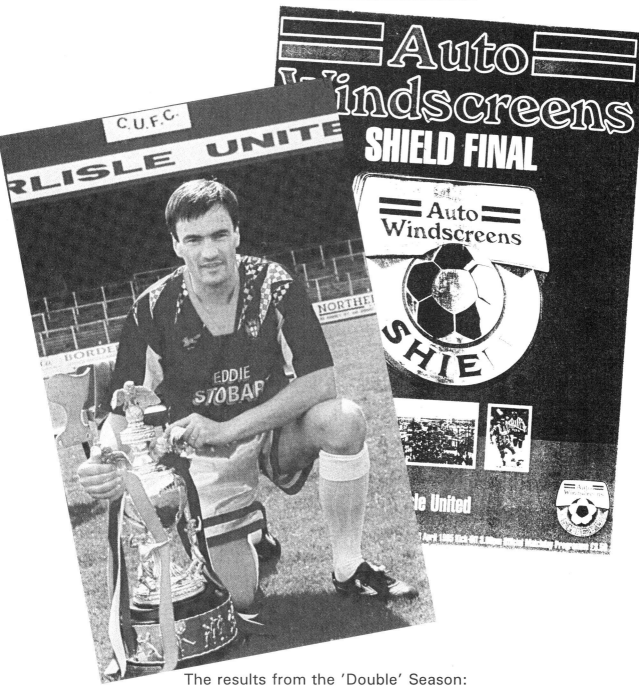

The results from the 'Double' Season:
A Wembley appearance and a Championship Trophy

THE MANAGERS

GEORGE BRISTOWE
1913 - March 1930

As such George Bristowe deserves perhaps the greatest credit awarded to any manager of Carlisle United, yet his role in the club's history has thus far been virtually forgotten in the passage of time. Before venturing any further, Bristowe is easily the longest serving manager the football club has ever had, a term in charge of team affairs which spanned some thirteen years.

It is curious to note that he was not actually afforded the title, 'team manager', but was in fact the General Secretary, the man who did just about everything for the club, perhaps 'dogs-body' would be a more accurate representation of his job description.

Bristowe knew the local game inside out and had a remarkable eye for talent. He would travel all over the United Kingdom to monitor future acquisitions, such was his enthusiasm for the job that many of these unofficial journeys were not supplemented by club expenses but came straight out of his own pocket. In one week he watched players in London, Norfolk and Oxfordshire, returning to Brunton Park armed with a full dossier of the individual strengths and weaknesses of the players he wanted. If they came available, then Bristowe's overpowering character and amiable personality could be relied upon to do the rest.

Success is the supporters guide to how a manager is shaping up. Bristowe brought the North-Eastern League Championship to Brunton Park in 1922, some 21 games were won, and just six lost out of a league total of 36 games played. This was to be an influential stepping stone as the club looked to greater things. The following season United finished sixth, and by their own standards finished in somewhat mediocre positions thereafter. However, at the end of the 1927/28 season which saw Bristowe's side remain unbeaten in their final eleven fixtures, they finished as runners up in the Championship. This was to be Bristowe's final season in the non-League game at Brunton Park, as the club were elected to the Football League the following season.

"This is the greatest achievement of my life, I am so pleased for everyone in Carlisle," said an elated Bristowe. There followed some tremendous signings including John (Jackie) Cape an electric winger from the local scene, Jimmy McConnell, a centre forward who finished the division's top scorer for two years in succession. Life in the Football League was a great deal tougher than Bristowe had appreciated, as it soon became clear that his desire and honest determination was not sufficient to take the team further. Thus the reign of the general secretary came to a sad end.

WILLIAM HAMPSON
March 1930 - May 1932

Born in Radcliffe, Lancashire, in 1882, Hampson progressed to become a fine defender and team manager to several clubs.

His playing career began with Rochdale in 1906, where, as a trialist he failed to make any impact. Later that same year he was taken on my Bury. A determined tackler he quickly made a name for himself and moved to Norwich City in 1907. He remained with the East Anglian side until January 1914, when he was involved in what was then a big money move.

His new club being the North-East giants, Newcastle United, who paid out the princely sum of £1,250 for Hampson's services. It was an astute signing, for the full back - once breaking into the first team - went on to make some 174 appearances for the Magpies, scoring just one goal.

His career was interrupted with the intervention of wartime activities, during this time he guested for Leeds City. He gained the reputation of being a tough but fair tackler, and was in 1924, the oldest ever footballer to win an F.A. Cup winners medal when Newcastle defeated Aston Villa 2-0. He was just 41 years and 8 months old!

In September 1927 he made a move to South Shields but was forced to retire from the physical playing side of the game in 1928, aged 46. Acting as a scout and taking up coaching roles in the North-East it was not too long before he was offered his first managerial role, with Carlisle United, arriving in the City in March 1930. The club had been elected to the Football League Division Three North the previous season, and Hampson was seen as the man to lead them to greater glories. United finished the 1929/30 campaign in 15th position, having conceded 101 goals. It was an abysmal record, one which Hampson openly stated he would improve upon. As good as his word, United did show signs of improvement, for Hampson introduced stars such as Bill Shankly, Arthur Sharp, and had an eye for up and coming talent.

He left United in May 1932, and eventually took up the managerial role at Ashington in 1934. Less than twelve months later he was at Leeds United where he reigned until May 1947, when the Yorkshire side earned just 18 points all season, finishing bottom of the First Division. He was reallocated to a chief scout's role, but his authority had been undermined and he eventually left to coach North-East schools.

Billy Hampson passed away in Congleton, Cheshire, in February 1966. His time at Carlisle was not a wasted one, for he should be admired for his wholesale clear-out of some nine United players during the summer of 1930; few managers would be confident enough to take such a gamble.

WILLIAM CLARKE
June 1932 - March 1935
May 1945 - August 1946

To be fair to Billy Clarke, he was employed in the capacity of club secretary, a good one at that. He remained with the club for almost twenty years in one capacity or another. A local man, he was first given the opportunity to take over as team manager with the departure of Billy Hampson in 1932.

Clarke was an honest, genuine chap, who loved the club and wanted whatever was best for Carlisle United and nothing else. Sadly, his knowledge of the game was limited to administration and what he had picked up from his predecessor. His first season in charge saw a mid-table finish, the following season - 1934/35 - United finished bottom of the pile with just 23 points. Clarke volunteered to stand down, such was the respect he commanded the club's supporters demanded that he remain as secretary.

His second spell as team manager came about in 1945, with no League football being played, it was down to Billy to get a side together in anticipation of the recommencement of activities. Always positive, always willing, he did so, only to hand over the reigns to Ivor Broadis in 1946.

There can be few managers or personnel involved with Carlisle United over the years who deserve as much credit as Billy Clarke, his commitment and dedication will never be forgotten.

ROBERT KELLY
March 1935 - November 1936

Bob Kelly the player was quick and possessed wonderful ball control, jinking his way round defences up and down the country, and eventually, all over the world. He was classed as one of the biggest names in the game between the First and Second World Wars and made some 14 appearances for England, at inside right, between 1920 and 1928.

His playing career began with Ashton White Star, before he progressed to Ashton Central, Earlestown, then St. Helens Town in 1912. Burnley signed him in November 1913 for a fee of £275, where he won Football League championship honours in 1921.

There followed a move to Sunderland in December 1925, at a then incredible fee of £6,550, and he remained at Roker Park for just two seasons before a further big money move to Huddersfield Town in February 1927, the fee commanded being £3,500. He appeared in two F.A. Cup finals for the Terriers, finishing on the losing side both times.

In July 1932 he moved to Preston North End before signing for Carlisle in March 1935 as player/manager. He actually played just 12 games for the club before hanging up his boots, thus completing a career total of 601 League appearances with 154 goals, one of those was netted for United. Kelly joined the club at a bad time, money was tight, and the team had failed to make any real impression in Division Three North. It was hoped that with Kelly's high profile and knowledge of the game, better quality players would join the club. In his first season he released the entire team, with the exception of Davie Lonsdale and Jimmy Parker, and assembled a new squad for less than £1,000. United finished the season in 13th position, a dramatic improvement.

His enterprising style and clear-cut image encouraged other financially better-off clubs to take an interest in his managerial skills, and when he left United for Stockport County it was no real surprise. At Edgeley Park he won the Division Three North Championship at the first attempt, although the club were relegated back again the following term! Kelly moved abroad in August 1946 to take up the head coach's position with Portuguese side Sporting Lisbon. This was followed by other coaching roles in Switzerland, and later, the Channel Islands. His final managerial role was with the Suffolk local non-League side, Bury Town, in December 1960.

FREDERICK WESTGARTH
December 1936 - March 1938

Born in the North-East, in South Shields in 1887, Fred Westgarth never actually played professional football nor any League soccer. He was however a fine coach, learning his trade in South Shields where he acted as coach-come-assistant trainer until 1926. That same year he joined Stockport County in a trainer's role and then became something of a footballing nomad, having coaching spells with Ebbw Vale, Workington, and Luton Town. In May 1934 he returned to Edgeley Park Stockport as manager and in a two year period rebuilt the side transforming them into real promotion candidates. Indeed, when he stood down as manager in September 1936, the club continued in this rich vein, and won promotion that same season.

Westgarth arrived in Carlisle in December 1936 and was to a certain extent somewhat ineffectual. The side were never higher than mid-table, and Westgarth's ability to motivate seemed to come into question. Granted, United were vastly improved upon previous seasons, as some form of consistency was introduced, but Westgarth clearly couldn't take them to a higher plane.

In March 1938 he resigned from his position to take the manager's chair at Bradford City. It was here that he achieved his only success in football, when Bradford won the Division Three North Cup in 1939.

Four years later he again moved, this time returning to the North-East with Hartlepools United, where he remained as manager for 14 years. It was during his time at the Victoria Ground, that Fred Westgarth had his finest years. Hartlepools prospered and had several good seasons, finishing fifth, then fourth in consecutive seasons, in Division Three North.

The 1956/57 season held high hopes for Westgarth and Hartlepools, that is until tragedy stuck, when on the 4th of February 1957, when Fred sadly passed away. It was a bitter blow to everyone at the club, however they went on to record their finest season, finishing as runners-up. Many people believed that had Fred lived on to fight another day, then the club could have won the Championship that same season.

DAVID TAYLOR
April 1938 - September 1939

Without doubt one of the most underestimated defenders (a right back) of his time, David Taylor had an illustrious career in the game, and always appeared to be on the verge of greater things. That is, until he arrived at Carlisle United F.C.

His early career was spent with Scottish club sides, Motherwell, and Glasgow Rangers, before Bradford City introduced him to the English game in 1910. He made 51 appearances for City, including an F.A. Cup final appearance and a winners medal in 1911, when the Yorkshire side defeated Newcastle United.

The following season, Burnley, then flying high in the First Division and one of the countries top clubs, signed him up. It was to be the first of his two spells at Turf Moor, where he made a total of 250 appearances, and won a further F.A. Cup winners medal in 1914. Burnley also finished as League Champions in 1921. In between these years, he made guest appearances for Chelsea in World War One football, and made a brief return to the Scottish game, with Glasgow Celtic in 1919, only to return to Burnley the following year. He eventually retired from playing in 1924.

Significantly, his retirement coincided with his appointment as manager of St. Johnstone in May 1924. The club had just been crowned Scottish Second Division champions and Taylor did a fine job in maintaining Scottish top flight football at Muirton Park. Alert to the pitfalls of stagnation when one remains in the same role for too long a period, he stood down as manager in 1930. Taylor was not out of the game too long, as Blackburn Rovers appointed him as first team coach, a position he held for a short time. Anxious to get back into the management role he returned to Scotland as manager of Dunfermline Athletic in 1936, and remained there until April 1938, whereupon he arrived at Brunton Park.

Taylor had a torrid time at Carlisle, his first and only full season saw the team finish fourth from bottom of Division Three North. They had some terrible hammerings inflicted upon them; 5-0 at Barrow, 7-1 at Crewe Alexandra, the record League defeat of 11-1 at Hull City, 7-1 at Southport, and 6-0 at Oldham Athletic.

Incredibly, although they conceded a massive 111 goals, the team provided the division's top scorer, Sam Hunt, who netted 33 times. Taylor had very little option but to stand down, his ideas were sound enough, but for a defender, his tactical strategy for the team left a great deal to be desired. He called it a day in September 1939, when with just two League fixtures of the 1939/40 campaign fulfilled, all football was suspended due to wartime activities. Taylor all but disappeared from the League game after his time at Carlisle, where his fine career had been blemished by the quantity of goals conceded, thus causing his awareness as a manager to come under scrutiny. In effect, nobody required his services as a top class manager again. A sad end indeed. David Taylor died in Scotland in 1949.

HUGH HARKNESS
1940 - 1945

With the advent of Adolf Hitler's nefarious activities, serious competitive football all but ceased. The Leagues were suspended, and eventually cancelled, as war broke out and the game was virtually forgotten.

Carlisle United, like every other League club relied on a quick end to the hostilities, as we now know, it never quite worked out that way. Many footballers found themselves at the front of the fighting, some would never play again. Back home in Carlisle, the club appointed a local league footballer to take charge of team affairs whilst the war was ongoing. His name was Harkness, something of an unknown, but a man who worked hard at keeping Brunton Park clean and tidy. Harkness worked as groundsman and general dogs-body, albeit he was officially classed as team manager. On the few occasions when representative matches were played, he selected the best team from guest players stationed in the Carlisle area.

In 1945, with the hostilities coming to an end, Harkness stood down, his reign up to that time being the longest of any official manager of the club. He was replaced by club secretary Bill Clarke, in an attempt to cut costs and raise funds for the re-start of competitive League football in this country.

IVAN ARTHUR 'IVOR' BROADIS
August 1946 - January 1949

Born in Poplar, East London, in 1922, Ivor became one of the most famous player/managers to ever don the blue and white of Carlisle United.

An England International, with 14 caps, he played in the 1954 World Cup finals, and appeared for some of the country's greatest football clubs.

His playing career began at Glengall Road School, Isle of Dogs, then to a school which favoured the oval ball as it's main sport - Coopers' Company School, Bow.

Moving from school football he signed for Finchley, then on to Northfleet, and a return to Finchley. During the war there were appearances for Tottenham Hotspur, Millwall and Carlisle United, all as an amateur.

August 1946 saw a permanent move to Carlisle at the tender age of just 23 years, and without any Football League appearance. Although his time as manager of the club could be regarded as being average, Broadis laid the foundations for the future, and when he left in January 1949, United were in a far healthier state than when he had taken over. Ivor is officially the first ever manager to transfer himself to another club. Still registered as a player, he sold himself to Sunderland for £18,000, claiming that it was in the best interests of the club that he leave, providing Carlisle with suitable financial reimbursement for the transfer. The fans were not convinced, but accepted his move out of respect for the money his move had produced.

His stay at Roker Park was to last less than two years as he moved to Manchester City in October 1951, this time a fee of £25,000 was involved. Newcastle United signed him two years later for the sum of £20,000. It was at the latter two clubs that he probably played his finest football, certainly the Geordie crowd accepted him as one of their own, and still do to this very day.

Ivor returned home in July 1955, when, the then United manager, Fred Emery, signed him as player/coach for a fee of £3,500. He remained at Brunton Park until June 1959, when he made a few brief appearances for local Scottish neighbours, Queen of the South, where he later acted as club coach.

In 1962 he retired from the game and took up a second career in journalism, writing about, football! It has to be said that he was equally as successful on this front as he was as an inside forward. Ivor is one of the most respected journalists covering the Northern game. Few footballers command respect after their playing days are over, Ivor is the exception to the rule.

WILLIAM SHANKLY O.B.E.
March 1949 - July 1951

It is very difficult to write anything which has not previously been penned about this great man. Bill Shankly was undoubtedly one of the greatest football club managers in the English game, if not the world. Born in Glenbuck, Scotland, in 1913, his playing days began with local side Cronberry. After proving his worth he signed for the gloriously named Glenbuck Cherrypickers, with few people at the time believing that the frail young man playing in 'Pickers' midfield was about to embark upon a fantastic career in the game.

Shankly was an uncompromising player, robust in the challenge yet delightful with his distribution, such skills attracted United who signed him in July 1932. Having made just 16 full appearances for the club he was sold to Preston North End, commanding a £500 transfer fee into the bargain. There followed a long spell with the Deepdale club, accompanied by Scottish full International recognition (5 caps). As was so often the case, the outbreak of war disrupted Shanks' playing career.

However he still managed to make guest appearances for, Northampton Town, Liverpool, Arsenal, Cardiff City, Bolton Wanderers, Luton Town and Partick Thistle. He retired from playing in March 1949. It was at this point that United again stepped in, this time to offer him the opportunity to take on his first managerial post. Shankly agreed to do so and found that a great deal of work was required at the club both on the pitch, and behind the scenes. Without further discussion, he took to clearing the terracing of weeds and grass, and completely repainted much of the ground providing, from the exterior, a smart well presented club. *"Keeping the fans happy is one of my priorities, these people keep me and my players in a job, it is for them we play, no football manager should ever forget this point."*

A great public relations speech, carefully worded, yet nothing rehearsed, Bill Shankly meant what he said. Before games at Brunton Park he would talk over the tannoy system, explaining to fans why he had made team changes, and other pertinent facts which were occurring behind the scenes. On one occasion he actually discussed a rumour which had linked him to a striker playing in the First Division. *"There is no way Bill Shankly or Carlisle United are interested in signing this player, he is not fit to play in our colours, the man plays as though his feet are tied together, so you can forget all talk of him coming here."*

Everything about United improved. On the field the club finished third in Division Three North at the end of the 1950/51 season. Shankly was adored by the Brunton Park faithful, although was no prima donna, just a working lad who had proved his worth and earned their respect. That respect turned to sadness and anger when the news broke that he had left the club, in July 1951, in favour of Grimsby Town. It was a bitter blow for everyone connected with Carlisle, as Shankly had led the club out of the wilderness and forced it into conceding that it was capable of greater things. That self belief had never before been evident. Shankly must take all the glory and praise for establishing United as a future footballing force. Some may laugh at such a statement, but United have, since Shankly's reign, been there, done the lot - and come back again. Not a solitary so called 'Big Club', has not fallen foul to Carlisle over the years, even Shanks' Liverpool were held to a 0-0 draw at Anfield in a classic F.A. Cup-tie.

Having left United, his reign at Grimsby lasted until January 1954, when he moved to Workington. Thereafter followed a spell as assistant manager with Huddersfield Town before being promoted to manager in November 1956. Finally the move to Liverpool came about in December 1959, the rest as they say, is history.

Bill Shankly O.B.E. died in September 1981. Football fans throughout the United Kingdom were united in sorrow, there were many in the City of Carlisle who spilled more than a few tears. Someone even placed a wreath at the club's main entrance, it bore the simple inscription, 'To Bill Shankly, thankyou for everything, we love you still. Supporters of Carlisle United A.F.C.'

FREDERICK DAVID EMERY
July 1951 - April 1958

To follow Bill Shankly the United board selected a relatively unheard of character in the form of Fred Emery. The new manager arrived from Bradford, then a struggling Second Division side.

It has to be said - in realistic terms - that Emery had, up to his arrival at Carlisle, little or no success, albeit as a player he won a Division Three North Championship medal with Doncaster Rovers.

What attracted the club to his managerial styles was presumably his ability to instil a fighting spirit into the team. Bradford had been struggling for much of the previous season, yet somehow, with rugged determination they battled it out and narrowly avoided relegation.

Fred's career in the game commenced with Lincoln City, then Bradford City, before a move to Doncaster Rovers, where he took over as manager for four years. In 1943 he managed Bradford, from where he moved to United.

In his first season in charge at Carlisle, United at one stage topped their division, but dropped back to finish in 7th position. Despite the lack of funds to support the purchase of better quality players, Emery did instil a 100% whole-hearted attitude in the team spirit, this ensured commitment which saw the club retain relative mediocrity and mid-table positions during his tenure.

Fred Emery's Carlisle United were uninspiring, and seemed to lack the fire of ambition which burned so fiercely in the supporters hearts. In April 1958 he stood down as team manager, and died just thirteen months later. Fred gave the appearance of being a morose character, but in fact he had a pleasing personality. It is difficult to assess what he could have achieved with a great financial budget, nevertheless, he did United no harm.

ANDREW BEATTIE
May 1958 - March 1960

Andy Beattie was your actual football odd-job man, there was hardly a position within the game which he did not hold at one time or another. As a player he was a Scottish International, with 7 full caps. A full back, he played for Preston North End, and guested for Leicester City, Notts County, Aldershot, Northampton Town, Derby County, Bradford City, Manchester City and Clapton Orient.

After the war he became the secretary/manager of Barrow F.C. then took over at Edgeley Park, Stockport in 1949. Then came a brief spell with Huddersfield Town before he arrived at Brunton Park in May 1958.

The serious thinking Scot had previously managed the Scotland national side, but resigned during the 1954 World Cup competition claiming that he had little support from the game's governing body. He was to later find himself in charge of the national side for a nineteen month spell between March 1959 and October 1960.

It was a difficult task which confronted Beattie, for Carlisle had just been relegated to the newly formed Fourth Division. The new manager proclaimed, *"This will be our only season in the Fourth Division, it is my intention to win it at the first attempt."* For a while it looked feasible, but a slump in form saw the club finish in 10th position. The following season was indeed a miserable one, lack of form and Beattie's apparent victory at all costs attitude cost United dearly. Attendances dropped when a dismal run after Christmas saw the club plummet down the League, and even worse, local rivals Workington achieved the double over the team. In what was an amicable agreement, Andy Beattie left, taking up an offer of the manager's job at Nottingham Forest. After this he held caretaker/manager positions with Plymouth Argyle and Wolverhampton Wanderers. He also held the impressive sounding position of professional advisor and general manager with Notts County. There was a time with Sheffield United as general manager, and scouting jobs for several clubs, including, Liverpool, Walsall, Brentford, Wolves and Notts County.

A real football nomad, Beattie was happiest screaming out instructions to his players from the touchline. At Carlisle he had a less than impressive time, but his undoubted tactical awareness could clearly, in different circumstances, have served the club well. Beattie died in September 1983, aged 70.

IVOR VERDUN POWELL
May 1960 - February 1963

The first Carlisle manager to attain any kind of real success in competitive first class League football, and for that he deserves great credit and recognition. Ivor was a Welsh International wing half, with 8 caps. A diminutive figure, he was a tireless workhorse for the clubs whom he served - Queens Park Rangers, Aston Villa, Port Vale and Bradford City as player/manager.

In July 1956 he took over as trainer/coach at Leeds United, a position he held until May 1960 when he was appointed as manager of Carlisle United. His introduction to League football at Brunton Park can hardly be described as stunning. He made major changes to the team, introducing 13 new faces, and naturally new players took time to settle, almost too long, as United finished in 19th position.

The following season saw a complete transformation as the players clicked and worked as a unit, the result, promotion to the Third Division as United finished in fourth position.

Expectations were high for the following season as Powell declared, *"I love it here, I think Carlisle and I were made for each other."* Confident of success he again changed his playing staff, this time though just 12 new faces came in. It was too many, United suffered a serious dip in form which lasted an entire season. Things were exasperated by a shattering and humiliating F.A. Cup defeat at the hands of Gravesend and Northfleet at Brunton Park. Powell was summonsed to the United boardroom immediately after the game and told his fate, sacked!

It was a great shame for the Welshman whose heart and soul was undoubtedly in the club. He later managed Bath City before retiring from the game completely in 1967.

GEORGE ALAN ASHMAN
February 1963 - June 1967   August 1972 - October 1975

What more can be said - the most successful manager of Carlisle United ever. Alan Ashman was, quite simply, Carlisle United. A playing career that was hardly memorable, Ashman played for Sheffield United and Nottingham Forest, both in the wartime leagues and as an amateur. In June 1951 he signed for United and made a total of 207 appearances, scoring 98 goals, before he retired in 1958.

It was then that Ashman embarked upon employment with which he is always linked, that of a poultry farmer, whilst carrying out these duties he also managed Penrith F.C. In February 1963 he was invited to take over as team manager of United. This offer was down to one of the club's directors, Mr Monkhouse, who owned the poultry farm where Ashman worked, and he gave him the opportunity to prove himself.

It was initially a trial period - United were bottom of the League and clearly going down. In came Ashman and for a few weeks he transformed the style of play into neat passing interchanges. Telling the players to do the easy thing, which they obeyed, albeit they were still relegated.

Ashman's position was made permanent, and the following season United were again promoted, this time as runners-up in the Fourth Division. The following season they were crowned as Third Division Champions. Things did not end there, as United almost took the Second Division by storm, eventually finishing third. Alan Ashman was proclaimed as a managerial genius, and hero worshipped at Carlisle where nothing was deemed as being beyond his ability. The club were gunning for First Division football.

Just when things seemed right, the inevitable happened. Ashman was invited to take over as manager of another club - West Bromwich Albion. At the end of his first season at the Hawthorns, the Baggies won the F.A.Cup, the following year they reached the quarter-finals of the European Cup Winners Cup, and were F.A. Cup semi-finalists. Football being what it is, Alan Ashman was on holiday in 1971 when a journalist contacted him and told him that he had been replaced at West Brom by Don Howe! Truly despicable treatment, but one which surprises no football supporter.

Ashman had no problems finding further employment, and he had a spell in Greece with Olympiakos Piraeur where the club finished League runners-up. In August 1972, Alan Ashman returned home and Brunton Park welcomed him back with open arms. Ultimately he led United to Division One, and for a proud few days the team topped the whole of the Football League. No matter what anyone may say or believe, you do not top any League without being the best, albeit shortlived - United were 'there'. It was heady days at Brunton Park. However, United struggled to score goals, and for some inexplicable reason Ashman refused to buy a proven young goalscorer, sticking with loyalty and the basic side which saw the team promoted, and which was to see them relegated. The following season Ashman resigned and later managed Workington and Walsall. He also acted as scout for Derby County and the Swallows of Walsall, and there were further brief spells as assistant manager at Derby and at Hereford United. A wonderful front man, he enjoyed getting out amongst the supporters and chatting to them about the game, the club, or football in general. An ambassador for the club, it was a great shame that he left them when he did, especially after the highlights of the previous season.

No matter what the future holds, Alan Ashman will always be remembered with fond memories at Brunton Park, and no praise is sufficient a reward for what he achieved for the club and its supporters.

126

TIMOTHY VICTOR WARD
September 1967 - September 1968

Tim Ward stepped into the void left by Ashman's departure, and faced a difficult task. Albeit everyone wanted him to succeed, as though to prove that the promotions had not been borne out of a fortunate couple of seasons.

An ex-England international, Ward had been a tough and industrious wing half, having played for Cheltenham Town, Derby County and Barnsley, There was also a guest appearance for Partick Thistle during the War.

At Barnsley, he retired from playing and took over as coach to the 'A' team.

Always keen to further his career he took on the manager's job at Exeter City, and his arrival at St. James' Park was greeted by Grecian supporters who saw him as a great prospect. Their elation was shortlived, for just eight days in fact, as Ward resigned and returned to Barnsley where he took over as team manager.

He was at the time, the youngest manager in the Football League, aged just 34. There came spells as manager of Grimsby Town and Derby County, before his arrival at Carlisle in September 1967. To his credit, Ward tried to force his own style on the team, but his leadership method failed to impress. Results were at best average, and the club never looked like mounting a promotion challenge. A sound 11th position was attained in Division Two, but things were far from happy. The fans found the manager aloof, almost uncaring, and slowly but surely the cries for 'Ward out' were chanted from the terraces. He succumbed to these pressures in September 1968, and duly returned to the Midlands, with Nottingham Forest, where he acted as scout. Tim Ward died in January 1993, his greatest achievements being with Derby County where supporters still recall him with some affection.

ROBERT STOKOE
October 1968 - January 1970
September 1970 - August 1985
October 1985 - May 1986

If any of United's managers were to be regarded as high profile, then Bob Stokoe would be that man. Not that he was extrovert, but Stokoe is the manager most football fans outside the area associate with the club, and quite rightly so.

This quiet and gentlemanly Geordie was a totally dedicated servant to every club he was involved with, and in particular Carlisle United.

As a player he was a solid centre half and an F.A. Cup winner in 1955. It was with Newcastle United that he made his name, making 287 appearances and scoring 5 goals for the Magpies. He later moved to Bury as player/manager in December 1961, before hanging up his boots in May 1964. In the managerial role, he moved on to Charlton Athletic and Rochdale, before arriving at Brunton Park in October 1968.

He took United to the semi-final of the Football League Cup in 1969 and introduced a new fresh style of football to the United faithful. Then, in 1970 he negotiated transfer terms with Blackpool and duly moved clubs, with United receiving a fee in exchange.

The spell at Bloomfield Road lasted 23 months before he returned to the North-East with Sunderland. Of his many achievements with the Roker Park side, the pinnacle was his 'out-managing' one of the greatest team managers of all time in the 1973 F.A. Cup Final, as his side returned to Sunderland with the Trophy. His reward for such success and for guiding the club to the Second Division Championship in 1976 was the sack!

There followed a spell with Bury, Blackpool, and Rochdale, before a return to Carlisle, where he acted as a scout, between August and November 1979. He stepped up into the manager's office again, in September 1980, where he remained, almost continuously, until May 1986.

Within this period, he stood down to allow 'Pop' Robson a chance to prove himself, however, he was forced to take charge when his successor resigned after less than two months in charge. He eventually handed over the role to Harry Gregg in 1986. The following season he took temporary charge of Sunderland before drifting out of the limelight for a few years. In 1991, Ian Porterfield persuaded him to take up the role as a scout for Chelsea. Bob Stokoe was a 'real' manager, a motivator who knew his players and the game inside out, a man who cared about Carlisle United and it's supporters. Greater credit cannot be paid for his services to the club.

IAN MacFARLANE
January 1970 - July 1972

Who would be a manager? No one could blame Ian MacFarlane for thinking such thoughts after his ridiculous dismissal from the Brunton Park hot seat in July 1972. This tall knowledgable Scot (known at Brunton Park as 'The Big Man') had all the credentials to lead United to greater things, only to find himself out in the cold.

MacFarlane played his football at Aberdeen, Chelsea, Leicester City and Bath City. Just 41 League appearances in England, with a further 17 in Scotland, he was hardly an experienced professional, yet he was an astute character who picked up many positive features from his managerial mentors.

He took on the role of assistant manager at Middlesbrough, then Manchester City, before being given his first full time managerial position with United in January 1970. His first League season in charge almost saw the club promoted, with a final position of fourth, after a run of five wins out of six in the last few fixtures. MacFarlane was the main reason the talented Stanley Bowles came to the club, as he believed in the man who told him he would kick-start his career.

Much was expected the following season, perhaps too much. MacFarlane had shown the football world that his Carlisle United side were able to compete with the best. They failed to live up to those expectations, for their form was indifferent, and resulted in a final League position of 10th. In July 1972, MacFarlane was, to the amazement of everyone, sacked.

He moved on to Sunderland where he acted as assistant manager, then caretaker/manager during October and November 1976. In 1977 he returned to Leicester City as assistant manager, a position he held for four seasons, which included a temporary spell in charge, for three months in 1978 (April - June). He acted as chief scout for Howard Wilkinson at Leeds United, standing down from the position in 1994.

RICHARD YOUNG
November 1975 - November 1976

A tremendous character, and a marvellous ambassador for Carlisle United. No doubt many fans will read about 'Dick', remembering him with great fondness and affection. The Author's memory of this 'gentleman' was being taken by the hand on a guided tour of the ground (at 10 years old), and being introduced to players and club officials, as some-one of great importance. Yet to Dick Young, all supporters were important. That is the sort of man he was, caring and loyal.

Born in Gateshead in 1918 he loved his football and played for Bolden Colliery before joining Sheffield United in November 1935. He was a six-footer and therefore a strong and powerful centre half, and his pace allowed him to be something of a utility player, for he often covered at right back. Injury ended his playing days whilst he was turning out for Lincoln City as player/coach after the Second World War, and he retired from playing in 1954.

Within twelve months he arrived at Carlisle as trainer/coach working with the then team manager Fred Emery. He served in this position for some twenty years, but his training methods could hardly be classed as methodical, indeed he was something of an innovator in this department. Dick would take players training on the beach at Silloth, or running along the dunes at Skinburness. Alternatively he would join them on cross-country runs in the Lake District or around Rickerby or Bitts Park in Carlisle. Whatever or wherever, Dick would be there training alongside them, encouraging and motivating.

In November 1975, he was made team manager, replacing Alan Ashman. He is in the record books as, on appointment, the oldest manager of a Football League club.

It was a difficult time for the club, for relegation from the First Division and poor form left Dick to fight an uphill battle. He signed the striker United needed in the First Division, Billy Rafferty, and brought in a towering centre half, Ian MacDonald. The club, as was expected, struggled, and after just one year in charge, Dick volunteered to resign. The club refused to allow him to leave and reinstated him as trainer/coach. He eventually retired from the game in 1982.

Dick Young passed away on 31st of January 1989, having seen it all in his days with the club. No one would have enjoyed the occasion of United competing for a trophy in a Wembley final more than him. It would be difficult to find someone who had a bad word to say about him, and other more eminent football authorities - managers, players, and officials - proclaimed him to be a football thoroughbred, impossible to replace. How right they were.

ROBERT MONCUR
November 1976 - February 1980

As a player, Bobby Moncur was a real gem, Scottish International, captain of both club and country, honours at all levels of the game, he was all things to the Newcastle United side of the sixties and early seventies. He left St. James' Park in June 1974, moving to Sunderland, then to Brunton Park as player/manager in November 1976.

Bobby arrived in the city and declared his intention to rebuild the side, *"it's a huge job, but we are all big enough to take it on, I expect your support,"* he said at one forum he chaired. He was a magnificent ambassador for the club and would regularly get out among the supporters, asking for their opinions, and seemingly listening to their complaints and criticism.

At the end of his first season, United were relegated to the Third Division, as Moncur struggled to inspire his side. The introduction of Peter Beardsley was about all he will be remembered for whilst at the club. His Carlisle was a robust and rugged one, and under his reign United became 'just another' Third Division team. He resigned in February 1980 to take over as manager of Hearts, and the move caused little concern amongst the club's support.

Since then he has managed Plymouth Argyle, 1981-1983 (sacked), and Hartlepool United, 1988-1989 (sacked) - with the club bottom of the Fourth Division. It only goes to prove that not all good players make good managers.

MARTIN HARVEY
February 1980 - September 1980

A fine defender for both club (Sunderland) and country (Northern Ireland), Harvey was seen as a solid and tough tackling player. As a person he was not so ruthless and he actually brought a smile back to Brunton Park, albeit for a short time.

One can only feel some sympathy for Martin Harvey, for he took over a struggling Third Division team from Bobby Moncur and literally transformed them into a stylish and entertaining side. The team finished the 1979/80 season in sixth place, mainly through his enthusiasm and motivation qualities.

The following season he found the going very difficult, results and form dipped, as the team struggled to get results. Harvey was asked to stand down as team manager and to take on a team coach's role. Naturally he refused and duly resigned altogether.

BRYAN STANLEY 'POP' ROBSON
August 1985 - October 1985

'Pop' Robson was an exquisite and exciting footballer, an out and out goalscorer with clubs such as Newcastle United, Sunderland, West Ham, Chelsea and Carlisle. He first came to United in March 1983 on loan from Chelsea. Two seasons later he returned as assistant manager to Bob Stokoe who was grooming him as his direct replacement. When his time did eventually arrive he failed to achieve the desired results and literally turned his back on the club and walked out after a handful of games.

It was a great disappointment to Stokoe and to all United fans who saw Robson as a bright managerial prospect. The step from assistant to manager, can be a daunting one and perhaps 'Pop' was not ready for it, the buck stopped with him and he didn't like it.

Many believed that the wrong man had in fact been groomed for the managerial role. Tommy Craig was a more influential figure in the United team yet was overlooked for Robson.

Had the pair worked together one can only imagine what we could have been achieved. Bryan 'Pop' Robson moved on to coach and play for Sunderland, plus Gateshead, and he acted as assistant manager at Hartlepool United. He has been successful as reserve team manager of none other than Manchester United.

HAROLD GREGG
May 1986 - November 1987

A tremendous goalkeeper who was at one time classed as the best in the world. Harry is a real hero, a survivor of the horrific Munich Disaster, he actually pulled people from the twisted wreckage, saving many lives.

As a goalkeeper he represented Coleraine, Doncaster Rovers, Manchester United, Stoke City and Northern Ireland.

He became manager of Shrewsbury Town in July 1968, before moving on to Swansea Town in November 1972, this was followed by a spell in charge of Crewe Alexandra in 1975. There followed a term back at Swansea as coach then assistant manager. Harry was introduced into the Brunton Park set up in May 1986 inheriting some fine players from his predecessor, Bob Stokoe.

To be fair to him, United had very little money and it was down to his managerial ability to encourage players to the club. Harry, like so many other before and after him, struggled to make any real impact. The club was relegated and Gregg's services were dispensed with, a matter which he greatly objected to and contested for a period of time.

CLIVE MIDDLEMASS
November 1987 - March 1991

Clive had a rather un-distinguished playing career, a defender with Workington he won no major honours within the game, albeit he did make some 170 League appearances between 1963 and 1970.

He had a spell as second in command at Bristol City between 1985 and 1987 before taking on the Carlisle job in November 1987.

Middlemass was not an extrovert type of manager, he would rather let the team's results speak for themselves. His first season in charge of United, saw them finish second bottom of the League, 19 points above Newport County!

The following season saw some improvement, with a mid-table position, the season after that was spoiled on the final day when Maidstone United wrecked any chances of a play-off place with a 5-2 destruction of United. To make matters worse, some four other results went against the club ensuring that United had played their last game of the season, and would remain a Fourth Division side.

Middlemass could not improve on this position. United again found themselves struggling as the fans began to call for his resignation, it never came. He was dismissed in March 1991, with the club stuck in the bottom three positions of the Fourth Division.

AIDEN McCAFFREY
April 1991 - September 1992

Aiden McCaffrey had acted as United coach for a period of three years, working closely with Clive Middlemass. It came as no surprise that the club looked within their ranks, and promoted Aiden to team manager, for he knew the club inside out, and knew what limited resources were available.

In his first full season in charge, United finished third bottom of the League and things hardly looked promising for the future. Money was dwindling, gates dropping, and eventually it was announced that the club would fold unless someone came in to buy it.

They did, and out went Aiden McCaffrey, the ex-England Youth International centre-half who had served the club well, but his predicament was a difficult one, few managers would have stuck it out for so long.

DAVID McCREERY
September 1992 - June 1993

A solid dependable midfielder, David McCreery first made his name at Old Trafford with Manchester United. This was followed by a spell with Queens Park Rangers, and later in 1981 a transfer to the NASL and Tulsa Roughnecks.

Newcastle United brought him back to England in October 1982 where his cultured football and

tenacity was of great importance in the rebuilding of the Magpies first team. Heart of Midlothian signed him in 1989 before he returned to the English game in 1992 with Hartlepool United.

There followed a brief spell with Coleraine in 1992, before he stepped into management with Hartlepool as assistant to Alan Murray.

David McCreery joined Carlisle as first team manager in September 1992. He task was a difficult one, to revitalise a side which had almost slipped out of League football and into the relative obscurity of the non-League game.

McCreery was an honest and hard working manager and he did give the job his very best, unfortunately, despite everything else he failed to inspire the club's support, and only rarely did United show glimpses of the endeavour every supporter wanted to see. McCreery resigned from his position at the end of the 1993/94 season, clearly disappointed that he had not achieved greater things. Despite this he will be remembered with some affection by most United supporters.

MICK WADSWORTH
June 1993 - To date

Born in Barnsley on the 3rd November 1950, Mick Wadsworth learned his trade in local football, and his often inspired performances as a striker aroused the interest of several local club sides. A move to Gainsborough proved to be the important one as it was from here that he attracted the attention of scouts from Scunthorpe United. As his form was closely monitored, Scunthorpe moved in to sign the slim athletic built striker in August 1976.

Some 19 League appearances, with a further 9 as substitute and 3 goals were bagged during that one season. Thereafter followed a successful career in coaching, until the call came from Carlisle United. Wadsworth accepted the role of Director of Coaching and duly appointed Mervyn Day and Joe Joyce as part of his coaching team.

The results have been incredible. In Mick's first full season in charge, United reached the Third (former Fourth) Division play-offs and the Northern area final of the Autoglass Trophy. Twelve months later, United had won the Third Division championship in some style, and reached Wembley for the first time in the club's history, this time as the Northern Area winners of the Autoglass Trophy.

Wadsworth is a straight-talking Yorkshireman, a professional who knows what he is talking about, and a man who has earned a great deal of respect from the Carlisle public. We can only wonder and dream of what further glories Mick Wadsworth may bring to the club.

THE CARLISLE UNITED SOCCER GRAVEYARD

Throughout the club's history, Carlisle United has never been categorised as a fashionable club, indeed, members of the national press have at one time or another termed the club as; the minnows - little Carlisle - the bumpkins - virtual aliens from the far North - and perhaps the most disrespectful term of all 'The Cumbrian No Hopers!' Of course all football clubs at one time or another suffer to the often biased criticism of the football reporter, yet Carlisle do appear to have suffered more than most.

To put matters straight, Carlisle have never been able to reap the recognition the club deserves. Outstanding victories over the so called soccer big boys tend to go unnoticed in the national press, yet there have been times when such clubs perished the thought of facing Carlisle United, especially at Brunton Park. This chapter then outlines how the mighty have fallen against the not so Little Carlisle United.

****

Saturday 6th January 1951
F.A. Cup Third Round

ARSENAL: Platt, Barnes, Smith, Forbes, Daniel, Mercer, Logie, Goring, Lewis, Roper, Cox.

CARLISLE: McLaren, Coupe, McIntosh, Kinloch, Twentyman, Waters, McCue, Turner, Billingham, Jackson, Hogan.

A real David and Goliath battle. United's regular centre forward, Jack Lindsay sustained a broken jaw in the week of the Arsenal cup-tie, thus keeping him out of the Highbury line-up. Centre half Geoff Twentyman, was another fitness doubt with a hamstring injury, but was cleared shortly before kick off. The team arrived in London the day before the game and went to the London Palladium to take in a show that evening. Sightseeing was definitely not on the agenda, as team manager Bill Shankly claimed that it would tire the players out!

An hour and a half before kick off, United arrived at Highbury stadium and were provided with a guided tour by their manager. *"This is the Arsenal goal in one half, and that's it in the other, lets make sure we know where it is,"* he told the team, the tour was little more than a confidence builder as

Shanks criticised everything he saw, from the pitch, to the stadium. The manager was confident his side would surprise the football world. *"It is eleven men against eleven men, they may be quicker, they may be more skilful, they may be stronger, but we have nothing to lose and everything to gain, I can tell you, the old men of Arsenal are worried about us."*

Before the game a pack of Cumberland hounds was paraded on the pitch as the screaming Cumbrian hordes revelled in the big match atmosphere, one London based reporter described the pre-match build up as: *"Amazing, the Carlisle support, several thousand of them were buoyant, there were foxes and hounds everywhere, scenes like this have never before been seen at Highbury. The Arsenal support seemed stunned by it all."*

In the dressing room, Bill Shankly inspected his side and gave individual personal messages to each one of the players, then as they set out from the 'away' dressing room, he yelled out, *"you can't lose, this lot are like a lot of cart-horses."*

Olga, with mascot George Baxter, greeting the fans at Highbury.

The game kicked off with the Gunners making most of the attacking, during an early Arsenal raid the ball appeared to be screaming into the United net only to be blocked on the line by Carlisle defender, Norman Coupe, who, with all the nonchalance of an experienced International, controlled the ball and belted it clear of the Carlisle penalty area.

The first ten minutes saw Arsenal strike a post and United keeper Jimmy McLaren pull off three outstanding saves. Team captain on the day, Alex McIntosh, recalls looking towards the clock end of Highbury and seeing the

McIntosh and Mercer toss-up at Highbury

time as 3.07 p.m., turning to fellow defender Geoff Twentyman he said, *"We are going to lose this 20-0 at this rate."*

Slowly but surely the Arsenal team found their opposition resilient and committed, time and again vital tackles would go in from Kinloch, Waters, and McCue. Arsenal's play became shoddy as the 50,000 plus crowd began to sense that 'lowly' Carlisle could spring a surprise.

Winger Billy Hogan ran the Gunners defence ragged, crossing and shooting from all angles, but none were too testing for Platt in the Arsenal goal. In the second half Platt pulled off the save of the game when he twisted in mid-air, to turn over a certain goal from Phil Turner. When the final whistle blew some of the Arsenal players fell to their knees exhausted, shocked, or just plain relieved that it was all over and a draw had been achieved.

The Carlisle team received a standing ovation from the crowd, yet Shanks, somewhat tongue in cheek told a reporter,

"I'm disappointed, we should have won, I'll give them what for in that dressing room." The manager was never one for showing his true feelings, he was to later recall the result as one of the greatest in his managerial career. That same evening the players were allowed a celebratory night on the town, just rewards for their efforts.

Result: (Mighty) Arsenal 0   (Little) Carlisle United 0.

****

> **Saturday 27th January 1968.**
> **F.A. Cup Third Round**

NEWCASTLE UNITED: McFaul, Craig, Burton, Clark, Moncur, Scott, Craggs, Bennett, Robson, Davies, Sinclair.

CARLISLE UNITED: Ross, Neil, Caldwell, McConnell, Garbutt, Marsland, McVitie, Murray, Rudge, Balderstone, Sharp.

"Lowly Carlisle United are the next visitors to Gallowgate in the cup, the challenge from Cumberland should not be sufficient as to cause the Magpies any serious problems, in fact the only concern troubling Mr. Harvey is home or away in the next round."

The North-East press were confident that their side would cruise into the fourth round of the competition. The previous week, the Magpies had hammered Coventry City at Highfield Road 4-1, Carlisle meanwhile had steamrollered Bolton Wanderers 3-0 at Brunton Park.

The majority of the First Division sides team were household names; Wyn Davies, Pop Robson, Ian McFaul, Bobby Moncur et al. In the public houses on Tyneside Newcastle fans were asking *"Who"*? when discussing the oppositions stars. One journalist, cornered by a group of Carlisle fans turned to leave the excited group, parting their company with the arrogant statement, *"I wouldn't be too upset if we put six or seven past you, this is the best side Newcastle have had for a long time."*

A crowd of 56,569 packed into St. James', and at least 8,000 of these had made the journey from Cumberland. The match kicked off to a cacophony of, *"C'mon Carlisle,"* echoing from the Gallowgate end, this cheer continued throughout the ninety minutes and long after.

The Tynesiders were outcheered, outplayed, and ousted from the cup by a tremendous header from the diminutive Murray who flashed the ball in past a flapping McFaul in the Newcastle goal. Tommy Murray was in fact the smallest player on the pitch.

Elsewhere, the mighty Wyn Davies was humbled by a titanic performance from Carlisle's Peter Garbutt. Some concern was expressed when Davies clearly feigned a foul in the Carlisle penalty area, collapsing to the ground between two defenders as though he had been poleaxed by a missile fired at close range from an elephant gun. The referee pointed to the penalty spot, and up stepped Ollie Burton.

"The confident Burton is not one to miss a penalty, as far as Carlisle are concerned, when this one hits the net they can kiss the fourth round goodbye." said one radio commentator. Burton struck the ball well, and was about to turn to celebrate when the Carlisle goalkeeper, Alan Ross flung himself at the ball and turned it away. St. James' Park fell into a deep silence.

The after-match appraisal was, as is generally the case when such results occur, typically subdued. *"It was one of those things... defensive mistakes let us down,"* said Joe Harvey frantically searching for an excuse as to why his side had been so professionally outplayed by their Cumberland neighbours.

To be fair, Alan Ross in the Carlisle goal had been outstanding, every ball he had to deal with stuck to his hands like glue, Tommy Murray had never stopped running and chasing, and Peter Garbutt was quite simply outstanding, clearing one ball off the line with a powerful header into touch.

Carlisle manager Tim Ward said of the result, *"I knew we could do it, I told the lads we could, it does no one any good to shout from the chimney tops, look at what it has done to Newcastle!"*

Seldom had such an unassuming manager made such an accurate statement.

Result: (Giant) Newcastle United 0   (Lowly) Carlisle United 1.

****

Tuesday 15th October 1969
Football League Cup Fourth Round

CARLISLE UNITED: Ross, Hemstead, Caldwell, Passmoor, Winstanley, O'Neill, McVitie, Ternent, Brown, Barton, Balderstone.

CHELSEA: Bonetti, Boyle, Harris, Hollins, Webb, Hinton, Cooke, Hudson, Osgood, Birchenall, Houseman.

Just take a look at the Chelsea line up, each and everyone of them household names. In the previous round the 'Pensioners' had knocked out League Champions Leeds United, and were installed as favourites to win the competition. Carlisle on the previous Saturday had destroyed Watford 3-1 at Vicarage Road, whilst Chelsea had drawn 2-2 with Derby County before a First Division crowd of 51,421.

Cup fever took the city by storm as the local press issued song sheets for the game, en-

couraging 'new' chants on the terraces. In the London press, at least one Chelsea star said of the tie, *"who and where is Carlisle?"* Team manager Dave Sexton knew the dangers such a draw held, *"I dislike playing little clubs, it is Carlisle's Cup Final, I'm sure they will try to make a game of it for twenty minutes or so."*

A crowd of 18,513 saw a cracking cup-tie, as Chelsea, wearing unfamiliar yellow, were well and truly beaten. Osgood, Hudson and Birchenall were non-existent as O'Neill,

Winstanley and Passmoor controlled the International line-up with consummate ease. Meanwhile, Chris Balderstone who could practically make a football talk, strolled majestically round the park, spraying passes to his United colleagues with unerring accuracy.

Chelsea and England 'keeper Peter Bonetti was felled by a slate thrown by an imbecile from the crowd gathered in the Warwick Road End of the ground. Match referee Kevin Howley announced that the ground would be cleared of all spectators should a similar mindless incident occur again. Thankfully no more hooliganism took place and Bonetti, although shocked, played on, having made a full recovery.

In the second half it was all Carlisle as Chelsea looked like the team from the lower league. The moment all United fans had been waiting for arrived from a free kick outside the Chelsea penalty area.

The kick was taken by United full back Derek Hemstead, a glorious grass-cutter, and the ball screamed past a hapless Peter Bonetti and into the Chelsea net to give United the lead. Then, and only then did Chelsea begin to play, but still they could find no way through a well marshalled and solid United defence.

When the final whistle sounded, hundreds of United supporters raced onto the pitch to rejoice with their heroes in blue. Chelsea trooped off, to a warm Brunton Park roar. One thing that is for certain, they certainly knew who Carlisle United were now! To his credit, Dave Sexton was complimentary of Carlisle's display, *"I think they could beat anyone on their day, tonight was all about Carlisle and not Chelsea, good luck to them."* Some of the Chelsea internationals refused to sign autographs for Carlisle youngsters, brushing them aside before and after the game as though they had no right to be on the same planet. Stars, I think not, goodbye Chelsea.

Result: (Who are) Carlisle United 1   (We are Chelsea Super) Chelsea 0.

* *

CARLISLE UNITED: Ross, Hemstead, Caldwell, Passmoor, Winstanley, Ternent, Brown, Barton, Hatton, Balderstone, McVitie.

WEST BROMWICH ALBION: Osborne, Fraser, Williams, Brown, Talbot, Kaye, Kryzwicki, Suggett, Astle, Hartford, Hope.

United's first ever major domestic competition semi-final appearance was another thriller. The game was billed locally as the 'battle of Ashman's twenty two', as ex-United manager Allan Ashman was then in charge of the Baggies. Albion who were the F.A. Cup winners in 1968 were one of the sides in the First Division, and they had already seen off the challenge of Villa, Ipswich, Bradford City and Leicester City, even worse, their manager knew United inside out.

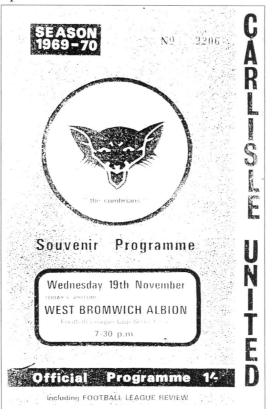

The Carlisle defence were hardly challenged, although livewire Astle did manage several powerful headers, but 'keeper, Alan Ross was more than equal to them.

The woodwork came to Albion's rescue on several occasions, as United peppered Osborne's goal, it was Frank Barton who finally broke the deadlock with a sweetly taken second half strike. It was enough to give Carlisle the first leg lead of 1-0, as yet another First Division scalp was added to the United gravestone.

Carlisle boss Bob Stokoe had a laid-back approach to the big game, as the players relaxed with games of golf and the odd running session along the beach at Silloth. With expert managerial guile, Ashman told the press, *"Make no mistake, West Brom are the underdogs, Carlisle relish clubs like us, they dismiss the big clubs' reputation, we will have our work cut out to get a result at Brunton Park."*

Some 20,322 persons witnessed what can only be described as a below par United performance, albeit West Brom were a determined bunch.

Bob Stokoe was disappointed with the 1-0 victory, *"We should have had three, it wasn't our night."* Star striker Bob Hatton said afterwards, *"I would not believe the saves John Osborne was pulling off, in another match we could have scored more, Ossie has kept them in the game."*

Meanwhile Allan Ashman was relieved with a 1-0 deficit. *"While I dislike losing any game, I am satisfied with 1-0, Carlisle played as I expected them to, with heart and commitment, they are a credit to the Second Division."*

Result: (Second Division) Carlisle United 1   (Allan Ashman's) West Brom. 0.

CARLISLE UNITED: Ross, Hemstead, Davis, Ternent, Winstanley, Balderstone, Murray, Barton, Hatton, Peddelty, McVitie.

NOTTINGHAM FOREST: Hill, Hindley, Winfield, Chapman, O'Kane, Newton, Rees, Lyons, Hilley, Richardson, Moore.

Three days earlier both sides had fought a goalless bore-draw at Forest's City ground. A snowbound pitch had spoiled the game, as First Division Forest were pushed all the way by United.

In the replay snow was still a problem, Matt Gillies the Forest manager was insistent that; *"little clubs get just one chance in the cup, Carlisle fought well on Saturday but we'll fight harder tonight."*

Winger Tommy Murray caused the Forest defence all kinds of trouble, as too did George McVitie as he weaved and danced his way through a below par Forest rearguard. Carlisle played neat passing football, possession being the name of the game, and goals by Murray and McVitie gave them a 2-1 victory, in what was no classic match

The result, all but unnoticed in the following mornings' nationals, was described in a short column in one newspaper as: *"A combination of the bad weather and a tired Forest, Carlisle nudged their way through to the next round in a fortunate manner."*

Result: (Fortunate) Carlisle United 2   (Cold, One League Higher) Nottingham Forest 1.

****

CARLISLE UNITED: Ross, Davis, Gorman, Ternent, Winstanley, Train, Barton, Martin, Owen, Bowles, Balderstone.

A.S. ROMA: Ginulfi, Bet, Peterilli, Salvori, Santarini, Del Sol, Cappellini, Vieri, Zigoni, Cordova, Amarildo.

The setting of the Olympic Stadium, Rome, is a far cry from Rochdale on a beautiful summer evening. This was the venue for Carlisle United's inaugural fixture in European competition, the might of Rome matched against Cumberland's best.

The atmosphere for the Carlisle following was electric, albeit the Anglo Italian was hardly the European Cup, but it mattered little, this was Europe and everyone connected with Carlisle United intended to enjoy themselves.

Few could have envisaged just what was to occur in the ninety minutes which followed. Roma, unbeaten at home in the Italian League for some considerable time, were a formidable side, players of International recognition - South Americans, and top class Italians filled their line-up.

Chris Balderstone was outstanding, the best player on the field, he pushed his team to the limit causing major panic in the Roma defence, he even managed a goal. The home fans, partisan and vociferous were silenced by a polished Carlisle performance, and the Cumbrians who came away with an incredible 3-2 victory.

The world famous coach of Roma, Henlenio Herrera said of Carlisle United, *"We have similar sides in the lower levels of our leagues."* It is difficult to believe that a club side such as Roma would know a great deal about the likes of Carlisle United, certainly when the final whistle blew they knew an awful lot more.

In the warmth of that summer evening the United players emerged from the Olympic Stadium with beaming smiles across their faces. The broadest of which came from Dick Young, *"Absolutely bloody marvellous, who could have believed this scoreline, I like Europe, give us more."*

Result: (European Giants) A.S. Roma 2   (Lower League) Carlisle United 3.

****

Saturday 3rd February, 1973
F.A. Cup Fourth Round

CARLISLE UNITED: Ross, Tiler, Gorman, Ternent, Winstanley, Delgado, Train, Martin, Wilson, O'Neill, Balderstone.

SHEFFIELD UNITED: McAlister, Badger, Hemsley, Flynn, Colquhoun, Eddy, Holmes, Salmons, Dearden, Currie, Speight.

To be fair, First Division Sheffield United came to Brunton Park for this cup-tie in fear that they too could find themselves buried beneath the Carlisle United gravestone.

This fear reflected in their play as they defended in numbers, leaving attacking to break-aways only.

Tony Currie was supremely marshalled by Ray Train who snapped at his heels wherever he went. Dennis Martin with his lazy looking style caused the Blades some serious grief as he jinked one way, then the other, before making pin-point crosses for Wilson, who looked ineffectual as a striker. Indeed had it not been for some alarming lack of ball control by Wilson, Carlisle could have had a three goal lead by half time. Kenny missed two clear headers and a loose ball opportunity as the home support grew frustrated with his abuse of the ball. The concern was eased with a Dennis Martin strike giving Carlisle a 1-0 half time lead.

In the second half it was a repeat performance although Dearden did pull one back for Sheffield, it was still one way traffic as a second Carlisle goal seemed inevitable. It was the tall elegant figure of Bob Delgardo who eventually forced the ball over the line in a goalmouth scramble at the Warwick Road End, to give Carlisle the lead and score what was ultimately the winning goal.

After the game, Sheffield manager Johnny Harris said: *"I knew this would happen, Carlisle never gave us an inch, they deserved the victory, they are a good Second Division side."*

SATURDAY, 3rd FEBRUARY, 1973

F.A. CUP FOURTH ROUND

United
(Blue Shirts)

1. A. ROSS
2. B. TILER
3. J. GORMAN
4. L. O'NEILL
5. R. DELGADO
6. S. TERNENT
7. D. MARTIN
8. R. TRAIN
9. R. OWEN
10. K. WILSON
11. C. BALDERSTONE
12.

Referee:
J. K. TAYLOR,
Wolverhampton.

Sheffield Utd.
(Red and White Shirts)

1. T. McALISTER
2. L. BADGER
3. T. HEMSLEY
4. J. FLYNN
5. E. COLQUHOUN
6. K. EDDY
7. A. WOODWARD
8. G. SALMONS
9. B. DEARDEN
10. T. CURRIE
11. M. SPEIGHT
12.

Linesmen:
R. Hodgson (Orange flag)
G. Courtney (Red flag)

Result:

(Good Second Division Side) Carlisle United 2
(Yorkshire First Division Giants) Sheffield United 1.

****

LIVERPOOL: Clemence, Smith, Lindsey, Thompson, Lloyd, Hughes, Keegan, Cormack, Toshack, Boersma, Callaghan.

CARLISLE UNITED: Ross, Carr, Gorman, O'Neill, Green, Balderstone, Martin, Train, Owen, Clarke, Laidlaw.

The pre-match publicity for this game outside the city of Carlisle was virtually non-existent. Everyone expected Bill Shankly's powerhouse Liverpool to wipe the floor with Carlisle United.

Before the game, in a Liverpool public house, one Reds' supporter asked another if he was going to the match, *"No,"* came the reply, *"I'll go in the next round."* Arrogance and confidence sufficient to arouse despair to the most ardent of supporters.

The Carlisle support was given half of the Anfield Road end of the ground, and some 7,000 plus made their way to Anfield and sang and sang. As the team took to the pitch, 'Twinkletoes' George Baxter, the long-time club mascot, ran onto the Anfield pitch and placed the fox on the centre spot only to find it removed almost immediately. Twinks skipped and danced and waved to each and every United supporter in the stadium.

Bill Shankly would not be drawn before the game, *"Carlisle are a competent side, on paper we should win easily, but this lot are determined, listen to that support, they are almost outsinging our kop."*

The game kicked off and for 89 minutes and 45 seconds it was like the alamo, as Keegan, Toshack and Co. did everything but score. Ross in the Carlisle goal was outstanding, using every part of his body to stop the Liverpool efforts! For fifteen seconds Carlisle could claim to be in control of the game, at the kick-off, and when Frank Clarke burst through the static Liverpool rearguard; he ballooned his shot high into the kop from around 40 yards out. Other than that it was all hands to the pump as just about every United player cleared a Liverpool effort from the goal line.

When the final whistle blew, all eleven Carlisle players dropped to the floor, exhausted. The kop and the Liverpool players applauded the Carlisle support, and congratulated United's players on a gritty performance. Liverpool skipper, Emlyn Hughes said of the game; *"Carlisle were magnificent, they refused to lay down and die. Chris Balderstone played one of the best games I have seen any footballer have here, I'm not looking forward to going to Carlisle."*

Taking everything into account, it was a fantastic result, especially when one considers that Liverpool dropped just four league points all season at Anfield!

Result: (See You In The Next Round) Liverpool 0, (Defiant) Carlisle United 0.

****

CHELSEA: Bonetti, Locke, Houseman, Hollins, Droy, Harris, Kember, Hay, Garland, Garner, Sissons.

CARLISLE UNITED: Ross, Carr, Gorman, O'Neill, Green, Parker, McIlmoyle, Train, Clarke, Balderstone, Laidlaw.

The big boys of London anticipated a glut of goals against the First Division new-comers. *"Look at our marvellous new East Stand,"* said Chelsea chairman Brian Mears prior to the game, *"It cost three maybe four times as much as the Carlisle side,"* he added.

The Pensioners manager Dave Sexton, a dedicated professional, was altogether carried away before the kick off. *"The Carlisle lads will take one look at this stand, listen to the noise and freeze, they are now in the big time, they must accept everything that goes with it."*

To be fair, Chelsea welcomed United onto the pitch and into the First Division, as did 6,000 United stalwarts amidst a crowd of 31,268.

As though playing psychological tennis, Allan Ashman, the Carlisle manager talked of the opponents as 'Giants', telling his side to work hard and fight for every ball. The national press had gathered in anticipation of a slaughter. Chelsea, always fashionable, are great media favourites. The rich and the high and mighty assembled at Stamford Bridge smiling at every mention of quaint Carlisle United. The late Hughie Neil later said, *"these people had gathered to see Carlisle destroyed, it was like lambs going to the slaughter, in the end it was Chelsea who was humbled."*

BBC Television's Grandstand had a 'Soccer Preview', and gave Carlisle a full twenty seconds. *"Frank Clarke will be the Cumbrians main threat up front"*, the shot then displayed a photograph of Newcastle United's Frank Clark! Chelsea meanwhile were afforded a full two minutes and quoted as, *"one of the top sides in the country".*

Three o'clock arrived and the 1974/75 football season kicked off, Carlisle United's first ever game in Division One of the Football League. Despite this deserved honour the club was still described as 'little Carlisle'.

It took just 108 seconds (1 minute and 48 seconds) for a football fairytale to start to take shape. After a terrible mix-up in the Chelsea defence, Bill Green left-footed the ball into an empty net, with Bonetti, Houseman, and Garner thrashing about like fish out of water. It was a fantastic moment, tears rolled down the faces of some of those who stood behind Bonetti's goal, incredibly, Carlisle United were leading Chelsea 1-0.

As the game wore on Carlisle began to dominate and it was Chelsea who appeared overawed by the occasion. The second half saw the expected Chelsea onslaught, and apart from a spectacular clearance by Peter Carr, which saw him slide in towards his own net from fully ten yards out and scoop the ball away from the goal, (the clearance appeared on the Match of the Day opening action shots all season), Chelsea did little to deserve a goal.

The match was wrapped up by a cool lob-cum-cross from Les O'Neill from the right edge of the Chelsea penalty area. Chris Balderstone, who dictated play, had an effort strike the home side's crossbar, and Bonetti did well to save from Joe Laidlaw. At 4.40 p.m., Peter Reeves, the match referee blew the final whistle. Chelsea were booed off, Carlisle received rapturous applause.

When pressed for a post match comment, Chelsea chairman Brian Mears, clearly disillusioned simply said, *"That team cost next to nothing, our players have big contracts and big egos. Carlisle's have big hearts and that was the difference between the two teams."*

As United fans unable to get to the game watched the teleprinter type out the final scores, many recall one presenter commenting, *"Chelsea have lost to Carlisle,"* then swiftly moved onto a different story.

Result: (Giant) Chelsea 0   (The Tiny Cumbrian Outfit) Carlisle United 2.

****

**Saturday 24th August, 1974
Football League Division One.**

CARLISLE UNITED: Ross, Carr, Winstanley, Green, Parker, O'Neill, Train, Balderstone, Martin, McIlmoyle, Laidlaw.

TOTTENHAM HOTSPUR: Jennings, Evans, Naylor, England, Osgood, Coates, McGrath, Perryman, Jones, Peters, Neighbour.

The euphoria of a fantastic start to the 1974/75 season and two straight away wins ensured a large crowd for United's first ever home League game in English football's top flight. Spurs had got off to a bad start, losing 1-0 at home to Ipswich, followed by a similar score at Manchester City. Brunton Park welcomed the First Division with 18,426 screaming souls, the majority desperate for further glory for the home side.

Tottenham Hotspur, make no mistake, are a big club. United could not have wished for more illustrious opponents to open their home campaign. At 1.00 p.m., Warwick Road, Carlisle, outside the stadium was buzzing with blue and white everywhere.

Shirts, scarves, pom-pom hats were selling out almost quicker than the manufacturer could supply them. United's home shirt, mainly blue, with a wide white front centre portion which had two parallel red lines in it's side border, was another big favourite.

Local businesses had used United's greatest ever achievement to their benefit; blue 'Carlisle United sausages' went on sale, car salesrooms advertised cars in United colours, there was a record produced 'Looking Good' - hardly a chart-topper but a catchy theme none the less. The first ever book dedicated to the club was published, a booklet style work entitled 'The Carlisle United Story'. All these things intimated one thing, the club had hit the big time. Media interest had never been greater, sitting proudly on top of the First Division after two games this was the dream so many United supporters had prayed for since 1904.

When referee Roy Capey signalled the kick-off at 3.00 p.m. the sun was shining, birds were singing, the Brunton Park pitch, always fine, looked like a velvet carpet, worthy of top class football.

At 4.40 p.m. the sun was still shining, but the birds could not be heard for the triumphant cheers of a celebrating Carlisle crowd who had witnessed yet another victory, a Chris Balderstone penalty, which had to be retaken as Jennings had moved, was perfectly executed before the travelling Tottenham crowd at the Waterworks End.

Had fate been kind to the home side, it could have been three, maybe four - nil. Another perfectly good penalty decision was overturned by Mr. Croysdale, an eagle eyed linesman who later claimed: *"The incident did not occur in the penalty area, it was a full two or three inches out!"* Mr. Capey, who initially pointed to the penalty spot was forced to give a free kick as an alternative. Despite the obvious tension such a decision created, the United players maintained good sense and refrained from pointless criticism of the official with the red flag.

Tottenham were outwitted, outclassed, and completely outplayed on the day. Ray 'Puffer' Train went close when he struck a thunderous shot against the underside of Jennings' crossbar, the ball ricocheted down towards the goal-line.

It was in, some claim, typical 1966 World Cup style, others more conservatively state that it didn't really matter as United won without any argument.

Pat Jennings, one of the worlds greatest goalkeepers, was given a torrid time by the United forwards, Dennis Martin tested him twice and Joe Laidlaw cracked a wicked dipping and swerving shot which looked a goal all the way, only for Jennings to calmly dive to his left and catch it as though it was something he did every day.

When the final whistle blew it was Jennings who was first to applaud the Carlisle crowd, warmly smiling and winking at the youngsters who cried his name, and signing autographs. The Irish International 'keeper commented, *"It's a nice set-up here, it will do the game good if Carlisle can maintain this challenge, I have no doubt that a number of teams will come unstuck to them this season, I can't remember having a busier game for many seasons."*

Spurs manager Bill Nicholson was equally as complimentary, *"Naturally I'm disappointed, some of my players lack discipline. Carlisle played some neat attractive football, Allan Ashman has done a good job here, the fans are a noisy lot, I could hardly hear myself think during the game and I've thought at some of the biggest stadiums in the world."* At teatime on the evening of Saturday 24th of August, 1974 Carlisle United sat proudly on top of the First Division, for ten whole days (since the opening Saturday of the season) the team was the best in England, a statistical fact which no one can ever dispute.

Result: (League Leaders) Carlisle United 1   (Outplayed) Tottenham Hotspur 0.

****

CARLISLE UNITED: Ross, Carr, McCartney, McDonald, Lathem, Parker, McVitie, Bonnyman, Tait, Rafferty, Hamilton.

MANCHESTER UNITED: Roche, Nicholl, Albiston, McIlroy, Greenhoff B., Buchan, Coppell, Greenhoff J., Pearson, Macari, Grimes.

Manchester United came to Brunton Park as F.A. Cup holders and holding down a respectable position in the First Division. Managed by Dave Sexton, who had suffered at the hands (or feet) of Carlisle on a number of previous occasions. Sexton's right hand man was ex-Carlisle inside forward Tommy Cavanagh.

The Red Devils were also one of the few teams whom Carlisle had never previously faced in first class competition. Demand for tickets was great as the club elected for allocation of a voucher system, issuing vouchers at a pre-selected (Sheffield Wednesday) home game, thus inflating the attendance figures twofold.

Despite the rush and demand for tickets, sufficient were issued as an official crowd of 25,500 gathered at Brunton Park.

Dave Sexton cautiously stated; *"Carlisle are a tough obstacle, Brunton Park has been a graveyard for top clubs, I believe we will be too strong for them."*

Carlisle manager, Bobby Moncur was professional enough not to be drawn on the subject of a Cup upset. *"I don't know what all the fuss is about, Manchester United are* 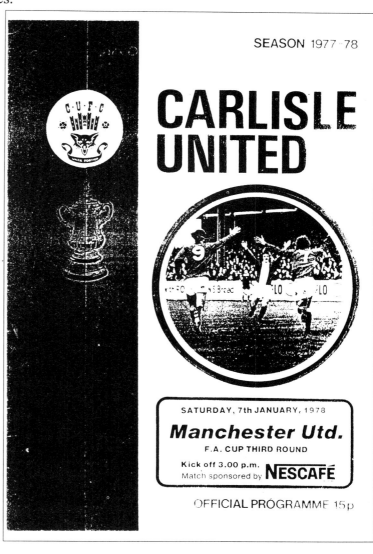 *the biggest club in the world, they should put six or seven past us shouldn't they?"*

To be fair, for twenty minutes or so, the Lancashire side looked yards quicker than their Third Division opposition. A close range Lou Macari goal looked like killing

149

the game dead, as Manchester went one nil up. George McVitie was tireless and went on one of his flying runs down the wing, he weaved through three United defenders before letting fly, causing Roche to save. The effort seemed to lift the crowd and the team as Carlisle took the game by the scruff of the neck and began to take control, causing their illustrious opponents to work, run and chase.

From a corner, Iain McDonald climbed high above the Manchester defence and nodded the ball into the bottom corner of Roche's goal, Brunton Park went wild as the smell of yet another big scalp filled the air.

The second half was a real blood and thunder affair, as Manchester began to panic. Brian Greenhoff, usually cool calm and collected, had been destroyed by George McVitie's fluent running and ball control. In a foolish display of immaturity the International defender lashed out. In floods of tears, Greenhoff walked from the pitch infuriated and embarrassed that he had been taken apart by an underrated winger from the Third Division.

As all Carlisle fans acknowledge, George McVitie could on his day hold his own against the world's best. With Carlisle attacking the Waterworks end it was McVitie who caused the most controversial moment of the game. Racing into the United penalty area he was felled by the outstretched leg of Jimmy Nicholl. 23,500 saw as clear a penalty decision as you could witness, everyone except the two thousand Manchester fans and the referee screamed out. The pleas were ignored as the game petered out to a 1-1 draw.

After the game, the majority of the nation's press concluded that it was a penalty, there was a belief that had the referee awarded it then trouble would have ensued from the Manchester United end of the ground, thus no decision had been made by the match official.

Bobby Moncur later confessed to being 'mortified' when no foul was given. A sincere Martin Buchan later stated: *"These things have a tendency to even themselves out during a season, you win some you lose some."* In the prophetic words of Carlisle striker Billy Rafferty, who was interviewed after the game, *"We were robbed."*

Result: (Tough Obstacle) Carlisle United 1   (Too Strong For Them) Manchester United 1.

****

**Tuesday 13th January 1986
F.A. Cup Third Round**

CARLISLE UNITED: Endersby, Lomax, McCartney, Ashurst, Saunders, Halsall, Hill, Cooke, Baker, Bishop, Halpin.

QUEENS PARK RANGERS: Hucker, Neil, Dawes, McDonald, Wicks, Fenwick, Walker, Fillery, Bannister, Byrne, Robinson.

Torrential rain had poured in Carlisle on the night of Friday 3rd January, the night before the Cup-tie. The persistent deluge had flooded the Brunton Park pitch resulting in the postponement of the game.

Eventually, after much deliberation, the match referee decided that the game could go ahead on Tuesday the 14th. The Saturday before had seen United go down 2-1 at home to Grimsby Town, leaving them stranded at the bottom of the Second Division table. Meanwhile QPR were sitting comfortably in the top half of the First Division table, and travelled to Cumbria as favourites to progress through to the next round.

Jim Smith otherwise known as 'Bald Eagle' stepped out onto the Brunton Park pitch and surveyed the quagmire before him. *"It is incredible that this match has been given the go ahead, but we have come here to do a job, the quicker we get it over and done with the quicker we can get home."* Rain continued to fall right up to kick-off time, when the skies cleared revealing a full moon and a drop in temperature. Just 5,080 were present, a handful of which were the Rangers' contingent, hardly the atmosphere one connects with a major cup upset.

Carlisle set off at a million miles an hour. Cooke and Bishop dominated the midfield, while Mick Halsall worked tirelessly throughout the ninety minutes. Winger John Halpin, was a constant threat, with some fine solo runs and exquisite crossing which

should have afforded United with a couple of goals, but the chances were woefully missed by the lumbering giant of a centre forward, Paul Baker. For the Rangers, John Byrne went close early on only to be defied by the woodwork and a splendid reaction save from Scott Endersby. It was a close affair with Carlisle doing most of the running, and a single goal always looking likely to be sufficient to clinch a victory.

That goal came from a moment of magic from John Cooke, a splendid lob cum shot, which left Hucker in the QPR goal at the Waterworks End of the ground stranded and clutching at thin air.

Somehow United managed to cling on to their lead, with Robinson and Byrne linking well, but again being defied by Endersby and some desperate clearances from United's centre half, Wes Saunders.

It was hardly the stuff dreams are made of, but it was without doubt the best result Carlisle had secured for several seasons. After the match, Jim Smith summed up the result, *"Carlisle United have always had a big reputation for dumping the bigger clubs, that reputation continued tonight, good luck to them."*

In the after match celebrations, Bob Stokoe, himself used to cup upsets, admitted to feeling satisfied with the result. *"I'm pleased for the lads, hopefully this will give us some confidence to climb up the league."*

Result: (Big Reputation) Carlisle United 1, (Job To Do) Queens Park Rangers 0.

****

There you have it, the list and memories are endless, each and every United supporter could retell a personal favourite, these few are perhaps the biggest and the best, from Rome to Liverpool the name of Carlisle United can rightfully stand proud, proving that even the biggest and the so called 'best' in Europe were no match for 'The Lads in Blue'.

1928/29 - 1994/95: Football League Record (Opponents)

Club	Home							Away							Total						
	Pl.	W.	D.	L.	F.	A.	%	Pl.	W.	D.	L.	F.	A.	%	Pl.	W.	D.	L.	F.	A.	%
Accrington Stanley	24	19	3	2	74	37	85.4	24	6	4	14	37	47	33.3	48	25	7	16	111	84	59.4
Aldershot	7	3	2	2	11	8	57.1	7	2	0	5	6	13	28.6	14	5	2	7	17	21	42.9
Arsenal	1	1	0	0	2	1	100	1	0	0	1	1	2	0	2	1	0	1	3	3	50
Ashington	1	1	0	0	5	1	100	1	1	0	0	4	0	100	2	2	0	0	9	1	100
Aston Villa	5	1	2	2	6	6	40	5	0	1	4	1	5	10	10	1	3	6	7	11	25
Barnet	3	1	0	2	5	4	33.3	3	1	0	2	4	6	33.3	6	2	0	4	9	10	33.3
Barnsley	13	6	3	4	27	22	57.7	13	3	3	7	15	25	34.6	26	9	6	11	42	47	46.2
Barrow	28	14	9	5	50	21	66.1	28	8	7	13	34	56	41.1	56	22	16	18	84	77	53.8
Birmingham City	9	5	2	2	15	13	66.7	9	2	1	6	9	16	27.8	18	7	3	8	24	29	47.2
Blackburn Rovers	12	5	2	5	14	11	50	12	4	0	8	12	20	33.3	24	9	2	13	26	31	41.7
Blackpool	14	7	2	5	21	16	57.1	14	2	4	8	8	24	28.6	28	9	6	13	29	40	42.8
Bolton Wanderers	12	8	3	2	23	9	70.8	12	4	2	6	11	22	41.7	24	11	5	8	34	31	56.3
Bournemouth	3	0	1	2	3	7	16.7	3	1	0	2	6	7	33.3	6	1	1	4	9	14	25
Bradford City	19	8	4	7	31	32	52.6	19	3	6	10	26	42	31.6	38	11	10	17	57	74	42.1
Bradford P.A.	13	7	2	4	25	17	61.5	13	6	4	3	22	16	61.5	26	13	6	7	47	33	61.5
Brentford	6	3	1	2	6	4	58.3	6	2	2	2	8	11	50	12	5	3	4	14	15	54.2
Brighton & H.A.	6	3	0	3	9	7	50	6	1	1	4	6	14	25	12	4	1	7	15	21	37.5
Bristol City	14	7	3	4	25	17	60.7	14	2	4	8	11	24	28.6	28	9	7	12	36	42	44.6
Bristol Rovers	6	3	0	3	14	9	50	6	2	1	3	6	12	41.7	12	5	1	6	20	21	45.8
Burnley	12	4	6	2	18	17	58.3	12	1	2	9	13	24	16.7	26	5	8	11	31	41	37.5
Bury	11	7	0	4	21	12	63.6	11	2	3	6	11	21	31.8	22	9	3	10	32	33	47.7
Cambridge United	6	2	4	0	9	6	66.7	6	3	1	2	8	8	58.3	12	5	5	2	18	14	62.5
Cardiff City	16	7	5	4	28	20	59.4	16	0	5	11	15	34	15.6	32	7	10	15	43	54	37.5
Charlton Athletic	14	6	6	2	28	16	64.3	14	0	6	8	12	23	21.4	28	6	12	10	40	39	42.9
Chelsea	5	2	1	2	5	5	50	5	1	1	3	6	9	30	10	3	2	5	11	14	40
Chester	32	18	8	6	62	40	68.7	32	8	8	16	40	68	37.5	64	26	16	22	102	108	53.1
Chesterfield	27	14	6	7	56	36	63.0	27	5	2	20	27	64	22.2	54	19	8	27	83	100	42.6
Colchester United	13	8	2	3	27	10	69.2	13	2	3	8	10	20	26.9	26	10	5	11	37	30	48.1
Coventry City	5	1	2	2	5	10	40	5	1	0	4	8	11	20	10	2	2	6	13	21	30
Crewe Alexandra	32	22	2	8	80	34	71.9	32	5	8	19	31	75	28.1	64	27	10	27	111	109	50
Crystal Palace	13	7	5	1	29	15	73.1	13	3	3	7	13	24	34.6	26	10	8	8	42	39	53.8
Darlington	35	16	9	10	64	51	58.6	35	13	7	15	54	60	47.1	70	29	16	25	118	111	52.9
Derby County	9	4	3	2	13	10	61.1	9	4	2	3	13	13	55.6	18	8	5	5	26	23	58.3
Doncaster Rovers	25	11	7	7	42	26	58	25	6	7	12	29	48	38	50	17	14	19	71	74	48
Everton	1	1	0	0	3	0	100	1	1	0	0	3	2	100	2	2	0	0	6	2	100
Exeter City	15	9	4	2	24	15	73.3	15	3	5	7	12	21	36.7	30	12	9	9	36	36	55
Fulham	14	8	3	3	28	17	67.9	14	6	1	7	15	21	46.4	28	14	4	10	43	38	57.1
Gateshead	23	15	6	2	56	26	78.3	23	4	5	14	29	46	28.3	46	19	11	16	85	72	53.3
Gillingham	18	8	2	8	23	22	50	18	3	6	9	12	23	33.3	36	11	8	17	35	45	41.7
Grimsby Town	13	4	4	5	22	20	46.1	13	1	3	9	9	21	19.2	26	5	7	14	31	41	32.7
Halifax Town	31	16	9	6	63	35	66.1	31	9	8	14	47	64	41.9	62	25	17	20	110	99	54
Hartlepool	33	22	6	5	75	34	75.8	33	10	6	17	50	54	39.4	66	32	12	22	125	88	57.6
Hereford United	10	6	2	2	15	7	70	10	2	3	6	6	13	25	20	7	5	8	21	20	47.5
Huddersfield Town	11	4	5	2	11	8	59.1	11	0	6	5	8	16	27.3	22	4	11	7	19	24	43.2
Hull City	27	10	9	8	32	29	53.7	27	6	6	15	25	61	33.3	54	16	15	23	57	90	43.5
Ipswich Town	4	4	0	0	11	4	100	4	1	0	3	4	8	25	8	5	0	3	15	12	62.5
Leeds United	5	1	2	2	7	8	40	5	0	2	3	3	10	20	10	1	4	5	10	18	30
Leicester City	4	0	1	3	2	5	12.5	4	1	2	1	5	10	50	8	1	3	4	7	15	31.3
Leyton Orient	9	7	0	2	14	5	77.8	9	1	2	6	6	14	22.2	18	8	2	8	20	19	50
Lincoln City	25	12	2	11	46	46	52	25	4	6	15	25	51	28	50	16	8	26	71	97	40
Liverpool	1	0	0	1	0	1	0	1	0	0	1	0	2	0	2	0	0	2	0	3	0
Luton Town	8	3	4	1	9	5	62.5	8	2	2	4	9	21	37.5	16	5	6	5	18	26	50
Maidstone United	3	3	0	0	7	2	100	3	0	1	2	3	10	16.7	6	3	1	2	10	12	58.3

Club	Home							Away							Total						
	Pl.	W.	D.	L.	F.	A.	%	Pl.	W.	D.	L.	F.	A.	%	Pl.	W.	D.	L.	F.	A.	%
Manchester City	4	1	2	1	3	2	50	4	2	0	2	7	7	50	8	3	2	3	10	9	50
Manchester United	-	-	-	-	-	-	-	-	-	-	-	-	-	-	-	-	-	-	-	-	-
Mansfield Town	25	15	5	5	55	26	70	25	7	2	16	28	53	32	50	22	7	21	83	79	51
Middlesbrough	14	6	4	4	17	14	57.1	14	6	1	7	15	15	46.4	28	12	5	11	32	29	51.8
Millwall	18	10	4	4	35	22	66.7	18	2	3	13	15	34	19.4	36	12	7	17	50	56	43.1
Nelson	3	2	1	0	14	3	83.3	3	1	1	1	4	4	50	6	3	2	1	18	7	66.7
New Brighton	16	7	7	2	26	17	65.6	16	3	2	11	17	37	25	32	10	9	13	43	54	45.3
Newcastle United	3	2	0	1	6	3	66.7	3	0	1	2	3	8	16.7	6	2	1	3	9	11	41.7
Newport County	5	1	3	1	11	12	50	5	2	1	2	7	9	50	10	3	4	3	18	21	50
Northampton Town	10	7	0	3	17	10	70	10	0	7	3	10	15	35	20	7	7	6	27	25	52.5
Norwich City	8	5	1	2	16	14	68.7	8	0	1	7	4	13	6.3	16	5	2	9	20	27	37.5
Nottingham Forest	4	1	2	1	5	5	50	4	0	0	4	2	13	0	8	1	2	5	7	18	25
Notts County	7	4	0	3	11	8	57.1	7	1	0	6	6	11	14.3	14	5	0	9	17	19	35.7
Oldham Athletic	26	16	7	3	52	24	73.6	26	6	5	15	34	60	32.7	52	22	12	18	86	84	53.4
Oxford United	14	6	5	3	19	17	60.7	14	4	4	6	11	20	42.9	28	10	9	9	30	37	51.8
Peterborough United	9	3	4	2	15	15	55.6	9	2	3	4	10	16	38.9	18	5	7	6	25	31	47.2
Plymouth Argyle	10	6	3	1	16	7	75	10	3	1	6	9	17	35	20	9	4	7	25	24	55
Portsmouth	16	9	5	2	29	11	71.9	16	3	21	11	17	32	25	32	12	7	13	46	43	48.4
Port Vale	10	4	4	2	16	13	60	10	3	3	4	8	12	45	20	7	7	6	24	25	52.5
Preston North End	12	6	4	2	19	9	66.7	12	5	1	6	15	16	45.8	24	11	5	8	34	25	56.2
Q.P.R.	9	5	0	4	17	17	55.6	9	1	3	5	6	15	27.8	18	6	3	9	23	32	41.7
Reading	5	1	3	1	7	7	50	5	1	1	3	5	10	30	10	2	4	4	12	17	40
Rochdale	35	21	8	6	85	29	71.4	35	11	6	18	40	63	40	70	32	14	24	125	92	55.7
Rotherham United	27	9	7	11	40	45	46.3	27	7	4	16	26	62	33.3	54	16	11	27	66	107	39.8
Scarborough	8	5	2	1	19	7	75	8	3	3	2	13	11	56.2	16	8	5	3	32	18	65.6
Scunthorpe United	17	8	2	7	35	23	52.9	17	5	5	7	18	28	44.1	34	13	7	14	53	51	48.5
Sheffield United	9	4	1	4	8	8	50	9	2	3	4	8	11	38.9	18	6	4	8	16	19	44.4
Sheffield Wednesday	9	3	5	1	14	10	61.1	9	0	4	5	3	12	22.2	18	3	9	6	17	22	41.7
Shrewsbury Town	12	7	3	2	16	11	70.8	12	3	5	4	16	16	45.8	24	10	8	6	32	27	58.3
Southampton	3	2	0	1	2	6	66.7	3	1	1	1	3	3	50	6	3	1	2	5	6	58.3
Southend United	6	4	1	1	15	7	75	6	0	2	4	2	8	16.7	12	4	3	5	17	15	45.8
Southport	28	17	7	4	64	30	73.2	28	7	5	16	33	57	33.9	56	24	12	20	97	87	53.6
South Shields	2	2	0	0	9	1	100	2	0	0	2	2	10	0	4	2	0	2	11	11	50
Stockport County	30	17	8	5	57	44	70	30	6	5	19	26	72	28.3	60	23	13	24	83	116	49.2
Stoke City	2	1	0	1	3	2	50	2	0	1	1	2	5	25	4	1	1	2	5	7	37.5
Sunderland	6	2	2	2	9	9	50	6	1	1	4	9	11	25	12	3	3	6	18	20	37.5
Swansea City	3	2	0	1	4	1	66.7	3	0	2	1	1	3	33.3	6	2	2	2	5	4	50
Swindon Town	12	6	5	1	21	12	70.8	12	0	8	4	8	15	33.3	24	6	13	5	29	27	52.1
Torquay United	10	5	2	3	14	9	60	10	2	3	5	8	13	35	20	7	5	8	22	22	47.5
Tottenham Hotspur	1	1	0	0	1	0	100	1	0	1	0	1	1	50	2	1	1	0	2	1	75
Tranmere Rovers	28	14	8	6	55	38	64.3	28	8	5	15	31	62	37.5	56	22	13	21	86	100	50.9
Walsall	18	9	5	4	31	30	63.9	18	4	4	10	15	34	33.3	36	13	9	14	46	64	48.6
Watford	8	7	1	0	16	3	93.8	8	2	3	3	9	14	43.8	16	9	4	3	25	17	68.8
West Bromwich A.	2	0	1	1	1	2	25	2	0	1	1	1	4	25	4	0	2	2	2	6	25
West Ham United	1	0	0	1	0	1	0	1	0	0	1	0	2	0	2	0	0	2	0	3	0
Wigan Athletic	3	2	0	1	5	3	66.7	3	2	0	1	4	2	66.7	6	4	0	2	9	5	66.7
Wigan Borough	3	3	0	0	13	2	100	3	1	1	1	4	11	50	6	4	1	1	17	13	75
Wimbledon	4	2	1	1	11	6	62.5	4	0	1	3	2	10	12.5	8	2	2	4	13	16	37.5
Wolverhampton W.	7	3	0	4	6	9	42.9	7	1	1	5	5	15	21.4	14	4	1	9	11	24	32.1
Workington	13	4	3	6	20	25	42.3	13	3	3	7	12	20	34.6	26	7	6	13	32	45	38.5
Wrexham	33	15	9	9	44	35	59.1	33	1	6	26	36	88	12.1	66	16	15	35	80	123	35.6
Wycombe Wands.	1	0	1	0	2	2	50	1	0	0	1	0	2	0	2	0	1	1	2	4	25
York City	33	16	13	4	64	41	68.2	33	6	11	16	36	70	34.8	66	22	24	20	100	111	51.5

MATCHES EXCLUDED:- 1931/2 Vs Wigan Borough, 1939/40 Vs Stockport & Oldham, 1961/2 Vs Accrington, 1991/2 Vs Aldershot, 1993/4 Vs Wycombe (play-offs). Percentage (%) calculation based on 2pts for a win.

NAME	Born: Place - Date	Transferred from:	Transferred to:	League & Cup App.	Sub	Gls.
ACKERMAN Alfred	South Africa - 5/1/29	Derby 11/56	Millwall 1/59	96		62
ADAMS William	Arlecdon - 8/1/19	Spurs 6/46	Workington 6/47	37		1
ADEY William	Dinnington - 6/7/09	Barnsley 10/36	Retired 1939	74		5
AGAR Alfred	Eshwinning - 28/8/04	Barrow 6/28	Accrington 6/30	50		11
ALLEN Melvyn	Bargoed - 1910	Hull City 8/34	Barrow 1/35	16		
ALMOND Alfred	Alderley Edge - 1907	Leed United 9/29	Barnsley 12/30	22		
ANDERSON George	Carlisle - 1914	Local 9/30	Local 10/30	2		
ANDERSON James	Felling - 26/5/13	Brentford 9/46	Retired 1946	10		
ARMES Samuel	New Seaham - 30/3/08	Howden 5/30	Chester 5/32	75		18
ARMSTRONG Derek	Carlisle - 16/3/39	Blackpool 8/61	Morecambe 1962	1		
ARMSTRONG Lee	Cockermouth - 19/10/72	Youth 1/89	Local 5/47	3		
ARNOLD Ian	Durham - 4/7/72	Middlesbrough 7/92	Kettering Town 11/94	34	12	11
ASHMAN Allan	Rotherham - 30/5/28	Nottingham Forest 6/51	Local 1959	207		98
ASHTON Edward	Kilnhurst - 19/1/06	Sheffield United 8/38	Barnsley 6/39	28		8
ASHURST John	Catbridge - 12/10/54	Blackpool 8/81	Leeds United 7/86	194		2
ASPINALL Warren	Wigan - 13/9/67	Bournemouth 3/95		6	1	1
ARTKINSON Ian	Carlisle - 19/12/32	Local 6/51	Exeter City 7/57	122		52
BAKER Paul	Newcastle - 5/1/63	Southampton 6/85	Hartlepool 7/87	66	5	11
BALDERSTONE Chris	Huddersfield - 16/11/40	Huddersfield 6/65	Doncaster Rovers 7/75	369	7	68
BANNON Paul	Dublin - 15/11/56	Bridgend 2/79	Bristol Rovers - 1/84	127	12	45
BARKAS Thomas	South Shields - 27/3/12	Stockport 2/49	Local 6/49	14	5	
BARNSLEY Andrew	Sheffield - 9/6/62	Rotherham 8/91	Non-League 5/93	53	2	5
BARRIE Walter	Kirkaldy - 1904	QPR 3/38	Retired 1939	10		
BARRY Michael	Hull - 22/5/53	Huddersfield 5/73	Bristol Rovers 9/77	73	8	10
BARTON Frank	Barton - 22/10/47	Scunthorpe 1/68	Blackpool 7/72	161	4	22
BATEY John	Carlisle - 1909	Local 12/34	Local 6/38	13		
BATEY Bob	Greenhead - 18/10/12	Local 10/33	Preston 3/34	23		
BAXTER Thomas	Worksop - 1910	Mansfield 9/33	Mansfield 10/33	5		
BEARDSLEY Peter	Newcastle - 18/11/61	Wallsend BC 8/79	Vancouver W 9/82	93	11	22
BECK William	London - 1905	Luton 12/35	Luton 1/36	2		
BELL David	Carlisle - 13/9/39	Local 3/57	Local 5/58	1		1
BELL Dornam	Newcastle - 1903	Colwyn Bay 8/33	Non-League 5/34	23		
BELL Graham	Middleton - 30/3/55	Preston 8/83	Bolton Wanderers 2/84	11	3	
BELL Robert	Glasgow - 23/3/35	Plymouth 6/59	Partick Thistle 10/59	1		
BELL Thomas	Sunderland - 1905	Portsmouth 9/30	Burton T. 8/31	13		
BENNETT Michael	Bolton - 24/12/62	Preston 7/90	Non-League 1991	21	3	
BERESFORD Frank	Chesterfield - 1907	Crystal Palace 11/37	Retired 5/39	68		10
BEVAN Brian	Exeter 20/3/37	Bristol City 3/60	Millwall 2/61	27		2
BILLINGHAM John	Daventry - 3/12/14	Burnley 9/49	Southport 3/51	64		17
BIRKETT William	Carlisle - 1903	Local 10/31	Local 5/32	13		
BISHOP Ian	Liverpool - 29/5/65	Everton 10/84	Bournemouth 7/88	131	4	14
BLACK Daniel	Whitehaven - 1909	Local 2/34	Local 5/35	21		
BLACKADDER Fred	Carlisle 13/1/16	Queens Park 5/37	Local 1937	3		
BLACKLEY Arthur	Carlisle 31/1/39	Chelsea 11/60	Local 1962	38		7
BLAIN James	Liverpool 9/4/40	Rotherham 1/64	Exeter City 10/65	41		7
BLAKE Gardiner	Clarenden - 1901	Airdrie 8/33	Local 5/34	33		1
BLANEY George	Workington - 1905	Local 10/38	Local 10/38	2		
BLOOMFIELD Edward	Wisbech - 28/6/32	Non-League 8/53	Southport 7/56	5		1
BLOTT John	Middlesbrough - 26/2/65	Manchester City 14/84	Mansfield Town 5/85	2		
BLUE Archibald	Glasgow - 8/4/40	Exeter City 7/62	Retired 1963	2		1
BOND Ernest	Preston - 4/5/29	Manchester United 9/52	Local 1959	191		24
BONNYMAN Phillip	Glasgow - 6/2/54	Hamilton 3/76	Chesterfield 3/80	149	3	26
BOWLES Stanley	Manchester - 24/12/48	Crewe 10/71	QPR 9/72	33		12
BOYD Brian	Carlisle - 4/1/38	Local 8/55	Local 7/58	6		
BRADLEY Gordon	Easington - 23/11/33	Bradford 9/57	Retired 1961	129		3
BRADLEY Robert	Washington - 1900	Non-League 8/32	Died 18/2/34	70		
BRAYTON Barry	Carlisle - 29/9/38	Local 1/60	Workington 2/67	158	1	34
BROADIS Ivor	Poplar 18/12/22	Spurs 8/46	Sunderland 2/49	91		52
		Newcastle 7/55	Queen of the South 7/59	159		32
BRODIE John	Ashington - 8/9/47	Non-League 12/67	Bradford 6/69	8	1	
BROWN Alex	Glasgow - 15/8/30	Preston 6/58	Non-League 5/61	104		
BROWN James	Cumnock - 16/2/24	Bradford City 9/50	Queen of the South 10/51	15		9

NAME	Born: Place - Date	Transferred from:	Transferred to:	League & Cup App.	Sub	Gls.
BROWN Owen	Liverpool - 4/9/60	Liverpool 6/80	Tranmere Rovers - 8/81	4		2
BROWN William	Dumfries - 1898	Kello R. 8/28	Local 9/28	1		
BROWN William	Falkirk - 5/2/50	Burnley 7/69	Newport County 8/70	16	3	8
BUCHAN Thomas	Edinburgh - 6/12/15	Blackpool 8/49	Non-League 4/50	30		
BUCHANAN William	Glasgow - 29/7/24	Motherwell 7/49	Barrow 10/49	9		
BUCKLEY Michael	Manchester - 4/11/53	Hartlepool 9/83	Middlesbrough 6/84	24	1	2
BURGESS David	Liverpool - 20/1/60	Blackpool (loan) 3/93		6		
		Blackpool 6/93		36	4	1
BURKE Richard	Ashton - 28/10/20	Newcastle 8/47	Non-League 5/49	78		8
BIRKINSHAW George	Barnsley - 1/10/22	Barnsley 9/46	Barnsley 6/47	25		
BURLEIGH Martin	Newcastle - 2/2/51	Darlington 6/75	Darlington 8/77	26		
BURN John	South Sheilds - 21/1/30	Chesterfield 6/55	Non-League 5/56	26		
CAIG Anthony	Whitehaven - 11/4/74	Youth 6/92		61		
CALDWELL Terry	Sharleston - 5/12/38	Leeds United 7/61	Barrow 7/70	340	4	1
CAMPBELL Alan	Arbroath - 21/1/48	Cardiff City 11/80	Non-League 3/82	29	2	2
CAPE John	Carlisle - 16/11/11	Penrith 5/29	Newcastle United 1/30	15		2
		Scarborough 10/46	Non-League 2/47	3		
CARLIN William	Liverpool - 6/10/40	Halifax Town 10/64	Sheffield United 9/67	92	1	21
CARR Kevin	Ashington - 6/11/58	Newcastle 8/85	Middlesbrough 12/86	17		
CARR Peter	Darlington - 25/8/51	Darlington 11/92	Hartlepool United 10/79	202	2	1
CARRUTHERS John	Dumfries - 2/8/26	Local 7/49	Workington 7/51	2		
CARTWRIGHT Phillip	Scarborough - 1909	Lincoln 9/34	Non-League 9/34	3		
CATON William	Stoke - 11/9/24	Stoke City 4/50	Chesterfield 10/52	64		16
CAVANAGH Thomas	Liverpool - 29/6/28	Bristol City 6/60	Retired 5/61	34		4
CAWLEY Edward	Hanley - 1904	Ashton N. 8/32	Non-League 6/33	27		1
CHARLTON John	Choppington - 1909	Frickley C. 9/29	Non-League 9/29	1		
CLARK Jon	Swansea - 12/11/58	Bury 8/87	Non-League 5/88	48	1	2
CLARKE Frank	Willenhall - 15/7/42	Ipswich Town 8/73	Non-League 5/77	121	5	30
CLARKE John	Edinburgh - 1905	Third Lanark 8/33	Third Lanark 5/34	28		1
CLARKE Thomas	Ardrossan - 12/4/46	Airdrie 7/70	Preston 7/75	23		
CLIFFE John	Lincoln - 1910	Barnsley 8/35	Non-League 5/39	108		16
CLAYTON John	Mansfield - 1907	Wrexham 8/32	Non-League 5/39	24		
CLAYTON Lewis	Royston - 7/6/24	Barnsley 9/46	Barnsley 6/47	24		
COADY Michael	Dipton - 1/10/58	Sunderland 7/80	Wolves 1/85	48	3	1
COLLINS Albert	Chesterfield - 15/4/23	Halifax Town 2/48	Barrow 12/48	20		3
COLLINS Andrew	Carlisle - 20/10/58	Spartans 9/77	Local 5/81	47	7	1
COLLINS James	Carlisle - 1906	Local 4/30	Local 1/31	8		
CONNOR Jack	Todmorden - 21/12/19	Ipswich 12/46	Ards 5/48	39		12
CONWAY Paul	London - 17/470	Oldham 7/93		40	2	10
COOK George	Shankhouse - 1900	Torquay 8/28	Non-League 5/29	23		
COOK George	Blyth - 1907	Tranmere Rovers 10/32	Tranmere rovers 5/33	5		
COOKE John	Salford - 25/4/62	Sheffield Wed. 10/85	Stockport COunty 7/88	105	1	11
COOPER Sidney	Carlisle - 1899	Local 11/28	5/28	11		2
COOPERTHWAITE John	Newcastle - 1898	Durham C. 2/29	Non-League 12/29	5		2
COUGHLIN Russell	Swansea - 15/2/63	Blackburn Rovers 10/80	Plymouth Argyle 7/84	114	16	13
COULTHARD Thomas	Darlington - 1902	Norwich 8/28	Local 5/31	97		1
COUPE Norman	Carlisle - 15/7/24	Swifts 9/47	Rochdale 10/51	31		
COUPLAND Joseph	Glasgow 10/4/20	Bradford City 7/52	Non-League 3/53	3		
COWPER Peter	Bolton - 1/9/02	Southport 7/32	Wigan Athletic 7/33	11		1
COWELL William	Hexham - 1897	Millwall 9/29	Non-League 5/30	1		
CRABBE John	Weymouth - 20/10/54	Gillingham 8/81	Hereford United 8/82	26		4
CRAIG Thomas	Glasgow - 21/11/50	Swansea 3/82	Retired 1984	92	6	10
CRANSTON Nicholas	Carlisle - 20/10/72	Youth 1/92	Local 5/92		2	
CRESSWELL Corbett	Sunderland - 3/8/32	Bishop A. 3/58	Local 5/59	14		2
CRICKETT Norman	Carlisle - 13/10/32	Local 11/52	Local 5/56	1		
CROMPTON Steven	Partington - 20/4/68	Manchester City 7/87	Stockport 2/88	10		
CROSS William	Dumfries - 1904	Queen South 9/33	Queen South 10/33	2		
CRUICKSHANK George	Malaya - 2/7/31	Queen South 8/57	Non-League 1/58	14		
CURRIE David	Stockton - 27/11/62	Barnsley 7/94		38		4
DAGGER Les	Preston - 25/4/33	Preston 6/61	Southport 7/63	74		9
DARNELL Len	Irchester - 1905	Reading 8/34	Non-League 10/34	7		
DALZIEL Ian	South Sheilds - 24/10/62	Hereford United 7/88	Non-League 5/93	90	1	2

NAME	Born: Place - Date	Transferred from:	Transferred to:	League & Cup App.	Sub	Gls.
DAVEY Simons	Swansea - 1/10/70	Swansea 8/92	Preston 2/95	105		18
DAVIDSON Jack	Throckley - 14/3/01	Local 3/31	Local 3/32	9		3
DAVIES Cyril	Swansea - 7/9/48	Swansea 6/68	Yeovil Town 5/69	1	1	
DAVIES Ian	Bristol - 29/3/57	Manchester City 8/84	Exeter City 12/84	4		
DAVIES Reginald	Cymmer - 27/5/29	Swansea 6/62	Non-League 5/64	65		13
DAVIS Joseph	Glasgow - 22/5/41	Hibs 12/69	Non-League 5/72	75	4	
DAWSON William	Newbiggin - 1905	Newbiggin 12/30	Local 5/31	18		
DAY Mervyn	Chelmsford - 26/6/55	Leeds United 7/93		16		
DEAKIN John	Stocksbridge - 29/9/66	Birmingham City 8/91	Non-League 5/92	3		
DEAN Joe	Manchester - 4/4/39	Bolton Wanderers 7/62	Barrow 7/70	137		
DELAP Rory	Coldfield - 6/7/76	Youth 8/92		2	3	
DELGADO Robert	Cardiff - 29/1/49	Luton Town 7/71	Rotherham United 12/73	25	10	3
DELLOW Ronald	Crosby - 13/7/14	Tranmere 8/39	Non-League 5/47	16		5
DERRETT Steve	Cardiff - 16/10/47	Cardiff 4/72	Rotherham United 12/73	13		
DEVLIN Joseph	Cleland - 12/3/31	Bradford 7/59	Non-League 5/60	5		
DEVLIN William	Glasgow - 30/5/31	Peterborough 8/56	Local 5/57	28		6
DICK George	Torphichen - 12-6/21	West Ham 7/49	Stockport County 10/50	52		23
DIXON Kevin	Conset - 27/7/60	Tow Law 8/83	Hartlepool United 8/84	5	4	
DOBIE Mark	Carlisle - 8/11/63	Workington 12/86	Local 4/87	4	2	
DODD Ray	Chester Le Street - 1900	Local 12/35	Local 12/35	1		
DORAN Robert	Carlisle - 26/12/33	Local 1/33	Local 5/62	107		
DOUGAL David	Eyemouth - 1907	Local 1/33	Local 5/35	28		5
DOUGALL James	Denny - 3/10/13	Preston 10/46	Halifax Town 10/48	70		15
DRURY James	Cumnock - 29/5/24	Rochdale 8/52	Southport 7/54	35		5
DUFFETT Edgar	Worcester - 29/8/26	Norwich 8/50	Non-League 5/53	47		8
DUNCAN William	Preston - 1904	Blackburn Rovers 2/35	Blackburn Rovers 5/53	13		
EDMONDSON Darren	Coniston - 4/11/71	Youth 7/90		146	6	7
EDWARDS Edmund	Spennymoor - 1911	Mossley 8/38	Non-League 5/39	2		
EDWARDS Rovert	Cockermouth - 1/7/72	Youth 4-90	Bristol City 3/91	48		5
ELLIOTT Anthony	Nuneaton - 30/11/69	Huddersfield Town 6/93		8	1	
ELLIOTT Eamonn	Belfast - 27/8/71	Youth 7/90	Non-League 8/91	3	1	
ELLIOTT Edward	Carlisle - 24/5/19	Local 12/37	Wolves 8/91	11		
ELLIOTT John	Eden Valley - 6/5/38	Youth 8/55	Local 5/58	2		1
ELLIOTT Robert	Carlisle - 1912	Local 5/34	Preston 12/34	10		1
EMBLETON George	Sarceton - 1910	Local 11/38	Local 5/39	10		1
ENDERSBY Scott	Lewisham - 20/2/60	Swindon Town 11/85	York City 7/87	52		
ENTWISTLE Wayne	Bury - 6/8/58	Bury 6/85	Bolton Wanderers 10/85	8	1	2
ERSKINE George	Dumfries - 1907	Local 5/38	Local 5/38	1		
EVANS John	Liverpool 13/3/38	Stockport 2/64	Exeter City 3/66	78		37
FAIRLEY Thomas	Houghton/Spring-12/10/32	Sunderland 5/56	Non-League 10/58	56		
FAIRWEATHER Carlton	Camberwell - 22/9/61	Wimbledon 8/93	Hong Kong 11/93	11	1	1
FAIRWEATHER John	Dornoch 12/8/24	Blackburn 11/48	Non-League 5/50	1		
FAREY John	Darlington - 22/7/22	Sunderland 11/47	Non-League 1/48	2		
FEATHERBY Stan	Richmond - 1906	Local 9/36	Local 9/36	2		
FELL Geoff	Carlisle - 8/5/60	Youth 6/77	Local 12/79		3	
FELTON Eric	Gateshead - 1906	Wardley C. 11/31	Darlington 3/33	20		3
FERGUSON Pearson	Coalburn - 1905	Ayr United 8/33	Local 5/35	67		19
FITZPATRICK Paul	Liverpool - 5/10/65	Bristol City 10/88	Leicester City 7/91	106	3	4
FLEMING George	Gourock - 25/2/35	Watford 6/60	Barrow 9/60	7		
FLETCHER Hugh	Lochgilphead - 8/4/33	Celtic 5/56	Local 5/61	124		18
FORBES William	Glasgow - 25/5/22	Preston 7/56	Non-League 11/57	25		
FORD Fred	Dartford - 10/12/16	Millwall 7/47	Non-League 5/48	28		
FORREST William	Bo'ness - 19/1/45	Hearts 7/62	Brighton 7/64	10		
FREW James	Stevenston - 1900	Southend 5/29	Non-League 5/30	24		2
FULBROOK Gary	Bath - 4/5/66	Bath City 9/87	Bath City 5/88	6		
FYFE Anthony	Carlisle - 23/2/62	Penrith 9/87	Halifax Town 1/90	28	20	12
GABBIADINI Riccardo	Newport - 11/3/70	Scarborough 8/92	Chesterfield 8/93	18	6	3
GALLACHER Brian	Oldham - 22/7/38	Bury 5/65	Stockport County 7/67	42	2	1
GALLOWAY David	Kirkaldy - 1910	Preston 8/35	Non-League	109		11
GALLIMORE Anthony	Crewe - 21/2/72	Stock City 3/93		104		7
GARBUTT Peter	Corbridge - 28/12/39	Crook T. 8/64	Local 10/70	134	2	12
GARRETT James	Dumfries - 15/3/39	Queen South 8/63	Local 5/64	1		

NAME	Born: Place - Date	Transferred from:	Transferred to:	League & Cup		
				App.	Sub	Gls.
GARVIE John	Bellshill - 16/10/27	Lincoln City 5/56	Non-League 5/57	25		6
GATES Eric	Feryhill - 28/6/55	Sunderland 6/90	Retired 5/91	33	5	8
GAVIN Mark	Baillieston - 10/12/63	Leeds United 7/85	Bolton Wanderers 3/86	12	1	1
GIBBS Geoffrey	Chester le Street - 1905	Worcester 8/32	Non-League 3/86	22	2	
GOMM Archibald	Beaconsfield - 1906	Millwall 8/31	Non-League 5/33	66		
GOLDSMITH Craig	Peterbrough - 27/8/63	Peterborough 12/89	Non-League 5/90	21	9	1
GOODALL Bernard	Slough - 4/10/37	Reading 7/63	Halifax Town 11/64	1		
GORDON William	Carlisle - 22/11/26	Local 8/48	Barrow 7/50	15		4
GORE Leslie	Fulham - 11/3/02	Stockport 9/37	Stockport 10/37	3		
GORMAN John	Winchburgh - 16/8/49	Celtic 9/70	Spurs 11/76	228	1	5
GORMAN Paul	Dublin - 6/8/63	Birmingham City 3/85	Shrewsbury Town 11/89	137	11	7
		Shrewsbury Town 12/91	Local 5/92	5		
GRAHAM Gordon	North Sheilds - 1900	South Shields 12/28	Non-League 3/29	7		1
GRAHAM Michael	Lancaster - 24/2/59	Mansfield 9/88	Non-League 5/91	137	1	3
GRAHAM William	Carlisle - 8/5/29	Consett - 1/54	Retired 5/60	35		2
GRANT Robert	Edinburgh - 25/9/40	St. Johnstone 7/62	Queen South 12/62	2		1
GRAY George	Glasgow - 6/10/29	Vale/Clyde 11/47	Vale/Clyde 12/47	1		1
GRAY Robert	Brambleside - 1903	Southport 1/33	Local 5/29	44		7
GREEN Michael	Carlisle - 8/9/46	Local 9/64	Gillingham 7/68	2		
GREEN William	Newcastle - 22/12/50	Hartlepool 7/73	West Ham 6/76	119		4
HAIGH Paul	Scarborough - 4/5/58	Hull 11/80	Hartlepool 7/87	228	5	4
HALPIN John	Broxburn - 15/11/61	Celtic 10/84	Rochdale 7/91	148	5	17
HAMILL Alex	Dumbarton - 1914	Barnsley 8/38	Retired 4/39	25		1
HALSALL Michael	Bootle - 21/7/61	Birmingham City 10/84	Grimsby Town 2/87	92		11
HAMILTON James	Uddingston - 14/6/55	Bristol Rovers 9/77	Gretna 5/82	150	4	12
HAMILTON James	Cumnock - 1910	Wrexham 8/38	Chester 5/39	28		
HAMILTON Sidney	Penrith - 1900	Local 10/37	Local 5/39	34		10
HAMPTON Peter	Oldham 12/9/54	Rochdale 12/87	Retired 5/88	12		
HARBACH Peter	Carlisle - 27/8/67	Newcastle 8/87	Local 5/88		7	
HARFORD George	London - 1910	Luton 8/38	Retired 2/40	26		
HARKNESS James	Edinburgh - 19/5/40	Hamilton 8/61	Local 6/63	17		
HARKNESS Steven	Carlisle - 27/8/71	Youth 3/89	Liverpool 7/89	12	1	
HARLAND Stanley	Liverpool - 19/6/40	Bradford City 6/64	Swindon 8/66	77		7
HARRISON Anthony	Gateshead - 9/1/54	Southport 6/78	Local 5/81	8		
HARRISON Graham	West Stanley - 1903	Darlington 8/28	Local 5/29	28		
HARRISON Robert	Manchester - 23/12/30	Local 2/53	Stockport County 7/56	66		16
HARRISON Wayne	Whitehaven - 16/10/57	Workington 8/87	Local 10/87	1	1	
HARTLE Barry	Salford - 8/8/39	Sheffield United 7/66	Stockport County 9/67	28	1	1
HARVEY Alex	Kirkconnel - 28/8/25	Queen South 8/46	Local 9/46	1		
HASSELL Richard	Coatbridge - 12/1/51	Youth 1/69	Local 5/70	3	3	
HATTON Robert	Hull 10/4/47	Northampton 7/69	Birmingham City 10/71	93		37
HAYTON Eric	Carlisle - 14/1/22	Local 8/45	Rochdale 5/51	49		5
HAYWARD Steve	Walsall - 8/9/71	Derby County 2/95		9		2
HEELBECK Leslie	Scarborough - 13/5/01	Newmarket 12/31	Wolves 5/32	12		1
HEGARTY Kevin	Edinburgh - 30/7/50	Hearts 9/71	Non-League 5/72	1	6	
HEIGH Robert	Bathgate - 1898	Grimsby Town 10/30	Non-League 5/31	6		
HEMSTEAD Derek	Scunthorpe - 22/5/43	Scunthorpe 7/69	Non-League 10/72	96	1	1
HENDERSON Joseph	Washington - 1902	Coventry 1/30	Local 5/30	9		2
HENSON Alan	Leeds - 1910	Local 12/34	Local 5/35	7		
HEPPLEWHITE Wilson	Washington - 11/6/64	Crook T. 3/65	Hartlepool United 7/67	3		
HESLOP Brian	Carlisle - 4/8/47	Youth 8/65	Sunderland 5/67	5		
HETHERINGTON Brent	Carlisle - 6/12/61	Workington 8/87	Local 1989	61		27
HICKIE George	Larkhall - 29/2/20	Barnsley 9/46	Non-League 10/46	1		
HIGGS Frank	Willington - 1905	Walsall 2/36	Non-League 5/37	49		
HILL Andrew	Ilkeston - 10/11/60	Derby County 9/83	Retired 5/86	73	12	15
HILL Georffrey	Carlisle - 31/8/29	Local 10/49	Local 5/59	188		
HILL Reginald	Gilbraltar - 1903	Local 1/31	Local 5/32	5		
HINDMARSH Edward	Sunderland - 7/9/21	Sunderland 7/45	Local 5/47	15		
HITCHON John	Carlisle - 30/8/19	Local 4/47	Local - 5/50	5		
HOGAN William	Salford - 9/1/24	Manchester City 9/49	Non-League 5/56	191		27
HOLDEN Stephen	Luton - 4/9/72	Leicester 10/92	Kettering Town 12/93	22		1
HOLDSWORTH Harold	Stockton - 1905	Notts County 9/29	Notts County 9/29	1		

NAME	Born: Place - Date	Transferred from:	Transferred to:	League & Cup App.	Sub	Gls.
HOLLAND John	Preston - 1905	Clapton Orient 8/29	Local 1931	34		13
HOLLIDAY John	Penrith - 13/3/70	Youth 9/89	Mansfield Town 10/92	19		
HOLMES Michael	Blackpool - 9/9/65	Torquay United 2/92	Northampton 2/93	34		4
HOLLICKIN Stephen	Manchester - 13/12/51	Bury 10/76	Hull 12/80	143		2
HOPPER Tony	Carlisle - 31/5/76	Youth 7/94		3	3	
HORNE George	Glasgow - 23/11/33	Maryhill 8/57	Non-League 4/58	4		2
HORNSBY Brian	Great Shelford - 10/9/54	Edmonton 8/83	Chesterfield 12/83	9	1	1
HORRIGAN Ken	Gravesend - 7/12/19	Imperial Paper 8//46	Non-League 5/47	16		1
HORSWILL Mick	Annfield Plain - 6/3/53	Hong Kong 8/83	Non-League 8/83	1		
HORTON Leslie	Salford - 12/7/21	Oldham Athletic 8/48	Rochdale 4/50	66		
HOUGHTON Keith	Backworth - 10/3/54	Blyth S. 1/80	Lincoln City 8/83	82	5	2
HOUSTON Graham	Gilbraltar - 24/2/60	Northwich 10/87	Non-League 3/88	8	8	1
HOWSHALL John	Longton - 12/7/12	Accrington 10/38	Non-League 1946	32		
HUNT Samuel	Doe Lea - 9/1/09	Accrington 10/38	Retired 8/39	31		33
HUNTER John	Coalburn - 26/5/34	Rotherham 7/57	Kings Lynn 2/58	1		
HUNTON Keith	Wellington - 18/7/61	Workington 2/87	Non-League 5/87	1		
HUTCHINSON David	Shotts - 1902	Motherwell 8/28	Luton Town 5/32	148		62
HUTTON Thomas	Gateshead - 10/9/22	Accrington 8/47	Rochdale 7/49	44		
ICETON Lloyd	Workington 30/3/20	Preston 10/46	Tranmere Rovers 6/50	77		18
IMRIE Adam	Dumfries - 1/10/33	Kilmarnock 5/57	Local 1/58	10		5
JACKSON James	Glasgow - 1/1/21	Bolton 7/50	Local 5/55	100		22
JACKSON Wilfred	Workington - 1905	Workington 9/35	Local 5/37	39		4
JEFFELS Simon	Barnsley - 18/1/66	Barnsley 7/88	Non-League 5/92	75	2	5
JOHNSON Jack	South Kirkby - 3/10/05	Barnsley 6/34	Accrington 6/38	139		1
JOHNSON James	Stockton - 26/2/23	Grimsby Town 3/51	Non-League 5/51	8		1
JOHNSTON Robert	Carlisle - 28/1/33	Local 11/51	Local 5/60	122		1
JOHNSTONE Eric	Newcastle - 22/3/43	Tow Law T. 6/63	Darlington 7/65	15		3
JONES Alex	Blackburn - 27/11/64	Preston 9/89	Rochdale 6/91	62		4
JONES David	Blaenau F. - 8/9/14	Stoke City 5/39	Non-League 5/48	66		
JONES Sidney	Gretna - 3/5/11	Local 2/35	Local 5/35	3		1
JOYCE Joe	Consett - 18/3/61	Scunthorpe 8/93		45	5	
KEATING Robert	Newcastle - 10/4/08	Bradford 10/37	Barnsley 5/38	5		1
KEEN Alan	Barrow - 29/5/30	Cheltenham Town 9/58	Local 5/60	7		
KEEN Stephen	Ealker - 1905	Everton 9/33	Tranmere 9/33	1		1
KELLY James	Drogheda - 16/2/25	Spurs 2/50	Non-League 5/52	43		6
KELLY Joseph	Cambuslang - 1900	Celtic 8/30	Non-League 5/31	32		
KELLY John	Wishaw - 1902	Spurs 8/30	Local 5/33	77		
KELLY Robert	Ashton - 1/4/07	Preston 3/35	Rochdale 10/35	12		
KEMP David	Harrow - 20/2/53	Portsmouth 3/78	Plymouth 9/79	60	1	22
KEMP Robert	Falkirk - 15/8/41	Falkirk 11/60	Queen South 12/60	1		
KENNEDY William	Larkhall - 12/03/03	Portsmouth 8/33	Non-League 5/34	8		
KENNY Vincent	Sheffield - 29/12/24	Sheffield Wednesday 7/55	Local 5/58	103		3
KENYON Fred	Carlisle - 14/1/22	Local 9/43	Local 5/49	1		
KERR Charles	Glasgow - 10/12/33	Morton 8/56	Barrow 7/59	9		3
KERR Thomas	Kelloholm - 22/5/10	Queen South 8/35	Local 5/39	136		
KINLOCH Thomas	Glasgow - 22/2/27	Falkirk 5/50	Workington 7/56	182		15
KINSELLA Leonard	Dumbarton 14/5/46	Burnley 9/70	Rochdale 9/71	10	4	
KIRKPATRICK John	Annan - 3/3/19	Local 11/37	Local 5/47	35		2
KIRKUP Frank	Spennymoor - 12/1/39	Workington 12/62	Notts County 6/65	76		15
KNIGHT Ian	Hartlepool - 26/10/66	Grimsby 8/92	Non-League 5/39	1		
KNOX Thomas	Ushan Moor - 11/11/05	Norwich City 9/37	Non-League 5/39	63		
LACKENBY George	Newcastle - 22/5/31	Exeter 7/57	Gateshead 7/59	46		
LAIDLAW Joseph	Whickham - 12/7/50	Middlesbrough 7/72	Doncaster 7/76	146	5	44
LAIDLER John	Windermere - 5/1/19	Netherfield 6/46	Local 5/47	27		3
LANDELLS John	Gateshead - 1905	Bristol City 8/35	Non-League 5/36	33		6
LANDSBOROUGH Murray	Thornhill - 30/12/15	Kilmarnock 8/47	Non-League 9/47	1		
LARGE Frank	Leeds - 26/1/40	Swindon Town 9/64	Oldham 12/65	51		18
LARKIN Anthony	Wrexham - 12/1/56	Shrewsbury 7/81	Hereford United 3/83	47	2	2
LATHAN John	Sunderland - 12/4/52	Mansfield Town 2/76	Portsmouth 3/78	55	6	8
LEACH Thomas	Wincobank - 23/9/03	Stockport County 2/37	Non-League 5/38	51		
LACKIE Jack	Alva - 1907	Local 8/37	Local 10/37	8		
LEE Robert	Melton Mowbray - 2/2/53	Bristol Rovers 8/81	Hong Kong 5/83	47	8	12

NAME	Born: Place - Date	Transferred from:	Transferred to:	League & Cup App.	Sub	Gls.
LEGGE Edward	Carlisle - 12/3/02	Local 8/32	Local 5/35	104		1
LINDSAY John	Cambuslang - 11/12/21	Bury 8/47	Southport 3/51	103		46
		Wigan Athletic 1/55	Non-League 5/55	13		2
LISLE Joseph	Dinnington - 14/7/10	Bury 9/36	Non-League 2/37	3		
LITTLE John	South Shields - 11/4/03	Local 2/29	Local 10/29	2		
LITTLE Ronald	Carlisle - 24/1/34	Local 5/55	Local 5/56	5		
LIVINGSTONE Joseph	Middlesbrough - 18/6/42	Middlesbrough 11/62	Hartlepool 5/66	79	1	42
LLOYD Edward	Oldham 25/7/05	Hull City 8/35	Scunthorpe United 6/36	42		
LOMAX Geoffrey	Droylsden 6/7/64	Manchester City 12/85	Rochdale 7/87	37		
LONGSTAFF James	Dumfries - 23/7/03	Local 12/32	Local 12/32	1		
LONSDALE David	Carlisle - 25/5/05	Local 1/31	Local 5/39	30		2
LORNIE John	Aberdeen - 2/3/39	Luton Town 6/63	Tranmere Rovers 6/64	4		
LUDLAM Steven	Chesterfield - 18/10/55	Sheffield United 5/77	Chester 7/80	90	6	11
LUMBY James	Grimsby 2/10/54	Scunthorpe 4/78	Tranmere Rovers 7/79	24	3	7
LYNAM Chris	Manchester 22/1/62	Ryoden (Hong Kong) 8/86	Non-League 8/86	1	1	
McARDLE Peter	Durham - 1904	Exeter City 8/36	Non-League 5/37	27		12
McAUGHTRIE David	Cumnock - 30/1/63	Stoke City 7/84	York City 6/85	28		1
McAULEY Hugh	Bootle - 8/1/53	Tranmere Rovers 7/79	Local 12/80	14	3	1
McBAIN Alan	Aberdeen - 10/2/40	Swansea City 6/60	Luton Town 6/63	70		
McBAIN Thomas	Wifflet - 1902	Newcastle 10/32	Local 5/34	38		12
McBRIDE William	Newtown - 8/11/13	Local 2/46	Local 5/47	15		1
McCAFFREY Aiden	Newcastle - 30/8/57	Non-League 1/88	Retired 1988	14		
McCAIG Robert	Dumfries - 15/8/23	Local 8/48	Blackburn Rovers 12/48	5		
McCALL Alexander	Annan 26/3/39	Local 9/58	Local 5/60	1		
McCARRON Frank	Glasgow - 1/10/43	Celtic 7/67	Non-League 5/68	7	2	1
McCARTNEY Michael	Edinburgh - 28/9/54	West Bromwich A. 5/73	Southampton 7/80	148	8	17
		Plymouth Argyle 3/83	Non-League 1987	130	1	7
McCLURE William	Shotts - 16/5/21	New Brighton 10/49	Hartlepool United 8/50	8		1
McCUE Alex	Greenoch - 25/11/27	Falkirk 10/50	Grimsby 7/51	32		11
MacCARTNEY Charles	Stamford - 1910	Wrexham 9/37	Non-League 11/37	4		
MacDONALD Garry	Middlesbrough - 26/3/62	Middlesbrough 7/84	Darlington 10/84	7	2	
McCONNELL James	Kilmarnock - 1900	USA 11/27	Crewe Alexandra 5/32	150	-	126
McCONNELL Peter	Stockport - 3/3/37	Leeds 8/62	Bradford City 7/69	272	1	27
McCREERY David	Belfast - 16/9/57	Hartlepool 10/92	Hartlepool 10/94	25	10	
McDONALD Ian	West Germany - 30/8/53	St. Johnstone 5/76	Dundee 5/81	186	1	7
McDONALD William	Longriggend - 30/8/18	Airdrie 8/46	Local 5/47	3		
McDOUGALL Laybourne	Tynemouth - 12/5/17	Non-League 6/37	Preston 3/38	3		
McGARR John	Carlisle - 3/6/10	Local 1/37	Local 5/38	5		3
McGARVEY Scott	Glasgow - 22/4/63	Portsmouth 7/86	Grimsby 3/87	35		11
McGILL Austin	Dumfries - 29/1/35	Queen South 8/59	Local 5/60	30		12
McGILL James	Gateshead - 14/11/1898	Non-League 12/31	Local 5/32	16		
McGORIAN Isaac	Silksworth - 1900	Notts County 2/30	Local 3/30	3		
McGROGAN Hugh	Dumbarton - 1/3/57	Oxford United 5/80	Non-League 3/81	1	1	
McHALE William	Fife - 9/8/29	Local 8/53	Halifax Town 3/55	1		
McILMOYLE Hugh	Cambuslang - 29/1/40	Rotherham 3/63	Wolves 10/64	77		44
		Bristol City 9/67	Middlesbrough 9/69	79		30
		Morton 7/74	Morton 5/75	15	3	2
McINTOSH Alex	Aberdeen - 19/10/23	Barrow 10/49	Local 5/55	228		4
McKELLAR David	Irvine - 22/5/56	Brentford 8/83	Hibs 7/85	82		
		Dunfermline 10/88	Kilmarnock 3/90	69		
McKENNA Frank	Blaydon - 8/1/33	Leeds United 2/58	Hartlepool United 7/59	45		11
MacLAREN James S.	Crieff - 26/11/21	Chester 12/48	Berwick R. 5/55	261		
McLAUGHLIN Hubert	Galston - 1895	Celtic 8/29	Scots League 5/30	31		
McLEAN David	Newcastle - 24/11/57	Newcastle United 3/78	Darlington 8/79	9	6	
McLEOD James	Glasgow - 31/8/1898	Partick Thistle 8/29	Scots League 5/30	9		1
McMAHON Steve	Glasgow - 22/4/70	Swansea 8/93		2		
McMILLAN Thomas	Auchinleck - 16/1/62	Watford 7/58	Non-League 2/61	89		7
McNEIL Robert	Hamilton - 1/11/62	Preston 8/87	Non-League 5/88	18	1	
McNICHOL Robert	Dumbarton - 13/2/33	Gravesend 10/63	Non-League 6/64	1		
McPARTLAND Desmond	Middlsbrough - 5/10/47	Middlesbrough 12/67	Northampton 7/69	5		
McPHAIL Donald	Hamilton - 1900	Middlesbrough 12/33	Local 4/34	5		
McVITIE George	Carlisle - 7/9/48	Local 12/65	West Bromwich A. 8/70	124	4	21

NAME	Born: Place - Date	Transferred from:	Transferred to:	App.	Sub	Gls.
MANNS Thomas	Rotherham - 2/5/08	Clapton Orient 8/35	Non-League 5/36	22		
MANTLE Joseph	Hetton le Hole - 1906	Chester 9/35	Local 2/37	55		38
MARSDEN John	Leeds - 17/12/31	Barrow 9/60	Doncaster Rovers 7/64	88		
MARSHALL Gary	Bristol - 20/4/64	Bristol City 7/88	Scunthorpe United 7/89	18	3	2
MARSLAND Gordon	Blackpool - 20/3/45	Blackpool 6/65	Bristol Rovers 6/69	62	1	4
MARTIN Dennis	Edinburgh - 27/10/47	West Bromwich A. 7/70	Newcastle United 10/77	271	4	48
MARTIN Geoff	Clay Cross - 9/3/40	Darlington 3/62	Workington 12/62	15		2
MASKILL Thomas	York - 12/4/02	Scarborough 8/30	Barnsley 5/31	37		1
MAXFIELD John	Carlisle - 17/6/19	Local 8/39	Workington 12/62	25		4
MAYES Alan	Edmonton - 11/12/53	Swindon Town 7/85	Blackpool 9/86	8	2	2
MEREDITH Robert	Swansea - 3/9/17	Non-League 1/47	Non-League 2/47	1		
METCALFE Stuart	Blackburn - 6/10/50	Blackburn 7/80	USA 5/81	23	2	3
MILLAR William	Ballymena - 21/6/03	Newport County 8/34	Non-League 5/35	33		9
MILLER Archibald	Larkhall - 5/9/13	Kilmarnock 9/50	Hearts 2/52	1		
MILLER David	Burnley - 8/1/64	Preston 9/89	Stockport 3/92	108	1	7
MILLER James	Felling - 11/7/03	Crewe 12/28	Local 5/34	160		6
MILLS Hugh	Alexandra - 13/4/12	Luton Town 3/37	Non-League 5/39	54		28
MILLS Keith	Newcastle - 30/12/63	North Shields 2/88	North Shields 4/88		1	
MITCHELL Robert	South Shields - 4/1/55	Grimsby Town 8/82	Rotherham 3/83	2		
MITTON Keith	Leyland - 30/12/28	Preston 6/54	Non-League 11/56	48		
MIXEN Harold	Westbury - 1904	Salisbury C. 9/32	Non-League 2/33	3		1
MOIR James	Newcastle - 23/3/18	Accrington 8/46	Non-League 5/48	42		18
MOLLOY Peter	Rossendale - 4/4/11	Stockport 5/37	Bradford City 5/38	33		
MONCUR Robert	Perth - 19/1/45	Sunderland 11/76	Retired 1977	11		
MONOGHAN William	Glasgow - 2/9/19	Bury 8/47	Non-League 12/49	19		
MOONEY Frank	Fauldhouse - 1/1/32	Blackburn 5/56	Non-League 5/60	124		23
MOORE David	Grimsby - 17/12/59	Grimsby Town 9/83	Blackpool 12/83	13		1
MORAN Thomas	Edinburgh - 5/2/30	Cowdenbeath - 5/54	Darlington 5/56	36		5
MORGAN Wendell	Gorseinon - 22/4/35	Newport County 6/60	Non-League 5/61	35		2
MORT Enoch	Ogmore Vale - 1909	Cardiff 8/38	Non-League 5/39	17		
MOSSOP Graham	Wellington - 11/1/58	Workington 7/79	Local 5/81	2		
MOUNTFIELD Derek	Liverpool - 22/11/62	Wolves 7/79		30	1	3
MURDOCH Robert	Liverpool - 25/1/36	Stockport 1/62	Southport 7/62	10		1
MURPHY James	Edinburgh - 1908	Leigh A. 8/38	Scots League 5/39	28		5
MURRAY Matthew	Paisley - 25/12/29	Barrow 7/59	Local 1/60	28		4
MURRAY Paul	Carlisle - 31/5/76	Youth 8/93		4	9	
MURRAY Thomas	Caldercruix - 1/6/43	Airdrie - 3/67	Hearts 3/71	123	10	37
MUTRIE Les	Newcastle - 1/4/52	Gateshead 6/77	Blyth Spartans	4	1	
NEIL Hugh	Cumnock - 2/10/36	St. Johnstone 6/61	Local 1968	246	1	2
NEVIN Paul	London 23/6/69	USA 9/91	Non-League 2/92	2	6	1
NICHOL Robert	Carlisle - 19/1/41	Juniors 6/58	Local 11/59	3		1
NICHOLSON Peter	Cleator Moor - 12/1/51	Lytham 3/83	Non-League 5/84	1	2	
NORRIS Stephen	Coventry - 22/9/61	Scarborough 12/89	Halifax Town 10/90	21	8	5
O'CONNELL Seamus	Carlisle - 1/1/30	Crook T. 2/58	Local 5/58	4		2
O'GRADY Henry	Tunstall - 16/3/07	Millwall 8/36	Accrington Stanley 5/37	28		9
O'HANLON Kelham	Saltburn - 16/5/62	Rotherham 8/91	Preston 6/93	83		
O'NEILL Les	Blyth - 4/12/43	Bradford C. 5/72	Local 5/76	148	7	20
O'NEILL William	Glasgow - 30/12/40	Celtic 5/69	Non-League 5/70	15		
O'RIORDAN Don	Dublin - 14/5/57	Preston 8/83	Middlesbrough 8/85	84		18
O'ROURKE John	Glasgow - 17/10/48	Arsenal 10/67	Non-League 1/68		1	
OGHANI George	Manchester - 2/9/60	Cyprus 8/92	Northwich Victoria 5/94	45	8	15
OGILVIE Howard	Carlisle - 1909	Local 4/39	5/39	2		
OGLEY Mark	Barnsley - 10/3/67	Barnsley 3/88	Aldershot 11/89	33		1
OLIPHANT David	Carlisle 29/1/42	Wolves 12/60	Local 10/64	109		11
OOSTHUIZEN Ron	South Africa - 16/3/36	Poole T. 9/59	Non-League 11/59	1		
OWEN Robert	Farnworth - 17/10/47	Manchester City 6/70	Doncaster Rovers 7/77	185	19	51
OXLEY Cyril	Wallsend - 2/5/04	Southend 9/29	Non-League 9/29	1		
PARKER Albert	Eccles - 1906	Bristol City 8/34	Non-League 5/35	18		
PARKER Charles	Seaham Harbour - 1898	Sunderland 8/29	Local 5/30	10		1
PARKER James	Carlisle - 17/5/14	Local 2/35	Local 9/35	2		
PARKER Robert	Coventry - 11/11/52	Coventry 6/74	Local 5/84	373	2	6
PARKER Wilson	Ryton on Tyne - 11/4/03	Scotswood 12/29	Non-League 6/35	58		

NAME	Born: Place - Date	Transferred from:	Transferred to:	League & Cup App.	Sub	Gls.
PASSMOOR Thomas	Chester le Street - 12/2/37	Scunthorpe 12/63	Non-League 5/70	242	16	
PATTERSON Mark	Leeds - 13/9/68	Youth 8/87	Derby County 11/87	24	9	3
PATTERSON Martin	Forest Hall - 1909	Local 10/37	Local 1/38	2		
PEACOCK Lee	Paisley - 9/10/76	Youth 3/95		2	6	
PEARSON John	Sheffield - 1/9/63	Barnsley 8/93	Mansfield 11/94	5		3
PEDDELTY Maurice	Carlisle - 23/5/50	Local 12/67	Darlington 7/70	9	5	1
PETERS Bob	Kensington - 8/5/71	Brentford 11/94		5	3	
PIERCE William	Howden on Tyne - 1908	QPR 8/31	Local 5/32	19		
PIGG William	Spen - 1897	QPR 8/26	Accrington Stanley 6/30	69		7
PLENDERLEITH Joseph	Carluke - 1902	Local 1/30	Local 3/30	1		
POLLOCK Thomas	Newcastle - 1900	Non-League 11/30	Non-League 11/30	1		
POND Harold	Kilnhurst - 19/4/17	Barnsley 9/38	Retired 10/45	11		
POSKETT Malcolm	Middlesbrough 19/7/53	Watford 8/82	Darlington 7/85	108	2	40
		Stockport County 8/86	Local 5/88	67	9	20
POTTS Craig	Carlisle - 25/3/74	Youth 7/90	Local 5/93	9	5	
PRESGRAVE Gordon	Kippax - 1913	Halifax 9/36	Non-League 11/36	5		1
PRIESTLEY Jason	Leeds - 25/10/70	Youth 7/89	Local 5/91	22		
PRINS Jason	Wisbech - 1/11/74	Youth 7/91	Non-League 5/94	7	11	
PROKAS Richard	Penrith - 22/1/76	Youth 7/94		37	2	1
PROUDLOCK Paul	Hartlepool - 25/10/62	Middlesbrough 3/89	Gateshead 7/93	137	18	20
PROUT George	Barrow - 3/11/02	Grimsby Town 8/28	Bath City 8/30	67		
PRUDHAM Edward	Gateshead - 12/4/52	Sheffield Wed. 11/74	Stockport County 7/77	15	2	2
PRUDHOE Mark	Washington - 11/11/63	Walsall 12/87	Darlington 3/89	34		
PURVIS Bartholomew	Gateshead - 15/10/21	Notts County 8/51	Local 11/51	4		
RAFFERTY William	Glasgow - 30/12/50	Plymouth Argyle 5/76	Wolves 3/78	72		27
RANSON John	London - 1905	Millwall 11/34	Millwall 4/35	15		9
RAWES Herbert	Frizington - 21/11/32	Local 9/53	Local 2/55	11		1
REDDISH Shane	Bolsover - 5/5/71	Doncaster 7/93	Hartlepool 11/94	35	2	1
REEVES David	Birkenhead - 19/11/67	Notts County 10/93		76		32
RICHMOND William	Kirkaldy - 1/3/1900	Montrose 8/29	Ayr U. 5/32	39		
RILEY William	Carlisle 19/10/1898	Non-League 9/28	Non-League 9/28	1		
RIVERS Walter	Throckley - 8/1/09	Aldershot 8/36	Accrington 10/36	2		1
ROBERTS Neville	Penhancho - 15/6/02	Barnsley 3/37	Local 5/38	30		6
ROBERTSON James	Gateshead - 24/11/69	Youth 7/88	Non-League 1989	10	3	
ROBINSON Andrew	Oldham - 10/3/66	Bury 3/87	Wycombe W. 6/88	43	3	3
ROBINSON Ernest	York - 21/1/10	Sheffield United 8/34	Local 5/35	38		
ROBINSON James	Liverpool - 26/2/72	Barnsley 1/94		22	8	2
ROBINSON William	Darlington - 24/8/03	Southend - 9/28	Non-League 10/28	4		1
ROBSON Arnold	Felling - 30/4/1897	Non-League 4/31	Non-League 5/31	8		
ROBSON Bryan	Sunderland - 11/11/45	Sunderland 3/81	Chelsea 8/82	48		21
		Sunderland 7/84	Retired 1985			
ROBSON William	Whitehaven - 13/10/31	Workington 11/59	Local 10/60	10		1
ROOKE Ronald	Carlisle - 12/12/26	Local 9/46	Local 10/49	1		
RORRISON Jim	Kirkconnel - 1897	St. Mirren 4/1	Local 5/31	2		
ROSS Alan	Glasgow - 26/5/42	Luton Town 6/63	Local 5/79	465	1	
ROSS Bryce	Edinburgh - 4/12/27	Newcastle 11/46	Non-League 3/48	3		
ROSS George	Deptford - 1/11/20	Millwall 5/47	Non-League 3/48	9		
ROSS Robert	Falkirk - 11/3/01	Falkirk 8/28	Scots League 5/29	22		2
ROUND John	Brierley Hill - 1911	Port Vale 8/35	Died 31/12/36	37		
ROUTLEDGE William	Choppington - 1911	York City 9/36	Local 3/31	16		
ROWELL Gary	Seaham - 6/6/57	Brighton H.A. 3/88	Burnley 8/88	7		
ROY James	Carlisle - 23/3/02	Local 9/28	Local 5/29	10		1
RUDGE John	Wolverhampton - 21/10/44	Huddersfield 12/66	Torquay United 1/69	45	5	16
RUDKIN George	Horncastle - 1/3/12	Mansfield Town 1/39	Chesterfield 5/39	16		1
RUSHBURY David	Wolverhampton - 20/2/56	Swansea 8/81	Gillingham 3/85	120	9	1
RYOTT William	Newcastle - 22/10/05	Non-League 12/30	Non-League 5/32	4		1
SADDINGTON Nigel	Sunderland - 9/12/65	Sunderland 2/88	Gateshead 5/90	91		15
SANDERSON John	Carlisle - 5/2/18	Local 5/38	Wolves 2/39	15		
SAUNDERS Wesley	Sunderland 23/2/63	Newcastle 8/85	Dundee 5/88	97		11
SAVILLE Peter	Dalbeattie - 29/8/48	Local 7/66	Harwick/Albert 1969	1		
SAWYERS Keith	Banbury - 11/6/60	Local 1/78	Local 5/80	5	4	
SCOTT Alex	St. Andrews - 17/11/22	Leicester City 1/50	Scots League 5/56	203		3

NAME	Born: Place - Date	Transferred from:	Transferred to:	League & Cup		
				App.	Sub	Gls.
SCOTT Alex	South Sheilds - 21/4/07	Non-League 2/37	Non-League 5/38	27		2
SCURR John	North Shields - 30/9/40	Arsenal 1/61	Local 5/62	15		1
SEED Terance	Preston - 3/9/23	Preston 12/4	Accrington Stanley 6/50	81		
SENDALL Richard	Stamford - 10/7/67	Blackpool 7/88	Retired 5/93	48	36	14
SHANKLY James	Douglas - 11/2/04	Barrow 8/35	Local 10/35	6		3
SHANKLY William	Glenbuck - 2/9/13	Non-League 7/32	Preston 7/33	16		
SHARP Arthur	Nottingham - 14/11/10	Non-League 8/35	Bristol City 5/32	68		14
SHARP Frank	Edinburgh - 28/5/47	Hearts 3/67	Cardiff City 2/69	31		
SHEPHERD Anthony	Glasgow - 16/11/66	Celtic 7/89	Motherwell 6/91	73	2	8
SHOULDER Alan	Bishop Auckland - 4/2/53	Newcastle United 8/82	Hartlepool United 6/85	110	2	32
SIDDALL Barry	Ellesmere Port - 12/954	Mossley 11/90	Chester City 7/91	24		
SIMPSON Reginald	Blackburn - 11/6/23	Preston 8/48	Local 5/49	36		
SIMPSON Ron	Carlisle - 25/2/34	Sheffield United 12/64	Queen South 5/66	45		6
SIMPSON William	Carlisle - 2/10/19	Spurs 8/46	Local 5/47	12		2
SINGLETON Jack	Egremont - 1909	Accrington 10/36	Bournemouth 5/37	1		
SLEIGHT Harold	Sleaford - 2/7/07	Non-League 11/36	Non-League 2/37	9		
SLINGER James	Leeds - 14/12/06	Non-League 4/32	Accrington 6/35	80		53
SMILES James	North Shields - 1900	Non-League 9/28	Non-League 12/30	43		
SMITH Albert	Glasgow - 1900	Dolphin FC 9/32	Scots League 7/33	39		1
SMITH Archibald	Larkhall - 23/10/24	Exeter City 8/52	Non-League 5/77	31		8
SMITH John	Liverpool 14/3/53	Everton 6/76	Non-League 5/77	4	1	
SMITH Kenneth	South Shields 21/5/32	Darlington 7/60	Canada 5/61	13		12
SMITH William	Boldon 12/3/07	Stockport County 2/37	Local 5/39	71		
SNEDDON Robert	Kilwinning - 1899	Kilmarnock 8/33	Scots League 5/34	17		3
SPEARITT Edward	Lowestoft - 31/1/47	Brighton 6/74	Gillingham 8/76	29	2	1
SPENCER Clarence	Nottingham - 1903	Barrow 8/34	Local 3/35	12		
SQUIRES Alan	Fleetwood - 26/2/23	Preston 12/46	Retired 2/48	25		
STANIFORTH Gordon	Hull - 23/2/57	York 10/79	Plymouth Argyle 3/83	118	8	33
STARK William	Glasgow - 27/5/37	Crewe 12/61	Colchester United 11/62	35		17
STEEN Alan	Glasgow - 26/6/22	Rochdale 12/51	Non-League 5/52	16		2
STEPHENS Archibald	Liverpool - 19/5/54	Middlesbrough 12/87	Darlington 3/89	20	4	3
STEVENSON John	Aberdeen - 1903	Bristol City 8/33	Local 5/35	65		11
STEWART George	Buckie - 17/2/27	Coventry 6/60	Scots League 6/61	7		2
STOKOE Dennis	Blyth - 6/6/25	Chesterfield 7/48	Workington 10/53	148		2
SULLIVAN Cornelius	Tynemouth - 1/9/1898	Bradford 9/30	Non-Leagie 5/31	10		
SUTTIE David	Blackburn - 1903	Nelson 9/33	Nelson 9/33	1		
SUTTON Michael	Norwich - 5/10/44	Chester 6/70	Non-League	51	2	1
SWEENEY Eric	Nantwich - 27/6/02	Crewe 8/32	Non-League 5/33	4		
SWEENEY William	St. Andrews - 23/10/18	Clyde 1/48	Scots League 5/49	37		
SWINBURNE Trevor	Houghton/Spring 20/6/53	Sunderland 5/77	Brentford 8/83	248		
SWORD Ronald	Dundee - 21/3/09	Dunfermline 10/38	Scots League 5/39	6		1
TAGG Ernest	Crewe - 15/9/17	Bournemouth 11/48	Non-League 3/49	5		1
TAIT Michael	Wallsend - 30/9/56	Oxford 1/77	Hull City 9/79	101	5	20
TATE William	Sunderland - 1908	Non-League 12/37	Non-League 5/38	14		3
TAYLOR Alex	Menstrie - 25/12/16	Stirling A/ 6/38	Scots League 5/47	24		
TAYLOR Joseph	West Bromwich - 23/7/09	Luton 9/35	Local 3/37	58		11
TAYLOR Samuel	Glasgow - 23/9/33	Preston 6/61	Southport 7/64	93		12
TEMPLE William	Blaydon - 12/12/14	Aldershot 5/37	Grimsby Town 9/38	11		4
TERNENT Stanley	Gateshead - 16/6/46	Burnley 5/68	Sunderland 5/74	186	2	5
TERRIS James	Chippenham - 25/7/33	Bristol City 4/59	Non-League 5/61	28		1
THOMAS Gwyn	Swansea - 26/9/57	Hull City 8/91	Non-League 5/62	35	2	1
THOMAS Roderick	London - 10/10/70	Watford 6/93		73	1	5
THOMPSON Geroge	Maltby - 15/9/26	Manchester City 6/57	Local 5/62	202		
THOMPSON John	Newbiggin - 23/2/03	Blackburn 2/29	Barrow 2/29	2		1
THOMPSON Ronald	Carlisle - 20/1/32	Local 7/51	Local 5/64	374		12
THOMSON James	Larkhall - 18/5/1895	T. Lanark 8/29	Scots League 5/30	15		3
THOMPSON Lawrence	Menstrie - 26/8/36	Partick Thistle 1/60	Scots League 5/60	12		1
THORPE Jeffrey	Cockermouth - 17/11/72	Youth 7/91		64	33	5
TICKELL Brian	Carlisle - 15/11/39	Huddersfield 5/59	Local 5/60	3		1
TILER Brian	Rotherham - 15/4/43	Aston Villa 10/72	Non-League 5/74	154	1	8
TOWERS Jack	Darlington - 1901	Southport 10/32	Hartlepool United 10/32	2		
TRAIN Raymond	Nuneaton - 10/2/51	Walsall 12/71	Sunderland 3/76	154	1	8

NAME	Born: Place - Date	Transferred from:	Transferred to:	App.	Sub	Gls.
TROOPS Harold	Sheffield - 10/2/26	Lincoln City 6/58	Non-League 5/60	60		1
TROTTER Alan	Keswick - 23/8/02	Local 9/28	Local 5/35	58		
TULLOCH Ronald	Haddington - 5/6/33	Southend 7/57	Local 5/60	73		22
TUPLING Stephen	Wensleydale - 11/7/64	Middlesbrough 7/84	Darlington 10/84	1		
TURNER Phillip	Chester - 20/2/27	Chester City 9/48	Bradford 6/51	79		23
TURNER Robert	Darlington - 1901	Swindon Town 11/33	Non-League 5/34	28		4
TWENTYMAN Geoffrey	Brampton - 19/1/30	Youth 2/47	Liverpool 12/53	149		2
		Ballymena U. 6/63	Local 5/64	10		
TYNAN Paul	Whitehaven - 15/7/69	Ipswich 8/87	Local 5/88	2	3	
VALENTINE Peter	Huddersfield - 16/4/63	Bury 8/93	Rochdale 11/94	27	2	2
VARTY William	Throckley - 25/6/06	Gateshead 2/36	Non-League 5/36	16		4
WAKENSHAW Robert	Ponteland - 22/12/65	Everton 9/85	Rochdale 9/86	62	2	2
WALKER George	Sunderland - 30/5/34	Bristol City 3/59	Non-League 5/64	164		51
WALLING Dean	Leeds - 17/4/69	Guisely 5/91		135	6	17
WALSH Derek	Hamilton - 24/10/67	Hamilton A. 8/88	Local 5/93	108	13	7
WALSHAW Kenneth	Tynemouth - 28/8/18	Lincoln C. 12/47	Bradford City 8/50	50		15
WALTON Ronald	Newcastle - 12/10/45	Crewe 1/66	Aldershot 8/66	1		
WALWYN Keith	Jamaica - 17/2/56	Blackpool 7/89	Kettering Town 8/91	59	3	15
WARD William	Carlisle - 1894	Local 8/20	Local 5/30	38		9
WATERS Patrick	Dublin - 31/1/22	Preston 12/50	Local 5/58	261		
WATSON Andrew	Leeds - 1/4/67	Swansea City 9/91	Blackpool 2/93	55	1	22
WATSON Gary	Easington - 2/3/61	Oxford United 5/80	Non-League 5/81	17	1	
WATSON William	Morpeth - 16/3/1899	Ashington 6/28	Rochdale 6/32	141		38
WEBB Stanley	Middlesbrough - 6/12/17	Middlesbrough 2/71	Brentford 10/72	16	10	5
WEBSTER Maurice	Blackpool - 12/3/04	Middlesbrough 8/35	Local 12/35	14		
WELSH Eric	Belfast - 1/5/42	Exeter 10/65	Torquay United 6/69	73	2	17
WESTMORLAND Joseph	Carlisle - 30/6/67	Local 2/59	Local 5/59	1		
WHEAT John	Worksop - 12/11/08	Barnsley 8/38	Bradford City 5/39	11		
WHARTON Kenneth	Newcastle - 28/11/60	Newcastle 8/89	Bradford City 8/89	1		
WHEELER William	Carlisle 27/9/20	Local 10/46	Local 5/47	4		
WHITE Robert	Newburn - 11/8/04	Watford 8/32	Watford 3/33	23		7
WHITE Walter	Fife - 26/7/02	Aldershot 8/34	Local 12/34	8		2
WHITEHOUSE James	West Bromwich - 19/9/24	Rochdale 10/51	Local 5/57	198	-	100
WHITELAW George	Paisley - 1/1/37	Halifax Town 2/61	Stockport County 1/62	34		10
WHITFIELD George	Penrith - 10/2/34	Local 4/56	Local 5/56	2		
WIGHTMAN John	Duns - 2/11/12	Blackburn Rovers 8/47	Scots League 5/48	36		
WILKES David	Barnsley - 10/3/64	Bridlington T. 11/90	Retired 1992	1	4	
WALLACY William	Annan - 1911	Local 3/32	Local 5/32	4		
WILLIAMS Joe	Rotherham - 1910	Middlesbrough 8/35	Local 3/37	20		2
WILLIAMS Neil	Waltham Abbey 23/10/64	Preston 8/92	Non-League 5/93	19		1
WILSON David	Wednesfield - 4/10/44	Nottingham Forest 10/65	Grimsby Town 3/67	54	1	23
WILSON Kenneth	Dumbarton - 15/9/47	Dumbarton 9/72	Scots League 5/73	14	6	1
WINSTANLEY Graham	Croxdale	Newcastle United 8/69	Brighton H.A. 10/74	165	1	8
		Brighton H.A. 7/79	Local 5/80			
WINSTER Carl	Shap - 11/4/1900	Local 3/29	Local 3/30	5		1
WINTER George	Carlisle - 1908	Local 11/35	Local 11/35	1		
WINTHROP Wilfred	Carlisle - 1909	Local 12/34	Local 5/35	2		
WOLF George	Newcastle - 23/4/03	Preston 8/33	Non-League 5/35	63		
WORRALL Gary	Salford - 4/11/61	Peterborough United 7/86	Non-League 5/87	32		
WRIGHT William	Liverpool - 28/4/58	Birmingham City 8/86	Local 5/88	87		3
YATES Richard	Queens Ferry 6/6/21	Wrexham 11/48	New Brighton 8/49	16		9
YOUNG William	Ferrybridge - 1898	Barnsley 9/32	Barnsley 5/33	3		

WHO'S WHO: LOAN SIGNINGS

NAME	Born: Place - Date	Transferred from:	Transferred to:	League & Cup App.	Sub	Gls.
BAILEY Ian	Middlesbrough - 2-0/1/56	Middlesbrough 2/77	3/77	7		1
BARNES Andrew	Croyden - 31/3/67	Crystal Palace 12/93	1/94	2		
BUTLER Martin	Hull - 3/3/66	York 12/88	12/88	1		
CALDWELL David	Aberdeen - 31/7/60	Mansfield 12/84	1/85	4		
CARNEY Stephen	Wallsend - 22/9/57	Newcastle 3/85	4/85	6		
CARTER Timothy	Bristol - 5/10/67	Sunderland 3/88	4/88	4		
CLARKE Derek	Willenhall - 19/2//50	Orient 10/78	11/78		1	
CORNELLY Dean	Glasgow - 6/1/70	Barnsley 8/92	12/93		3	
COOKE John	Salford - 25/4/62	Sunderland 11/84	12/84	5	1	2
CULLEN Tony	Gateshead - 30/9/69	Sunderland 12/89	12/89	2		1
DAVIES Alan	Manchester - 5/12/61	Newcastle - 11/86	12/86	4		1
DEANS John (Dixie)	Johnstone - 30/7/46	Luton 2/77	2/77	4		2
FINLAY Alan	Liverpool - 10/12/67	Stockport 1/93	1/93	1		
FLOUNDERS Andrew	Hull - 13/12/63	Rochdale 10/93	12/93	5		1
		Rochdale 2/94	3/94	1	2	
FREEMAN Clive	Leeds - 12/9/62	Swansea 1/92	2/92	4		
GRAHAM Deniol	Cannock - 4/10/69	Barnsley 12/93	12/93	2		1
HAWKE Warren	Durham 20/9/70	Sunderland 10/92	11/92	8		2
HINDSON Graham	Stanley - 8/1/50	Luton 9/75	9/75	1	2	
HOLDSWORTH Dean	Walthamstow - 8/11/68	Watford 2/88	3/88	4		1
HUGHES Bily	Coatbridge - 30/12/48	Leicester 9/79	10/79	5		
HUTCHINSON Mark	Stoke - 2/11/63	Leicester 8/84	10/84	6		
HUTCHINSON Robert	Glasgow - 19/6/53	Walsall 1/88	4/88	12	1	2
LEMON Paul	Middlesbrough - 3/6/66	Sunderland 12/84	12/84	2		
LILLIS Jason	Chatham - 1/10/69	Maidstone 2/91	3/91	4		1
LOWE Kenneth	Sedgefield - 6/11/61	Birmingham 9/94	10/94	1	1	
LOWERY Tony	Wallsend - 6/7/61	Mansfield 10/91	11/91	6	1	
McCALL Steve	Carlisle - 15/10/60	Sheffield Wednesday 2/90	3/90	6		
METHVEN Colin	India - 10/12/55	Blackpool 9/90	11/90	12		
NIXON Eric	Manchester - 4/10/62	Manchester City 1/87	3/87	16		
NUTTELL Mickey	Boston - 22/11/68	Peterborough 11/88	11/88	1	2	
OWEN Gordon	Barnsley - 14/6/59	Blackpool 10/90	11/90	4	1	
RITCHIE Thomas	Edinburgh - 2/1/52	Sunderland 3/82	5/82	14	1	
ROBSON Bryan	Sunderland - 11/11/45	Chelsea 3/83	5/83	11	4	
ROBSON Keith	Hetton-Le-Hole - 15/11/53	Leicester City 3/83	5/83	10	1	4
ROSE Kevin	Evesham - 23/11/60	Bolton Wanderers 3/90	5/90	11		
RUSSELL Guy	Birmingham - 28/9/67	Birmingham City 3/87	3/87	9	3	2
STONEHOUSE Kevin	Bishop Auckland - 20/9/59	Darlington 3/89	4/89		3	
TAYLOR Martin	Tamworth - 9/12/66	Derby County 9/87	11/87	10		
TOLMIE James	Glasgow - 20/11/60	Manchester City 3/86	5/86	7	1	1
WHITE Winston	Leicester - 26/10/58	West Brom.Albion 2/93	3/93	6		

KEY TO WHO'S WHO

The tables are generally self-explanatory. The second column shows the place and date (or month and year) of birth. The third and fourth columns show the club the player came from (to Carlisle), and was transferred to (from Carlisle) respectively with dates (month and year). Where a player has been transferred to Carlisle more than once then the details given on two (or three) lines refer to clubs involved each time, and appearances and goals on each occasion. Appearances and goals refer to Football League, F.A.Cup and Football League Cup (and subsequent sponsors names), therefore the above is a complete listing of players that have made at least one appearance (or substitute appearance).

STATISTICAL NOTES

The seasonal statistical pages that follow have been designed for easy reference, and are generally self explanatory, however the following notes are added to avoid confusion: Left hand (first) column: Signifies the League match number, or the round number in a Cup Competition (R = round proper - e.g. 1R = 1st round proper, Rr = round replay - e.g. 2Rr = 2nd round replay, 2R2r = 2nd round 2nd replay, 1R1 = 1st round, 1st leg, 1R2 = 1st round, 2nd leg, etc. SF = Semi-final). Second column: Provides the date (Months abbreviated). Third column: Provides the opposition ('Home' matches in upper case - capital letters). Fourth column: ('Res.') is the final score. Fifth column: ('H.T.') is the half-time score (extra-time time details are indicated separately). Sixth column: ('Att.') The attendance. Seventh column: The goalscorers. O.G. indicates a goal scored by an opposition player, and 'pen' indicates a goal scored from a penalty (n.b. where space is limited players' names may be abbreviated).
The numbers used in the charts (right-hand 'players' table) refer to the normally accepted position for that period (numbered shirts did not appear until the 1939/40 season), e.g. 1 = goalkeeper, 2 = right-back ...., 11 = left-winger, etc. Substitutes are included, i.e. 12 and/or 14; 12 replaced the asterisk suffixed player (e.g. 4*), and 14 replaced the hash suffixed player (e.g.6#).

SEASON 1928/29

DIVISION 3 NORTH

No.	Date	Opposition	Res.	H.T.	Att.	Goalscorers	Prout	Coulthard	Cook	Harrison	Ross	Pigg	Agar	Hutchinson	McConnell	Ward	Watson	Smile	Cooper	Cooperthwaite	Graham	Brown	Little	Miller	Riley	Robinson	Roy	Thompson	Troughear	Winster
1	25 Aug	Accrington Stanley	3-2	2-0	6714	McConnell, Ward, Agar	1	2	3	4	5	6	7	8	9	10	11													
2	30	BRADFORD CITY	2-2	1-1	11771	Ross, McConnell	1	2	3	4	5	6	7	8	9	10	11													
3	1 Sep	HARTLEPOOLS UNITED	8-0	5-0	7346	McCnnell(3),Htchinsn(2),Rbinsn,Ward,Agar	1		3		5	6	7	8	9	10	11	2							4					
4	3	Bradford City	2-4	1-3	17161	McConnell(2)	1		3	4	5	6		8	9	10	11				2				7					
5	8	Darlington	0-0	0-0	5006		1	3		4	5	6	7	8	9	10	11	2												
6	13	SOUTHPORT	4-2	2-0	9707	McConnell(3), Pigg(pen)	1	3		4	5	6	7	8	9	10	11	2												
7	15	Rotherham United	0-4	0-2	8075		1	2	3	4		6	7	8	9	10	11									5				
8	22	WIGAN BOROUGH	2-1	1-1	9529	McConnell, Ward	1	2	3	4		6	7	8	9	10	11									5				
9	29	Crewe Alexandra	1-1	0-1	5754	McConnell	1	3	2	4		6	7	8	9	10	11												5	
10	6 Oct	TRANMERE ROVERS	4-1	3-0	8440	McConnell(2), Hutchinson, O.G.	1	2	3	4		6	7	8	9	10	11												5	
11	13	Stockport County	2-2	1-2	14563	McConnell, Ward	1	2	3	4		6	7	8	9	10	11												5	
12	20	NELSON	4-0	1-0	2321	McConnell(2), Ward, Watson	1	2	3	4		6	7	8	9	10	11												5	
13	27	South Shields	0-5	0-2	9157		1	2	3	4			7	8	9	10	11									6			5	
14	3 Nov	ASHINGTON	5-1	3-0	6267	Agar(2), Ward(2), McConnell	1		3			6	7		9	10	11	2	8											
15	10	Doncaster Rovers	0-3	0-1	6391		1	2	3	4	5	6	7	8	9		11		10											
16	17	Barrow	1-1	1-1	8508	Agar	1	3		4	5	6	7	8	9	10	11	2												
17	1 Dec	WREXHAM	1-1	0-0	11801	McConnell	1	3		4	5	6	7	8	9	10	11	2												
18	12	New Brighton	0-1	1-1	2061		1	2	3	4	5		7		9	10	11		8			6								
19	15	ROCHDALE	4-2	1-1	5838	McConnell(2), Cooper, Agar	1	2	3		5	6			9	10			8		11	4								
20	22	Southport	3-4	2-2	2533	McConnell(3)	1	2	3		5	6			9	10	11		8			4								
21	25	HALIFAX TOWN	2-1	0-1	10394	McConnell, Pigg(pen)	1	3				6	7	8	9	10	11	2				4					5			
22	26	Halifax Town	2-5	0-1	8599	McConnell, Agar	1		3			6	7	8	9	10					11	4								
23	29	ACCRINGTON STAN.	4-3	2-0	6662	McConnell(2), Pigg(pen), Cooper	1		3	5		6	7	8	9		11	2	10		2	4								
24	1 Jan	LINCOLN CITY	3-1	0-1	10539	McConnell(2), Graham	1	3			5	6	7		9	10		2	8		11	4								
25	5	Hartlepools United	0-1	0-1	3000		1	3			5	6	7	8	9	10		2			11	4								
26	12	Rochdale	0-4	0-2	5115		1	3			5	6	7		9	10	11	2	8			4								
27	19	DARLINGTON	3-0	1-0	5263	Agar(2), McConnell	1	3		4	5	6	7		9	10		2			11	4								
28	26	ROTHERHAM UNITED	1-1	1-1	6251	Pigg	1	3		4	5	6	7		9	10		2			11	4								
29	2 Feb	Wigan Borough	2-2	2-2	4707	Thompson, O.G.	1	3			5	6	7		9	10		2				4						8		
30	9	CREWE ALEXANDRA	1-0	0-0	6949	Ross	1	3			5	6	7		9	10	11	2				4						8		
31	16	Tranmere Rovers	2-1	1-1	4299	Cooperthwaite(2)		3			5	6	7		9		11	2	8	10		4	1							
32	23	STOCKPORT COUNTY	0-5	0-2	10779		1	3			5	6	7	8	9			2		10	11	4								
33	2 Mar	Nelson	0-1	0-0	4107		1	3					7		9		11	2	8		10	4								
34	9	SOUTH SHIELDS	5-0	2-0	7559	McConnell(2),Hutchinsn,Ward,O.G.	1	3		4		6		8	9	10	11	2								5				7
35	13	Chesterfield	2-1	1-0	2589	Miller, Watson	1	2	3	4		6	7	8	9		11							10		5				
36	16	Ashington	4-0	2-0	2219	McConnell(3), Roy	1	3		4		6	7	8	9	10	11	2								5				
37	23	DONCASTER ROVERS	1-2	1-1	7358	McConnell	1	3				6	7		9	10	11	2	8							5				
38	29	Lincoln City	0-3	0-2	8734		1	2	3	4		6		8	9		11							10		5				7
39	30	BARROW	4-1	2-0	7441	McConnell(2), Ward, Miller	1	3				6		8	9	10	11	2				4				5				7
41	6 Apr	CHESTERFIELD	1-2	1-1	6059	McConnell	1	3				6		8	9	10	11	2				4				5				7
41	13	Wrexham	1-5	0-2	5489	McConnell(pen)	1	2	3	4			7	8	9	10	11	2				6				5				
42	20	NEW BRIGHTON	2-1	0-0	5441	McConnell, Hutchinson	1	3				6	7	8	9	10	11	2				4				5				

F.A. CUP

No.	Date	Opposition	Res.	H.T.	Att.	Goalscorers	Prout	Coulthard	Cook	Harrison	Ross	Pigg	Agar	Hutchinson	McConnell	Ward	Watson	Smile
1R	24 Nov	Wrexham	1-0	0-0	7600	Ward	1	3		4	5	6	7	8	9	10	11	2
2R	8 Dec	Lincoln City	0-1	0-0	13701		1	3		4	5	6	7	8	9	10	11	2

Final League Table

		Pl.	Home W	D	L	F	A	Away W	D	L	F	A	F.	A.	Pts
1	Bradford City	42	17	2	2	82	18	10	7	4	46	25	128	43	63
2	Stockport County	42	19	0	0	77	23	9	4	8	34	35	111	58	62
3	Wrexham	42	17	2	2	59	25	4	8	9	32	44	91	69	52
4	Wigan Borough	42	16	4	1	55	16	5	5	11	27	33	82	49	51
5	Doncaster Rovers	42	14	3	4	39	20	6	7	8	37	46	76	66	50
6	Lincoln City	42	15	3	3	58	18	6	3	12	33	49	91	67	48
7	Tranmere Rovers	42	15	3	3	55	21	7	0	14	24	56	79	77	47
8	Carlisle United	42	15	3	3	61	27	4	5	12	25	50	86	77	46
9	Crewe Alexandra	42	11	6	4	47	23	7	2	12	33	45	80	68	44
10	South Shields	42	13	5	3	57	24	5	3	13	26	50	83	74	44
11	Chesterfield	42	13	2	6	46	28	5	3	13	25	49	71	77	41
12	Southport	42	13	5	3	52	27	3	3	15	23	58	75	85	40
13	Halifax Town	42	11	7	3	42	24	2	6	13	21	38	63	62	39
14	New Brighton	42	11	3	7	40	28	4	6	11	24	43	64	71	39
15	Nelson	42	14	1	6	48	28	3	4	14	29	62	77	90	39
16	Rotherham United	42	12	5	4	44	23	3	4	14	16	54	60	77	39
17	Rochdale	42	12	4	5	55	34	1	6	14	24	62	79	96	36
18	Accrington Stanley	42	11	5	5	42	22	2	3	16	26	60	68	82	34
19	Darlington	42	12	6	3	47	26	1	1	19	17	62	64	88	33
20	Barrow	42	7	6	8	42	37	3	2	16	22	56	64	93	28
21	Hartlepools United	42	9	4	8	35	38	1	2	18	24	74	59	112	26
22	Ashington	42	6	5	10	31	52	2	2	17	14	63	45	115	23

- 1928/29 Season -

(Back): Coulthard, Prout, Cook, Hetherington(Trainer).   (Middle): Robinson, Harrison, Coulthard, Ross, Pigg.   (Front): Agar, Hutchinson, McConnell, Matthews, Watson

- 1929/30 Season -

(Back): Harrison, Thompson, Richmond, Almond, Pigg, Watson, Charlton.
(Middle): Frew, Parker, Prout, McLoughlan, McConnell, Little, Holdsworth, Coulthard, Hetherington (Trainer).   (Front): Agar, Hutchison, Miller.

SEASON 1929/30
DIVISION 3 NORTH

No.	Date	Opposition	Res.	H.T.	Att.	Goalscorers	Prout	Coulthard	Frew	Watson	Holland	McConnell	Hutchison	McLaughlan	Miller	Pigg	Ward	Agar	Almond	Ames	Cape	Charlton	Cooperthwaite	Coxwell	Henderson	Holdsworth	Little	McGorian	McLeod	Oxley	Parker C.W.	Parker W.	Plenderleith	Richmond	Smiles	Thomson J.	Winster	Collins
1	31 Aug	CREWE ALEXANDRA	2-0	2-0	9478	Hutchinson, Thompson	1	2			10	9	8		3	4		7											5					6			11	
2	3 Sep	Southport	3-4	1-3	5314	Hutchinson(2), Frew		2	5		10	9	8		3	4		7																6			11	
3	7	York City	2-2	2-1	7462	Hutchinson, McConnell	1	2			10	9	8		3	4		7											5					6			11	
4	12	SOUTHPORT	4-0	1-0	8502	Hutchinson(2), Agar, McConnell		2	5			9	8		3	4		7									1		10					6			11	
5	14	STOCKPORT COUNTY	1-5	0-2	10204	Hutchinson	1	3	5			9	8		4			7								9			10					6	2		11	
6	21	New Brighton	1-2	0-0	3865	Holland		2	3		10	9	8		4			7			9						1							5	6		11	
7	25	Wigan Athletic	0-8	0-6	5263			2	3			9	8		4			7			3	1							10	9	5			6			11	
8	28	PORT VALE	1-4	1-2	8784	McConnell		2	5		10	9	8		4	6			3			7					1										11	
9	5 Oct	Barrow	2-0	0-0	6982	Hutchinson, McConnell	1	2	5	11	10	9	8		4	6			3			7																
10	12	WREXHAM	5-1	5-1	8861	McConnell(4), Holland	1	2	5	11	10	9	8		3	4	6					7																
11	19	Darlington	0-3	0-1	5042		1	2	5	11	10	9	8		3	4	6					7																
12	26	HARTLEPOOLS	5-2	0-1	6228	Hutchinson(2),Holland(2),McConnll	1	2	5	11	10	9	8		3	4	6					7																
13	2 Nov	Doncaster Rovers	4-1	2-0	3966	McConnll(2), Hutchinson, Holland	1	2	5	11	10	9	8		4	6						7	3															
14	9	CHESTERFIELD	6-0	3-0	7250	McConnll(3),Hutchinsn(2),Pigg(pen)	1	2	5	11	10	9	8		3	4	6					7																
15	16	Lincoln City	1-4	1-1	5298	McConnell	1	2	5	11	10	9	8		3	4	6					7																
16	23	TRANMERE ROVERS	4-3	4-1	6406	McConnell(2), Hutchinson, Holland	1	2	5	11	10	9	8		3	4	6					7																
17	7 Dec	ROTHERHAM UNITED	3-1	1-1	4820	Holland(2), Hutchinson	1	2	5	11	10	9	8		3	4	6					7																
18	21	SOUTH SHIELDS	4-1	0-0	5570	Parker, Cape, Hutchinson, Holland	1	2		11	10	9	8		3	4	6					7												5				
19	25	Nelson	2-2	1-1	3454	Cape, Holland	1	2		11	10	9	8		3	4	6					7												5				
20	28	Crewe Alexandra	2-1	1-0	5271	McConnell(2)	1	2	5	11	10	9	8		3	4	6					7																
21	1 Jan	Accrington Stanley	2-7	1-3	4138	Pigg, Watson	1	2	5	11	10	9	8		3	4	6					7																
22	4	YORK CITY	2-2	0-1	7149	McConnell, Watson		2	5	11	10	9	8		3	4	6					7											1					
23	18	Stockport County	1-7	0-3	11701	Hutchinson		2	5	11	10	9	8		3	4									7	1							6				
24	23	NELSON	2-2	2-1	3960	Pigg(pen), Watson				11	10		8		3	4	6		7						9	1					5					2		
25	25	NEW BRIGHTON	2-2	1-1	5580	Thompson, Holland			5	11	10	9	8		3	4															6	1				2	7	
26	1 Feb	Port Vale	0-4	0-2	9279					11	10	9	8		3	4	6														1	5				2	7	
27	8	BARROW	7-1	4-1	5262	McConnell(4),Watson(2),Thompson				11	10	9	8		3	4	6														1	5				2	7	
28	15	Wrexham	3-3	1-2	3482	Hutchinson(2), Watson				11	10	9	8		3	4	6														1	5				2	7	
29	20	Halifax Town	0-1	0-0	1709			2		11	10	9	8		3	4	6														1	5				7		
30	22	DARLINGTON	1-4	0-3	5813	Winster	1			11		9	8		3	4												6	10			5			2		7		
31	1 Mar	Hartlepools United	0-1	0-0	4816		1		5	11	10	9			3	4	6																	8	2	7		
32	8	DONCASTER ROVERS	1-1	1-1	4850	Hutchinson(pen)	1		5	11	10	9	8		3	4	6																	6	2	7		
33	15	Chesterfield	1-3	0-3	1864	McConnell	1			11	10	9	8		3		6		7								4				5			2				
34	22	LINCOLN CITY	2-4	1-3	4191	McLeod, Frew	1		5	11		9	8		3		6		7								4		10					2				
35	29	Tranmere Rovers	0-3	0-0	3757		1			11	10	9	8		3	4	6		7															2				5
36	5 Apr	HALIFAX TOWN	2-0	0-0	3833	McConnell, Holland	1		5	11	10	9	8		3	4	6								7									2				
37	12	Rotherham United	1-4	1-1	4214	Holland	1		5	11	10	9	8		3	4	6								7									2				
38	18	ACCRINGTON STAN.	2-1	1-1	5682	Henderson, McConnell		2			10	9	8		4				3						7								1		6		11		5
39	19	ROCHDALE	2-0	2-0	2987	Henderson, Hutchinson			11			9	8		4			7	3						8				10			1		6	2			5
40	26	South Shields	2-5	2-1	2082	Hutchinson, Agar			11			8			4	6		7	3						8				10			1			2			5
41	29	Rochdale	0-2	0-0	1758			2	11			8			4	6	9		3						7				10			1						5
42	3 May	WIGAN ATHLETIC	5-0	2-0	3851	Hutchinson(3,1pen), Armes(2)		2	11			8			4	6			3	7					9				10			1						5

F.A. CUP

No.	Date	Opposition	Res.	H.T.	Att.	Goalscorers	Prout	Coulthard	Frew	Watson	Holland	McConnell	Hutchison	McLaughlan	Miller	Pigg	Ward	Agar	McLeod
1R	30 Nov	HALIFAX	2-1	1-1	8190	McConnell, McLeod	1	2	5	11		9	8		3	4	6	7	10
2R	14 Dec	CREWE	4-2	2-2	10864	Hutchinson(2), Watson, Cape	1	2	5	11	10	9	8		3	4	6	7	
3R	11 Jan	EVERTON	2-4	1-3	20000	McConnell, Watson		2	5	11	10	9	8		3	4	6	7	

Final League Table

		Pl.	Home W	D	L	F	A	Away W	D	L	F	A	F.	A.	Pts
1	Port Vale	42	17	2	2	64	18	13	5	3	39	19	103	37	67
2	Stockport County	42	15	3	3	67	20	13	4	4	39	24	106	44	63
3	Darlington	42	14	2	5	71	29	8	4	9	37	44	108	73	50
4	Chesterfield	42	18	1	2	53	15	4	5	12	23	41	76	56	50
5	Lincoln City	42	12	8	1	54	23	5	6	10	29	38	83	61	48
6	York City	42	11	7	3	43	20	4	9	8	34	44	77	64	46
7	South Shields	42	11	6	4	49	32	7	4	10	28	42	77	74	46
8	Hartlepools United	42	13	4	4	50	24	4	7	10	31	50	81	74	45
9	Southport	42	11	5	5	49	31	4	8	9	32	43	81	74	43
10	Rochdale	42	14	3	4	57	30	4	4	13	32	61	89	91	43
11	Crewe Alexandra	42	12	5	4	55	28	5	3	13	27	43	82	71	42
12	Tranmere Rovers	42	12	4	5	57	35	4	5	12	26	51	83	86	41
13	New Brighton	42	13	4	4	48	22	3	4	14	21	57	69	79	40
14	Doncaster Rovers	42	13	5	3	39	22	2	4	15	23	47	62	69	39
15	Carlisle United	42	13	4	4	63	34	3	3	15	27	67	90	101	39
16	Accrington Stanley	42	11	4	6	55	30	3	5	13	29	51	84	81	37
17	Wrexham	42	10	5	6	42	28	3	3	15	25	60	67	88	34
18	Wigan Borough	42	12	4	5	44	26	1	3	17	16	62	60	88	33
19	Nelson	42	9	4	8	31	25	4	3	14	20	55	51	80	33
20	Rotherham United	42	9	4	8	46	40	2	4	15	21	73	67	113	30
21	Halifax Town	42	7	4	7	27	26	3	1	17	17	53	44	79	28
22	Barrow	42	9	4	8	31	28	2	1	18	10	70	41	98	27

SEASON 1930/31
DIVISION 3 NORTH

No.	Date	Opposition	Res.	H.T.	Att.	Goalscorers	Kelly John	Coulthard	Almond	Miller	Kelly Jerry	Maskell	Armes	Hutchinson	McConnell	Sharp	Watson	Sullivan	Anderson	Pollock	Richmond	Troughear	Lonsdale	Collins	Bell	Dawson	Smiles	Parker	Heigh	Rorrison	Robson	Birkett	Davidson	Hill
1	30 Aug	Chesterfield	1-2	0-1	5524	Armes	1	2	3	4	5	6	7	8	9	10	11																	
2	1 Sep	Tranmere Rovers	0-2	0-1	7031		1	2	3	4	5	6	7	8	9	10	11																	
3	6	BARROW	0-1	0-0	6530		1	2	3	4	5	6	7	8	9	10	11																	
4	11	STOCKPORT COUNTY	5-1	3-0	8597	McConnell(4), Armes	1	2	3	4	5	6	7	8	9	10	11																	
5	13	Southport	2-1	2-0	2863	Hutchinson, McConnell	1	2	3	4	5	6	7	8	9	10	11																	
6	15	Stockport County	0-3	0-2	5424		1	2		4		5		7	8	9	11	6	10						3									
7	20	ACCRINGTON STAN.	7-3	3-1	6704	Hutch'n(2),Armes,Wat'n(2),McC.,And'n	1	2	3	4	5	6	7	8	9		11		10															
8	27	Rochdale	3-1	0-1	3165	Hutchinson(2), McConnell	1	2	3	4	5	6	7	8	9	10	11																	
9	4 Oct	CREWE ALEXANDRA	4-1	2-0	7308	McConnell(3), Miller	1	2	3	4	5	6	7	8	9	10	11																	
10	11	Wrexham	1-2	0-0	8757	Hutchinson	1	2		4	5	6	7	8	9	10	11								3									
11	18	NEW BRIGHTON	2-0	1-0	5748	McConnell, Armes	1	2	3	4	5	6	7	8	9	10	11																	
12	25	Gateshead	0-1	0-0	14823		1	2	3	4	5	6	7	8	9		11													10				
13	1 Nov	DARLINGTON	2-1	1-1	5504	McConnell, Sharp	1	2	3	4	5	6		8	9	10	11			7														
14	8	Nelson	2-1	1-1	2703	McConnell, Armes	1		3	4	5		7	8	9	10	11											2						
15	15	WIGAN BOROUGH	6-1	1-1	7243	Htchinsn(2),McCnnll,Armes,Shrp,Watsn	1		3		5	6	7	8	9	10	11		4									2						
16	22	Hartlepools United	5-3	2-1	2140	Armes(2), Hutchinson(2), Watson	1	2	3		5	6	7	8	9	10	11		4															
17	6 Dec	Hull City	1-1	0-1	6176	Ryott	1	2	3	4	5	6	7	8	9	10	11																	
18	20	Halifax Town	5-1	0-0	3869	Hutchinson(2),McConnell(2),Watsn	1	2		4	5	6	7	8	9	10	11								3									
19	25	York City	0-4	0-1	4663		1	2		4	5	6	7	8	9	10	11								3									
20	26	YORK CITY	2-0	0-0	7772	Sharp, Maskell	1			4	5	6	7	8	9	10	11								2	3								
21	27	CHESTERFIELD	0-0	0-0	7361		1	2		4		6	7	8	9	10	11							5	3									
22	1 Jan	DONCASTER ROVERS	1-1	1-1	8073	Watson	1	2				6	7	8	9	10	11		4					5	3									
23	3	Barrow	2-7	2-2	6670	Armes, McConnell	1	2		4			7	8	9		11				6			5	3									10
24	15	LINCOLN CITY	3-6	2-2	4261	McConnell(3)	1			4	5	6	7	8	9	10	11								2	3								
25	17	SOUTHPORT	4-3	2-1	5331	McConnell(2), Hutchinson, Sharp	1			4		6	7	8	9	10	11					5			2	3								
26	24	Accrington Stanley	0-3	0-3	1680		1	2		4	5	6	7	8	9	10	11									3								
27	31	ROCHDALE	7-1	4-0	2224	McConnll(4),Htchinsn,Coulthrd,Armes	1	2		4	5	6	7	8	9		11									3			10					
28	7 Feb	Crewe Alexandra	5-3	3-2	4986	McConnell(3), Armes, Watson		2		4			7	8	9		11	6				5				3	1		10					
29	14	WREXHAM	1-1	0-1	6626	Hutchinson		2		4			7	8	9		11	6					5			3	1		10					
30	21	New Brighton	0-2	0-0	2740			2		4			7	8	9		11	6				5				3	1		10					
31	28	GATESHEAD	2-2	1-1	9680	Sharp, Watson	1	2		4	5	6	7	8	9	10	11									3								
32	7 Mar	Darlington	0-3	0-2	1766		1	2		4	5	6	7	8	9	10	11									3								
33	14	NELSON	8-1	6-1	3468	McConnll(3),Shrp(3),Htchinsn,Watsn	1	2			5	6	7	8	9	10	11		4							3								
34	21	Wigan Borough	2-1	2-1	3529	McConnell, Watson	1	2			5	6	7	8	9	10	11		4							3								
35	28	HARTLEPOOLS UNITED	3-0	2-0	3303	Armes, Davidson, Watson	1	2			5	6	7		9	10	11		4							3							8	
36	3 Apr	ROTHERHAM UNITED	1-2	0-2	5190	Sharp	1	2		4	5	6	7	8	9	10	11									3								
37	4	Lincoln City	1-5	1-5	9011	McConnell	1	2		4	5	6	7	8	9	10	11									3								
38	6	Rotherham United	0-1	0-0	4814			2		4		6	7	8	9	10	11					5				3	1							
39	11	HULL CITY	1-5	0-3	4560	Davidson		2				6	7		9	10	11					5				3	1				4		8	
40	18	Doncaster Rovers	0-2	0-2	2528			2		4	5	6	7	8	9	10	11							3			1							
41	25	HALIFAX TOWN	6-2	4-0	2160	Htchinsn(2),McConnll(2),Watsn,Shrp				4	5	6		8	9	10	11									2		1		7	3			
42	2 May	TRANMERE ROVERS	3-0	2-0	3990	Hutchinson(2,1pen), Watson	1			4		6		8		10	11									2				9	7	5	3	

F.A. CUP

No.	Date	Opposition	Res.	H.T.	Att.	Goalscorers	Kelly John	Coulthard	Almond	Miller	Kelly Jerry	Maskell	Armes	Hutchinson	McConnell	Sharp	Watson	Bell
1R	29 Nov	NEW BRIGHTON	3-1	0-1	9300	McConnell, Maskell	1	2	3	4	5	6	7	8	9	10	11	
2R	13 Dec	TUNBRIDGE WELLS R	4-2	1-0	11500	McConnell(2), Hutchinson(2,1pen)	1	2	3	4	5	6	7	8	9	10	11	
3R	10 Jan	Bolton Wanderers	0-1	0-1	23029		1	2		4	5	6	7	8	9	10	11	3

Final League Table

		Pl.	Home W	D	L	F	A	Away W	D	L	F	A	F.	A.	Pts
1	Chesterfield	42	19	1	1	66	22	7	5	9	36	35	102	57	58
2	Lincoln City	42	16	3	2	60	19	9	4	8	42	40	102	59	57
3	Wrexham	42	16	4	1	61	25	5	8	8	33	37	94	62	54
4	Tranmere Rovers	42	16	3	2	73	26	8	3	10	38	48	111	74	54
5	Southport	42	15	3	3	52	19	7	6	8	36	37	88	56	53
6	Hull City	42	12	7	2	64	20	8	3	10	35	35	99	55	50
7	Stockport County	42	15	5	1	54	19	5	4	12	23	42	77	61	49
8	Carlisle United	42	13	4	4	68	32	7	1	13	30	49	98	81	45
9	Gateshead	42	14	4	3	46	22	2	9	10	25	51	71	73	45
10	Wigan Borough	42	14	4	3	48	25	5	1	15	28	61	76	86	43
11	Darlington	42	9	6	6	44	30	7	4	10	27	29	71	59	42
12	York City	42	15	3	3	59	30	3	3	15	26	52	85	82	42
13	Accrington Stanley	42	14	2	5	51	31	1	7	13	33	77	84	108	39
14	Rotherham United	42	9	6	6	50	34	4	6	11	31	49	81	83	38
15	Doncaster Rovers	42	9	8	4	40	18	4	3	14	25	47	65	65	37
16	Barrow	42	13	4	4	45	23	2	3	16	23	66	68	89	37
17	Halifax Town	42	11	6	4	30	16	2	3	16	25	73	55	89	35
18	Crewe Alexandra	42	13	2	6	52	35	1	4	16	14	58	66	93	34
19	New Brighton	42	12	4	5	36	25	1	3	17	13	51	49	76	33
20	Hartlepools United	42	10	2	9	47	37	2	4	15	20	49	67	86	30
21	Rochdale	42	9	1	11	42	50	3	5	13	20	57	62	107	30
22	Nelson	42	6	7	8	28	40	0	0	21	15	73	43	113	19

- 1930/31 Season -

(Unnamed team group)

- 1931/32 Season -

(Unnamed team group)

SEASON 1931-32

DIVISION 3 NORTH

No.	Date	Opposition	Res.	H.T.	Att.	Goalscorers	Kelly	Pierce	Henderson	Miller	Gomm	Richmond	Armes	Hutchinson	McConnell	Sharp	Watson	Birkett	Kelly	Troughear	McGill	Heelbeck	Robson	Lonsdale	Hill	Felton	Davidson	Slinger	Willaoy	Bell	Parker	Ryott
1	29 Aug	Hartlepools	2-2	0-1	5295	McConnell(2)	1	2	3	4	5	6	7	8	9	10	11															
2	2 Sep	Accrington Stanley	3-5	2-3	3288	McConnell(2), Watson	1	2	3	4	5	6	7	8	9	10	11															
3	5	CREWE ALEXANDRA	2-1	2-0	6685	Armes, Watson	1	2	3	4	5	6	7	8	9	10	11															
4	10	WREXHAM	2-2	0-1	6848	Hutchinson (2, 1 pen)	1	2	3	4	5	6	7	8	9	10	11															
5	12	Rochdale	3-4	1-1	4383	Watson(2), McConnell	1	2	3	4	5	6	7	8	9	10	11															
6	14	Wrexham	0-1	0-1	6999			2	3	4	5	6	7	8	9	10	11														1	
7	19	DONCASTER ROVERS	5-1	3-1	5011	Watson(3), McConnell(2)		2	3	4	5	6	7	8	9	10	11														1	
8	26	Southport	0-2	0-1	5692			2	3	4	5	6	7	8	9	10	11														1	
9	3 Oct	YORK CITY	1-1	0-1	5809	Hutchinson(pen)	1	2	3	4	5	6	7	8	9	10													11			
10	10	Tranmere Rovers	0-3	0-2	6646		1	2	3	4	5	6	7	8	9	10	11															
11	17	Wigan Borough *	2-3	2-1	2667	McConnell, Miller		2	3	10	5	6	7		9			11				4				8					1	
12	24	DARLINGTON	0-2	0-2	4163			2	3		5	6	7	10	9			11				4				8					1	
13	31	Halifax Town	1-1	0-1	4379	McConnell		2	3		5	6		8	9	10	11					4				7					1	
14	7 Nov	WALSALL	4-0		3678	McConnell(2), Davidson, Sharp		2	3		5	6		8	9	10	11					4				7					1	
15	14	Gateshead	0-4	0-3	9910			2	3		5	6		8	9	10	11					4				7					1	
16	21	NEW BRIGHTON	0-0	0-0	3577			3			5	6		8	9	10	11	3				4				7					1	
17	5 Dec	HULL CITY	0-1	0-1	4674			2		4	5	6	7	8	9	10					3										1	
18	19	CHESTER	4-3	1-2	4220	McConnell, Watson, Miller, Armes		2	8			10	7		9		6	11		4	3	5									1	
19	25	Stockport County	0-0	0-0	7142				8		5	6	7		9	10	11		2	3	4										1	
20	26	STOCKPORT COUNTY	1-1	1-0	8106	Watson					5	6	7		9		11		2	3	4					8	10				1	
21	1 Jan	TRANMERE ROVERS	1-1	1-1	5544	Sharp		2		4	5	6	7		9	10	11			3						8					1	
22	2	HARTLEPOOLS UNITED	3-2	2-1	3867	Armes(2), Sharp		2		4	5	6	7		9	10	11			3						8					1	
23	9	Barrow	1-4	0-1	5654	Miller		2		4	5		7		9	10	11			3		6				8					1	
24	16	Crewe Alexandra	1-5	0-3	6119	Hutchinson				4		6	7	8	9	10	11		2	3	5										1	
25	23	ROCHDALE	4-0	4-0	3872	McConnell(3), Hutchinson				4	5		7	8	9	10	11		2	3		6									1	
26	30	Doncaster Rovers	3-3	1-1	4536	Watson(3)		2					7	8	9	10	11		5	3		6									1	
27	6 Feb	SOUTHPORT	2-2	1-1	5304	Hutchinson, Watson				4	5		7	8	9	10	11		2	3		6									1	
28	13	York City	4-2	2-1	2476	McConnell(2), Watson(2)				4	5		7	8	9	10	11		2	3		6									1	
29	24	Lincoln City	1-3	0-3	5384	McConnell		2		4	5		7	8	9	10	11			3		6									1	
30	5 Mar	Darlington	1-0	0-0	2267	Hutchinson				4	5		7	8		10			2			6				9			11		1	
31	12	HALIFAX TOWN	4-0	2-0	3453	Hutchinsn(2,1pen),Heelbeck,Watsn				4	5		7	8		10	11		2			6				9					1	
32	19	Walsall	1-3	0-1	2229	Armes				4	5	6	7	8	9		11	3	2									10			1	
33	25	ROTHERHAM UNITED	1-2	1-0	4962	McConnell				4	5	6	7	8	9	10	11	3	2											1	
34	26	GATESHEAD	0-0	0-0	5401					4	5		7		9	10			2	3			6						11		1	8
35	28	Rotherham United	1-4	1-1	4645	Hutchinson				4			7		9	10			2	3			6	5					11		1	8
36	2 Apr	New Brighton	1-4	1-2	2455	Sharp				4	5		7	8		10			2	3			6						11		1	
37	9	BARROW	3-1	1-1	2710	McConnell, Hutchinson, Sharp	1		3	4	5		7	8	9		11		2				6				10					
38	16	Hull City	0-2	0-1	2392		1		3	4	5		7	8	9		11		2				6				10					
39	23	LINCOLN CITY	0-3	0-1	3412		1		3	4	5		7	8	9		11		2					6	10							
40	30	Chester	1-4	0-1	4618	Watson	1			4	5	6	7	8		10	11	2		3									9			
41	7	ACCRINGTON STAN.	3-0	2-0	2540	Hutchinson(2), Felton	1		3		5	6	7	8			11	2					4			9		10				

* Wigan Borough Resigned 26/10/1931 - record expunged.

F.A. CUP

	Date	Opposition	Res.	H.T.	Att.	Goalscorers	Kelly	Pierce	Henderson	Miller	Gomm	Richmond	Armes	Hutchinson	McConnell	Sharp	Watson	Birkett	Kelly	Troughear	McGill	Heelbeck	Robson	Lonsdale	Hill	Felton	Davidson	Slinger	Willaoy	Bell	Parker	Ryott
1R	28 Nov	Yorkshire Amateurs	3-1	3-1	2000	Richmond, McConnell, Sharp		2			5	6	7	8	9	10	11	3		4											1	
3R	12 Dec	DARLINGTON	0-2	0-1	8954			2		4		6	7	8	9	10	11	3		5											1	

Final League Table

		Pl.	Home					Away					F.	A.	Pts
			W	D	L	F	A	W	D	L	F	A			
1	Lincoln City	40	16	2	2	65	13	10	3	7	41	34	106	47	57
2	Gateshead	40	15	3	2	59	20	10	4	6	35	28	94	48	57
3	Chester	40	16	2	2	54	22	5	6	9	24	38	78	60	50
4	Tranmere Rovers	40	15	4	1	76	23	4	7	9	31	35	107	58	49
5	Barrow	40	16	1	3	59	23	8	0	12	27	36	86	59	49
6	Crewe Alexandra	40	15	3	2	64	24	6	3	11	31	42	95	66	48
7	Southport	40	14	5	1	44	15	4	5	11	14	38	58	53	46
8	Hull City	40	14	1	5	52	21	6	4	10	30	32	82	53	45
9	York City	40	14	3	3	49	24	4	4	12	27	57	76	81	43
10	Wrexham	40	14	2	4	42	25	4	5	11	22	44	64	69	43
11	Darlington	40	12	1	7	41	27	5	3	12	25	42	66	69	38
12	Stockport County	40	12	3	5	31	15	1	8	11	24	38	55	53	37
13	Hartlepools United	40	10	4	6	47	37	6	1	13	31	63	78	100	37
14	Accrington Stanley	40	14	4	2	56	20	1	2	17	19	60	75	80	36
15	Doncaster Rovers	40	12	3	5	38	27	4	1	15	21	53	59	80	36
16	Walsall	40	12	3	5	42	30	4	0	16	15	55	57	85	35
17	Halifax Town	40	11	6	3	36	18	2	2	16	25	69	61	87	34
18	Carlisle United	40	9	7	4	40	23	2	4	14	24	56	64	79	33
19	Rotherham United	40	10	3	7	41	23	4	1	15	22	49	63	72	32
20	New Brighton	40	8	5	7	25	23	0	3	17	13	53	38	76	24
21	Rochdale	40	4	2	14	33	63	0	1	19	15	72	48	135	11

Wigan Borough resigned during season

SEASON 1932/33

DIVISION 3 NORTH

No.	Date	Opposition	Res.	H.T.	Att.	Goalscorers	Kelly	Bradley	Legge	Cawley	Miller	Henderson	Troughear	Shankly	Batey	Gomm	Clayton	Towers	Cowper	Smith	White	Sweeney	Gibbs	Felton	Young	McBain	Slinger	Dougal	Gray	Cook	Parker	Mizen	Longstaff
1	27 Aug	Rochdale	1-0	1-0	4898	White	1	2	3	4						5	6		7	8	9	10	11										
2	1 Sep	CREWE ALEXANDRA	2-0	1-0	6723	White, Cowper	1	2	3	4						5	6		7	8	9	10	11										
3	3	SOUTHPORT	0-0	0-0	7602		1	2	3	4						5	6		7	8	9	10	11										
4	5	Crewe Alexandra	0-1	0-0	5192		1	2	3	4						5	6		7	8	9	10	11										
5	10	Mansfield Town	1-3	0-2	7573	Gibbs	1	2		4	3					5	6		7	8	9	10	11										
6	17	ROTHERHAM UNITED	0-0	0-0	6286		1	2		4	3					5	6		7		9	8	11	10									
7	24	Accrington Stanley	1-3	1-1	3518	Gibbs	1	2		4	3					5	6		7		9	8	11		10								
8	29	STOCKPORT COUNTY	2-1	1-0	5169	White(2)	1	2		4	3					5	6		7	8	10		11		9								
9	1 Oct	NEW BRIGHTON	1-3	1-2	5054	Cawley	1	2	3	4						5		6	7	8	9	10	11										
10	8	Chester	0-4	0-2	5722		1	2	3	4						5		6	7	8	9		11	10									
11	15	BARROW	0-1	0-0	6161		1	2	3	4	6				5				7	8			11	10	9								
12	22	WALSALL	1-1	1-0	4125	White	1	2		4	6	3							7	8			11	10	9					5			
13	29	Wrexham	1-2	0-2	4090	Felton	1	2		4	6	3				5			7	8			11	10	9								
14	5 Nov	TRANMERE ROVERS	0-1	0-0	5054		1	2		4	6	3				5			7	8			11	10		9							
15	12	Halifax Town	1-3		4890	Slinger	1	2	3	4						5	6		7	8				10		9	11						
16	19	HARTLEPOOLS	3-1	2-1	4594	Slinger, White, Felton	1	2	3	4						5	6		7	8				10		9	11						
17	3 Dec	HULL CITY	1-1	1-1	4073	Legge	1	2	3						4	5	6		7	8				10		9	11						
18	24	Stockport County	1-0	0-0	4068	White		2	3						4		6		7	8	9			10			11				1		
19	26	GATESHEAD	1-2	1-1	10177	McBain		2	3						4	5	6		7	8					10	11					1		
20	27	Gateshead	0-1	0-0	9283			2	3						4	5	6		7	8				10	11	9					1		
21	31	ROCHDALE	2-2	1-2	4093	Slinger(2)		2	3					4	5		6		7	8							9		10	1			11
22	2 Jan	Barnsley	1-4	0-3	5663	Slinger		2	3					4	5		6		7	8					11		9		10	1			
23	7	Southport	0-4	0-3	2893			2	3		6				4	5			7	8				11			9		10	1			
24	21	MANSFIELD TOWN	3-1	1-0	4328	Dougal, Gray, Miller(pen)		2			6	3			4	5			7					8			11	9	10	1			
25	28	Rotherham United	0-1	0-0	2738			2			6	3			4	5			7					8			11	9	10	1			
26	4 Feb	ACCRINGTON STAN.	2-2	1-1	1927	Mizen, Gray		2	3						4	5	6			8							11	9	10	1		7	
27	11	New Brighton	0-2	0-2	2780			2	3						4	5	6				9	8					11		10	1		7	
28	18	CHESTER	1-1	0-0	4490	Smith		2	3						4	5	6		7		9	8					11		10	1			
29	25	Barrow	1-2	0-2	999	O.G.		2	3						4	5	6		7	8							11	9	10	1			
30	4 Mar	Walsall	0-5	0-4	5637		1	2	3						4	5	6		7	8							11	9	10				
31	11	WREXHAM	2-1	1-0	5403	Sweeney(2)	1	2	3		6			5	4							8					11	9	10			7	
32	18	Tranmere Rovers	2-1	1-0	3430	Slinger, Gray	1	2	3		6			5	4				7			8					11	9	10				
33	25	HALIFAX TOWN	5-3	3-1	4605	Slinger(3), McBain(2)	1	2	3		6			5	4							8				7	11	9	10				
34	1 Apr	Hartlepools	1-2	1-1	3232	Slinger	1	2	3		6			5	4							8				7	11	9	10				
35	8	BARNSLEY	0-1	0-1	5145		1	2	3		6			5	4							8				7	11	9	10				
36	14	YORK CITY	5-1	2-1	6256	Slinger(3), McBain, O.G.	1	2	3		6				4	5						8				7	11	9	10				
37	15	Hull City	1-6	0-4	12023	McBain	1	2	3						4	5	6					8	11			7		9	10				
38	17	York City	1-0	0-0	4250	Slinger	1	2	3						4	5	6					8	11			7		9	10				
39	22	DONCASTER ROVERS	0-2	0-1	4429		1	2	3						4	5	6					8	11			7		9	10				
41	27	DARLINGTON	3-0	3-0	3721	McBain(2), Gray	1	2	3		6				4	5						8	11			7		9	10				
41	29	Darlington	2-5	1-3	750	McBain, Gray	1	2	3		6				4	5						8				7		9	10	11			
42	4 May	Doncaster Rovers	2-4	0-3	3324	Sweeney, Slinger	1	2	3		6				4	5						8	11			7		9	10				

F.A. CUP

Rd	Date	Opposition	Res.	H.T.	Att.	Goalscorers	Kelly	Bradley	Legge	Cawley	Miller	Henderson	Troughear	Shankly	Batey	Gomm	Clayton	Towers	Cowper	Smith	White	Sweeney	Gibbs	Felton	Young	McBain	Slinger	Dougal	Gray	Cook	Parker	Mizen	Longstaff
1R	26 Nov	DENABY UNITED	1-0	1-0	3076	Slinger	1	2	3	4						5	6		7	8				10		9	11						
2R	10 Dec	HULL CITY	1-1	0-1	10365	Felton	1	2	3	4						5	6		7	8				10		9	11						
2Rr	15	Hull City	1-2	0-2	12000	White		2	3	4					5		6		7	8				10		9	11				1		

Final League Table

	Pl.	Home					Away					F.	A.	Pts
		W	D	L	F	A	W	D	L	F	A			
1 Hull City	42	18	3	0	69	14	8	4	9	31	31	100	45	59
2 Wrexham	42	18	2	1	75	15	6	7	8	31	36	106	51	57
3 Stockport County	42	16	2	3	69	30	5	10	6	30	28	99	58	54
4 Chester	42	15	4	2	57	25	7	4	10	37	41	94	66	52
5 Walsall	42	16	4	1	53	15	3	6	12	22	43	75	58	48
6 Doncaster Rovers	42	13	8	0	52	26	4	6	11	25	53	77	79	48
7 Gateshead	42	12	5	4	45	25	7	4	10	33	42	78	67	47
8 Barnsley	42	14	3	4	60	31	5	5	11	32	49	92	80	46
9 Barrow	42	12	3	6	41	24	6	4	11	19	36	60	60	43
10 Crewe Alexandra	42	16	3	2	57	16	4	0	17	23	68	80	84	43
11 Tranmere Rovers	42	11	4	6	49	31	6	4	11	21	35	70	66	42
12 Southport	42	15	3	3	54	20	2	4	15	16	47	70	67	41
13 Accrington Stanley	42	12	4	5	55	29	3	6	12	23	47	78	76	40
14 Hartlepools United	42	15	3	3	56	29	1	4	16	31	87	87	116	39
15 Halifax Town	42	12	4	5	39	23	4	4	14	32	67	71	90	38
16 Mansfield Town	42	13	4	4	57	22	1	3	17	27	78	84	100	35
17 Rotherham United	42	14	3	4	42	21	0	3	18	18	63	60	84	34
18 Rochdale	42	9	4	8	32	33	4	3	14	26	47	58	80	33
19 Carlisle United	42	8	7	6	34	25	5	0	16	17	50	51	75	33
20 York City	42	10	4	7	51	38	3	2	16	21	54	72	92	32
21 New Brighton	42	8	6	7	42	36	3	4	14	21	52	63	88	32
22 Darlington	42	9	6	6	42	32	1	2	18	24	77	66	109	28

- 1932/33 Season -

The team in which Tommy McBain played. Back row (l. to r.)—
T. Troughear, J. Kelly, W. Shankly, Cawley, Gomm, Legge, Slinger,
T. Curry (trainer).
Front row—T. McBain, Sweeney, Bradley (captain), Gray, Smith.

- 1933/34 Season -

(Back): Directors - Henderson, Laidlaw, Blyth.
(Middle): Blake, Bell, Baty, Sneddon, Kennedy, Legge.
(Front): Clark (Sec.), Bradley, Stevenson, Wolf, Baxter, McBain, Currie (Trainer).

SEASON 1933/34

DIVISION 3 NORTH

No.	Date	Opposition	Res.	H.T.	Att.	Goalscorers	Wolf	Bradley	Legge	Blake	Clarke	Bell	Stevenson	Sneddon	Slinger	McGain	Ferguson	Batey	Black	Baxter	Cross	Dougal	Gray	Henderson	Kennedy	Keen	Miller	McPhail	Suttie	Throughear	Trotter	Turner	Elliott
1	26 Aug	HALIFAX	1-0	0-0	7198	Slinger	1	2	3	4	5	6	7	8	9	10	11																
2	31	BARROW	0-0	0-0	6607		1	2	3	4	5			8	9	10	11																
3	2 Sep	Crewe	0-4	0-2	4787		1	2	3	4	5	6		8	9	10									7	6							
4	4	Barrow	0-2	0-1	4862		1	2	3	4		6		8		9				11	10				7			5					
5	9	NEW BRIGHTON	1-2	1-2	5679	Sneddon	1	2	3	4	5	6	10	8		9				11					7								
6	16	ROTHERHAM	1-0	1-0	3828	Keen	1	2	3	4	5	6	10	8	9					11				7									
7	23	WALSALL	3-2	1-1	5008	Slinger(3)	1	2	3	4	5	6	7	8	9	10	11																
8	30	York	1-4	0-3	5179	Slinger	1	2	3	4	5	6		8	9	10	11								7								
9	7 Oct	CHESTER	1-0	0*0	5473	Slinger	1	2	3	4	5		7		9	10	11										6						8
10	14	Doncaster	1-2	1-1	3074	Stevenson	1	2	3	4	5		7		9	10	11			8							6						
11	21	DARLINGTON	3-3	1-1	4411	Slinger, Ferguson, Clark	1	2	3	4	5		7		9	10	11					8					6						
12	28	Southport	1-1	0-0	2495	Stevenson	1	2	3	4			7		9	10				11	5	8					6						
13	4 Nov	WREXHAM	0-0	0-0	5036		1	2	3	4			7		9			5				8					6					10	11
14	11	Hartlepools	2-3	1-0	4706	Stevenson, Turner	1	2	3	4	6		7					5		9		8										10	11
15	18	MANSFIELD	3-2	1-0	3335	McBain, Dougal, Turner	1	2	3	4			7			10		5		9		8	11									6	
16	2 Dec	TRANMERE	2-1	0-1	4068	McBain, Slinger	1	2	3	4	5		7		9		11	10		8												6	
17	16	CHESTERFIELD	1-1	1-1	4393	Slinger	1	2	3	4	5		7	8	9			10							11							6	
18	23	Accrington	1-2	1-0	2967	Slinger	1	2	3	4	5		7	8	9			10							11							6	
19	25	Stockport	0-4	0-1	9781		1	2	3	4	5		7	8	9			10							11							6	
20	26	STOCKPORT	2-2	1-1	7364	Slinger, Stevenson	1	2	3	4	5		7	8	9	10	11															6	
21	30	Halifax	2-3	0-3	4303	McBain, Slinger	1	2	3	4	5		7	8	9	10	11															6	
22	6 Jan	CREWE	6-1	4-0	3342	Slinger(4), McBain, Ferguson	1	2	3	4	5		7		9	10	11	8														6	
23	13	Barnsley	0-1	0-1	7045		1	2	3	4	5		7		9	10	11	8														6	
24	20	New Brighton	1-2	1-0	2634	Slinger	1	2	3	4	5		7		9	10	11	8														6	
25	27	ROTHERHAM	0-1	0-1	3828		1	2	3	4	5		7		9		11	8														6	
26	3 Feb	Walsall	2-3	0-2	5425	Slinger, Ferguson	1		3	4		6	7		9		11	5				10					8	2					
27	6	Rochdale	1-0	0-0	1261	Dougal	1	2	3	4		6	7		9		11	5				10					8						
28	10	YORK	3-2	0-1	3319	Stevenson, Ferguson, Blake		2	3	4		6	7		9		11	5	1			10					8						
29	17	Chester	3-3	3-0	4454	Dougal(2), Slinger		2	3	4		6	7		9		11	5	1			10					8						
30	24	DONCASTER	0-1	0-0	3074		1		3	4		6	7		9		11	5				10					8	2					
31	3 Mar	Darlington	2-1	1-0	2997	Slinger(2)	1		3	4		6	7		9		11	5				10					8				2		
32	10	SOUTHPORT	0-0	0-0	2566		1		3	4		6	7		9	10	11	5				4						2					
33	17	Wrexham	1-8	1-2	3556	Stevenson	1		3	4		6	7		9	10	11	5				7						2					
34	24	HARTLEPOOLS	4-1	0-1	3119	Slinger(2), Ferguson, Turner		3		5			7	8	9		11	10	1			2		4								6	
35	30	GATESHEAD	6-0	4-0	5502	Slinger(3), Sneddon(2), Ferguson	1	3		5	6			8	9		11					10	2	4								7	
36	31	Mansfield	0-6	0-0	3301		1	3		5	6			8	9		11					10	2	4								7	
37	2 Apr	Gateshead	3-2	1-2	2624	Henderson, Slinger, Turner	1	3			6				9	8	11					10	2	4				5				7	
38	7	BARNSLEY	1-4	1-1	4969	Slinger		3	4	5	6			8	9		11		1			10		2								7	
39	14	Tranmere	1-3	1-1	2245	Gray	1			5	6	7			9		11					10	2	4				3				8	
40	21	ROCHDALE	3-0	2-0	2762	Slinger(2), Ferguson	1	3		5	6	7			9		11					10	2	4								8	
41	28	Chesterfield	0-4	0-4	6351		1	3			6	7			9		11					2	10	4				5				8	
42	5 May	ACCRINGTON	3-0	2-0	2716	Slinger, Ferguson, Gray	1	3		5	6	7			9		11					8	2	10	4								

F.A. CUP

No.	Date	Opposition	Res.	H.T.	Att.	Goalscorers	Wolf	Bradley	Legge	Blake	Clarke	Bell	Stevenson	Sneddon	Slinger	McGain	Ferguson	Batey	Black	Baxter	Cross	Dougal	Gray	Henderson	Kennedy	Keen	Miller	McPhail	Suttie	Throughear	Trotter	Turner	Elliott
1R	25 Nov	WREXHAM	2-1	0-1	3927	Stevenson, Slinger	1	2	3	4			10		9	7				5		8	6									11	
2R	9 Dec	CHELTENHAM	1-2	1-1	4721	Slinger	1	2	3	4	5		10		9	7				8		6										11	

Final League Table

		Pl.	Home					Away					F.	A.	Pts
			W	D	L	F	A	W	D	L	F	A			
1	Barnsley	42	18	3	0	64	18	9	5	7	54	43	118	61	62
2	Chesterfield	42	18	1	2	56	17	9	6	6	30	26	86	43	61
3	Stockport County	42	18	3	0	84	23	6	8	7	31	29	115	52	59
4	Walsall	42	18	2	1	66	18	5	5	11	31	42	97	60	53
5	Doncaster Rovers	42	17	1	3	58	24	5	8	8	25	37	83	61	53
6	Wrexham	42	14	1	6	68	35	9	4	8	34	38	102	73	51
7	Tranmere Rovers	42	16	2	3	57	21	4	5	12	27	42	84	63	47
8	Barrow	42	12	5	4	78	45	7	4	10	38	49	116	94	47
9	Halifax Town	42	15	2	4	57	30	5	2	14	23	61	80	91	44
10	Chester	42	11	6	4	59	26	6	0	15	30	60	89	86	40
11	Hartlepools United	42	14	3	4	54	24	2	4	15	35	69	89	93	39
12	York City	42	11	5	5	44	28	4	3	14	27	46	71	74	38
13	Carlisle United	42	11	6	4	43	23	4	2	15	23	58	66	81	38
14	Crewe Alexandra	42	12	3	6	54	38	3	3	15	27	59	81	97	36
15	New Brighton	42	13	3	5	41	25	1	5	15	21	62	62	87	36
16	Darlington	42	11	4	6	47	35	2	5	14	23	66	70	101	35
17	Mansfield Town	42	9	7	5	49	29	2	5	14	32	59	81	88	34
18	Southport	42	6	11	4	35	29	2	6	13	28	61	63	90	33
19	Gateshead	42	10	3	8	46	40	2	6	13	30	70	76	110	33
20	Accrington Stanley	42	10	6	5	44	38	3	1	17	21	63	65	101	33
21	Rotherham United	42	5	7	9	31	35	5	1	15	22	56	53	91	28
22	Rochdale	42	7	5	9	34	30	2	1	18	19	73	53	103	24

SEASON 1934/35

DIVISION 3 NORTH

No.	Date	Opposition	Res.	H.T.	Att.	Goalscorers	Wolf	Legge	Allen	Darnell	Parker A.	Spencer	Miller	White	Slinger	Stevenson	Ferguson	Troughear	Ranson	Batey	Dougal	Henderson	Lonsdale	Henson	Jones	Johnson	Elliott	Black	Cartwright	Kelly	Parker J.	Robinson	Winthrop
1	25 Aug	Tranmere	1-3	0-1	6159	Slinger	1	2	3	4	5	10	7	8	9		11												6				
2	30	ACCRINGTON	2-0	0-0	6203	Spencer, White	1	2	3	4	5	10	7	8	9		11												6				
3	1 Sep	WREXHAM	0-2	0-2	6716		1	2	3	4	5	10	7		9	8	11												6				
4	8	Halifax	0-4	0-1	7808		1	2	3	4	5	10		8			11					9				6			7				
5	15	ROTHERHAM	2-1	2-1	5154	Miller, White	1	2		4	5	10	7	8	9											6				11		3	
6	22	Walsall	0-1	0-1	4394		1	2	3	4		10	7	8	9											6				11		5	
7	25	Accrington	0-1	0-1	3039		1	2	3	4		10	7	8								9				6				11		5	
8	29	CHESTERFIELD	3-1	2-0	3960	Slinger(2), Miller	1	2	3		5		7		9	8	11									6	10		4				
9	6 Oct	Mansfield	0-3	0-2	8424		1	2	3		5		7			9	8	11								6	10		4				
10	13	BARROW	0-0	0-0	4867		1	2	3		5		7	9		8	11									6	10		4				
11	20	GATESHEAD	5-4	4-1	4351	Slinger(2),Stevenson,Miller,Elliott	1	2	3		5		7		9	8	11									6	10		4				
12	27	Stockport	0-2	0-2	7078		1	2	3		5		7			9	8	11								6	10		4				
13	3 Nov	CREWE	1-3	0-1	3112	Slinger	1	2	3		5		7			9	8	11								6	10		4				
14	10	Hartlepools	2-5	1-2	1586	Slinger, O.G.	1	2	3		5		7			9	8	11								6	10		4				
15	17	DONCASTER	1-1	0-1	3784	Ferguson	1		3		5				9	10	11			8			2			6	7		4				
16	1 Dec	CHESTER	1-3	1-2	3711	Lonsdale							7					4	9	3		2	5	10		6	11	1					8
17	15	YORK	4-0	3-0	2629	Ranson(2), Ferguson, Lonsdale							7				8	11	9	3		10	2	5		6		1				4	
18	22	Darlington	0-5	0-2	3726								7				8	11	4	9			10	2	5	6		1				3	
19	26	Lincoln	2-4	1-1	8592	Miller, Ranson							7				8	11	4	9			10	2	5	6		1				3	
20	29	TRANMERE	1-1	1-0	4305	Stevenson							7				8	11	4	9			10	2	5	6		1				3	
21	1 Jan	LINCOLN	2-1	1-0	3773	Stevenson, Miller							7				8	11	4	9			10	2	5	6		1				3	
22	5	Wrexham	2-4	0-1	3695	Ranson(2)			3				7			9	8	11					10	2	5	6		1				4	
23	12	Southport	3-0	2-0	1928	Stevenson(2), Miller			3				7				8	11		9			10	2	5	6		1				4	
24	19	HALIFAX	2-4	2-3	4657	Miller, Ranson							7			9	8	11	4				2	5	10	6		1				3	
25	26	Rotherham	1-4	0-3	3626	Ferguson							7				8	11	4	9			2	5	10	6		1				3	
26	2 Feb	WALSALL	1-6	1-1	2907	Ranson		2			5		7				8	11	9				3			6		1			4	10	
27	9	Chesterfield	0-3	0-2	4007			2					7				8	11	9				3	5		6		1			4		10
28	23	Barrow	1-2	1-0	2466	Ferguson		2									8	11	9				3	5	7	6		1		4	5		10
29	21	New Brighton	1-5	1-3	852	Ranson		2									8	11	4	9	6			5	7			1			3		10
30	2 Mar	Gateshead	2-3	2-2	2894	Ranson, Jones		2									8	11	4	9	6			5				1		10	3		7
31	9	STOCKPORT	1-2	1-1	5968	Ferguson		2									8	11	4		6			5	7			1			3		9
32	16	Crewe	1-1	1-0	3683	Ferguson	1	2			5	10					8	11	4		6								9	3		7	
33	23	HARTLEPOOLS	2-2	1-0	4091	Ferguson(2,1pen)	1	2				10					8	11	4		6		3	5					9			7	
34	30	Doncaster	0-3	0-2	10784		1	2				10	7				8	11	4			9	3	5		6							
35	6 Apr	SOUTHPORT	0-1	0-0	3410		1	2			5	10	7				8	11	4		6		3			9							
36	19	Chester	0-3	0-1	3986		1	2					7			9	8	11					10	3					4		5		6
37	19	ROCHDALE	0-0	0-0	4417								7			9	8	11	9	3	10	2	5			6		1	4			
38	20	NEW BRIGHTON	4-1	3-0	2674	Ferguson(2), Miller(2)	1	2					7			9	8	11			10					6			3		5		4
39	22	Rochdale	1-3	0-2	5711	Ferguson	1	2					7			9		11	4		8			10		6					5		3
40	25	MANSFIELD	1-1	0-0	2622	Slinger	1	2					7		9			11		3				10		6			4		5		8
41	27	York	0-7	0-2	2864		1	2			5		7		9			11	4					10		6					3		8
42	4 May	DARLINGTON	1-2	0-1	2021	Kelly	1	2			5		7					11			3			10		6			9		4		8

F.A. CUP

No.	Date	Opposition	Res.	H.T.	Att.	Goalscorers	Wolf	Legge	Allen	Darnell	Parker A.	Spencer	Miller	White	Slinger	Stevenson	Ferguson	Troughear	Ranson	Batey	Dougal	Henderson	Lonsdale	Henson	Jones	Johnson	Elliott	Black	Cartwright	Kelly	Parker J.	Robinson	Winthrop
1R	24 Nov	WIGAN ATH.	1-6	0-3	3196	Ranson	1	3	6		5			8	10	7			9							4	11				2		

Final League Table

		Pl.	Home					Away					F.	A.	Pts
			W	D	L	F	A	W	D	L	F	A			
1	Doncaster Rovers	42	16	0	5	53	21	10	5	6	34	23	87	44	57
2	Halifax Town	42	17	2	2	50	24	8	3	10	26	43	76	67	55
3	Chester	42	14	4	3	62	27	6	10	5	29	31	91	58	54
4	Lincoln City	42	14	3	4	55	21	8	4	9	32	37	87	58	51
5	Darlington	42	15	5	1	50	15	6	4	11	30	44	80	59	51
6	Tranmere Rovers	42	15	4	2	53	20	5	7	9	21	35	74	55	51
7	Stockport County	42	15	2	4	57	22	7	1	13	33	50	90	72	47
8	Mansfield Town	42	16	3	2	55	25	3	6	12	20	37	75	62	47
9	Rotherham United	42	14	4	3	56	21	5	3	13	30	52	86	73	45
10	Chesterfield	42	13	4	4	46	21	4	6	11	25	31	71	52	44
11	Wrexham	42	12	5	4	47	25	4	6	11	29	44	76	69	43
12	Hartlepools United	42	12	4	5	52	34	5	3	13	28	44	80	78	41
13	Crewe Alexandra	42	12	6	3	41	25	2	5	14	25	61	66	86	39
14	Walsall	42	11	7	3	51	18	2	3	16	30	54	81	72	36
15	York City	42	12	5	4	50	20	3	1	17	26	62	76	82	36
16	New Brighton	42	9	6	6	32	25	5	2	14	27	51	59	76	36
17	Barrow	42	11	5	5	37	31	2	4	15	21	56	58	87	35
18	Accrington Stanley	42	11	5	5	44	36	1	5	15	19	53	63	89	34
19	Gateshead	42	12	4	5	36	28	1	4	16	22	68	58	96	34
20	Rochdale	42	9	5	7	39	35	2	6	13	14	36	53	71	33
21	Southport	42	6	6	9	27	36	4	6	11	28	49	55	85	32
22	Carlisle United	42	7	6	8	34	36	1	1	19	17	66	51	102	23

- 1934/35 Season -

Stripes, back row: Batey, Troughear, Black, Lonsdale, Smith.
Front row: Dixon, A.N. Other, Henderson, Dougal, Kennedy, Baxter.

- 1935/36 Season -

(Back): Lloyd, James, Hill, Round, Harford, Manns, Webster, Henderson, Clarke (Sec.)Kelly (Manager)
(Front): Kerr, Williams, Landells, Shankley, Galloway, Cliffe, Johnston

SEASON 1935/36
DIVISION 3 NORTH

No.	Date	Opposition	Res.	H.T.	Att.	Goalscorers	Harford	Kerr	Lloyd	Webster	Round	Mannes	Williams	Galloway	Shankly J.	Landells	Cliffe	Kelly	James	Higgs	Henderson	Johnson	Beck	Dodd	Varty	Taylor	Mantle	Lonsdale	Parker	Winter
1	31 Aug	DARLINGTON	3-0	1-0	9911	Shankly(2), Cliffe	1	2	3	4	5	6	7	10	9	8	11													
2	2 Sep	Halifax	0-1	0-1	8709		1	2	3	4	5	6		10		9	11	7	8											
3	7	Gateshead	1-1	0-0	8430	Shankly	1	2	3	4	5	6		10	9	8	11	7												
4	12	HALIFAX	0-0	0-0	9563		1	2	3	4	5	6	7	10	9	8	11													
5	14	TRANMERE	0-1	0-0	9394		1	2	3	4	5	6		10	9	8	11													7
6	19	OLDHAM	2-1	1-1	7548	Landells(2)	1	2	3	4	5	6	7	8	9	10	11													
7	21	Walsall	0-3	0-1	7377		1	2	3	4	5	6	7	8	9	10	11													
8	28	STOCKPORT	2-1	1-0	8338	Mantle, Taylor	1	2	3		5			8		10		7				4				11	9	6		
9	5 Oct	HARTLEPOOLS	0-0	0-0	7618		1	2	3	4	5		7	8		10						6				11	9			
10	12	Mansfield	1-1	1-1	4228	Mantle	1	2	3	4	5		7	8		10						6				11	9			
11	19	Crewe	0-2	0-1	3649		1	2	3	4	5		7	8		10						6				11	9			
12	26	ACCRINGTON	3-1	2-0	6083	Taylor(2), Mantle	1	2	3	4	5	6	7	8			11									10	9			
13	2 Nov	Southport	3-0	2-0	2148	Mantle, Taylor, Cliffe	1	2	3	4	5	6	7	8			11									10	9			
14	9	CHESTER	1-3	1-1	8778	Mantle	1	2	3					8			7									10	9	6		11
15	16	Lincoln	0-2	0-1	5415		1	2	3	4	5	6		10		8	7									11	9			
16	23	ROCHDALE	4-3	2-1	6029	Mantle(2), Williams, Taylor	1	2	3		5	6	7	8			11					4				10	9			
17	14 Dec	New Brighton	0-3	0-2	1719		1	2	3		5	6	7	8		10	11					4				9				
18	21	CHESTERFIELD	2-1	2-0	4161	Taylor, Cliffe	1	2	3		5		7	8			11					4				10	9	6		
19	26	Rotherham	0-4	0-2	4497		1	2	3		5			10		8	7					4	6			11	9			
20	28	Darlington	1-4	1-3	3831	Taylor	1	2	3		5			10		8	7					4	6	9		11				
21	1 Jan	ROTHERHAM	1-1	1-0	8456	Taylor	1	2	3		5	6		10		8	11					4				9	7			
22	4	GATESHEAD	2-0	1-0	5389	Mantle, Taylor	1	2	3		5	6		10		8	11					4				9	7			
23	11	York	0-2	0-1	4134		1	2	3		5	6	11	10			7					4				9	8			
24	18	Tranmere	1-4	1-2	7851	Mantle	1	2	3		5		7	8			11				10	4				6	9			
25	25	WALSALL	2-1	2-0	5151	Mantle(2)	1	2	3		5	6	7				11				10	4				8	9			
26	1 Feb	Stockport	0-2	0-0	7065		1	2	3		5	6	7				11			8		4				10	9			
27	8	Hartlepools	1-1	1-0	4107	Mantle		2	3			6		10			7	4	1			5			11	8	9			
28	15	MANSFIELD	3-0	2-0	4918	Galloway(2), Mantle		2	3			6		8			7	4	1			5			11	10	9			
29	22	CREWE	1-2	1-0	6011	Mantle		2	3			6		8			7	4	1			5			11	10	9			
30	29	Chester	2-3	1-0	3675	Mantle, Varty		2	3					8		10	7	4	1			5			11	6	9			
31	7 Mar	SOUTHPORT	4-0	1-0	3550	Mantle, Landells, Varty(2)		2	3					8		10	7	4	1			5			11	6	9			
32	14	Accrington	0-0	0-0	3560			2	3					8		10	7	4	1			5			11	6	9			
33	21	LINCOLN	4-1	2-0	5642	Mantle(3), Cliffe		2	3					10		8	7	4	1			5			11	6	9			
34	28	Rochdale	0-0	0-0	3722			2	3		5			10		8	7	4	1						11	6	9			
35	4 Apr	York	0-0	0-0	5134			2	3		5			10		8	7	4	1						11	6	9			
36	10	WREXHAM	5-1	1-1	6535	Landells(2),Mantle(p),Jmes(p),Tylor		2	3					10		8	7	4	1			5			11	6	9			
37	11	Barrow	1-1	0-1	3594	Landells		2	3					10		8	7	4	1			5			11	6	9			
38	13	Wrexham	1-1	1-0	3278	Galloway		2	3					10		8	7	4	1			5			11	6	9			
39	18	NEW BRIGHTON	3-0	3-0	3592	Cliffe, Varty, Mantle		2	3					10		8	7	4	1			5			11	6	9			
40	25	Chesterfield	0-5	0-2	8225			2	3					10		8	7	4	1			5			11	6	9			
41	30	BARROW	2-2	1-1	4893	Mantle, Galloway		2	3				7	10		8		4	1			5			11	6	9			
42	2 May	Oldham	0-3	0-2	2891			2	3				7	10		8		4	1			5			11	6	9			

F.A. CUP

Round	Date	Opposition	Res.	H.T.	Att.	Goalscorers	Harford	Kerr	Lloyd	Webster	Round	Mannes	Williams	Galloway	Shankly J.	Landells	Cliffe	Kelly	James	Higgs	Henderson	Johnson	Beck	Dodd	Varty	Taylor	Mantle	Lonsdale	Parker	Winter
1R	30 Nov	Tranmere	0-3	0-1	6992		1	2	3		5		7	8	9	4	11					6				10				

Final League Table

		Pl.	Home					Away					F.	A.	Pts
			W	D	L	F	A	W	D	L	F	A			
1	Chesterfield	42	15	3	3	60	14	9	9	3	32	25	92	39	60
2	Chester	42	14	5	2	69	18	8	6	7	31	27	100	45	55
3	Tranmere Rovers	42	17	2	2	75	28	5	9	7	18	30	93	58	55
4	Lincoln City	42	18	1	2	64	14	4	8	9	27	37	91	51	53
5	Stockport County	42	15	2	4	45	18	5	6	10	20	31	65	49	48
6	Crewe Alexandra	42	14	4	3	55	31	5	5	11	25	45	80	76	47
7	Oldham Athletic	42	13	5	3	60	25	5	4	12	26	48	86	73	45
8	Hartlepools United	42	13	6	2	41	18	2	6	13	16	43	57	61	42
9	Accrington Stanley	42	12	5	4	43	24	5	3	13	20	48	63	72	42
10	Walsall	42	15	2	4	58	13	1	7	13	21	46	79	59	41
11	Rotherham United	42	14	3	4	52	13	2	6	13	17	53	69	66	41
12	Darlington	42	16	3	2	60	26	1	3	17	14	53	74	79	40
13	Carlisle United	42	13	5	3	44	19	1	7	13	12	43	56	62	40
14	Gateshead	42	11	10	0	37	18	2	4	15	19	58	56	76	40
15	Barrow	42	9	9	3	33	16	4	3	14	25	49	58	65	38
16	York City	42	10	8	3	41	28	3	4	14	21	67	62	95	38
17	Halifax Town	42	12	3	6	34	22	3	4	14	23	39	57	61	37
18	Wrexham	42	12	3	6	39	18	3	4	14	27	57	66	75	37
19	Mansfield Town	42	13	5	3	55	25	1	4	16	25	66	80	91	37
20	Rochdale	42	8	10	3	35	26	2	3	16	23	62	58	88	33
21	Southport	42	9	8	4	31	26	2	1	18	17	64	48	90	31
22	New Brighton	42	8	5	8	29	33	1	1	19	14	69	43	102	24

- 1936/37 Season -

Stripes, back row: McDonnell, Routledge, Round, Gray, McIlraith.
Front row: Traynor, Waterbrook, Lisle, Lonsdale, Jackson, Kerr.

Blues, back row: James, Bradford, Cuthbert, Higgs, Johnson, Taylor.
Front row: Cliffe, Galloway, Tait, Rivers, McArdle.

SEASON 1936/37

DIVISION 3 NORTH

No.	Date	Opposition	Res.	H.T.	Att.	Goalscorers	Higgs	Kerr	Rivers	James	Round	Taylor	McArdle	Mantle	Johnson J.	Cliffe	Galloway	Routledge	Roberts	Sleight	Scott	Williams	Smith	Singleton	Presgrave	O'Grady	Mills	McGarr	Leach	Lonsdale	Lisle	Adey	Featherby
1	29 Aug	Tranmere	1-5	1-3	8310	Mantle	1	2	10	4	5	3	11	9	6	7	8																
2	3 Sep	SOUTHPORT	1-1	1-0	7413	Rivers	1	2	10	4	5	3		9	6	7	8														11		
3	5	HALIFAX	1-2	0-2	5864	Johnson	1	2			5	3		7	6		8	4								9					11		10
4	8	Southport	1-2	1-1	5066	McArdle	1	2				3	11	9	5	7	8	4								6							10
5	12	Mansfield	4-1	1-1	6665	Mantle(2), Presgrove, James	1	2		6		3	11	9	5		10	4							7	8							
6	19	CREWE	4-0	3-0	7053	McArdle(2), Mantle(2,1pen)	1	2		6		3	11	9	5		10	4							7	8							
7	26	Chester	0-4	0-2	8932		1	2		6		3	11	9	5		10	4							7	8							
8	3 Oct	ROCHDALE	1-0	0-0	6916	Mantle	1	2		6			11	9	5		10	4							7	8						3	
9	10	Barrow	0-5	0-2	4935		1	2		6			11		5	8	10	4							7	9						3	
10	17	PORT VALE	5-2	4-1	4691	Mantle(2), McArdle, Taylor, Cliffe	1	2		10	5	6	11	9		4	7	8														3	
11	24	Rotherham	1-0	—	5916	McArdle	1	2		10	5	6	11	9		4	7	8														3	
12	31	STOCKPORT	1-0	0-0	7946	Mantle	1	2		10	5	6	11	9		4	7	8														3	
13	7 Nov	Wrexham	0-1	0-1	3871		1			10	5	6	11	9		4	7	8		2												3	
14	14	DARLINGTON	2-0	1-0	5785	Cliffe, James	1			10	5	6	11	9		4	7	8		2												3	
15	21	Gateshead	0-1	—	2903			2		10	5	6		9		4	7	8				1									11	3	
16	5 Dec	New Brighton	1-1	1-0	2353	Mantle		2		10		6	11	9	5		7	8				1				4						3	
17	19	Accrington	1-2	0-1	3285	Mantle		2		10			11	9	5		7	8				1				4		6				3	
18	25	OLDHAM	2-1	2-0	10598	Mantle(2)				10		6	11	9	5		7	8		2		1				4						3	
19	26	TRANMERE	3-1	—	10582	Mantle, James, McArdle		2		10		6	11	9	5		7	8				1				4						3	
20	28	Oldham	1-2	0-1	4355	Mantle		2				6	11	9	5		7	10				1		8		4						3	
21	1 Jan	YORK	1-1	1-1	9940	Williams		2		10		6		9	5		11	8			1	7				4						3	
22	2	Halifax	1-6	1-3	4946	Mantle(1pen)		2		10		6		9	5		11	8			1	7				4						3	
23	9	MANSFIELD	1-2	1-2	6162	Galloway		2		10		6	11	9			7	8		5	1					4						3	
24	21	HULL	1-1	1-0	2678	O'Grady	1	2		10		6			5		7	8	4							9						3	
25	23	Crewe	2-1	1-1	2512	O'Grady(2)	1	2				6	11		5			8	4		7					9	10					3	
26	4 Feb	CHESTER	1-1	1-0	3362	McArdle	1					6	11			4	7	10	8		9	2									5	3	
27	6	Rochdale	0-3	0-2	4428		1						11			8	7	10	4		9	2									5	3	
28	13	BARROW	2-2	2-1	4675	Adey(pen), McArdle	1			10			11			6	9	8	4		7	2									5	3	
29	20	Port Vale	0-1	0-0	6585		1	2					11			4	7	8			9	6				10					5	3	
30	27	ROTHERHAM	4-1	2-1	2982	Galloway(2), McArdle, O'Grady	1	2					11			4	7	8			9	6				10					5	3	
31	6 Mar	Stockport	2-1	0-1	12365	McArdle(2)	1	2					11			4	7	8			9	6				10					5	3	
32	13	WREXHAM	2-1	2-0	5872	O'Grady, McArdle	1	2					11			4	7	8			6					10	9				5	3	
33	20	Darlington	5-1	2-0	2817	Roberts(2), Cliffe, Mills, O'Grady	1	2								4	7	8	11		6					10	9				5	3	
34	26	HARTLEPOOLS	2-0	1-0	8366	Roberts, Mills	1	2								4	7	8	11		6					10	9				5	3	
35	27	GATESHEAD	2-1	0-0	5934	Galloway, O'Grady	1	2								4	7	8	11		6					10	9				5	3	
36	29	Hartlepools	0-3	0-2	4748		1	2								4	7	8	11		6					10	9				5	3	
37	3 Apr	Hull	1-1	0-1	4355	Mills	1	2								4	7	8	11		6						9	10			5	3	
38	10	NEW BRIGHTON	1-1	—	5246	Mills	1	2								4	7	8	11		6						9	10			5	3	
39	15	LINCOLN	3-1	1-1	8710	Mills, Galloway, O'Grady	1	2								4	7	8	11		6					10	9				5	3	
40	17	Lincoln	0-3	0-1	7582		1	2								4	7	8	11		6					10	9				5	3	
41	24	ACCRINGTON	2-0	1-0	5470	Adey(pen), O'Grady	1	2								4	7	8	11		6					10	9				5	3	
42	1 May	York	2-5	0-3	3147	Adey(pen), Cliffe	1	2								4	7	8	11		6					10	9				5	3	

F.A. CUP

No.	Date	Opposition	Res.	H.T.	Att.	Goalscorers	Higgs	Kerr	Rivers	James	Round	Taylor	McArdle	Mantle	Johnson J.	Cliffe	Galloway	Routledge	Roberts	Sleight	Scott	Williams	Smith	Singleton	Presgrave	O'Grady	Mills	McGarr	Leach	Lonsdale	Lisle	Adey	Featherby
1R	28 Nov	STOCKPORT	2-1	1-1	12394	Mantle, McArdle		2		10	5	6	11	9		4	7	8			1											3	
2R	12 Dec	CLAPTON ORIENT	4-1	2-0	13318	McArdle(2), James, O'Grady		2		10		6	11	9	5		7	8			1					4						3	
3R	16 Jan	Swansea	0-1	0-0	8790		1	2		10		6	11	9	5		7	8	4													3	

Final League Table

		Pl.	Home					Away					F.	A.	Pts
			W	D	L	F	A	W	D	L	F	A			
1	Chesterfield	42	15	3	3	60	14	9	3	3	32	25	92	39	60
2	Chester	42	14	5	2	69	18	8	6	7	31	27	100	45	55
3	Tranmere Rovers	42	17	2	2	75	28	5	9	7	18	30	93	58	55
4	Lincoln City	42	18	1	2	64	14	4	8	9	27	37	91	51	53
5	Stockport County	42	15	2	4	45	18	5	6	10	20	31	65	49	48
6	Crewe Alexandra	42	14	4	3	55	31	5	5	11	25	45	80	76	47
7	Oldham Athletic	42	13	5	3	60	25	5	4	12	26	48	86	73	45
8	Hartlepools United	42	13	6	2	41	18	2	6	13	16	43	57	61	42
9	Accrington Stanley	42	12	5	4	43	24	5	3	13	20	48	63	72	42
10	Walsall	42	15	2	4	58	13	1	7	13	21	46	79	59	41
11	Rotherham United	42	14	3	4	52	13	2	6	13	17	53	69	66	41
12	Darlington	42	16	3	2	60	26	1	3	17	14	53	74	79	40
13	Carlisle United	42	13	5	3	44	19	1	7	13	12	43	56	62	40
14	Gateshead	42	11	10	0	37	18	2	4	15	19	58	56	76	40
15	Barrow	42	9	9	3	33	16	4	3	14	25	49	58	65	38
16	York City	42	10	8	3	41	28	3	4	14	21	67	62	95	38
17	Halifax Town	42	12	3	6	34	22	3	4	14	23	39	57	61	37
18	Wrexham	42	12	3	6	39	18	3	4	14	27	57	66	75	37
19	Mansfield Town	42	13	5	3	55	25	1	4	16	25	66	80	91	37
20	Rochdale	42	8	10	3	35	26	2	3	16	23	62	58	88	33
21	Southport	42	9	8	4	31	26	2	1	18	17	64	48	90	31
22	New Brighton	42	8	5	8	29	33	1	1	19	14	69	43	102	24

SEASON 1937/38

DIVISION 3 NORTH

No.	Date	Opposition	Res.	H.T.	Att.	Goalscorers	Leckie	Kerr	Adey	Molloy	Leach	Johnson	Roberts	Scott	Mills	Galloway	Cliffe	Hamilton	Knox	Smith	Temple	McGarr	Keating	Gore	Beresford	Batey	Blackadder	McCartney	McDougall	Patterson	Tate	Elliott	Erskine
1	28 Aug	Accrington	4-1	1-0	7970	Galloway, Cliffe, Roberts	1	2	3	6	5	4	11	10	9	8	7																
2	2 Sep	CHESTER	1-3	1-2	11377	Mills	1	2	3	6	5	4	11	10	9	8	7																
3	4	LINCOLN	0-1	0-1	7766		1	2	3	6	5	4	11		9	8					7		10										
4	8	Chester	0-1	0-0	5372		1	2	3		5	4	11	10	9	8	7			6													
5	11	HALIFAX	5-2	2-2	5974	Mills(5)	1	2	3		5	4	11	10	9	8	7			6													
6	13	Rotherham	1-0	1-0	6393	Scott	1	2		4	3	5	11	10	9	8	7			6													
7	18	Tranmere	0-5	0-1	9517		1	2		4	3	5	11	10		8	7			6					9								
8	25	YORK	2-1	1-0	6467	Cliffe, Temple	1	2		4	3	5	11	10	9		7			6	8												
9	2 Oct	Bradford	0-4	0-1	6606			2	3	4	3		11	10	9		7		1	6	8												
10	9	SOUTHPORT	1-0	0-0	6474	Mills		2	4	3	5			10	9		7		1	6	8		11										
11	16	Hull	1-2	1-1	10837	Keating		2	4	3	5				9		7		1	6	8		11										
12	23	NEW BRIGHTON	1-1	0-0	3911	O.G.		2	4	3	5		11	10		8			1	6	7			9									
13	30	Gateshead	1-2	0-2	10514	Temple		2	4	3	5		11			8	7		1	6		10		9									
14	6 Nov	OLDHAM	1-1		6608	Adey(pen)		2	4						9	8	7		1	6		10	11						3				
15	13	Darlington	1-3	0-1	3913	Cliffe		2		6	5	4			9	8	7		1				11		10				3				
16	20	PORT VALE	3-1	2-0	4959	Beresford, Scott, Roberts		2			5	4	11	10					1					9	8				3	6	7		
17	4 Dec	BARROW	2-1	1-0	2770	Hamilton(2)			3		5	4			9	8	7		1				11		10	2		6					
18	18	HARTLEPOOLS	3-1	0-1	3855	Mills(2), Hamilton		2	3	6	5	4			9		10	11	1						8						7		
19	25	DONCASTER	2-2	1-1	10821	Mills, Tate		2	3	6	5	4			9		10	11	1						8						7		
20	27	Doncaster	3-1	1-0	17446	Mills, Tate, Hamilton		2	3	6		4			9		10	11	1	5					8						7		
21	1 Jan	ACCRINGTON	3-1	2-0	9492	Hamilton(2), Johnson		2	3	6		4			9		10	11	1	5					8						7		
22	8	Crewe	1-4		3545	Temple		2	3	6	5	4			9			11	1		10				8						7		
23	15	Lincoln	1-0	1-0	5845	Roberts		2	3	6	5	4	11		9	10			1						8						7		
24	22	Halifax	0-0	0-0	6228			2	3	6	5	4			9			11	1		10				8						7		
25	29	TRANMERE	0-0	0-0	7216			2	3	6	5	4			9		10	11	1						8						7		
26	5 Feb	York	1-3		6284	Tate		2	3	6	5	4			9			11	1						8						7		
27	12	BRADFORD	2-0	2-0	6372	Mills, Beresford		2	3	6	5	4			9		10	11	1						8						7		
28	19	Southport	1-1	1-0	4295	Galloway		2	3	6	5	4			9		10	11	1						8						7		
29	26	HULL	0-1	0-1	7525			2	3	6	5	4			9		10	11	1						8						7		
30	5 Mar	New Brighton	1-5	0-0	4075	Cliffe		2	3	6	5	4	11			9	10		1					5	8								
31	12	GATESHEAD	1-0	0-0	9139	Cliffe		2	3	6	5	4				9	10	7	1				11		8								
32	19	Oldham	0-3	0-2	10669				3	6	5	4					10	7	1				11	9	8	2							
33	26	DARLINGTON	3-0	2-0	4911	Mills(2), McGarr		2	3	6	5	4	11		9			7	1			8	10										
34	2 Apr	Port Vale	2-2	1-1	6463	McGarr, Adey(pen)		2	3		5	4	11		9			7	1	6		8	10										
35	9	CREWE	5-1	3-1	5429	Mills(3), McGarr, Hamilton		2	3		5	4	11		9			7	1	6		8			10								
36	15	Rochdale	1-3	1-2	4648	Temple		2	3		5	4	11		9			7	1	6		8			10								
37	16	Barrow	2-4	1-2	4934	Cliffe, Beresford		2	3		5	4	11	10				7	1	6		9			8								
38	18	ROCHDALE	0-1	0-1	5609			2	3			4	11		9	8	7		1	6					10		5						
39	23	WREXHAM	0-0	0-0	4145			2	3	6			11			9	10		1	4			11	7	8		5						
40	25	Wrexham	0-0	0-0	2237			2	3	4	5		11			10			1	6		9			8						7		
41	30	Hartlepools	1-4	0-1	2766	Beresford		2	3	4	5				9		10	7	1	6			11		8								
42	7 May	ROTHERHAM	0-1	0-1	3748				3	4			11		9		10	7		6					8	2						1	5

F.A. CUP

No.	Date	Opposition	Res.	H.T.	Att.	Goalscorers	Leckie	Kerr	Adey	Molloy	Leach	Johnson	Roberts	Scott	Mills	Galloway	Cliffe	Hamilton	Knox	Smith	Temple	McGarr	Keating	Gore	Beresford	Batey	Blackadder	McCartney	McDougall	Patterson	Tate	Elliott	Erskine
1R	27 Nov	Tranmere	1-2	1-1	7932	Leach			3		5	4	11	10					1	2		9			8					6	7		

Final League Table

		Pl.	Home					Away					F.	A.	Pts
			W	D	L	F	A	W	D	L	F	A			
1	Stockport County	42	17	3	1	59	18	6	11	4	25	21	84	39	60
2	Lincoln City	42	18	1	2	65	20	7	6	8	38	37	103	57	57
3	Chester	42	15	5	1	68	21	7	4	10	19	36	87	57	53
4	Oldham Athletic	42	13	7	1	49	25	7	4	10	28	34	77	59	51
5	Hull City	42	13	6	2	39	22	4	6	11	29	47	68	69	46
6	Hartlepools United	42	16	1	4	53	21	3	6	12	22	48	75	69	45
7	Halifax Town	42	12	4	5	40	20	6	5	10	28	43	68	63	45
8	Wrexham	42	12	3	6	41	21	4	9	8	30	36	71	57	44
9	Mansfield Town	42	13	1	7	64	35	5	7	9	27	41	91	76	44
10	Carlisle United	42	13	6	2	42	19	5	2	14	23	49	65	68	44
11	Port Vale	42	12	6	3	39	23	5	4	12	19	41	58	64	44
12	York City	42	13	3	5	54	27	3	8	10	25	43	79	70	43
13	Accrington Stanley	42	14	2	5	51	26	2	7	12	25	43	76	69	41
14	Southport	42	10	8	3	39	28	2	5	14	34	59	73	87	37
15	New Brighton	42	10	8	3	36	16	3	3	15	19	54	55	70	37
16	Barrow	42	11	5	5	42	25	2	5	14	28	61	70	86	36
17	Rotherham United	42	11	7	3	52	28	3	0	18	26	63	78	91	35
18	Rochdale	42	12	3	6	44	27	1	6	14	25	59	69	86	35
19	Tranmere Rovers	42	10	8	3	52	30	2	1	18	19	58	71	88	33
20	Crewe Alexandra	42	6	8	7	31	31	4	4	13	24	52	55	83	32
21	Gateshead	42	9	8	4	40	31	2	2	17	23	67	63	98	32
22	Darlington	42	6	8	7	42	46	2	6	13	24	50	66	96	30

- 1937/38 Season -

(Back): Hamilton, Mort, Sanderson, Smith Cliffe
(Middle): Clarke (Sec.), Elliott, Hamill, Barrie, Wheat, Edwards, Knox, Webster (Trainer)
(Front): Beresford, Mills, Kerr, Ashton, Rudkin

- 1938/39 Season -

(Back): Hamilton, Mort, Sanderson, Smith, Cliffe. (Middle): Clarke (Sec.), Elliott, Hamill, Barrie, Wheat, Edwards, Knox, Webster (Trainer). (Front): Beresford, Mills, Kerr, Ashton, Rudkin.

SEASON 1938/39

DIVISION 3 NORTH

No.	Date	Opposition	Res.	H.T.	Att.	Goalscorers	Knox	Kerr	Barrie	Wheat	Mort	Smith	Hamill	Edwards	Mills	Beresford	Ashton	Cliffe	Hamilton J.	Hamilton S.	Howshall	Hunt	Murphy	Pond	Rudkin	Sanderson	Sword	Taylor	Ogilvie	Lonsdale	Embleton	Elliott	Blaney
1	27 Aug	HARTLEPOOLS	2-0	1-0	7014	Mills(2)	1	3	2	4	5	6	7	10	9	8	11																
2	30	Rochdale	3-2	2-2	5217	Ashton(2,1pen), Murphy	1	2		4	5	6	7		9	8	11				3		10										
3	3 Sep	Darlington	1-2	1-2	3977	Beresford	1	2		4	5	6	7		9	8	11				3		10										
4	8	GATESHEAD	2-2	2-1	11813	Ashton(2,1pen)	1	2		4	5		7		9	8	11				3		10							6			
5	10	HULL	1-2	0-2	7236	Murphy	1	2		4		6	7		9	8	11				3		10				5						
6	17	CREWE	1-0	1-0	4518	Beresford	1	2		5	4				9	8	11	7			3		10							6			
7	24	Southport	1-7	1-3	5295	Ashton(pen)	1	2		5	4				9	8	7		3		11		10							6			
8	1 Oct	DONCASTER	2-3	1-1	5258	O.G., Mills	1	2			4				9	8	11		7				10				5	3					6
9	8	Rotherham	0-4	0-1	7110			2					7		9	8	11						10				3	5	4			1	6
10	15	Lincoln	1-2	0-0	5085	Mills		2	6	5	4				9	8		7			11		10				3					1	
11	22	STOCKPORT	3-2	1-1	5776	Hunt(2), Mills(pen)		2	4	5					11	8		7				6	9	10			3					1	
12	29	Accrington	1-1	0-0	3765	Hunt		3	2	4	5			10		8	11	7				6	9									1	
13	5 Nov	BARNSLEY	3-1	0-0	6770	Ashton(pen), Hunt, Cliffe		3	2	5	4					8	11	7				6	9	10								1	
14	12	Oldham	0-6	0-4	9325			3	2	5	4					8	11	7				6	9	10								1	
15	19	HALIFAX	1-2		4606	Murphy				4	5					8	11	7	2		3	6	9	10								1	
16	3 Dec	BARROW	3-0	1-0	4118	Hunt(3,1pen)	1			4	5			8		10				2		11	6	9			3			7			
17	10	New Brighton	3-2	1-1	3991	Hunt(2), S.Hamilton	1			4	5			8		10				2		11	6	9			3			7			
18	17	BRADFORD C.	0-2	0-1	4272		1			4	5			8		10				2		11	6	9			3			7			
19	24	Hartlepools	1-2	1-0	2435	Hunt	1			4	5			8		10				2		11	6	9			3			7			
20	26	Wrexham	5-2	2-1	7372	S.Hamiltn(2), Berefrd, Embleton, Hnt	1			4	5			8		10				2		11	6	9			3			7			
21	27	WREXHAM	1-1	1-0	6865	Hunt				4	5			8		10				2		11	6	9			3			7			1
22	31	DARLINGTON	1-1	1-1	3977	Murphy				4	5			8		10				2		11	6	9			3			7			1
23	14 Jan	Hull	1-11	1-4	5278		1					6		8						2	5	11	10	9			3	4		7			
24	21	Crewe	1-7	0-4	3803	Hamill(pen)		2			5		4		9	8		7				11	6	10			3					1	
25	28	SOUTHPORT	1-1	1-0	3690	Hunt	1	2			4	6				8		7	3		11	5	10	9									
26	4 Feb	Doncaster	0-1	0-1	9614		1	2			4	6				8	11	7			5		10	9			3						
27	11	ROTHERHAM	3-1	1-0	3027	Hunt, Beresford, Rudkin	1	2			4	6				8	11				5		10	9	7		3						
28	18	LINCOLN	4-3	0-1	3869	Hunt(4,1pen)	1	2			4	6				8	11				5		10	9	7		3						
29	25	Stockport	0-3	0-1	6712		1	2			4					8	11		3		5		10	9	7	6							
30	29	Chester	1-6	0-2	1735	Hunt	1	2			4					8	11		3		5		10	9	7	6							
31	4 Mar	ACCRINGTON	6-4	4-1	3859	Hunt(4,1pen), Murphy, Ashton	1	2			4					8	11		3		5		10	9	7	6							
32	11	Barnsley	0-3	0-2	13104		1	2			4					8	11		3		5		10	9	7	6							
33	18	OLDHAM	2-0	1-0	3573	Hunt(2)	1	2								8	11		3		5		10	9	7	6	4						
34	25	Halifax	1-5	1-1	3772	Hunt	1	2								8	11		3		5		10	9	7	6	4						
35	1 Apr	NEW BRIGHTON	1-1	1-1	3998	Hunt	1	2	4							8	11		3		5		10	9	7	6							
36	7	YORK	1-3	0-2	5285	Sword	1	2								8	11		3		5		10	9	7	6	4						
37	8	Barrow	0-5	0-3	5167		1				4	6				8	11	7	3		5		10	9				2					
38	10	York	1-4		5479	Beresford		2						10		8	11	7	3		5			9		6		4					1
39	15	CHESTER	1-3	1-3	2601	Hunt		2				5		10		8	11				4			9	7		3	1	6				
40	22	Bradford C.	0-2	0-1	4791		1	2				5				8	11	7			4		10	9		6	3						
41	29	ROCHDALE	5-1	2-0	2800	Hunt(3,1pen), Beresford, Ashton	1	2				5				8	11	7			3	4	10	9		6							
42	6 May	Gateshead	1-1	1-0	3483	Hunt	1	2				5				8	11	7			3	4	10	9		6							

F.A. CUP

No.	Date	Opposition	Res.	H.T.	Att.	Goalscorers	Knox	Kerr	Barrie	Wheat	Mort	Smith	Hamill	Edwards	Mills	Beresford	Ashton	Cliffe	Hamilton J.	Hamilton S.	Howshall	Hunt	Murphy	Pond	Rudkin	Sanderson	Sword	Taylor	Ogilvie	Lonsdale	Embleton	Elliott	Blaney
1R	26 Nov	Walsall	1-4	0-2	11036	Hamill		2		5	4		7			8					3	11	6	9	10							1	

Final League Table

		Pl.	Home					Away					F.	A.	Pts
			W	D	L	F	A	W	D	L	F	A			
1	Tranmere Rovers	42	15	4	2	57	21	8	6	7	24	20	81	41	56
2	Doncaster Rovers	42	15	4	2	48	16	6	8	7	26	33	74	49	54
3	Hull City	42	11	8	2	51	19	9	5	7	29	24	80	43	53
4	Oldham Athletic	42	16	4	1	48	18	3	9	9	19	28	67	46	51
5	Gateshead	42	15	5	1	53	20	5	6	10	31	39	84	59	51
6	Rotherham United	42	13	6	2	45	21	7	4	10	23	35	68	56	50
7	Lincoln City	42	14	3	4	48	17	5	5	11	18	33	66	50	46
8	Crewe Alexandra	42	14	3	4	47	17	4	6	11	24	36	71	53	45
9	Chester	42	13	4	4	54	31	3	8	10	23	41	77	72	44
10	Wrexham	42	14	4	3	37	15	2	7	12	21	48	58	63	43
11	York City	42	11	4	6	40	25	5	6	10	30	43	70	68	42
12	Carlisle United	42	11	5	5	35	19	4	4	13	22	48	57	67	39
13	New Brighton	42	12	5	4	43	18	3	3	15	17	43	60	61	38
14	Bradford City	42	12	6	3	46	21	2	4	15	20	48	66	69	38
15	Port Vale	42	11	8	2	45	27	1	6	14	20	46	65	73	38
16	Southport	42	8	8	5	30	26	4	6	11	23	56	53	82	38
17	Rochdale	42	7	10	4	38	27	6	1	14	29	51	67	78	37
18	Halifax Town	42	9	7	5	24	19	3	5	13	20	47	44	66	36
19	Darlington	42	10	4	7	37	31	1	6	14	17	48	54	79	32
20	Hartlepools United	42	10	8	3	36	20	0	4	17	17	60	53	80	32
21	Barrow	42	9	6	6	28	20	2	4	15	13	51	41	71	32
22	Accrington Stanley	42	9	2	10	31	32	2	5	14	14	43	45	75	29

- 1945/46 Season -

(Back): Harkness, Armstrong, Elliott, McPherson, Patrick, Woolacott, McGoody
(Front): Lawson, Hayton, Turnbull, Mills, Desborough, Meredith

- 1946/47 Season -

(Back): Harkness (Trainer), Corrieri, Adams, Taylor, Binns, Hindmarsh, Reed (Chairman), Reay,
Forsyth, Blythe.   Front: Dellow, Broadis, Bakas, Cape, Kirkpatrick, McKarrill

SEASON 1946/47

DIVISION 3 NORTH

No.	Date	Opposition	Res.	H.T.	Att.	Goalscorers	Jones	Adam	McBride	Horrigan	Taylor	Hindmarsh	Dellow	Broadis	Moir	Simpson	Laidler	Kirkpatrick	Harvey	McDonald	Clayton	Iceton	Burkinshaw	Squires	Anderson	Hitchson	Seed	Wheeler	Dougal	Connor	Maxfield	Armstrong	Cape	Hickey	Blackadder	Twentyman	Hayton	Meredick
1	31 Aug	Oldham	2-0	1-0	7696	Broadis, Moir	1	2	3	4	5	6	7	8	9	10	11																					
2	7 Sep	STOCKPORT	1-1	0-1	12555	Horrigan	1	2	3	4	5			8	9		11	7	10	6																		
3	14	Wrexham	1-2	1-1	9053	Broadis	1	2		4	5		7	8	9	10	11	6							3													
4	19	BRADFORD	4-3	3-0	10467	Kirkpatrick, Broadis, McBride, Moir	1	2	3	4	5		7	10	9		11	8		6																		
5	21	DONCASTER	2-3	1-2	12888	Kirkpatrick, Moir	1	2	3	4	5		7	10	9		11	8		6																		
6	24	Accrington	3-4	0-2	5556	Dellow, Simpson, Laidler	1	2	3	4	5		7		9	10	11	8		6																		
7	28	Rochdale	0-6	0-4	7414		1			4	2		7		9	10	11	8																3	5			
8	5 Oct	NEW BRIGHTON	3-2	1-0	10118	Broadis(2), Moir	1	3		2	5		7	8	9		11	10					6		4													
9	12	Halifax	1-0	1-0	3420	Dellow	1	3		2	5	4	7	8	9		11	10					6															
10	19	Gateshead	3-1	2-1	7037	Broadis(2), Moir	1	2	3		5	4	7	8	9		11	10					6															
11	26	HARTLEPOOLS	5-1	3-0	10775	Broadis(3), Hayton, Moir	1	2			5			8	9		11	10					6		4	3											7	
12	2 Nov	Crewe	0-2	0-0	6519		1		2		5			8	9		11	10					6		4	3											7	
13	9	LINCOLN	1-0	1-0	11821	Hayton	1	2	3		5			8	9		11	10					6		4												7	
14	16	Southport	2-0	1-0	4921	Broadis, Iceton	1	2	3		5			8				10				7	6	11	4				9									
15	23	ROTHERHAM	1-1	1-0	14816	Broadis	1	2	3		5			8				10				7	6	11	4				9									
16	7 Dec	YORK	1-2	1-1	11144	Hayton	1	2		4				8				10					6	11	5	3			9								7	
17	21	DARLINGTON	1-5	1-3	8342	Adams	1	7		4					9			8					6	11	5	2	3		10									
18	25	BARROW	4-1	2-0	9576	Broadis, Moir, Iceton, Dougal	1	2					6	8	9									11	5	3			10									
19	26	Barrow	1-3	0-2	8379	Moir	1	2					6		9		11	10					4		5	3											7	
20	28	Oldham	1-2	0-2	7696	Broadis	1						6	10	9								4	11	5	3				8	2						7	
21	1 Jan	ACCRINGTON	4-2	2-0	11522	Connor, Maxfield, Broadis, Moir	1						4	8	11								6		5	3				10	7	9	2					
22	4	Stockport	0-2	0-0	10006		1	11					6	8									4		5	3				10	7	9	2					
23	25	Doncaster	2-9	0-5	14051	Moir, Broadis	1	2			4			8	7			10					6	11	5	3			9									
24	1 Feb	ROCHDALE	1-3	1-1	9140	Iceton(pen)	1	2														10	6	11	5	3				8	9							7
25	15	HALIFAX	1-0	0-0	8449	Moir	1							8	7			11	4				6		5	3				10	9							
26	22	GATESHEAD	3-1	2-1	7196	Connor, Simpson, Laidler	1	2							7	10	11		4				6		5	3				8	9							
27	1 Mar	Hartlepools	1-4	1-2	4372	Moir	1	2							7			11	4				6		5	3				8	9							
28	8	CREWE	3-3	3-1	8303	Connor(2), Broadis	1				5			10	7			11	4					2	3					8	9							
29	15	Lincoln	1-1	0-0	6267	Moir	1	2	3	4					7	10	11						6		5					8	9							
30	22	SOUTHPORT	1-1	0-1	8687	Moir	1	2	3						7	8				4			6	11	5					10	9							
31	29	Rotherham	0-4	0-2	10180		1	2			4				7		11	10					6		5	3				8	9							
32	4 Apr	HULL	0-2	0-1	11704		1	2			4			8	7		11	10					6		5	3				9								
33	5	CHESTER	3-2	2-1	6810	Dellow, Broadis, Moir	1	2			4		7	8	9								6		5	3												
34	7	Hull	0-2	0-1	21854		1	2			4		7		9	10	11			6					5	3							8					
35	12	York	2-2	0-1	6090	Moir, Iceton	1	2						8	7							4		11		3			6	10		9	5					
36	19	TRANMERE	4-2	3-2	9997	Laidler, Broadis, Dougal, O.G.		2			4			8	9							7		11		3	1	5	6	10								
37	26	Darlington	1-2	1-1	4779	Moir		2			4				9							7	8	11		3		5	6	10								
38	3 May	Bradford	2-2	1-2	4565	Dellow, Moir		2			4		7	8	9									11		3		5	6	10								
39	7	WREXHAM	1-1	0-1	9431	Broadis		2			4	6	7	8	9									11		3		5		10								
40	24	Tranmere	1-1	1-0	5546	O.G.		2					7	8		6													9	10			5	11		4		
41	26	New Brighton	2-2	0-2	4561	Dellow, O.G.		2					7	8		6													9	10			5	11	4	6		
42	31	Chester	0-4	0-2	4037			2					7			10						6							9			3		11	8	4		

Additional player: Ross = match 19/position 8, match 27/position 10

F.A. CUP

Round	Date	Opposition	Res.	H.T.	Att.	Goalscorers	Jones	Adam	McBride	Horrigan	Taylor	Hindmarsh	Dellow	Broadis	Moir	Simpson	Laidler	Kirkpatrick	Harvey	McDonald	Clayton	Iceton	Burkinshaw	Squires	Anderson	Hitchson	Seed	Wheeler	Dougal	Connor	Maxfield	Armstrong	Cape	Hickey	Blackadder	Twentyman	Hayton	Meredick
1R	30 Nov	RUNCORN	4-0	2-0	11196	Iceton(2), Broadis, Dougal	1	2		4				8				10					6	11	5	3			9								7	
2R	14 Dec	South Liverpool	3-2	1-1	6193	Iceton(2,1pen), Moir	1	2		4				8	9								6	11	5	3			10								7	
3R	11 Jan	Sheffield United	0-3	0-1	28549		1	2					7	8	11	10							4		5	6	3		9									

Final League Table

		Pl.	Home					Away					F.	A.	Pts
			W	D	L	F	A	W	D	L	F	A			
1	Doncaster Rovers	42	15	5	1	67	16	18	1	2	56	24	123	40	72
2	Rotherham United	42	20	1	0	81	19	9	5	7	33	34	114	53	64
3	Chester	42	17	2	2	53	13	8	4	9	42	38	95	51	56
4	Stockport County	42	17	0	4	50	19	7	2	12	28	34	78	53	50
5	Bradford City	42	12	5	4	40	20	8	5	8	22	27	62	47	50
6	Rochdale	42	9	5	7	39	25	10	5	6	41	39	80	64	48
7	Wrexham	42	13	5	3	43	21	4	7	10	22	30	65	51	46
8	Crewe Alexandra	42	12	4	5	39	26	5	5	11	31	48	70	74	43
9	Barrow	42	10	2	9	28	24	7	5	9	26	38	54	62	41
10	Tranmere Rovers	42	11	5	5	43	33	6	2	13	23	44	66	77	41
11	Hull City	42	9	5	7	25	19	7	3	11	24	34	49	53	40
12	Lincoln City	42	12	3	6	52	32	5	2	14	34	55	86	87	39
13	Hartlepools United	42	10	5	6	36	26	5	4	12	28	47	64	73	39
14	Gateshead	42	10	3	8	39	33	6	3	12	23	39	62	72	38
15	York City	42	6	4	11	35	42	8	5	8	32	39	67	81	37
16	Carlisle United	42	10	5	6	45	38	4	4	13	25	55	70	93	37
17	Darlington	42	12	4	5	48	26	3	2	16	20	54	68	80	36
18	New Brighton	42	11	3	7	37	30	3	5	13	20	47	57	77	36
19	Oldham Athletic	42	6	6	10	29	31	6	3	12	26	49	55	80	32
20	Accrington Stanley	42	8	3	10	37	38	6	1	14	19	54	56	92	32
21	Southport	42	6	5	10	35	41	1	6	14	18	44	53	85	25
22	Halifax Town	42	6	3	12	28	36	2	3	16	15	56	43	92	22

SEASON 1947/48

DIVISION 3 NORTH

No.	Date	Opposition	Res.	H.T.	Att.	Goalscorers	Jones	Hutton	Burke	Wightman	Seed	Ross G.	Moir	Dougal	Lindsay	Broadis	Iceton	Connor	Ford	Hayton	Monaghan	Walshaw	Twentyman	Sweeney	Collis	Squires	Kenyon	Farey	Gray	Ross B.	Landsborough	Maxfield	Gordon
1	23 Aug	DARLINGTON	4-2	3-1	13280	Lindsay(2), Broadis, Iceton	1	2	3	6	5	4	7	8	9	10	11																
2	26	York	2-2	1-1	8681	Dougal, Lindsay	1	2	3	6	5	4	7	8	9	10	11																
3	30	Gateshead	3-1	2-0	8831	Lindsay, Connor, Iceton	1	2			5	4		8	9	10	11	7						6		3							
4	4 Sep	YORK	1-1	1-1	17317	Broadis	1	2	3		5	4		8	9	10	11	7						6									
5	6	HARTLEPOOLS	1-1	1-0	14223	Lindsay	1	2	3					8	9	10	11	7	5					6		4							
6	8	Mansfield	3-2	2-1	8272	Lindsday(2), Dougal	1	2	3	6	5			8	9	10	11	7	4														
7	13	Rotherham	2-7	1-3	11631	Lindsay(2,1pen)	1	2	3	6	5			8	9		11	7	4											10			
8	20	STOCKPORT	4-0	2-0	13327	Lindsay,Dougal,Broadis, Burke(pen)	1	2	3		5	6		8	9	10	11		4	7													
9	27	CREWE	5-2	2-1	13986	Lindsay(4), Hayton	1	2	3	6	5			8	9	10	11		4	7													
10	4 Oct	Chester	1-4		7910	Broadis	1		3	6				8	9	10	11		4	7	2												
11	11	Bradford	1-1	1-0	10645	Broadis	1	2	3	6	5	4		10	9	7	11		8														
12	18	BARROW	1-2	0-1	14237	Connor	1	2	3	6	5	4		8	9	10	11	7															
13	25	Wrexham	1-2	0-0	11641	Connor	1	2	3	6				10	9	8	11	7	4														
14	1 Nov	HALIFAX	5-2	5-1	11784	Iceton(2),Burke(pen),Lindsay,Connr	1	2	3	6				10	9	8	11	7	4														
15	8	Rochdale	1-2	1-1	8777	Iceton	1	2		6	5			10	9	8	11	7	4												3		
16	15	NEW BRIGHTON	2-1	0-0	11829	Gray, Broadis	1	2	3	6				10	9	8	11	4	5										7				
17	22	Southport	4-0	2-0	6730	Lindsay(3,1pen), Broadis	1			6	5			10	9	8	11	7	4							3							
18	6 Dec	Accrington	2-1	1-1	4867	Broadis(2)			3	6	5	4		8		11	9	10			2						1						
19	13	ACCRINGTON	2-3	1-1	11514	Broadis, Moir			3	6	5		7	11	9	8		10	4		2						1						
20	20	Darlington	3-4	2-0	7138	Lindsay(2), Dougal	1		3	6	5	4		10	9	8	11	7			2												
21	26	Tranmere	3-0	1-0	10999	Broadis(2), Walshaw	1		3	6	5		7	10		8	11		4		2	9											
22	27	TRANMERE	4-3	1-3	12084	Lindsay(2), Iceton, Dougal	1		3	6	5	4	7		9	8	11				2	10											
23	1 Jan	MANSFIELD	3-1	0-0	9997	Broadis(3)	1		3	6	5		7		9	8	11		4		2	10											
24	3	GATESHEAD	1-1	0-0	14771	Lindsay	1		3	6	5		7		9	8	11		4		2	10											
25	10	LINCOLN	2-5	1-2	14068	Lindsay, Walshaw	1		3	6	5		7		9	8	11		4		2	10											
26	17	Hartlepools	1-1	1-1	7522	Lindsay	1	2		6	5			8	9		11	7	4	10						3							
27	24	HULL	0-0	0-0	17339			2	3	6	5			7	9	8	11		4	10					1								
28	31	ROTHERHAM	0-3	0-2	14344			2	3		5			7	9	8	11	6	4	10					1								
29	7 Feb	Stockport	3-2	1-1	11135	Broadis(2), Iceton		2	3		5			10	9	8	11	7	4					6	1								
30	14	Crewe	2-0	2-0	7456	Broadis, Iceton		2	3					10	9	8	11	5	7					6	1							4	
31	21	CHESTER	2-0	1-0	11720	Hayton, Iceton		2	3	4				10	9	8	11	5	7					6	1								
32	28	BRADFORD	1-2	0-1	13971	Lindsay		2	3	4				10	9	8	11	5						6	1	7							
33	6 Mar	Barrow	0-2	0-0	10890			2	3	4				9	10	11	8				5			6	1								
34	13	WREXHAM	1-2	1-1	11148	Moir		2	3	6	5		9	10			11		4			8			1	7							
35	20	Halifax	1-2	0-1	9802	Dougal		2	3	4	5		7	8	9		11				10	6			1								
36	26	OLDHAM	4-1	2-0	14026	Dougal(3), Broadis	1	2	3	6				10	9	8	11	7	4											5			
37	27	ROCHDALE	5-0	3-0	10912	Connor(3), Iceton, O.G.		2	3	6	5			10	8	11	9		4	7					1								
38	29	Oldham	1-2	1-1	11136	Burke(pen)		2	3	6	5			10		11	9	8	4	7					1								
39	3 Apr	New Brighton	3-1	1-1	3935	Walshaw(2), Iceton		2	3	6	5			10			11	7	4			8			1								9
40	10	SOUTHPORT	2-3	2-2	9801	Connor, O.G.		2	3	6	5				9		11	10	4			8			1	7							
41	17	Lincoln	0-3	0-0	15337			2	3	6	5		7		9	8	11		4			10			1								
42	1 May	Hull	1-3	0-2	25123	Broadis		2	3	6	5			10	9	8	11		4						1	7							

F.A. CUP

	Date	Opposition	Res.	H.T.	Att.	Goalscorers	Jones	Hutton	Burke	Wightman	Seed	Ross G.	Moir	Dougal	Lindsay	Broadis	Iceton	Connor	Ford	Hayton	Monaghan
1R	29 Nov	Barrow	2-3	2-1	14801	Broadis, Lindsay	1		3	6	5			10	9	8	11	7	4		2

Final League Table

		Pl	Home					Away					F.	A.	Pts
			W	D	L	F	A	W	D	L	F	A			
1	Lincoln City	42	14	3	4	47	18	12	5	4	34	22	81	40	60
2	Rotherham United	42	15	4	2	56	18	10	5	6	39	31	95	49	59
3	Wrexham	42	14	3	4	49	23	7	5	9	25	31	74	54	50
4	Gateshead	42	11	5	5	48	28	8	6	7	27	29	75	57	49
5	Hull City	42	12	5	4	38	21	6	6	9	21	27	59	48	47
6	Accrington Stanley	42	13	1	7	36	24	7	5	9	26	35	62	59	46
7	Barrow	42	9	4	8	24	19	7	9	5	25	21	49	40	45
8	Mansfield Town	42	11	4	6	37	24	6	7	8	20	27	57	51	45
9	Carlisle United	42	10	4	7	50	35	8	3	10	38	42	88	77	43
10	Crewe Alexandra	42	12	4	5	41	24	6	3	12	20	39	61	63	43
11	Oldham Athletic	42	6	10	5	25	25	8	3	10	38	39	63	64	41
12	Rochdale	42	12	4	5	32	23	3	7	11	16	49	48	72	41
13	York City	42	8	7	6	38	25	5	7	9	27	35	65	60	40
14	Bradford City	42	10	4	7	38	27	5	6	10	27	39	65	66	40
15	Southport	42	10	4	7	34	27	4	7	10	26	36	60	63	39
16	Darlington	42	7	8	6	30	31	6	5	10	24	39	54	70	39
17	Stockport County	42	9	6	6	42	28	4	6	11	21	39	63	67	38
18	Tranmere Rovers	42	10	1	10	30	28	6	3	12	24	44	54	72	36
19	Hartlepools United	42	10	6	5	34	23	4	2	15	17	50	51	73	36
20	Chester	42	11	6	4	44	25	2	3	16	20	42	64	67	35
21	Halifax Town	42	4	10	7	25	27	3	3	15	18	49	43	76	27
22	New Brighton	42	5	6	10	20	28	3	3	15	18	53	38	81	25

- 1947/48 Season -

(unnamed team group)

- 1948/49 Season -

Carlisle United's team which beat Chester on Saturday. Left to right:—Back row: Monaghan, Seed, Sweeney, Burke, Horton, Stokoe. Front row: Collins, Broadis, Lindsay, Dougal, Iceton.

SEASON 1948/49

DIVISION 3 NORTH

No.	Date	Opposition	Res.	H.T	Att.	Goalscorers	Sweeney	Monaghan	Burke	Horton	Stokoe	Seed	Collins	Dougal	Lindsay	Broadis	Iceton	Gordon	Twentyman	Simpson	Turner	McClaren	Maxfield	Hayton	Hutton	Barkas	McCaig	Tagg	Walshaw	Yates	Kenyon	Coupe
1	21 Aug	CHESTER	2-1	1-1	11941	Lindsay, Dougal	1	2	3	4	6	5	7	10	9	8	11															
2	25	New Brighton	0-2	0-1	7178		1	2	3	8	6	5	7	11	9	10				4												
3	28	Southport	2-2	0-2	8935	Broadis, Burke(pen)	1		3	4	6	2	7	10	9	8		11		5												
4	2 Sep	NEW BRIGHTON	2-2	1-1	13216	Broadis, Maxfield	1		3	4	6	2		10	9	8				5			11			7						
5	4	CRWEE	6-2	2-0	14020	Gordon(3),Maxfield,Broadis,Dougal	1		3	4	6	2		10		8		9		5			11			7						
6	7	Rochdale	0-1	0-1	8343		1		3	4	6	2		10		8		9		5			11			7						
7	11	York	0-6	0-3	8041		1		3	4		2		10		8		9		5	11		6			7						
8	16	ROCHDALE	1-1	0-0	12539	Walshaw	1		3	4	6					8		9		5	11					2		7	10			
9	18	STOCKPORT	2-1	0-1	12701	Broadis(2)	1		3	4	6		7	10		8				5	11					2			9			
10	25	Doncaster	0-2	0-1	11934		1		3	4	6		7	10		8				5	11					2			9			
11	2 Oct	Gateshead	0-3	0-1	11674		1		3	4	6		7	10		8				5	11					2			9			
12	9	BRADFORD C.	3-2	1-1	11349	Turner, Broadis, Burke(pen)	1		3		6	10	5	7		8			4		11	9				2						
13	16	Halifax	4-3	2-2	11544	Broadis(2), Lindsay, Turner	1		3		6	10	5	7	9	8			4		11					2						
14	23	WREXHAM	3-2	0-1	11640	Collins(2), Broadis	1		3	10		5	7			8	9		6	4	11					2						
15	30	Barrow	0-0	0-0	10597		1		3		6	10	5	7	9	8				4	11					2						
16	6 Nov	MANSFIELD	3-1	1-0	13726	Collins, Broadis, Yates	1		3		6		5	7		8			4				11			2			10	9		
17	13	Tranmere	1-2	0-1	5850	Broadis	1		3		6		5	7		8			4				11			2			10	9		
18	20	OLDHAM	2-0	0-0	11036	Broadis, Tagg	1		3		6		5	7		8			4							2		10		9		
19	4 Dec	ROTHERHAM	1-8	1-3	14639	Iceton	1		3		6		5	7		8	11		4							2			10	9		
20	18	Chester	1-2	1-1	4628	O.G.	1	2	3	4			7			8	11	6		5									10	9		
21	25	Darlington	2-2	2-1	9317	Yates, Burke(pen)	1		3	4			5				11	6	2	7					8				10	9		
22	27	DARLINGTON	0-2	0-0	13587		1		3	4			5				11	6	2	7					8				10	9		
23	1 Jan	SOUTHPORT	4-2	2-1	9496	Yates(2), Walshaw, O.G.			3	4		5				8	11	6	2			1	7						10	9		
24	15	Crewe	0-3	0-1	4631				3	7						8	11	6		5		1				2		4	10	9		
25	22	YORK	3-3	2-2	9035	Yates(2,1pen), Broadis			3	4		5				8	11	6	2			1	7						10	9		
26	29	Accrington	1-2	1-1	7844	Burke(pen)			3	4		5				8	11	6	2			1	7						10	9		
27	5 Feb	Stockport	0-2	0-0	9384				3	4		5				8		9	6	2		1		11	7				10			
28	19	DONCASTER	3-0	2-0	11934	Yates, Barkas, Walshaw			3	4		5				8			6	2		1	7			10			11	9		
29	26	GATESHEAD	2-1	1-0	10375	Yates, Walshaw			3	4		5				8			6	2		1	7			10			11	9		
30	5 Mar	Bradford C.	2-1	1-1	5627	Yates, Burke(pen)			3	4		5				8			6	2		1	7			10			11	9		
31	12	HALIFAX	0-0	0-0	9734					4		5				8			6	2	11	1	7						10	9		3
32	19	Wrexham	0-4	0-3	7340					4		5				8			6	2	7	1							10	9		3
33	23	Hull	0-3	0-0	36864				3	4	6	5						9	2	7		1							10	11		
34	26	BARROW	2-0	2-0	8093	Walshaw(2)			3	4	6	5						9	2	7		1		8					10	11		
35	2 Apr	Mansfield	0-2	0-1	8615				3	4	6	5				8		9	2	7		1							10	11		
36	9	TRANMERE	2-2	1-1	7014	Walshaw, Turner			3	4	6	5				8		9	2	7		1							10	11		
37	15	Hartlepools	0-1	0-1	8874				3	4	6	5				9				2	7	1	11						10			
38	16	Oldham	0-1	0-0	17915				3	4		5				9			6	2	7	1	11	8					10			
39	18	HARTLEPOOLS	0-0	0-0	7055			2	3	4					9		8	6		7		1	11						10		5	
40	23	ACCRINGTON	4-1	2-1	6613	Barkas(3), Lindsay		2	3	4					9	8		6	5	7		1				10				11		
41	30	Rotherham	1-1	0-1	9085	Barkas		2		4	6				9	8		5	3	7		1				10				11		
42	7 Mar	HULL	1-1	1-1	15519	Walshaw		2		4	6				9	8		5	3			1	7						10	11		

F.A. CUP

No.	Date	Opposition	Res.	H.T	Att.	Goalscorers	Sweeney	Monaghan	Burke	Horton	Stokoe	Seed	Collins	Dougal	Lindsay	Broadis	Iceton	Gordon	Twentyman	Simpson	Turner	McClaren	Maxfield	Hayton	Hutton	Barkas	McCaig	Tagg	Walshaw	Yates	Kenyon	Coupe
1R	27 Nov	New Brighton	0-1	0-1	3496		1		3		6		5	7		8	11		4							2			10	9		

Final League Table

		Pl.	Home					Away					F.	A.	Pts
			W	D	L	F	A	W	D	L	F	A			
1	Hull City	42	17	1	3	65	14	10	10	1	28	14	93	28	65
2	Rotherham United	42	16	4	1	47	17	12	2	7	43	29	90	46	62
3	Doncaster Rovers	42	10	8	3	26	12	10	2	9	27	28	53	40	50
4	Darlington	42	10	3	8	42	36	10	3	8	41	38	83	74	46
5	Gateshead	42	10	6	5	41	28	6	7	8	28	30	69	58	45
6	Oldham Athletic	42	12	4	5	49	28	6	5	10	26	39	75	67	45
7	Rochdale	42	14	3	4	37	16	4	6	11	18	37	55	53	45
8	Stockport County	42	13	5	3	44	16	3	6	12	17	40	61	56	43
9	Wrexham	42	12	6	3	35	22	5	3	13	21	40	56	62	43
10	Mansfield Town	42	13	6	2	39	15	1	8	12	13	33	52	48	42
11	Tranmere Rovers	42	8	9	4	23	19	5	6	10	23	38	46	57	41
12	Crewe Alexandra	42	13	4	4	31	18	3	5	13	21	56	52	74	41
13	Barrow	42	10	8	3	27	13	4	4	13	14	35	41	48	40
14	York City	42	11	3	7	49	28	4	6	11	25	46	74	74	39
15	Carlisle United	42	12	7	2	46	32	2	4	15	14	45	60	77	39
16	Hartlepools United	42	10	5	6	34	25	4	5	12	11	33	45	58	38
17	New Brighton	42	10	4	7	25	19	4	4	13	21	39	46	58	36
18	Chester	42	10	7	4	36	19	1	6	14	21	37	57	56	35
19	Halifax Town	42	8	4	9	26	27	4	7	10	19	35	45	62	35
20	Accrington Stanley	42	11	4	6	39	23	1	6	14	16	41	55	64	34
21	Southport	42	6	5	10	24	29	5	4	12	21	35	45	64	31
22	Bradford City	42	7	6	8	29	31	3	3	15	19	46	48	77	29

SEASON 1949/50
DIVISION 3 NORTH

No.	Date	Opposition	Res.	H.T.	Att.	Goalscorers	McClaren	Buchanan	Buchan	Twentyman	Stokoe	Horton	Turner	Maxfield	Lindsay	Dick	Hogan	Hill	Iceton	Hayton	Billingham	Carruthers J.	Caton	McClure	McIntosh	Kelly	Fairweather	Hitchon	Monaghan	Seed	Rooke	Scott	Walshaw	Coure
1	20 Aug	ACCRINGTON	2-1	1-1	13747	Dick, Walshaw	1	3	4	5	6	2	11	7	9	8																	10	
2	24	Wrexham	1-1	0-0	13506	Maxfield	1	3	4	5	6	2	11	7	9	8																	10	
3	27	Mansfield	1-4	1-2	15165	Dick(pen)	1	3	4	5	6	2	11	7	9	8																	10	
4	1 Sep	WREXHAM	1-0	1-0	15170	Lindsay	1	3	4	5	6	2			8	10	7				9												11	
5	3	STOCKPORT	2-0	1-0	14670	Hogan, Billingham	1	3	4	5	6	2			8	10	7				9												11	
6	6	Tranmere	0-0	0-0	9338		1	3	4	5	6	2			8	10	7				9												11	
7	10	ROTHERHAM	3-1	3-1	14621	Billingham, Dick, O.G.	1	3	4	5	6	2			8	10	7				9												11	
8	17	Lincoln	1-2	0-2	11166	Turner	1	3	4	5	6	2	11			8	7				9												10	
9	24	BARROW	2-0	1-0	14164	Walshaw, Turner	1	3	4	5	6	2	11			8	7				9												10	
10	1 Oct	Crewe	1-2	1-2	9777	Billingham	1		4	5	6	2	11			10	8	7			9		3											
11	8	Doncaster	0-0	0-0	17342		1		4	5	6	2	11			10	8	7			9		3											
12	15	GATESHEAD	4-2	2-1	16578	Billingham(2), Turner, Dick	1		4		6	2	11		8	10	7				9		3							5				
13	22	Hartlepool	5-1	3-0	10145	Turner(2), Billingham, Dick, Hogan	1		4		6	2	11		8	10	7				9		3							5				
14	29	DARLINGTON	0-1	0-0	14572		1		4		6	2	11		8	10					9		3							5		7		
15	5 Nov	New Brighton	2-3	2-2	4978	Dick, Walshaw	1		4		6	2	11			10	7				9		3							5			8	
16	12	HALIFAX	0-2	0-1	7347		1		4		6				8	10	7				9		3					2		5			11	
17	19	Rochdale	0-1	0-1	7323		1		4		6	2	11		8		7				9		3							5			10	
18	3 Dec	Chester	4-2		4494	Billingham(2), Hogan, Dick	1		4		6	2	11		8	10	7			5	9		3											
19	17	Accrington	1-1	1-0	2802	Hogan(pen)	1		4		6	2	11		8	10	7			5	9		3											
20	24	MANSFIELD	1-1	1-0	12495	Lindsay	1		4		6	2	11		8	10	7			5	9		3											
21	26	York	1-1	0-1	11648	Stokoe	1		4		6	2	11		8	10	7			5	9		3											
22	27	YORK	4-3	2-3	14298	Dick(3), Billingham	1		4		6	2	11		8	10	7			5	9		3											
23	31	Stockport	0-2	0-0	13026		1		4		6	2	11		8	10	7			5	9		3											
24	14 Jan	Rotherham	1-1	1-0	12893	Iceton	1		4	5	6				9	10	7		11		8		3	2										
25	21	LINCOLN	0-2	0-1	12892		1		4	5	6				9	10	7		11		8		3	2										
26	28	BRADFORD C.	3-0	1-0	9094	Billingham(2), Turner	1		4	5	6		7		9	10			11		8		3	2										
27	4 Feb	Barrow	3-1	1-0	4243	Dick(2,1pen), Hogan	1		4	5	6				8	10	7				9		3	2								11		
28	11	SOUTHPORT	3-3	2-2	10192	Dick(2), Billingham	1		4	5	6				8	10	7				9		3	2		11								
29	18	CREWE	2-2	2-1	10102	Turner(2)	1		4	5	6		7		8	10					9		3	2		11								
30	25	ROCHDALE	2-0	2-0	9525	Billingham(2)				5					8	10	7			4	9		3		2	11	1							6
31	4 Mar	Bradford C.	2-3	1-1	12903	Billingham, Dick			4	5					8	10	7				9		3		2	11	1							6
32	11	HARTLEPOOL	2-1	0-0	8219	Lindsay(2)	1			5	6				8	10	7				9		3		2	11			4					
33	18	Darlington	1-1	0-0	5174	Lindsay	1		4	5					8	10	7				9		3		2	11								6
34	25	NEW BRIGHTON	0-0	0-0	8451		1		4	5					8	10	7				9		3		2	11								6
35	1 Apr	Halifax	1-1	0-1	4179	Billingham	1			5					8	10	7		6	4	9		3		2	11								
36	7	OLDHAM	3-0	1-0	10490	Turner, Lindsay, Kelly	1			5			7		8	10			6	4	9		3		2	11								
37	8	DONCASTER	0-0	0-0	11503		1			5					8	10	7		6	4	9		3		2	11								
38	10	Oldham	1-1	1-1	9060	Hogan	1			5					8	10	7		6	4	9		3		2	11								
39	15	Gateshead	1-2	1-1	12067	Lindsay	1			5					8	10	7		6	4	9		3		2	11								
40	22	CHESTER	5-1	2-1	9559	Dick(2,1pen), Lindsay, Caton, Kelly	1			5					8	9	7		6	4			3	10	2	11								
41	29	Southport	2-1	2-0	2360	Dick(2)	1			5					8	9	7		6	4			3	10	2	11								
42	6 May	YORK	0-0	0-0	14298		1			5					8	9	7		6	4			3	10	2	11								

F.A. CUP

No.	Date	Opposition	Res.	H.T.	Att.	Goalscorers	McClaren	Buchanan	Buchan	Twentyman	Stokoe	Horton	Turner	Maxfield	Lindsay	Dick	Hogan	Hill	Iceton	Hayton	Billingham	Carruthers J.	Caton	McClure	McIntosh	Kelly	Fairweather	Hitchon	Monaghan	Seed	Rooke	Scott	Walshaw	Coure
1R	26 Nov	LINCOLN C.	1-0	1-0	11372	Dick	1		4		6	2	11		8	10	7			5	9		3											
2R	10 Dec	SWINDON	2-0	1-0	18604	Lindsay(2)	1		4		6	2	11		8	10	7			5	9		3											
3R	7 Jan	LEEDS	2-5	1-4	22832	Lindsay, Dick	1		4		6	2	11		8	10	7			5	9		3											

Final League Table

		Pl	Home W	D	L	F	A	Away W	D	L	F	A	F.	A.	Pts
1	Doncaster Rovers	42	9	9	3	30	15	10	8	3	36	23	66	38	55
2	Gateshead	42	13	5	3	51	23	10	2	9	36	31	87	54	53
3	Rochdale	42	15	3	3	42	13	6	6	9	26	28	68	41	51
4	Lincoln City	42	14	5	2	35	9	7	4	10	25	30	60	39	51
5	Tranmere Rovers	42	15	3	3	35	21	4	8	9	16	27	51	48	49
6	Rotherham United	42	10	6	5	46	28	9	4	8	34	31	80	59	48
7	Crewe Alexandra	42	10	6	5	38	27	7	8	6	30	28	68	55	48
8	Mansfield Town	42	12	4	5	37	20	6	8	7	29	34	66	54	48
9	Carlisle United	42	12	6	3	39	20	4	9	8	29	31	68	51	47
10	Stockport County	42	14	2	5	33	21	5	5	11	22	31	55	52	45
11	Oldham Athletic	42	10	4	7	32	31	6	7	8	26	32	58	63	43
12	Chester	42	12	3	6	47	33	5	3	13	23	46	70	79	40
13	Accrington Stanley	42	12	5	4	41	21	4	2	15	16	41	57	62	39
14	New Brighton	42	10	5	6	27	25	4	5	12	18	38	45	63	38
15	Barrow	42	9	6	6	27	20	5	3	13	20	33	47	53	37
16	Southport	42	7	10	4	29	26	5	3	13	22	45	51	71	37
17	Darlington	42	9	8	4	35	27	2	5	14	21	42	56	69	35
18	Hartlepools United	42	10	3	8	37	35	4	2	15	15	44	52	79	33
19	Bradford City	42	11	1	9	38	32	1	7	13	23	44	61	76	32
20	Wrexham	42	8	7	6	24	17	2	5	14	15	37	39	54	32
21	Halifax Town	42	9	5	7	35	31	3	3	15	23	54	58	85	32
22	York City	42	6	7	8	29	33	3	6	12	23	37	52	70	31

- 1949/50 Season -

(Back): Buchan, Twentyman, McLaren, Stokoe, Buchanan, Horton
(Front): Hogan, Lindsay, Billingham, Dick, Walshaw

- 1950/51 Season -

(Back): Billingham, McIntosh, Twentyman, McLaren, Caton, Stokoe
(Front): Hogan, Turner, Jackson, Dick, Kelly

SEASON 1950/51

DIVISION 3 NORTH

No.	Date	Opposition	Res.	H.T.	Att.	Goalscorers	McLaren	McIntosh	Coupe	Twentyman	Stokoe	Caton	Dick	Hogan	Jackson	Billingham	Kelly	Turner	Brown	Duffett	Hayton	Hill	Johnson	Kinlock	Lindsay	Maxfield	McCue	Scott	Waters	Miller
1	19 Aug	Scunthorpe	0-1	0-0	9288		1	2		5	3	6	10	7	9	4	11	8												
2	24	GATESHEAD	3-0	1-0	12016	Hogan, Jackson, Caton	1	2	3	5		11	10	7	9	4				8		6								
3	26	TRANMERE	3-1	3-1	13640	Hogan, Duffett, Caton	1	2	3	5		11	10	7	9	4				8		6								
4	28	Gateshead	3-4	1-0	14896	Dick(2), Billingham	1		3	5		11	10	7	9	4				8		6						2		
5	2 Sep	Bradford	2-0	0-0	16655	Hogan(2)	1		3	5			10	8	7	9	4	11				6						2		
6	7	HARTLEPOOL	1-0	0-0	14780	Kelly	1		3	5			10	8	7	9	4	11				6						2		
7	9	OLDHAM	1-0	0-0	13838	Lindsay	1		3	5			10	8	7	4		11				6			9			2		
8	11	Hartlepool	3-3	2-2	8654	Dick(2,1pen), Turner	1		3	5		11	10	7		4		8				6			9			2		
9	16	Wrexham	1-2	1-1	10334	Lindsay	1		3	5		11	10	7		4		8				6			9			2		
10	23	SCUNTHORPE	3-1	2-1	11961	Jackson, Dick, Turner	1		3			6	10	7	9		5	11		8	4							2		
11	30	Mansfield	1-2	1-0	6686	Diffett	1		3			6	10	7	9		5	11		8	4							2		
12	7 Oct	Chester	1-1	0-0	7671	Caton	1		3		6	10		7		4		8					5		9	11		2		
13	14	SHREWSBURY	2-2	1-1	10843	Caton(2,1pen)	1		3		6	10		7		4	11	8					5		9					3
14	21	Bradford C.	4-2	2-0	16481	McCue, Brown, Hogan, Caton	1	2	3	5		10		7		4		8	9			6					11			
15	28	ROCHDALE	4-0	2-0	13295	McCue(2), Turner, Brown	1	2	3	5		10		7		4		8	9			6					11			
16	4 Nov	Crewe	1-1	1-0	8782	Brown	1	2	3	5		10				4		8	9			6				7	11			
17	11	NEW BRIGHTON	1-0	0-0	12629	Brown	1	2	3	5		10		7		4		8	9			6					11			
18	18	Lincoln	1-1	0-0	9480	McCue	1	2	3	5		10		7		4		8				6			9		11			
19	2 Dec	Stockport	2-1	1-1	9288	Lindsay, McCue	1	2	3	5		10		7				8						4	9		11		6	
20	16	SOUTHPORT	3-1	2-0	10360	Lindsay(2), McCue	1	2	3	5				7				8					10	4	9		11		6	
21	23	Tranmere	2-2	2-0	8208	Turner	1	2	3	5				7		10		8						4	9		11		6	
22	25	ACCRINGTON	3-1	2-1	13943	Lindsay(2), McCue	1	2	3	5				7		10		8						4	9		11		6	
23	26	Accrington	4-0	2-0	4947	McCue(2), Turner, Hogan	1		3					7		10		8		6				4	9		11	2	5	
24	30	BRADFORD	1-0	0-0	10656	Turner	1	2	3					7		10		8		6				4	9		11		5	
25	1 Jan	BARROW	1-1	1-1	12512	McCue	1	2	3					7		10		8		6				4	9		11		5	
26	13	Oldham	1-1	0-1	14397	Turner	1	2	3					7		10	9	8		6				4			11		5	
27	20	WREXHAM	0-2	0-2	10860		1	2	3					7		10	9	11	8	6				4					5	
28	27	York	1-1	0-0	7677	Hogan	1	2	3					7		10		8						4	9		11		6	
29	3 Feb	Scunthorpe	1-1	0-0	9288	Jackson	1	2	3	5				7		10	4				9				8		11		6	
30	10	Barrow	2-1	0-1	11270	Brown(2)	1	2	3	5	4			7		10					9				8		11		6	
31	17	MANSFIELD	2-0	1-0	10734	Lindsay, Jackson	1	2	3		4			7		10	8				5				9		11		6	
32	24	CHESTER	2-1	1-0	11012	Lindsay, Jackson	1	2	3		4			7		10	8				5				9		11		6	
33	3 Mar	Shrewsbury	3-0	1-0	9795	Hogan, Caton, Jackson	1	2		5	4	8		7		10					9						11	3	6	
34	10	BRADFORD C.	2-1	0-1	11297	Hogan, Brown	1	2		5	4	8		7		10					9						11	3	6	
35	17	Rochdale	1-4	1-2	6190	Jackson	1	2		5	4	10		7	8						9						11	3	6	
36	23	ROTHERHAM	0-0	0-0	20454		1	2		5	4			7		10		8			9						11	3	6	
37	24	CREWE	2-1	0-0	10508	Hogan(2)	1	2		5	4			7		10		8			9						11	3	6	
38	26	Rotherham	0-3	0-1	17309		1	2		5	4	10		7				8			9						11	3	6	
39	31	New Brighton	1-0	0-2	2668	McCue	1	2			4	6		7		10		8			9						11	3	5	
40	7 Apr	LINCOLN	2-0	1-0	8859	Jackson, Turner	1	2				6		7		10		8			9						11	3	4	
41	14	Darlington	0-1	1-0	4026		1	2				6		7		10		8			5	9					11	3	4	
42	19	DARLINGTON	2-1	0-0	9365	Turner, Brown	1		2			6					8	10	7	9	5						11	3	4	
43	21	STOCKPORT	2-2	1-1	10154	Jackson, Brown	1		2			6					8	10	7	9	5						11	3	4	
44	26	HALIFAX	1-0	0-0	7954	Turner	1	2			4	6	10	7				8									11	3	5	
45	28	Halifax	0-1	0-0	4720		1	2			4	6	10					8	7			9					11	3	5	
46	3 Mar	YORK	3-2	2-1	7335	Turner(2), Scott	1	2				6		7		10		8		9				4			11	3	5	

F.A. CUP

			Res.	H.T.	Att.	Goalscorers	McLaren	McIntosh	Coupe	Twentyman	Stokoe	Caton	Dick	Hogan	Jackson	Billingham	Kelly	Turner	Brown	Duffett	Hayton	Hill	Johnson	Kinlock	Lindsay	Maxfield	McCue	Scott	Waters	Miller
1R	25 Nov	BARROW	2-1	1-1	13273	McCue, Turner	1	2	3	5		10		7		4		8	9			6					11			
2R	9 Dec	Southport	3-1	1-1	8193	Turner(2), Lindsay	1	2	3	5		10		7				8				6		4	9		11			
3R	6 Jan	Arsenal	0-0	0-0	57932		1	2	3	5				7		10	9	8						4			11		6	
3Rr	11	ARSENAL	1-4	0-2	20900	McCue	1	2	3	5				7		10	9	8						4			11		6	

Final League Table

		Pl.	Home					Away					F.	A.	Pts
			W	D	L	F	A	W	D	L	F	A			
1	Rotherham United	46	16	3	4	55	16	15	6	2	48	25	103	41	71
2	Mansfield Town	46	17	6	0	54	19	9	6	8	24	29	78	48	64
3	Carlisle United	46	18	4	1	44	17	7	8	8	35	33	79	50	62
4	Tranmere Rovers	46	15	5	3	51	26	9	6	8	32	36	83	62	59
5	Lincoln City	46	18	1	4	62	23	7	7	9	27	35	89	58	58
6	Bradford Park Ave.	46	15	3	5	46	23	8	5	10	44	49	90	72	54
7	Bradford City	46	13	4	6	55	30	8	6	9	35	33	90	63	52
8	Gateshead	46	17	1	5	60	21	4	7	12	24	41	84	62	50
9	Crewe Alexandra	46	11	5	7	38	26	8	5	10	23	34	61	60	48
10	Stockport County	46	15	3	5	45	26	5	5	13	18	37	63	63	48
11	Rochdale	46	11	6	6	38	18	6	5	12	31	44	69	62	45
12	Scunthorpe United	46	10	12	1	32	9	3	6	14	26	48	58	57	44
13	Chester	46	11	6	6	42	30	6	3	14	20	34	62	64	43
14	Wrexham	46	12	6	5	37	28	3	6	14	18	43	55	71	42
15	Oldham Athletic	46	10	5	8	47	36	6	3	14	26	37	73	73	40
16	Hartlepools United	46	14	5	4	55	26	2	2	19	9	40	64	66	39
17	York City	46	7	12	4	37	24	5	3	15	29	53	66	77	39
18	Darlington	46	10	8	5	35	29	3	5	15	24	48	59	77	39
19	Barrow	46	12	3	8	38	27	4	3	16	13	49	51	76	38
20	Shrewsbury Town	46	11	3	9	38	30	4	4	15	15	44	43	74	37
21	Southport	46	9	4	10	29	25	4	6	13	27	47	56	72	36
22	Halifax Town	46	11	6	6	36	24	0	6	17	14	45	50	69	34
23	Accrington Stanley	46	10	4	9	28	29	1	6	16	14	72	42	101	32
24	New Brighton	46	7	6	10	22	32	4	2	17	18	58	40	90	30

SEASON 1951/52

DIVISION 3 NORTH

No.	Date	Opposition	Res.	H.T.	Att.	Goalscorers	McClaren	McIntosh	Scott	Waters	Twentyman	Stokoe	Hogan	Jackson	Ashman	Caton	Kelly	Whitehouse	Thompson R.	Steen	Purvis	Kinloch	Johnson	Hill	Duffett	Brown
1	18 Aug	Rochdale	4-0	1-0	6026	Ashman(3), Hogan	1	2	3	4	5	6	7	8	9	10	11									
2	23	HALIFAX	2-2	1-1	14545	Ashman(2)	1	2	3	4		6	7	8	9	10	11							5		
3	25	ACCRINGTON	4-1	3-0	12015	Ashman(2), Caton(2)	1	2	3	4	5	6	7	8	9	10	11									
4	1 Sep	Crewe	1-1	0-0	6339	Jackson	1	2	3	4	5	6	7	10	9		11									8
5	6	BRADFORD P.A.	1-0	0-0	14793	Kelly	1	2	3	4	5	6	7	8	9	10	11									
6	8	Stockport	1-1	0-1	11914	Duffett	1	2		5		6	7	8	9		11			3	4				10	
7	10	Halifax	2-1	0-0	8287	Duffett, Kelly	1	2		5		6	7	8	9		11			3	4				10	
8	15	WORKINGTON	0-1	0-1	14629		1	2		5		6	7	8	9	10	11			3	4					
9	17	Bradford P.A.	1-0	0-0	17652	Ashman	1	2		5		6	7	8	9	10	11			3	4					
10	22	Barrow	1-0	1-0	11901	Hogan	1	2	3	5		6	7	8	9	10	11				4					
11	29	GRIMSBY	1-2	0-2	14144	Jackson	1	2	3	5		6	7	8	9	10	11				4					
12	6 Oct	DARLINGTON	1-1	0-0	11240	Scott	1	2	3	4	5	6	7	8	9	10	11									
13	13	Oldham	0-2	0-1	22315		1	2	3	4	5		7	8	9	6	11								10	
14	20	HARTLEPOOL	2-1	2-1	8893	Jackson(2)	1	2	3	4	5	6	7	8	9										10	
15	27	Bradford C.	2-1	1-0	13701	Whitehouse(2)	1	2	3		5	6	7	10	9			11		8	4					
16	3 Nov	YORK	2-1	2-0	10662	Whitehouse(2)	1	2	3		5		7	10	9	6		11		8	4					
17	10	Chester	2-4	0-2	6082	Ashman, Kelly	1	2	3	4	5		7	10	9			11		8						
18	17	LINCOLN	1-4	0-3	11099	Hogan	1	2	3	4	5	6	7	10	9		11									
19	1 Dec	TRANMERE	1-0	1-0	8727	Whitehouse	1	2	3		5	6	7		9			11		8	4				10	
20	8	Southport	1-2	1-1	3662	McIntosh(pen)	1	2	3		5	6	7		9			11		8	4				10	
21	22	Accrington	2-0	1-0	3873	Whitehouse, Ashman	1	2	3		5	6	7		9			8			11	4			10	
22	25	Gateshead	1-1	0-1	8848	Whitehouse	1	2	3		5	6	7		9			8			11	4			10	
23	26	GATESHEAD	0-0	0-0	13021		1	2	3		5	6	7		9			8			11	4			10	
24	29	CREWE	2-0	1-0	10406	Hogan(2)	1	2	3		5	6	7		9	10		8			11	4				
25	1 Jan	CHESTERFIELD	2-3	1-0	10390	Ashman, Caton	1	2	3		5	6	7		9	10		8			11	4				
26	5	STOCKPORT	2-1	1-0	10744	Whitehouse, Steen	1	2	3	5		6	7		9	10		8			11	4				
27	12	Mansfield	2-1	1-0	8497	Whitehouse, Caton	1	2	3	5		6	7		9	10		8			11	4				
28	19	Workington	2-1	0-1	17165	Ashman(2)	1	2	3	5		6	7		9	10		8			11	4				
29	26	BARROW	0-1	0-0	9781		1	2	3	5		6	7		9	10		8			11	4				
30	2 Feb	MANSFIELD	0-0	0-0	8946		1	2	3	5		6	7		9	10		8			11	4				
31	9	Grimsby	1-4	0-2	16148	Twentyman	1	2	3	5	4	6	7	10	9			8			11					
32	16	Darlington	2-1	1-0	5881	Ashman, Steen	1	2	3	5		6	7	10	9			8	4		11					
33	23	Chesterfield	0-3	0-0	10331		1	2	3	5			7	10	9			8	4		11		6			
34	1 Mar	OLDHAM	3-3	1-0	9231	Whitehouse, Ashman(2)	1	2	3	5		6	7	10	9			8			11	4				
35	6	ROCHDALE	1-1	1-0	3978	Whitehouse	1	2	3	5		6	7	10	9			8			11	4				
36	8	Hartlepool	0-1	0-0	9233		1	2	3	5		6	7		9			8	4		11				10	
37	15	BRADFORD C.	1-3		8609	Scott	1	2	10	5	3	6	7		9				4		11			8		
38	22	York	0-0	0-0	7577		1	2	8	5	3	6	7		9				4		11				10	
39	29	CHESTER	0-0	0-0	4351		1	2	3	5		6	7		9	10			4		11			8		
40	5 Apr	Lincoln	2-2	0-2	12093	Ashman, Caton	1	2	3	5		6	7	8	9			11							10	
41	11	WREXHAM	2-0	1-0	8748	Ashman, Caton	1	2	3	5		6	7	8	9			11							10	
42	12	SCUNTHORPE	3-0	2-0	6398	Ashman, Caton, Jackson	1	2	3	5		6	7	8	9			11				4				
43	14	Wrexham	1-3	1-2	7056	Duffett	1	2	3	5		6	7	8	9			11				4				
44	19	Tranmere	2-3	0-1	5790	Ashman, Duffett	1	2	3	5	4	6	7	8	9			11							10	
45	24	Scunthorpe	1-1	1-0	7453	Thompson	1	2	3	5		6	7	8	9			11				4				
46	26	SOUTHPORT	0-2	0-1	6398		1	2	3	5		6	7	10	9			11		8	4					

F.A. CUP

No.	Date	Opposition	Res.	H.T.	Att.	Goalscorers	McClaren	McIntosh	Scott	Waters	Twentyman	Stokoe	Hogan	Jackson	Ashman	Caton	Kelly	Whitehouse	Thompson R.	Steen	Purvis	Kinloch	Johnson	Hill	Duffett	Brown
1R	24 Nov	Bradford C.	1-6	0-3	16706	Brown	1	2	3	4	5	6	7			10	11	8								9

Final League Table

		Pl.	Home					Away					F.	A.	Pts
			W	D	L	F	A	W	D	L	F	A			
1	Lincoln City	46	19	2	2	80	23	11	7	5	41	29	121	52	69
2	Grimsby Town	46	19	2	2	59	14	10	6	7	37	31	96	45	66
3	Stockport County	46	12	9	2	47	17	11	4	8	27	23	74	40	59
4	Oldham Athletic	46	19	2	2	65	22	5	7	11	25	39	90	61	57
5	Gateshead	46	14	7	2	41	17	7	4	12	25	32	66	49	53
6	Mansfield Town	46	17	3	3	50	23	5	5	13	23	37	73	60	52
7	Carlisle United	46	10	7	6	31	24	9	6	8	31	33	62	57	51
8	Bradford Park Ave.	46	13	6	4	51	28	6	6	11	23	36	74	64	50
9	Hartlepools United	46	17	3	3	47	19	4	5	14	24	46	71	65	50
10	York City	46	16	4	3	53	19	2	9	12	20	33	73	52	49
11	Tranmere Rovers	46	17	2	4	59	29	4	4	15	17	42	76	71	48
12	Barrow	46	13	5	5	33	19	4	7	12	24	42	57	61	46
13	Chesterfield	46	15	7	1	47	16	2	4	17	18	50	65	66	45
14	Scunthorpe United	46	10	11	2	39	23	4	5	14	26	51	65	74	44
15	Bradford City	46	12	5	6	40	32	4	5	14	21	36	61	68	42
16	Crewe Alexandra	46	12	6	5	42	28	5	2	16	21	54	63	82	42
17	Southport	46	12	6	5	36	22	3	5	15	17	49	53	71	41
18	Wrexham	46	14	5	4	41	22	1	4	18	22	51	63	73	39
19	Chester	46	13	4	6	46	30	2	5	16	26	55	72	85	39
20	Halifax Town	46	11	4	8	31	23	3	3	17	30	74	61	97	35
21	Rochdale	46	10	5	8	32	34	1	8	14	15	45	47	79	35
22	Accrington Stanley	46	6	8	9	30	34	4	4	15	31	58	61	92	32
23	Darlington	46	10	5	8	39	34	1	4	18	25	69	64	103	31
24	Workington	46	8	4	11	33	34	3	3	17	17	57	50	91	29

- 1951/52 Season -

(Back): McBain (Asst.Trainer), McIntosh, Scott, McLaren, Waters, Stokoe, Ford (Trainer)
(Back): Hogan, Jackson, Emery (Manager), Ashman, Caton, and kelly (Inset: Twentyman)

- 1952/53 Season -

(Back): McIntosh, Scott, MacLaren, Kinloch, Waters, Stokoe
(Front): Hogan, Ashman, Whitehouse, Jackson, Drury

SEASON 1952/53

DIVISION 3 NORTH

No.	Date	Opposition	Res.	H.T.	Att.	Goalscorers	McLaren	McIntosh	Scott	Thompson	Waters	Stokoe	Hogan	Ashman	Smith	Jackson	Drury	Bond	Duffett	Atkinson	Whitehouse	Harrison	Twentyman	Hill	Coupland	Johnston	Kinloch
1	23 Aug	Gateshead	0-2	0-0	11390		1	2	3	4	5	6	7	8	9	10	11										
2	27	Accrington	0-1	0-1	7117		1	2	3			6	7	8	9		11										
3	30	HARTLEPOOL	4-1	1-0	10876	Smith(2), Whitehouse, Ashman	1	2	3	4		6	7	8	9		11				10	5					
4	4 Sep	ACCRINGTON	4-4	2-2	10897	Whitehouse,Ashman,Smith,Drury	1	2	3	4		6	7	8	9		11				10	5					
5	6	Workington	1-1	0-1	14138	Ashman	1	2	3			6	7	8	9					11	10	5					4
6	11	DARLINGTON	4-2	2-1	9021	Whitehouse,Kinloch,Ashman,Hogan	1	2	3			6	7	8	9		11				10			5			4
7	13	Southport	0-2	0-1	5750		1	2	3			6	7	8	9		11				10	5					4
8	17	Darlington	0-0	0-0	5081		1	2	3			6	7	8	9		11				10			5			4
9	20	CREWE	1-2	0-1	8823	Smith	1	2				6	7	8	9		11				10	3	5				4
10	25	GRIMSBY	3-0	0-0	9528	McIntosh(pen), Whitehouse, Smith	1	2	3		5	6			9	10	11		7		8						4
11	27	Port Vale	0-0	0-0	10803		1	2	3		5	6			9	10	11		7		8						4
12	29	Stockport	0-3	0-2	3639		1	2	3	7	5	6			9	10	11				8						4
13	4 Oct	CHESTER	1-1	0-1	9421	Harrison	1	2	3		5	6			9	10	11				8	7					4
14	11	HALIFAX	1-2	1-2	7213	Smith	1	2	3		5	6			9	10	11				8	7					4
15	18	Mansfield	1-2	1-2	7500	Smith	1	2	3		4	6	7	10	9		11				8	5					
16	25	OLDHAM	0-0	0-0	10188		1	2	3		4	6	7	8	9		11				10	5					
17	1 Nov	Bradford P.A.	2-2	2-2	13834	Stokoe, Bond	1	2	3		4	6	7	8	9		11				10	5					
18	8	WREXHAM	1-0	1-0	9058	Ashman	1	2	3		4	6	7	8	9		11				10	5					
19	15	Barrow	0-0	0-0	6979		1	2	3		4	6	7	9	10		11				8	5					
20	29	York	0-1	0-1	6589		1	2	3		4	6		9	10		11				8	7	5				
21	6 Dec	WORKINGTON	3-1	0-1	9340	Ashman(2), Harrison	1	2	3		4	6		9			11				10	8	7	5			
22	13	Chesterfield	2-4	1-1	4991	Whitehouse(2)	1	2	3		4	6		9			11				10	8	7	5			
23	20	GATESHEAD	2-2	2-2	4465	Whitehouse, Duffett	1		3		4	6		9			11				10	8	7	5		2	
24	25	SCUNTHORPE	8-0	5-0	9518	Whitehouse(5),Ashman(2),Harrison	1		3		4	6		9			11				10	8	7	5		2	
25	27	Scunthorpe	2-1	1-1	7325	Whitehouse, Harrison	1		3		4	6		9			11				10	8	7	5		2	
26	1 Jan	STOCKPORT	2-1	2-0	8919	Harrison, Ashman	1		3		5	6		9			11				10	8	7			2	4
27	3	Hartlepool	0-1	0-0	10876		1		3		4	6		9			11				10	8	7	5		2	
28	10	ROCHDALE	5-0	2-0	7282	Whitehouse(4), Ashman	1		3		4	6		9			11				10	8	7	5		2	
29	24	SOUTHPORT	2-0	0-0	6425	Ashman(2)	1		3		4	6		9			11				10	8	7	5		2	
30	31	Rochdale	2-1	0-0	3447	Whitehouse, Ashman	1		3		4	6		9			11				10	8	7	5		2	
31	7 Feb	Crewe	2-2	1-1	7101	Twentyman, Ashman	1		3		4	6		9			11				10	8	7	5		2	
32	14	PORT VALE	2-0	2-0	10419	Harrison, Duffett	1		3		4	6		9			11				10	8	7	5		2	
33	21	Chester	2-1	2-0	5987	Harrison, Whitehouse	1		3		4	6		9			11				10	8	7	5		2	
34	28	Halifax	1-2	1-1	7635	Ashman	1		3		4	6		9			11				10	8	7	5		2	
35	7 Mar	MANSFIELD	1-0	1-0	8309	Bond	1		3		4	6		9			11	7			10	8		5		2	
36	12	TRANMERE	4-0	2-0	4069	Whitehouse,Atkinsn,Harrisn,Ashmn	1		3			6		9			11			10	8	7		5		2	4
37	14	Oldham	4-2	3-0	20397	Whitehouse(2), Harrison, Ashman	1		3			6		9				11			10	8	7	5		2	4
38	21	BRADFORD P.A.	1-3	1-1	8923	Whitehouse	1		3			6		9				11			10	8	7	5		2	4
39	28	Wrexham	0-3	0-2	10744		1		3			6		9				11			10	8	7	5		2	4
40	3 Apr	BRADFORD C.	4-4	2-3	8222	Whitehouse(2,1pen),Harrison,Drury	1				4			9			11				8	7		5	3	2	6
41	4	BARROW	0-0	0-0	6383		1					6		9		10	11				8	7		5	3	2	4
42	7	Bradford C.	2-7	0-2	12836	Whitehouse, Ashman	1		3		4	6		9		10	11				8	7		5		2	
43	11	Grimsby	3-2	2-2	10260	Whitehouse, Ashman(2)	1		3			6		9		10	11				8	7		5		2	4
44	18	YORK	1-1	1-0	4805	Drury	1		3			6		9		10	11				8	7		5		2	4
45	25	Tranmere	1-4	0-2	6155	Whitehouse	1		3			6		9			11				10	8	7	5		2	4
46	30	CHESTERFIELD	3-0	1-0	4258	Whitehouse, Ashman, Jackson	1	2	3			6		9		10	11				8	7		5			4

F.A. CUP

No.	Date	Opposition	Res.	H.T.	Att.	Goalscorers	McLaren	McIntosh	Scott	Thompson	Waters	Stokoe	Hogan	Ashman	Smith	Jackson	Drury	Bond	Duffett	Atkinson	Whitehouse	Harrison	Twentyman	Hill	Coupland	Johnston	Kinloch
1R	21 Nov	Scunthorpe	0-1	0-0	9028		1	2	3		4	6	7	9	10		11				8	5					

Final League Table

		Pl.	Home					Away					F.	A.	Pts
			W	D	L	F	A	W	D	L	F	A			
1	Oldham Athletic	46	15	4	4	48	21	7	11	5	29	24	77	45	59
2	Port Vale	46	13	9	1	41	10	7	9	7	26	25	67	35	58
3	Wrexham	46	18	3	2	59	24	6	5	12	27	42	86	66	56
4	York City	46	14	5	4	35	16	6	8	9	25	29	60	45	53
5	Grimsby Town	46	15	5	3	47	19	6	5	12	28	40	75	59	52
6	Southport	46	16	4	3	42	18	4	7	12	21	42	63	60	51
7	Bradford Park Ave.	46	10	8	5	37	23	9	4	10	38	38	75	61	50
8	Gateshead	46	13	6	4	51	24	4	9	10	25	36	76	60	49
9	Carlisle United	46	13	7	3	57	24	5	6	12	25	44	82	68	49
10	Crewe Alexandra	46	13	5	5	46	28	7	3	13	24	40	70	68	48
11	Stockport County	46	13	8	2	61	26	4	5	14	21	43	82	69	47
12	Tranmere Rovers	46	16	4	3	45	16	5	1	17	20	47	65	63	47
13	Chesterfield	46	13	6	4	40	23	5	5	13	25	40	65	63	47
14	Halifax Town	46	13	5	5	47	31	3	10	10	21	37	68	68	47
15	Scunthorpe United	46	10	6	7	38	21	6	8	9	24	35	62	56	46
16	Bradford City	46	14	7	2	54	29	0	11	12	21	51	75	80	46
17	Hartlepools United	46	14	6	3	39	16	2	8	13	18	45	57	61	46
18	Mansfield Town	46	11	9	3	34	25	5	5	13	21	37	55	62	46
19	Barrow	46	15	6	2	48	20	1	6	16	18	51	66	71	44
20	Chester	46	10	7	6	39	27	1	8	14	25	58	64	85	37
21	Darlington	46	13	4	6	33	27	1	2	20	25	69	58	96	34
22	Rochdale	46	12	5	6	41	27	2	0	21	21	56	62	83	33
23	Workington	46	9	5	9	40	33	2	5	16	15	58	55	91	32
24	Accrington Stanley	46	7	9	7	25	29	1	2	20	14	60	39	89	27

SEASON 1953/54
DIVISION 3 NORTH

No.	Date	Opposition	Res.	H.T.	Att.	Goalscorers	MacLaren	McIntosh	Scott	Kinloch	Waters	Johnston	Hogan	Whitehouse	Ashman	Atkinson	Drury	Hill	Coupland	Twentyman	Stokoe	Bloomfield	Harrison	Graham	Smith	McHave	Jackson	Bond	Doran	Rawes	Thompson
1	22 Aug	ROCHDALE	7-0	5-0	8378	Whtehse(2),Atkinsn(2),Jhnstn,Drury,Ashmn	1	2	3	4	5	6	7	8	9	10	11														
2	26	Grimsby	2-3	1-2	14516	Ashman, Drury	1	2	3	4			7	8	9		11		5						10						6
3	29	Wrexham	2-4	1-1	10321	Ashman, Smith	1		3					8	9		11	2							10						
4	1 Sep	GRIMSBY	3-3	0-1	10267	Whitehouse, Ashman, O.G.	1	2	3	4		6	7	8	9		10	5							11						
5	5	MANSFIELD	5-0	3-0	8482	Whitehouse(3), Ashman(2)	1	2	3	4		10	7	8	9		11	5													6
6	7	Stockport	2-3	0-1	10157	Whitehouse, Bloomfield	1	2	3	4				8	9		5					7				10		11			6
7	12	Barrow	1-1	0-1	6817	Ashman	1	2	3	4				8	9	10	5					7						11			6
8	15	STOCKPORT	2-0	1-0	9387	Ashman, McIntosh(pen)	1	2	3	4	5			8	9	10	11			6	7										
9	19	BRADFORD C.	2-0	1-0	8822	Ashman(2)	1	2	3	4	5		7	8	9	10	11					6									
10	22	ACCRINGTON	2-1	1-0	6153	Atkinson(2)	1	2	3	4	5		7	8	9	10	11					6									
11	26	Chesterfield	0-5	0-3	8683		1	2	3	4	5		7	8	9	10	11					6									
12	28	Accrington	2-2	1-1	8758	Ashman, Atkinson	1	2	3	4		6		8	9	10	11		5					7							
13	3 Oct	TRANMERE	0-2	0-0	8168		1	2	3	4		6		8	9	10	11		5					7							
14	10	DARLINGTON	1-1	1-1	6566	Ashman	1	2	3	4		6		8	9	10			5					7				11			
15	17	Barnsley	1-1	1-1	11369	Ashman	1	2	3	4		6		8	9				5					7			10	11			
16	24	BRADFORD P.A.	0-1	0-1	7873		1	2	3	4				8	9				5	6							10	11	7		
17	31	Port Vale	0-1	0-1	12454		1		3	4		6		10	9	8		2	5									11	7		
18	7 Nov	CREWE	5-0	2-0	4934	Whtehse(2),McIntsh(p),Ashmn,Bnd	1		3	4		6		10	9	8		2	5									11	7		
19	14	Chester	1-0	0-0	5104	Whitehouse	1		3	4		6		10	9	8		2	5				7					11			
20	28	York	3-1	2-0	5752	Whitehouse, Atkinson, Bond	1		3	4	5	6		10		8		2					7		9			11			
21	5 Dec	SCUNTHORPE	5-1	2-1	6169	Whitehouse(2),Atkinson(2),Ashman	1			4		6		10	9	8		2	3	5			7					11			
22	19	Rochdale	1-2	1-2	4654	Bond	1	2	3	4	5	6		8	9		10						7					11			
23	25	Gateshead	2-2	1-1	8534	Kinloch, Adhman	1	2	3	4	5	6		10	9	8							7					11			
24	26	GATESHEAD	1-0	1-0	7210	Whitehouse	1	2	3	4	5	6		10	9	8							7					11			
25	1 Jan	WORKINGTON	2-2	1-1	13648	Ashman(2)	1	2	3	4	5			10	9	8							7					11			6
26	2	WREXHAM	0-0		7014		1	2	3	4	5	6		10	9	8							7					11			
27	9	Workington	2-2	1-1	12974	Harrison(2)	1	2	3	4		6		10	9	8			5				7					11			
28	16	Mansfield	1-2	1-1	6386	Scott	1	2	3	4		6		10	9	8			5				7					11			
29	23	BARROW	2-2	2-2	5498	Whitehosue, Ashman	1	2	3	4		6		10	9	8			5				7					11			
30	30	HARTLEPOOL	2-3	1-1	5024	Whitehouse, Atkinson	1	2	3	4		6		10	9	8			5				7					11			
31	6 Feb	Bradford C.	0-1	0-1	8413		1	2	3	4	5	6		8	9								7		10			11			
32	13	CHESTERFIELD	2-3	1-1	4917	Whitehouse, Ashman	1	2	3	4	5	6		8	9								7		10			11			
33	20	Tranmere	2-1	1-1	5546	Kinloch, Ashman	1	2	3	4	5	6		10	9	8							7					11			
34	27	Darlington	2-3	1-3	4560	Graham, Bond	1	2	3	4	5	6		8	9								7	10				11			
35	6 Mar	BARNSLEY	2-4	1-2	4954	Ashman(2)	1	2	3	4	5	6		10	9	8							7					11			
36	13	Bradford P.A.	4-2	3-2	6346	Ashman(3), Atkinson	1	2		4	3	6		8	9	10							7					11	5		
37	20	PORT VALE	0-0	0-0	9995		1	2	3	4		6		8	9	10							7					11	5		
38	27	Crewe	0-0	0-0	3617		1	2	3	4		6		8	9								7		10			11	5		
39	3 Apr	CHESTER	1-1	1-1	2329	Ashman	1		3	4		6		8	9				2				7		10			11	5		
40	10	Southport	0-3	0-1	2910		1		3	4		6		8	9	10	11		2										5	7	
41	12	Hartlepool	1-1	1-0	5398	Whitehouse	1		3	4		6		8	9	10	7		2									11	5		
42	16	HALIFAX	5-0	4-0	5188	Whitehouse(4), Ashman	1		3	4	5	6		8	9	10	7		2									11			
43	17	YORK	1-1	1-1	4411	Atkinson	1		3	4	5	6		8	9	10	7		2									11			
44	19	Halifax	0-2	0-0	3514		1		3	4		6		8	9		7		2						10			11	5		
45	24	Scunthorpe	1-2	0-1	7731	Ashman	1		3	4		6		8	9				2				7			10		11	5		
46	27	SOUTHPORT	3-2	2-1	3251	Atkinson(2), Harrison	1		3	4		6		8	9	10			2				7					11	5		

F.A. CUP

No.	Date	Opposition	Res.	H.T.	Att.	Goalscorers	MacLaren	McIntosh	Scott	Kinloch	Waters	Johnston	Hogan	Whitehouse	Ashman	Atkinson	Drury	Hill	Coupland	Twentyman	Stokoe	Bloomfield	Harrison	Graham	Smith	McHave	Jackson	Bond	Doran	Rawes	Thompson
1R	21 Nov	Southport	0-1	0-0	7063		1		3	4		6		8	9				2		5					10	11		7		

Final League Table

		Pl.	Home					Away					F.	A.	Pts
			W	D	L	F	A	W	D	L	F	A			
1	Port Vale	46	16	7	0	48	5	10	10	3	26	16	74	21	69
2	Barnsley	46	16	3	4	54	24	8	7	8	23	33	77	57	58
3	Scunthorpe United	46	14	7	2	49	24	7	8	8	28	32	77	56	57
4	Gateshead	46	15	4	4	49	22	6	9	8	25	33	74	55	55
5	Bradford City	46	15	6	2	40	14	7	3	13	20	41	60	55	53
6	Chesterfield	46	13	6	4	41	19	6	8	9	35	45	76	64	52
7	Mansfield Town	46	15	5	3	59	22	5	6	12	29	45	88	67	51
8	Wrexham	46	16	4	3	59	19	5	5	13	22	49	81	68	51
9	Bradford Park Ave.	46	13	6	4	57	31	5	8	10	20	37	77	68	50
10	Stockport County	46	14	6	3	57	20	4	5	14	20	47	77	67	47
11	Southport	46	12	5	6	41	26	5	7	11	22	34	63	60	46
12	Barrow	46	12	7	4	46	26	4	5	14	26	45	72	71	44
13	Carlisle United	46	10	8	5	53	27	4	7	12	30	44	83	71	43
14	Tranmere Rovers	46	11	4	8	40	34	7	3	13	19	36	59	70	43
15	Accrington Stanley	46	12	7	4	41	22	4	3	16	25	52	66	74	42
16	Crewe Alexandra	46	9	8	6	30	26	5	5	13	19	41	49	67	41
17	Grimsby Town	46	14	5	4	31	15	2	4	17	20	62	51	77	41
18	Hartlepools United	46	10	8	5	40	21	3	6	14	19	44	59	65	40
19	Rochdale	46	12	5	6	40	20	3	5	15	19	57	59	77	40
20	Workington	46	10	9	4	36	22	3	5	15	23	58	59	80	40
21	Darlington	46	11	3	9	31	27	1	11	11	19	44	50	71	38
22	York City	46	8	7	8	39	32	4	6	13	25	54	64	86	37
23	Halifax Town	46	9	6	8	26	21	3	4	16	18	52	44	73	34
24	Chester	46	10	7	6	39	22	1	3	19	9	45	48	67	32

- 1953/54 Season -

(Back): Hill, McIntosh, Kinloch, McLaren, Johnson, Doran, Reed (Director)
(Front): Graham, Whitehouse, Ashman, Bond, Atkinson

- 1954/55 Season -

(Back): Hill, Jackson, Kinloch, Mitton, MacLaren, Waters, McIntosh
(Front): Thompson, Harrison, Hogan, Graham, Whitehouse, Rawes, Atkinson, Ashman, Sealeo, Scott, Bond

SEASON 1954/55
DIVISION 3 NORTH

No.	Date	Opposition	Res.	H.T.	Att.	Goalscorers	McLaren	Hill	McIntosh	Kinloch	Waters	Johnston	Graham	Whitehouse	Rawes	Atkinson	Bond	Mitton	Scott	Lindsay	Doran	Thompson	Hogan	Harrison	Ashman	Jackson	Moran	Crickett
1	21 Aug	Stockport	2-5	1-3	9817	Whitehouse, Atkinson	1	2	3	4	5	6	7	8	9	10	11											
2	24	ACCRINGTON	1-0	0-0	9004	Whitehouse	1	2	3	4	5	6	7	8	9	10	11											
3	28	HARTLEPOOL	3-2	0-0	7425	Atkinson, Bond, Kinloch(pen)	1	2	3	4	5	6	7	8	9	10	11											
4	1 Sep	Accrington	2-3	1-1	9818	Ashman, Atkinson	1	2	3	4			6	8	7	10	11				5				9			
5	4	Gateshead	0-0	0-0	7361		1	2	3	4		6	7	8		10	11				5				9			
6	6	Bradford P.A.	2-0	1-0	8792	Whitehouse, Ashman	1	2	3	4	5		7	8		10	11					6			9			
7	11	DARLINGTON	0-1	0-1	7438		1	2	3	4	5	8	7			10	11					6			9			
8	14	BRADFORD P.A.	3-2	3-0	7120	Jackson(2), Rawes	1	2	3	4	5				9	10	11					6	7		8			
9	18	Chesterfield	1-2	0-2	11649	Jackson	1	2	3	4	5		7	8	9		11					6				10		
10	21	CHESTER	1-2	1-2	5607	Atkinson	1	2	3	4	5			8	9		11					6	7			10		
11	25	CREWE	4-0	2-0	6252	Atkinson(2), Whitehouse, Harrison	1	2	3	4	5			8	9		11					6		7		10		
12	29	Chester	2-1	0-0	5354	Whitehouse, Jackson	1	5	3	4		6		8	9		11	2						7		10		
13	2 Oct	Wrexham	1-1	1-0	8752	Whitehouse	1	5	3	4		6		8	7		11	2							9	10		
14	9	MANSFIELD	1-2	0-1	6158	Atkinson	1	5	3	4				8	9		11	2				6		7		10		
15	16	Workington	0-1	0-0	13400		1	2	3	4	5			8	9		11					6		7		10		
16	23	BARROW	4-0	1-0	4262	Whitehouse(2), Ashman(2)	1	2	3	4	5			8		10						6		7	9		11	
17	30	Southport	1-4	1-3	3288	Atkinson	1	2	3	4	5			8		10						6		7	9		11	
18	6 Nov	YORK	4-5	0-3	5616	Whitehouse(3), Moran	1	2	3	4	5			8		10						6		7	9		11	
19	13	Halifax	3-5	1-3	6930	Whitehouse, Harrison, Atkinson		2		4	5			8		10			1	3		6		7	9		11	
20	27	Bradford C.	0-2	0-0	6874			5	3	4				8		10	11		1	2		6		7	9			
21	4 Dec	BARNSLEY	2-4	2-2	5153	Whitehouse, Atkinson			3	4				8		10	11		1	2	5	6		7	9			
22	18	Stockport	3-3	1-1	3596	Whitehouse, Ashman, Kinloch(pen)		5	3	4		6		8			11		1	2			7		9	10		
23	25	ROCHDALE	7-2	2-1	6556	Atk'son(2), Bond, Kin'ch(pen), O.G.(3)		2	3	4				8	9		11		1		5	6	7			10		
24	27	Rochdale	2-1	1-0	8274	Whitehouse, Jackson		2	3	4			7	8	9		11		1		5	6				10		
25	1 Jan	Hartlepool	0-1	0-0	12445			2	3	4				8	7	9	11		1		5	6				10		
26	29	GRIMSBY	3-1	1-0	5082	Atkinson(2), Bond		2	3	4	5			8	9		11		1			6	7			10		
27	5 Feb	CHESTERFIELD	1-2	0-2	6130	Hogan		2	3	4	5			8			11		1	9		6	7			10		
28	12	Crewe	1-4	0-2	2824	O.G.		2	3	4	5			8					1			6	7		9	10	11	
29	19	WREXHAM	1-0	0-0	4812	Whitehouse			3	4	5			8	9			1		2		6		7		10	11	
30	26	Mansfield	1-1	0-0	4070	Atkinson		5	3	4		6		8		9		1		2				7		10	11	
31	5 Mar	WORKINGTON	0-4	0-2	8906				3	4	5			8		10		1		2		6		7	9		11	
32	8	Grimsby	0-2	0-0	3690			5	3	4				8	9		11	1		2		6		7		10		
33	12	Barrow	1-2	0-2	4800	Atkinson		5	3	4				8		9	11	1		2		6		7		10		
34	19	SOUTHPORT	2-1	0-0	3815	Jackson(2)			3	4				8	9			1		2	5	6		7		10	11	
35	2 Apr	HALIFAX	4-0	3-0	4134	Whitehouse(3), Kinloch(pen)			3	4				8	9			1		2	5	6		7		10	11	
36	8	TRANMERE	1-2	0-1	6326	Whitehouse	1		3	4				8	9					2	5	6		7		10	11	
37	9	Oldham	1-2	1-0	7259	Jackson	1		3	4				8	9					2	5	6		7		10	11	
38	11	Tranmere	1-6	1-4	5760	Lindsay			3	4	5			8	9			1		2	7	6				10	11	
39	13	York	1-2	0-2	8874	Harrison		2	3	4	5	6		8		10		1						7	9		11	
40	16	BRADFORD C.	1-0	1-0	4360	Whitehouse		2		4	5	6		8		10		1	3	9				7			11	
41	18	Scunthorpe	1-1	1-1	7263	Moran		2		4	5	6		8		10		1	3	9				7			11	
42	20	Darlington	1-1	0-1	4004	Whitehouse		2		4	5	6		8		10		1	3	9				7			11	
43	23	Barnsley	1-3	0-3	13581	Atkinson		2	5			6		8		10	11	1	3	9		4		7				
44	26	OLDHAM	5-2	2-0	4123	Whitehse, Atkinsn(2), Knloch, Lndsay		5		4		2		8		10	11	1	3	9		6		7				
45	30	SCUNTHORPE	1-2	1-1	4636	Atkinson		5		4		2		8		10	11	1	3	9		6		7				
46	3 May	GATESHEAD *	1-2	0-1	2719	Whitehouse(pen)		2		4	5	6		8		10	11	1	3					7	9			

* Gateshead fixture first played, January 15 - abandoned, attendance 4321

F.A. CUP

	Date	Opposition	Res.	H.T.	Att.	Goalscorers	McLaren	Hill	McIntosh	Kinloch	Waters	Johnston	Graham	Whitehouse	Rawes	Atkinson	Bond	Mitton	Scott	Lindsay	Doran	Thompson	Hogan	Harrison	Ashman	Jackson	Moran	Crickett
1R	20 Nov	Stockport	1-0	1-0	10591	Bond		5	3	4				8		10	11		1	2		6		7	9			
2R	11 Dec	WATFORD	2-2	1-1	13576	Whitehouse, Ashman		5	3	4				8		10	11		1	2		6		7	9			
2Rr	15	Watford	1-4	0-2	5500	Ashman		5		4				8		10	11		1	2		6		7	9			3

Final League Table

		Pl.	Home					Away					F.	A.	Pts
			W	D	L	F	A	W	D	L	F	A			
1	Barnsley	46	18	3	2	51	17	12	2	9	35	29	86	46	65
2	Accrington Stanley	46	18	2	3	65	32	7	9	7	31	35	96	67	61
3	Scunthorpe United	46	14	6	3	45	18	9	6	8	36	35	81	53	58
4	York City	46	13	5	5	43	27	11	5	7	49	36	92	63	58
5	Hartlepools United	46	16	3	4	39	20	9	2	12	25	29	64	49	55
6	Chesterfield	46	17	1	5	54	33	7	5	11	27	37	81	70	54
7	Gateshead	46	11	7	5	38	26	9	5	9	27	43	65	69	52
8	Workington	46	11	7	5	39	23	7	7	9	29	32	68	55	50
9	Stockport County	46	13	4	6	50	27	5	8	10	34	43	84	70	48
10	Oldham Athletic	46	14	5	4	47	22	5	5	13	27	46	74	68	48
11	Southport	46	10	9	4	28	18	6	7	10	19	26	47	44	48
12	Rochdale	46	13	7	3	39	20	4	7	12	30	46	69	66	48
13	Mansfield Town	46	14	5	4	40	28	4	5	14	25	43	65	71	45
14	Halifax Town	46	9	5	9	41	27	6	4	13	22	40	63	67	43
15	Darlington	46	10	7	6	41	28	4	7	12	21	45	62	73	42
16	Bradford Park Ave.	46	11	7	5	29	21	4	4	15	27	49	56	70	41
17	Barrow	46	12	4	7	39	34	5	2	16	31	55	70	89	40
18	Wrexham	46	9	6	8	40	35	4	6	13	25	42	65	77	38
19	Tranmere Rovers	46	9	6	8	37	30	4	5	14	18	40	55	70	37
20	Carlisle United	46	12	1	10	53	39	3	5	15	25	50	78	89	36
21	Bradford City	46	9	5	9	30	26	4	5	14	17	29	47	55	36
22	Crewe Alexandra	46	8	10	5	45	35	2	4	17	23	56	68	91	34
23	Grimsby Town	46	10	4	9	28	32	3	4	16	19	46	47	78	34
24	Chester	46	10	3	10	23	25	2	6	15	21	52	44	77	33

SEASON 1955/56

DIVISION 3 NORTH

No.	Date	Opposition	Res.	H.T.	Att.	Goalscorers	Burn	Hill	Kenny	Kinloch	Waters	Thompson	Hogan	Whitehouse	Atkinson	Broadis	Bond	Moran	Mitton	Scott	Graham	Johnston	Little	Crickett	Ashman	Elliott	Doran	Bloomfield
1	20 Aug	CHESTERFIELD	1-1	1-1	10478	Atkinson	1	2	3	4	5	6	7	8	9	10	11											
2	22	Halifax	2-2	0-1	7741	Atkinson, Whitehouse	1	2	3	4	5	6	7	8	9	10	11											
3	27	Tranmere	1-0	1-0	8282	Whitehouse	1	2	3	4	5	6	7	8	9	10	11											
4	30	HALIFAX	2-2	1-1	10553	Atkinson, Kinloch(pen)	1	2	3	4	5	6	7	8	9		10	11										
5	3 Sep	SOUTHPORT	4-0	2-0	9513	Whitehse,Atkinsn,Broadis,Kinloch(p)	1	2	3	4	5	6	7	8	9		10	11										
6	6	Grimsby	0-1		12494			2	3	4	5	6	7				10	11	1						9			8
7	10	Gateshead	3-2	1-0	6400	Ashman(2), Broadis		2	3	4	5	6	7	8			10	11	1						9			
8	13	GRIMSBY	1-2	1-2	12244	Ashman		2	3	4	5	6	7	8			10	11	1						9			
9	17	DARLINGTON	2-0	1-0	9635	Atkinson, Moran		2	3	4	5	6	7	8			10	11	1						9			
10	24	Accrington	0-1		9805			2	3	4	5	6	7	8			10	11	1						9			
11	28	Chester	3-3	2-2	7916	Kinloch(2), Atkinson		2	3	4	5	6	7	8	9	10	11		1									
12	1 Oct	BARROW	2-0	1-0	9719	Atkinson, Bond		2	3	4	5	6	7	8	9	10	11		1									
13	8	Scunthorpe	0-4	0-1	8623			2	3	4	5	6	7	8		10	11		1						9			
14	15	WREXHAM	0-1	0-1	8255			2	3	4	5	6	7	8		10	11		1						9			
15	22	Workington	0-4	0-3	13045			2		4	5	6		8		10		11	1	3					9		7	
16	29	YORK	3-1	1-0	6240	Atkinson(2), Whitehouse	1	2		4	5	6	7	8	9	10	11			3								
17	2 Nov	Derby	0-3	0-1	17036		1	2		4	5	6	7	8	9	10	11			3								
18	12	CREWE	4-1	3-0	6290	Thompson(2), Atkinson, Ashman	1	2		4	5	6	7	8		10	11			3					9			
19	26	STOCKPORT	4-1	3-1	6301	Whitehouse(2), Broadis, Hogan	1	5	2	4		6	7	8		10	11			3					9			
20	3 Dec	Mansfield	1-0	0-0	6042	Atkinson	1	2	3		5	4		7	9	10	11					6			8			
21	17	Chesterfield	1-2	0-1	5340	Moran	1	2	3		5	4		7	9	10	11					6			8			
22	24	TRANMERE	0-3	0-2	5309		1	2	3		5	4		7	9	10	11						6		8			
23	26	Rochdale	2-5	1-1	4698	Whitehouse, Bond	1	5	2	4		6	7	8		10	11			3					9			
24	27	ROCHDALE	1-2	1-1	4429	Ashman	1	5	2	4		6	7	8		10	11			3					9			
25	31	Southport	0-3	0-0	5356		1	2	5	4		6	7	8		10	11			3					9			
26	2 Jan	BRADFORD P.A.	4-1	3-0	6188	Ashman(3), Broadis	1	2	5	4		6	7		9	10	11			3					8			
27	14	GATESHEAD	2-1	0-1	3337	Ashman(2)	1	2	5	4		6			9		10	11		3				7	8			
28	21	Darlington	5-3	3-1	4026	Whtehse(2),Ashmn,Broads,Knlch(p)	1	2	5	4		6		8			10	11		3				7	9			
29	28	OLDHAM	3-1	1-0	5762	Whitehouse(2), Ashman	1	2	5	4		6		8			10	11		3				7	9			
30	4 Feb	ACCRINGTON	0-4	0-3	5725		1	2	5	4		6		8			10			3				7	9			
31	11	Barrow	0-0	0-0	7210		1	2	5	4		6		8			10	11		3				7	9			
32	18	SCUNTHORPE	1-2	1-0	4228	Atkinson	1	2	5	4		6	7	8			11	10		3					9			
33	25	Wrexham	2-5	1-4	5004	Ashman(2)	1	2	5	4		6		8			10			3					9			
34	3 Mar	WORKINGTON	2-4	1-1	8354	Whitehouse, Atkinson	1	5	3	4		6		8	9	10	11			2			7					
35	10	York	1-3	1-1	9782	Atkinson	1		3	4		6	7		10	8	11			2					9	5		
36	17	HARTLEPOOL	0-3	0-1	4718		1		3	4	5	6	7			10	11			2					9		8	
37	24	Crewe	1-3	0-1	5214	Ashman			3	4	5	6	7	8		10	11	1		2					9			
38	30	BRADFORD C.	0-0	0-0	5288				3	4	5	6	7			10	8	11	1	2					9			
39	31	DERBY	0-3	0-1	7835				3	4	5	6	7			10	8	11	1		2				9			
40	2 Apr	Bradford C.	0-0	0-0	7945			2	5	4			7	8			11	10	6	1	3				9			
41	7	Stockport	1-8	1-4	4957	Whitehouse		2	5	4			7	8			11	10	6	1	3				9			
42	12	MANSFIELD	5-2	3-1	4145	Ashman(2),Atkinson,Kinloch,O.G.		2	3	4	5		7			10	8	11	1		6				9			
43	21	Oldham	2-2	2-1	5119	Broadis, Bond		2	3	4	5		7			10	8	11	1		6				9			
44	24	CHESTER	4-1	3-0	3872	Atkinson, Graham, Ashman, Bond		2	3	4	5		7			10	8	11	1		6				9			
45	28	Bradford P.A.	1-2	1-0	5320	Kinloch(pen)		2	3	4	5		7			10	8	11	1		6				9			
46	30	Hartlepool	0-3	0-0	5445			2	3	4	5					10	8	11	7	1	6				9			

F.A. CUP

No.	Date	Opposition	Res.	H.T.	Att.	Goalscorers	Burn	Hill	Kenny	Kinloch	Waters	Thompson	Hogan	Whitehouse	Atkinson	Broadis	Bond	Moran	Mitton	Scott	Graham	Johnston	Little	Crickett	Ashman	Elliott	Doran	Bloomfield
1R	19 Nov	Darlington	0-0	0-0	12418		1	2		4	5	6	7			10	8	11		3					9			
1Rr	22	DARLINGTON	0-0	0-0	19305		1	2		4	5	6	7			10	8	11		3					9			
1R2r	28	Darlington *	1-3	0-1	34250	Kinloch(pen)	1	2		4	5	6	7	8		10		11		3					9			

* Played at Newcastle Utd.

Final League Table

		Pl.	Home					Away					F.	A.	Pts
			W	D	L	F	A	W	D	L	F	A			
1	Grimsby Town	46	20	1	2	54	10	11	5	7	22	19	76	29	68
2	Derby County	46	18	4	1	67	23	10	3	10	43	32	110	55	63
3	Accrington Stanley	46	17	4	2	61	19	8	5	10	31	38	92	57	59
4	Hartlepools United	46	18	2	3	47	15	8	3	12	34	45	81	60	57
5	Southport	46	12	9	2	39	18	11	2	10	27	35	66	53	57
6	Chesterfield	46	18	1	4	61	21	7	3	13	33	45	94	66	54
7	Stockport County	46	16	4	3	65	22	5	5	13	25	39	90	61	51
8	Bradford City	46	16	5	2	57	25	2	8	13	21	39	78	64	49
9	Scunthorpe United	46	12	4	7	40	26	8	4	11	35	37	75	63	48
10	Workington	46	13	4	6	47	20	6	5	12	28	43	75	63	47
11	York City	46	12	4	7	44	24	7	5	11	41	48	85	72	47
12	Rochdale	46	13	5	5	46	39	4	8	11	20	45	66	84	47
13	Gateshead	46	15	4	4	56	32	2	7	14	21	52	77	84	45
14	Wrexham	46	11	5	7	37	28	5	5	13	29	45	66	73	42
15	Darlington	46	11	6	6	41	28	5	3	15	19	45	60	73	41
16	Tranmere Rovers	46	11	4	8	33	25	5	5	13	26	59	59	84	41
17	Chester	46	10	8	5	35	33	3	6	14	17	49	52	82	40
18	Mansfield Town	46	13	6	4	59	21	1	5	17	25	60	84	81	39
19	Halifax Town	46	10	6	7	40	27	4	5	14	26	49	66	76	39
20	Oldham Athletic	46	7	12	4	48	36	3	6	14	28	50	76	86	38
21	Carlisle United	46	11	3	9	45	36	4	5	14	26	59	71	95	38
22	Barrow	46	11	6	6	44	25	1	3	19	17	58	61	83	33
23	Bradford Park Ave.	46	13	4	6	47	38	0	3	20	14	84	61	122	33
24	Crewe Alexandra	46	9	4	10	32	35	0	6	17	18	70	50	105	28

- 1955/56 Season -

CARLISLE UNITED F.C.

BACK ROW (*l. to r.*) G. Hill, P. Waters, T. Kinloch, K. Mitton,
V. Kenny, R. Thompson.
FRONT (*l. to r.*) W. Hogan, J. Whitehouse, I. Atkinson, I. Broadis, E. Bond

- 1956/57 Season -

Back: Dick Young (trainer), Forbes, Whitfield, Fletcher, Fairley, Mitton,
Hill, Johnston, Waters. Front row (left to right): Kerr, Garvie, Broadis,
Atkinson, Bond, Devlin.

SEASON 1956/57
DIVISION 3 NORTH

No.	Date	Opposition	Res.	H.T.	Att.	Goalscorers	Fairley	Fletcher	Kenny	Thompson	Waters	Forbes	Mooney	Garvie	Ashman	Broadis	Devlin	Hill	Whitehead	Johnston	Kerr	Whitehouse	Atkinson	Ackerman	Bond	Mitton	Doran	Graham
1	18 Aug	OLDHAM	2-2	0-0	9027	Garvie, broadis	1	2	3	4	5	6	7	8		10	11						9					
2	22	Darlington	1-0	0-0	8317	Garvie	1	2	3	4	5	6	7	8		10	11						9					
3	25	Mansfield	1-5	0-2	8057	Atkinson	1	2	3	4	5	6	8		7	10	11						9					
4	1 Sep	SOUTHPORT	1-2	1-2	8072	Broadis	1	9		4	5	6	7	8		10	11	2	3									
5	3	York	0-2	0-2	11709		1		3	4	5	6	7			8	10	2					9		11			
6	8	Chesterfield	2-2	1-2	8890	Broadis, Devlin			3	4	5	6	7		9	8	10	2							11			1
7	15	CHESTER	3-0	0-0	6306	Mooney(3)	1		3	4	5	6	7		9	8	10	2							11			
8	17	Stockport	0-2	0-1	8455		1		3	4	5	6	7		9		10	2					8		11			
9	22	Hartlepools	1-2	0-0	12267	Kerr	1		3	4	5	6	9				11	2			7		8		10			
10	25	STOCKPORT	3-3	2-2	5614	Mooney, Broadis, Atkinson	1	3		4	5	6	7			8	11	2					9		10			
11	29	BRADFORD C.	1-4	0-1	6487	Mooney	1	3		4	5	6	7			8	11	2					9		10			
12	6 Oct	BRADFORD P.A.	2-1	0-0	4713	Mooney, Atkinson	1	3		6	5	4	7			8	11	2					9		10			
13	9	DARLINGTON	1-2	1-0	7005	Bond	1	3		6	5	4	7			8	11	2					9		10			
14	13	Gateshead	2-4	1-4	6034	Kerr, Bond	1	3		6	5	10				9		2		4	7				11			8
15	20	WORKINGTON	1-1	1-1	7500	Kerr	1	3		9	5	6				8	11	2		4	7				10			
16	27	Derby	0-3	0-0	15205		1		3	6	5		9			8	11	2		4	7				10			
17	3 Nov	CREWE	2-1	1-0	7131	Broadis, Mooney	1		3	6	5		8			10		2		4	7		9		11			
18	10	Scunthorpe	2-1	1-0	5546	Broadis(2)	1		3	6	5		7	10		8		2		4			9		11			
19	24	Halifax	3-1	1-0	4515	Ackerman(2), Garvie	1		3	6	5		7	10		8		2		4				9	11			
20	1 Dec	WREXHAM	2-2	1-1	7838	Broadis(2)	1		3	6	5		7	10		8		2		4				9	11			
21	15	Oldham	2-2	0-0	3023	Whitehouse, Ackerman	1		3	6	5		7	10				2		4		8		9	11			
22	22	MANSFIELD	6-1	0-1	4989	Ackerman(4), Broadis, Garvie	1		3	6	5		7	10		8		2		4				9	11			
23	25	BARROW	1-1	0-1	7483	Mooney	1		3	6	5		7	10		8		2		4		9			11			
24	26	Barrow	0-3	0-1	6065		1		3	6	5		7	10		8		2		4		9			11			
25	29	Southport	1-4	1-2	3528	Atkinson	1		3	6	5	4	7	10		8		2					9		11			
26	1 Jan	YORK	2-0	0-0	6240	Ackerman, Kenny(pen)	1	2	3	6	5		7	10		8				4				9	11			
27	12	CHESTERFIELD	4-2	2-1	8611	Ackerman(2), Mooney, Bond	1	2	3	6	5		7	10		8				4				9	11			
28	19	Chester	2-1	1-0	6533	Ackerman, Garvie	1		3	6	5		7	10		8		2		4				9	11			
29	26	Accrington	2-1	1-0	6915	Ackerman(2)	1		3	6	5		7			8		2		4			10	9	11			
30	2 Feb	HARTLEPOOLS	2-1	2-1	12121	Ackerman, Mooney	1		3	6	5		7	10		8		2		4			11	9				
31	9	Bradford C.	2-3	2-2	13842	Broadis, Devlin	1		3	6	5		7	10		8	11	2		4				9				
32	16	Bradford P.A.	3-1	2-0	7376	Ackerman(2), Devlin	1		3	6	5		7	10		8	11	2		4				9				
33	23	GATESHEAD	3-2	3-0	5000	Ackerman, Garvie, Devlin	1		3	6	5		7	10		8	11	2		4				9				
34	2 Mar	Workington	0-2	0-2	18601		1		3	6	5		7	10		8	11	2		4				9				
35	9	DERBY	1-3	0-3	11406	Kenny(pen)	1		3	6	5		7	8			11	2		4			10	9				
36	16	Crewe	2-2	1-2	4803	Broadis, Devlin	1		3	6	5		7	10		8	11	2		4				9				
37	19	ACCRINGTON	2-2	1-1	7734	Broadis, O.G.	1	2	3	6	5		7	10		8	11			4				9				
38	23	SCUNTHOPRE	0-0	0-0	8165		1	2	3	6	5		7	10		8	11			4				9				
39	30	Rochdale	1-2	0-1	5521	Bond	1	2	3	6	5	4		10		8	7							9	11			
40	6 Apr	HALIFAX	0-0	0-0	5845		1	2	3	6		4		10		8	7							9	11	5		
41	9	HULL	1-3	1-1	6297	Broadis	1							10		8	7			4				9	11	5		
42	13	Wrexham	4-6	4-2	5378	Ashman, Broadis, Devlin, Kenny(pen)	1	2	3	6	5				10	8	7			4				9	11			
43	19	TRANMERE	2-2	0-0	11612	Ackerman(2)	1	3			5	6			10	8	7	2		4				9	11			
44	22	Tranmere	1-0	0-0	5336	Bond	1		3	6	5				10	8		2		4	7			9	11			
45	27	Hull	0-0	0-0	13010		1		3	6	5				10	8		2		4	7			9	11			
46	30	ROCHDALE	2-1	0-0	3499	Broadis, Ashman	1	2	3	6	5				10	8				4	7			9	11			

F.A. CUP

	Date	Opposition	Res.	H.T.	Att.	Goalscorers	Fairley	Fletcher	Kenny	Thompson	Waters	Forbes	Mooney	Garvie	Ashman	Broadis	Devlin	Hill	Whitehead	Johnston	Kerr	Whitehouse	Atkinson	Ackerman	Bond	Mitton	Doran	Graham
1R	17 Nov	BILLINGHAM SYNTH	6-1	3-1	11000	Garvie(3), Ackerman(2), Broadis	1		3	6	5		7	10		8		2		4				9	11			
2R	8 Dec	DARLINGTON	2-1	2-1	14761	Ackerman(2)	1		3	6	5		7	10		8		2		4				9	11			
3R	5 Jan	BIRMINGHAM	3-3	0-1	27164	Ackerman(3)	1	2	3	6	5		7	10		8				4				9	11			
3Rr	9	Birmingham	0-4	0-1	56500		1	2	3	6	5		7	10		8				4				9	11			

Final League Table

		Pl.	Home					Away					F.	A.	Pts
			W	D	L	F	A	W	D	L	F	A			
1	Derby County	46	18	3	2	69	18	8	8	7	42	35	111	53	63
2	Hartlepools United	46	18	4	1	56	21	7	5	11	34	42	90	63	59
3	Accrington Stanley	46	15	4	4	54	22	10	4	9	41	42	95	64	58
4	Workington	46	16	4	3	60	25	8	6	9	33	38	93	63	58
5	Stockport County	46	16	3	4	51	26	7	5	11	40	49	91	75	54
6	Chesterfield	46	17	5	1	60	22	5	4	14	36	57	96	79	53
7	York City	46	14	4	5	43	21	7	6	10	32	40	75	61	52
8	Hull City	46	14	6	3	45	24	7	4	12	39	45	84	69	52
9	Bradford City	46	14	3	6	47	31	8	5	10	31	37	78	68	52
10	Barrow	46	16	2	5	51	22	5	7	11	25	40	76	62	51
11	Halifax Town	46	16	2	5	40	24	5	5	13	25	46	65	70	49
12	Wrexham	46	12	7	4	63	33	7	3	13	34	41	97	74	48
13	Rochdale	46	14	6	3	38	19	4	6	13	27	46	65	65	48
14	Scunthorpe United	46	9	5	9	44	36	6	10	7	27	33	71	69	45
15	Carlisle United	46	9	9	5	44	36	7	4	12	32	49	76	85	45
16	Mansfield Town	46	13	3	7	58	38	4	7	12	33	52	91	90	44
17	Gateshead	46	9	6	8	42	40	8	4	11	30	50	72	90	44
18	Darlington	46	11	5	7	47	36	6	3	14	35	59	82	95	42
19	Oldham Athletic	46	9	7	7	35	31	3	8	12	31	43	66	74	39
20	Bradford Park Ave.	46	11	2	10	41	40	5	1	17	25	53	66	93	35
21	Chester	46	8	7	8	40	35	2	6	15	15	49	55	84	33
22	Southport	46	7	8	8	31	34	3	4	16	21	60	52	94	32
23	Tranmere Rovers	46	5	9	9	33	38	2	4	17	18	53	51	91	27
24	Crewe Alexandra	46	5	7	11	31	46	1	2	20	12	64	43	110	21

SEASON 1957/58
DIVISION 3 NORTH

No.	Date	Opposition	Res.	H.T.	Att.	Goalscorers	Fairley	Hill	Fletcher	Lackenby	Forbes	Mooney	Broadis	Johnston	Ackerman	Ashman	Bond	Thompson R.	Kenny	Thompson G.	Bradley	Waters	McKenna	Imrie	Cruickshank	Kerr	Tulloch	Horne	Hunter	Cresswell	Doran	Elliott	O'Connell
1	24 Aug	Oldham	0-1	0-0	11339		1	2	3	5	6	7	8	4	9	10	11																
2	27	MANSFIELD	3-4	1-3	11149	Ackerman(2), Bond	1	2	3	5	6		8	4	9	10	11									7							
3	31	BURY	0-2	0-0	10872			2	3	5	6	7	8		9		11	4									10						
4	2 Sep	Mansfield	0-2	0-0	9674			2	3		6		8		9		11	4						7	10						5		
5	7	Accrington	2-2	2-3	7674	Imrie, Ackerman			2		6		8		9		10	4	3		1		5	7	11								
6	10	YORK	2-1	1-1	9557	Broadis(2)			2		6		8		9		10	4	3		1		5	7	11								
7	14	CHESTER	3-2	2-1	8764	Imrie(2), Bond			2		6		8		9		10	4	3		1		5	7	11								
8	16	York	5-0	2-0	6711	Imrie(2), Ackerman(2), Tulloch			2						9	8		6	3		1	4	5	7	11		10						
9	21	Chesterfield	3-1	2-1	9679	Ackerman(2), Ashman			2						9	8		6	3		1	4	5	7	11		10						
10	24	Southport	0-2	0-2	1959				2						9	8		6	3		1	4	5	7	11		10						
11	28	TRANMERE	3-1	3-1	7926	Ashman(2), Tulloch			2				8		9	7		6	3		1	4	5		11		10						
12	1 Oct	SOUTHPORT	4-0	1-0	9082	Ackerman(3), Broadis			2				8		9	7	11	6	3		1	4	5				10						
13	5	Hartlepool	1-0	0-0	10119	Horne			2				8		9	7	11	6	3		1	4	5					10					
14	12	HULL	0-1	0-1	11178				2				8		9	7	11	6	3		1	4	5				10						
15	19	Darlington	2-1	0-0	6769	Broadis, Tulloch			2		5		8		9	7	11	6	3		1	4					10						
16	26	SCUNTHORPE	3-4	3-2	10579	Ackerman, Bradley, Broadis			2		5		8		9	7	11	6	3		1	4					10						
17	2 Nov	Wrexham	0-1	0-0	8042			3	2		5		8		9		11	6			1	4			7		10						
18	9	CREWE	2-0	2-0	7843	Ackerman, Elliott		2	3		4				9		11	6			1		5		10							7	
19	23	HALIFAX	2-1	1-1	8134	Mooney, Ackerman		3	2			7	8		9		11	6			1	4	5				10						
20	30	Stockport	1-4	0-1	9572	Mooney		3	2			7	8		9	10	11	6			1	4	5										
21	14 Dec	Bradford C.	1-1	1-1	12509	Ackerman		3	2		5	7	8	10	9			6			1	4			11								
22	21	OLDHAM	1-1	1-0	6282	Mooney		3	2		5	7			9			6			1			8	11		10						
23	25	WORKINGTON	2-2	1-1	12462	Ackerman(2)		3	2			7	8		9		11	6			1	4	5				10						
24	26	Workington	1-2	0-1	13250	Ackerman		2	3		4	7			9			6			1		5	10	11								
25	28	Bury	0-3	0-0	12082			2	3		4		8		9			6			1		5			7	10		11				
26	1 Jan	BRADFORD P.A.	2-3	2-2	7202	Tulloch(2)		3	2		5	7	8		9			6			1	4					10						
27	4	Bradford P.A.	1-4	0-3	5849	Ackerman			2		5	7	8		9			6	3			4					10						
28	11	ACCRINGTON	6-1	3-1	6854	Ackerman(3),Broadis,Tulloch,Horne			2		5		8	4	9			6	3		1		7				10	11					
29	18	Chester	0-0	0-0	4949				2		5		8	4	9			6	3		1		7				10	11					
30	1 Feb	CHESTERFIELD	2-2	0-1	6763	Ackerman, Tulloch			2		5		8	4	9			6	3		1		7				10	11					
31	8	Tranmere	1-0	1-0	7265	Ackerman			2		5		8	4	9			6	3		1		7				10						
32	15	HARTLEPOOL	1-2	0-1	7670	Ackerman			2		5	11	8	4	9			6	3		1		7				10						
33	18	GATESHEAD	5-1	4-1	8913	Ackerman(3), O'Connell, Broadis			2		5		8	4	9			6	3		1		7										10
34	22	Halifax	0-5	0-1	5059				2				8	4	9			6	3		1		5	7			10						
35	1 Mar	DARLINGTON	5-2	5-1	7675	Tulloch(2),Broadis,Bond,McKenna			2		5		8	4	9			6	3		1		7				10						
36	11	Rochdale	0-1	0-0	4079				2		5		8	4	9			6	3		1		7				10						
37	15	WREXHAM	4-0	1-0	7169	Ackerman(3), O'Connell			2		5		8	4	9			6	3		1		7										10
38	22	Hull	0-4	0-3	9917				2					4	9			6	3		1		7						8	5			10
39	29	ROCHDALE	1-0	1-0	3991	Ackerman	1		2		5		8	4	9			6	3				7		11		10						
40	5 Apr	Gateshead	2-3	0-2	4278	Ackerman, Tulloch	1		2		5		8	4	9			6	3				7				10						
41	7	Barrow	3-2	2-0	6884	Tulloch(2), Ackerman			2		5		8	4	9			6	3		1		7				10						
42	12	STOCKPORT	3-1	1-0	7421	Ackerman(2), Tulloch			2		5		8	4	9			6	3		1		7				10						
43	14	BARROW	2-1	2-1	10089	Broadis, Tulloch		2	3		5		8	4	9			6			1		7				10						
44	19	Crewe	0-0	0-0	3409			2	3		5		8	4	9			6			1		7				10						11
45	26	BRADFORD C.	0-3	0-2	8555			2	3		5	11	8	4	9			6			1		7				10						
46	1 May	Scunthorpe	1-3	0-2	12555	Tulloch			2		5		8		9			6			1	4	7				10						

F.A. CUP

No.	Date	Opposition	Res.	H.T.	Att.	Goalscorers	Fairley	Hill	Fletcher	Lackenby	Forbes	Mooney	Broadis	Johnston	Ackerman	Ashman	Bond	Thompson R.	Kenny	Thompson G.	Bradley	Waters	McKenna	Imrie	Cruickshank	Kerr	Tulloch	Horne	Hunter	Cresswell	Doran	Elliott	O'Connell
1R	16 Nov	RHYL	5-1	0-0	13233	Broadis(2), Bond(2), Ackerman			3		2		7	8	9		11	6			1	4	5				10						
2R	7 Dec	ACCRINGTON	1-1	0-0	13171	Ackerman			3		2		7	8	9	10	11	6			1	4	5										
2Rr	11	Accrington	2-3	1-1	11413	Ackerman, Johnston			3		2		7	8	9	10	11	6			1	4	5										

Final League Table

		Pl.	Home					Away					F.	A.	Pts
			W	D	L	F	A	W	D	L	F	A			
1	Scunthorpe United	46	16	5	2	46	19	13	3	7	42	31	88	50	66
2	Accrington Stanley	46	16	4	3	53	28	9	5	9	30	33	83	61	59
3	Bradford City	46	13	7	3	42	19	8	7	3	31	30	73	49	57
4	Bury	46	17	4	2	61	18	6	6	11	33	44	94	62	56
5	Hull City	46	15	6	2	49	20	4	9	10	29	47	78	67	53
6	Mansfield Town	46	16	3	4	68	42	6	5	12	32	50	100	92	52
7	Halifax Town	46	15	5	3	52	20	5	6	12	31	49	83	69	51
8	Chesterfield	46	12	8	3	39	28	6	7	10	32	41	71	69	51
9	Stockport County	46	15	4	4	54	28	3	7	13	20	39	74	67	47
10	Rochdale	46	14	4	5	50	25	5	4	14	29	42	79	67	46
11	Tranmere Rovers	46	12	6	5	51	32	6	4	13	31	44	82	76	46
12	Wrexham	46	13	8	2	39	18	4	4	15	22	45	61	63	46
13	York City	46	11	8	4	40	26	6	4	13	28	50	68	76	46
14	Gateshead	46	12	5	6	41	27	3	10	10	27	49	68	76	45
15	Oldham Athletic	46	11	7	5	44	32	3	10	10	28	52	72	84	45
16	Carlisle United	46	13	7	3	56	35	6	3	14	24	43	80	78	44
17	Hartlepools United	46	11	6	6	45	26	5	6	12	28	50	73	76	44
18	Barrow	46	9	7	7	36	32	4	8	11	30	42	66	74	41
19	Workington	46	11	6	6	46	33	3	7	13	26	48	72	81	41
20	Darlington	46	15	3	5	53	25	2	4	17	25	64	78	89	41
21	Chester	46	7	10	6	38	26	6	3	14	35	55	73	81	39
22	Bradford Park Ave.	46	8	6	9	41	41	5	5	13	27	54	68	95	37
23	Southport	46	8	3	12	29	40	3	3	17	23	48	52	88	28
24	Crewe Alexandra	46	6	5	12	29	41	2	2	19	18	52	47	93	23

- 1957/58 Season -

(Back): Hill, Forbes, Fairley, Thompson, Kenny, Waters
(Front): Mooney, Broadis, Ackerman, Garvie, Bond.

- 1958/59 Season -

(Back): Bradley, Lackenby, Thompson, Brown, G.Thompson, Troops
(Front): Mooney, Broadis, Ackerman, Tulloch, McMillan.

SEASON 1958/59
DIVISION 4

No.	Date	Opposition	Res.	H.T.	Att.	Goalscorers	Thompson G.	Brown	Troops	Bradley	Lackenby	Thompson R.	Mooney	Broadis	Ackerman	Tulloch	McMillan	Bell	Bond	Boyd	Cresswell	Doran	Fairley	Fletcher	Graham	Johnston	Keen	McKenna	Nicholl	Westmorland	Walker
1	23 Aug	ALDERSHOT	1-0	1-0	9912	Ackerman	1	2	3	4	5	6	7	8	9	10	11														
2	26	GILLINGHAM	1-2	1-1	10759	Mooney		2	3	4	5	6	7	8	9	10	11						1								
3	30	Millwall	0-1	0-0	14024			2	3	4		6	7	8	9	10	11				5	1									
4	1 Sep	Gillingham	1-1	1-1	8106	McKenna		2	3	4		6	7	8	9	10					5	1						11			
5	6	WALSALL	1-1	1-1	7554	Broadis		2	3	4		6	7	8	9	10					5	1						11			
6	9	NORTHAMPTON	2-1	1-0	11238	McKenna(2)	1	2	3	4		6	7	8	9	10					5							11			
7	13	Darlington	1-0	1-0	7515	McKenna	1	2	3	4		6	7	8	9	10					5							11			
8	20	SHREWSBURY	0-0	0-0	10465		1	2	3	4		6	7	8	9	10					5							11			
9	23	BARROW	1-0	0-0	8846	McKenna	1	2	3	4		6	7	8	9	10					5							11			
10	27	Coventry	2-1	1-1	19153	Ackerman, Tulloch	1	2	3	4		6	7	8	9	10					5							11			
11	29	Barrow	3-1	2-0	4947	Ackerman, Tulloch(2)	1	2	3	4		6	7	8	9	10					5							11			
12	4 Oct	EXETER	1-2	0-1	10372	McKenna	1	2	3	4		6		8	9	10	7				5							11			
13	11	York	1-1	0-0	9373	Ackerman	1	2	3	4		6	7	8	9	10					5							11			
14	18	BRADFORD P.A.	1-1	0-0	8844	Tulloch	1	2	3	4		6	7			10					5				8			11			
15	25	Port Vale	1-1	1-0	12984	Ackerman	1	2	3	4		6	7	8	9	10					5							11			
16	1 Nov	CYRSTAL PALACE	3-3	2-1	7384	Bell, Fletcher, Tulloch	1	2	3	4		6	7			10		8			5			9				11			
17	8	Chester	1-2	1-1	7351	Fletcher	1	2	3			6	7		9	10					5			8	4			11			
18	22	Hartlepool	2-1	1-0	4064	Fletcher(2)	1	2	3			6	7	8	9						5			10	4			11			
19	29	SOUTHPORT	5-0	3-0	6515	Fltchr(2),Ackrmn,McKnna,Troops(p)	1	2	3			6	7	8	9						5			10	4			11			
20	13 Dec	CREWE	2-0	0-0	5183	Fletcher, R.Thompson	1	2	3	4		6	7	8	9						5			10	11						
21	20	Aldershot	0-4		3483		1		3	4		6	7	8	9						5			10		2		11			
22	26	WORKINGTON	3-2	2-1	11659	Fletcher(2), Ackerman	1	2	3			6	7	8	9						5			10	4			11			
23	27	Workington	1-0	0-0	8765	Fletcher	1	2	3			6	7	8	9						5			10	4			11			
24	3 Jan	MILLWALL	0-2	0-2	7725		1	2	3			6	7	8	9						5			10	4			11			
25	7 Feb	Shrewsbury	1-4		5259	Fletcher	1	2	3			6		8	9						5			7	4			11			
26	14	COVENTRY	1-6	0-4	5289	Tulloch	1	2	3			6		8	9				10		5			7	4			11			
27	17	Crewe	1-3	0-2	5302	Fletcher	1	2	3			6	7	8					4		10			5	9			11			
28	21	Exeter	1-2	1-0	10006	Bond	1	2	3			6	7	8					4		10			5	9	11					
29	25	Torquay	0-0	0-0	3120		1	2	3			6	7	8					4		10			5	9	11					
30	28	YORK	0-0	0-0	3076		1	2	3			6	7	8					4		10			5	9	11					
31	3 Mar	OLDHAM	3-0	2-0	5403	Walker(2), Bond	1	2	3				7	8					4	9	5			11	6						10
32	7	Bradford	3-0		6329	Fletcher(3)	1	2	3				7		9				4	8	5			11	6						10
33	11	DARLINGTON	1-1	1-1	5898	Walker	1	2	3			6	7		9				4	8	5			11							10
34	14	PORT VALE	0-3	0-1	6110		1	2	3	4			7	8					6	9	5			11							10
35	16	WATFORD	2-0	0-0	4965	Cresswell(2)	1	2		4			7		9				6		3	5						11		8	10
36	21	Crystal Palace	2-0		15319	Tulloch, O.G.	1	2		4			7		9				6		3	5						11			10
37	27	Gateshead	1-4	1-1	7623	Bradley	1	2	3	4			7		9				6			5		8				11			10
38	28	CHESTER	4-3	2-2	4522	McKenna(2), Fletcher, Walker	1	2	3				7	8					6			5		9				11			10
39	30	GATESHEAD	4-2	2-2	5029	Mooney(2), Fletcher, Broadis	1	2	3				7	8					6			5		9				11			10
40	4 Apr	Watford	2-2	1-1	7219	Mooney, McKenna	1	2	3				7	8					6			5		9				11			10
41	6	Northampton	0-0	0-0	3450		1	2				6	7		9				4			5		8		3		11			10
42	11	HARTLEPOOL	1-0	1-0	4828	Mooney	1	2	3				7	8					4			5		9	6			11			10
43	14	Walsall	0-5	0-4	10085		1	2	3	4		6	7	8					5					9				11			10
44	18	Southport	1-0	0-0	2663	Walker	1	2		4			7		8							5		9	6			11		3	10
45	25	TORQUAY	0-1	0-0	3376		1	2		4			7									5		9	6			11		3	10
46	28	Oldham	0-2	0-2	3011		1	2	3			6	7	8					9			5						11			10

F.A. CUP

	Date	Opposition	Res.	H.T.	Att.	Goalscorers	Thompson G.	Brown	Troops	Bradley	Lackenby	Thompson R.	Mooney	Broadis	Ackerman	Tulloch	McMillan	Bell	Bond	Boyd	Cresswell	Doran	Fairley	Fletcher	Graham	Johnston	Keen	McKenna	Nicholl	Westmorland	Walker
1R	15 Nov	Heanor Town	5-1	2-0	5000	Ackerman(2), Mooney, Fletcher(2)	1	2	3			6	7	8	9						5			10	4			11			
2R	6 Dec	CHESTERFIELD	0-0	0-0	13031		1	2	3	4		6	7	8	9						5			10		11					
2Rr	9	Chesterfield	0-1	0-0	11049		1	2	3	4		6	7	8	9						5			10		11					

Final League Table

		Pl.	Home W	D	L	F	A	Away W	D	L	F	A	F.	A.	Pts
1	Port Vale	46	14	6	3	62	30	12	6	5	48	28	110	58	64
2	Coventry City	46	18	4	1	50	11	6	8	9	34	36	84	47	60
3	York City	46	12	10	1	37	17	9	8	6	36	35	73	52	60
4	Shrewsbury Town	46	15	5	3	59	24	9	5	9	42	39	101	63	58
5	Exeter City	46	16	4	3	55	24	7	7	9	32	37	87	61	57
6	Walsall	46	13	5	5	56	25	8	5	10	39	39	95	64	52
7	Crystal Palace	46	12	8	3	54	27	8	4	11	36	44	90	71	52
8	Northampton Town	46	14	5	4	48	25	7	4	12	37	53	85	78	51
9	Millwall	46	13	6	4	46	23	7	4	12	30	46	76	69	50
10	Carlisle United	46	11	6	6	37	30	8	6	9	25	35	62	65	50
11	Gillingham	46	14	6	3	53	27	6	3	14	29	50	82	77	49
12	Torquay United	46	11	5	7	45	32	5	7	11	33	45	78	77	44
13	Chester	46	10	5	8	39	33	6	7	10	33	51	72	84	44
14	Bradford Park Ave.	46	15	1	7	51	29	3	6	14	24	48	75	77	43
15	Watford	46	10	6	7	46	36	6	4	13	35	43	81	79	42
16	Darlington	46	7	8	8	37	36	6	8	9	29	32	66	68	42
17	Workington	46	9	10	4	40	32	3	7	13	23	46	63	78	41
18	Crewe Alexandra	46	11	5	7	52	32	4	5	14	18	50	70	82	40
19	Hartlepools United	46	11	4	8	50	41	4	6	13	24	47	74	88	40
20	Gateshead	46	11	3	9	33	30	5	5	13	23	55	56	85	40
21	Oldham Athletic	46	15	0	8	39	29	1	4	18	20	55	59	84	36
22	Aldershot	46	8	4	11	37	45	6	3	14	26	52	63	97	35
23	Barrow	46	6	6	11	34	45	3	4	16	17	59	51	104	28
24	Southport	46	7	8	8	26	25	0	4	19	15	61	41	86	26

SEASON 1959/60
DIVISION 4

No.	Date	Opposition	Res.	H.T.	Att.	Goalscorers
1	22 Aug	CRYSTAL PALACE	2-2	2-1	7011	McGill, Walker
2	26	Chester	1-0	0-0	7800	Murray
3	29	Bradford P.A.	1-1	1-0	8357	McGill
4	1 Sep	CHESTER	2-1	1-1	9344	Walker, R.Thompson
5	5	STOCKPORT	0-4	0-2	6604	
6	10	Walsall	1-0	0-0	15403	Walker
7	12	Exeter	3-1	2-1	7431	Tulloch, Mooney, Murray
8	15	WALLSALL	1-1	0-1	8733	McGill
9	19	WATFORD	1-0	0-0	7045	Walker
10	23	Crewe	0-3	0-1	9171	
11	26	Oldham	1-0	0-0	5956	Fletcher
12	29	CREWE	4-2	2-2	7571	McGill(2), Walker, Murray
13	3 Oct	Rochdale	0-3	0-1	4897	
14	6	NOTTS COUNTY	2-0	1-0	9004	McMillan, Walker
15	10	DONCASTER	2-0	2-0	7019	Mooney, Nichol
16	15	Notts County	1-2	1-2	12232	McGill
17	17	Northampton	2-2	1-1	8789	R.Thompson(2)
18	24	TORQUAY	2-0	1-0	1811	R.Thompson, Walker
19	31	Millwall	1-1	1-1	8792	McGill
20	7 Nov	SOUTHPORT	1-0	0-0	6311	McGill
21	21	BARROW	0-2	0-2	5009	
22	28	Aldershot	2-0	0-0	4292	Terris, McGill
23	12 Dec	Gateshead	0-1	0-1	2442	
24	19	Crystal Palace	1-2	0-1	9045	Murray
25	26	WORKINGTON	0-1	0-0	8638	
26	29	Workington	0-1	0-0	6593	
27	2 Jan	BRADFORD P.A.	0-3	0-2	4076	
28	9	Gillingham	1-3	1-2	3469	Tickell
29	16	Stockport	0-0	0-0	5203	
30	23	EXETER	0-4	0-0	4366	
31	30	DARLINGTON	1-0	0-0	1914	Brayton
32	6 Feb	Watford	1-3	1-1	12242	Robson
33	13	OLDHAM	0-1	0-0	2144	
34	20	ROCHDALE	1-1	1-0	2258	Thomson
35	27	Doncaster	1-4	1-2	4426	Bevan
36	5 Mar	NORTHAMPTON	0-2	0-1	3503	
37	12	Torquay	1-2	0-1	6974	Mooney
38	19	MILLWALL	3-3	2-2	3126	Mooney, Walker(2)
39	26	Southport	1-1	0-1	2388	R.Thompson
40	2 Apr	GILLINGHAM	0-1	0-0	2538	
41	9	Barrow	1-5	1-3	4241	Mooney
42	15	HARTLEPOOLS	1-1	0-0	3164	Mooney
43	16	ALDERSHOT	0-0	0-0	3200	
44	18	Hartlepools	2-1	1-0	3603	McMillan, Walker
45	23	Darlington	1-2	0-1	3726	McGill
46	30	GATESHEAD	4-0	2-0	2303	Bevan, McGill(2), Walker

Player appearances (shirt numbers)

No.	Thompson G.	Brown	Troops	Bradley	Fletcher	Thompson R.	Mooney	Walker	Tulloch	McMillan	Bevan	McGill	Murray	Terris	Thomson	Johnston	Brayton	Robson	Doran	Devlin	Tickell	Oosthuizen	Nichol	McCall	Keen	Graham	Bell
1	1	2	3				7	8		10	9	11				4			5							6	
2	1	2	3	4				8	9	10			11	7					5		6						
3	1	2	3	4				8	9	10			11	7					5		6						
4	1	2	3	4		6		8		10		9		7					5			11					
5	1			4	2	6	7	8		10		9	11		3				5								
6	1	2	3	4			7	8	9	10		6	11						5								
7	1	2	3	4			7	8	9	10		6	11						5								
8	1	2	3	4			7	8	9	10		6	11						5								
9	1	2	3	4			7	8	9	10		6	11						5								
10	1	2		4	3		7	8	9	10		6	11						5								
11	1	2		4	3		7	8			9						6					11					10
12	1	2		4	3	6	7	8		10		9	11						5								
13	1	2		4	3		7	8	9	10		6	11						5								
14	1	2		4	3		7	8		10		9							5				6				
15	1	2		4	3		7	8		10		9							5				6				
16	1	2		4	3		7	8		10		9	11	6					5								
17	1	2		4	3	6	7	8		10		9	11						5								
18	1	2		4	3	6	7	8		10		9	11						5								
19	1	2		4	3		7	8	9	10		6	11						5								
20	1	2		4	3		7	8	9	10		6	11						5								
21	1	2		4	3			8		10		9	11						5		7	6					
22	1	2		4	5			8		10		9	11	3		6		7									
23	1	2		4				8		10		9	11	3		6		5									
24	1	2		4	5			8		10			11	3			6	9									
25	1	2		4	5			8		10			11	3			6	9									
26	1	2		4	5			8		10			11	3			6	9									
27	1	2		4	5	6		8		10			11	3			7	9									
28	1	2		4				8		10			11	3	7	6	9				5						
29	1	2		4				8		10			11	3	7	6	9				5						
30	1	2		4		6	7	8				9		3	10		11		5								
31	1	2		4		6	7	8				9		3	10		11		5								
32	1	2		4		6		8				9		3	10		11	7	5	3							
33	1	2		4		6		8				9		3	10		11	7	5	3							
34	1		3	4		6		8				11		2	10		9	7	5								
35	1		3	4	5	6		8	9	10	11		2				7										
36	1	2	3	4	5	6	7	8	9	10	11																
37	1	2	3	4	5	6	7	8	9	10	11																
38	1	2	3	4	5	6	7	8		10	11																
39	1	2	3	4	5	6	7	8		10	11						9										
40	1	2	3	4	5	6		8		10	11						9		7								
41	1		3	4	5	6	7	8		10	11						9			2							
42	1		3	4	5		7	8		10	11						9			2			6				
43	1		3	4	5	6		8		10	11					7	9			2							
44	1		3	4	5	6		8		10	11					7	9			2							
45	1			4		6				10	11	9				3	7	8	5								2
46	1			4		6				10	11	9				3	7		5	2							

F.A. CUP

	Date	Opposition	Res.	H.T.	Att.	Goalscorers
1R	14 Nov	Rochdale	2-2	1-1	5811	McGill, Walker
1Rr	17	ROCHDALE	1-3	1-0	13330	Devlin

	Thompson G.	Brown	Troops	Bradley	Mooney	Walker	McMillan	McGill	Murray	Doran	Devlin
1R	1	2	6	3	7	8	4	9	10	5	11
1Rr	1	2	6	3	7	8	4	9	10	5	11

Final League Table

		Pl	Home W	D	L	F	A	Away W	D	L	F	A	F.	A.	Pts
1	Walsall	46	14	5	4	57	33	14	4	5	45	27	102	60	65
2	Notts County	46	19	1	3	66	27	7	7	9	41	42	107	69	60
3	Torquay United	46	17	3	3	56	27	9	5	9	28	31	84	58	60
4	Watford	46	17	2	4	62	28	7	7	9	30	39	92	67	57
5	Millwall	46	12	8	3	54	28	6	9	8	30	33	84	61	53
6	Northampton Town	46	13	6	4	50	22	9	3	11	35	41	85	63	53
7	Gillingham	46	17	4	2	47	21	4	6	13	27	48	74	69	52
8	Crystal Palace	46	12	6	5	61	27	7	6	10	23	37	84	64	50
9	Exeter City	46	13	7	3	50	30	6	4	13	30	40	80	70	49
10	Stockport County	46	15	6	2	35	10	4	5	14	23	44	58	54	49
11	Bradford Park Ave.	46	12	10	1	48	25	5	5	13	22	43	70	68	49
12	Rochdale	46	15	4	4	46	19	3	6	14	19	41	65	60	46
13	Aldershot	46	14	5	4	50	22	4	4	15	27	52	77	74	45
14	Crewe Alexandra	46	14	3	6	51	31	4	6	13	28	57	79	88	45
15	Darlington	46	11	6	6	40	30	6	3	14	23	43	63	73	43
16	Workington	46	10	8	5	41	20	4	6	13	27	40	68	60	42
17	Doncaster Rovers	46	13	3	7	40	23	3	7	13	29	53	69	76	42
18	Barrow	46	11	8	4	52	29	4	3	16	25	58	77	87	41
19	Carlisle United	46	9	6	8	28	28	6	5	12	23	38	51	66	41
20	Chester	46	10	8	5	37	26	4	4	15	22	51	59	77	40
21	Southport	46	9	7	7	30	32	1	7	15	18	60	48	92	34
22	Gateshead	46	12	3	8	37	27	0	6	17	21	59	58	86	33
23	Oldham Athletic	46	5	7	11	20	30	3	5	15	21	53	41	83	28
24	Hartlepools United	46	9	2	12	40	41	1	5	17	19	68	59	109	27

- 1959/60 Season -

(Back): Doran, Westmorland, Fletcher, Oosthuizen, G.Thompson, Fairley, Bradley, Johnston, R.Thompson, Keen, Dick, Young(Train) (Middle): Tulloch, Graham, Blamire, Nichol, Mooney, Brown, Topping(Sec), Reed(Dir)
(Full details of front row not known)

- 1960/61 Season -

(Back): Marsden, Doran, O'Connor, Cavanagh, G.Thompson, Brown, Walker
(Middle): Powell (Manager), R.Thompson, Graham, Stewart, Terris, Morgan, Bevan, Young (Trainer)
(Front): McMillan, Fleming, Smith, Bradley

SEASON 1960/61

DIVISION 4

No.	Date	Opposition	Res.	H.T.	Att.	Goalscorers	Thompson G.	Bradley	McBain	Oliphant	Marsden	Thompson R.	Brayton	Blackley	Whitelaw	Walker	Morgan	Cavanagh	Doran	McMillan	Fletcher	Brown	Bevan	Smith	Fleming	Stewart	Graham	Terris	Scurr
1	20 Aug	Exeter	0-0	0-0	9933		1	4			6					10	7	8			5	2	11	9			3		
2	23	STOCKPORT	1-4	0-2	9261	Smith	1	4			6					10	7	8			5	2	11	9			3		
3	27	PETERBOROUGH	3-3	2-2	8334	Walker, Stewart, Cavanagh	1	4	3							10	7	8	6		5	2	11			9			
4	29	Stockport	0-2	0-0	9033		1	4	3							10	7	8	6		5	2	11			9			
5	3 Sep	Southport	0-3	0-2	4452		1	4								10	7	8		3	5	2	11			9	6		
6	6	ROCHDALE	1-2	1-1	5262	Smith	1	4	11						9	10	7	8		3	5	2		6					
7	10	DARLINGTON	4-4	2-3	4803	Smith(2), Morgan, R.Thompson	1	4	11			10	9				7	8		3	5	2		6					
8	13	Rochdale	1-2	1-1	4023	Smith	1	4							9	10		8		5	3	2	7	6				11	
9	17	Crystal Palace	1-1	0-1	15867	Smith	1	4							9	10		8		5	3	2	7	6				11	
10	19	Mansfield	3-1	2-0	3110	Brayton, Walker, Smith	1	4							9	10		8		5	3	2	7	6				11	
11	24	DONCASTER	2-1	2-0	5340	McMillan, Smith	1	4							9	10	7	8		5	3	2		6				11	
12	27	MANSFIELD	3-1	1-1	6135	Walker, Smith(2)	1	4							9	10	7	8		5	3	2		6				11	
13	1 Oct	Hartlepools	1-0	1-0	3259	Morgan	1	4							9	10	7	8		5	3	2		6				11	
14	5	Wrexham	1-2	0-0	6171	McMillan	1	4							9	10	7	8		5	3	2		6				11	
15	8	CREWE	0-1	0-0	4365		1	4							9	10	7	8		5	3	2		6				11	
16	15	York	0-4	0-2	4957		1	4		5					9	10	7	8		3		2		6				11	
17	22	ACCRINGTON S.	3-1	2-1	3849	Smith(2), Stewart	1	4	11	5					9	10		8		3		2		6		7			
18	29	Millwall	2-4	2-2	6732	Cavanagh, O.G.	1	4	11							10		8	5	3		2	7	6					9
19	12 Nov	Gillingham	1-1	1-1	5604	Walker	1	4	11	5			7			10		8		3		2		6					9
20	19	BRADFORD P.A.	2-2	1-0	4160	Blackley, Bradley	1	4	11	5			7			10		8		3		2		6					9
21	3 Dec	ALDERSHOT	2-2	2-2	3040	Cavanagh, Walker	1	4	11	5			7			10		8		3		2		6					9
22	10	Oldham	2-5	1-3	11800	Brayton, Walker	1		4	5			7		9	10	11	8		3		2		6					
23	17	EXETER	2-2	1-0	2484	Brayton, Blackley	1	6	4	5			7		9	10	11			3		2							8
24	26	Workington	1-2	1-1	3672	Blackley	1	6	4	5			7		9	10	11	8		3		2							
25	27	WORKINGTON	2-4	1-2	5290	Oliphant, Walker	1	6	4				7		9	10	11	8	5	3		2							
26	31	Peterborough	0-5	0-3	11539		1			4			7			10		8	5	3		2	6			9		11	
27	2 Jan	GILLINGHAM	1-3	1-0	3364	Cavanagh	1	6		4			7			10		8	5	3		2				9		11	
28	14	SOUTHPORT	1-0	1-0	2422	Walker	1	3	4		6		7			10	11	8			5	2							9
29	21	Darlington	0-0	0-0	6407		1	3	4		6		7			10	11	8			5	2							9
30	28	BARROW	1-0	0-0	2646	Blackley	1	3	4		6		7			10	11	8			5	2							9
31	4 Feb	CRYSTAL PALACE	2-0	1-0	4464	Brayton, McMillan	1	3	4		6		7	8	9	10	11				5	2							
32	11	Doncaster	0-1	0-1	3818		1	3	4		6		7	8	9	10	11				5	2							
33	18	HARTLEPOOLS	2-2	1-2	3667	McMillan, Whitelaw	1	3	4		6		7		9	10	11	8			5	2							
34	25	Crewe	0-3	0-2	4200		1	3	4		6		7		9	10	11	8			5	2							
35	4 Mar	YORK	1-1	0-1	3050	McMillan	1	3	4		6		7		9	10	11	8			5	2							
36	11	Accrington S.	0-1	0-0	2771		1	11	3	4	5	6	7		9	10		8				2							
37	18	MILLWALL	1-2	1-0	3096	Whitelaw	1	2	3	4	5	6		8	7	9	10	11											
38	21	Northampton	0-0	0-0	17282		1	2	3	4	5	6		8	7	9	10	11											
39	25	Barrow	2-0	1-0	3422	Walker(2)	1	2	3	4	5	6		8	7	9	10	11											
40	31	CHESTER	3-1	2-0	4381	Brayton, Whitelaw, Walker	1	2	3	4	5	6		8	7	9	10	11											
41	3 Apr	Chester	2-3	2-1	3908	Walker(2)	1	2	3	4	5	6		8	7	9	10	11											
42	8	Bradford P.A.	0-0	0-0	10467		1	2	3	4	5	6		8	7	9	10	11											
43	11	WREXHAM	1-0	0-0	4574	Walker	1	2	3	4	5	6		8	7	9	10	11											
44	15	NORTHAMPTON	2-1	1-1	3985	Blackley	1	2	3	4	5	6		8	7	9	10	11											
45	22	Aldershot	1-2	1-1	3826	Whitelaw	1	2	3	4	5	6		8	7	9	10	11											
46	29	OLDHAM	3-0	2-0	4292	Walker, Brayton, Whitelaw	1	2	3	4	5	6		8	7	9	10	11											

F.A. CUP

Rd	Date	Opposition	Res.	H.T.	Att.	Goalscorers	Thompson G.	Bradley	McBain	Oliphant	Whitelaw	Brayton	Walker	Cavanagh	McMillan	Brown	Smith
1R	5 Nov	Chester	1-0	1-0	5899	Bevan	1	4	11	5	9	7	10	8	3	2	6
2R	26	Port Vale	1-2	1-1	6392	Walker	1	4	11	5	9	7	10	8	3	2	6

LEAGUE CUP

Rd	Date	Opposition	Res.	H.T.	Att.	Goalscorers	Thompson G.	Bradley	McBain	Brayton	Walker	Morgan	Cavanagh	Doran	Smith	Stewart	Graham
1R	10 Oct	Stockport	0-2	0-1	8173		1	4	2	7	11	8	5	6	9	10	3

Final League Table

		Pl.	Home					Away					F.	A.	Pts
			W	D	L	F	A	W	D	L	F	A			
1	Peterborough Utd.	46	18	3	2	85	30	10	7	6	49	35	134	65	66
2	Crystal Palace	46	16	4	3	64	28	13	2	8	46	41	110	69	64
3	Northampton Town	46	16	4	3	53	25	9	6	8	37	37	90	62	60
4	Bradford Park Ave.	46	16	5	2	49	22	10	3	10	35	52	84	74	60
5	York City	46	17	3	3	50	14	4	6	13	30	46	80	60	51
6	Millwall	46	13	3	7	56	33	8	5	10	41	53	97	86	50
7	Darlington	46	11	7	5	41	24	7	6	10	37	46	78	70	49
8	Workington	46	14	3	6	38	28	7	4	12	36	48	74	76	49
9	Crewe Alexandra	46	11	4	8	40	29	9	5	9	21	38	61	67	49
10	Aldershot	46	16	4	3	55	19	2	5	16	24	50	79	69	45
11	Doncaster Rovers	46	15	0	8	52	33	4	7	12	24	45	76	78	45
12	Oldham Athletic	46	13	4	6	57	38	6	3	14	22	50	79	88	45
13	Stockport County	46	14	4	5	31	21	4	5	14	26	45	57	66	45
14	Southport	46	12	6	5	47	27	7	0	16	22	40	69	67	44
15	Gillingham	46	9	7	7	45	34	6	6	11	19	32	64	66	43
16	Wrexham	46	12	4	7	38	22	5	4	14	24	34	62	56	42
17	Rochdale	46	13	7	3	43	19	4	1	18	17	47	60	66	42
18	Accrington Stanley	46	12	4	7	44	32	4	4	15	30	56	74	88	40
19	Carlisle United	46	10	7	6	43	37	3	6	14	18	42	61	79	39
20	Mansfield Town	46	10	3	10	39	34	6	3	14	32	44	71	78	38
21	Exeter City	46	12	3	8	39	32	2	7	14	27	62	66	94	38
22	Barrow	46	10	6	7	33	28	3	5	15	19	51	52	79	37
23	Hartlepools United	46	10	4	9	46	40	2	4	17	25	63	71	103	32
24	Chester	46	9	7	7	38	35	2	2	19	23	69	61	104	31

SEASON 1961/62

DIVISION 4

No.	Date	Opposition	Res.	H.T.	Att.	Goalscorers	Harkness	Neil	Caldwell	Oliphant	Marsden	Thompson R.	Dagger	Brayton	Murdoch	Walker	Martin	Thompson G.	Whitelaw	Taylor	Stark	Scurr	Doran	Blackley	Armstrong	McBain
1	19 Aug	ALDERSHOT	2-1	0-1	6795	Oliphant, Walker		2	3	4	5	6	7			10		1	9	11	8					
2	21	Colchester	0-2	0-0	4979			2	3	4	5	6	7			8		1	9	11	10					
3	26	Stockport	2-1	0-0	4617	Whitelaw, Taylor		2	3	4	5	6	7			10		1	9	11	8					
4	29	COLCHESTER	1-1	0-1	8547	Whitelaw		2	3	4	5	6	7			10		1	9	11	8					
5	2 Sep	OLDHAM	2-0	0-0	6044	Whitelaw, Oliphant		2	3	4	5	6	7			10		1	9	11	8					
6	6	Chester	1-1	1-0	6974	Scurr		2	3	4	5	6	7			10		1	9	11	8					
7	9	Accrington	0-1	0-0	2905			2	3	4	5	6	7			10		1	9	11	8					
8	16	DARLINGTON	1-0	0-0	6247	Oliphant(pen)		2	3	4	5	6	7			10		1	9	11	8					
9	18	York	1-1	1-1	8171	Blackley		2	3	4	5	6	7			10		1	9	11				8		
10	23	Hartlepools	3-0	2-0	3931	Taylor(2), Walker		2	3	4		6	7			10		1	9	11		5		8		
11	27	YORK	3-2	2-1	8490	Walker(2), Oliphant(pen)		2	3	4	5	6	7			10		1	9	11				8		
12	30	SOUTHPORT	2-1	1-1	7558	Oliphant(pen), O.G.	1	2	3	4	5	6	7			10			9	11				8		
13	2 Oct	Tranmere	3-0	1-0	10050	Walker(2), Taylor	1	2		4	5	6	7			10			9	11				8		3
14	7	Chesterfield	3-1	2-1	3250	Walker(3)	1	2		4	5	6	7			10			9	11				8		3
15	10	TRANMERE	0-3	0-1	11460		1	2		4	5	6	7			10			9	11				8		3
16	14	GILLINGHAM	1-2		7713	Blackley	1	2	3	4	5	6	7			9				11				8	10	
17	21	Millwall	0-3	0-3	11421			2	3	4	5	6	7			10		1	9	11				8		
18	28	MANSFIELD	1-0	0-0	5099	Taylor		2	3	4		6	7	8		10		1		11	9	5				
19	11 Nov	ROCHDALE	2-2	2-0	5263	Brayton, Taylor		2	3	4	5	6	7	8		10		1	9	11						
20	18	Crewe	0-3	0-2	7048			2	3	4	5	6	7	8		10		1	9	11						
21	2 Dec	Wrexham	2-2	1-0	11044	Walker(2)		2	3	4	5	6	7	8		10		1	9	11						
22	9	DONCASTER	1-0	0-0	4639	Stark		2	3	4		6	7	8		10		1		11	9	5				
23	16	Aldershot	1-0	0-0	5345	Walker		2	3	4	5	6	7	8		10		1		11	9					
24	23	STOCKPORT	1-0	0-0	4658	Brayton		2	3	4	5	6	7	8		10		1		11	9					
25	26	WORKINGTON	1-2	1-1	8967	Brayton		2	3	4	5	6	7	8		10		1		11	9					
26	13 Jan	Oldham	0-5	0-2	11693			2	3	4	5	6	7	11		10		1			9	8				
27	20	ACCRINGTON	2-0	1-0	4500	Stark, Walker		2	3	4	5	6	7	11	8	10		1			9					
28	27	EXETER	2-1	0-1	4993	Stark(2)		2	3	4	5	6	7	11	8	10		1			9					
29	3 Feb	Darlington	1-2	1-0	4103	Brayton		2	3	4	5	6	7	11	8	10		1			9					
30	10	HARTLEPOOLS	1-0	0-0	4208	Taylor		2	3	4	5	6	7	8		10		1		11	9					
31	16	Southport	0-0		3533			2	3	4	5	6	7	8				1		11	9				10	
32	24	CHESTERFIELD	3-1	2-0	3866	Dagger, Murdoch, Stark		2	3	4	5	6	7	8		10		1		11	9					
33	3 Mar	Gillingham	1-4	0-1	5483	Walker		2	3	4	5	6	7	8		10		1		11	9					
34	6	Workington	1-2	1-0	5239	Walker		2	3	4		6	7			10	11	1			9	8	5			
35	10	MILLWALL	3-2	1-2	4225	Start, Brayton, Oliphant(pen)		2	3	4	5	6	7	8		10	11	1			9					
36	13	WREXHAM	1-0	1-0	8230	Walker		2	3	4	5	6	7	8		10	11	1			9					
37	17	Mansfield	2-5	0-3	5558	Stark(2)		2	3	4	5	6	7	8		10	11	1			9					
38	24	BARROW	0-0	0-0	4862		1	2	3	4		6	7	8		10	11				9		5			
39	26	Barrow	3-0		4874	Stark(3)	1	2	3	4		6	7	8		10	11				9		5			
40	31	Rochdale	1-1	1-0	2453	Martin	1	2	3	4		6	7	8		10	11				9		5			
41	6 Apr	CREWE	3-0	0-0	6456	Dagger, Brayton, Martin	1	2	3	4		6	7	8		10	11				9		5			
42	14	Exeter	0-4		3278		1	2	3	4		6	7	8		10	11				9		5			
43	20	BRADFORD	2-4	1-2	7702	Walker, Murdoch	1	2	3	4		6	7	8	9	10	11						5			
44	23	Bradford	2-3	0-1	8411	Brayton, Oliphant	1	2	3	4	5	6	7	8	9	10	11									
45	28	Doncaster	2-1	2-1	2349	Walker(2)	1	2	3	4	5	6	7	8	9	10	11									
46	1 May	CHESTER	2-0	1-0	12660	Brayton, Walker	1	2	3	4	5	6	7	8	9	10	11									

F.A. CUP

	Date	Opposition	Res.	H.T.	Att.	Goalscorers	Harkness	Neil	Caldwell	Oliphant	Marsden	Thompson R.	Dagger	Brayton	Murdoch	Walker	Martin	Thompson G.	Whitelaw	Taylor	Stark	Scurr	Doran	Blackley	Armstrong	McBain
1R	4 Nov	Darlington	4-0	0-2	7355	Whitelaw(2), Brayton, Taylor		2	3	4	5	6	7	8		10		1		11	9					
2R	25 Nov	Barnsley	2-1	1-0	6931	Walker, Taylor		2	3	4	5	6	7	8		10		1		11	9					
3R	6 Jan	Wolves	1-3		14113	R.Thompson		2	3	4	5	6	7	11		10		1	9		8					

LEAGUE CUP

	Date	Opposition	Res.	H.T.	Att.	Goalscorers	Harkness	Neil	Caldwell	Oliphant	Marsden	Thompson R.	Dagger	Brayton	Murdoch	Walker	Martin	Thompson G.	Whitelaw	Taylor	Stark	Scurr	Doran	Blackley	Armstrong	McBain
1R	12 Sep	HUDDERSFIELD	1-1	1-0	4893	Oliphant(pen)		2	3	4	5	6	7			10		1	9	11				8		
1Rr	25	Huddersfield	0-3	0-2	8695			2	3	4	5	6	7			10		1	9	11				8		

Final League Table

		Pl.	Home					Away					F.	A.	Pts
			W	D	L	F	A	W	D	L	F	A			
1	Millwall	44	16	3	3	47	18	7	7	8	40	44	87	62	56
2	Colchester United	44	17	4	1	78	24	6	5	11	26	47	104	71	55
3	Wrexham	44	12	6	4	56	23	10	3	9	40	33	96	56	53
4	Carlisle United	44	15	3	4	35	22	7	5	10	29	41	64	63	52
5	Bradford City	44	14	5	3	58	32	7	4	11	36	54	94	86	51
6	York City	44	17	2	3	62	19	3	8	11	22	34	84	53	50
7	Aldershot	44	16	4	2	56	20	6	1	15	25	40	81	60	49
8	Workington	44	12	6	4	40	23	7	5	10	29	47	69	70	49
9	Barrow	44	12	7	3	49	20	5	7	10	25	38	74	58	48
10	Crewe Alexandra	44	16	3	3	53	24	4	3	15	26	46	79	70	46
11	Oldham Athletic	44	12	7	3	47	26	5	5	12	30	44	77	70	46
12	Rochdale	44	14	3	5	47	28	5	4	13	24	43	71	71	45
13	Darlington	44	13	5	4	37	24	5	4	13	24	49	61	73	45
14	Mansfield Town	44	14	3	5	51	19	5	3	14	26	47	77	66	44
15	Tranmere Rovers	44	15	2	5	53	37	5	2	15	17	44	70	81	44
16	Stockport County	44	13	3	6	42	27	4	6	12	28	42	70	69	43
17	Southport	44	13	5	4	36	25	4	4	14	25	46	61	71	43
18	Exeter City	44	11	5	6	43	32	2	6	14	19	45	62	77	37
19	Chesterfield	44	11	3	8	43	38	3	6	13	27	49	70	87	37
20	Gillingham	44	10	6	6	48	30	3	5	14	25	64	73	94	37
21	Doncaster Rovers	44	8	5	9	34	29	3	2	17	26	56	60	85	29
22	Hartlepools United	44	6	5	11	27	35	2	6	14	25	66	52	101	27
23	Chester	44	5	9	8	36	37	2	3	17	18	59	54	96	26

Accrington Stanley resigned during season.

- 1961/62 Season -

Back row: *Oliphant, Neil, Marsden. Thompson (G), Caldwell, Thompson (R).*
Front row: *Dagger, Scurr, Whitelaw. Walker. Taylor.*

- 1962/63 Season -

(Back): Stark, Dagger, Thompson, Brayton, Walker, Forrest, Caldwell
(Middle): Young(Trainer), Davies, Marsden, Richardson, Harkness, Dean, Green, Neil, Nicholson
(Front): McBain, Oliphant, Grant, Powell(Manager), Blue, Martin, Taylor

SEASON 1962/63

DIVISION 3

No.	Date	Opposition	Res.	H.T.	Att.	Goalscorers	Dean	Caldwell	McBain	Oliphant	Marsden	McConnell	Taylor	Brayton	Livingstone	McIlmoyle	Kirkup	Neil	Dagger	Thompson R.	Davies	Walker	Stark	Forrest	Blue	Harkness	Grant	Martin
1	21 Aug	PETERBOROUGH	1-4	1-1	12238	Stark		3		4	5		11					2	7	6	8	10	9		1			
2	24	QPR	2-5	1-2	8116	Stark, Taylor			3	4	5	6	11					2	7		8	10	9		1			
3	27	Peterborough	2-2	1-1	13668	Stark, Walker	1		3		5	4	11					2	7	6	8	10	9					
4	31	Hull	1-3	1-2	8325	Stark	1		3		5	4	11					2	7	6	8	10	9					
5	8 Sep	CRYSTAL PALACE	2-2	1-1	6591	Grant, Dagger	1		3					8				2	7	6		5	9	4			10	11
6	12	Bradford P.A.	1-3	0-3	7429	Dagger	1		3	10		4	11					2	7	6	8	5	9					
7	15	Wrexham	1-2	1-2	9378	Dagger	1		3	10		4	11					2	7	6	8	5	9					
8	18	SWINDON	0-0	0-0	6602		1		3		4	5	11					2	7	6	8	10	9					
9	22	HALIFAX	1-0	0-0	4895	Walker	1		3		4	5	11					2	7	6	8	10	9					
10	29	Bristol Rovers	1-1	1-0	9104	Stark	1		3		4	5	11					2	7	6	8	10	9					
11	2 Oct	BRIGHTON	1-0	0-0	7865	Dagger	1		3		4	5	11					2	7	6	8	10	9					
12	5	BRISTOL CITY	2-5	1-2	8229	Dagger, Davies	1		3		4	5	11					2	7	6	8	10	9					
13	9	Brighton	0-1	0-1	6556		1		3			5	11					2	7	6	8	10		4			9	
14	12	Reading	0-2	0-0	12922		1		3			5	11					2	7	6	8	10	9	4				
15	20	PORT VALE	1-1	1-1	5627	Stark	1		3		5	6		8				2	7			10	9	4				11
16	27	Shrewsbury	1-1	1-1	5368	Stark	1		3			5	4	11	8			2	7			10	9					
17	10 Nov	Southend	0-2	0-0	8856		1		3			5	4	11	8			2	7			10	9					
18	11	COLCHESTER	3-1	0-1	3518	Brayton, Taylor, Thompson	1		3			5	4	11	8	9		2	7	4		10						
19	30	BOURNEMOUTH	0-3	0-0	6903		1		3			5	4	11	8			2	7	6		10						
20	8 Dec	Coventry	2-3	1-1	8853	Blue, Taylor	1	2	3			5	4	11	8	9					6	10			7			
21	15	NORTHAMPTON	1-2	0-1	3933	McConnell(pen)	1	3	4		2	5		8	9		11				6	10			7			
22	22	Q.p.r.	2-2	1-1	9733	Livingstone(2)	1	2	3	4	5	6	7	8	9		11					10						
23	26	WATFORD	2-1	1-1	5479	Brayton, Livingstone	1	2	3	4	5	6	7	8	9		11					10						
24	29	Watford	1-5	1-3	8397	McConnell(pen)	1	2	3	4	5	6	7	8	9		11					10						
25	23 Feb	Bristol City	2-2	0-0	8413	Brayton(2)	1	2	3	4	5	6	7	8	9		11					10						
26	9 Mar	Port Vale	0-2	0-2	6308		1	5	3	4		6	7	8	9		11	2				10						
27	12	NOTTS COUNTRY	4-2	2-2	6732	Braytn,Kirkup,Livingstne,McIlmoyle	1	5	3	4		6	7	8	9	10	11	2										
28	16	SHREWSBURY	2-1	2-1	4825	Livingstone, McConnell	1	5	3	4		6	7	8	9	10	11	2										
29	21	Notts County	0-1	0-0	3455		1	5	3			6		8	9	10	11	2	7									
30	23	Millwall	0-2	0-0	10005		1	5	3		2			8	9	10	11		7	6				4				
31	26	Halifax	4-2	1-2	2735	Kirkup, Livingstone, McIlmoyle(2)	1	5	3	4		6		7	9	8	11	2				10						
32	30	SOUTHEND	1-2	1-0	5435	Livingstone	1	5	3	4		6	7	9	8		11	2				10						
33	2 Apr	BRISTOL ROVERS	4-0	2-0	5354	Livingstone,McIlmyle,Braytn,Dgger	1	5	3	4		6		9	8	10	11	2	7									
34	6	Colchester	1-2	1-0	4282	Livingstone	1	5	3	4		6		9	8	10	11	2	7									
35	12	BARNSLEY	2-1	1-0	5944	Davies, Livingstone	1	5	3	4		6		8	9		11	2	7		10							
36	14	Barnsley	0-2	0-1	8146		1	6	3	4	5			8	9	10	11	2	7									
37	20	Bournemouth	1-5	0-1	8899	Dagger	1	5	3	4		6		8	9	10	11	2	7									
38	23	BRADFORD P.A.	3-0	2-0	4845	Brayton, Davies, Oliphant(pen)	1	2	3	4	5	6		8	9		11		7			10						
39	27	COVENTRY	0-1	0-1	4751		1	2	3	10	5	6		8		9	11		7	4								
40	30	Swindon	0-2	0-1	14221		1	2	3	4	5	6		8	10	9			7									
41	6 May	READING	1-1	1-0	4305	Kirkup	1	2	3	4	5	6		9	8	10	11		7									
42	9	Northampton	0-2	0-2	15062		1	5	3	4		6		7	9	8	11	2				10						
43	11	HULL	2-1	1-1	2519	Livingstone, McIlmoyle	1	5	3	4		6	7	8	9	10	11	2										
44	14	MILLWALL	4-3	2-1	3292	Brayton,Livingstone,Kirkup,Oliphnt	1	5	3	4			10	7	8	9	11	2					6					
45	18	Crystal Place	0-3	0-1	10242		1		3	4	5		10	7	8	9	11	2					6					
46	23	WREXHAM	2-2	2-1	3092	McIlmoyle(2)	1	2	3	4	5	6	7	8	9	10	11											

F.A. CUP

No.	Date	Opposition	Res.	H.T.	Att.	Goalscorers	Dean	Caldwell	McBain	Oliphant	Marsden	McConnell	Taylor	Brayton	Livingstone	McIlmoyle	Kirkup	Neil	Dagger	Thompson R.	Davies	Walker	Stark	Forrest	Blue	Harkness	Grant	Martin
1R	3 Nov	HARTLEPOOLS	2-1	1-1	6627	Brayton, O.G.	1		3			5	4	11	8			2	7	6	10	9						
2R	24	Blyth Spartans	2-0	1-0	5928	Walker, Brayton	1		3			5	4	11	8	9		2	7	6		10						
2R	5 Jan	GRVSEND & NTHFLEET	0-1	0-0	9115		1	2	3	4	5	6	7	8	9		11					10						

LEAGUE CUP

No.	Date	Opposition	Res.	H.T.	Att.	Goalscorers	Dean	Caldwell	McBain	Oliphant	Marsden	McConnell	Taylor	Brayton	Livingstone	McIlmoyle	Kirkup	Neil	Dagger	Thompson R.	Davies	Walker	Stark	Forrest	Blue	Harkness	Grant	Martin
1R	3 Sep	Tranmere	3-2	3-1	5546	Grant(3)	1		3					8				2	7	6		5	9	4			10	11
2R	26	Torquay	2-1	1-1	3899	Walker, Taylor	1		3	4	5		11					2	7	6	8	10	9					
3R	16 Oct	NORWICH	1-1	0-1	8105	Brayton	1		3			5	6	11				2	7		8	10	9	4				
3Rr	24	Norwich	0-5	0-3	14210		1		3			5	4	11	8			2	7	6	10	9						

Final League Table

		Pl.	Home					Away					F.	A.	Pts
			W	D	L	F	A	W	D	L	F	A			
1	Northampton Town	46	16	6	1	64	19	10	4	9	45	41	109	60	62
2	Swindon Town	46	18	2	3	60	22	4	12	7	27	34	87	56	58
3	Port Vale	46	16	4	3	47	25	7	4	12	25	33	72	58	54
4	Coventry City	46	14	6	3	54	28	4	11	8	29	41	83	69	53
5	Bournemouth	46	11	12	0	39	16	7	4	12	24	30	63	46	52
6	Peterborough Utd.	46	11	5	7	48	33	9	6	8	45	42	93	75	51
7	Notts County	46	15	3	5	46	29	4	10	9	27	45	73	74	51
8	Southend United	46	11	7	5	38	24	8	5	10	37	53	75	77	50
9	Wrexham	46	14	6	3	54	27	6	3	14	30	56	84	83	49
10	Hull City	46	12	6	5	40	22	7	4	12	34	47	74	69	48
11	Crystal Palace	46	10	7	6	38	22	7	6	10	30	36	68	58	47
12	Colchester United	46	11	6	6	41	35	7	5	11	32	58	73	93	47
13	Queen's Park Rgs.	46	9	6	8	44	36	8	5	10	41	40	85	76	45
14	Bristol City	46	10	9	4	54	38	6	4	13	46	54	100	92	45
15	Shrewsbury Town	46	13	4	6	57	41	3	8	12	26	40	83	81	44
16	Millwall	46	11	6	6	50	32	4	7	12	32	55	82	87	43
17	Watford	46	12	3	8	55	40	5	5	13	27	45	82	85	42
18	Barnsley	46	12	6	5	39	28	3	5	15	24	46	63	74	41
19	Bristol Rovers	46	11	8	4	45	29	4	3	16	25	59	70	88	41
20	Reading	46	13	4	6	51	30	3	4	16	23	48	74	78	40
21	Bradford Park Ave.	46	10	9	4	43	36	4	3	16	36	61	79	97	40
22	Brighton & Hove A.	46	7	6	10	28	38	5	6	12	30	46	58	84	36
23	Carlisle United	46	12	4	7	41	37	1	5	17	20	52	61	89	35
24	Halifax Town	46	8	3	12	41	51	1	9	13	23	55	64	106	30

SEASON 1963/64

DIVISION 4

No.	Date	Opposition	Res.	H.T.	Att.	Goalscorers	Ross	Neil	Caldwell	McConnell	Passmoor	Thompson R.	Taylor	Evans	McIlmoyle	Livingstone	Kirkup	Brayton	Dean	Marsden	Oliphant	Twentyman	Lornie	Johnstone	Forrest	Garrett	Goodall	McNichol	Davies
1	24 Aug	DARLINGTON	3-3	2-2	5782	McIlmoyle(2), Livingstone		2	3	6					8	9	11		1	5	4	7							
2	26	EXETER	3-0	1-0	6454	McIlmoyle(2), Livingstone		2	3	6					8	9	11		1	5	4	7							10
3	30	Tranmere	1-6	0-3	9086	McIlmoyle			3	6					8	9	11		1	5	4	7						2	10
4	7 Sep	HALIFAX	3-0	1-0	5224	Livingstone(2), Davies		2	3	6	4		7		8	9			1	5				11					10
5	11	Exeter	0-1	0-1	5671			2	3	6	4		7		8	9			1	5				11					10
6	14	Torquay	1-3	0-1	4680	McIlmoyle		2	3	6	4		7		8	9	11		1	5									10
7	16	Hartlepools	6-0	2-0	3815	McIlmyle(2),Johnstne,Dvies,Braytn,OG		2	3	6	4				9		11	8	1	5				7					10
8	20	OXFORD	2-1	0-0	7196	McIlmoyle, O.G.		2	3	6	4		7		9			8	1	5				11					10
9	27	ALDERSHOT	4-0	3-0	3144	Kirkup(3), McIlmoyle	1	2	3	6	4		7		9	11	8			5									10
10	1 Oct	HARTLEPOOLS	7-1	6-0	7075	McIlmoyle(4),Brayton(2),McConnell	1	2	3	6	4		7		9	11	8			5									10
11	5	Bradford	2-2	1-2	3658	McIlmoyle, Brayton	1	2	3	6	4		7		9	11	8			5									10
12	9	Gillingham	0-2	0-1	17421		1	2	3	6	4		7		9	11	8			5									10
13	12	Newport	4-1	2-1	5489	McConnell(2), McIlmoyle, Kirkup	1	2	3	8	4		7		9	11				5				6					10
14	15	GILLINGHAM	3-1	1-0	11900	McIlmoyle(3)	1	2	3	8	4		7		9	11				5				6					10
15	18	STOCKPORT	0-0	0-0	9507		1	2	3	8	4		7		9	11				5				6					10
16	22	LINCOLN	5-0	2-0	10257	Livingstone(3), Davies, O.G.	1	2	3		4		7		9	8	11			6	5								10
17	26	Bradford P.A.	1-1	1-0	6448	Livingstone	1	2	3		4		7		9	8	11			6	5								10
18	30	Lincoln	2-0	0-0	7013	McIlmoyle(2)	1	2	3	6	4		7		9	8	11			5									10
19	2 Nov	CHESTERFIELD	1-0	1-0	8223	Kirkup	1	2	3	6	4		7		9	8	11			5									10
20	9	Doncaster	1-1	0-1	5397	Davies(pen)	1	2	3	6	4		7		9	8				5		11							10
21	23	Chester	2-4	0-3	8223	Livingstone, McIlmoyle	1	2	3	6	4		7		9	8	11			5									10
22	30	YORK	4-0	2-0	5884	McIlmoyle(2), Brayton, Davies	1	2	3	6	4				9	8	11	7										5	10
23	14 Dec	Darlington	6-1	1-0	3075	Livingstne(3),McIlmoyle(2),McCnnell	1	2	3	6	5	4	7		9	8	11												10
24	21	TRANMERE	5-2	4-1	6671	McIlmoyle(3), Livingstone, Brayton	1	2	3	6	5	4	7		9	8	11	10											
25	26	Workington	2-2	2-1	18633	Livingstone(2)	1	2	3	6	5	4	7		9	8	11												
26	28	WORKINGTON	3-1	3-0	16347	McIlmoyle, Taylor, Davies	1	2	3	6	5	4	7		9	8	11												10
27	11 Jan	Halifax	2-1	1-0	3389	Livingstone, Kirkup	1	2	3	6	5	4	7		9	8	11												10
28	18	TORQUAY	0-1	0-1	9844		1	2	3	6	5	4	7		9	8	11												10
29	1 Feb	Oxford	2-1	1-1	10546	McIlmoyle, Davies(pen)	1	2	3	6	5	4	7		9		11												10
30	4	BRADFORD	1-2	0-0	9914	Evans	1	2	3	6	5	4		7	9		11												10
31	7	Aldershot	2-3	0-1	5135	McConnell, O.G.	1	2	3	8	5		10		9					4	6				7				
32	22	NEWPORT	3-3	2-2	7528	McIlmoyle(2), Livingstone	1	2	3	6	5	4	7		9	8	11												10
33	24	BRIGHTON	0-1	0-1	8506		1	2	3	6	5	4	7		9	8								11					10
34	29	Stockport	3-0	2-0	3645	Thompson, McIlmoyle, Evans	1	2	3	6	5	4		11	9		8												10
35	7 Mar	BRADFORD P.A.	4-0	2-0	7175	Evans(2), McIlmoyle, McConnell	1	2	3	4	5	6		8	9		11	7											10
36	14	Chesterfield	0-2	0-2	3435		1	2	3	4	5	6		10	9	8	11	7											
37	16	Barrow	2-2	2-0	2385	Evans, Davies	1	2	3	4	5	6	7	8	9		11												10
38	21	DONCASTER	6-0	3-0	4753	Evans(3),McIlmoyle,Davies,Taylor		2	3	4	5	6	7	8	9		11		1										10
39	27	SOUTHPORT	5-2	1-2	9557	Evns(2),Dvies(p),McCnnell,Lvngstne		2	3	4	5	6	7	8	9		11		1										10
40	28	Rochdale	1-1	1-0	2736	Livingstone		2	3	4		6	7	8	10	9		11	1	5									
41	30	Southport	0-3	0-2	3778			2	3	4		6	7	9	8		11		1	5									10
42	4 Apr	CHESTER	3-1	2-1	6940	McIlmoyle(2), Evans	1	2	3	4	5	6	7	8	9	10	11												
43	11	York	0-0	0-0	3151		1	2	3	4	5	6	7	8	9	10	11												
44	17	BARROW	4-1	3-0	9538	Evans(2), Livingstone(2)	1	2	3	4	5	6	7	8	9	10	11												
45	21	ROCHDALE	1-0	1-0	11556	Evans	1	2	3	4	5	6	7	8	9	10	11												
46	25	Brighton	3-1	3-0	8773	Evans(2), McIlmoyle	1	2	3	4	5	6		8	9		11	7											10

F.A. CUP

	Date	Opposition	Res.	H.T.	Att.	Goalscorers	Ross	Neil	Caldwell	McConnell	Passmoor	Thompson R.	Taylor	Evans	McIlmoyle	Livingstone	Kirkup	Brayton	Dean	Marsden	Oliphant	Twentyman	Lornie	Johnstone	Forrest	Garrett	Goodall	McNichol	Davies
1R	16 Nov	York	5-2	3-0	7343	Lvingstne,McIlmyle,Dvies(p),Krkup,Tylor	1	2	3	6			4	7	9	8	11											5	10
2R	7 Dec	GATESHEAD	4-3	3-0	12719	McIlmoyle(3), Taylor	1	2	3	6	5	4	7		9	8	11												10
3R	4 Jan	QPR	2-0	1-0	15359	Livingstone, McIlmoyle	1	2	3	6	5	4	7		9	8	11												10
4R	25 Jan	Bedford Town	3-0	2-0	18000	Livingstone, Kirkup, Davies(pen)	1	2	3	6	5	4	7		9	8	11												10
5R	15 Feb	Preston	0-1	0-0	37100		1	2	3	8	5		10		9		11			4	6				7				

LEAGUE CUP

	Date	Opposition	Res.	H.T.	Att.	Goalscorers	Ross	Neil	Caldwell	McConnell	Passmoor	Thompson R.	Taylor	Evans	McIlmoyle	Livingstone	Kirkup	Brayton	Dean	Marsden	Oliphant	Twentyman	Lornie	Johnstone	Forrest	Garrett	Goodall	McNichol	Davies
1R	4 Sep	CREWE	3-2	2-1	5874	Johnstone, Livingstone, McIlmoyle		2	3	6	4		7		8	9			1	5				11					10
2R	25	Manchester City	0-2	0-0	37916			2	3	6	4		7		9		11	8	1	5									10

Final League Table

		Pl	Home W	D	L	F	A	Away W	D	L	F	A	F.	A.	Pts
1	Gillingham	46	16	7	0	37	10	7	7	9	22	20	59	30	60
2	Carlisle United	46	17	3	3	70	20	8	7	8	43	38	113	58	60
3	Workington	46	15	6	2	46	19	5	9	9	30	33	76	52	59
4	Exeter City	46	12	9	2	39	14	8	9	6	23	23	62	37	58
5	Bradford City	46	15	3	5	45	24	10	3	10	31	38	76	62	56
6	Torquay United	46	16	6	1	60	20	4	5	14	20	34	80	54	51
7	Tranmere Rovers	46	12	4	7	46	30	8	7	8	39	43	85	73	51
8	Brighton & Hove A.	46	13	3	7	45	22	6	9	8	26	30	71	52	50
9	Aldershot	46	15	3	5	58	28	4	7	12	25	50	83	78	48
10	Halifax Town	46	14	4	5	47	28	3	10	10	30	49	77	77	48
11	Lincoln City	46	15	2	6	49	31	4	7	12	18	44	67	75	47
12	Chester	46	17	3	3	47	18	2	5	16	18	42	65	60	46
13	Bradford Park Ave.	46	13	5	5	50	34	5	4	14	25	47	75	81	45
14	Doncaster Rovers	46	11	8	4	46	23	4	4	15	24	52	70	75	42
15	Newport County	46	12	3	8	35	24	5	5	13	29	49	64	73	42
16	Chesterfield	46	8	6	9	29	27	7	3	13	28	44	57	71	42
17	Stockport County	46	12	7	4	32	19	5	5	15	18	49	50	68	42
18	Oxford United	46	10	7	6	37	27	4	6	13	22	36	59	63	41
19	Darlington	46	8	9	6	40	37	6	3	14	26	56	66	93	40
20	Rochdale	46	9	8	6	36	24	3	7	13	20	35	56	59	39
21	Southport	46	12	6	5	42	29	3	3	17	21	59	63	88	39
22	York City	46	9	3	11	29	26	5	4	14	23	40	52	66	35
23	Hartlepools United	46	8	7	8	30	36	4	2	17	24	57	54	93	33
24	Barrow	46	4	10	9	30	36	2	8	13	21	57	51	93	30

- 1963/64 Season -

(Back): Johnson, Lornie, Taylor, Oliphant, Forrest, Davies. (Middle): Sharp, Nicholson(Physo), Twentyman, Neil, Ross, Dean, Garrett, Green, Kirkup, Young(Train), Dent(Sec.)
(Front): Caldwell, McIlmoyle, Goodall, Ashman (Manager), McConnell, Livingstone, Marsden

- 1964/65 Season -

● *Third Division Champions 1964-1965. Back Row (left to right): D. Young (trainer), H. Neil. T. Caldwell, J. Dean, P. McConnell, T. Passmoor, S. Harland. Front Row: J. Blain, W. Carlin, F. Large, J. Evans, R. Simpson.*

SEASON 1964/65

DIVISION 3

No.	Date	Opposition	Res.	H.T.	Att.	Goalscorers	Dean	Neil	Caldwell	McConnell	Passmoor	Harland	Blain	Carlin	Large	Evans	Simpson	Ross	Brayton	Livingstone	McIlmoyle	Johnstone	Kirkup	Garbutt	Oliphant	Murray
1	22	Colchester	1-0	1-0	4420	McIlmoyle		2	3	4	5	6				10		1	8	11	9		7			
2	24	PORT VALE	1-1	1-0	11809	Oliphant		2	3		5	6				8		1	10	7	9	11			4	
3	28	BRENTFORD	0-1	0-1	11023			2	3	4		6				8		1	10	7	9	11			5	
4	31	Port Vale	3-1	3-1	8003	Brayton, Johnstone, McConnell		2	3	4		6	7					1	10	8	9	11			5	
5	5 Sep	Bristol Rovers	2-5	1-2	12580	Livingstone(2)		2	3	4	5	6	7					1	10	8	9	11				
6	8	WATFORD	1-1	1-0	8817	O.G.		2	3	4	5	6	7					1	10	8	9	11				
7	12	OLDHAM	2-0	0-0	9618	Brayton, Harland		2	3	4	5	6	7					1	10	8	9	11				
8	17	Watford	0-0	0-0	9387			2	3	4	5	6	7			8		1	10		9	11				
9	19	Exeter	0-0	0-0	7368			2	3	4	5	6	7			8		1	10		9	11				
10	26	BOURNEMOUTH	3-4	3-2	8708	Brayton, Johnstone, McConnell		2	3	4	5	6		8		10		1	7		9	11				
11	1 Oct	Luton	1-1	0-1	7745	Large		2	3	4	5	6		8	9	10		1	7			11				
12	3	Peterborough	2-1	0-1	11012	Brayton, Evans		2	3	4	5	6		8		10		1	7		9	11				
13	7	LUTON	1-1	0-1	9038	Evans		2	3	4	5	6		8		10		1	7		9	11				
14	9	Hull	0-1	0-0	10931			2	3	4	5	6		8		10		1	7		9	11				
15	17	GILLINGHAM	3-1	0-1	7342	Evans, Large, McConnell	1	2	3	4	5	6	7	8	9	10	11									
16	21	Grimsby	1-1	0-0	5345		1	2	3	4	5	6		8	9	10			7			11				
17	23	Bristol City	2-1	1-0	10303	Evans, Kirkup		2	3	4	5	6		8	9	10		1	7				11			
18	27	WALSALL	2-1	1-0	10188	Evans, Kirkup		2	3	4	5	6		8	9	10		1	7				11			
19	30	Q.P.R.	2-0	1-0	9483	Blain, Kirkup		2	3	4	5	6	7	8	9	10		1					11			
20	7 Nov	Shrewsbury	2-2	2-1	5416	Large, McConnell		2	3	4	5	6	7	8	9	10		1					11			
21	21	Southend	0-1	0-1	6422			2	3	4	5	6	7	8	9	10		1					11			
22	28	BARNSLEY	4-0	2-0	6723	Carlin, Evans, Large, Neil	1	2	3	4	5	6	7	8	9	10							11			
23	5 Dec	Walsall	0-1	0-0	5578		1	2	3	4	5	6	7	8	9	10				11						
24	12	COLCHESTER	4-1	1-1	5747	Large(2), Blain, McConnell	1	2	3	4	5	6	7	8	9	10	11									
25	19	Brentford	1-6	1-2	8400	Large	1	2	3	4	5	6	7	8	9	10	11									
26	26	WORKINGTON	1-0	1-0	14142	Large	1	2	3	4	5	6	7		9	10	11		8							
27	28	Workington	1-0	1-0	11900	McConnell	1	2	3	4	5	6	7		9	10	11		8							
28	2 Jan	BRISTOL ROVERS	1-2	1-2	11311	Evans	1	2	3	4	5	6	7	8	9		11			10						
29	9	GRIMSBY	3-1	2-0	7144	Blain, McConnell, Simpson	1	2	3	4	5	6	7	8	9	10	11									
30	16	Oldham	3-2	2-1	4950	Evans(2), Simpson	1	2	3	4	5	6	7	8	9	10	11									
31	29	Scunthorpe	1-0	0-0	6710	Carlin	1		3	4	5	6	7	8	9	10	11							2		
32	6 Feb	Bournemouth	4-0	1-0	6841	Evans(2), Large, O.G.	1		3	4	5	6	7	8	9	10	11							2		
33	13	PETERBOROUGH	2-1	1-0	9845	Blain, Simpson	1	2	3	4	5	6	7	8	9	10	11									
34	20	HULL	0-0	0-0	17174		1	2	3	4	5	6	7	8	9	10	11									
35	27	Gillingham	0-1	0-0	14384		1	2	3	4	5	6	7	8	9	10	11									
36	6 Mar	SCUNTHORPE	3-1	1-1	9481	Evans, Harland, Large	1	2	3	4	5	6	7	8	9	10	11									
37	9	EXETER	2-1	1-0	11544	Carlin, Large	1	2	3	4	5	6	7	8	9	10	11									
38	12	Q.p.r.	2-1	0-1	5934	Blain, Evans	1	2	3	4	5	6	7	8	9	10	11									
39	16	READING	1-2	0-2	11864	Large	1	2	3	4	5	6	7	8	9	10	11									
40	19	SHREWSBURY	2-1	1-0	10435	Large, Livingstone	1	2	3	4	5	6	7		9		11		8	10						
41	27	Reading	2-1	2-0	6356	Carlin, Evans	1	2	3	4	5	6	7	8	9	10	11							2		
42	2 Apr	SOUTHEND	4-3	3-1	12050	Evans(2), Large, Simpson	1	2	3		5	6	7	8	9	10	11							4		
43	10	Barnsley	2-1	1-1	2919	Caldwell, Carlin	1	2	3	4	5	6	7	8	9	10	11									
44	16	BRISTOL CITY	1-1	0-1	16069	Harland	1	2	3	4	5	6	7	8	9	10	11									
45	19	Mansfield	0-2	0-2	13832		1	2	3	4	5	6	7	8	9	10	11									
46	20	MANSFIELD	3-0	3-0	18764	Large(2), Evans	1	2	3	4	5	6	7	8	9	10	11									

F.A. CUP

No.	Date	Opposition	Res.	H.T.	Att.	Goalscorers	Dean	Neil	Caldwell	McConnell	Passmoor	Harland	Blain	Carlin	Large	Evans	Simpson	Ross	Brayton	Livingstone	McIlmoyle	Johnstone	Kirkup	Garbutt	Oliphant	Murray
1R	14 Nov	Crook Town	0-1	0-0	4600		1	2	3	4	5	6	7	8	9	10	11									

LEAGUE CUP

No.	Date	Opposition	Res.	H.T.	Att.	Goalscorers	Dean	Neil	Caldwell	McConnell	Passmoor	Harland	Blain	Carlin	Large	Evans	Simpson	Ross	Brayton	Livingstone	McIlmoyle	Johnstone	Kirkup	Garbutt	Oliphant	Murray
1R	2 Sep	Southport	0-0	0-0	6321			2	3	4	5	6	7					1	10	8	9	11				
1Rr	14	SOUTHPORT	1-0	0-0	8349	Livingstone		2	3	4	5	6	7					1	10	8	9	11				
2R	23	BRISTOL CITY	4-1	2-0	10055	McIlmoyle(2), Murray, Johnstone		2	3	4	5	6				8		1	7		9	11				10
3R	10 Oct	Chesterfield	1-3	1-1	7321	McConnell		2	3	4	5	6		8		10		1	7		9	11				

Final League Table

		Pl.	Home W	D	L	F	A	Away W	D	L	F	A	F.	A.	Pts
1	Carlisle United	46	14	5	4	46	24	11	5	7	30	29	76	53	60
2	Bristol City	46	14	6	3	53	18	10	5	8	39	37	92	55	59
3	Mansfield Town	46	17	4	2	61	23	7	7	9	34	38	95	61	59
4	Hull City	46	14	6	3	51	25	9	6	8	40	32	91	57	58
5	Brentford	46	18	4	1	55	18	6	5	12	28	37	83	55	57
6	Bristol Rovers	46	14	7	2	52	21	6	8	9	30	37	82	58	55
7	Gillingham	46	16	5	2	45	13	7	4	12	25	37	70	50	55
8	Peterborough Utd.	46	16	3	4	61	33	6	4	13	24	41	85	74	51
9	Watford	46	13	8	2	45	21	4	8	11	26	43	71	64	50
10	Grimsby Town	46	11	10	2	37	21	5	7	11	31	46	68	67	49
11	Bournemouth	46	12	4	7	40	24	6	7	10	32	39	72	63	47
12	Southend United	46	14	4	5	48	24	5	4	14	30	47	78	71	46
13	Reading	46	12	8	3	45	26	4	6	13	25	44	70	70	46
14	Queen's Park Rgs.	46	15	5	3	48	23	2	7	14	24	57	72	80	46
15	Workington	46	11	7	5	30	22	6	5	12	28	47	58	69	46
16	Shrewsbury Town	46	10	6	7	42	38	5	6	12	34	46	76	84	42
17	Exeter City	46	8	7	8	33	27	4	10	9	18	25	51	52	41
18	Scunthorpe United	46	9	8	6	42	27	5	4	14	23	45	65	72	40
19	Walsall	46	9	4	10	34	36	6	3	14	21	44	55	80	37
20	Oldham Athletic	46	10	3	10	40	39	3	7	13	21	44	61	83	36
21	Luton Town	46	6	8	9	32	36	5	3	15	19	58	51	94	33
22	Port Vale	46	7	6	10	27	33	2	8	13	14	43	41	76	32
23	Colchester United	46	7	6	10	30	34	3	4	16	20	55	50	89	30
24	Barnsley	46	8	5	10	33	31	1	6	16	21	59	54	90	29

SEASON 1965/66

DIVISION 2

No.	Date	Opposition	Res.	H.T.	Att.	Goalscorers	Dean	Neil	Caldwell	McConnell	Passmoor	Harland	Blain	Carlin	Balderstone	Gallacher	Evans	Welsh	Wilson	Simpson	Large	Brayton	Livingstone	Heslop	Marsland	McVitie	Garbutt	Green	Hepplewhite	Walton
1	21 Aug	NORWICH C.	4-1	3-0	11954	Simpson(2,1 pen),Balderstone,Large	1		3	4	5	6	7		10		2	8		11	9									
2	25	Southampton	0-1	0-0	21928		1		3	4	5	6	7		10		2	8		11	9									
3	28	Wolves	0-3	0-1	18943		1		3	4	5	6	7		10		2	8		11	9									
4	31	SOUTHAMPTON	1-0	0-0	15260	Harland	1		3	4	5	6	7		10		2	8		11	9									
5	3 Sep	ROTHERHAM	1-0	0-0	12551	Balderstone	1		3	4	5	6	7		10		2	8		11	9									
6	7	DERBY C.	2-1		16566	Blain,Large	1		3	4	5	6	7		10		2	8		11	9									
7	11	Manchester C.	1-2	0-1	22891	Evans	1	2	3	4	5	6	7		10			8		11	9									
8	15	Derby C.	1-3	1-1	11047	Evans	1	2	3	4	5	6	7		10			8		11	9									
9	17	BRISTOL C.	5-0	1-0	10694	Living'ne(2),Balder'ne,Harl'd,Blain	1		3	4	5	6	7		10		2	8		11	9*		12							
10	25	Coventry C.	2-3	1-2	20672	Balderstone (2)	1	2		4	5	6	7		10			8		11			9				3			
11	2 Oct	PRESTON N.E.	0-2	0-0	14729		1	2	3	4	5	6	7		10			8		11	9									
12	9	Charlton A.	2-3	1-3	11369	Balderstone, Livingstone	1	2		4	5	6	11		10			8		3			9			7				
13	16	PLYMOUTH A.	1-3	1-1	10471	Livingstone	1	2		4	5	6		7	10	3		8			11		9							
14	23	Portsmouth	1-4	0-1	14406	Balderstone	1			4	5	6			8	9	3	10		7					4					11
15	30	BOLTON W.	1-1	0-0	11114	Evans	1	3		2	5	6			8		10	7		9	11				4					
16	6 Nov	Ipswich T.	0-1	0-0	10772		1			2	5	6			11		3	10	7		8		9		4					
17	13	BIRMINGHAM C.	1-0	1-0	10243	Welsh	1			4	5	6				2	10	7	8	11	9								3	
18	20	Leyton O.	1-2		3678	Wilson	1		3	4	5	6			11	2	10	7	8		9									
19	4 Dec	Huddersfield T.	0-2	0-0	15517		1	2	3	4	5	6			10			7	8	11			9							
20	11	C. PALACE	3-1	1-0	9577	Livingstone, Wilson, Welsh	1	2	3	4	5	6			10	12		7*	8	11			9							
21	27	BURY	4-1	2-0	12019	Wilson(2), Livingstone,Balderstone	1	2	3	4	5	6		11	10			7	9			8								
22	1 Jan	CHARLTON A.	3-1	2-1	11489	Balderstone, Harland, Welsh	1	2	3	4	5			11	10			7	8				9	6						
23	8	Birmingham C.	1-2	0-1	14989	Wilson	1	2	3	4	5	6			10			7	8	11			9							
24	15	PORTSMOUTH	2-1	1-1	9636	Wilson, Balderstone (pen)	1	2		4	5	6			10				8	11			9						3	7
25	29	Norwich C.	0-2	0-0	16231		1	2		4	5	6			10			7	8	11			9							
26	5 Feb	WOLVES	2-1	1-1	13838	Harland, Garbutt	1	2	3	4	5	6			10	11		7	8				9							
27	26	MANCHESTER CITY	1-2	0-2	9327	Wilson	1		3	4	5	6			10	11	2	7	8				9							
28	8 Mar	MIDDLESBROUGH	2-1	0-0	13459	Wilson, Carlin	1	2	3	4	5	6			10			7	8	11			9							
29	12	Bristol C.	0-2	0-1	14721		1		3	4	5				10	9	2	7	8					11	6					
30	14	Plymouth A.	0-0	0-0	12104		1		3	4	5	6			10	11	2	7	8				9							
31	18	COVENTRY C.	2-2	1-1	13167	Welsh, Carlin	1		3	4	5				10	9	2	7	8				11		6					
32	1 Apr	IPSWICH T.	3-1	0-1	7555	McConnell, Welsh, Brayton	1		3	4	5				10	9	2	7		8	11	7			6					
33	5	Bolton W.	0-4	0-2	6506		1		3	4	5				10	8	2	7			9	7			6					
34	8	Cardiff C.	1-1	1-1	8003	Carlin	1		3	4	5			8	10		2	7		9	11				6					
35	12	CARDIFF C.	2-0	1-0	11252	McConnell, Wilson	1		3	4	5				10	8	2		9	7	11				6					
36	15	LEYTON O.	1-0	0-0	9811	McConnell	1		3	4	5				10	8	2		9	11	7				6					
37	23	Middlesbrough	2-0		15564	Wilson(2)	1		3	8	5				10	11	2			7	4				6					
38	25	Preston N.E.	1-2	1-0	13766	Balderstone	1		3	4	5				10	8	2	7		9	11				6					
39	30	HUDDERSFIELD T.	2-0	0-0	13688	Balderstone, Carlin	1		3	4	5	6			10	8	2	7		9	11									
41	7 May	C. Palace	0-2	0-1	9413		1		3	4	5				10	8	2	7		9	11				6					
41	10	Bury	1-2	1-1	4747	Carlin	1		3	4	5	6			10	8	2	7			11					9				
42	12	Rotherham U.	3-3	3-2	4798	Wilson(2), Brayton	1		3	4	5	6			10	8	2	7		9	11									

F.A. CUP

Rd	Date	Opposition	Res.	H.T.	Att.	Goalscorers	Dean	Neil	Caldwell	McConnell	Passmoor	Harland	Blain	Carlin	Balderstone	Gallacher	Evans	Welsh	Wilson	Simpson	Large	Brayton	Livingstone
3R	22 Jan	CRYSTAL P.	3-0	2-0	13640	McConnell Welsh Wilson	1	2	3	4	5	6			10			7	9	11			8
3R	12 Feb	Shrewsbury T.	0-0	0-0	13967		1	2	3	4	5	6			10	8		7	9	11			
3Rr	15	SHREWSBURY T.	1-1	0-1	17841	O.G.	1	2	3	4	5	6			10	8		7	9	11			
3R2r	21	Shrewsbury T. *	3-4	1-3	18678	Balderstone Wilson Carlin	1		3	4	5	6			10	11	2	7	8				9

* Played at Preston

LEAGUE CUP

Rd	Date	Opposition	Res.	H.T.	Att.	Goalscorers	Dean	Neil	Caldwell	McConnell	Passmoor	Harland	Blain	Carlin	Balderstone	Gallacher	Evans	Welsh	Wilson	Simpson	Large
2R	21 Sep	Charlton A.	1-4	0-2	11627	Balderstone	1	2	3	4	5	6	7		10			8		11	9

Final League Table

		Pl.	Home					Away					F.	A.	Pts
			W	D	L	F	A	W	D	L	F	A			
1	Manchester City	42	14	7	0	40	14	8	8	5	36	30	76	44	59
2	Southampton	42	13	4	4	51	25	9	6	6	34	31	85	56	54
3	Coventry City	42	14	5	2	54	31	6	8	7	19	22	73	53	53
4	Huddersfield Town	42	12	7	2	35	12	7	6	8	27	24	62	36	51
5	Bristol City	42	9	10	2	27	15	8	7	6	36	33	63	48	51
6	Wolverhampton W.	42	15	4	2	52	18	5	6	10	35	43	87	61	50
7	Rotherham United	42	12	6	3	48	29	4	8	9	27	45	75	74	46
8	Derby County	42	13	2	6	48	31	3	9	9	23	37	71	68	43
9	Bolton Wanderers	42	12	2	7	43	25	4	7	10	19	34	62	59	41
10	Birmingham City	42	10	6	5	41	29	6	3	12	29	46	70	75	41
11	Crystal Palace	42	11	7	3	29	16	3	6	12	18	36	47	52	41
12	Portsmouth	42	13	4	4	47	26	3	4	14	27	52	74	78	40
13	Norwich City	42	8	7	6	33	27	4	8	9	19	25	52	52	39
14	Carlisle United	42	16	2	3	43	19	1	3	17	17	44	60	63	39
15	Ipswich Town	42	12	6	3	38	23	3	3	15	20	43	58	66	39
16	Charlton Athletic	42	10	6	5	39	29	2	8	11	22	41	61	70	38
17	Preston North End	42	7	10	4	37	23	4	5	12	25	47	62	70	37
18	Plymouth Argyle	42	7	8	6	37	26	5	5	11	17	37	54	63	37
19	Bury	42	12	5	4	45	25	2	2	17	17	51	62	76	35
20	Cardiff City	42	10	3	8	37	35	2	7	12	34	56	71	91	34
21	Middlesbrough	42	8	8	5	36	28	2	5	14	22	58	58	86	33
22	Leyton Orient	42	3	9	9	19	36	2	4	15	19	44	38	80	23

- 1965/66 Season -

(Back): Neill, Gallacher, Dean, Ross, Green, Caldwell
(Middle): Nicholson(Physo), Marsland, McConnell, Passmoor, Ashman(Man), Garbutt, Heslop, Harland, Young(Train)
(Front): Carlin, Brayton, Blain, Evans, Large, Livingstone, Balderstone, McVitie, Hepplewhite, Simpson

- 1966/67 Season -

(Back): Smith, Reddelty, Neil, Gallagher, Dean, Ross, Hepplewhite, Caldwell, McClelland, Peacock
(Middle): Young (Trainer), Green, Heslop, McConnell, Dent (Sec) Passmoor, Marsland, Garbutt, Nicholson (Physo)
(Front): McVitie, Loyden, Welsh, Carlin, Ashman (Manager) Brayton, Balderstone, Wilson, Saville

SEASON 1966/67

DIVISION 2

No.	Date	Opposition	Res.	H.T.	Att.	Goalscorers	Ross	Gallacher	Caldwell	McConnell	Passmoor	Garbutt	Welsh	Murray	Rudge	Balderstone	McVitie	Carlin	Hartle	Neil	Wilson	Dean	Marsland	Brayton	Sharpe	Heslop
1	20 Aug	Crystal Palace	2-4	0-2	11374	Welsh(2)		2	3	4	5		7			10		8	11			1	6	9		
2	23	DERBY	0-0	0-0	13347			2	3	4	5		7			10		8	11		9	1	6			
3	27	HUDDERSFIELD	2-1	0-0	10322	Carlin(2)		2	3	4	5		7			10		8	11		9	1	6			
4	31	Derby	1-0	0-0	12296	Welsh		2	3	4	5		7			10		8	11		9	1	6			
5	3 Sep	Cardiff	2-4	0-4	7014	McConnell, Welsh		2	3	4	5		7			10		8	11		9	1	6			
6	7	Bolton	0-3	0-1	15105			2	3	4	5		7			10		8	11		9	1	6			
7	10	WOLVES	1-3	0-2	11359	Wilson		2	3	4	5		7			10		8	11		9	1	6			
8	17	Ipswich	2-1	0-1	14317	Marsland, Carlin	1	3		4	5		7			10		8	11	2	9		6			
9	24	BRISTOL CITY	2-1	1-0	9948	McVitie, Carlin	1	3		4	5		9			10	7	8	11*	2	12		6			
10	27	NORWICH	1-0	1-0	10329	Wilson	1	3		4	5		7			10		8	11	2	9		6			
11	1 Oct	Bury	2-0	0-0	5552	Wilson(2)	1	3		4	5		7			12	10	8	11	2*	9		6			
12	8	COVENTRY	2-1	1-0	10885	Garbutt, Wilson	1	3		4	5	6	7			10		8	11	2	9					
13	15	Norwich	0-2	0-1	11540		1	3		4	5	6	7			10		8	11	2*	9	1		12		4
14	22	BIRMINGHAM	2-0	1-0	10900	Carlin, Wilson	1	3			5	6	7			4	10	8	11	2	9					
15	29	Portsmouth	1-2	0-0	11674	Balderstone	1	3		4	5	6				10	7	8	11	2	9					
16	5 Nov	HULL	2-0	1-0	14157	Carlin, Wilson	1	3		4	5	6				10	7	8	11	2	9					
17	12	Plymouth	2-1	1-0	13354	Carlin(2)	1	3		4	5	6				10	7	8	11	2	9					
18	19	NORTHAMPTON	2-0	1-0	11946	McVitie, Garbutt	1	3		4	5	6				10	7	8	11	2				9		
19	26	Millwall	1-2	0-0	15895	Welsh	1	3		4	5	6	7			10		8	11	2	9					
20	3 Dec	BROTHERHAM	2-3	1-2	10766	Garbutt, Welsh	1	3		4	5	6	7			10		8	11	2	9					
21	10	Preston	3-2	0-1	15869	Balderstone(2), Caplin	1	12	3	4	5	6	7			10		8	11	2*	9					
22	17	CRYSTAL PALACE	3-0	1-0	10324	Neil, Carlin, Wilson	1	3		4	5	6	7			10		8	11	2	9					
23	26	BLACKBURN	1-2	1-1	17523	Welsh	1	3		4	5	6	7			10		8	11	2	9					
24	27	Blackburn	0-2	0-0	20219		1	3			5	6	7	10		4	11		8	2	9					
25	31	Huddersfield	1-1	0-1	18606	Rudge	1	3			5	6	7	10		4	11		8	2	9					
26	7 Jan	CARDIFF	3-0	2-0	10295	Welsh(2), Wilson	1	3	12		5	6	7	10*		4	11		8	2	9					
27	14	Wolves	1-1	0-0	23522	McVitie	1	3		4	5	6	7			10	11		8	2	9					
28	21	IPSWICH	2-1	0-1	11812	Balderstone, Hartle	1	2*	3	4	5	6	7			10	11		8	12	9					
29	4 Feb	Bristol City	0-3	0-1	23206		1	2	3	4	5	6	7			10	11*		8	12	9					
30	11	BURY	2-0	1-1	11534	McConnell, McVitie	1	3		4	5	6	7			4	10	8	11	2	9					
31	25	Coventry	1-2	0-0	29965	McVitie	1	3		4	5	6	7			10	11	8		2	9					
32	4 Mar	PORTSMOUTH	5-1	2-1	11104	McCnnell,Blderstne,Wlsh,Rdge,McVtie	1	3		4	5	6	7		9	10	11			2						
33	18	Birmingham	2-1	0-0	17613	Welsh, McVitie	1	3		4	5	6	7	8	9	10	11			2						
34	24	Charlton	0-1	0-0	15075		1	3		4	5	6	7	8	9	10	11			2						
35	28	CHARLTON	1-0	1-0	11607	Murray	1	3		4	5	6	7	8	9	10	11			2						
36	1 Apr	Hull	2-1	1-1	19029	Garbutt, Welsh	1	2	3	4	5	6	7	8	9	10	11									
37	8	PLYMOUTH	0-0		11391		1	3		4	5	6	7	8	9	10				2						
38	15	Northampton	3-3	1-1	10752	Murray, Rudge, Balderstone	1	3		4	5	6	7	8	9	10				2					11	
39	22	MILLWALL	2-1	1-1	8493	Balderstone(pen), McVitie	1	2	3	4	5	6	7	8	9	10	11									
40	29	Rotherham	3-2	3-2	7641	McConnell, Murray, Rudge	1	2	3	4	5	6	7	8	9	10	11									
41	6	PRESTON	1-1		9443	Welsh	1	2	3	4	5	6	7	8	9	10	11									
42	13	BOLTON	6-1	1-1	7732	Rudge(3),Murray,Welsh,Gallacher	1	2	3	4	5	6	7	8	9	10	11									

F.A. CUP

Rnd	Date	Opposition	Res.	H.T.	Att.	Goalscorers	Ross	Gallacher	Caldwell	McConnell	Passmoor	Garbutt	Welsh	Balderstone	McVitie	Carlin	Neil	Wilson
3R	28 Jan	Blackburn	2-1	2-1	23312	Wilson, Carlin	1	2	3	4	5	6	7	10	11	8		9
4R	18 Feb	Ipswich	0-2	0-0	22911		1		3	4	5	6	7	10	11	8	2	9

LEAGUE CUP

Rnd	Date	Opposition	Res.	H.T.	Att.	Goalscorers	Ross	Gallacher	Caldwell	McConnell	Passmoor	Garbutt	Welsh	Balderstone	McVitie	Carlin	Hartle	Neil	Wilson	Dean	Marsland
2R	14 Sep	TRANMERE	1-1	1-0	6076	Marsland		2	3	4	5		7	10		8	11		9	1	6
2Rr	21	Tranmere	2-0	1-0	5422	Balderstone, Welsh	1	2	3	4	5		7	10		8	11	2	9		6
3R	5 Oct	Southampton	3-3	2-1	13317	Balderstone, Hartle, Wilson	1	3		4	5	12	7	10		8	11	2	9		6*
3Rr	12	SOUTHAMPTON	2-1	1-1	13275	Balderstone(2)	1	3		4	5		7	10		8	11	2	9		
4R	26	BLACKBURN	4-0	2-0	14054	Balderstone, Carlin, Wilson(2)	1	3			5	6	7	4	10	8	11	2	9		
5R	7 Dec	Qeens Park Rangers	1-2	1-1	19146	Carlin	1	3		4	5	6	7	10		8	11	2	9		

Final League Table

		Pl.	Home					Away					F.	A.	Pts
			W	D	L	F	A	W	D	L	F	A			
1	Coventry City	42	17	3	1	46	16	6	10	5	28	27	74	43	59
2	Wolverhampton W.	42	15	4	2	53	20	10	4	7	35	28	88	48	58
3	Carlisle United	42	15	3	3	42	16	8	3	10	29	38	71	54	52
4	Blackburn Rovers	42	13	6	2	33	11	6	7	8	23	35	56	46	51
5	Ipswich Town	42	11	8	2	45	25	6	8	7	25	29	70	54	50
6	Huddersfield Town	42	14	3	4	36	17	6	6	9	22	29	58	46	49
7	Crystal Palace	42	14	4	3	42	23	5	6	10	19	32	61	55	48
8	Millwall	42	14	5	2	33	17	4	4	13	16	41	49	58	45
9	Bolton Wanderers	42	10	7	4	36	19	4	7	10	28	39	64	58	42
10	Birmingham City	42	11	5	5	42	23	5	3	13	28	43	70	66	40
11	Norwich City	42	10	7	4	31	21	3	7	11	18	34	49	55	40
12	Hull City	42	11	5	5	46	25	5	2	14	31	47	77	72	39
13	Preston North End	42	14	3	4	44	23	2	4	15	21	44	65	67	39
14	Portsmouth	42	7	5	9	34	37	6	8	7	25	33	59	70	39
15	Bristol City	42	10	8	3	38	22	2	6	13	18	40	56	62	38
16	Plymouth Argyle	42	12	4	5	42	21	2	5	14	17	37	59	58	37
17	Derby County	42	8	6	7	40	32	4	6	11	28	40	68	72	36
18	Rotherham United	42	10	5	6	39	28	3	5	13	22	42	61	70	36
19	Charlton Athletic	42	11	4	6	34	16	2	5	14	15	37	49	53	35
20	Cardiff City	42	9	7	5	43	28	2	2	16	18	59	61	87	33
21	Northampton Town	42	8	6	7	28	33	4	0	17	19	51	47	84	30
22	Bury	42	9	3	9	31	30	2	3	16	18	53	49	83	28

SEASON 1967/68
DIVISION 2

No.	Date	Opposition	Res.	H.T.	Att.	Goalscorers	Ross	Neil	Caldwell	McConnell	Passmoor	Barbutt	Rudge	Murray	McIlmoyle	Balderstone	McVitie	Marsland	Sharpe	Barton	Brodie	Carlin	Dean	McPartland	McCarran	Hartle	Saville	O'Rourke
1	19 Aug	Hull	0-1	0-0	17123		1	2	3	4	5	6	9	12		10	7*				8					11		
2	23	Blackburn	0-0	0-0	17740		1	2	3		5	6	9	7		10					8				4	11		
3	26	MIDDLESBROUGH	2-2	1-2	12389	Garbutt, Balderstone	1	2	3	4	5	6	9	7*		10			11		8				12			
4	29	BLACKBURN	1-0	0-0	11668	Garbutt	1	2	3	4	5	8	7			10			11		9				6			
5	2 Sep	Bristol City	0-1	0-1	13842		1	2	3	4	5				12	10			11		8				6		7*	
6	5	ROTHERHAM	4-1	3-1	9496	McCarron, Murray, Garbutt, O.G.	1	2	3	4	5			7		10			11		9				6			
7	9	BIRMINGHAM	1-1	1-0	11200	Garbutt	1	2	3	4	5	8		7		10			11		9				6			
8	16	Bolton	3-2	1-0	12809	McConnell(2), Murray	1	2	3	4	5	8		7		10		6	11		9							
9	23	HUDDERSFIELD	2-1	1-0	13511	Marsland(pen), McIlmoyle	1	2	3	4	5	8			7	9		10	6	11								
10	30	Ipswich	1-3	1-2	14183	Murray	1	2	3	4	5	8			7	9		10	6	11								
11	7 Oct	Portsmouth	1-2	0-0	21865	McIlmoyle	1	2	3	4	5	6	8		7	9		10		11								
12	14	PRESTON	4-1	1-0	11228	McIlmyle, Balderstne, Marslnd, Rudge	1	2	3		5	6	8		7	9		10	4	11								
13	21	Charlton	2-2	0-1	13645	McIlmoyle, Balderstone	1	2	3	4	5	6	8		7	9		10		11								
14	28	CRYSTAL PALACE	3-0	2-0	11399	Rudge(2), McIlmoyle	1	2	3	4	5	6	8		7	9		10		11								
15	4 Nov	Aston Villa	0-1	0-0	17767		1	2	3	4	5	6	8		7	9		10		11								
16	11	Q.PARK RANGERS	3-1	2-1	12544	Rudge, McIlmoyle(2)	1	2	3	4	5	6	8		7	9		10		11								
17	18	Derby	1-0	1-0	20850	Balderstone	1	2	3	4	5	6	9		7	9		10		11								
18	25	CARDIFF	1-3	0-1	10966	McIlmoyle	1	2	3	4	5	6	8		7	9		10		11								
19	2 Dec	Plymouth	1-3	0-2	8791	Rudge	1	2	3	4	5	6	8		7	9	10	11*										12
20	9	NORWICH	2-2	0-2	8076	Murray(2)	1	2	3	4*	5	6	8		7	9		10		11					12			
21	16	HULL	1-1	1-0	9063	Murray	1	2	3	4	5	6			8	9		10	7	11								
22	23	Middlesbrough	0-4	0-0	27952			2	3	4	5	6	12	8		10*	7		11			1						
23	26	Blackpool	1-1	1-1	20732	McVitie		2	3	4	5	6	12	8	9	10	7		11			1*						
24	30	BLACKPOOL	1-3	1-3	12679	Murray		2	3	4	5	6	12	8	9	10*	7		11			1						
25	6 Jan	BRISTOL CITY	0-0	0-0	8261			2	3	4		5	7	8	9	10	11	6				1						
26	13	Birmingham	3-1	2-0	21686	Rudge, Murray, McVitie		2	3	4	12	5	7	8		10	11	6		9*		1						
27	20	BOLTON	3-0	1-0	11065	Rudge, Murray, Barton		2	3	4		5	7	8		10	11	6		9		1						
28	3 Feb	Huddersfield	1-1	1-0	9071	O.G.	1	2	3	4		5	9	8		10	7	6		11								
29	10	IPSWICH	4-1	1-1	17111	Murray(2), Balderstone, Barton	1	2	3	4	12	5		8*		10	7	6	11	9								
30	23	PORTSMOUTH	1-1	1-0	11976	Rudge	1	2	3	4		5	7	8		10	11	6		9								
31	2 Mar	Preston	2-0	0-0	13481	Murray(2)	1	2	3	4		5	7	8		10	11	6		9								
32	16	CHARLTON	0-0	0-0	7440		1		3	4		5	12		9*	10	7	6	11	8	2							
33	23	Crystal Palace	1-1	1-1	9219	Marsland	1		3	4		5	7			10		6	11	8	2							
34	30	ASTON VILLA	1-2	1-2	8861	Garbutt	1		3	4		5	12			10	7	6	11	8*	2							
35	6 Apr	Q.Park Rangers	0-1	0-0	18103		1		3	4	5	8				9	10	11	6		7	2						
36	13	DERBY	1-1	0-0	8009	McIlmoyle	1		3	4	5	8			9	10	11	6		7				2				
37	15	Millwall	0-1	0-1	11854				3	4	5	8	7		9	10	11	6	12				1	2*				
38	16	MILLWALL	1-1	0-1	5810	McIlmoyle	1		3	4	5	8	7		9	10	11	6			2							
39	20	Cardiff	0-1	0-1	13926		1		3	4	5	6	7			10		8	11	9	2							
40	27	PLYMOUTH	2-0	0-0	5938	Murray, McVitie	1		3	2	5	4	7	8	9	10	11	6										
41	4 May	Norwich	1-2	0-1	11429	Rudge	1		3	2	5		7	8	9	10	11	4										
42	11	Rotherham	2-1	2-1	6950	McIlmoyle, Murray	1	2	3	4	5	6	7	8	9	10	11											

F.A. CUP

	Date	Opposition	Res.	H.T.	Att.	Goalscorers	Ross	Neil	Caldwell	McConnell	Passmoor	Barbutt	Rudge	Murray	McIlmoyle	Balderstone	McVitie	Marsland	Sharpe	Barton	Brodie	Carlin
3R	27 Jan	Newcastle	1-0	0-0	56550	Murray	1	2	3	4		5	7	8		10	11	6		9		
4R	17 Feb	EVERTON	0-2	0-1	25000		1	2	3	4		5	7	8		10	11	6		9		

LEAGUE CUP

	Date	Opposition	Res.	H.T.	Att.	Goalscorers	Ross	Neil	Caldwell	McConnell	Passmoor	Barbutt	Rudge	Murray	McIlmoyle	Balderstone	McVitie	Marsland	Sharpe	Barton
2R	13 Sep	Workington	0-2	0-1	10746		1	2	3	4	5	8		7		10		6	11	9

Final League Table

		Pl.	Home					Away					F.	A.	Pts
			W	D	L	F	A	W	D	L	F	A			
1	Ipswich Town	42	12	7	2	45	20	10	8	3	34	24	79	44	59
2	Queen's Park Rgs.	42	18	2	1	45	9	7	6	8	22	27	67	36	58
3	Blackpool	42	12	6	3	33	16	12	4	5	38	27	71	43	58
4	Birmingham City	42	12	6	3	54	21	7	8	6	29	30	83	51	52
5	Portsmouth	42	13	6	2	43	18	5	7	9	25	37	68	55	49
6	Middlesbrough	42	10	7	4	39	19	7	5	9	21	35	60	54	46
7	Millwall	42	9	10	2	35	16	5	7	9	27	34	62	50	45
8	Blackburn Rovers	42	13	5	3	34	16	3	6	12	22	33	56	49	43
9	Norwich City	42	12	4	5	40	30	4	7	10	20	35	60	65	43
10	Carlisle United	42	9	9	3	38	22	5	4	12	20	30	58	52	41
11	Crystal Palace	42	11	4	6	34	19	3	7	11	22	37	56	56	39
12	Bolton Wanderers	42	8	6	7	37	28	5	7	9	23	35	60	63	39
13	Cardiff City	42	9	6	6	35	29	4	6	11	25	37	60	66	38
14	Huddersfield Town	42	10	6	5	29	23	3	6	12	17	38	46	61	38
15	Charlton Athletic	42	10	6	5	43	25	2	7	12	20	43	63	68	37
16	Aston Villa	42	10	3	8	35	30	5	4	12	19	34	54	64	37
17	Hull City	42	6	8	7	25	23	6	5	10	33	50	58	73	37
18	Derby County	42	8	5	8	40	35	5	5	11	31	43	71	78	36
19	Bristol City	42	7	7	7	26	25	6	3	12	22	37	48	62	36
20	Preston North End	42	8	7	6	29	24	4	4	13	14	41	43	65	35
21	Rotherham United	42	7	4	10	22	32	3	7	11	20	44	42	76	31
22	Plymouth Argyle	42	5	4	12	26	36	4	5	12	12	36	38	72	27

- 1967/68 Season -

(Back): Neil, Caldwell, Passmoor, Rudge, McVitie, McConnell
(Middle): Marsland, McCarron, Green, Dean, Ross, Garbutt, Balderstone, Nicholson (Physo)
(Front): Young (Trainer), Carlin, Murray, Welsh, Hartle, Saville, Sharp, Doyle (Asst. Trainer)

- 1968/69 Season -

CARLISLE UNITED F.C.
Division Two 1968-1969

Back Row:— GORDON MARSLAND ☐ HUGH NEIL ☐ TERRY CALDWELL ☐ ALLAN ROSS
PETER McCONNELL (Captain) ☐ TOM PASSMOOR ☐ PETER GARBUTT ☐ CYRIL DAVIES
Front Row:— ERIC WELSH ☐ TOMMY MURRAY ☐ HUGH McILMOYLE ☐ CHRIS BALDERSTONE
GEORGE McVITIE

SEASON 1968/69

DIVISION 2

No.	Date	Opposition	Res.	H.T.	Att.	Goalscorers	Ross	Marsland	Caldwell	Ternent	Passmoor	Garbutt	Welsh	Barton	McIlmoyle	Balderstone	McVitie	McConnell	Neil	Rudge	Sharpe	Hassell	Brodie	Murray	Davies
1	10 Aug	Bury	2-3	1-2	8952	McIlmoyle, Murray	1		3			5	6	7	9	10	11	4	2					8	
2	13	PORTSMOUTH	0-0	0-0	9748		1		3			5	6	7	9	10	11	4	2					8	
3	17	CHARLTON	1-1	1-0	8621	McIlmoyle	1		3			5	6	12	9	10	7*	4	2		11			8	
4	19	Preston	2-2	1-2	14984	McVitie, McIlmoyle	1	2	3			5	6		9	10	11	4		7				8	
5	24	Middlesbrough	0-1	0-0	22392		1	2	3			5	6		9	10	11	4		7				8	
6	27	OXFORD	0-2	0-1	9396		1	2	3	4		5	6		9	10	11			7				8	
7	31	HUDDERSFIELD	0-0	0-0	7935		1	2*	3	4		5	6	7	9	10	11		12					8	
8	7 Sep	Crystal Palace	0-5	0-3	15169		1	5	3	4			6	7	12	9	11*		2					8	
9	14	NORWICH	0-4	0-2	7353		1	10*	3	4		6	12	7*	9		11	5		8	12		2		
10	21	Cardiff	1-2	1-1	10809	Murray	1		3	4		5	6	12	9	10	11*	2			7			8	
11	28	BIRMINGHAM	2-3	2-1	7623	Murray, McIlmoyle	1		3	4		5	6	12	9	10*	11	2			7			8	
12	5 Oct	BOLTON	1-1	1-1	8846	Garbutt	1		3	4		5	6	12	9	10	11*	2			7			8	
13	9	Oxford	1-0	1-0	10256	Balderstone	1		3	4		5	6	7	9	10	11	2						8	
14	12	Blackburn	2-0	1-0	12101	McIlmoyle(2)	1		3	4		5	6	7	9	10	11	2						8	
15	19	BLACKPOOL	1-0	0-0	10519	McVitie	1		3	4		5	6	7	9	10	11	2						8	
16	26	Aston Villa	0-0	0-0	14971		1		3	4		5	6	7	9	10	11	2						8	
17	2 Nov	HULL	1-0	0-0	9374	Murray	1		3	4		5	6	12	7*	9	10	11	2					8	
18	9	Sheffield	1-0	1-0	13158	McIlmoyle	1		3	4		5	6	12	7*	9	10	11	2					8	
19	16	FULHAM	2-0	2-0	9644	Balderstone, McIlmoyle	1		3	4		5	6	7	9	10	11	2						8	
20	23	Derby	3-3	2-2	23395	McVitie, Garbutt, Murray	1		3	4		5	6	7	9	10	11	2						8	
21	30	BRISTOL CITY	3-0	1-0	9263	McIlmoyle(2), Garbutt	1		3	4		5	6	7	9	10	11	2						8	
22	7 Dec	Millwall	1-1	0-1	12767	Balderstone	1		3	4		5	6	7	9	10	11	2						8	
23	14	BLACKBURN	4-1	3-1	9160	Balderstone, McVitie, Murray(2)	1		3	4		5	6	7	9	10	11	2						8	
24	21	Blackpool	0-1	0-1	11169		1		3	4		5	6	7	9	10	11	2						8	
25	26	Bolton	1-0	1-0	13922	McIlmoyle	1	12	3	4		5	6	7	9	10	11	2*						8	
26	28	ASTON VILLA	0-1	0-0	12554		1	12	3	4		5	6	7	9	10	11	2*						8	
27	11 Jan	Hull	2-1	1-1	12389	McIlmoyle, Balderstone	1	2	3	4		5	6	7	9	10	11							8	
28	18	SHEFFIELD	0-1	0-1	9717		1	2	3	4		5	6	7	9	10	11							8	
29	1 Feb	Fulham	2-0	1-0	12863	Murray(2)	1	2	3	4		5	6	7	9	10	11							8	
30	15	Bristol City	0-3	0-2	13785		1	2	3	4		5	6*	7	9	10	11				12			8	
31	22	MILLWALL	1-0	1-0	7937	McVitie	1	2	3	4		5	6	7	9	10	11							8	
32	1 Mar	BURY	2-0	1-0	7937	McVitie, McIlmoyle	1	2	3	4		5	6	7	9	10	11							8	
33	8	Charlton	1-1	1-1	19439	Barton	1	2		4		5	6	7	10	9	3	11						8	
34	11	DERBY	1-1	1-0	12844	McIlmoyle	1	2	3	4		5	6	7	9	10	11							8	
35	15	MIDDLESBROUGH	3-0	2-0	13920	Barton, Welsh, McIlmoyle	1	2		4		5	6	7	10	9	3	11						8	
36	22	Huddersfield	0-2	0-0	8560		1	2		4		5	6	7	10	9	3	11						8	
37	29	CRYSTAL PALACE	1-2	1-1	8172	Murray	1	2		4		5	6	7	10	9	3	11						8	
38	5 Apr	Birmingham	0-3	0-1	22397		1	2	3	4		5	6	7	8*	9	10	11						12	
39	7	PRESTON	1-0	1-0	7349	McIlmoyle	1	2	3			5	6	7	10	9	11	2						12	
40	9	Portsmouth	1-2	1-1	18130	Murray	1	2	3			5	6	7	8	9	10	11			4*			12	
41	12	CARDIFF	1-0	1-0	5546	McIlmoyle	1		3			5	7	4	9	10	11					2		8	6
42	19	Norwich	1-2	1-0	8313	Murray	1	2	3	4		5		7*	9	10	11						6	8	12

F.A. CUP

Round	Date	Opposition	Res.	H.T.	Att.	Goalscorers	Ross	Marsland	Caldwell	Ternent	Passmoor	Garbutt	Welsh	Barton	McIlmoyle	Balderstone	McVitie	McConnell	Neil	Rudge	Sharpe	Hassell	Brodie	Murray	Davies
3R	4 Jan	Chelsea	0-2	0-2	37322		1	2	3	4		5	6	7	9	10	11							8	

LEAGUE CUP

Round	Date	Opposition	Res.	H.T.	Att.	Goalscorers	Ross	Marsland	Caldwell	Ternent	Passmoor	Garbutt	Welsh	Barton	McIlmoyle	Balderstone	McVitie	McConnell	Neil	Rudge	Sharpe	Hassell	Brodie	Murray	Davies
2R	4 Sep	CARDIFF	2-0	2-0	7720	McIlmoyle, McVitie	1	6	3	4	2	5		7*	9	10	11							8	12
3R	24	LEICESTER	0-3	0-1	10985		1		3	12		5			9	6	7	4	2	10*	11			8	

Final League Table

		Pl.	Home					Away					F.	A.	Pts
			W	D	L	F	A	W	D	L	F	A			
1	Derby County	42	16	4	1	43	16	10	7	4	22	16	65	32	63
2	Crystal Palace	42	14	4	3	45	24	8	8	5	25	23	70	47	56
3	Charlton Athletic	42	11	8	2	39	21	7	6	8	22	31	61	52	50
4	Middlesbrough	42	13	7	1	36	13	6	4	11	22	36	58	49	49
5	Cardiff City	42	13	3	5	38	19	7	4	10	29	35	67	54	47
6	Huddersfield Town	42	13	6	2	37	14	4	6	11	16	32	53	46	46
7	Birmingham City	42	13	3	5	52	24	5	5	11	21	35	73	59	44
8	Blackpool	42	9	8	4	33	20	5	7	9	18	21	51	41	43
9	Sheffield United	42	14	4	3	41	15	2	7	12	20	35	61	50	43
10	Millwall	42	10	5	6	33	23	7	4	10	24	26	57	49	43
11	Hull City	42	10	7	4	38	20	3	9	9	21	32	59	52	42
12	Carlisle United	42	10	5	6	25	17	6	5	10	21	32	46	49	42
13	Norwich City	42	7	6	8	24	25	8	4	9	29	31	53	56	40
14	Preston North End	42	8	8	5	23	19	4	7	10	15	25	38	44	39
15	Portsmouth	42	11	5	5	39	22	1	9	11	19	36	58	58	38
16	Bristol City	42	9	9	3	30	15	2	7	12	16	38	46	53	38
17	Bolton Wanderers	42	8	7	6	29	26	4	7	10	26	41	55	67	38
18	Aston Villa	42	10	8	3	22	11	2	6	13	15	37	37	48	38
19	Blackburn Rovers	42	9	6	6	30	24	4	5	12	22	39	52	63	37
20	Oxford United	42	8	5	8	21	23	4	4	13	13	32	34	55	33
21	Bury	42	8	4	9	35	33	3	4	14	16	47	51	80	30
22	Fulham	42	6	7	8	20	28	1	4	16	20	53	40	81	25

SEASON 1969/70
DIVISION 2

No.	Date	Opposition	Res.	H.T.	Att.	Goalscorers	Ross	Hemstead	Davis	Ternent	Winstanley	Garbutt	McVitie	Peddelty	Barton	Hatton	Balderstone	Caldwell	Brown	Passmoor	O'Neil	Murray	McIlmoyle	Dean	Hassel
1	9 Aug	CARDIFF	2-3	0-2	10506	McIlmoyle, McVitie	1	2		4	6		12		7	9	11				5	3	8	10	
2	16	Swindon	2-2	1-0	17055	Balderstone, Murray	1	2		4*		6	11		7	9	10				5	3	12	10	
3	19	ASTON VILLA	1-1	0-0	12509	McVitie	1	2				4	7		8	9	11	3			5	6		10	
4	23	MIDDLESBROUGH	1-0	0-0	12578	Balderstone(pen)	1	2				4*	7		11	9	6	12			5	3	8	10	
5	26	BOLTON	2-1	2-1	11682	Balderstone	1	2		4	6		7		8	9	11				5	3		10	
6	30	Norwich	0-1	0-1	14659		1	2		4*	6		7		8	9	11				5	3	12	10	
7	6 Sep	HULL	2-1	1-0	10049	Hatton(2)	1	2		4	6		7		8*	9	11				5	3	12	10	
8	13	Millwall	2-4	2-1	10345	Hatton(2)	1	2		4	6		7*		8	9	11	3			5		12	10	
9	17	Leicester	2-1	0-0	24434	McIlmoyle(2)	1	2		8	4				7	9	11	3			5	6		10	
10	20	PRESTON	1-0	1-0	9782	Barton	1	2			4				7	9	11	3			5	6	8	10	
11	27	Birmingham	1-1	0-1	28765	Balderstone(pen)	1	2		8	4		11		7	9	10	3			5*	6	12		
12	4 Oct	HUDDERSFIELD	0-2	0-1	9721		1	2		4	5		7			10	9	11	3			6	8		
13	7	SWINDON	2-2	0-0	9723	Hatton, Brown	1	2		4	5		11*		7	9	10	3	12			6	8		
14	11	Watford	2-1	0-1	16125	Hatton(2)	1	2		4	6					9	10	3	7	5	11	8			
15	18	Q. P. RANGERS	3-2		11900	Brown(2), Winstanley	1	2		10	5				7	9	11	3	8	4	6				
16	25	Bristol City	0-0	0-0	15161		1	2		10	5				7	9	6	3	8	4		11			
17	1 Nov	PORTSMOUTH	3-3	1-2	9804	Winstanley, Barton, Brown	1			4	6				11	8	9	2	3	7	5		10		
18	8	Oxford	0-1	0-0	8374		1			6	5				11	7	9	2	3	8	4		10		
19	12	Aston Villa	0-1	0-0	24447		1	2		10	5				7	9	6	3	8	4					
20	15	BLACKBURN	0-1	0-0	14481		1	2		10	5				12	6	9	11	3	7	4		8*		
21	22	Charlton	1-2	1-0	10175	Barton	1	2		4	6				11	8	9	10	3	7*	5		12		
22	29	SHEFFIELD UNITED	0-1	0-1	7365		1	2		4	5				11	8	9	10	3			6	7		
23	6 Dec	Blackpool	1-1	1-0	9766	Murray	1	2	3	4	5				11	8	9	6		7			10		
24	13	MILLWALL	4-0	2-0	6214	Balderstone, Brown, Hatton, O.G.	1	2	3	4	5				11	8	9	6		7			10		
25	20	Hull	4-2	1-0	9295	Brown(2), Hatton(2)	1	2	3	4	5				11	8	9	6		7			10		
26	26	Middlesbrough	2-0	1-0	29703	Hatton, Barton	1	2	3	4	5*		11	12	9	8	6			7			10		
27	27	NORWICH	2-1	0-0	9668	Balderstone(2)	1	2	3	4	5		11	12	8	9	6			7*			10		
28	10 Jan	Preston	1-3	1-2	9586	Balderstone	1	2	3	4	5		11	10*	8	9	6						7		12
29	17	BIRMINGHAM	4-3	3-1	7912	Barton(2), Peddelty, Murray(pen)	1	2	3	4	5		11	10	8	9	6						7		
30	31	Huddersfield	0-1	0-1	17370		1	2	3	4	5		11*	12	8	9	6						7		
31	10 Feb	WATFORD	5-0	3-0	7660	Balderstne(2),Mrray,McVtie,Hatton	1		3	4	5	6	7		8	9	11	2					10		
32	14	Cardiff	1-1	1-0	20143	Balderstone	1		3	4	5	6	7		8	9	11	2					10		
33	21	OXFORD	1-1	1-1	7377	Balderstone			3	4	5	6	7		8	9	11	2					10	1	
34	28	Portsmouth	0-4	0-1	10952		12		3	4	5	6*	7		8	9	11	2					10	1	
35	7 Mar	CHARLTON	1-1	0-0	7143	Murray		2*	3	4	5		7	12	8	9	11	6					10	1	
36	13	Sheffield United	0-1	0-1	22005		1		2	4	5	6	7*	8		10	11	3	9				12		
37	21	BLACKPOOL	1-2	1-2	8212	Barton	1	3	2	4	5	6	7	10	8	9	11						8		
38	27	Q. Park Rangers	0-0	0-0	16343		1	2	3	4	5		7	6	9	10*	11	12					8		
39	28	Blackburn	0-1	0-0	8394		1	2	3	4		5	7	6*	8		11	12	9				10		
40	31	BRISTOL CITY	2-1	2-1	6219	McVitie, Brown	1	2	3	4		5	7	6	8		11		9				10		
41	4 Apr	Bolton	2-1	0-0	9120	Barton, Balderstone	1	2	3	4	5		7	6	8		11		9				10		
42	14	LEICESTER	2-2	0-1	6657	Winstanley, McVitie		2	4	5		7	6		8	9	11	3					10		

F.A. CUP

	Date	Opposition	Res.	H.T.	Att.	Goalscorers	Ross	Hemstead	Davis	Ternent	Winstanley	Garbutt	McVitie	Peddelty	Barton	Hatton	Balderstone	Caldwell	Brown	Passmoor	O'Neil	Murray	McIlmoyle	Dean	Hassel
3R	3 Jan	Nottingham F.	0-0	0-0	23419		1	2	3	4	5		11	10	7	9	6						8		
3Rr	6	NOTTINGHAM F.	2-1	1-0	12840	Murray, McVitie	1	2	3	4	5		11	10	8	9	6						7		
4R	24	ALDERSHOT	2-2	2-1	15634	Hatton, Balderstone	1	2	3	4	5		11	10*	8	9	6			12			7		
4Rr	27	Aldershot	4-1	3-0	19138	Murray, McVitie, Caldwell, Barton	1	2	3	4	5		11		8	9	6	10					7		
5R	7 Feb	MIDDLESBROUGH	1-2	0-0	27500	Winstanley	1	2*	3	4	5		11		8	9	6	10	12				7		

LEAGUE CUP

	Date	Opposition	Res.	H.T.	Att.	Goalscorers	Ross	Hemstead	Davis	Ternent	Winstanley	Garbutt	McVitie	Peddelty	Barton	Hatton	Balderstone	Caldwell	Brown	Passmoor	O'Neil	Murray	McIlmoyle	Dean	Hassel
2R	2 Sep	HUDDERSFIELD	2-0	1-0	11198	McIlmoyle(2)	1	2		4	6				8	9	11				5	3		10	
3R	24	BLACKBURN	2-1	0-1	11748	Hatton, McVitie	1	2		4	5		11		7	9	10	3			6	8			
4R	14 Oct	CHELSEA	1-0	0-0	18513	Hempstead	1	2		8	5		7		10		11	3	9	4	6				
5R	29	Oxford	0-0	0-0	17965		1		2	5			11		7	9	6	3	8	4	6	10			
5Rr	4 Nov	OXFORD	1-0	0-0	16303	Balderstone(pen)	1		10	5					7	9	2	3	8	4	6	11			
SF	19	WEST BROM. ALB.	1-0	0-0	20322	Barton	1	2		6	5		11		8	9	10	3	7	4					
SFr	3 Dec	West Bromwich Alb.	1-4	0-0	32971	Barton	1	2		6	5		11		8	9	10	3	7	4					

Final League Table

		Pl.	Home W	D	L	F	A	Away W	D	L	F	A	F.	A.	Pts
1	Huddersfield Town	42	14	6	1	36	10	10	6	5	32	27	68	37	60
2	Blackpool	42	10	9	2	25	16	10	4	7	31	29	56	45	53
3	Leicester City	42	12	6	3	37	22	7	7	7	27	28	64	50	51
4	Middlesbrough	42	15	4	2	36	14	5	6	10	19	31	55	45	50
5	Swindon Town	42	13	7	1	35	17	4	9	8	22	30	57	47	50
6	Sheffield United	42	16	2	3	50	10	6	3	12	23	28	73	38	49
7	Cardiff City	42	12	7	2	38	14	6	6	9	23	27	61	41	49
8	Blackburn Rovers	42	15	2	4	42	19	5	5	11	12	31	54	50	47
9	Queen's Park Rgs.	42	13	5	3	47	24	4	6	11	19	33	66	57	45
10	Millwall	42	14	4	3	38	18	1	10	10	18	38	56	56	44
11	Norwich City	42	13	5	3	37	14	3	6	12	12	32	49	46	43
12	Carlisle United	42	10	6	5	39	28	4	7	10	19	28	58	56	41
13	Hull City	42	11	6	4	43	28	4	5	12	29	42	72	70	41
14	Bristol City	42	11	7	3	37	13	2	6	13	17	37	54	50	39
15	Oxford United	42	9	9	3	23	13	3	6	12	12	29	35	42	39
16	Bolton Wanderers	42	9	6	6	31	23	3	6	12	23	38	54	61	36
17	Portsmouth	42	8	4	9	39	35	5	5	11	27	45	66	80	35
18	Birmingham City	42	9	7	5	33	22	2	4	15	18	56	51	78	33
19	Watford	42	6	8	7	26	21	3	5	13	18	36	44	57	31
20	Charlton Athletic	42	6	8	6	23	28	0	9	12	12	48	35	76	31
21	Aston Villa	42	7	8	6	23	21	1	5	15	13	41	36	62	29
22	Preston North End	42	7	6	8	31	28	1	6	14	12	35	43	63	28

- 1969/70 Season -

CARLISLE UNITED F.C.
DIVISION TWO 1969-70

Left to right :
Back row: FRANK BARTON   WILLIE O'NEIL   MAURICE PEDDELTY   STAN TERNENT
TERRY CALDWELL
Centre row: PETER GARBUTT   GRAHAM WINSTANLEY   ALLAN ROSS   JOE DEAN
TOMMY PASSMORE   DEREK HEMSTEAD
Front row: GEORGE McVITIE   WILLIE BROWN   CHRIS BALDERSTONE   BOB HATTON
TOMMY MURRAY   RICKY HASSELL
Picture by Bill Walker, "Cumberland Evening News and Star."

- 1970/71 Season -

(Back): O'Neill, Clarke, Ross, Ternent
(Middle): Young (Trainer), Garbutt, Winstanley, Hemstead, Davis, Sutton, Balderstone, Stokoe (Manager)
(Front): McVitie, Murray, Owen, Hatton, Barton, Martin

SEASON 1970/71
DIVISION 2

No.	Date	Opposition	Res.	H.T.	Att.	Goalscorers	Ross	Hemstead	Davis	Ternent	Winstanley	Sutton	McVitie	Murray	Owen	Hatton	Barton	Balderstone	Martin	Gorman	Kinsella	Webb	Garbutt
1	15 Aug	Middlesbrough	1-2	0-1	21228	Sutton	1	2	3	4	5	6	7	8	9	10	11						12
2	22	BIRMINGHAM	0-3	0-1	9244		1	2	11	4	5	6	12		9	10	8	3*	7				
3	29	Leicester	2-2	1-0	20809	Barton, Hatton	1	2	11	4	5	6			9	10	8	3	7				
4	1 Sep	HULL	2-0	1-0	8847	Balderstone(pen), Owen	1	2	11	4	5	6			9	10*	8	3	7				12
5	5	ORIENT	2-0	0-0	8143	Barton, Owen	1	2	11	4	5	6		10	9		8	3	7				
6	12	Watford	0-0	0-0	10462		1	2	11	4	5	6			9	10*	8	3	7	12			
7	19	SWINDON	2-1	0-0	10073	Martin, Hatton	1	2	11	4	5	6			9	10	8	3	7				
8	26	Sheffield Wednesday	0-3	0-3	12881		1	2	11	4	5	6			9*	10	8	3	7	12			
9	29	Charlton	1-1	0-1	9007	Balderstone	1	2	11	4	5	6			9		8	3	7	10			
10	2 Oct	MILLWALL	3-0	2-0	8424	Martin, Hatton, Owen	1	2	11	4	5	6		10	9		8	3	7				
11	10	Norwich	1-0	1-0	10883	Hatton	1	2	11	4	5	6			9	10	8	3	7				
12	17	MIDDLESBROUGH	1-0	0-0	15863	Owen	1	2	11	4	5	6		10	9		8	3	7				
13	20	SUNDERLAND	0-0	0-0	16263		1	2	11	4	5	6		10	9		8	3	7				
14	24	CARDIFF	1-1	0-0	10955	Balderstone	1	2	11	4	5	6			9	10	8	3	7				
15	31	Sheffield United	2-2	0-2	19268	Balderstone, Ternent	1	2	11	4	5	6		12	9		8	3	7*	10			
16	7 Nov	OXFORD	3-2	2-0	8090	Owen, Balderstone(2,1pen)	1	2	11	4	5	6		10	9		8	3	7				
17	17	Luton	3-3	0-0	14837	Hemstead, Balderstone, Martin	1	2	11	4	5	6		10	9		8	3	7				
18	21	BLACKBURN	1-0	0-0	7305	Balderstone	1	2	11	4	5	6		10	9		8	3	7				
19	28	Bristol City	1-2	0-0	13561	Hatton	1	2	11*	4	5	6		10	9		8	3	7		12		
20	5 Dec	PORTSMOUTH	6-0	4-0	7540	Owen(2), Hatton(4)	1		11	4	5			7	10	9	8	2			3	6	
21	12	Q. Park Rangers	1-1	0-0	8884	Murray	1		11	4	5			7	9	10	8	2			3	6	
22	19	Birmingham	0-1	0-0	15670		1		11	4	5			7	9	10	8*	2	12		3	6	
23	26	BOLTON	1-0	1-0	11132	Hatton	1		11	4	5	6			9			2	7		3	10	
24	9 Jan	CHARLTON	1-1	0-0	12266	Martin	1		11	4	5	6		8*	9	10		2	7		3	12	
25	16	Sunderland	0-2	0-2	16336		1	12	11	4	5	6		7	9	10		2*			8	3	
26	30	BRISTOL CITY	2-1	1-1	7764	Hatton, Owen	1		11	4	5	6		7	9	10		2			8	3	
27	2 Feb	Portsmouth	4-1	1-1	13219	Winstanley, Owen, Hatton, Murray	1		11	4	5	6		7	9	10		2			8	3	
28	13	Q.PARK RANGERS	3-0	3-0	9074	Martin(2), Hatton	1		11	4	5	6		7*	9	10	12	2			8	3	
29	20	Blackburn	2-0	1-0	9195	Balderstone, Martin	1		11	4	5	6			9	10	8	2	7		3		
30	27	SHEFFIELD UNITED	1-0	0-0	19678	Owen	1		11	4	5	6			9	10	8	2	7		3		
31	6 Mar	Cardiff	0-4	0-4	22371		1		11	4	5	6			9	10	8	2	7		3		
32	13	LUTON	1-0	1-0	13681	Owen	1		11	4	5	6			9	10	8	2	7		3		
33	20	Oxford	1-1	0-0	8116	Martin	1		11	4	5				9	10	8	2	7*	3		6	12
34	27	Orient	1-1	0-0	2998	Barton	1		11	4	5				9	10	8	2	7	3		6	
35	3 Apr	LEICESTER	0-1	0-0	15325		1	2	11	4	5			7	9	10	6				8	3	
36	5	Millwall	1-2	1-0	8238	Barton	1	2	11	4	5	6				10	7				8	3	9
37	10	Bolton	3-0	1-0	8038	Webb, Martin, Ternent	1	2	11	4	5	6				10	7				8	3	9
38	13	WATFORD	2-1	2-0	9484	Ternent, Hatton	1	2	11	4	5	6				10	7				8	3	9
39	17	NORWICH	4-2	2-0	8771	Hatton(2), Winstanley, Martin	1	2	11	4	5	6				10	7				8	3	9
40	24	Swindon	0-0	0-0	11780		1	2	11	4	5	6				10	7				8	3	9
41	28	Hull	2-1	1-0	14363	Hatton, Webb	1	2	11	4	5	6				10	7				8	3	9
42	1 May	SHEFFIELD WED.	3-0	2-0	9512	Hatton, Webb(2)	1	2	11	4	5	6			12	10*	7				8	3	9

F.A. CUP

Round	Date	Opposition	Res.	H.T.	Att.	Goalscorers	Ross	Hemstead	Davis	Ternent	Winstanley	Sutton	McVitie	Murray	Owen	Hatton	Barton	Balderstone	Martin	Gorman	Kinsella	Webb	Garbutt
3R	11 Jan	Southend	3-0	2-0	16729	Owen, Hatton(2)	1	2		4	5	6*		7	9	10			11	8	3	12	
4R	23	TOTTENHAM	2-3	1-1	25400	Martin, Owen	1	12	2	4	5	6		7*	9	10			11	8	3		

LEAGUE CUP

Round	Date	Opposition	Res.	H.T.	Att.	Goalscorers	Ross	Hemstead	Davis	Ternent	Winstanley	Sutton	McVitie	Murray	Owen	Hatton	Barton	Balderstone	Martin	Gorman	Kinsella	Webb	Garbutt
2R	9 Sep	MANCHESTER C.	2-1	1-0	17942	Martin, Hatton	1	2	3	4	5	6			9	10	8		11	7			
3R	6 Oct	OXFORD	3-1	2-1	13849	Hatton(3)	1	2	3	4	5	6			9	10	8		11	7			
4R	28	Aston Villa	0-1	0-0	26779		1	2	3	4	5	6		12	9		8		11	7*	10		

Final League Table

		Pl.	Home					Away					F.	A.	Pts
			W	D	L	F	A	W	D	L	F	A			
1	Leicester City	42	12	7	2	30	14	11	6	4	27	16	57	30	59
2	Sheffield United	42	14	6	1	49	18	7	8	6	24	21	73	39	56
3	Cardiff City	42	12	7	2	39	16	8	6	7	25	25	64	41	53
4	Carlisle United	42	16	3	2	39	13	4	10	7	26	30	65	43	53
5	Hull City	42	11	5	5	31	16	8	8	5	23	25	54	41	51
6	Luton Town	42	12	7	2	40	18	6	6	9	22	25	62	43	49
7	Middlesbrough	42	13	6	2	37	16	4	8	9	23	27	60	43	48
8	Millwall	42	13	5	3	36	12	6	4	11	23	30	59	42	47
9	Birmingham City	42	12	7	2	30	12	5	5	11	28	36	58	48	46
10	Norwich City	42	11	8	2	34	20	4	6	11	20	32	54	52	44
11	Queen's Park Rgs.	42	11	5	5	39	22	5	6	10	19	31	58	53	43
12	Swindon Town	42	12	7	2	38	14	3	5	13	23	37	61	51	42
13	Sunderland	42	11	6	4	34	21	4	6	11	18	33	52	54	42
14	Oxford United	42	8	8	5	23	23	6	6	9	18	25	41	48	42
15	Sheffield Wed.	42	10	7	4	32	27	2	5	14	19	42	51	69	36
16	Portsmouth	42	9	4	8	32	28	1	10	10	14	33	46	61	34
17	Orient	42	5	11	5	16	15	4	5	12	13	36	29	51	34
18	Watford	42	6	7	8	18	22	4	6	11	20	38	38	60	33
19	Bristol City	42	9	6	6	30	28	1	5	15	16	36	46	64	31
20	Charlton Athletic	42	7	6	8	28	30	1	8	12	13	35	41	65	30
21	Blackburn Rovers	42	5	8	8	20	28	1	7	13	17	41	37	69	27
22	Bolton Wanderers	42	6	5	10	22	31	1	5	15	13	43	35	74	24

SEASON 1971/72

DIVISION 2

No.	Date	Opposition	Res.	H.T.	Att.	Goalscorers	Ross	Davis	Gorman	Ternent	Winstanley	Sutton	Barton	Martin	Owen	Webb	Balderstone	Hatton	Hemstead	Kinsella	Hegarty	Bowles	Train	Delgardo	Clark
1	14 Aug	PRESTON	0-0	0-0	11063		1	2	3	4		6	7	8		5	9	11	10						
2	21	Birmingham	2-3	0-0	26245	Webb, Hatton	1	2	3	4		6	7	8		5	9	11	10						
3	28	SWINDON	0-0	0-0	9963		1		3	4	5	6	7	8	12	9*	11	10	2						
4	1 Sep	Sunderland	3-0	2-0	20998	Hatton, Balderstone, Martin	1		3	4	5	6	7	8	9		11	10	2						
5	4	Norwich	0-1	0-1	11477		1	12	3	4	5	6	7	8	9		11	10	2						
6	11	WATFORD	2-0	0-0	9743	Barton, Hatton	1		3	4	5	6	7	8	9		11	10	2						
7	18	Orient	1-2	1-1	7068	Hatton	1		3	4	5	6	7	8	9		11	10	2						
8	25	HULL	2-1	1-1	9879	Hatton, Martin	1		3	4	5	6	7	8	9		11	10	2		12				
9	28	CHARLTON	5-2	1-1	9724	Owen(3), Hatton, Balderstone	1		3	4	5	6	7	8	9		11	10	2						
10	2 Oct	Millwall	1-2	1-1	11546	Winstanley	1	12	3	4	5	6	7	8*	9		11	10	2						
11	9	BURNLEY	0-3	0-0	11625		1		3	4	5	6	7	8*	9	12	11	10	2						
12	16	Preston	0-3	0-2	15340		1		3	8	4	5	6	7		9	12	10	2		11*				
13	20	Sheffield Wednesday	1-2	1-1	15672	Martin	1	2*	3	4	5	12	7		9		11	10			6				
14	23	Luton	2-0	1-0	11963	Hatton, Balderstone	1		3	4*	5	6	7	8	9	12	11	10	2						
15	30	OXFORD	2-1	0-1	8497	Owen(2)	1		3	4	5	6	7	8	9	12	11		2		10*				
16	6 Nov	Blackpool	0-2	0-2	12769		1		3	4	5	6	7	8	9		11		2		10				
17	13	PORTSMOUTH	1-0	0-0	7955	Martin	1		3	4	5	12	7	8	9*	10	6		2		11				
18	19	Bristol City	4-1	3-1	13123	Barton, Bowles, Owen(2)	1	12	3	4	5	6	7	8	9		11*		2		10				
19	27	CARDIFF	2-1	1-0	6835	Owen, Martin	1		3	4	5		7	8	9	10	6		2		11				
20	4 Dec	Fulham	1-0	0-0	8101	Bowles	1		3	4	5		7	8	9	10	6		2		11				
21	11	Q.PARK RANGERS	1-4	0-3	9243	Ternent	1		3	4	5		7	8	9	10	6		2		12	11			
22	18	NORWICH	3-0	2-0	9081	Bowles(3)	1		3	4	5		7	8	9		11		2		6	10			
23	27	Middlesbrough	2-2	2-2	24696	Bowles, Balderstone	1	12	3	4	5		7	8	9		11		2		6	10*			
24	1 Jan	ORIENT	2-0	1-0	11449	Barton, Owen	1		3	4	5		7	8	9		11		2		6	10			
25	8	Swindon	0-0	0-0	13089		1		3	4	5		7	8	9		11		2		6	10			
26	22	Charlton	1-1	0-0	8180	Bowles	1		3	4	5		7	8	9		11		2		6	10			
27	29	SHEFFIELD WED.	2-2	1-1	9011	Martin, Balderstone(pen)	1		3	4	5		7	8	9		11		2		6	10			
28	12	LUTON	0-0	0-0	8731		1		3	4	5		7	8	9		11		2		6	10			
29	19	Oxford	1-3	1-2	7629	Balderstone	1		3	4			7	8	5	9*	11		2		6	10	12		
30	26	BLACKPOOL	2-0	0-0	9985	Bowles(2)	1		3	4			7	8	5	12	11		2			10	9*	6	
31	4 Mar	Portsmouth	0-1	0-0	9098		1		3	4			7	8	9	12	11		2		6*	10	5		
32	11	Burnley	1-3	0-1	10314	Barton	1		3	4			7	8	9*		11		2		12	6	10	5	
33	14	MIDDLESBROUGH	3-0	2-0	10316	Delgardo, Barton, Balderstone		2	3	4			7	8	9		11					10	6	5	1
34	21	BIRMINGHAM	2-2	1-1	12281	Martin, Bowles		2	3	4			7	8	9*		11				12	10	6	5	1
35	25	Watford	2-1	1-0	6004	Owen, Martin		2	3	4			7	8	9		11					10	6*	5	1
36	3 Apr	Hull	0-2	0-1	16403			2	3	4	5		7	8	9	12	11					10	6*	5	1
37	4	MILLWALL	3-3	1-1	10692	Balderstone(pen), Martin, Barton		2	3	4	5		7	8	9		11*				12	10	6		1
38	8	BRISTOL CITY	2-0	1-0	6596	Owen, Gorman		2	3	4	5		7	8	9	11*					12	10		6	1
39	15	Cardiff	1-3	0-0	17734	Barton		2	3	4	5		7	8	9							10	11	6	1
40	22	FULHAM	3-1	1-0	6067	Gorman, Martin, Barton	1	2	3	4	5		7*	8	9	12	11					10	6		
41	25	SUNDERLAND	1-2	1-0	10326	Bowles	1	2	3	4	5		7	8	9		11					10	6		
42	29	Q.Park Rangers	0-3	0-1	7616		1		3	4	5		7	8	9		11		2			10	6		

F.A. CUP

No.	Date	Opposition	Res.	H.T.	Att.	Goalscorers	Ross	Davis	Gorman	Ternent	Winstanley	Sutton	Barton	Martin	Owen	Webb	Balderstone	Hatton	Hemstead	Kinsella	Hegarty	Bowles	Train	Delgardo	Clark
3R	15 Jan	Tottenham	1-1	1-1	33702	Bowles	1		3	4	5		7	8	6	9	11		2			10			
3Rr	18	TOTTENHAM	1-3	1-1	21560	Martin	1	12	3	4	5		7	8	9	10*	11		2		6				

LEAGUE CUP

No.	Date	Opposition	Res.	H.T.	Att.	Goalscorers	Ross	Davis	Gorman	Ternent	Winstanley	Sutton	Barton	Martin	Owen	Webb	Balderstone	Hatton	Hemstead	Kinsella	Hegarty	Bowles	Train	Delgardo	Clark
2R	7 Sep	SHEFFIELD WED.	5-0	3-0	10338	Hatton(2), Martin(2), Barton	1		3	4	5	6	7	8	9		11	10	2						
3R	6 Oct	Norwich	1-4	0-2	17726	Winstanley	1		3	4	5	6	7	8	9		11	10	2						

Final League Table

		Pl.	Home					Away					F.	A.	Pts
			W	D	L	F	A	W	D	L	F	A			
1	Norwich City	42	13	8	0	40	16	8	7	6	20	20	60	36	57
2	Birmingham City	42	15	6	0	46	14	4	12	5	14	17	60	31	56
3	Millwall	42	14	7	0	38	17	5	10	6	26	29	64	46	55
4	Queen's Park Rgs.	42	16	4	1	39	9	4	10	7	18	19	57	28	54
5	Sunderland	42	11	7	3	42	24	6	9	6	25	33	67	57	50
6	Blackpool	42	12	6	3	43	16	8	1	12	27	34	70	50	47
7	Burnley	42	13	4	4	43	22	7	2	12	27	33	70	55	46
8	Bristol City	42	14	3	4	43	22	4	7	10	18	27	61	49	46
9	Middlesbrough	42	16	4	1	31	11	3	4	14	19	37	50	48	46
10	Carlisle United	42	12	6	3	38	22	5	3	13	23	35	61	57	43
11	Swindon Town	42	10	6	5	29	16	5	6	10	18	31	47	47	42
12	Hull City	42	10	6	5	33	21	4	4	13	16	32	49	53	38
13	Luton Town	42	7	8	6	25	24	3	10	8	18	24	43	48	38
14	Sheffield Wed.	42	11	7	3	33	22	2	5	14	18	36	51	58	38
15	Oxford United	42	10	8	3	28	17	2	6	13	15	38	43	55	38
16	Portsmouth	42	9	7	5	31	26	3	6	12	28	42	59	68	37
17	Orient	42	12	4	5	32	19	2	5	14	18	42	50	61	37
18	Preston North End	42	11	4	6	32	21	1	8	12	20	37	52	58	36
19	Cardiff City	42	9	7	5	37	25	1	7	13	19	44	56	69	34
20	Fulham	42	10	7	4	29	20	2	3	16	16	48	45	68	34
21	Charlton Athletic	42	9	7	5	33	25	3	2	16	22	52	55	77	33
22	Watford	42	5	5	11	15	25	0	4	17	9	50	24	75	19

- 1971/72 Season -

Back row, left to right : MIKE SUTTON   DEREK HEMSTEAD   STAN WEBB   DENNIS MARTIN   ALLAN ROSS   TOM CLARKE   STAN TERNENT   STAN BOWLES   GRAHAM WINSTANLEY   CHRIS BALDERSTONE

Front row, left to right : FRANK BARTON   KEVIN HEGARTY   RAY TRAIN   JOHN GORMAN   JIM FLEMING   JOE DAVIS   BOBBY OWEN

Picture by Peter Robinson

- 1972/73 Season -

Standing: F. Clarke, M. Sutton, D. Hempstead, S. Ternent, D. Martin, S. Webb, C. Balderstone, G. Winstanley, R. Delgado, A. Ross
Front: F. Barton, J. Fleming, J. Gorman, K. Hegarty, J. Davis, R. Train, R. Owen, S. Bowles.

SEASON 1972/73

DIVISION 2

No.	Date	Opposition	Res.	H.T.	Att.	Goalscorers	Ross	Hemstead	Gorman	Laidlaw	Winstanley	Delgardo	Train	Martin	Owen	Bowles	Balderstone	Ternent	O'Neill	Derrett	Webb	Wilson	Clarke	Tiler	Carr
1	12 Aug	Burnley	2-2	1-0	9804	Martin, Owen	1	2	3	4	5	6	7	8	9	10	11								
2	19	SWINDON	3-0	0-0	7747	Owen, Balderstone(2)	1	2	3	4	5	6	7	8	9	10	11								
3	26	Huddersfield	1-1	1-1	9483	Bowles	1	2	3	4	5		7	8	9	10	11	6							
4	29	Aston Villa	0-1	0-0	29047		1	2	3	4	5		7	8	9	10	11	6							
5	2 Sep	NOTTINGHAM FOREST	1-2	1-1	7626	Owen	1	2	3	4	5		7	8	9	10*	11	6	12						
6	9	Middlesbrough	0-1	0-1	9799		1		3	4	5		7*	10	9		11	6	8	2	12				
7	16	CARDIFF	4-0	3-0	5911	Laidlaw, Train, Balderstone, Owen	1		3	4	5		7	10	9		11	6	8	2					
8	23	Preston	0-1	0-1	10957		1		3	4	5	12	7	8	9		11	6	10*	2					
9	26	BLACKPOOL	2-3	1-2	10969	Owen, Laidlaw	1		3	4	5	12	7	8*	9		11	6		2		10			
10	30	SHEFFIELD WED.	1-1	0-0	7306	Laidlaw	1		3	4	5	12	7*	8	9		11	6		2		10			
11	7 Oct	Q.Park Rangers	0-4	0-0	11755				3	6	5	2	8	7	9		11	4				10	1		
12	14	FULHAM	2-1	0-1	6221	Laidlaw, Delgardo			3	4	5	2	10	7	9		11	6				8	1		
13	21	Orient	1-2	1-1	4695	Laidlaw			3	4	5	2	7	8	9		11					10	1	6	
14	28	PORTSMOUTH	1-0	0-0	6361	Balderstone			3	11	5		7	8	9		2	6				10	1	4	
15	4 Nov	Blackpool	0-0	0-0	9564				3	11	5		7	12	9		8	6		2		10*	1	4	
16	11	SUNDERLAND	4-3	3-1	8884	Owen, Martin, Gorman, Ternent			3	11	5		7	8	9		10	6		2			1	4	
17	18	OXFORD	2-1	2-0	5919	Laidlaw, Balderstone(pen)	1		3*	11	5	12	7	8	9		10		6	2				4	
18	25	Luton	1-0	0-0	10091	Owen	1		3	11	5		7	8	9		10		6	2				4	
19	2 Dec	BRISTOL CITY	1-2	0-1	6526	Owen	1		3	11	5		7	8	9		10		6	2				4	
20	9	Hull	1-1	1-1	7075	Laidlaw	1		3	11	5		7	8	9		10		6					4	2
21	16	BRIGHTON	5-1	3-0	5671	Owen(3), O'Neill, Winstanley	1		3	11	5		7	8	9		10		6					4	2
22	23	Millwall	0-1	0-1	7933		1		3	11	5	12	7	8	9*		10		6					4	2
23	26	PRESTON	6-1	3-1	9939	Balderstne,Wilsn,Mrtin(2),Laidlw(2)	1		3	11	5		7	8			10		4			9		6	2
24	6 Jan	HUDDERSFIELD	0-0	0-0	6986		1		3	11	5		7	8			10	12	4			9		6	2
25	20	Nottingham Forest	1-2	1-1	6866	Martin	1		3	11		5	7	9*			10	8	6			12		4	2
26	27	MIDDLESBROUGH	1-1	0-1	7653	O'Neill	1		3	11		5	10	8	9*		7		6			12		4	2
27	10 Feb	Cardiff	0-1	0-0	7819		1		3		5	6	10	7	8				4			11		9	2
28	17	BURNLEY	1-1	0-1	18000	Martin	1		3	11	5	12	8	7	9		10		4*					6	2
29	3 Mar	Q.PARK RANGERS	1-3	0-0	8729	Delgardo	1		3	11	5		8	7	9		10		4					6	2
30	10	Fulham	0-1	0-0	9835		1		3	11	5	9*	8	7			10		4			12		6	2
31	12	Swindon	0-2	0-2	7942		1		3	11	5	9	8	7			10*		4			12		6	2
32	17	ORIENT	1-0	0-0	5696	Laidlaw	1		3	11	5		7	8*	9		10		4			12		6	2
33	21	Brighton	0-1	0-0	11008		1		3	11	5		8	7	12		10		4			9		6	2*
34	24	Portsmouth	0-0	0-0	5346		1		3	11	5		8	7	9		10		4					6	2
35	27	Sunderland	1-2	1-0	39930	Laidlaw	1		3	11	5		8	7	9		10*		4			12		6	2
36	31	LUTON	2-0	2-0	5517	Gorman, Owen	1		3	11	5		7	8	9		10		4					6	2
37	7 Apr	Bristol City	1-4	1-3	10530	Laidlaw	1		3	11	5		8	7	9		10*	12	4					6	2
38	14	HULL	0-1	0-1	5870		1		3	11	5		7		9*		10	4	6			8		12	2
39	21	Oxford	1-1	0-0	4627	Laidlaw	1			11	5	4	7	8*	12		10		9	2				6	3
40	23	Sheffield Wednesday	0-0	0-0	8895		1			11	5	4	8				10		7	2		9		6	3
41	24	MILLWALL	0-1	0-1	6178		1			11	5		8		9		7	4		2		10		6	3
42	28	ASTON VILLA	2-2	2-1	6178	Tiler, Laidlaw	1		3	11	5		7	8	9		10		4					6	2

F.A. CUP

No.	Date	Opposition	Res.	H.T.	Att.	Goalscorers	Ross	Hemstead	Gorman	Laidlaw	Winstanley	Delgardo	Train	Martin	Owen	Bowles	Balderstone	Ternent	O'Neill	Derrett	Webb	Wilson	Clarke	Tiler	Carr
3R	13 Jan	HUDDERSFIELD	2-2	0-0	9550	Gorman, Laidlaw	1		3	11	5*	12	7	8			10	4	6			9		2	
3Rr	15	Huddersfield	1-0	1-0	13555	O.G.	1		3	11		5	7	8			10	6	4			9		2	
4R	3 Feb	SHEFFIELD UNITED	2-1	1-0	13241	Martin, Delgardo	1		3		5	6	7	8			11	4*	10	12		9		2	
5R	24	ARSENAL	1-2	1-1	24000	Martin	1		3	11	2	5	8	7	9*		10		4			12		6	

LEAGUE CUP

No.	Date	Opposition	Res.	H.T.	Att.	Goalscorers	Ross	Hemstead	Gorman	Laidlaw	Winstanley	Delgardo	Train	Martin	Owen	Bowles	Balderstone	Ternent	O'Neill	Derrett	Webb	Wilson	Clarke	Tiler	Carr
2R	5 Sep	LIVERPOOL	1-1	0-1	16257	O'Neill	1		3	4	5		7	8	9	10	11*	6	12	2					
2Rr	19	Liverpool	1-5	0-2	22182	Owen	1		3	4	5		7	8	9		11	6	10	2					

Final League Table

		Pl.	Home					Away					F.	A.	Pts
			W	D	L	F	A	W	D	L	F	A			
1	Burnley	42	13	6	2	44	18	11	8	2	28	17	72	35	62
2	Queen's Park Rgs.	42	16	4	1	54	13	8	9	4	27	24	81	37	61
3	Aston Villa	42	12	5	4	27	17	6	9	6	24	30	51	47	50
4	Middlesbrough	42	12	6	3	29	15	5	7	9	17	28	46	43	47
5	Bristol City	42	10	7	4	34	18	7	5	9	29	33	63	51	46
6	Sunderland	42	12	6	3	35	17	6	5	10	24	32	59	49	46
7	Blackpool	42	12	6	3	37	17	6	4	11	19	34	56	51	46
8	Oxford United	42	14	2	5	36	18	5	5	11	16	25	52	43	45
9	Fulham	42	11	6	4	32	16	5	6	10	26	33	58	49	44
10	Sheffield Wed.	42	14	4	3	40	20	3	6	12	19	35	59	55	44
11	Millwall	42	12	5	4	33	18	4	5	12	22	29	55	47	42
12	Luton Town	42	6	9	6	24	23	9	2	10	20	30	44	53	41
13	Hull City	42	9	7	5	39	22	5	5	11	25	37	64	59	40
14	Nottingham Forest	42	12	5	4	32	18	2	7	12	15	34	47	52	40
15	Orient	42	11	6	4	33	18	1	8	12	16	35	49	53	36
16	Swindon Town	42	8	9	4	28	23	2	7	12	18	37	46	60	36
17	Portsmouth	42	7	6	8	21	22	5	5	11	21	37	42	59	35
18	Carlisle United	42	10	5	6	40	24	1	7	13	10	28	50	52	34
19	Preston North End	42	6	8	7	19	25	5	4	12	18	39	37	64	34
20	Cardiff City	42	11	4	6	32	21	0	7	14	11	37	43	58	33
21	Huddersfield Town	42	7	9	5	21	20	1	8	12	15	36	36	56	33
22	Brighton & Hove A.	42	7	8	6	32	31	1	5	15	14	52	46	83	29

SEASON 1973/74

DIVISION 2

No.	Date	Opposition	Res.	H.T.	Att.	Goalscorers	Ross	Carr	Gorman	Green	Winstanley	O'Neill	Train	Ternent	Clarke F.	Laidlaw	Martin	Delgado	Owen	Tiler	Barry	Balderstone	Clarke T.	McCartney
1	25 Aug	CARDIFF	1-1	1-0	6863	F.Clarke	1	2	3	4	5	6	7	8	9*	10	11	12						
2	1 Sep	Luton	1-6	0-6	7231	Owen	1	2	3	4	5		6*	8	9	11	7	12	10					
3	8	NOTTS COUNTY	0-3	0-0	6109	Martin, O'Neill(2)	1	2	3	5		4			9	11*	7	10	8			6	12	
4	11	Middlsbrough	0-1	0-0	16837		1	2	3	5		4			9	10	11					6	8	
5	15	Sheffield Wednesday	0-1	0-0	15080		1	2	3	5		8*		6	9	10	7	12		4	11			
6	18	PORTSMOUTH	0-2	0-0	6416		1	2	3	5		7		4	9	10				6	8	11		
7	22	OXFORD	2-1	0-0	5093	F.Clarke, Martin	1	2	3	5		4			9	10	7			6	8	11		
8	29	Millwall	2-1	0-0	8907	O.G., Green	1	2	3	5		6				10	7	12	9	4	8	11*		
9	2 Oct	Portsmouth	1-2	0-1	10796	Owen	1	2	3	5		4			9*	11	7	10	12	6	8			
10	6	BOLTON	1-0	1-0	8365	Owen	1	2	3	5		4				11	7		9	6	8	10		
11	13	West Bromwich Albion	1-1	1-0	12528			2	3	5		4				10	11	7	9	6	8		1	
12	20	Crystal Palace	1-0	0-0	19678	Laidlaw	1	2	3	5		4		8	10	11	7		9	6				
13	23	MIDDLESBROUGH	1-1	0-1	11152	Martin	1	2	3	5		4		8	10	11	7		9	6				
14	27	FULHAM	3-0	2-0	7147	F.Clarke, Martin, O'Neill	1	2	3	5		4		8	10	11	7		9	6				
15	3 Nov	Swindon	2-2	2-1	6480	F.Clark(2)	1	2	3	5		4			10	11	7		9*	6	8	12		
16	10	HULL	4-0	1-0	6563	Owen, Martin, Laidlaw(2)	1	2	3		5	6		4	10	11	7		9			8		
17	17	Nottingham Forest	0-2	0-2	11153		1	2		5		4		6	8	11	7		9			10		
18	24	BRISTOL CITY	2-1	1-1	6020	Winstanley, O'Neill	1	2		5	4	12		6	10*	11	7		9			8		
19	8 Dec	BLACKPOOL	2-3	1-1	6641	Train, O'Neill	1	2		5		4	10			11	7		9	6		8		
20	15	Orient	1-0	0-0	7645	Martin	1		3	5	2	4	8			11	7		9	6*		10		12
21	22	MILLWALL	1-1	1-0	8300	Owen	1		3	5	2		6		9	11	7		8	4		10		
22	26	Preston	1-0	0-0	11446	Train	1		3	5	2	4	8		10	11	7		9	6				
23	29	Notts County	3-0	2-0	10209	Laidlaw(2), O.G.	1		3	5	2	4	8		10	11	7		9	6				
24	1 Jan	LUTON	2-0	0-0	9255	Green, Martin	1		3	5	2	4*	8		10	11	7		9	6		12		
25	12	SHEFFIELD WED.	2-2	1-2	7332	Laidlaw, Owen	1	2	3	5		4	8		10	11	7*		9			6		12
26	19	Cardiff	2-2	0-1	10797	Train, F.Clarke	1	2	3	5		4	8		10	11	7		9			6		
27	2 Feb	ORIENT	3-0	2-0	9422	F.Clarke(2), Laidlaw	1	2	3	5		4	8		10	11	7		9			6		
28	23	Bolton	0-2	0-0	16675		1	2	3	5			8	4	10	11	7		9			6		
29	25	WEST BROM. ALB.	0-1	0-1	6407		1	2	3	5			8	4	10*	11	7		9			6		12
30	3 Mar	PRESTON	2-2	0-2	7671	O'Neill, Owen	1	2	3	5		4	7		10	11			9			6		
31	9	Fulham	2-0	1-0	6731	Laidlaw, F.Clarke	1	2	3	5		4	8		10	11	7		9	6				
32	13	Aston Villa	1-2	0-1	12007	F.Clarke	1	2	3	5		4	8		10	11	7		9	6				
33	16	CRYSTAL PALACE	1-0	1-0	6964	F.Clarke	1	2	3	5		4	8		10	11	7		9			6		
34	23	Hukll	1-1	1-0	6137	Owen	1	2	3	5		4	8		10	11	7		9			6		
35	30	SWINDON	5-1	2-0	6544	F.Clarke(4,1pen), Laidlaw	1	2	3	5		4	8		10	11	7		9			6		
36	6 Apr	Bristol City	0-2	0-1	9570		1	2		5	3		8		10	11	7		9			6		4
37	12	Sunderland	1-2	0-0	34179	Laidlaw	1	2		5	3	4	8		10	11	7		9			6		
38	13	NOTTINGHAM FOREST	2-1	0-1	9258	Owen, Laidlaw	1	2	10	5	3	4	8			11	7		9			6		
39	16	SUNDERLAND	1-0	0-0	19692	Balderstone(pen)	1	2	3	5		4	8		10	11	7		9			6		
40	20	Blackpool	0-4	0-2	15777		1	2	3	5	12	4	8		10*	11	7		9			6		
41	23	Oxford	1-0	0-0	9675	Owen	1	2	3		5	4	8		10	11	7		9			6		
42	27	ASTON VILLA	2-0	1-0	12494	Laidlaw, F.Clarke	1	2	3		5	4	8		10	11	7		9			6		

F.A. CUP

	Date	Opposition	Res.	H.T.	Att.	Goalscorers	Ross	Carr	Gorman	Green	Winstanley	O'Neill	Train	Ternent	Clarke F.	Laidlaw	Martin	Delgado	Owen	Tiler	Barry	Balderstone	Clarke T.	McCartney
3R	5 Jan	SUNDERLAND	0-0	0-0	20595		1		3	5	2	4	8		10	11	7		9	6*			12	
3Rr	9	Sunderland	1-0	0-0	25710	Martin	1	2	3	5		4	8		10	11	7		9			6		
4R	26	Liverpool	0-0	0-0	47211		1	2	3	5		4	8		10	11	7		9			6		
4Rr	29	LIVERPOOL	0-2	0-2	21262		1	2	3	5		4	8*		10	11	7		9	12		6		

LEAGUE CUP

	Date	Opposition	Res.	H.T.	Att.	Goalscorers	Ross	Carr	Gorman	Green	Winstanley	O'Neill	Train	Ternent	Clarke F.	Laidlaw	Martin	Delgado	Owen	Tiler	Barry	Balderstone	Clarke T.	McCartney
1R1	28 Aug	WORKINGTON	2-2	0-2	7040	Owen(2)	1	2	3	5	6		7	4	9	10	11		8					
1R2	5 Sep	Workington	1-0	1-0	4931	O'Neill	1	2	3	5		7			9	10	11	4	8	6				
2R	10 Oct	Gillingham	2-1	1-1	7871	Balderstone, Martin	1	2	3	5		4				11	7	12	9	6	8	10*		
3R	6 Nov	MANCHESTER CITY	0-1	0-0	14472		1	2	3	5		4			10	11	7	12	9	6*		8		

Final League Table

		Pl.	Home					Away					F.	A.	Pts
			W	D	L	F	A	W	D	L	F	A			
1	Middlesbrough	42	16	4	1	40	8	11	7	3	37	22	77	30	65
2	Luton Town	42	12	5	4	42	25	7	7	7	22	26	64	51	50
3	Carlisle United	42	13	5	3	40	17	7	4	10	21	31	61	48	49
4	Orient	42	9	8	4	28	17	6	10	5	27	25	55	42	48
5	Blackpool	42	11	5	5	35	17	6	8	7	22	23	57	40	47
6	Sunderland	42	11	6	4	32	15	8	3	10	26	29	58	44	47
7	Nottingham Forest	42	12	6	3	40	19	3	9	9	17	24	57	43	45
8	West Bromwich Alb.	42	8	9	4	28	24	6	7	8	20	21	48	45	44
9	Hull City	42	9	9	3	25	15	4	8	9	21	32	46	47	43
10	Notts County	42	8	6	7	30	35	7	7	7	25	25	55	60	43
11	Bolton Wanderers	42	12	5	4	30	17	3	7	11	14	23	44	40	42
12	Millwall	42	10	6	5	28	16	4	8	9	23	35	51	51	42
13	Fulham	42	11	4	6	26	20	5	6	10	13	23	39	43	42
14	Aston Villa	42	8	9	4	33	21	5	6	10	15	24	48	45	41
15	Portsmouth	42	9	8	4	26	16	5	4	12	19	46	45	62	40
16	Bristol City	42	8	9	4	23	21	5	5	11	22	34	47	54	38
17	Cardiff City	42	8	7	6	27	20	2	9	10	22	42	49	62	36
18	Oxford United	42	8	5	8	27	21	2	8	11	8	25	35	46	36
19	Sheffield Wed.	42	6	6	9	33	24	3	5	13	18	39	51	63	35
20	Crystal Palace	42	6	7	8	24	24	5	5	11	19	32	43	56	34
21	Preston North End	42	7	8	6	24	23	2	6	13	16	39	40	62	31
22	Swindon Town	42	6	7	8	22	27	1	4	16	14	45	36	72	25

- 1973/74 Season -

(Back): Owen, Ternent, Clarke, Ross, Tiler, Carr
(Middle): Derrett, Martin, Delgado, Green, Winstanley, McCartney, Wilson
(Front): Barry, Gorman, Laidlaw, O'Neill, Train

- 1974/75 Season -

(Back): McCartney, Clarke, McClaughlin, Ross, T.Clarke, Owen, Barry
(Middle): Nicholson(Physio), Young(Train), Spearitt, Martin, Balderstone, Ashman(Man), Laidlaw, Winstanley, McIlmoyle,
Neil(Scout)   (Front): Train, Gorman, O'Neill, Green, Carr, Parker

SEASON 1974/75

DIVISION 1

No.	Date	Opposition	Res.	H.T.	Att.	Goalscorers	Ross	Carr	Gorman	O'Neill	Green	Parker	McIlmoyle	Train	Clarke F.	Balderstone	Laidlaw	Martin	Winstanley	Barry	Owen	Clarke T.	Spearritt	Prudham	McCartney
1	17 Aug	Chelsea	2-0	1-0	31268	Green, O'Neill	1	2	3	4	5	6	7	8	9*	10	11	12							
2	20	Middlesbrough	2-0	1-0	28719	O'Neill(2)	1	2	3*	4	5	6	9	7	12	10	11	8							
3	24	TOTTENHAM	1-0	1-0	18426	Balderstone(pen)	1	2		4	5	6	9*	8	12	10	11	7	3						
4	27	MIDDLESBROUGH	0-1	0-1	18473		1	2	3	4	5	6	9	8		10	11	7							
5	31	Leicester	1-1	1-0	20658	McIlmoyle	1	2	3	4	5	6	9	8		10	11	7							
6	7 Sep	STOKE	0-2	0-1	14507		1	2	3	4	5	6	9	8		10	11			7*	12				
7	14	Newcastle	0-1	0-0	37075		1	2	3	4	5	6	9	8	7	10	11								
8	21	BIRMINGHAM	1-0	0-0	12691	O'Neill	1	2	3	4	5	6	9	8	7	10	11								
9	24	MANCHESTER CITY	0-0	0-0	17900		1	2	3	4	5	6	9	8		10	11	7							
10	28	Luton	1-3	1-1	12987	Laidlaw	1	2	3	4	5	6	9	8		10	11	7							
11	5 Oct	LIVERPOOL	0-1	0-1	20844		1	2	3	4	5	6	10	8			11	7			9				
12	12	Wolves	0-2	0-1	18918			2	3		5	6		8		10	11	7		12	9	1	4*		
13	16	Tottenham	1-1	1-1	12823	Owen	1	2	3		5	6		8	9	4		7		11	10				
14	19	DERBY	3-0	1-0	13353	Train, Martin, F.Clarke		2	3		5	6		8	9	4		7		11	10	1			
15	26	Coventry	1-2	1-1	17070	F.Clarke		2	3		5	6	12	8	9*		11	7		4	10	1			
16	2 Nov	Sheffield United	1-2	1-2	17679	McIlmoyle		2	3		5	6	11	8	9	4		7		12	10*	1			
17	9	WEST HAM	0-1	0-0	14141			2	3	4	5	6	10	8	9		11	7				1			
18	16	Q.Park Rangers	1-2	0-2	15700	Parker(pen)	1	2	3	4	5	6		8	9*	10	11	7			12				
19	23	LEEDS	1-2	1-0	19975	Martin	1	2	3	4	5	6		8	9		11	7						12	10*
20	30	Ipswich	1-3	0-2	20122	O'Neill	1	2	3	4	5	6		8	9		12	7						11	10
21	7 Dec	ARSENAL	2-1	1-0	12926	Prudham, Martin	1	2	3	4	5	6		8	9			7						11	10*
22	14	CHELSEA	1-2	1-2	12854	Martin	1	2	3	4	5	6		8	9		12	7						11	10*
23	21	Everton	3-2	0-1	33489	Laidlaw(2), O'Neill	1	2	3	4	5	6	12	8	9*	10	11	7							
24	26	NEWCASTLE	1-2	0-1	25000	Owen	1	2	3	4	5	6	9*	8		11	10	7			12				
25	28	Burnley	1-2	1-1	19382	Martin	1	2		4	5	6		8		11	10	7			9				3
26	11 Jan	Arsenal	1-2	1-2	21538	O'Neill	1			4	5	2		8		11	6	10	7		9		3		
27	18	IPSWICH	2-1	1-1	13054	F.Clarke, Laidlaw	1		3	4	5	6		8		11	10	7			9		2		
28	1 Feb	West Ham	0-2	0-2	26805		1		3	4	5	6		8		11	10	7		12	9		2		
29	8	SHEFFIELD UNITED	0-1	0-1	12023		1	2		4	5	6	12	8		11*	10	7			9		3		
30	22	Q.PARK RANGERS	1-2	1-1	13176	Owen	1	2		4	5	6		8		11	10	7			9		3		
31	25	Leeds	1-3	0-1	32346	Laidlaw	1	2		4	5	6		8		11	12	10	7*		9		3		
32	1 Mar	Leicester	0-1	0-0	12676		1	2	12	4	5	6		8		11*	10	7			9		3		
33	15	Luton	0-1	0-0	8339	Laidlaw	1	2	3	4	5	6		8		11	10	7			9				
34	19	Manchester City	2-1	2-1	24047	Laidlaw(2)	1	2		4	5	6		8		11	10	7			9		3		
35	22	Stoke	2-5	1-1	20545	Laidlaw, Carr	1	2		4*	5	6		8		11	12	10	7		9		3		
36	25	Birmingham	0-2	0-1	33761		1	2		4	5	6		8		11	12	10	7			9*	3		
37	29	EVERTON	3-0	3-0	16049	Laidlaw(pen), Martin, F.Clarke		2	3	4	5	6		8	9*	11	10	7				1			12
38	1 Apr	BURNLEY	4-2	2-1	12793	O'Neill, Train, Laidlaw(2,1pen)		2	3	4*	5	6		8	9	11	10	7					1	12	
39	5	COVENTRY	0-0	0-0	10857			2	3		5	6		8	11*	4	10	7				9*	1	12	
40	12	Liverpool	0-2	0-0	46073			2	3	4	5	6		8	9*	11	10	7			12	1			
41	19	WOLVES	1-0	1-0	9707	Martin	1	2		4	5	6		8		11	10	7					3	9	
42	26	Derby	0-0	0-0	38000		1	2		4	5	6		8	9	11	10	7					3		

F.A. CUP

Round	Date	Opposition	Res.	H.T.	Att.	Goalscorers	Ross	Carr	Gorman	O'Neill	Green	Parker	McIlmoyle	Train	Clarke F.	Balderstone	Laidlaw	Martin	Winstanley	Barry	Owen	Clarke T.	Spearritt	Prudham	McCartney
3R	4 jan	Preston	1-0	1-0	18682	Laidlaw	1	2	3	4	5	6		8		11	10		7		9				
4R	24	WEST BROM. ALB.	3-2	2-1	14843	F.Clarke, Laidlaw, Owen	1		3	4	5	6		8		11	10	7			9		2		
5R	15 Feb	Mansfield	1-0	1-0	18293	Owen	1	2		4	5	6		8		11	10	7			9		3		
6R	8 Mar	FULHAM	0-1	0-0	21570		1	2	3	4	5	6		8		11	10	7			9				

LEAGUE CUP

Round	Date	Opposition	Res.	H.T.	Att.	Goalscorers	Ross	Carr	Gorman	O'Neill	Green	Parker	McIlmoyle	Train	Clarke F.	Balderstone	Laidlaw	Martin	Winstanley	Barry	Owen	Clarke T.	Spearritt	Prudham	McCartney
2R	11 Sep	Bradford	1-0	1-0	6969	O'Neill	1	2	3	4	5	6	9	8	7	10	11								
3R	9 Oct	Colchester	0-2	0-0	7842			2	3		5	6		8	9	10		7		4			1	11	

Final League Table

		Pl.	Home					Away					F.	A.	Pts
			W	D	L	F	A	W	D	L	F	A			
1	Derby County	42	14	4	3	41	18	7	7	7	26	31	67	49	53
2	Liverpool	42	14	5	2	44	17	6	6	9	16	22	60	39	51
3	Ipswich Town	42	17	2	2	47	14	6	3	12	19	30	66	44	51
4	Everton	42	10	9	2	33	19	6	9	6	23	23	56	42	50
5	Stoke City	42	12	7	2	40	18	5	8	8	24	30	64	48	49
6	Sheffield United	42	12	7	2	35	20	6	6	9	23	31	58	51	49
7	Middlesbrough	42	11	7	3	33	14	7	5	9	21	26	54	40	48
8	Manchester City	42	16	3	2	40	15	2	7	12	14	39	54	54	46
9	Leeds United	42	10	8	3	34	20	6	5	10	23	29	57	49	45
10	Burnley	42	11	6	4	40	29	6	5	10	28	38	68	67	45
11	Queen's Park Rgs.	42	10	4	7	25	17	6	6	9	29	37	54	54	42
12	Wolverhampton W.	42	12	5	4	43	21	2	6	13	14	33	57	54	39
13	West Ham United	42	10	6	5	38	22	3	7	11	20	37	58	59	39
14	Coventry City	42	8	9	4	31	27	4	6	11	20	35	51	62	39
15	Newcastle United	42	12	4	5	39	23	3	5	13	20	49	59	72	39
16	Arsenal	42	10	6	5	31	16	3	5	13	16	33	47	49	37
17	Birmingham City	42	10	4	7	34	28	4	5	12	19	33	53	61	37
18	Leicester City	42	8	7	6	25	17	4	5	12	21	43	46	60	36
19	Tottenham Hotspur	42	8	4	9	29	27	5	4	12	23	36	52	63	34
20	Luton Town	42	8	6	7	27	26	3	5	13	20	39	47	65	33
21	Chelsea	42	4	9	8	22	31	5	6	10	20	41	42	72	33
22	Carlisle United	42	8	2	11	22	21	4	3	14	21	38	43	59	29

SEASON 1975/76
DIVISION 2

No.	Date	Opposition	Res.	H.T.	Att.	Goalscorers	Burleigh	Carr	Gorman	O'Neill	Green	Parker	Martin	Train	Owen	Laidlaw	Clarke F.	Barry	Spearritt	Prudham	McCartney	Hindson	Ross	McVitie	Latham	Bonnyman
1	16 Aug	OXFORD	1-1	1-1	8505	Laidlaw(pen)	1	2	3	4	5	6	7	8	9	10	11									
2	20	Fulham	0-3	0-1	7445		1	2	3	4	5	6	11	8	7	10	9									
3	23	Chelsea	1-3	0-1	19165	Barry	1	2	3	4	5	6	7	8	9	10	11*	12								
4	30	BLACKBURN	0-1	0-0	8683		1	2	11	4	5	6*	7		12	10		8			3	9				
5	6 Sep	Notts County	0-1	0-1	8005		1	2	3	4	5	6	7		9	11		8			10*	12				
6	13	PORTSMOUTH	2-1	1-1	7316	Prudham, Clarke	1	6	3	12	5		7			10	11	4		2	9	8*				
7	20	Bristol Rovers	1-0	0-0	8225	Barry	1	6	3	4	5		7			10	11	8		2	9					
8	23	SUNDERLAND	2-3	0-2	28185	Barry, Laidlaw(pen)	1	6	3	10	5		7				11	9		4	2	8*			12	
9	27	WEST BROM. ALB.	1-1	0-0	6625	Laidlaw	1	6	3	4	5		7*			10	11	8		2	9				12	
10	4 Oct	Plymouth	1-2	0-1	12875	Clarke	1		3	4	5	6	7		12	11	10	8*		2	9					
11	11	LUTON	1-1	1-1	6621	Clarke	1	6	3	4	5				7	10	11	8		2	9					
12	18	Orient	0-1	0-1	4600		1	6	3	4	5	2				12	10	11	8		9*	7				
13	25	CHARLTON	1-1	0-1	7008	O'Neill	1	6	3	4	5	2	7	8		10	9					11				
14	1 Nov	Nottingham Forest	0-4	0-2	18894		1	6	3	10	5	2	7	4		11	9					8				
15	4	OLDHAM	2-1	2-0	6389	McCartney, Clarke		2	3	10	5	6	8	4		11	9			12	7*	1				
16	8	YORK	1-0	1-0	7021	Laidlaw		2	3*	10	5	6	7	4	12	11	9				8	1				
17	15	Bolton	0-0	0-0	14556			2	3	10*	5	6	7	4		11	9	12			8	1				
18	22	ORIENT	1-2	0-0	6502	Laidlaw(pen)		2	3	10	5	6	7	4		11	9				8	1				
19	27	SOUTHAMPTON	1-0	0-0	6977	Clarke		2	3*		5	6	7	4	12	11	9				10	1				
20	6 Dec	Bristol City	0-0	0-0	12466			2	3		5		6	8	4	12	9*	10			11	1	7			
21	12	CHELSEA	2-1	1-1	8065	McCartney(2)		2	3		5		6	11	8		9	4			10	1	7			
22	20	Oxford	0-0	0-0	4241			2	3		5		6	11	4		9	8	12		10*	1	7			
23	26	BLACKPOOL	1-0	0-0	11532	Train		2	3	12	5		6	11	8		9*	4			10	1	7			
24	27	HULL	3-2	3-0	7056	Green, Clarke, O'Neill		2	3	4	5		6	11			9	10				1	7			
25	10 Jan	Portsmouth	0-1	0-0	11430			2	3	4	5		6	11	8	12	9				10*	1	7			
26	17	NOTTS COUNTY	1-2	0-1	7600	Martin		2	3	4*	5		6	11	8	10	9				12	1	7			
27	31	FULHAM	2-2	1-1	6247	Barry, Owen		2	3		5		6	11	8	10	12	9			4*	1	7			
28	7 Feb	Oldham	2-2	1-1	8870	Clarke(2)		6	3				11	8		10	9	4	2			1	7			
29	14	York	2-1	0-0	3850	Barry, McVitie		6	3		5		11	8	12	10*	9	4	2			1	7			
30	21	BOLTON	3-2	1-1	12809	O.G., Lathan, Spearritt		3			5		11	8	6	10	9	4	2			1	7			
31	24	SUNDERLAND	2-2	1-2	20001	Train, Barry	12	3			5		11	8	6	10	9*	4	2			1	7			
32	27	Chrlton	2-4	2-2	10370	Owen, Martin	5	3					11	8	6	10	9	4	2			1	7			
33	6 Mar	NOTTINGHAM FOREST	1-1	0-1	7153	Martin		3	12	5			11	8	6	10	9	4	2			1		7*	9	
34	13	Luton	0-3	0-1	8856			3			8		11		6	10	9	4	2*			1		12	7	5
35	20	Southampton	1-1	0-1	18304	Lathan		2	3	4	5		11		6	10	9					1			7	8
36	27	BRISTOL CITY	0-1	0-1	7563			2	3	4*	5		11		6	10	9					1		12	7	8
37	3 Apr	West Bromwich Albion	0-3	0-2	17136			2	3		5		10		6		9	4				1	7		11	8
38	10	BRISTOL ROVERS	4-2	1-1	5928	Barry, Owen, Lathan, Martin		2	3	6	5		10		12		9*	4				1	7		11	8
39	16	Blackburn	0-1	0-1	11215			2	3	8	5		11		12		9					1	7	10*		6
40	17	Blackpool	1-2	1-0	8382	Laidlaw		2	3	8	5		11			9	10	4				1	7*	12		6
41	20	HULL	0-0	0-0	8185				3	8	5		11			9	10	4	2			1	7			6
42	24	PLYMOUTH	2-0	1-0	7038	Clarke, McVitie		2	3	8	5		11			10	9	4				1	7			6

F.A. CUP

No.	Date	Opposition	Res.	H.T.	Att.	Goalscorers	Burleigh	Carr	Gorman	O'Neill	Green	Parker	Martin	Train	Owen	Laidlaw	Clarke F.	Barry	Spearritt	Prudham	McCartney	Hindson	Ross	McVitie	Latham	Bonnyman
3R	1 Jan	West Bromwich A.	1-3	1-0	16478	O.G.	1	5	3	4*		6	11	8	12	10	9		2				7			

LEAGUE CUP

No.	Date	Opposition	Res.	H.T.	Att.	Goalscorers	Burleigh	Carr	Gorman	O'Neill	Green	Parker	Martin	Train	Owen	Laidlaw	Clarke F.	Barry	Spearritt	Prudham	McCartney	Hindson	Ross	McVitie	Latham	Bonnyman
2R	2 Sep	GILLINGHAM	2-0	2-0	5274	Laidlaw, O.G.	1	2	3	4	5	6	7			10	9	8			11					
3R	8 Oct	Everton	0-2	0-1	20010		1	6	3	10	5		7		8		9		4	2	11					

Final League Table

		Pl.	Home					Away					F.	A.	Pts
			W	D	L	F	A	W	D	L	F	A			
1	Sunderland	42	19	2	0	48	10	5	6	10	19	26	67	36	56
2	Bristol City	42	11	7	3	34	14	8	8	5	25	21	59	35	53
3	West Bromwich Alb.	42	10	9	2	29	12	10	4	7	21	21	50	33	53
4	Bolton Wanderers	42	12	5	4	36	14	8	7	6	28	24	64	38	52
5	Notts County	42	11	6	4	33	13	8	5	8	27	28	60	41	49
6	Southampton	42	18	2	1	49	16	3	5	13	17	34	66	50	49
7	Luton Town	42	13	6	2	38	15	6	4	11	23	36	61	51	48
8	Nottingham Forest	42	13	1	7	34	18	4	11	6	21	22	55	40	46
9	Charlton Athletic	42	11	5	5	40	34	4	7	10	21	38	61	72	42
10	Blackpool	42	9	9	3	26	22	5	5	11	14	27	40	49	42
11	Chelsea	42	7	9	5	25	20	5	7	9	28	34	53	54	40
12	Fulham	42	9	8	4	27	14	4	6	11	18	33	45	47	40
13	Orient	42	10	6	5	21	12	3	8	10	16	27	37	39	40
14	Hull City	42	9	5	7	29	23	5	6	10	16	26	45	49	39
15	Blackburn Rovers	42	8	6	7	27	22	4	8	9	18	28	45	50	38
16	Plymouth Argyle	42	13	4	4	36	20	0	8	13	12	34	48	54	38
17	Oldham Athletic	42	11	8	2	37	24	2	4	15	20	44	57	68	38
18	Bristol Rovers	42	7	9	5	20	15	4	7	10	18	35	38	50	38
19	Carlisle United	42	9	8	4	29	22	3	5	13	16	37	45	59	37
20	Oxford United	42	7	7	7	23	25	4	4	13	16	34	39	59	33
21	York City	42	8	3	10	28	34	2	5	14	11	37	39	71	28
22	Portsmouth	42	4	6	11	15	23	5	1	15	17	38	32	61	25

- 1975/76 Season -

(Back): Neil(Chief Scout), Ashman(Man), Parker, Owen, Martin, Ross, Burleigh, McCartney, Prudham, Gorman, Nicholson(Physo), Young(Train).   (Front): Train, Spearritt, Laidlaw, Green, Clarke, Carr, O'Neill

- 1976/77 Season -

Back row: H. Nicholson (physio), G. McVitie, R. Parker, W. Green, R. Owen, M. Barry, H. Neil (chief scout).
Middle row: D. Martin, P. Bonnyman, M. Burleigh, I. McDonald, A. Ross, W. Rafferty, F. Clarke.
Front row: J. Smith, J. Lathan, L. O'Neill, R. Young (manager), E. Prudham, M. McCartney, J. Gorman.

SEASON 1976/77

DIVISION 2

No.	Date	Opposition	Res.	H.T.	Att.	Goalscorers	Ross	Carr	Gorman	Bonnyman	MacDonald	Parker	McVitie	McCartney	Owen	Rafferty	Martin	Barry	F.Clarke	Lathan	Smith	Hoolickin	O'Neill	Prudham	Burleigh	Moncur	Tait	Deans	Bailey
1	21 Aug	Southampton	2-1	1-0	18695	Rafferty(2)	1	2	3	4	5	6	7	8	9	10	11												
2	28	Chelsea	1-2	0-1	18681	McVitie	1	2	3	4	5	6	7	8	9	10	11												
3	4 Sep	HULL	1-1	1-0	6000	Barry	1	2	3	4	5	6	7			10	11	8	9										
4	11	Sheffield United	0-3	0-2	13666		1	2	3	4	5	6	7*	12		10	11	8	9										
5	14	HEREFORD	2-2	1-2	7371	Martin, Rafferty	1	2	3	4	5	6	7			10	11	8		9									
6	18	BURNLEY	2-1	1-0	8945	Lathan, Rafferty	1	2	3	4	5	6	7			10	11	8		9									
7	25	Nottingham Forest	1-5	1-1	12479	Barry	1	2	3	4	5	6	7			10	11	8		9									
8	2 Oct	CHARLTON	4-2	2-0	6274	Rfferty,Bonnyman,McVtie,Gorman	1	2	3	4*	5	6	7	12		10	11	8		9									
9	12	BLACKPOOL	1-1	1-1	8427	MacDonald	1	2*	3	4	5	6	7			10	11	8		12	9								
10	16	LUTON	1-1	1-1	6972	Rafferty	1		3	2	5	6			11	10	7	8			9	4							
11	23	Wolves	0-4	0-2	15563		1		3	4	5*	6				10	11	8		9	7	2	12						
12	30	Notts County	1-2	1-1	8327	Rafferty	1		3	4	5	6	7*	8		9		10		12	11	2							
13	6 Nov	BOLTON	0-1	0-0	8811		1		3	4	5	6	7	12		9*	11	8			2		10						
14	13	Oldham	1-4	0-1	9166	Hoolickin	1	3		4	5	6		8		9	11	10			7	2							
15	16	Fulham	0-2	0-1	9215			3		4	5	6		11		10	7	8*		9		2	12		1	6			
16	20	MILLWALL	0-1	0-0	6998			3		4	5					10		8		11	9	2	7		1	6			
17	27	Plymouth	1-0	0-0	10204	F.Clarke		3		4	5					10		8	11		9	2	7		1	6			
18	4 Dec	ORIENT	1-0	0-0	5294	McVitie		3		4	5		12			10		8	9	11*		2	7		1	6			
19	11	Bristol Rovers	1-2	1-1	5496	Rafferty		3		4	5					10		8	11	9		2	7		1	6			
20	18	CARDIFF	4-3	1-0	5924	McVitie, Rafferty(3)		3		4	5		11*			10		8	9	12		2	7		1	6			
21	27	Blackpool	0-0	0-0	17075			3		4	5					10		8	9	11		2	7		1	6			
22	29	BLACKBURN	1-1	1-0	8852	Barry(pen)		3		4	5		11			10		8	9			2	7		1	6			
23	3 Jan	NOTTS COUNTY	0-2	0-1	8323			3		4	5		11			10		8	9	12		2	7*		1	6			
24	22	SOUTHAMPTON	0-6	0-2	9617			3		4	5		11			10		8	9	7		2			1	6			
25	5 Feb	Chelsea	0-1	0-1	11356			3			8					10	11					2	7		1	6	4	9	
26	12	Hull	1-3	0-2	6524	Deans		3	12		5		7*	11		10		8				2			1	6	4	9	
27	19	SHEFFIELD UNITED	4-1	3-1	6821	Deans, Parker, Rafferty, Bailey	1	8			5	6	7			10	4		11			2						9	3
28	26	Burnley	0-2	0-0	10814		1	4	12		5	6	7*			10	11	8				2						9	3
29	5 Mar	NOTTINGHAM FOREST	1-1	0-0	7603	Martin	1	4			5	6	7			10	11	8				2					9		3
30	11	Charlton	0-1	0-0	7113		1	8			5	6	7			10	4		11			2					9		3
31	19	FULHAM	1-2	0-0	6243	McVitie	1	8			5	6	7			10	4		11			2					9		3
32	22	Bolton	4-3	2-0	18471	McVitie(2), Rafferty, Tait	1	2			5	6	7	11		10	4			12							9*		3
33	26	Luton	0-5	0-2	11735		1	2			8*	5	6	7	11	10	4						12				9		3
34	6 Apr	Blackburn	3-1	1-0	6851	Martin, MacDonald, Rafferty	1	2			8	5	6	7	3	10	4						11				9		
35	12	OLDHAM	1-1	0-0	6831	Martin	1	2			8	5	6	7	3	10	4						11				9		
36	16	Millwall	1-1	0-0	6237	Tait	1	2*			8	5	6	7	3	12	10	4					11				9		
37	19	WOLVES	2-1	1-1	8533	Rafferty, O'Neill	1				8	5	6	7	3	10	4					2	11				9		
38	23	PLYMOUTH	3-1	2-0	7751	Rafferty, McCartney(pen), Tait	1				8	5	6	7	3	10	4					2	11				9		
39	30	Orient	0-0	0-0	4183		1				8	5	6	7	3	9	11			4		2	10						
40	4 May	Hereford	0-0	0-0	4448		1				8	5	6	7	3	10				9		2	11						
41	7	BRISTOL ROVERS	2-3	2-0	7396	Lathan, O.G.	1				8	5	6	7	3	10	4			9		2	11						
42	14	Cardiff	1-1	1-1	15801	O'Neill	1				8	5	6	7*	3	10	4			12		2	11				9		

F.A. CUP

Rnd	Date	Opposition	Res.	H.T.	Att.	Goalscorers	Ross	Carr	Gorman	Bonnyman	MacDonald	Parker	McVitie	McCartney	Owen	Rafferty	Martin	Barry	F.Clarke	Lathan	Smith	Hoolickin	O'Neill	Prudham	Burleigh	Moncur	Tait	Deans	Bailey
3R	8 Jan	MATLOCK	5-1	2-0	10361	Rafferty(2),McVitie,Clrke,Bnnyman		3		4	5		7			10		8	9		11	2			1	6			
4R	29	Liverpool	0-3	0-2	45358			3		4	5					10	11	8	9			2	7		1	6			

LEAGUE CUP

Rnd	Date	Opposition	Res.	H.T.	Att.	Goalscorers	Ross	Carr	Gorman	Bonnyman	MacDonald	Parker	McVitie	McCartney	Owen	Rafferty	Martin	Barry	F.Clarke	Lathan	Smith	Hoolickin	O'Neill	Prudham	Burleigh	Moncur	Tait	Deans	Bailey
1R1	14 Aug	Southport	2-1	1-1	2700	Rafferty(2)	1	2	3	4	5	6	7	11	9	10	8												
1R2	17	SOUTHPORT	0-1	0-0	6176		1	2	3	4	5	6	7	8	9	10	11												
2R	30	Arsenal	2-3	2-3	21550	Bonnyman, Clarke	1	2	3	4	5	6	7		9	11	8	10											

Final League Table

		Pl.	Home					Away					F.	A.	Pts
			W	D	L	F	A	W	D	L	F	A			
1	Wolverhampton W.	42	15	3	3	48	21	7	10	4	36	24	84	45	57
2	Chelsea	42	15	6	0	51	22	6	7	8	22	31	73	53	55
3	Nottingham Forest	42	14	3	4	53	22	7	7	7	24	21	77	43	52
4	Bolton Wanderers	42	15	2	4	46	21	5	9	7	29	33	75	54	51
5	Blackpool	42	11	7	3	29	17	6	10	5	29	25	58	42	51
6	Luton Town	42	13	5	3	39	17	8	1	12	28	31	67	48	48
7	Charlton Athletic	42	14	5	2	52	27	2	11	8	19	31	71	58	48
8	Notts County	42	11	5	5	29	20	8	5	8	36	40	65	60	48
9	Southampton	42	12	6	3	40	24	5	4	12	32	43	72	67	44
10	Millwall	42	9	6	6	31	22	6	7	8	26	31	57	53	43
11	Sheffield United	42	9	8	4	32	25	5	4	12	22	38	54	63	40
12	Blackburn Rovers	42	12	4	5	31	18	3	5	13	11	36	42	54	39
13	Oldham Athletic	42	11	6	4	37	23	3	4	14	15	41	52	64	38
14	Hull City	42	9	8	4	31	17	1	9	11	14	36	45	53	37
15	Bristol Rovers	42	8	9	4	32	27	4	4	13	21	41	53	68	37
16	Burnley	42	8	9	4	27	20	3	5	13	19	44	46	64	36
17	Fulham	42	9	7	5	39	25	2	6	13	15	36	54	61	35
18	Cardiff City	42	7	6	8	30	30	5	4	12	26	37	56	67	34
19	Orient	42	4	8	9	18	23	5	8	8	19	32	37	55	34
20	Carlisle United	42	7	7	7	31	33	4	5	12	18	42	49	75	34
21	Plymouth Argyle	42	5	9	7	27	25	3	7	11	19	40	46	65	32
22	Hereford United	42	6	9	6	28	30	2	6	13	29	48	57	78	31

SEASON 1977/78
DIVISION 3

No.	Date	Opposition	Res.	H.T.	Att.	Goalscorers	Swinburne	Carr	McCartney	Bonnyman	MacDonald	Parker	McVitie	Ludlam	Latham	Rafferty	Martin	Tait	Hoolickin	Mutrie	Ross	Hamilton	Clarke F.	Collins	Fell	Kemp	Sawyers	McLean	Lumby
1	20 Aug	Tranmere	2-3	1-2	2136	O.G., Tait	1	2	3	4*	5	6	7	8	9	10	11	12											
2	27	PLYMOUTH	0-0	0-0	4853		1	2	3		5	6	7	8	9	10	11	4											
3	3 Sep	Rotherham	0-0	0-0	4052		1	11	3		5	6	7	8	9*	10		4		2	12								
4	10	PRESTON	3-1	1-1	5743	Rafferty(2), Tait	1	4	3		5	6	7	11	12	10		8		2	9*								
5	13	Peterborough	1-2	0-1	4496	Latham	1	4	3		5	6	7	11	9	10		8		2									
6	17	OXFORD	2-2	0-1	4676	Rafferty, McCartney(pen)	1	4	3		5	6	7	8		10	11	9		2									
7	20	CHESTER	0-0	0-0	4941		1	4	3		5	6	7	8*	12	10	11	9		2									
8	24	Hereford	0-1	0-1	3750		1	4	3	12	5	6	7	8	11*	10		9		2									
9	26	Exeter	1-0	0-0	5106	Rafferty	1	4	3		5	6	7	8	11	10		9		2									
10	1 Oct	COLCHESTER	1-3	0-1	4611	McVitie	1	4	3		5	6	7	8	11	10	12	9*		2									
11	4	LINCOLN	2-3	2-0	4041	Bonnyman, MacDonald		4	3	8	5		7	6*		10	11			2	1	12	9						
12	8	Cambridge	0-2		3984			2	3	8	5	4	7	6		10	11				1	9							
13	15	BRADFORD	1-1	1-0	4234	Rafferty		2	3		5	6	7	4	8	10					1	11	9						
14	22	Gillingahm	1-1	1-1	6822	Rafferty		5	3			6	7	4	8	10		12			1	11	9	2*					
15	29	CHESTERFIELD	2-1	0-0	4088	Rafferty, Tait		5	3			6	7	4	8	10		12			1	11	9*	2					
16	5 Nov	Sheffield Wednesday	1-3	0-3	12285	Hamilton		5	3			6	7	8	4	10		12			1	11	9*	2					
17	12	PORTSMOUTH	3-1	1-1	3878	Tait, McVitie, Bonnyman		5	3	4		6	7		8	10		9			1	11		2					
18	19	Shrewsbury	3-0	2-0	3701	Latham, Tait, Rafferty		5	3	4		6	7		8	10		9			1	11		2					
19	3 Dec	PORT VALE	1-1	0-0	4318	McCartney		5	3	8		6	7		4	10		9			1	11		2					
20	10	Swindon	2-2	1-1	5889	Rafferty, Tait		5	3	8		6	7		4	10		9			1	11		2					
21	26	WALSALL	2-0	0-0	10326	O.G., Tait		4	3	8		6	7		5	10		9			1	11		2					
22	27	Wrexham	1-3	0-3	10589	McCartney(pen)		4	3	8		6	7		5	10		9			1	11		2					
23	31	Bury	1-1		4468	Hamilton		3	8	5		6	7		4	10		9			1	11		2					
24	2 Jan	SHEFFIELD WED.	1-0	0-0	11309	Rafferty	12	3	8	4		6	7		5	10		9			1	11		2*					
25	14	TRANMERE	2-2	0-1	6281	Bonnyman, Hamilton		2	3	8	4	6	7		5	10		9			1	11							
26	21	Plymouth	1-0	1-0	4744	Hamilton	1	2	3	8	4	6	7		5	10		9				11							
27	4 Feb	Preston	1-2		9095	Tait	1	6	3	8	4		7		5	10		9				11	2						
28	7	ROTHERHAM	2-1	0-1	5386	O.G., Bonnyman	1	2	3	8	4	6	7		5	10		9				11							
29	11	Oxford	0-0	0-0	3854		1	2	3	8	4	6	7		5	10		9				11							
30	25	Colchester	2-2	0-2	3867	Rafferty, Latham	1	4	3	8		6	7		5	10		9				11	2						
31	1 Mar	Chester	2-2		2934	Bonnyman, Parker	1	4	3	8		6	7		5			9	10*			11	2	12					
32	4	CAMBRIDGE	1-1	0-0	5336	Parker	1	3	2	8	4	6	7		5			9	10			11							
33	7	PETERBOROUGH	0-0	0-0	4563		1	2	3	8	4	6	7		5			9	10*			11		12					
34	11	Bradford	2-2	2-2	6386	McCartney, MacDonald	1	2	5	8*	4	6	7					9				11	12	3		10			
35	18	GILLINGHAM	1-0	1-0	5095	Kemp	1	2	5		4	6	7					9				11	10	3		8			
36	25	Walsall	0-0	0-0	5907		1	2	5	8	4	6	7					9				11		3		10			
37	27	WREXHAM	1-4	1-3	8731	McVitie	1	2	5	8	4	6	7					9				11		3		10			
38	28	Chesterfield	1-2	1-1	4248	McCartney(pen)	1		3	8	4	6	7					5				11	9*	2		10	7	12	
39	1 Apr	BURY	0-3	0-0	4405		1		2	8	4	6	7					9				11*		3		10	5	12	
40	3	EXETER	2-0	1-0	3693	Kemp, Bonnyman	1		3	8	4	6	7					9				11		2		10	5*	12	
41	8	Portsmouth	3-3	1-2	5937	McCartney(pen), Tait, Kemp	1		3	8	4	6	7					9				11		2		10	12	5*	
42	11	HEREFORD	2-0		3846	McVitie(2)	1		3	8	4	6	7					9				11		2		10	12	5*	
43	15	SHREWSBURY	1-0	0-0	4247	Tait	1		3	8	4	6	7					9				11		2		10	5		
44	22	Port Vale	1-0	1-0	3942	Bonnyman	1		3	8	4	6	7					9				11		2		10	5		
45	26	Lincoln	1-2	1-1	3384	Kemp	1		3	8	5	6	7					4				11		2		10			9
46	29	SWINDON	2-2	1-1	4351	yman, Lumby	1		3	8		6	7					4				11		2		10		5	9

F.A. CUP

No.	Date	Opposition	Res.	H.T.	Att.	Goalscorers	Swinburne	Carr	McCartney	Bonnyman	MacDonald	Parker	McVitie	Ludlam	Latham	Rafferty	Martin	Tait	Hoolickin	Mutrie	Ross	Hamilton	Clarke F.	Collins	Fell	Kemp
1R	20 Nov	STAFFORD R.	2-0	0-0	5443	Rafferty(2)		5	3	8		6	7		4	10		9			1	11		2		
2R	17 Dec	CHESTER	3-1	1-1	5577	Rafferty(2), McVitie		5	3	8		6	7		4	10		9			1	11		2		
3R	6 Jan	MANCHESTER U.	1-1	1-1	25500	MacDonald			3	8	4	6	7	12	5	10		9			1	11		2		
3Rr	11	Manchester United	2-4	0-2	54156	Tait, Rafferty		2	3	8	4	6	7		5	10		9			1	11				

LEAGUE CUP

No.	Date	Opposition	Res.	H.T.	Att.	Goalscorers	Swinburne	Carr	McCartney	Bonnyman	MacDonald	Parker	McVitie	Ludlam	Latham	Rafferty	Martin	Tait	Hoolickin	Mutrie	Ross	Hamilton
1R1	13 Aug	Huddersfield	1-1	0-0	3774	Ludlam		2	3	4	5	6	7	8	12	10	11	9			1	
1R2	16	HUDDERSFIELD	2-2	0-0	5447	Martin, Rafferty	1	2	3	4	5	6	7	8	12	10	11	9*				

Final League Table

		Pl.	Home					Away					F.	A.	Pts
			W	D	L	F	A	W	D	L	F	A			
1	Wrexham	46	14	8	1	48	19	9	7	7	30	26	78	45	61
2	Cambridge United	46	19	3	1	49	11	4	9	10	23	40	72	51	58
3	Preston North End	46	16	5	2	48	19	4	11	8	15	19	63	38	56
4	Peterborough Utd.	46	15	7	1	32	11	5	9	9	15	22	47	33	56
5	Chester	46	14	8	1	41	24	2	14	7	18	32	59	56	54
6	Walsall	46	12	8	3	35	17	6	9	8	26	33	61	50	53
7	Gillingham	46	11	10	2	36	19	4	10	9	31	39	67	60	50
8	Colchester United	46	10	11	2	36	16	5	7	11	19	28	55	44	48
9	Chesterfield	46	14	6	3	42	18	3	12	8	17	31	59	49	48
10	Swindon Town	46	12	7	4	40	22	4	9	10	27	38	67	60	48
11	Shrewsbury Town	46	11	7	5	42	23	5	8	10	21	34	63	57	47
12	Tranmere Rovers	46	13	7	3	39	19	3	8	12	18	33	57	52	47
13	Carlisle United	46	10	9	4	32	26	4	10	9	27	33	59	59	47
14	Sheffield Wed.	46	13	7	3	28	14	2	9	12	22	38	50	52	46
15	Bury	46	7	13	3	34	22	6	6	11	28	34	62	56	45
16	Lincoln City	46	8	8	5	35	26	5	7	11	18	35	53	61	45
17	Exeter City	46	11	8	4	30	18	4	6	13	19	41	49	59	44
18	Oxford United	46	11	10	2	38	21	2	4	17	26	46	64	67	40
19	Plymouth Argyle	46	7	8	8	33	28	4	9	10	28	40	61	68	39
20	Rotherham United	46	11	5	7	28	22	3	9	13	25	49	51	68	39
21	Port Vale	46	7	11	5	28	23	1	9	13	18	44	46	67	36
22	Bradford City	46	11	6	6	40	29	1	4	18	16	57	56	86	34
23	Hereford United	46	9	9	5	28	22	0	5	18	6	38	34	60	32
24	Portsmouth	46	4	11	8	31	38	3	6	14	10	37	41	75	31

- 1977/78 Season -

(Back): Fell, McCartney, Carr, Hoolickin, McVitie, Barry, Lathan, Ludlam
(Middle): Nicholson (Physo), Harvey (Coach), Tait, Ross, Swinburne, Clarke, Neil (Chief Scout), Moncur (Manager)
(Front): Martin, Rafferty, MacDonald, Bonnyman, Parker, Mutrie

- 1978/79 Season -

(Back): McLean, McVitie, Tait, Bonnyman, MacDonald, Lumby, Hoolickin
(Middle): Neil(Scout), Harvey(Asst Man), Crombie, Swinburne, Harrison, Hamilton, Moncur(Man), Nicholson(Physio)
(Front): Parker, Sawyers, Fell, McCartney, Collins, Kemp, Ludlam

SEASON 1978/79
DIVISION 3

No.	Date	Opposition	Res.	H.T.	Att.	Goalscorers	Swinburne	Hoolickin	McCartney	MacDonald	Tait	Parker	McVitie	Bonnyman	Kemp	Ludlam	Hamilton	Lumby	Ross	Sawyers	Collins	Clarke D.	Bannon	McLean
1	19 Aug	Hull	1-1	1-1	5062	Tait	1	2	3	4	5	6	7	8	9	10	11							
2	22	CHESTERFIELD	1-1	0-0	5232	Kemp	1	2	3		5	6	7	8	9	4	11	10						
3	26	WALSALL	1-0	1-0	4781	Lumby	1	2	3	4	5*	6	7	8	9	12	11	10						
4	2 Sep	Blackpool	1-3	0-0	7789	Kemp	1	2	3	4	5	6	7	8	9		11	10						
5	8	COLCHESTER	4-0	4-0	4430	McCrtney(p),Bonnymn,Tait,Hamiltn	1	2	3	4	5	6	7	8	9		11	10						
6	12	Peterborough	0-0	0-0	6283		1	2	3	4	5	6	7	8	9		11	10						
7	16	Lincoln	1-1	0-0	2577	McVitie	1	2	3	4	5	6	7	8	9		11	10						
8	23	SOUTHEND	0-0	0-0	5263		1	2	3	4	5	6	7	8	9		11	10						
9	25	SWANSEA	2-0		8489	McCartney(pen), Kemp	1	2	3	4	5	6	7	8	9	10	11							
10	30	Mansfield	0-1	0-1	4716		1	2	3	4	5	6	7	8	9	10	11							
11	7 Oct	PLYMOUTH	1-1	0-0	5731	Bonnyman	1	2	3	4	5	6	7	8	9	10	11							
12	14	Sheffield Wednesday	0-0	0-0	10980		1	2	3	4	5	6	7	8	9	10	11							
13	17	Watford	1-2	0-2	12444	O.G.	1	2	3	4	5	6	7	8	9	10	11							
14	21	ROTHERHAM	1-1	0-0	5085	Kemp	1	2	3	4	5	6	7	8	9	10	11							
15	28	SWINDON	2-0	1-0	5141	Kemp, McCartney(pen)		2	3	4	5	6	7	8	9	10	11		1					
16	4 Nov	Shrewsbury	0-0	0-0	4656		1	2	3	4*	5	6	7	8	9	10	11			12				
17	11	BLACKPOOL	1-1	0-0	6505	Parker	1	2	3		5	6	7	8*	9	10	11				4	12		
18	18	Walsall	2-1	1-0	4441	Kemp, O.G.	1	2	3		5	6	7	8	9	4	11	10						
19	2 Dec	Gillingham	0-0	0-0	4322		1	2	3		5	6	7	8	9	4	11	10						
20	9	EXETER	1-1		5468	Kemp	1	2	3	4	10	6	7	8	9	5	11*	12						
21	26	Chester	2-1	1-1	4690	Kemp, McVitie	1	2	3		5	6	7	8	10	4	11	9						
22	30	Brentford	0-0	0-0	6480		1	2	3*	4	5	6	7	8	10	9	11	12						
23	1 Jan	LINCOLN	2-0	1-0	3892	Ludlam, Kemp	1	2	3	4	5	6	7	8	10	9	11							
24	2 Feb	Swansea	0-0	0-0	10821		1	2	3	4	5	6	7	8	10	9	11							
25	10	MANSFIELD	1-0	1-0	4934	Bonnyman	1	2	3	4	5	6	7	8	10	9	11							
26	13	BURY	1-2	0-1	5447	Bonnyman(pen)	1	2		4	5	6	7	8	10*	9	11				3	12		
27	17	Plymouth	0-2	0-2	6294		1	2		4	5	6	7	8	10	9	11				3			
28	24	SHEFFIELD WED.	0-0	0-0	5675		1	2	3	4	5	6	7	8		9	11						10	
29	3 Mar	Rotherham	3-1	0-1	3908	Kemp(2), Tait	1	2	3	4	5	6	7	8	9	10								11
30	6	TRANMERE	2-0	1-0	4330	McCartney(pen), Bonnyman	1	2	3	4	5	6	7	8	10	9								11
31	10	Swindon	0-0	0-0	8386		1	2	3	4	5	6	7	8	10	9		12						11*
32	12	Southend	1-1	0-1	5457	Tait	1	2	3	4	5	6	7	8	10	9								11
33	17	SHREWSBURY	1-1	0-0	5057	Ludlam	1	2	3	4	5	6	7	8	10	9		12						11*
34	20	PETERBOROUGH	4-1	1-1	5471	Lumby(2), Kemp(2)	1	2	3	4	5	6	7	8	10	11		9						
35	24	Chesterfield	3-2	0-0	4152	Kemp, Lumby, Tait	1	2	3	4	5	6	7*	8	9	11		10						12
36	27	HULL	2-2	0-0	6254	Kemp, McCartney(pen)	1	2	3	4	5	6	7	8	10	9		11						
37	31	Oxford	1-5	0-2	3439	Kemp	1	2	3	4	5	6	7	8	11	9		10*						12
38	2 Apr	Colchester	1-2	1-0	2608	Lumby	1	2	3	4	5	6	7	8	10	11		9						
39	7	GILLINGHAM	1-0	0-0	5130	Kemp	1	2	3	4	5	6	7	8	9	11		9						
40	13	Bury	2-2	2-1	4838	Tait, Kemp	1	2	3	4	5	6	7	8	10	11		9						
41	14	CHESTER	1-1	1-0	5309	MacDonald	1	2	3	4	5	6	7	8	9	11		10						
42	16	Tranmere	1-1	0-1	1504	Lumby	1	2	3	4	12	6	7	8	10	11		9						5*
43	21	BRENTFORD	1-0	0-0	3967	Ludlam	1	2	3	4	5	6	7	8	9	11		10*						12
44	24	WATFORD	1-0	1-0	7141	Bonnyman	1	2	3	4	5	6	7	8	10	11	9							
45	28	Exeter	2-3	1-2	4299	Bonnyman, Tait	1	2	3	4	5	6	7	8	9	10	11							
46	5 May	OXFORD	0-1	0-0	3811		1	2	3	4	5	6	7	8	9	10	11							

F.A. CUP

Rd	Date	Opposition	Res.	H.T.	Att.	Goalscorers	Swinburne	Hoolickin	McCartney	MacDonald	Tait	Parker	McVitie	Bonnyman	Kemp	Ludlam	Hamilton	Lumby
1R	25 Nov	HALIFAX T.	1-0	0-0	5060	LUMBY	1	2	3		5	6	7	4	9	8	11	10
2R	16 Dec	HULL	3-0	0-0	5335	LUMBY, McCartney(pen), Kemp	1	2	3	4	5	6	7	8	9	10		11
3R	10 Jan	Ipswich	2-3	1-2	19036	Tait, Kemp	1	2	3	4	5	6	7	8	10	9	11	

LEAGUE CUP

Rd	Date	Opposition	Res.	H.T.	Att.	Goalscorers	Swinburne	Hoolickin	McCartney	MacDonald	Tait	Parker	McVitie	Bonnyman	Kemp	Ludlam	Hamilton	Lumby
1R1	12 Aug	BLACKPOOL	2-2	1-1	5100	Kemp, Bonnyman	1	2	3	4	5	6	7	8	9		11	10
1R2	16	Blackpool	2-1	1-1	6617	Lumby	1	2	3	4	5	6	7	8	9		11	10

Final League Table

		Pl.	Home					Away					F.	A.	Pts
			W	D	L	F	A	W	D	L	F	A			
1	Shrewsbury Town	46	14	9	0	36	11	7	10	6	25	30	61	41	61
2	Watford	46	15	5	3	47	22	9	7	7	36	30	83	52	60
3	Swansea City	46	16	6	1	57	32	8	6	9	26	29	83	61	60
4	Gillingham	46	15	7	1	39	15	6	10	7	26	27	65	42	59
5	Swindon Town	46	17	2	4	44	14	8	5	10	30	38	74	52	57
6	Carlisle United	46	11	10	2	31	13	4	12	7	22	29	53	42	52
7	Colchester United	46	13	9	1	35	19	4	8	11	25	36	60	55	51
8	Hull City	46	12	9	2	36	14	7	2	14	30	47	66	61	49
9	Exeter City	46	14	6	3	38	18	3	9	11	23	38	61	56	49
10	Brentford	46	14	4	5	35	19	5	5	13	18	30	53	49	47
11	Oxford United	46	10	8	5	27	20	4	10	9	17	30	44	50	46
12	Blackpool	46	12	5	6	38	19	6	4	13	23	40	61	59	45
13	Southend United	46	11	6	6	30	17	4	9	10	21	32	51	49	45
14	Sheffield Wed.	46	9	8	6	30	22	4	11	8	23	31	53	53	45
15	Plymouth Argyle	46	11	9	3	40	27	4	5	14	27	41	67	68	44
16	Chester	46	11	9	3	42	21	3	7	13	15	40	57	61	44
17	Rotherham United	46	13	3	7	30	23	4	7	12	19	32	49	55	44
18	Mansfield Town	46	7	11	5	30	24	5	8	10	21	28	51	52	43
19	Bury	46	6	11	6	35	32	5	9	9	24	33	59	65	42
20	Chesterfield	46	10	5	8	35	34	3	9	11	16	31	51	65	40
21	Peterborough Utd.	46	8	7	8	26	24	3	7	13	18	39	44	63	36
22	Walsall	46	7	6	10	34	32	3	6	14	22	39	56	71	32
23	Tranmere Rovers	46	4	12	7	26	31	2	4	17	19	47	45	78	28
24	Lincoln City	46	5	7	11	26	38	2	4	17	15	50	41	88	25

SEASON 1979/80

DIVISION 3

No.	Date	Opposition	Res.	H.T.	Att.	Goalscorers	Swinburne	Hoolickin	McCartney	MacDonald	Tait	Parker	Bannon	Bonnyman	Ludlam	Kemp	McAuley	McVitie	Beardsley	Hamilton	Collins	Hughes	Winstanley	Staniforth	Sawyers	Fell	Houghton
1	18 Aug	Southend	0-1	0-1	4140		1	2	3	4	5	6	7	8	9	10	11										
2	21	BLACKBURN	1-1	1-1	5801	Bannon	1	2	3	4	5	6	9	8*	7			11	12	10							
3	25	BURY	1-0	1-0	4635	Bannon	1	2	3	4	5	6	9	8	7			11		10							
4	1 Sep	Millwall	0-1	0-0	5153		1	2	3	4	5	6	9	8	7	12	11*			10							
5	8	GILLINGHAM	1-2	0-2	3411	Hamilton	1	2	3	4		6		9		5	10	11*	12	7	8						
6	15	Reading	0-2	0-0	4925		1	2		4		6	9*	8	12		11		5	10	3	7					
7	18	ROTHERHAM	3-1	2-1	3916	Bannon, Bonnyman(pen), O.G.	1	2		4		6	9	8	12		11		5	10	3*	7					
8	22	Exeter	2-1	0-1	3409	Bonnyman, Bannon	1	2		4		6	9	8	12		11		5	10	3*	7					
9	29	CHESTER	2-2	0-0	4324	Bonnyman, Beardsley	1	2	3	4		6	9	8			11*		5	10	3*	7					
10	2 Oct	Rotherham	1-4	1-1	6024	Bannon	1	2	3	4		6	9	8	11		12		5	10		7*					
11	6	WIMBLEDON	1-1	1-1	4476	Bonnyman	1	2		4		6	9	8				7	5	10			3	11			
12	10	Blackburn	2-1	1-0	7204	O.G., Bannon	1	2		4		6	9	8				7	5	10			3	11			
13	13	Hull	0-2	0-1	5838		1	2		4		6	9	8				7	5	10			3*	11	12		
14	20	BARNSLEY	3-1	1-0	5107	Bonnyman, Bannon, McVitie	1	2		4		6	9	8				7	5	10			3	11			
15	23	MANSFIELD	1-1	1-0	4898	Bonnyman	1	2		4		6	9	8*				7	5	10			3	11		12	
16	27	Oxford	0-1	0-0	4007		1	2		4		6	9		8			7	5	10			3	11			
17	3 Nov	SOUTHEND	4-0	1-0	3744	Bannon, Staniforth, Ludlam(2)	1	2		4		6	9*	8	12			7	5	10			3	11			
18	6	Mansfield	1-2	0-0	3000	Ludlam	1	2		4		6	9	8	5					10			3	11			
19	10	Plymouth	2-4	1-1	5216	Ludlam, Bannon	1	2		4		6	9	8	5			7*	12	10			3	11			
20	17	SHEFFIELD UNITED	1-0	1-0	6347	Staniforth	1	2		4		6	9	8	5			7		10			3	11			
21	1 Dec	BRENTFORD	3-1	1-0	4272	Bannon, Staniforth(2)	1	2		4		6	9	8	5			7		10			3	11			
22	7	Colchester	1-1	0-1	4104	Beardsley	1	2		4		6	9*	8	5			7	12	10			3	11			
23	21	GRIMSBY	0-2	0-1	4633		1	2		4		6	9	8	5			7		10	3			11			
24	26	Chesterfield	2-3	1-2	5002	MacDonald, Bonnyman	1	2		4		6	9	8	5			7	11	10	3						
25	12 Jan	MILLWALL	4-0	1-0	4867	Bonnymn,Hoolickn,Beardsley,Ldlam	1	2		4		6		8	5			7	9	10			3	11			
26	19	Gillingham	1-1	1-0	5106	Beardsley	1	2		4		6	9	8	5			7	11	10			3				
27	9 Feb	EXETER	4-1	4-0	7085	Hamilton(2), McVitie, Beardsley	1	2	3	4		6	12	8	5			7	9	10				11*			
28	20	Chester	0-1	0-0	3765		1	2	3	4			12	8	5			7	9*	10		6		11			
29	23	HULL	3-2	3-2	4263	Hamilton, Bonnyman, Ludlam	1	2	3	4			12	8	5			7	9*	10		6		11			
30	26	SHEFFIELD WED.	0-2	0-2	6223		1	2	3	4			11	8*	5			7	9	10		6					12
31	1 Mar	Barnsley	1-1	0-0	10116	Beardsley	1	2	3	4			9		5			7	10	11		6					8
32	4	Bury	2-0	1-0	2894	Bannon(2)	1	2	3	4			9		5			7	11	10		6					8
33	8	OXFORD	2-2	1-0	3384	Ludlam, Bonnyman	1	2	3	4			9	8	5*			7	11			6					10
34	11	Swindon	0-0	0-0	9752		1	2	3	4			9		5			7	11	10		6					8
35	14	Wimbledon	0-0	0-0	2093		1	2	3	4					5			7	9	10	12	6		11			8
36	18	BLACKPOO[L]	2-0	0-0	3793	Bannon, McVitie	1	2	3	4			12		5			7	11	10		6		9*			8
37	22	PLYMOUTH	2-1	1-0	3611	Beardsley, Bannon	1	2	3	4			9		5			7	11	10*	12	6					8
38	29	Sheffield United	2-0	0-0	11971	McCartney(pen), McVitie	1	2	3	4			9		5			7	11	10		6					8
39	4 Apr	Grimsby	0-2	0-1	15121		1	2	3	4*			9		5			7	11	10	12	6					8
40	5	CHESTERFIELD	0-2	0-1	5164		1	2	3			6	9		4			7	11	10		5					8
41	7	Blackpool	1-2	1-2	6054	Ludlam	1	2	3	4			9		5			7	11*	10		6		12			8
42	12	SWINDON	2-1	2-1	3472	Bannon(2)	1	2	3	4			9		5			7	8	10	12	6		11*			
43	15	READING	3-3	1-2	3287	Beardsley,McCartney(pen),Bannon	1	2	3	4			9		5			7	11	10		6					8
44	19	Brentford	3-0	1-0	6130	Winstanley, Collins, Hamilton	1	2	3	4			9		5			7	10	11		6					8
45	26	COLCHESTER	2-0	1-0	3702	Bannon(2)	1		3	4			9		5			7	11	10	2	6					8
46	3 May	Sheffield Wednesday	0-0	0-0	32734		1	2	3	4		6	9*		5				11	10		7	12				8

F.A. CUP

No.	Date	Opposition	Res.	H.T.	Att.	Goalscorers	Swinburne	Hoolickin	McCartney	MacDonald	Tait	Parker	Bannon	Bonnyman	Ludlam	Kemp	McAuley	McVitie	Beardsley	Hamilton	Collins	Hughes	Winstanley	Staniforth	Sawyers	Fell	Houghton
1R	24 Nov	HULL	3-3	2-0	4970	Bonnyman(pen), Ludlam, Bannon	1	2		4		6	9	8	5			7		10			3	11			
1Rr	28	Hull	2-0	1-0	9000	Winstanley, Bonnyman	1	2		4		6	9	8	5			7		10			3	11			
2R	15 Dec	SHEFFIELD WED.	3-0	2-0	7823	Staniforth, Beardsley, Bannon	1	2		4		6	9	8		12		7*	5	10			3	11			
3R	5 Jan	BRADFORD	3-2	1-1	6480	Bonnyman(pen), Ludlam, Hoolickin	1	2		4		6	12	8	5			7	9	10			3	11*			
4R	26	WREXHAM	0-0	0-0	13136		1	2		4		6		8	5			7	9	10			3	11			
4Rr	29	Wrexham	1-3	1-2	14643	Bonnyman	1	2		4		6	12	8	5*			7	9	10			3	11			

LEAGUE CUP

No.	Date	Opposition	Res.	H.T.	Att.	Goalscorers	Swinburne	Hoolickin	McCartney	MacDonald	Tait	Parker	Bannon	Bonnyman	Ludlam	Kemp	McAuley
1R1	1 Aug		1-1	0-0	5878	Kemp	1	2	3	4	5	6	7	8	10	9	11
1R2	14	WREXHAM	1-2	1-0	6500	O.G.	1	2	5	3	6	4	9	8	7	10	11

Final League Table

		Pl.	Home					Away					F.	A.	Pts
			W	D	L	F	A	W	D	L	F	A			
1	Grimsby Town	46	18	2	3	46	16	8	8	7	27	26	73	42	62
2	Blackburn Rovers	46	13	5	5	34	17	12	4	7	24	19	58	36	59
3	Sheffield Wed.	46	12	6	5	44	20	9	10	4	37	27	81	47	58
4	Chesterfield	46	16	5	2	46	16	7	6	10	25	30	71	46	57
5	Colchester United	46	10	10	3	39	20	10	2	11	25	36	64	56	52
6	Carlisle United	46	13	6	4	45	26	5	6	12	21	30	66	56	48
7	Reading	46	14	6	3	43	19	2	10	11	23	46	66	65	48
8	Exeter City	46	14	5	4	38	22	5	5	13	22	46	60	68	48
9	Chester	46	14	6	3	29	18	3	7	13	20	39	49	57	47
10	Swindon Town	46	15	4	4	50	20	4	4	15	21	43	71	63	46
11	Barnsley	46	10	7	6	29	20	6	7	10	24	36	53	56	46
12	Sheffield United	46	13	5	5	35	21	5	5	13	25	45	60	66	46
13	Rotherham United	46	13	4	6	38	24	5	6	12	20	42	58	66	46
14	Millwall	46	14	6	3	49	23	2	7	14	16	36	65	59	45
15	Plymouth Argyle	46	13	7	3	39	17	3	5	15	20	38	59	55	44
16	Gillingham	46	8	9	6	26	18	6	5	12	23	33	49	51	42
17	Oxford United	46	10	4	9	34	24	4	9	10	23	38	57	62	41
18	Blackpool	46	10	7	6	39	34	5	4	14	23	40	62	74	41
19	Brentford	46	10	6	7	33	26	5	5	13	26	47	59	73	41
20	Hull City	46	11	7	5	29	21	1	9	13	22	48	51	69	40
21	Bury	46	10	4	9	30	23	6	3	14	15	36	45	59	39
22	Southend United	46	11	6	6	33	23	3	4	16	14	35	47	58	38
23	Mansfield Town	46	9	9	5	31	24	1	7	15	16	34	47	58	36
24	Wimbledon	46	6	8	9	34	38	4	6	13	18	43	52	81	34

- 1979/80 Season -

(Back): Ludlam, Kemp, Parker, Sawyers, Collins, McCartney
(Middle): Nicholson(Physio), Hamilton, MacDonald, Swinburne, Harrison, Bannon, Winstanley, Harvey(Asst Man)
(Front): McVitie, Fell, Tait, Moncur(Man), Collins, Hoolickin, Lumby

- 1980/81 Season -

(Back): Watson(Sec), Parker, McVitie, Hamilton, Pickering(Coach), Collins, Brown, McAuley, Nicholson(Physio)
(Middle): Gate, MacDonald, Bannon, Swinburne, Harrison, Houghton, Watson, Coady
(Front): Metcalfe, Staniforth, McGrogan, Harvey(Man), Fell, Beardsley, Thompson

SEASON 1980/81
DIVISION 3

No.	Date	Opposition	Res.	H.T.	Att.	Goalscorers	Swinburne	Coady	Watson	MacDonald	Houghton	Parker	McVitie	Metcalfe	Bannon	Hamilton	Brown	Beardsley	Campbell	McGrogan	Robson	Coughlin	McAuley	Haigh	Collins	Staniforth	Harrison	Hoolickin
1	16 Aug	SHEFFIELD UNITED	0-3	0-1	5248		1	2	3	4	5	6	7	8*	9	10	11	12										
2	19	Huddersfield	1-1	1-1	7674	Houghton	1	6	3	4	5			7	8	9	10*	12								11		2
3	23	Chester	0-1	0-0	2007		1	2	3*	4	5	6	7	8	9	10										12		11
4	30	NEWPORT	1-4	1-2	2859	Hamilton	1			4	5	6	7	8	12	10		9							3	11		2
5	6 Sep	Plymouth	1-4	1-2	4854	Staniforth	1	12		4	5	6	7	8		10		9							3	11		2
6	13	GILLINGHAM	0-0	0-0	3029		1	5	3	4		6	7	8	9	10		12								11		2
7	16	MILLWALL	2-1	2-1	3418	O.G., Metcalfe	1	5	3	4		6	7	8	9	10		12								11		2
8	20	Oxford	2-1	1-1	2712	Staniforth, Beardsley	1	5	3	4		6	7	8	12	10		9								11		2
9	27	CHESTERFIELD	2-6	2-3	4256	Coady, Staniforth(pen)	1	5		4		6	7	8	9	3		10					12			11		2
10	30	Millwall	0-3	0-1	3168		1	5	3	4		6	7	8	9	10		12								11		2
11	4 Oct	Walsall	3-4	1-2	3185	MacDonald, Hamilton, Staniforth	1	5	3	4		6	7	8	12	10		9								11		2
12	7	BARNSLEY	2-2	2-1	2828	Hamilton(pen), Bannon	1	5	3	4		6	7	8	9	10		11					12					2
13	11	BRENTFORD	1-2	0-0	3030	Beardsley	1	5	3	4		6	7	8	12	10		9								11		2
14	18	Swindon	1-1	0-0	5989	McAuley	1		3	4		6	7	8		10		9		5			12			11		2
15	21	Hull	1-0	0-0	3603	Metcalfe	1		3	4		6	7	8	9	10		5	12							11		2
16	28	BLACKPOOL	2-0	2-0	3588	Bannon(2)	1		3	4		6	12	8	9	10		5					7			11		2
17	1 Nov	Portsmouth	1-2	0-1	13913	Beardsley	1		3	4		6		8	9	5		10					7		12	11		2
18	4	Barnsley	1-3	0-2	9191	Metcalfe	1		3	4		6		8	9	5		10					7		12	11		2
19	8	FULHAM	2-2	1-1	3665	Staniforth(pen), O.G.	1		3	4		6		8	12	9		10		5			7			11		2
20	11	HUDDERSFIELD	1-1	1-0	3998	Coughlin			3	4		6		8	9		12	10	5			7				11	1	2
21	15	Sheffield United	2-2	2-1	11031	Staniforth, Bannon		5		4		6	12	8	9	10						7		3		11	1	2
22	29	Exeter	0-2	0-2	3940			2		4		6		8	9	10						7		3	12	11	1	
23	6 Dec	COLCHESTER	4-0	2-0	3196	Beardsley(2), Brown, Staniforth		3		4		6		8			9	10	5			7		2	12	11	1	
24	20	Charlton	1-2	1-0	5444	Brown		3		4		6	12	8			9	10	5			7		2		11	1	
25	26	BURNLEY	3-2	3-0	7137	Campbell, Coughlin, Beardsley		3		4		6		8	9		12	10	5			7		2		11	1	
26	27	Rotherham	0-3	0-2	8450			3		4		6		8	12	9		10	5			7		2		11	1	
27	10 Jan	Reading	1-3	1-2	3957	Coughlin		3		4	5	6		8	12	9		10				7		2		11	1	
28	31	CHESTER	3-0	3-0	3283	Campbell, Staniforth(2)	1	3			5	6		8	9	4		10				12	7		2	11		
29	7 Feb	Gillingham	1-0	0-0	4927	Staniforth(pen)	1	3	12		5	6		8	9	4		10					7		2	11		
30	10	READING	0-0	0-0	3889		1	3			5	6		8	9	4		10				12	7		2	11		
31	14	PLYMOUTH	2-0	0-0	3924	Staniforth, Beardsley	1	3	12		5	6		8		4	9	10					7		2	11		
32	21	Chesterfield	0-1	0-1	5750		1	3	12		5	6		8	9	4		10					7		2	11		
33	28	OXFORD	0-0	0-0	3552		1	3	12		5	6		8		4		10					7	9	2	11		
34	7 Mar	WALSALL	1-1	1-0	4485	Robson	1	3	12		5	6				4		10			9		7	8	2	11		
35	14	Brentford	1-1	0-0	6211	Staniforth(pen)	1	2	3	12	5	6				4		10	8		9		7			11		
36	17	SWINDON	2-1	2-1	4104	Robson(2)	1	2	3		5	6	12			4		10	8		9		7			11		
37	21	HULL	2-0	0-0	4098	Robson, Beardsley	1	2	3		5	6	12			4		10	8		9		7			11		
38	28	Blackpool	1-0	0-0	4531	Beardsley	1	2	3	12	5	6				4		10	8		9		7			11		
39	31	EXETER	1-1	1-0	4385	Robson	1	2	3		5	6	12	11		4		10	8		9		7					
40	4 Apr	PORTSMOUTH	0-0	0-0	4299		1	2	3	12	5	6				4		10	8		9		7			11		
41	11	Fulham	3-2	1-1	4193	Beardsley, Staniforth, Robson	1	2	3		5	6				4		10	8		9	12	7			11		
42	18	Rotherham	0-1	0-1	6798		1	2			5	6	12			4		10	8		9		7	3		11		
43	21	Burnley	3-0	1-0	5100	Staniforth(3)	1	2		12	5	6			9	4		10	8				7	3		11		
44	25	CHARLTON	1-2	0-2	4397	Bannon	1	2			5	6			9	4		10	8				7	3		11		
45	2 May	Colchester	0-1	0-1	1430		1	2			5	6			9	4		10	8				7	3		11		
46	5	Newport	0-4	0-2	3747		1	2			5	6			9	4		10	8				7	3		11		

F.A. CUP

No.	Date	Opposition	Res.	H.T.	Att.	Goalscorers	Swinburne	Coady	Watson	MacDonald	Houghton	Parker	McVitie	Metcalfe	Bannon	Hamilton	Brown	Beardsley	Campbell	McGrogan	Robson	Coughlin	McAuley	Haigh	Collins	Staniforth	Harrison	Hoolickin
1R	20 Nov	Workington	0-0	0-0	8000			5		4		6			9	10		8					7	3		11	1	2
1Rr	25	WORKINGTON	4-1	1-1	5356	Brown(2), Beardsley(2)		5		4		6		8			9	10					7	3		11	1	2
2R	13 Dec	WALSALL	3-0	1-0	4778	Beardsley(2), Brown			3	4		6	11	8			9	10	5				7			2	1	
3R	3 Jan	Mansfield	2-2	1-2	5598	Bannon, O.G.		12	3	4		6		8	9			10	5				7			11	1	2
3Rr	6	MANSFIELD	2-1	1-0	6929	Beardsley, MacDonald			3	4		6		8*	9			10	5		12		7			11	1	2
4R	24	BRISTOL CITY	1-1	1-0	10057	Coady	1	5	3	4		6			9		12	10	8*				7		2	11		
4Rr	28	Bristol City	0-5	0-4	12081		1		3	4	5	6			9		12	10	8*				7		2	11		

LEAGUE CUP

No.	Date	Opposition	Res.	H.T.	Att.	Goalscorers	Swinburne	Coady	Watson	MacDonald	Houghton	Parker	McVitie	Metcalfe	Bannon	Hamilton	Brown	Beardsley	Campbell	McGrogan	Robson	Coughlin	McAuley	Haigh	Collins	Staniforth	Harrison	Hoolickin
1R1	9 Aug	ROCHDALE	2-0	2-0	2257	Bannon, Brown	1	5	3	4		6		8	9	10*12	11					7				2		
1R2	12	Rochdale	1-1	0-1	1806	Brown	1	5	3	4		6		8*	9	10	12	11					7			2		
2R1	26	CHARLTON	1-2	1-1	2673	Hamilton	1	2		4	5	6	7	8*	9	10		12						3		11		
2R2	2 Sep	Charlton	1-2	1-1	5160	Hamilton	1			4	5	6	7	8	12	10		9						3		11		2

Final League Table

		Pl.	Home					Away					F.	A.	Pts
			W	D	L	F	A	W	D	L	F	A			
1	Rotherham United	46	17	6	0	43	8	7	7	9	19	24	62	32	61
2	Barnsley	46	15	5	3	46	19	6	12	5	26	26	72	45	59
3	Charlton Athletic	46	14	6	3	36	17	11	3	9	27	27	63	44	59
4	Huddersfield Town	46	14	6	3	40	11	7	8	8	31	29	71	40	56
5	Chesterfield	46	17	4	2	42	16	6	6	11	30	32	72	48	56
6	Portsmouth	46	14	5	4	35	19	8	4	11	20	28	55	47	53
7	Plymouth Argyle	46	14	5	4	35	18	5	9	9	21	26	56	44	52
8	Burnley	46	13	5	5	37	21	5	9	9	23	27	60	48	50
9	Brentford	46	7	9	7	30	25	7	10	6	22	24	52	49	47
10	Reading	46	13	5	5	39	22	5	5	13	23	40	62	62	46
11	Exeter City	46	9	9	5	36	30	7	4	12	26	36	62	66	45
12	Newport County	46	11	6	6	38	22	4	7	12	26	39	64	61	43
13	Fulham	46	8	7	8	28	29	7	6	10	29	35	57	64	43
14	Oxford United	46	7	8	8	20	24	6	9	8	19	23	39	47	43
15	Gillingham	46	9	8	6	23	19	3	10	10	25	39	48	58	42
16	Millwall	46	10	9	4	30	21	4	5	14	13	39	43	60	42
17	Swindon Town	46	10	6	7	35	27	3	9	11	16	29	51	56	41
18	Chester	46	11	5	7	25	17	4	6	13	13	31	38	48	41
19	Carlisle United	46	8	8	7	29	24	6	4	13	24	41	56	70	41
20	Walsall	46	8	9	6	43	35	5	6	12	16	31	59	74	41
21	Sheffield United	46	12	6	5	38	20	2	6	15	27	43	65	63	40
22	Colchester United	46	12	7	4	35	22	2	4	17	10	43	45	65	39
23	Blackpool	46	9	9	5	39	28	4	5	14	26	47	65	75	32
24	Hull City	46	7	8	8	23	22	1	8	14	17	49	40	71	32

SEASON 1981/82

DIVISION 3

No.	Date	Opposition	Res.	H.T.	Att.	Goalscorers	Swinburne	Ashurst	Haigh	Rushbury	Coady	Houghton	Parker	Coughlin	Campbell	Beardsley	Lee	Crabbe	Bannon	Staniforth	Ritchie	Craig	Larkin	Collins	Robson
1	29 Aug	BRISTOL CITY	2-2	2-0	3930	Lee, Robson	1	2		3	4	5	6	7	8		9	11							10
2	5 Sep	Exeter	1-2	0-0	3533	Robson	1	2	7	3	4	5	6		8		9	11							10
3	12	SOUTHEND	3-2	1-2	3596	Robson, Crabbe(pen), O.G.	1	2	5	3	4				7	8	9	11				6			10
4	19	Lincoln	0-0	0-0	3623		1	5	4	3			2	7		8	9	10		11		6			
5	22	Chesterfield	0-1	0-1	4710		1	5	4	3			2	7		8	9	10		11		6			
6	26	OXFORD	2-1	0-0	3085	Lee, Beardsley	1	5	4	3			2	7		8	9	10		11		6			
7	29	BURNLEY	1-0	0-0	3983	Staniforth	1	5	4	3			2	7		8	9	10		11		6			
8	3 Oct	Brentford	2-1	0-0	4690	Lee, Staniforth	1	5	4	3			2	7		8	9	10		11		6			
9	10	Swindon	1-2	1-0	5265	Beardsley	1	5	4	3			2	7		8	9	10		11		6			
10	17	PLYMOUTH	3-1	1-0	3630	Staniforth(3)	1	5	4	3			2	7		8	9			11		6			10
11	20	Huddersfield	1-2	1-2	7185	Robson	1	5	4	3			2			10	9	7		11		6			8
12	24	WALSALL	2-1	1-0	3956	Crabbe, Beardsley	1	5	4	3			2			10	9	7		11		6			8
13	31	Newport	0-2	0-2	3972		1	5		3			2		4	10	9	7		11		6			8
14	3 Nov	DONCASTER	2-0	1-0	3725	Coughlin, Staniforth	1	5		3			2	4		10	9	7		11		6			8
15	7	FULHAM	1-2	0-2	4385	Robson	1	5		3		10	2	4			9	7		11		6			8
16	14	Portsmouth	2-1	1-0	8858	Robson, Lee	1	5		3			2	4		10	9	7		11		6			8
17	28	GILLINGHAM	2-0	2-0	4196	Bannon, Crabbe	1	5	4	3			2			10	9	7	11			6			8
18	5 Dec	Millwall	2-1	1-1	4740	Bannon(2)	1	5	4	3			2			10	9	7	11			6			8
19	19	Bristol Rovers	1-0	1-0	3759	Lee	1	5		3			2		4		9	7	10	11		6			8
20	30 Jan	LINCOLN	1-0	1-0	3893	Bannon	1	5		3		4	2	7			10	9		11		6			8
21	2 Feb	PRESTON N.E.	1-0	1-0	5044	Houghton	1	5	2	3		4		7			10	6	9	11					8
22	6	Southend	1-1	0-1	4911	Lee	1	5	2	3		4		7			10	6	9	11					8
23	9	CHESTERFIELD	3-0	0-0	5575	Robson, Lee, Crabbe	1	5		3		4	2	7			11	10	6	9					8
24	13	BRENTFORD	1-0	0-0	4942	Bannon	1	5		3		4	2		7		11	10	6	9					8
25	20	Oxford	1-2	1-2	4797	Lee	1	5	8	3		4	2		7		10	6	9	11					
26	27	SWINDON	1-1	1-1	4633	Beardsley	1	5	11	3		4	2		7	9	10	6							8
27	6 Mar	Plymouth	0-1	0-0	3272		1	5		3		4	2	7			10	6	9	11					8
28	9	HUDDERSFIELD	2-2	1-1	3643	Staniforth(2)	1	5		3		4	2	7			10		9	11			6		8
29	13	Walsall	1-1	0-0	3507	Robson	1	5		3		4	2	8			10			11	7	6			9
30	16	Doncaster	1-1	1-1	3431	Bannon	1	5		3		4	2	8			10		7	11		6			9
31	20	NEWPORT	2-2	2-0	4042	Bannon, Coughlin	1	5		3		4	2	8			10		7	11		6			9
32	23	READING	2-1	2-0	4557	Coughlin, Robson	1	5		3		4	2	8			10			11	7	6			9
33	27	Fulham	1-4	0-3	7477	Robson	1	5		3		4	2	8			10			11	7	6			9
34	3 Apr	PORTSMOUTH	2-0	2-0	3919	Staniforth, Ashurst	1	5	8	3			2				10			11	7	6	4		9
35	6	Bristol City	1-1	1-0	4329	Lee	1	5	8	3			2				10			11	7	6	4		9
36	10	Preston N.E.	1-0	1-0	7802	Robson	1	5		3			2	8			10		11		7	6	4		9
37	13	CHESTER	3-0	1-0	5340	Craig, Bannon, Lee	1	5		3			2	8			10		11		7	6	4		9
38	17	MILLWALL	2-1	0-0	4917	Craig, Bannon	1	5		3			2	8			10		11		7	6	4		9
39	20	EXETER	3-2	2-1	5220	Robson(3)	1	5		3			2	8						10	11	7	6	4	9
40	24	Gillingham	0-0	0-0	5809		1	5		3			2	8						10	11	7	6	4	9
41	1 May	WIMBLEDON	2-1	1-0	4466	Staniforth, O.G.	1	5		3			2	8			10			11	7	6	4		9
42	4	Burnley	0-1	0-0	9899		1	5		3			2	8			10		11		7	6	4		9
43	8	Reading	2-2	1-1	2715	Craig, Coughlin	1	5		3			2	8			10		11		7	6	4		9
44	11	Wimbledon	1-3	0-1	2002	Coughlin	1	5		3			2	8			10		11		7	6	4		9
45	15	BRISTOL ROVERS	1-2	1-2	6653	Staniforth(pen)	1	5		3		4	2	8			10			11	7	6			9
46	19	Chester	1-0	1-0	2535	Robson	1	5		3		4	2	8			10			11	7	6			9

F.A. CUP

No.	Date	Opposition	Res.	H.T.	Att.	Goalscorers	Swinburne	Ashurst	Haigh	Rushbury	Coady	Houghton	Parker	Coughlin	Campbell	Beardsley	Lee	Crabbe	Bannon	Staniforth	Ritchie	Craig	Larkin	Collins	Robson
1R	21 Nov	Darlington	2-2	1-1	4005	Staniforth, Robson	1	5		3			2	4		10	9	7	12	11		6			8
1Rr	12 Dec	DARLINGTON	3-1	2-1	4582	Robson, Beardsley, Bannon	1	5	4	3			2			10	9	7*	12	11		6			8
2R	9 Jan	BISHOP AUCKLAND	1-0	0-0	4536	Lee	1	5		3		12	2	4			9	7	10	11		6*			8
3R	23	HUDDERSFIELD	2-3	1-2	6345	Bannon, Robson	1	5	12	3			2	7			10	4*	9	11		6			8

LEAGUE CUP

No.	Date	Opposition	Res.	H.T.	Att.	Goalscorers	Swinburne	Ashurst	Haigh	Rushbury	Coady	Houghton	Parker	Coughlin	Campbell	Beardsley	Lee	Crabbe	Bannon	Staniforth	Ritchie	Craig	Larkin	Collins	Robson
1R1	1 Sep	Bury	3-3	1-2	2247	Coady, Haigh, Lee	1	2	7	3	4	5	6		8		9	11							10
1R2	15	BURY	2-1	2-1	3392	Lee, O.G.	1	5	2	3	4				7	8	9	10		11		6			
2R1	6 Oct	BRISTOL CITY	0-0	0-0	4111		1	5	4	3			2	7		8	9	10		11		6			
2R2	27	Bristol City	1-2	0-0	5220	Staniforth(pen)	1	5		3			2		4	10	9*	7	12	11		6			8

Final League Table

		Pl.	Home					Away					F.	A.	Pts
			W	D	L	F	A	W	D	L	F	A			
1	Burnley	46	13	7	3	37	20	8	10	5	29	25	66	45	80
2	Carlisle United	46	17	4	2	44	21	6	7	10	21	29	65	50	80
3	Fulham	46	12	9	2	44	22	9	6	8	33	29	77	51	78
4	Lincoln City	46	13	7	3	40	16	8	7	8	26	24	66	40	77
5	Oxford United	46	10	8	5	28	18	9	6	8	35	31	63	49	71
6	Gillingham	46	14	5	4	44	26	6	6	11	20	30	64	56	71
7	Southend United	46	11	7	5	35	23	7	8	8	28	25	63	51	69
8	Brentford	46	8	6	9	28	22	11	5	7	28	25	56	47	68
9	Millwall	46	12	4	7	36	28	6	9	8	26	34	62	62	67
10	Plymouth Argyle	46	12	5	6	37	24	6	6	11	27	32	64	56	65
11	Chesterfield	46	12	4	7	33	27	6	6	11	24	31	57	58	64
12	Reading	46	11	6	6	43	35	6	5	12	24	40	67	75	62
13	Portsmouth	46	11	10	2	33	14	3	9	11	23	37	56	51	61
14	Preston North End	46	10	7	6	25	22	6	6	11	25	34	50	56	61
15	Bristol Rovers	46	12	4	7	35	28	6	5	12	23	37	58	65	61
16	Newport County	46	9	10	4	28	21	5	6	12	26	33	54	54	58
17	Huddersfield Town	46	10	5	8	38	25	5	7	11	26	34	64	59	57
18	Exeter City	46	14	4	5	46	33	2	5	16	25	51	71	84	57
19	Doncaster Rovers	46	10	7	6	35	31	4	8	11	24	44	55	68	56
20	Walsall	46	10	7	6	32	23	3	7	13	19	32	51	55	53
21	Wimbledon	46	10	5	8	37	33	4	5	14	28	48	61	75	53
22	Swindon Town	46	9	5	9	37	36	4	8	11	18	35	55	71	52
23	Bristol City	46	7	6	10	24	29	4	7	12	16	36	40	65	46
24	Chester	46	2	10	11	16	30	5	1	17	20	48	36	78	32

- 1981/82 Season -

(Back): Coady, Parker, Haigh, Collins, Larkin, Crabbe.
(Middle): Young (Coach), Houghton, Bannon, Swinburne, Pickering (Trainer), Harrison, Lee, Ashurst, Nicholson (physio).
(Front): Ritchie, Coughlin, Robson, Stokoe (Manager), Stainforth, Campbell, Hamilton. (Sitting - apprentices)

- 1982/83 Season -

(Back): Park, Hornsby, Haigh, Bannon, Larkin, Rushbury.   (Middle): Nicholson(Physo), Lee, Poskett, Swinburne, Rush, Ashurst, Houghton.   (Front): Coughlin, Shoulder, Stokoe(Manager), Craig(Player/Coach), Staniforth, Mitchell

SEASON 1982/83
DIVISION 2

No.	Date	Opposition	Res.	H.T.	Att.	Goalscorers	Swinburne	Haigh	Rushbury	Ashurst	Houghton	Craig	Staniforth	Coughlin	Poskett	Hornsby	Shoulder	Lee	Larkin	Mitchell	Parker	Bannon	Robson B.	Robson K.	McCartney	Nicholson
1	28 Aug	Derby	3-0	2-0	11206	Shoulder(2), Poskett	1	2	3	4	5	6	7	8	9	10	11									
2	4 Sep	GRIMSBY	2-3	0-0	4683	Shoulder, Staniforth(pen)	1	2	3	4	5	6	7	8	9	10	11	12								
3	7	Burnley	1-1	0-0	7645	Poskett	1	2	3	4		6	7	8	9		11	12	5	10						
4	11	Leicester	0-6	0-2	8440		1	2	3	4	5	6	7	8	9		11	12		10*						
5	18	CRYSTAL PALACE	4-1	2-0	4390	Poskett(4)	1		3	4		6	7	8	9		11		5		2	10				
6	25	Cambridge	1-1	1-0	3051	Coughlin	1		3	4		6	7	8	9		11		5		2	10				
7	28	SHEFFIELD WED.	4-2	0-0	6127	Craig(2), Bannon, Shoulder	1	3		4	12	6	7	8	9		11		5		2	10				
8	2 Oct	WOLVES	0-2	0-2	7723		1	3		4		6	7	8	9		11		5		2	10				
9	9	CHARLTON	4-1	0-0	4606	Poskett(2), Larkin, Bannon	1	3		4		6	7	8	9		11		5		2	10				
10	16	Leeds	1-1	1-1	14141	Shoulder	1	3		4	12	6	7	8	9		11		5		2	10				
11	23	Oldham	3-4	1-0	4211	Shoulder, Larkin, Staniforth(pen)	1	3	12	4		6	7		9	8	11		5		2	10*				
12	30	CHELSEA	2-1	2-0	7141	Shoulder, Poskett	1	3	12	4		6*	7	8	9		11		5		2	10				
13	6 Nov	Blackburn	2-3	2-1	5204	Shoulder(2)	1	3	12	4		6*	7	8	9		11		5		2	10				
14	13	ROTHERHAM	2-2	1-1	5294	Poskett, Bannon	1	3	12	4		6	7	8	9		11		5		2	10				
15	20	NEWCASTLE	2-0	1-0	16276	Hornsby, Lee	1	3		4	6		7	8		9*	11	12	5		2	10				
16	27	Q.p.r.	0-1	1-0	9697		1	3	6	4	12		7	8			11	9	5		2	10				
17	4 Dec	SHREWSBURY	2-3	2-2	4226	Poskett, Bannon	1	3	12	4			7	8	9	6	11		5		2	10				
18	11	Barnsley	2-2	2-1	10226	Craig, Lee	1	3	5	4	6	10		8*	9		11	7			2	12				
19	18	FULHAM	3-2	0-1	4859	Shoulder(2), Bannon	1	3	5	4	6		12		9	8	11	7			2	10				
20	27	Bolton	0-1	0-0	8171		1	3	5	4	6	10*	12		9	8	11	7			2					
21	28	MIDDLESBROUGH	1-3	0-1	8181	Shoulder(pen)	1	3	5	4	6	8	7	12	9		11				2	10				
22	1 Jan	Newcastle	2-2	1-1	29154	Shoulder, Bannon	1	3	5	4	6	8		7	9		11	12			2	10				
23	3	Grimsby	1-2	1-1	6377	Bannon	1	3	5	4	6	8			9	12	11	7			2	10				
24	15	DERBY	3-0	2-0	4732	Poskett, Shoulder, Bannon	1	3		4	12	6	7	8*	9		11		5		2	10				
25	22	Sheffield Wednesday	1-1	1-1	12874	Shoulder(pen)	1	3		4		6	7	8	9		11		5		2	10				
26	5 Feb	LEICESTER	0-1	0-1	4402		1	3	12	4		6	7	8	9		11		5		2	10				
27	12	Wolves	1-2	1-1	13171	Bannon	1	3	5	4	6	8		7	9		11				2	10				
28	19	Charlton	0-0	0-0	4940		1	3	5	4	6	8		7			11	9			2	10				
29	26	LEEDS	2-2	0-2	6419	Shoulder, Bannon	1	3	5	4	6	8		7		9	11	12			2	10				
30	5 Mar	OLDHAM	0-0	0-0	4045		1	3	5	4	6	8	9	7			11	12			2	10				
31	12	Chelsea	2-4	1-2	6677	Haigh, Shoulder(pen)	1	3	5		6	8	7	4			11	9	12		2	10				
32	19	BLACKBURN	3-1	3-1	4756	B.Robson, Poskett, Coughlin	1	3	5		6		12	4	9		11				2	10	8	7		
33	26	Rotherham	2-1	0-0	5486	Poskett, K.Robson	1	3	5		6		12	4	9		11				2	10*	8	7	6	
34	2 Apr	Middlesbrough	0-1	0-1	9965		1	3	5		6	10		4	9		11				2*		8	7		12
35	5	BOLTON	5-0	3-0	5615	Craig,Shoulder,Bannon,B.Robson(2)	1	2	5		6*	12		4	9		11					10	8	7	3	
36	9	Crystal Palace	1-2	1-0	5696	Shoulder	1	2	5		6	12		4	9		11					10*	8	7	3	
37	16	BURNLEY	1-1	0-0	5081	Shoulder	1	2	5		6	12		4	9		11					10	8	7	3	
38	23	Shrewsbury	1-2	0-0	3220	Shoulder	1	2	5		6	10		4	9		11				12		8	7	3	
39	30	Q.P.R.	1-0	1-0	5724	K.Robson	1	2	5		6	12		4	9		11*					10	8	7	3	
40	3 May	CAMBRIDGE	2-2	1-1	4630	B.Robson, K.Robson	1	2	5		6			4	9		11					10	8	7	3	
41	7	Fulham	0-2	0-1	10045		1	2	5		6	12		10	9		11				4		8	7	3	
42	14	BARNSLEY	2-2	2-1	5898	K.Robson	1	2	5		6	7		4	9*		11					10*	8	12	3	

F.A. CUP

No.	Date	Opposition	Res.	H.T.	Att.	Goalscorers	Swinburne	Haigh	Rushbury	Ashurst	Houghton	Craig	Staniforth	Coughlin	Poskett	Hornsby	Shoulder	Lee	Larkin	Mitchell	Parker	Bannon	Robson B.	Robson K.	McCartney	Nicholson
3R	8 Jan	BURNLEY	2-2	1-1	6998	Bannon, Poskett	1	3	5	4	6	8	7#		9		11	12			2	10				
3Rr	11	Burnley	1-3	0-1	9439	Poskett	1	3	5	4	6*	8		7	9		11	12			2	10				

LEAGUE CUP

No.	Date	Opposition	Res.	H.T.	Att.	Goalscorers	Swinburne	Haigh	Rushbury	Ashurst	Houghton	Craig	Staniforth	Coughlin	Poskett	Hornsby	Shoulder	Lee	Larkin	Mitchell	Parker	Bannon	Robson B.	Robson K.	McCartney	Nicholson
1R1	31 Aug	BOLTON	3-3	1-2	4314	Staniforth, Ashurst, Coughlin	1	2	3	4	5	6	7	8	9	10	11									
1R2	13 Sep	Bolton	0-4	0-1	4039		1	2#	3	4	6	5	7	8	9		11	10		12						

Final League Table

		Pl.	Home					Away					F.	A.	Pts
			W	D	L	F	A	W	D	L	F	A			
1	Queen's Park Rgs.	42	16	3	2	51	16	10	4	7	26	20	77	36	85
2	Wolverhampton W.	42	14	5	2	42	16	6	10	5	26	28	68	44	75
3	Leicester City	42	11	4	6	36	15	9	6	6	36	29	72	44	70
4	Fulham	42	13	5	3	36	20	7	4	10	28	27	64	47	69
5	Newcastle United	42	13	6	2	43	21	5	7	9	32	32	75	53	67
6	Sheffield Wed.	42	9	8	4	33	23	7	7	7	27	24	60	47	63
7	Oldham Athletic	42	8	10	3	38	24	6	9	6	26	23	64	47	61
8	Leeds United	42	7	11	3	28	22	6	10	5	23	24	51	46	60
9	Shrewsbury Town	42	8	9	4	20	15	7	5	9	28	33	48	48	59
10	Barnsley	42	9	8	4	37	28	5	7	9	20	27	57	55	57
11	Blackburn Rovers	42	11	7	3	38	21	4	5	12	20	37	58	58	57
12	Cambridge United	42	11	7	3	26	17	2	5	14	16	43	42	60	51
13	Derby County	42	7	10	4	27	24	3	9	9	22	34	49	58	49
14	Carlisle United	42	10	6	5	44	28	2	6	13	24	42	68	70	48
15	Crystal Palace	42	11	7	3	31	17	1	5	15	12	35	43	52	48
16	Middlesbrough	42	8	7	6	27	29	3	8	10	19	38	46	67	48
17	Charlton Athletic	42	11	3	7	40	31	2	6	13	23	55	63	86	48
18	Chelsea	42	8	5	8	31	22	3	6	12	20	39	51	61	47
19	Grimsby Town	42	9	7	5	32	26	3	4	14	13	44	45	70	47
20	Rotherham United	42	6	7	8	22	29	4	8	9	23	39	45	68	45
21	Burnley	42	10	4	7	38	24	2	4	15	18	42	56	66	44
22	Bolton Wanderers	42	10	2	9	30	26	1	9	11	12	35	42	61	44

SEASON 1983/84

DIVISION 2

No.	Date	Opposition	Res.	H.T.	Att.	Goalscorers	McKellar	Moore	Rushbury	Ashurst	O'Riordan	McCartney	Bell	Coughlin	Poskett	Dixon	Shoulder	Haigh	Horswill	Parker	Craig	Bannon	Hill	Buckley	Hornsby	Nicholson
1	27 Aug	CAMBRIDGE	0-0	0-0	3738		1	2	3	4	5	6	7	8	9	10	11	12								
2	29	BLACKBURN	0-1	0-1	4470		1	2	3	4	5		7	8	9	10	11	12	6							
3	3 Sep	Sheffield Wednesday	0-2	0-1	14544		1	2	3	4	5		7	8*	9	10	11		6	12						
4	6	Charlton	0-1	0-0	3770		1	2	3	4	5		7		9	12	11		6		8		10*			
5	10	SHREWSBURY	1-0	1-0	3164	O'Riordan	1	2	3	4	5	10			9	7	11		6		8					
6	17	Brighton	1-1	0-1	11735	Shoulder	1	2	3		5	10	7	4	9	12	11		6		8					
7	24	HUDDERSFIELD	0-0	0-0	5461		1	2	3	4	5	10			9		11		6		8			7		
8	1 Oct	Derby	4-1	2-0	12041	Poskett(4)	1	2		4	5				9		11		6	3	8			7		
9	8	Cardiff	0-2	0-0	4596		1	2	12	4	5		8		9		11		6	3				7	10	
10	15	FULHAM	2-0	1-0	3992	O'Riordan, Buckley	1	2		4	5		8		9		11		6	3				7	10	
11	22	CHELSEA	0-0	0-0	6774		1	2		4	5		8	12	9		11		6	3				7	10	
12	29	Oldham	3-2	2-2	4087	Moore, O'Riordan, Shoulder	1	2		4	5		12		9		11		6	3	8			7	10	
13	5 Nov	Swansea	0-0	0-0	6838		1	2		4	5				9		11		6	3	8			7	10	
14	12	PORTSMOUTH	0-0	0-0	4814		1	2		4	5			12	9		11		6	3	8			7	10	
15	19	MANCHESTER CITY	2-0	1-0	8745	Poskett, Shoulder	1	2		4	5			12	9		11		6	3	8			7	10	
16	26	Grimsby	1-1	0-0	5665	Buckley	1	2		4	5		12		9		11		6	3	8			7	10	
17	3 Dec	LEEDS	1-0	0-0	6845	Poskett	1	2		4	5		10	12	9		11		6	3	8			7	10	
18	11	Crystal Palace	2-1	1-0	6460	O'Riordan, Shoulder	1	2		4	5		12		9		11		6	3	8			7	10	
19	17	BARNSLEY	4-2	2-1	4812	Rushbury, Bannon, Poskett(2)	1	2		4	5		10*	7	9		11		6	3	8	12				
20	26	Middlesbrough	1-0	0-0	11147	Ashurst	1	2		4	5		10	7	9		11		6	3	8					
21	27	NEWCASTLE	3-1	1-1	14756	Coughlin, Craig, Shoulder	1	2		4	5		12	7	9		11		6	3	8		10*			
22	31	SHEFFIELD WED.	1-1	0-1	10475	O'Riordan	1	2		4	5			7	9		11		6	3	8	12				
23	2 Jan	Huddersfield	0-0	0-0	10131		1	2		4	5			7	9		11		6	3	8		10			
24	14	Cambridge	2-0	1-0	2203	Poskett, Hill	1	2		4	5			7	9		11		6	3	8		10			
25	21	BRIGHTON	1-2	0-2	5169	Poskett	1	2		4	5			7	9		11		6	3	8		10	12		
26	4 Feb	DERBY	2-1	1-1	4915	Hill, Shoulder	1	2		4	5	6			9		11			3	8		10	7		
27	11	Shrewsbury	0-0	0-0	3439		1	2		4	5	6			9		11			3	8		10	7		
28	18	OLDHAM	2-0	0-0	4389	Poskett, Shoulder	1	2		4	5	6		12	9		11			3	8		10*	7		
29	25	Chelsea	0-0	0-0	16543		1	2		4	5	6			9		11			3	8		10	7		
30	3 Mar	SWANSEA	2-0	1-0	4280	Poskett(2)	1	2		4	5	6		12	9		11			3	8		10*	7		
31	10	Portsmouth	1-0	0-0	10748	Shoulder	1	2		4	5	6	10		9		11			3	8			7		
32	17	CHARLTON	3-0	1-0	4375	O'Riordan, Craig, Poskett	1	2		4	5	6	10		9		11			3	8			7		
33	24	Blackburn	1-4	0-3	6171	Parker	1	2		4	5	6	10		9		11			3	8			7		
34	31	Fulham	0-0	0-0	6018		1			4	5	6	10		9		11	2		3	8			7		
35	7 Apr	CARDIFF	1-1	0-1	4704	Poskett	1			4	5	6	10		9		11	2		3	8			7		
36	14	Manchester City	1-3	1-1	20760	Hill	1			4	5	6	10		9	12	11	2		3			8	7		
37	20	MIDDLESBROUGH	1-1	0-0	5674	O'Riordan	1			4	5	6	12		9		11	2		3	10	8		7		
38	23	Newcastle	1-5	0-3	33386	Coughlin	1			4	5	6	10		9		11	2		3	8			7		
39	28	GRIMSBY	1-1	1-0	3512	Coughlin	1			4	5	6	10		9		11	2		3	8			7		
40	5 Mar	Leeds	0-3	0-0	8279		1			4	5	6	10		9	12		2		3	8			7		11
41	7	CRYSTAL PALACE	2-2	2-0	3013	Poskett(2)	1			4	5	6	10		9		11	2		3	8			7		12
42	12	Barnsley	1-2	1-0	4512	O'Riordan	1			4	5	6	8					2		3	7		11			10

F.A. CUP

No.	Date	Opposition	Res.	H.T.	Att.	Goalscorers	McKellar	Moore	Rushbury	Ashurst	O'Riordan	McCartney	Bell	Coughlin	Poskett	Dixon	Shoulder	Haigh	Horswill	Parker	Craig	Bannon	Hill	Buckley	Hornsby	Nicholson
3R	7 Jan	SWINDON	1-1	1-0	5778	Ashhurst	1		2	4	5		12	7	9		11		6	3	8		10*			
3Rr	10	Swindon	1-3	0-1	8077	Shoulder(pen)	1		2	4	5		10	7	9		11	3			8			12	6*	

LEAGUE CUP

No.	Date	Opposition	Res.	H.T.	Att.	Goalscorers	McKellar	Moore	Rushbury	Ashurst	O'Riordan	McCartney	Bell	Coughlin	Poskett	Dixon	Shoulder	Haigh	Horswill	Parker	Craig	Bannon	Hill	Buckley	Hornsby	Nicholson
2R1	4 Oct	SOUTHAMPTON(N)	2-0	1-0	8570	Poskett(2)	1	2		4	5		8	10	9		11		6	3				7		
2R2	25	Southampton	0-3	0-1	12483		1	2		4	5		8	10	9	11*			6	3	12			7		

Final League Table

	Pl.		Home					Away				F.	A.	Pts
		W	D	L	F	A	W	D	L	F	A			
1 Chelsea	42	15	4	2	55	17	10	9	2	35	23	90	40	88
2 Sheffield Wed.	42	16	4	1	47	16	10	6	5	25	18	72	34	88
3 Newcastle United	42	16	2	3	51	18	8	6	7	34	35	85	53	80
4 Manchester City	42	13	3	5	43	21	7	7	7	23	27	66	48	70
5 Grimsby Town	42	13	6	2	36	15	6	7	8	24	32	60	47	70
6 Blackburn Rovers	42	9	11	1	35	19	8	5	8	22	27	57	46	67
7 Carlisle United	42	10	9	2	29	13	6	7	8	19	28	48	41	64
8 Shrewsbury Town	42	13	5	3	34	18	4	5	12	15	35	49	53	61
9 Brighton & Hove A.	42	11	6	4	42	17	6	3	12	27	43	69	60	60
10 Leeds United	42	13	4	4	33	16	3	8	10	22	40	55	56	60
11 Fulham	42	9	6	6	35	24	6	6	9	25	29	60	53	57
12 Huddersfield Town	42	8	6	7	27	20	6	9	6	29	29	56	49	57
13 Charlton Athletic	42	13	4	4	40	26	3	5	13	13	38	53	64	57
14 Barnsley	42	9	6	6	33	23	6	1	14	24	30	57	53	52
15 Cardiff City	42	11	3	7	32	27	4	3	14	21	39	53	66	51
16 Portsmouth	42	8	3	10	46	32	6	4	11	27	32	73	64	49
17 Middlesbrough	42	9	8	4	26	18	3	5	13	15	29	41	47	49
18 Crystal Palace	42	8	5	8	18	18	4	6	11	24	34	42	52	47
19 Oldham Athletic	42	10	6	5	33	27	3	2	16	14	46	47	73	47
20 Derby County	42	9	5	7	26	26	2	4	15	10	46	36	72	42
21 Swansea City	42	7	4	10	20	28	0	4	17	16	57	36	85	29
22 Cambridge United	42	4	7	10	20	33	0	5	16	8	44	28	77	24

- 1983/84/ Season -

(Back): Nicholson(Physio), Dixon, O'Riordan, McCartney, Parker, Hornsby
(Middle): Ashurst, Moore, McKellar, Bannon, Poskett, Hough
(Front): Coughlin, Ball, Stokoe(Manager), Craig(Assistant Manager), Ruchbury, Shoulder

- 1984/85 Season -

(Back): Haigh, O'Riordan, Poskett, MacDonald, Tupling, Rushbury
(Middle): Stokoe(Manager), Hill, Ashurst, McKellar, , McAughtrie, Hutchinson(Managing Director)
(Front): Shoulder, Robson, Jenkins(Chairman), Craig, McCartney

SEASON 1984/85

DIVISION 2

No.	Date	Opposition	Res.	H.T.	Att.	Goalscorers	McKellar	Davies	Ashorst	O'Riordan	Rushbury	Hutchinson	Poskett	Craig	Hill	McCartney	McAlightrie	Haigh	Shoulder	Bishop	Halsall	Cooke	Lemon	Caldwell	Halpin	Blott	Carney	Gorman	Robson	Tupling	Blackhall	MacDonald
1	25 Aug	BRIGHTON	0-3	0-3	4721		1	3	4	5	6	8*	9	11	12														10	2		7
2	27	Barnsley	3-1	1-1	5681	Craig(pen), Robson, O.G.	1		4	5	3	8	9	11		2	6												10			7
3	1 Sep	Blackburn	0-4	0-1	5121		1		4	5			9	11		2	6												10	8		7
4	4	SHREWSBURY	2-0	0-0	3321	O'Riordan, Poskett	1	11	4	5	3		9	8		2	6												10			7
5	8	MANCHESTER CITY	0-0	0-0	6461		1	11	4	5	3		9	8	12	2	6												10			7
6	15	Birmingham	0-2	0-2	11740		1	11	4	5	3		9	8	12	2	6												10			7
7	22	SHEFFIELD UNITED	1-1	0-0	5204	Poskett	1		4	5	3	7	9	8		2		6	11										10			
8	29	Oxford	0-4	0-3	7427		1		4	5	3		9	8	7	2		6	11										10			12
9	6 Oct	Wimbledon	0-3	0-1	2876		1		4	5	3		9	8	7*	2		6	11										10			12
10	13	CRYSTAL PALACE	1-0	1-0	3156	McCartney(pen)	1		4	5		8				7	6	3	2		11	10										9
11	20	Grimsby	0-1	0-1	4832		1		4	5		8		11		7*	6	3	2	9	10											
12	27	HUDDERSFIELD	0-1	0-0	3775		1		4	5	12	8				7*	6	3	2	9	10			11								
13	10 Nov	Leeds	1-1	1-1	13327	Shoulder	1		4	5			9				6	3	2	7	10	8		11								
14	17	Cardiff	1-2	1-1	3005	Bishop	1		4	5*			9				6	3	2	7	10	8		11								
15	20	FULHAM	3-0	1-0	2994	Halsall, McAughtrie, O'Riordan	1		4	5			9				6	3	2	7	10	8		11								
16	24	NOTTS COUNTY	1-0	1-0	3165	McCartney(pen)	1		4	5			9				6	3	2	7	10	8		11								
17	30	Charlton	1-1	0-0	4073	Halsall	1		4	5			9				6	3	2	7	10	8		11								
18	8 Dec	PORTSMOUTH	3-0	1-0	4006	Cooke, Poskett, Shoulder	1		4	5			9				6	3	2	7	10	8		11								
19	15	Oldham	3-2	1-2	3007	Cooke, Halsall, O.G.	1		4	5			9*			12	6	3	2	7	10	8		11								
20	23	BLACKBURN	0-1	0-0	10835		1		4	5	12					11	6	3	2	7	10	8				9						
21	26	MIDDLESBROUGH	0-3	0-1	4423		1		4	5							6	3	2	7	10	8		11*	9		12					
22	29	Shrewsbury	2-4	1-1	3649	McCartney(pen), O.G.	1		4	5		11	9			12	6	3	2	7		8			10*							
23	1 Jan	Wolves	2-0	2-0	6264	O'Riordan, Poskett	1		4	5	10		9		11		6	3	2	7		8										
24	2 Feb	OXFORD	0-1	0-1	4056		1		4	5			9		12		6	3	2		10	8		7	11*							
25	5	Brighton	1-4	0-1	7610	O'Riordan	1		4	5	3		9		12		6		2	11	10	8		7*								
26	9	Manchester City	3-1	1-1	21374	Poskett(2), Bishop			4	5	11		9		7		6	3	2	8	10						1					
27	23	Fulham	2-0	0-1	5229	O'Riordan, Halpin			4	5	11		9		7*		6	3	2	8	10				12	1						
28	26	LEEDS	2-2	1-0	5484	O'Riordan(2)	1		4	5	3				7		6		2	9	10	8		11								
29	2 Mar	Huddersfield	0-2	0-0	5263		1		4	5					12		7		6	2	9*	10	8		11								
30	9	GRIMSBY	1-1	0-1	3218	Haigh	1		4	5	3					7*	6		2	12	10	8		11								
31	12	BIRMINGHAM	2-1	0-1	4099	O'Riordan, Shoulder	1		4	5	3		9					6	2	7	10	8		11								
32	17	Crystal Palace	1-2	1-2	4330	Halsall	1		4	5			9			12	6		2	7	10	8		11*								
33	23	WIMBLEDON	6-1	1-0	2779	Hill(3), Poskett(2), McCartney(pen)	1		4	5			9			10		3	2	7				11				6				
34	30	BARNSLEY	2-0	1-0	2784	McCartney(pen), Poskett	1		4	5			9			10		3	2	7	12	8		11*				6				
35	6 Apr	Middlesbrough	2-1	0-0	5275	Haigh, Hill	1		4	5			9					3	2	7	10	8		11				6				
36	8	WOLVES	0-1	0-0	4021		1		4	5			9					3	2	7	10	8		11*				6	12			
37	13	Sheffield United	0-0	0-0	8945		1		4	5			9		7			3	2		10	8		11				6	12			
38	20	CARDIFF	0-1	0-0	2621		1		4	5			9		7*			3	2		10	8		11				6	11	12		
39	27	Notts County	0-3	0-0	4051		1		4	5			9		7		3	6	2		10			11			8					
40	3 May	CHARLTON	1-1	0-1	2368	O'Riordan	1		4	5	12				7		3	6	2		10			11			8		9*			
41	6	Portsmouth	1-3	1-1	12401	Halsall	1		4	5			9*			12	3	6	2		10			11			7					
42	11	OLDHAM	2-5	1-1	2470	Gorman, O'Riordan	1		4	5			9*				3	6	2	12	10	8		11			7					

F.A. CUP

			Res.	H.T.	Att.	Goalscorers	McKellar	Davies	Ashorst	O'Riordan	Rushbury	Hutchinson	Poskett	Craig	Hill	McCartney	McAlightrie	Haigh	Shoulder	Bishop	Halsall	Cooke	Lemon	Caldwell	Halpin	Blott	Carney	Gorman	Robson	Tupling	Blackhall	MacDonald
3R	4 Jan	DAGENHAM	1-0	0-0	4509	Poskett	1		4	5	11		9			10	6	3	2	7		8										
4R	26	Leicester	0-1	0-1	14635		1		4	5	11*		9				7	6	3	2	10	8		12								

LEAGUE CUP

			Res.	H.T.	Att.	Goalscorers	McKellar	Davies	Ashorst	O'Riordan	Rushbury	Hutchinson	Poskett	Craig	Hill	McCartney	McAlightrie	Haigh	Shoulder	Bishop	Halsall	Cooke	Lemon	Caldwell	Halpin	Blott	Carney	Gorman	Robson	Tupling	Blackhall	MacDonald
2R1	25 Sep	Fulham	0-2	0-0	3340		1		4	5			9	8	7	2	6	3		11									10			
2R2	9 Oct	FULHAM	1-2	1-0	2818	Hill	1		4	5	3		9	8	7		6		2	11*									10			12

Final League Table

		Pl.	Home					Away					F.	A.	Pts
			W	D	L	F	A	W	D	L	F	A			
1	Oxford United	42	18	2	1	62	15	7	7	7	22	21	84	36	84
2	Birmingham City	42	12	6	3	30	15	13	1	7	29	18	59	33	82
3	Manchester City	42	14	4	3	42	16	7	7	7	24	24	66	40	74
4	Portsmouth	42	11	6	4	39	25	9	8	4	30	25	69	50	74
5	Blackburn Rovers	42	14	3	4	38	15	7	7	7	28	26	66	41	73
6	Brighton & Hove A.	42	13	6	2	31	11	7	6	8	23	23	54	34	72
7	Leeds United	42	12	7	2	37	11	7	5	9	29	32	66	43	69
8	Shrewsbury Town	42	12	6	3	45	22	6	5	10	21	31	66	53	65
9	Fulham	42	13	3	5	35	26	6	5	10	33	38	68	64	65
10	Grimsby Town	42	13	1	7	47	32	5	7	9	25	32	72	64	62
11	Barnsley	42	11	7	3	27	12	3	9	9	15	30	42	42	58
12	Wimbledon	42	9	8	4	40	29	7	2	12	31	46	71	75	58
13	Huddersfield Town	42	9	5	7	28	29	6	5	10	24	35	52	64	55
14	Oldham Athletic	42	10	4	7	27	23	5	4	12	22	44	49	67	53
15	Crystal Palace	42	8	7	6	25	27	4	5	12	21	38	46	65	48
16	Carlisle United	42	8	5	8	27	23	5	3	13	23	44	50	67	47
17	Charlton Athletic	42	8	7	6	34	30	5	5	13	17	33	51	63	45
18	Sheffield United	42	7	6	8	31	28	3	8	10	23	38	54	66	44
19	Middlesbrough	42	6	8	7	22	26	4	2	15	19	31	41	57	40
20	Notts County	42	6	5	10	25	32	4	2	15	20	41	45	73	37
21	Cardiff City	42	5	3	13	24	42	4	5	12	23	37	47	79	35
22	Wolverhampton W.	42	5	4	12	18	32	3	5	13	19	47	37	79	33

SEASON 1985/86

DIVISION 2

No.	Date	Opposition	Res.	H.T.	Att.	Goalscorers	Carr	Haigh	McCartney	Ashurst	Baker	Halsall	Gorman	Bishop	Entwistle	Hill	Gavin	Robson	Halpin	Mayes	Maunders	Wakenshaw	Cooke	Endersby	Lomax	McGarvey	Tolmie
1	17 Aug	Bradford	1-2	0-0	5086	Entwistle	1	2	3	4	5	6	7*	8	9	10	11	12									
2	24	Portsmouth	0-4	0-3	12595		1	2	3	4	5		12	6	9	10	7		11	8*							
3	27	CRYSTAL PALACE	2-2	1-1	3080	Entwistle, Halpin	1	2	3	4	5	10	8	6	9				11	7							
4	31	Blackburn	0-2	0-0	5959		1	2	3		5	10	4	6	9				7	11	8						
5	7 Sep	BARNSLEY	1-1	0-0	2418	Bishop	1	2	3	4		6	8	10	9				11	7	12	5*					
6	13	Grimsby	0-1	0-0	4098		1	2	3	4	5	6	8		9	10	11		7								
7	17	OLDHAM	3-1	1-0	3309	Hill(2), Gavin	1	2	3	4		6	8			9	11		7			5	10				
8	21	Hull	0-4	0-0	6117		1	2	3		4	6	8*		9				11	7	12	5	10				
9	28	SHREWSBURY	0-2	0-1	2559		1	2	3		4	6	8		9*		11	12	7			5	10				
10	5 Oct	Brighton	1-6	0-2	8608	Wakenshaw	1	2	3		4	6	8				11		7			5	9	10			
11	12	NORWICH	0-4	0-1	2907		1	2	3	4		6	8		12		11		7			5	9	10			
12	19	SUNDERLAND	1-2	0-1	9249	Halpin	1	2	3	4	12	6		10		9	7*		11			5		8			
13	22	Millwall	1-3	0-1	4522	O.G.	1	2	3	4	12	6	7*	10		9			11			5		8			
14	26	Huddersfield	3-3	0-0	5012	Wakenshaw, McCartney, Halpin		2*	3	4	7	6		10		9			11			5		8			
15	3 Nov	Wimbledon	1-4	1-0	3882	Hill	1		3	4	2	6		10		9			11			5	7	8			
16	9	STOKE	3-0	2-0	2813	Mayes(2), Hill			3	4	9	6	2	10					11	7		5		8	1		
17	23	LEEDS	1-2	0-0	3504	Baker			3	4	9*	6	2	10		12			11	7		5		8	1		
18	30	Charlton	0-3	0-1	3059				3	4	9	6	2	10		12			11	7		5		8	1		
19	7 Dec	MILLWALL	1-0	0-0	2497	Bishop			3	4	9	6		10					11	7		5		8	1	2	
20	13	Bradford	0-1	0-0	5212				3	4	9	6	7	10					11			5	12	8	1	2	
21	22	PORTSMOUTH	0-1	0-0	4225				3	4	9	6		10		12			11	7*		5		8	1	2	
22	26	MIDDLESBROUGH	1-0	0-0	4238	Halpin			3	4	9	6		10					11			5		8	1	2	
23	1 Jan	Sheffield United	0-1	0-0	10561				3	4	9*	6	12	10					11			5		8	1	2	
24	11	GRIMSBY	1-2	0-2	2483	Hill			3	4	9*	6		10		7	12		11			5		8	1	2	
25	18	BLACKBURN	2-1	1-0	3801	Hill, Halpin			3	4	9	6		10		7			11			5	12	8	1	2	
26	1 Feb	Crystal Palace	1-1	0-1	3744	McCartney			3	4	9	6		10		7			11			5		8	1	2	9
27	8	Sunderland	2-2	0-0	12689	McGarvey, Bishop	12		3	4	5	6		10		7			11					8	1	2	9
28	1 Mar	Shrewsbury	0-0	0-0	2364		3				5	6	4	10		7			11					8	1	2	9
29	11	HULL	2-1	1-0	3248	Baker, Halsall			3	4	7	6		10		7			11			5		8	1	2	9
30	15	Norwich	1-2	0-1	13852	McGarvey	12		3		4	6		10		7			11			5		8	1	2*	9
31	18	HUDDERSFIELD	2-0	0-0	3334	Halsall, Hill		2	3		4	6		10		7			11			5		8	1		9
32	22	Barnsley	2-1	0-1	4400	Hill, Halpin		2	3	4	7*	6		10		12			11			5		8	1		9
33	29	SHEFFIELD UNITED	1-0	1-0	4579	Bishop		2	3	4		6	12	10					11	7*		5		8	1		9
34	31	Middlesbrough	3-1	1-1	7603	Cooke(2), O.G.		2	3	4		6	12	10		7			11*			5		8	1		9
35	6 Apr	WIMBLEDON	2-3	1-1	5593	Cooke, McGarvey(pen)		2	3	4		6		10		7						5		8	1	9	11
36	8	Fulham	1-0	1-0	2134	Hill		2	3	4	9	6		10		7						5		8	1		11
37	12	Stoke	0-0	0-0	7159			2	3	4	9	6	12	10		7						5		8	1		11*
38	19	FULHAM	2-1	2-1	3817	Bishop, Saunders		2	3	4	9	6	12	10		7						5		8	1		11*
39	26	Leeds	0-2	0-1	13868			2	3	4	9	6		10		7						5		8	1		11
40	29	BRIGHTON	2-0	1-0	4854	Cooke, Tolmie(pen)		2	3	4	9	6		10		7						5		8	1		11
41	3 May	CHARLTON	2-3	2-1	6526	Saunders(2)		2	3	4	9	6	12	10		7						5		8	1		11*
42	5	Oldham	1-2	1-0	4493	Bishop		2		4	9	6	11	10		7						5		8	1	3	12

F.A. CUP

	Date	Opposition	Res.	H.T.	Att.	Goalscorers	Carr	Haigh	McCartney	Ashurst	Baker	Halsall	Gorman	Bishop	Entwistle	Hill	Gavin	Robson	Halpin	Mayes	Maunders	Wakenshaw	Cooke	Endersby	Lomax	McGarvey	Tolmie
3R	13	Q. PARK RANGERS	1-0	1-0	5080	Cooke			3	4	9	6		10		7				11		5		8	1	2	
4R	25	Peterborough	0-1	0-1	8311				3	4		6	12	10		7				11		5	9*	8	1	2	

LEAGUE CUP

	Date	Opposition	Res.	H.T.	Att.	Goalscorers	Carr	Haigh	McCartney	Ashurst	Baker	Halsall	Gorman	Bishop	Entwistle	Hill	Gavin	Robson	Halpin	Mayes	Maunders	Wakenshaw	Cooke	Endersby	Lomax	McGarvey	Tolmie
1R1	20 Aug	Crewe	3-3	2-2	1732	Gavin, Mayes(2)	1	2	3		5		4	6	9	10	11		7	8							
1R2	3 Sep	CREWE	3-4	2-1	2520	Halpin(2), Bishop	1	2	3		5	10	8	6	9				11	7		4					

Final League Table

		Pl.	Home				Away					F.	A.	Pts
			W	D	L	F	A	W	D	L	F	A			
1	Norwich City	42	16	4	1	51	15	9	5	7	33	22	84	37	84
2	Charlton Athletic	42	14	5	2	44	15	8	6	7	34	30	78	45	77
3	Wimbledon	42	13	6	2	38	16	8	7	6	20	21	58	37	76
4	Portsmouth	42	13	4	4	43	17	9	3	9	26	24	69	41	73
5	Crystal Palace	42	12	3	6	29	22	7	6	8	28	30	57	52	66
6	Hull City	42	11	7	3	39	19	6	6	9	26	36	65	55	64
7	Sheffield United	42	10	7	4	36	24	7	4	10	28	39	64	63	62
8	Oldham Athletic	42	13	4	4	40	28	4	5	12	22	33	62	61	60
9	Millwall	42	12	3	6	39	24	5	5	11	25	41	64	65	59
10	Stoke City	42	8	11	2	29	16	6	4	11	19	34	48	50	57
11	Brighton & Hove A.	42	10	5	6	42	30	6	3	12	22	34	64	64	56
12	Barnsley	42	9	6	6	29	26	5	8	8	18	24	47	50	56
13	Bradford City	42	14	1	6	36	24	2	5	14	15	39	51	63	54
14	Leeds United	42	9	7	5	30	22	6	1	14	26	50	56	72	53
15	Grimsby Town	42	11	4	6	35	24	3	6	12	23	38	58	62	52
16	Huddersfield Town	42	10	6	5	30	23	4	4	13	21	44	51	67	52
17	Shrewsbury Town	42	11	5	5	29	20	3	4	14	23	44	52	64	51
18	Sunderland	42	10	5	6	33	29	3	6	12	14	32	47	61	50
19	Blackburn Rovers	42	10	4	7	30	20	2	9	10	23	42	53	62	49
20	Carlisle United	42	10	2	9	30	28	3	5	13	17	43	47	71	46
21	Middlesbrough	42	8	6	7	26	23	4	3	14	18	30	44	53	45
22	Fulham	42	8	3	10	29	32	2	3	16	16	37	45	69	36

- 1985/86 Season -

BACK ROW (L to R): Paul Haigh, Paul Baker, Dave McKellar, Kevin Carr, Jack Ashurst (team capt.), Andy Hill.
MIDDLE ROW (L to R): Bob Stokoe (Team Manager), Paul Gorman, Ian Bishop, Mick Halsall, Mick McCartney, Bryan Robson (now with Gateshead).
FRONT ROW (L to R): Alan Mayes, Wayne Entwistle, Andrew Jenkins (Chairman), Mark Gavin, John Halpin.

- 1986/87 Season -

Back Row: Paul Haigh, Mick Halsall, Mick McCartney, Geoff Lomax, John Cooke.
Centre: Ken Oliver, Paul Gorman, Paul Baker, Kevin Carr, Scott Endersby, Andy Hill, Wes Saunders, Scott McGarvey.
Front Row: Ian Bishop, Garry Worrall, Harry Gregg (Team Manager), John Halpin, Bob Wakenshaw, Alan Mayes (Not on picture).

SEASON 1986/87

DIVISION 3

No.	Date	Opposition	Res.	H.T.	Att.	Goalscorers	Endersby	Lomax	McCartney	Wright	Saunders	Halsall	Baker	Cooke	McGarvey	Bishop	Worrall	Poskett	Haigh	Groman	Carr	Lynam	Patterson	Halpin	Davies	Nixon	Dobie	Russell	Robinson	Hunton
1	23 Aug	Chester	2-2	2-1	3425	McGarvey(pen), Baker	1	2	3	4	5	6*	7	8	9	10	11	12												
2	30	YORK	2-2	1-0	3593	McGarvey, Poskett	1		3	4	5		7	8	9*	10	11	12	2	6										
3	6 Sep	Blackpool	2-1	2-1	4188	Poskett(2)			3	4	5	6*	7	8		10	11	9	2		1									
4	13	WALSALL	0-3	0-1	3281		1		3	4	5	6	7*	8		10	11	9	2	12										
5	16	BRENTFORD	0-0	0-0	2904		1		3	4		6	5	8		10	11	9	2			7								
6	20	Bristol City	0-3	0-2	7040		1		3	4	5*	6	7	8		10	11	9	2				12							
7	27	MANSFIELD	1-2	1-1	2817	Cooke	1		3	4		6	5	8		10	11	9	2				7							
8	11 Oct	DARLINGTON	1-0	0-0	3087	Saunders	1		3	4	5	6		8	9	10	11	7	2											
9	14	Doncaster	0-2	0-1	2134		1		3	4	5	6	7	8	9	10	11*	12	2											
10	18	Gillingham	0-1	0-0	4207		1		3	4	5	6	7	8	9	10	11*	12	2											
11	21	BURY	2-1	1-1	2444	Baker, Saunders	1		3	4	5		7	8	9	10	11		2	6										
12	25	BRISTOL ROVERS	2-0	1-0	2799	Baker, Saunders	1		3	4	5		7	8	9	10	11		2	6										
13	28	Newport	1-1	1-1	1540	Cooke	1		3*	4	5	6	7	8	9	10			2	11										
14	1 Nov	Wigan	0-2	0-2	2982		1		3	4	5	6	7*		9	10	11	12	2	8										
15	4	PORT VALE	2-0	0-0	2748	McGarvey, Halsall	1		3	4	5	6			9	10	11	7	2	8										
16	8	Bournemouth	1-2	0-0	4284	Bishop	1		3	4	5	6			9	10	11	7	2	8										
17	22	FULHAM	1-3	0-0	2462	Poskett	1		3	4	5	6	12		9	10*		7	2	8					11					
18	29	Swindon	0-2	0-0	6194		1		3	4	5		7			10	8	9	2	6					11					
19	13 Dec	Chesterfield	2-3	0-0	1973	McGarvey, Halsall	1		3	4	5	6			9	10			2	8					11	7				
20	21	NOTTS COUNTY	0-2	0-0	2811		1			4	5	6	3	8	9	10			2						11	7				
21	26	Middlesbrough	0-1	0-0	14216		1		3	4	5	6*	12	8	9	10			2						11	7				
22	27	ROTHERHAM	3-5	1-3	2381	Baker(2), Davies	1		5	3	8	4	6			10		7	2							9	11			
23	3 Jan	Fulham	0-3	0-0	3700			2		4	5	6	7	8	9*	10				12	3	1			11					
24	24	BLACKPOOL	3-1	2-1	3048	McGarvey, Baker, Haigh		2		5	6	7	8	9	10	11			4	3			1							
25	3 Feb	BOLTON	0-0	0-0	2535			2		5	6	7	8	9	10	11			4	3			1							
26	7	Brentford	1-3	1-1	3032	McGarvey		2	5		6	7*	8	9	10	11	12		4	3			1							
27	14	BRISTOL CITY	1-2	0-2	2500	McGarvey(pen)		2	5*		6	7	8	9	10	11	12		4	3			1							
28	21	Mansfield	0-2	0-0	2082			2			6	5	8	9	10	11	7		4	3			1							
29	28	NEWPORT	2-2	0-1	2192	McGarvey, Bishop		2	6			5	8	9	10	11	7*		4	3			1					12		
30	3 Mar	WIGAN	0-2	0-0	2278			2	6			5	7	9*	8	11	10		4	3			1					12		
31	14	GILLINGHAM	2-4	2-0	2117	Baker, Poskett		2	6			5	8		11	7	10		4	3			1					12	9*	
32	17	Bury	0-0	0-0	1927			2	6	5			8		10	11	7		3	4			1					9		
33	21	Darlington	1-0	0-0	2029	Poskett		2	6	5			8		10	11	7		3	4			1					9		
34	28	DONCASTER	1-0	1-0	2002	Baker		2	6	5			9	8	10	11*	7		3	4			1			12				
35	31	York	0-2	0-1	2557			2	6	5			9	8	10*	11	7		3	4			1			12				
36	4 Apr	BOURNEMOUTH	0-0	0-0	2005			2	6	5			7			9			3	4			1					11	8	10
37	7	Walsall	0-3	0-1	4102			2	6	5			7			9			3	4		12	1					11	8*	10
38	11	Port Vale	1-0	0-0	2449	Russell		2	6	5			7	8		11*	9		3	4			1					12		10
39	18	Bolton	0-2	0-1	4241			2	6	5			7	8		11*	9		3	4			1					12		10
40	20	MIDDLESBROUGH	0-1	0-1	5929		1	2	6	5			12	8		10			3	4								11*		7
41	22	Bristol Rovers	0-4	0-2	2435		1	2	6	5			7	8		10			3	4								11		7
42	26	Notts County	1-2	1-1	4808	Russell	1		6	5			7	8		10			3	4								11		2
43	2 May	SWINDON	0-3	0-1	2082		1	2	6	5			7			10			3	4*		12						11		8
44	4	Rotherham	1-2	0-2	2598	Poskett		2								10	11	9	3	4			7						8	1
45	6	CHESTER	0-2	0-1	1287			2								10	11	9	3	4			7						6	1
46	9	CHESTERFIELD	3-0	1-0	1436	Bishop, Poskett, Baker		2		4			7		9	11	8	10*	3	5		12							6	1

F.A. CUP

	Date	Opposition	Res.	H.T.	Att.	Goalscorers	Endersby	Lomax	McCartney	Wright	Saunders	Halsall	Baker	Cooke	McGarvey	Bishop	Worrall	Poskett	Haigh	Groman	Carr	Lynam
1R	15 Nov	Notts County	1-1	0-0	4629	Bishop	1		3	4	5	6			9	10	11	7	2	8		
1Rr	18	NOTTS COUNTY	0-3	0-1	3742		1		3	4	5	6	9			10	11*	7	2	8		12

LEAGUE CUP

	Date	Opposition	Res.	H.T.	Att.	Goalscorers	Endersby	Lomax	McCartney	Wright	Saunders	Halsall	Baker	Cooke	McGarvey	Bishop	Worrall	Poskett	Haigh	Groman	Carr
1R1	2 Sep	GRIMSBY	1-0	1-0	2861	Baker	1		3	4	5	6	7	8		10	11	9	2		
1R2	9	Grimsby	0-2	0-0	3902		1		3	4	5	6	7	8		10	11	9	2		1

Final League Table

		Pl.	Home					Away					F.	A.	Pts
			W	D	L	F	A	W	D	L	F	A			
1	Bournemouth	46	19	3	1	44	14	10	7	6	32	26	76	40	97
2	Middlesbrough	46	16	5	2	38	11	12	5	6	29	19	67	30	94
3	Swindon Town	46	14	5	4	37	19	11	7	5	40	28	77	47	87
4	Wigan Athletic	46	15	5	3	47	26	10	5	8	36	34	83	60	85
5	Gillingham	46	16	5	2	42	14	7	4	12	23	34	65	48	78
6	Bristol City	46	14	6	3	42	15	7	8	8	21	21	63	36	77
7	Notts County	46	14	6	3	52	24	7	7	9	25	32	77	56	76
8	Walsall	46	16	4	3	50	27	6	5	12	30	40	80	67	75
9	Blackpool	46	11	7	5	35	20	5	9	9	39	39	74	59	64
10	Mansfield Town	46	9	9	5	30	23	6	7	10	22	32	52	55	61
11	Brentford	46	9	7	7	39	32	6	9	8	25	34	64	66	60
12	Port Vale	46	8	6	9	43	36	7	6	10	33	34	76	70	57
13	Doncaster Rovers	46	11	8	4	32	19	3	7	13	24	43	56	62	57
14	Rotherham United	46	10	6	7	29	23	5	6	12	19	34	48	57	57
15	Chester City	46	7	9	7	32	28	6	8	9	29	31	61	59	56
16	Bury	46	9	7	7	30	26	5	6	12	24	34	54	60	55
17	Chesterfield	46	11	5	7	36	33	2	10	11	20	36	56	69	54
18	Fulham	46	8	8	7	35	41	4	9	10	24	36	59	77	53
19	Bristol Rovers	46	7	8	8	26	29	6	4	13	23	46	49	75	51
20	York City	46	11	8	4	34	29	1	5	17	21	50	55	79	49
21	Bolton Wanderers	46	8	5	10	29	26	2	10	11	17	32	46	58	45
22	Carlisle United	46	5	11	7	26	35	3	3	17	13	43	39	78	38
23	Darlington	46	6	10	7	25	28	1	6	16	20	49	45	77	37
24	Newport County	46	4	9	10	26	34	4	4	15	23	52	49	86	37

SEASON 1987/88
DIVISION 4

No.	Date	Opposition	Res.	H.T.	Att.	Goalscorers
1	15 Aug	Peterborough	0-1	0-1	4000	
2	22	SCUNTHOPRE	3-1	0-0	2074	Robinson, Hetherington, O.G.
3	29	Burnley	3-4	1-3	5781	Cooke, Poskett(2,1pen)
4	31	HEREFORD	3-1	1-1	2708	Hetherington, Poskett, Cooke
5	4 Sep	Stockport	0-3	0-1	2257	
6	12	HARTLEPOOL	1-3	0-2	2463	Bishop
7	16	Exeter	1-1	1-1	3347	Bishop
8	19	Cardiff	2-4	2-1	2659	Hetherington, Saunders
9	26	SCARBOROUGH	4-0	1-0	2693	Hetheringtn,Saundrs,Wrght,Pskett
10	29	DARLINGTON	3-3	2-2	2996	Clark, Bishop, Poskett
11	3 Oct	Rochdale	2-1	0-0	1940	Poskett(2)
12	10	WOLVES	0-1	0-1	2620	
13	17	Bolton	0-5	0-2	4184	
14	20	Colchester	0-1	0-1	1328	
15	24	TRANMERE	3-2	0-1	2160	Hetherington, Cooke, Houston
16	31	Crewe	1-4	0-3	2124	Hetherington
17	3 Nov	LEYTON ORIENT	1-2	1-1	2139	Hetherington
18	7	NEWPORT	3-1	2-0	1766	Hetherington, Saunders, Cooke
19	21	Wrexham	0-4	0-1	1485	
20	28	TORQUAY	3-3	3-2	2017	Robinson, Hetherington, Poskett
21	12 Dec	Swansea	1-3	0-1	3876	Robinson
22	18	CAMBRIDGE	2-1	2-0	1843	Saunders, Halpin
23	26	Scarborough	1-3	0-1	3261	Poskett
24	1 Jan	BURNLEY	3-4	2-2	4262	Poskett, Stephens, Halpin
25	2	Hartlepool	0-0	0-0	3153	
26	9	Darlington	1-2	0-1	2517	Stephens
27	16	CARDIFF	0-0	0-0	2344	
28	23	EXETER	0-0	0-0	1699	
29	30	Hereford	0-2	0-2	1904	
30	6 Feb	STOCKPORT	2-0	1-0	1842	Saunders, Wright(pen)
31	20	PETERBOROUGH	0-2	0-2	2026	
32	27	ROCHDALE	2-0	2-0	1983	Holdsworth, Wright
33	5 Mar	BOLTON	0-2	0-1	2796	
34	12	Wolves	1-3	0-1	9262	Hutchinson
35	19	CREWE	0-1	0-1	1834	
36	26	Tranmere	0-3	0-2	3093	
37	2 Apr	Newport	2-1	2-1	1376	Poskett(2)
38	4	WREXHAM	0-4	0-2	2284	
39	9	Leyton Orient	1-4	0-2	2861	Hutchinson
40	12	Scunthorpe	0-3	0-0	3514	
41	19	HALIFAX	1-1	0-0	1517	Fyfe
42	23	COLCHESTER	4-0	2-0	1496	Fyfe(2), Saddington, Halpin
43	26	Halifax	1-1	0-1	1005	Cooke
44	30	Torquay	0-1	0-1	3537	
45	2 May	SWANSEA	0-1	0-1	1854	
46	7	Cambridge	2-1	0-1	1738	Hetherington, Fyfe

Player appearances (shirt numbers by match)

Player columns: Crompton, Patterson, McNeil, Gorman, Wrighton, Sanders, Robinson, Cooke, Poskett, Bishop, Hetherington, Clarke, Harbach, Taylor, Fulbrook, Tynan, Harrison, Houston, Robertson, Prudhoe, Hampton, Halpin, Stephens, McCaffery, Saddington, Holdsworth, Mills, Carter, Rowell, Fyfe, Ogley

No	Cromp	Patt	McNe	Gorm	Wrig	Sand	Robi	Cook	Posk	Bish	Heth	Clar	Harb	Tayl	Fulb	Tyna	Harr	Hous	Robe	Prud	Hamp	Halp	Step	McCa	Sadd	Hold	Mill	Cart	Rowe	Fyfe	Ogle
1	1	2	3*	4	5	6	7	8	9	10	11	12																			
2	1	2		4	5	6	7	8	9	10	11	3																			
3	1	2		4	5	6	7	8	9	10	11*	3	12																		
4	1	2	3	4*	5	6		8	9	10	11	7	12																		
5	1	2	3	4	5	6		8	9	10	11	7																			
6	1	2	3	4*	5	6		8	9	10	11	7	12																		
7	1	2	3	4	5	6		8	9	10	11	7																			
8	1	2	3#	4	5	6	14	8	9*	10	11	7	12																		
9		2	3		5	6	4	8	9	10	11	7				1															
10		2	3		5	6	4	8	9	10	11	7				1															
11		2			5	6	4	8	9	10	11	7				1	3														
12		2	3		5	6	4*	8	9	10	11	7				1		12													
13		2	3	7	5		4	8	9		11			12		1	10*	6#	14												
14	1	2			5	3	4	8	9		11	7		14			10#	12	6*												
15	1	2	3*	4	5		12	8	9	10	11	7						6													
16		2			5	6		8	9	10	11	7				1	3				4										
17				12	5	6	2	8	9	10	11	7				1	3				4*										
18			2	12	5	6	3	8	9		11	7				1	10	14			4*										
19			2	4#	5	6	7	8	9		11				12	1	3				10*										
20			2	4	5*	6	7	8	9		11					1	3	12			10										
21			2		5	6	4	8	9		11	7				1	3				10										
22			2		5	6	4	8	9		11	7				1	3	12				10									
23			2	6	5		4	8	12		11	7				1	3					10	9								
24			2	6	5		4	8	11*		12	7				1	3					10	9								
25			2		5	6	4	8	11			7				1	3					10	9								
26			14	2	5	6	4	8	11*		12					1	3					10	9	7							
27			2		5	6	4	8			11#					1	3	12				10	9*	7							
28			2		5*	6	4	8			12	9				1	3					10		7	11						
29			2		5	6	4				8	9				1	3	12				10		7*	11						
30			9		5	6		8			11	2				1	3					10		7			4				
31			2		5		7				11	3				1						10		6	8	4	9*	12			
32			2		5		8	7	11			3				1						10		6		4	9				
33			2		5		8*	7	11			3				1						10		6	12	4	9				
34			2		5		12	7	11*			3				1						10		6	8	4	9				
35			9		5		7*				11	2					3					10		6	8	4			1		
36			9		5					11	3#						14	2				10		6*	8	4			1	7	
37					5			9		11*	2						3					10		6	8	4			1	7	
38					5			9	7	12	3											10		6*	8	4			1	11	2
39			3		5	6		9#	7	12	2					1	14					10			8	4				11	
40			3		5	6		9	7	12	2					1						10			8	4				11	
41			3		5	6		9	7		2					1						10			8	4				11	12
42			3		5	6	12	9	7							1						10				4				11	8
43			3		5	6	11	9	7		10				2	1										4					8
44			3		5	6	11*	9	7		2				12	1						10				4					8
45			3		5	6		9*	7		10				11	2	1								12					8	4
46			3		5	6*		9	7	11	10				12	2	1													8	4

F.A. CUP

Rd	Date	Opposition	Res.	H.T.	Att.	Goalscorers
1R	14 Nov	Macclesfield	2-4	1-0	2385	Hetherington, Fulbrook

Appearances: Patterson 2, Gorman 4, Wrighton 5, Sanders 6, Robinson 3, Cooke 8, Poskett 9*, Hetherington 11, Clarke 7, Tynan 1, Harrison 10, Houston 12

LEAGUE CUP

Rd	Date	Opposition	Res.	H.T.	Att.	Goalscorers
1R1	18 Aug	Stockport	1-0	1-0	1476	Hetherington
1R2	25	STOCKPORT	3-0	0-0	2174	Hetherington(2), Cooke
2R1	22 Sep	OLDHAM	4-3	1-1	2271	Htheringtn,Pskett,Cooke,Wrght(p)
2R2	6 Oct	Oldham	1-4	0-1	4353	Cooke

Appearances:
- 1R1: Crompton 1, Patterson 2, Gorman 4, Wrighton 5, Sanders 6, Robinson 7, Cooke 8, Poskett 9, Bishop 10, Hetherington 11, Clarke 3
- 1R2: Crompton 1, Patterson 2*, McNeil 12, Gorman 4, Wrighton 5, Sanders 6, Robinson 7, Cooke 8, Poskett 9, Bishop 10, Hetherington 11, Clarke 3
- 2R1: Crompton 1, Patterson 2, McNeil 3, Wrighton 5, Sanders 6, Robinson 4, Cooke 8, Poskett 9, Bishop 10, Hetherington 11, Clarke 7
- 2R2: Patterson 2, Gorman 12, Wrighton 5, Sanders 6, Robinson 4, Cooke 8, Poskett 9, Bishop 10, Hetherington 11#, Clarke 7, Tynan 1, Houston 3*, Robertson 14

Final League Table

		Pl.	Home W	D	L	F	A	Away W	D	L	F	A	F.	A.	Pts
1	Wolverhampton W.	46	15	3	5	47	19	12	6	5	35	24	82	43	90
2	Cardiff City	46	15	6	2	39	14	9	7	7	27	27	66	41	85
3	Bolton Wanderers	46	15	6	2	42	12	7	6	10	24	30	66	42	78
4	Scunthorpe United	46	14	5	4	42	20	6	12	5	34	31	76	51	77
5	Torquay United	46	10	7	6	34	16	11	7	5	32	25	66	41	77
6	Swansea City	46	9	7	7	35	28	11	3	9	27	28	62	56	70
7	Peterborough Utd.	46	10	5	8	28	26	10	5	8	24	27	52	53	70
8	Leyton Orient	46	13	4	6	55	27	6	8	9	30	36	85	63	69
9	Colchester United	46	10	5	8	23	22	9	5	9	24	29	47	51	67
10	Burnley	46	12	5	6	31	22	8	2	13	26	40	57	62	67
11	Wrexham	46	13	3	7	46	26	7	3	13	23	32	69	58	66
12	Scarborough	46	12	8	3	38	19	5	6	12	18	29	56	48	65
13	Darlington	46	13	6	4	39	25	5	5	13	32	44	71	69	65
14	Tranmere Rovers	46	14	2	7	43	20	5	7	11	18	33	61	53	64
15	Cambridge United	46	10	6	7	32	24	6	7	10	18	28	50	52	61
16	Hartlepool United	46	9	7	7	25	26	7	5	11	25	32	50	57	59
17	Crewe Alexandra	46	7	11	5	25	19	6	8	9	32	34	57	53	58
18	Halifax Town	46	11	7	5	37	25	3	7	13	17	34	54	59	55
19	Hereford United	46	8	7	8	25	27	6	5	12	16	32	41	59	54
20	Stockport County	46	7	7	9	26	26	5	8	10	18	32	44	58	51
21	Rochdale	46	7	9	7	28	34	6	6	11	19	42	47	76	48
22	Exeter City	46	8	6	9	33	29	3	7	13	20	39	53	68	46
23	Carlisle United	46	9	5	9	38	33	3	7	11	19	53	57	86	44
24	Newport County	46	4	5	14	19	36	2	2	19	16	69	35	105	25

- 1987/88 Season -

CARLISLE UNITED A.F.C. – 1987–88

Back Row (L to R): John Cooke, Mark Patterson, Malcolm Poskett, Paul Gorman, Steve Crompton, Brent Hetherington, Peter Harbach, Paul Tynan.
Middle Row (L to R): Neil Wrightson, Ian Bishop, Bobby McNeil, Andy Robinson, Wes Saunders, Billy Wright, Ian Milburn
Front Row (L to R): Alan Stewart, John McNamee, Jason Priestley, Jim Robertson, Brian Sweeney, Steve Harkness, (all YTS trainees).

- 1988/89 Season -

(Back): Robertson, Hetherington, Holdsworth, Prudhoe, Walsh, Sendall, Dalziel.
(Second Row): Ogley, Marshall, Clark, Saddington, Gorman, Jeffries, Stephens, Fyfe.
(Third Row): Hampton (Physio), McNamee, Priestley, Middlemass (Manager), Jeffries (Chairman), Harkness, Milburn, McCaffey (Coach).   (Front): Elliott, Beal, Eagling, Heaney.

SEASON 1988/89
DIVISION 4

No.	Date	Opposition	Res.	H.T.	Att.	Goalscorers
1	27 Aug	PETERBOROUGH	2-2	1-1	2650	Hetherington(2)
2	3 Sep	York	1-1	1-0	2303	Walsh
3	10	TRANMERE	1-1	0-0	2384	Clark
4	16	Halifax	3-3	3-1	1546	Hetherington, Marshall, Sendall
5	20	Scunthorpe	1-1	0-1	3113	Gorman(pen)
6	24	ROTHERHAM	0-2	0-0	2862	
7	30	Cambridge	2-3	1-1	2043	Saddington, Walsh
8	4 Oct	COLCHESTER	1-2	0-0	2193	Sendall
9	8	Hereford	1-2	1-1	2127	Hetherington
10	15	TORQUAY	2-1	1-1	2164	Hetherington, Fyfe
11	22	Exeter	0-3	0-1	2235	
12	25	BURNLEY	0-0	0-0	4543	
13	29	Lincoln	2-0	0-0	3727	Hetherington(2)
14	5 Nov	SCARBOROUGH	0-1	0-1	2617	
15	8	Leyton Orient	0-2	0-0	2879	
16	12	DARLINGTON	1-2	0-2	2194	Dalziel(pen)
17	26	GRIMSBY	2-1	0-1	2175	Marshall, Hetherington
18	3 Dec	Wrexham	1-2	1-2	1892	O.G.
19	17	Hartlepool	2-0	2-0	1974	Saddington, Halpin
20	26	ROCHDALE	1-0	0-0	10013	Stephens
21	31	STOCKPORT	1-1	1-0	3724	O.G.
22	2 Jan	Crewe	0-1	0-1	4626	
23	10	Doncaster	3-1	1-0	2128	Gorman(3)
24	14	YORK	0-0	0-0	3462	
25	21	Peterborough	4-1	2-0	2537	Hetherington(2), Halpin, Graham
26	28	HALIFAX	3-1	0-0	3007	Halpin(2), Gorman
27	4 Feb	SCUNTHORPE	0-3	0-1	2627	
28	11	Rotherham	1-2	1-1	4111	Graham
29	18	HEREFORD	3-0	1-0	2548	Fyfe(2), Walsh
30	4 Mar	EXETER	1-0	0-0	2601	Sendall
31	11	Scarborough	1-0	0-0	2354	Saddington
32	14	LINCOLN	2-1	2-0	2691	Fyfe, Halpin
33	17	Tranmere	0-0	0-0	5143	
34	21	Burnley	0-0	0-0	5258	
35	25	CREWE	0-1	0-1	4866	
36	27	Rochdale	0-0	0-0	2145	
37	1 Apr	HARTLEPOOL	2-1	2-0	3158	Halpin(2)
38	4	DONCASTER	0-1	0-1	2991	
39	7	Stockport	1-1	0--1	2543	Saddington
40	15	CAMBRIDGE	1-1	1-0	2579	Sendall
41	21	Colchester	1-1	1-0	3908	Proudlock
42	29	Grimsby	0-0	0-0	3833	
43	1 May	LEYTON ORIENT	2-1	2-1	2410	Sendall, Hetherington
44	3	Torquay	0-1	0-1	1603	
45	6	Wrexham	1-2	0-0	2427	Sendall
46	13	Darlington	3-2	3-1	3049	Proudlock(2), Gorman

Player appearances (shirt numbers)

Column order: Prudhoe · Robertson · Dalziel · Saddington · Ogley · Clark · Marshall · Gorman · Sendall · Hetherington · Halpin · Walsh · Stephens · Graham · Fyfe · Fitzpatrick · McKellar · Nuttell · Jeffels · Butler · Harkness · Proudlock · Stonehouse

No.	Pru	Rob	Dal	Sad	Ogl	Clk	Mar	Gor	Sen	Het	Hal	Wal	Ste	Gra	Fyf	Fit	McK	Nut	Jef	But	Hrk	Pro	Sto
1	1	2	3	4	5	6	7	8	9	10	11												
2	1	2	3	4	5	6	11	8	9	10*		7	12										
3	1		3	4	5	6	7	8	9	14	11#	12	10*			2							
4	1		3	4	5	6	7	8	9	10	11					2							
5	1		3	4	5	6	11	8	9	10		7				2							
6	1		3	4	5	6	11	8	9	10			7*			2							
7	1	12	3*	4	5	6	11	8	9	10		7				2							
8	1			4	5	6	11	8	9		7		3			2		10					
9	1		3	4	5		11	8	9		7					6		10					
10			3	4	5		11	8		10		7		2	9	6	1						
11			3	4	5		11	8		12	10	7		2	9*	6	1						
12			3	4	5		11	8		10		7		2	9	6	1						
13			3	4	5		11	8		12	10	7		2	9*	6	1						
14			3	4	5		11	8		10		7		2	9*	6	1					12	
15			3	4	5		11	8			7			2	9	6	1	10					
16			3	4	5*		11	8#		10		7		2	9	6	1				12	14	
17		14		4			7	8		12	10	11	3	2	9*	6	1	5#					
18			3	4	5		7	8			11			2	9*	6	1			12			
19	1		3	4	5			8		12	7	11		2	9*	6				10			
20	1		3	4				8		12	7	11		2	9	6			5			10*	
21	1		3	4				8		10	7	11		2	9	6			5				
22			3	4				8	9	10	11			2		6	1		5	7			
23			3	4				8	12	10	11		7	2	9*	6	1		5				
24			3	4				8	12	10	11		7	9*	2	14	6#	1	5				
25			3	4				8		10	11		7	9*	2	12	6	1	5				
26			3	4				8		10	11		7	9*	2	12	6	1	5				
27			3	4				8		10	11		7	9*	2	12	6	1	5				
28			3	4				8		10	11		7	2	9	6	1		5				
29			3	4			12	8			11	7		2	9	6	1		5*		10		
30			3	4						10				9*	2	12	6	1	5		8		
31			3	4	7			8#		14	11		12	2	9*	6	1	5			10		
32			3	4				8		10	11			2	9	6	1		5	7			
33			3	4				8		10	11	12		2	9*	6	1		5	7			
34			3	4				8		10	11			2	9	6	1		5	7			
35			3	4				8#		14	11			2	9*	6	1		5	7		10	12
36			3	4*				8		12	11	7		2	9	6	1		5			10	
37				4				8			11	3		2	9	6	1		5	7		10	
38				4				8		12	11	3		2	9	6*	1		5	7		10	
39			3	4				8	9	12	11			2		6	1		5*	7		10	14
40			3	4				8	9#	12	11*	7		2		6	1		5			10	14
41			3	4				8	9					2		6	1		5			10	
42		2	3	4				8		10	12	11	7		6*	9	1		5				
43		2	3	4				9		10	11	7				6	1		5		8		
44	2#		3	4			14	8	9	12	11	7*				6	1		5		10		
45			3	4			14	8	9	7*	11			2		6#	1		5			12	10
46			3	4	6			8	9		11			2			1		5	7		10*	

F.A. CUP

	Date	Opposition	Res.	H.T.	Att.	Goalscorers
1R	19 Nov	Telford	1-1	0-0	2163	Walsh
1Rr	22	TELFORD	4-1	1-1	2833	Saddington, Fitzpatrick, Grman, Hlpin
2R	10 Dec	Scarborough	1-0	0-0	2849	O.G.
3R	7 Jan	LIVERPOOL	0-3	0-1	18556	

F.A. Cup player numbers:

	Sad	Mar	Gor	Het	Hal	Gra	Fyf	Fit	McK	Jef
1R	4		7	8	12	10	11	3	9*	2	6	1	5
1Rr	4		7	8		10	11	3	9	2	6	1	5
2R	3 4 5	7*	8	12	11	6	9	2	10	1
3R	7# 3 4		8	12	10	11		9*	2	14	6	1	5

LEAGUE CUP

	Date	Opposition	Res.	H.T.	Att.	Goalscorers
1R1	30 Aug	BLACKPOOL	1-1	0-1	2336	Gorman
1R2	6 Sep	Blackpool	0-3	0-1	2945	

League Cup player numbers:

	Pru	Rob	Dal	Sad	Ogl	Clk	Mar	Gor	Sen	Het	Hal	Ste	Gra
1R1	1	2	3	4	5	6	7	8	9*	10	11		12
1R2	1	2	3	4	5	6	11	8	9	10#		7	12		14

Final League Table

		Pl.	Home W	D	L	F	A	Away W	D	L	F	A	F.	A.	Pts
1	Rotherham United	46	13	6	4	44	18	9	10	4	32	17	76	35	82
2	Tranmere Rovers	46	15	6	2	34	13	6	11	6	28	30	62	43	80
3	Crewe Alexandra	46	13	7	3	42	24	8	8	7	25	24	67	48	78
4	Scunthorpe United	46	11	9	3	40	22	10	5	8	37	35	77	57	77
5	Scarborough	46	12	7	4	33	23	9	7	7	34	29	67	52	77
6	Leyton Orient	46	16	2	5	61	19	5	10	8	25	31	86	50	75
7	Wrexham	46	12	7	4	44	28	7	7	9	33	35	77	63	71
8	Cambridge United	46	13	7	3	45	25	5	7	11	26	37	71	62	68
9	Grimsby Town	46	11	9	3	33	18	6	6	11	32	41	65	59	66
10	Lincoln City	46	12	6	5	39	26	6	4	13	25	34	64	60	64
11	York City	46	10	8	5	43	27	7	5	11	19	36	62	63	64
12	Carlisle United	46	9	6	8	26	25	6	9	8	27	27	53	52	60
13	Exeter City	46	14	4	5	46	23	4	2	17	19	45	65	68	60
14	Torquay United	46	15	2	6	32	23	2	6	15	13	37	45	60	59
15	Hereford United	46	11	8	4	40	27	3	8	12	26	45	66	72	58
16	Burnley	46	12	6	5	35	20	2	7	14	17	41	52	61	55
17	Peterborough Utd.	46	10	3	10	29	32	4	9	10	23	42	52	74	54
18	Rochdale	46	10	10	3	32	26	3	4	16	24	56	56	82	53
19	Hartlepool United	46	10	6	7	33	33	4	4	15	17	45	50	78	52
20	Stockport County	46	8	10	5	31	20	2	11	10	23	32	54	52	51
21	Halifax Town	46	10	7	6	42	27	3	4	16	27	48	69	75	50
22	Colchester United	46	8	7	8	35	30	4	7	12	25	48	60	78	50
23	Doncaster Rovers	46	9	6	8	32	32	4	4	15	17	44	49	78	49
24	Darlington	46	3	12	8	28	38	5	6	12	25	38	53	76	42

SEASON 1989/90

DIVISION 4

No.	Date	Opposition	Res.	H.T.	Att.	Goalscorers	McKellar	Graham	Wharton	Saddington	Ogley	Gorman	Shepherd	Walsh	Walwyn	Proudlock	Halpin	Dalziel	Fyfe	Fitzpatrick	Hetherington	Jones	Miller	Sendall	Cullen	Goldsmith	Norris	McCall	Edwards	Robertson	Rose
1	19 Aug	Hereford	2-2	1-1	2285	Ogley, Walsh	1	2	3	4	5	6	7	8	9	10	11														
2	26	CHESTERFIELD	4-3	1-2	3059	Fyfe(2), Proudlock, Walwyn	1	2		4	5*		7	8	9	10	11	3	12	6											
3	2 Sep	Exeter	0-0	0-0	3338		1	2		4	5		7		9	10	11	3	8	6											
4	9	GRIMSBY	1-1	0-0	3360	Fyfe	1	2		4	5#	8	7		9*	10	11	3	12	6	14										
5	15	Halifax	1-1	0-0	2121	Walwyn	1	2		4			7		9	10	11	3		6		5	8								
6	23	GILLINGHAM	3-0	1-0	3185	Proudlock, Fitzpatrick, Miller	1	2		4					9	8*	11	3	10	6	12	5	7								
7	26	Cambridge	2-1	0-0	2607	Dalziel, Walwyn	1	2		4					9	8	11	3	10	6		5	7								
8	30	COLCHESTER	1-0	1-0	3979	Fyfe	1	2		4				12	9	8*	11	3	10	6		5	7								
9	7 Oct	WREXHAM	1-0	0-0	3699	Hetherington	1	2		4				8	9		11	3	10*	6	12	5	7								
10	14	Doncaster	1-1	0-1	2419	Proudlock	1	2		4				8#	9*	10	11	3	12	6	14	5	7								
11	17	SCUNTHORPE	0-1	0-0	4793		1	2		4				8#	9*	10	11	3	12	6	14	5	7								
12	21	Scarborough	1-2	1-1	2592	Walwyn	1	2#		4				8	9*	10	11	3	12	6	14	5	7								
13	28	HARTLEPOOL	1-0	0-0	3699	Hetherington	1	2#		4				8	9*	10	11	3		6	14	5	7	12							
14	31	Aldershot	0-1	0-0	2123		1	2		4				8	9*	10	11	3#		6		5	7	12							
15	4 Nov	MAIDSTONE	3-2	1-0	3395	Proudlock, Sendall, O.G.	1	2		4			7	8#		10	11		9*	6		5		3	12						
16	11	Torquay	2-1	0-0	2266	Sendall(2)	1	2		4			7	12		10#	11	3*		6		5	8	9							
17	25	Rochdale	2-1	1-0	1920	Saddington, Miller	1	2		4			7		12	10	11*	3		6		5	8	9							
18	2 Dec	PETERBOROUGH	0-0	0-0	4608		1	2		4			7	14	9			3	12	6		5	8			10*					
19	17	STOCKPORT	3-1	1-1	4971	Proudlock, Miller, Cullen	1	2		4			7		9*	10		3	12	6		5	8		11						
20	26	Burnley	1-2	1-1	12276	Proudlock	1	2#		4				8	9*	10		3		6		5	7	12	11	14					
21	30	Lincoln	3-1	1-1	4793	Saddington, Shepherd	1	2		4			8		9			3		6		5	7				11	10			
22	1 Jan	YORK	2-1	0-1	6510	Jones, Saddington(pen)	1	2		4			8*	12	9			3		6		5	7				11	10			
23	6	SOUTHEND	3-0	1-0	6198	Walwyn(2), Norris	1	2		4			8	12	9			3		6		5*	7				11	10			
24	13	Chesterfield	0-3	0-3	4801		1	2		4	5		8		9	12		3		6			7				11	10			
25	20	HEREFORD	2-1	0-0	4726	Fitzpatrick, Walwyn	1	5		4			8	2	9	12		3		6		7*					11	10			
26	27	Grimsby	0-1	0-0	4657		1	5		4			8	2	9	12		3*		6			7				11	10			
27	10 Feb	HALIFAX	1-1	0-0	4844	Fitzpatrick	1			4			7	2	9*					6		5	8	14			11	10*	3		
28	13	EXETER	1-0	0-0	8461	Shepherd	1			4			7	2	9					6		5	8				11		3		
29	17	Peterborough	0-3	0-1	4088		1	2		4			7		9				10*	6		5	8#				11	12	3		
30	24	ROCHDALE	0-1	0-0	4904		1	2		4			7	12	9				10*	6		5	8				11	12	3		
31	27	Gillingham	1-2	1-2	3177	Sendall	1	2		4			7							6		5	8	12			11		3*		
32	3 Mar	Southend	0-2	0-0	3465		1	5		4			7	2	9#		11			6			8	10		12	14	3*			
33	6	Colchester	0-4	0-2	3752		1	5		4			7	2		10							8	9		11*	12		3		
34	17	Wrexham	0-1	0-0	3409		1	5		4			7			10							8	9		11	10*		3	2	
35	20	DONCASTER	1-0	0-0	3970	Jones	1	2		4			12		7					6		5	8	9			11	10*			
36	24	Scunthorpe	3-2	0-1	3406	Saddington(pen), Jones, Norris		2		4			9		7					6		5	8				11	10		3	1
37	31	SCARBOROUGH	3-1	0-0	4304	Saddington(2,1pen), Goldsmith		2		4			12	9#	7*					6		5	8	14			11	10		3	1
38	4 Apr	CAMBRIDGE	3-1	2-0	4890	Walwyn(2), Walsh		2		4			7		9					6		5	8				11	10		3	1
39	7	Hartlepool	0-1	0-0	3769			2		4			7		9	12				6		5	8				11*	10		3	1
40	10	ALDERSHOT	1-3	1-1	4998	Saddington(pen)		2		4			7		9	12				6		5	8				11	10*		3	1
41	14	York	1-0	1-0	2805	Jones		2		4			7		9		11			6		5	8	10						3	1
42	16	BURNLEY	1-1	0-0	6736	Fitzpatrick		2		4			3#	7	9	10*				6		5	8	14		11#	12				1
43	20	Stockport	1-3	1-2	3819	Walwyn		2		4			3#	7	9	10				6		5	8	14		12	11*				1
44	24	LINCOLN	1-2	0-2	5064	Saddington(pen)				4			7		9*	10				6		5	2	12		11	8		3		1
45	28	TORQUAY	2-0	0-0	3997	Norris, Walsh				4			7		9	10				6		5	2			11	8		3		1
46	5 May	Maidstone	2-5	1-3	5008	Walwyn, Saddington				4			7		9	10				6		5	2	11		12	8*		3		1

F.A. CUP

No.	Date	Opposition	Res.	H.T.	Att.	Goalscorers	McKellar	Graham	Wharton	Saddington	Ogley	Gorman	Shepherd	Walsh	Walwyn	Proudlock	Halpin	Dalziel	Fyfe	Fitzpatrick	Hetherington	Jones	Miller	Sendall	Cullen
1R	18 Nov	WREXHAM	3-0	1-0	4588	Proudlock(2), Sendall	1	2		4			7	3		10	11			6		5	8	9	
2R	9 Dec	Wigan	0-2	0-0	4151		1	2		4			7	6	9	10		3	12		14	5	8#	11*	

LEAGUE CUP

No.	Date	Opposition	Res.	H.T.	Att.	Goalscorers	McKellar	Graham	Wharton	Saddington	Ogley	Gorman	Shepherd	Walsh	Walwyn	Proudlock	Halpin	Dalziel	Fyfe	Fitzpatrick	Hetherington	Jones	Robertson
1R1	22 Aug	Halifax	1-3	1-1	1604	Shepherd	1	6	3	4	5		8	7	9	10*	11					12	2
1R2	29	HALIFAX	1-0	0-0	3054	Walwyn	1	2	14	4	5		7*	8	9	10	11	3	12	6			

Final League Table

		Pl.	Home					Away					F.	A.	Pts
			W	D	L	F	A	W	D	L	F	A			
1	Exeter City	46	20	3	0	50	14	8	2	13	33	34	83	48	89
2	Grimsby Town	46	14	4	5	41	20	8	9	6	29	27	70	47	79
3	Southend United	46	15	3	5	35	14	7	6	10	26	34	61	48	75
4	Stockport County	46	13	6	4	45	27	8	5	10	23	35	68	62	74
5	Maidstone United	46	14	4	5	49	21	8	3	12	28	40	77	61	73
6	Cambridge United	46	14	3	6	45	30	7	7	9	31	36	76	66	73
7	Chesterfield	46	12	9	2	41	19	7	5	11	22	31	63	50	71
8	Carlisle United	46	15	4	4	38	20	6	4	13	23	40	61	60	71
9	Peterborough Utd.	46	10	8	5	35	23	7	9	7	24	23	59	46	68
10	Lincoln City	46	11	6	6	30	27	7	8	8	18	21	48	48	68
11	Scunthorpe United	46	9	9	5	42	25	8	6	9	27	29	69	54	66
12	Rochdale	46	11	4	8	28	23	9	2	12	24	32	52	55	66
13	York City	46	10	5	8	29	24	6	11	6	26	29	55	53	64
14	Gillingham	46	9	8	6	28	21	8	3	12	18	27	46	48	62
15	Torquay United	46	12	9	2	33	29	3	10	10	20	37	53	66	57
16	Burnley	46	6	10	7	19	18	8	4	11	26	37	45	55	56
17	Hereford United	46	7	4	12	31	32	8	6	9	25	30	56	62	55
18	Scarborough	46	10	5	8	35	28	5	5	13	25	45	60	73	55
19	Hartlepool United	46	12	4	7	45	33	3	6	14	21	55	66	88	55
20	Doncaster Rovers	46	7	7	9	29	29	7	2	14	24	31	53	60	51
21	Wrexham	46	8	8	7	28	28	5	4	14	23	39	51	67	51
22	Aldershot	46	8	7	8	28	26	4	7	12	21	43	49	69	50
23	Halifax Town	46	6	9	9	31	29	7	1	14	26	36	57	65	49
24	Colchester United	46	9	3	11	26	25	2	7	14	22	50	48	75	43

- 1989/90 Season -

Back row: Paul Proudlock, Mike Graham, Tony Fyfe, Keith Walwyn, Jimmy Robertson, Richard Sendall, Brent Hetherington
Middle row: Simon Jeffels, Paul Gorman, Dave McKellar, Paul Fitzpatrick, Jason Priestley, Mark Ogley, Nigel Saddington
Front row: Peter Hampton (Physio), Tony Shepherd, Ian Dalziel, Clive Middlemass (Manager), Andrew Jenkins (Chairman), John Halpin, Derek Walsh, Aidan McCaffery (Coach)

- 1990/91 Season -

Back Row Left to Right: Tony Shepherd, Robert Edwards, Mike Graham, Ian Taylor, Jason Priestley, Anthony Caig, Dave Miller, Ian Dalziel, John Halpin.

3rd Row Left to Right: Simon Jeffels, Paul Fitzpatrick, Darren Edmonson, Richard Sendall, Paul Proudlock, Keith Walwyn, Craig Goldsmith, Steve Norris, Nigel Saddington, John Holliday, Alex Jones.

2nd Row Left to Right: Geoff Bell, Jeff Thorpe, Peter Hampton (Asst. Manager), Eric Gates, Mike Bennett, Clive Middlemass (Manager), Mr. A. H. Jenkins (Chairman), Derek Walsh, Eamonn Elliott, Aidan McCaffery (Youth Team Coach), David Wilkes (Community Football Officer), Marcus Thompson, Derek Townsley.

Front Row Left to Right: Lee Armstrong, Richard Nugent, Simon Todd, Craig Potts, Simon Reay, Gary Parker, Nicky Cranston, Calum Graham.

SEASON 1990/91

DIVISION 4

No.	Date	Opposition	Res.	H.T.	Att.	Goalscorers	Priestley	Miller	Edwards	Graham	Jones	Fitzpatrick	Walsh	Shepherd	Walwyn	Gates	Proudlock	Goldsmith	Norris	Sendall	Methven	Jeffels	Edmondson	Fyfe	Owen	Thorpe	Bennett	Siddall	Elliott	Wilkes	Halpin	Dalziel	Holliday	Lillis	Armstrong
1	25 Aug	DONCASTER	2-3	1-2	4218	Walwyn, Shepherd	1	2	3	4	5	6	7*	8	9	10#	11	12	14																
2	1 Sep	Peterborough	1-1	1-1	3675	Norris	1	2	3	4#	5	6	7	8	9	10*	11				14	12													
3	8	MAIDSTONE	1-0	1-0	3808	Edwards(pen)	1	2	3			6	7	8	9*	10	11				12	5													
4	15	Hereford	2-4	0-2	2773	Proudlock, Edwards	1	2	3	4		6*	7	8		10#	11	12	14	9	5														
5	17	Stockport	1-3	0-1	3118	Norris	1	2	3			6	7	8		10*	11	12	9		5	4													
6	22	HARTLEPOOL	1-0		3303	Gates	1	2	3			6	7	8	12	10	11		9*		5	4													
7	27	BURNLEY	1-1	1-0	5205	Walwyn	1	2	3			6	7	8	9	10	11			5	4														
8	2	Gillingham	1-2	1-2	3022	Walwyn	1	2	3			6	7	8	9	10	11			5	4														
9	6	Walsall	1-1	1-0	4248	Gates	1	2	3			6	7	8	9	10	11			5	4														
10	13	HALIFAX	0-3	0-3	3697		1	2	3			6#	7	8	9*	10	11			5	4	12	14												
11	20	CHESTERFIELD	1-0	1-0	3029	Gates	1	2	3			6	7	8		10*	11			5	4	12	9												
12	24	Scarborough	1-1	0-1	1329	Shepherd	1	2#	3			6	7	8	9*	12	10			5	4	11	14												
13	27	Torquay	0-3	0-0	3269		1		3			6	7	8		10	11			5	4	2*	9	12											
14	3 Nov	LINCOLN	0-0	0-0	3095		1		3	4		6	8	12	10	11*				5	2	9													
15	10	YORK	1-0	0-0	2888	Gates	1		4	5	6	7	8	9	10					2	11	3													
16	24	Rochdale	1-0	0-0	1733	Gates			4	5	6	7	8	9	10	11				2		3	1												
17	1 Dec	Wrexham	0-3	0-2	1682			3		5		2	8	9	10	11	14		12	6	7*			1	4#										
18	15	NORTHAMPTON	4-1	2-0	2873	Proudlock, Walwyn, Gates, Jeffels	6	3		5		7	8	9	10	11			4	2				1												
19	23	BLACKPOOL	1-0	1-0	5195	Edwards(pen)	6	3		5	12	7*	8	9	10	11			4	2				1												
20	26	Cardiff	1-3	0-1	2281	Jeffels	6	3		5	12		8	9*	10	11			4	2				14	7#	1									
21	29	Scunthorpe	0-2	0-0	2971		7	3		5			8	9*	10	11			4	2				14	6	1	12								
22	1 Jan	ALDERSHO	1-2	0-1		Miller	7#	3		5	6		8	9	10	11			4	2				12		1									
23	5	Darlington	1-3	0-1	3726	Shepherd	2	3		5	6		8	9*	10#	7			12	4				11		1			14						
24	12	PETERBOROUGH	3-2	1-1	2744	Jeffels, Halpin, Gates	2	3		5	6		8	9*	10	7			12	4				1					11						
25	19	Doncaster	0-4	0-0	2447		8	3		5	6#			9	10	7			4	2	12	14		1					11						
26	26	HEREFORD	0-1	0-1	2572		2	3		5			9*		10	7			4	6	12			1					11	8				
27	2 Feb	STOCKPORT	1-0	1-0	2750	O.G.	2	3	4	5			8		10*	12			9		6			1					11	7				
28	5	Hartlepool	1-4	0-2	2670	Edwards(pen)	2	3	4*	5			8		10	12			9		6			1					11	7				
29	16	ROCHDALE	1-1	0-0	2505	Miller	7	3	4		6		8		10				9		2			1					11	5				
30	23	York	0-2	0-0	2002		7	3	4		6		8		12	10			9*		2	14		1					11	5				
31	26	DARLINGTON	0-2	0-1	2895		2	3	4		6		8		10	7*			9#		14			1		5	13		11					
32	2 Mar	WREXHAM	2-0	0-0	2207	Lillis, Gates	2	3	4		6		8		10	7			12		5			1					11				9*	
33	9	Northampton	1-1	0-1	3216	Proudlock	2	3	4		6		8		10*	7			12		1			11					5			9		
34	12	GILLINGHAM	0-4	0-2	2633		2	3	4		6*		8		10#	7			9		12	14		1					11	5				
35	16	Burnley	1-2	1-0	6635	Proudlock	1	2	3	4#		14	8		12	7			5	10	1	11		6								9*		
36	19	Halifax	1-1	1-1	1004	Edwards(pen)	1	2	3	4			8			7			12	5	10			11						6		9*		
37	23	Walsall	0-3	0-3	2433		1	2		4#			8		12	7*			9	5	14			3					11	6				
38	30	CARDIFF	3-2	1-0	2264	Shepherd, Proudlock(2)	1	2		4			8			7			9	5	10			3					11	6				
39	2 Apr	Blackpool	0-6	0-3	5368		1	2		4			8			7			9*	5#	10	14		3					11	6				12
40	6	SCUNTHORPE	0-3	0-3	1909		1	2		4			8*		12	7			9#	5	14			3					10	11	6			
41	13	Aldershot	0-3	0-2	1813			4		5		12	9			7			6	8#	10			1		2*			11	3				
42	20	Chesterfield	1-4	1-2	2708	Shepherd(pen)		4		5	2*		10		9#	7			14	6		8			11	3	1							12
43	27	SCARBOROUGH	4-1	2-0	1762	Fyfe(2), Sendall, Miller		4		5			10			7			9		6	8	11*	3	1					12				2
44	1 May	Maidstone	0-0	0-0	1111			4		5			10			7			9		6	8	11	3	1								2
45	4	TORQUAY	3-1	1-1	2175	Fyfe, Miller, Sendall		4		5			10			7			9		6	8	11	3	1								2
46	11	Lincoln	2-6	1-2	2333	Proudlock, Shepherd	1	4*		5			10			7			9		6	8	11	3	1					12				2

F.A. CUP

No.	Date	Opposition	Res.	H.T.	Att.	Goalscorers	Priestley	Miller	Edwards	Graham	Jones	Fitzpatrick	Walsh	Shepherd	Walwyn	Gates	Proudlock	Goldsmith	Norris	Sendall	Methven	Jeffels	Edmondson	Fyfe	Owen
1R	17 Nov	Wigan	0-5	0-3	3947		1			4		5	6	7		9	10#		12		14		8*	2	11

(Edwards column: 3)

LEAGUE CUP

No.	Date	Opposition	Res.	H.T.	Att.	Goalscorers	Priestley	Miller	Edwards	Graham	Jones	Fitzpatrick	Walsh	Shepherd	Walwyn	Gates	Proudlock	Goldsmith	Norris	Sendall	Methven	Jeffels
1R1	28 Aug	SCUNTHORPE	1-0	1-0	2531	Fitzpatrick	1	2	3	4	5	6	7*	8	9	10#	11	12	14			
1R2	4 Sep	Scunthorpe	1-1	0-1	2130	Walwyn	1	2	3	4		6	7	8	9	10	11				5	
2R1	25	DERBY	1-1	1-0	7628	Proudlock	1	2	3			6	7	8	9*	10	11	12	14		5	4#
2R2	10 Oct	Derby	0-1	0-1	12253		1	2	3			6	7	8	9	10*	11#	14			5	4

(2R2: Jeffels/Edmondson column: 12)

Final League Table

		Pl.		Home				Away			F.	A.	Pts
			W	D	L	F	A	W	D	L	F	A	
1	Darlington	46	13	8	2	36	14	9	9	5	32	24	68 38	83
2	Stockport County	46	16	6	1	54	19	7	7	9	30	28	84 47	82
3	Hartlepool United	46	15	5	3	35	15	9	5	9	32	33	67 48	82
4	Peterborough Utd.	46	13	9	1	38	15	8	8	7	29	30	67 45	80
5	Blackpool	46	17	3	3	55	17	6	7	10	23	30	78 47	79
6	Burnley	46	17	5	1	46	16	6	5	12	24	35	70 51	79
7	Torquay United	46	14	7	2	37	13	4	11	8	27	34	64 47	72
8	Scunthorpe United	46	17	4	2	51	20	3	7	13	20	42	71 62	71
9	Scarborough	46	13	5	5	36	21	6	7	10	23	35	59 56	69
10	Northampton Town	46	14	5	4	34	21	4	8	11	23	37	57 58	67
11	Doncaster Rovers	46	12	5	6	36	22	5	9	9	20	24	56 46	65
12	Rochdale	46	10	6	7	26	23	5	8	10	21	31	50 53	62
13	Cardiff City	46	10	6	7	26	23	5	9	9	17	31	43 54	60
14	Lincoln City	46	10	7	6	32	27	4	10	9	18	34	50 61	59
15	Gillingham	46	9	9	5	35	27	3	9	11	22	33	57 60	54
16	Walsall	46	7	12	4	25	17	5	5	13	23	34	48 51	53
17	Hereford United	46	9	10	4	32	19	4	4	15	21	39	53 58	53
18	Chesterfield	46	8	12	3	33	26	5	2	16	14	36	47 62	53
19	Maidstone United	46	9	5	9	42	34	4	7	12	24	37	66 71	51
20	Carlisle United	46	12	3	8	30	30	1	6	16	17	59	47 89	48
21	York City	46	8	6	9	21	23	3	7	13	24	34	45 57	46
22	Halifax Town	46	9	6	8	34	29	3	4	16	25	50	59 79	46
23	Aldershot	46	8	7	8	38	43	2	4	17	23	58	61 101	41
24	Wrexham	46	8	7	8	33	34	2	3	18	15	40	48 74	40

SEASON 1991/92

DIVISION 4

No.	Date	Opposition	H.T.	Res.	Att.	Goalscorers	O'Hanlon	Armstrong	Barnsley	Miller	Jeffels	Graham	Thomas	Sendall	Walling	Fyfe	Proudlock	Thorpe	Wilkes	Edmondson	Potts	Deakin	Bennett	Nevin	Watson	Gallimore	Lowery	Holliday	Walsh	Gorman	Holmes	Prins
1	17 Aug	Doncaster	3-0	1-0	2639	Sendall, Fyfe, Proudlock	1	2	3	4	5	6	7*	8	9	10	11	12														
2	24	BLACKPOOL	1-2	1-2	4369	Walling	1		3	4	5	6	7		9	10*	8	11#	12	2	14											
3	31	Cardiff	0-1	0-0	4096		1	14	3	4	5	6	7		9*	10	8	12		2	11#											
4	3 Sep	ROTHERHAM	1-3	1-1	2346	Barnsley(pen)	1		3	4	5	6	7			10	8	9*	12	2	11											
5	14	LINCOLN	0-2	0-2	2149		1	12	3	4	5	6	8			9	10	7#	14	11*	2											
6	17	MANSFIELD	1-2	0-0	1803	Edmondson	1	12	2	4	5	6	7				8	11		10			3		9							
7	21	Northampton	2-2	1-1	2656	Watson(2)	1		2	4	5	6	7			9	11	12		10*			3		8							
8	28	WALSALL	3-3	1-0	2148	Fyfe(2), Barnsley(pen)	1		2	4	5	6	7*		12	9	11			10			3		8							
9	5 Oct	Burnley	0-2	0-1	6157		1		2	4	5	6	7*		12	9#	11			10					8	3	14					
10	12	SCUNTHORPE	0-0	0-0	1988		1	2		4	5	6	7		9	10	12								11*	3	8					
11	19	Wrexham	0-3	0-1	1266		1	2		4		6	7		9	10	12							3	11*	8	5					
12	26	CREWE	2-1	0-0	1905	Watson, Fyfe	1		2	4			7		9	10		12		6					11	3	8	5*				
13	2 Nov	GILLINGHAM	0-0	0-0	1672		1		2	4	5		7		9*	10		12		6					11	3	8					
14	5	Barnet	2-4	1-0	2983	Fyfe(pen), O.G.	1		2	4			7		9	10		12		6					11	3	8	5*				
15	9	Scarborough	2-2	0-2	1501	Thorpe, Graham	1		2	4#		14	7		9	10		12		6					11	3	8	5*				
16	23	HEREFORD	1-0	0-0	2032	Walling	1		2	4	5	6	7		9	10	8	11*							12	3						
17	30	MAIDSTONE	3-0	2-0	2146	Watson(2), Barnsley(pen)	1		2	4	5	6	7*		9	10	8							12	11	3						
18	21 Dec	Blackpool	0-1	0-0	3440		1		2	4	5	6			9	10	8	3							11			7				
19	26	DONCASTER	1-0	0-0	3174	Jeffels	1		2	4	5	6			9	10	8	3							11			7				
20	28	CARDIFF	2-2	0-0	3080	Watson, Jeffels	1		2	4	5	6*			9		8	3						12	11			7	10			
21	1 Jan	Rotherham	0-1	0-0	4856		1		2	4	5				9		8	3						6	11			7	10			
22	4	Chesterfield	0-0	0-0	2892		1		2	4	5	6			9		8	3							11			7	10			
23	11	ROCHDALE	0-0	0-0	2494		1		2	4	5	6			9	10		11							8			7	3			
24	18	York	0-2	0-0	1953		1	12	2	4	5	6			9	10	7	11*							8				3			
25	25	HALIFAX	1-1	0-1	2091	Watson(pen)	1	12	3	2	5		7		9	10	11			6*					8					4		
26	7 Feb	Crewe	1-2	1-1	3232	Watson	1	2	3	4			7		9	10*	12	11#		6				14	8		5					
27	12	Maidstone	1-5	0-3	944	Watson	1	2	3	4			7		9	10	12	11		6*				14	8							
28	22	Rochdale	1-3	1-2	1691	Watson	1		3		2		8		12	10*	7#	11		6				14	9		5			4		
29	29	CHESTERFIELD	1-2	0-2	2038	Edmondson	1	6*	2		5		8			10		11		7				12	9	3				4		
30	3 Mar	YORK	1-1	1-1	1681	Watson	1	6	2		5			12				11		7				9*	8	3				4		
31	7	Halifax	2-3	1-0	1015	Walling, Watson	1	6	2						9	10		11		7					8	3				4	5	
32	10	BARNET	1-3	0-2	1888	Holmes	1	6	2						9	10		11		7					8	3				4	5	
33	14	Gillingham	2-1	1-0	2179	Holmes, Watson	1	6	2	4			7			10		11		2					9	3				8	5	
34	21	SCARBOROUGH	2-2	0-0	1813	Walling, Holmes	1	6	12	4			7		9	10		11		14	2*					3				8	5#	
35	24	WREXHAM	0-1	0-0	1826		1	6	2*	4	5				10#		12	11							9	3		14		8		
36	28	Hereford	0-1	0-1	1810		1	6	2	4	5						12	11							9	3			7*	8		
37	1 Apr	Lincoln	0-1	0-0	2118		1	2	6		5		8		14	10*	12	11							9			4#	3		7	
38	11	Mansfield	1-2	0-0	3085	Walling	1	2*	6			14	8		4	10		11#							9		5		3		7	12
39	18	NORTHAMPTON	2-1	1-0	1935	Watson, Holmes	1	6		4			8			10					5	3		12	9	2					7	11
40	21	Walsall	0-0	0-0	2406		1	6					3*		8	10				4	12				9	5	2				7	11
41	25	BURNLEY	1-1	0-1	9051	Thomas	1	14	6				8			10				3*	4	12			9	5	2				7	12
42	2 May	Scunthorpe	0-4	0-2	3853		1	14	6				8		9					3*	4	11		12		5	2				7	10

F.A. CUP

No.	Date	Opposition	H.T.	Res.	Att.	Goalscorers	O'Hanlon	Armstrong	Barnsley	Miller	Jeffels	Graham	Thomas	Sendall	Walling	Fyfe	Proudlock	Thorpe	Wilkes	Edmondson	Potts	Deakin	Bennett	Nevin	Watson	Gallimore	Lowery	Holliday	Walsh	Gorman	Holmes	Prins
1R	16 Nov	CREWE	1-1	0-1	3106	Watson	1	14	2	4	5		7		12	10	9	3		6					11*	8#						
1Rr	26	Crewe	3-5	0-2	3733	Barnsley(2pens), Fyfe	1		3	4	5	2	7		9	10	8			6*				12	11							

LEAGUE CUP

No.	Date	Opposition	H.T.	Res.	Att.	Goalscorers	O'Hanlon	Armstrong	Barnsley	Miller	Jeffels	Graham	Thomas	Sendall	Walling	Fyfe	Proudlock	Thorpe	Wilkes	Edmondson	Potts	Deakin	Bennett	Nevin	Watson	Gallimore	Lowery	Holliday	Walsh	Gorman	Holmes	Prins
1R1	20 Aug	Rochdale	1-5	1-5	1650	Barnsley	1	2	3	4	5	6	7		9	10	8	11*	12													
1R2	27	ROCHDALE	1-1	0-0	1572	Barnsley	1		3	4	5	6	7		9	10	8	11*	12	2												

Final League Table

		Pl.	Home					Away					F.	A.	Pts
			W	D	L	F	A	W	D	L	F	A			
1	Burnley	42	14	4	3	42	16	11	4	6	37	27	79	43	83
2	Rotherham United	42	12	6	3	38	16	10	5	6	32	21	70	37	77
3	Mansfield Town	42	13	4	4	43	26	10	4	7	32	27	75	53	77
4	Blackpool	42	17	3	1	48	13	5	7	9	23	32	71	45	76
5	Scunthorpe United	42	14	5	2	39	18	7	4	10	25	41	64	59	72
6	Crewe Alexandra	42	12	6	3	33	20	8	4	9	33	31	66	51	70
7	Barnet	42	16	1	4	48	23	5	5	11	33	38	81	61	69
8	Rochdale	42	12	6	3	34	22	6	7	8	23	31	57	53	67
9	Cardiff City	42	13	3	5	42	26	4	12	5	24	27	66	53	66
10	Lincoln City	42	9	5	7	21	24	8	6	7	29	20	50	44	62
11	Gillingham	42	12	5	4	41	19	3	7	11	22	34	63	53	57
12	Scarborough	42	12	5	4	39	28	3	7	11	25	40	64	68	57
13	Chesterfield	42	6	7	8	26	28	8	4	9	23	33	49	61	53
14	Wrexham	42	11	4	6	31	26	3	5	13	21	47	52	73	51
15	Walsall	42	5	10	6	28	28	6	7	8	20	32	48	58	49
16	Northampton Town	42	5	9	7	25	23	6	4	11	21	34	46	57	46
17	Hereford United	42	9	4	8	31	24	3	4	14	13	33	44	57	44
18	Maidstone United	42	6	9	6	24	22	2	9	10	21	34	45	56	42
19	York City	42	6	9	6	26	23	2	7	12	16	35	42	58	40
20	Halifax Town	42	7	5	9	23	23	3	3	15	11	40	34	75	38
21	Doncaster Rovers	42	6	2	13	21	35	3	6	12	19	30	40	65	35
22	Carlisle United	42	5	9	7	24	27	2	4	15	17	40	41	67	34

- 1991/92 Season -

(Back): Graham, Deakin, Dalziel, Walling, Sendall, Thorpe, Edmondson,
(Middle): Fyfe, Miller, Priestley, Taylor, O'Hanlon, Jeffels, Holliday
(Front): Hampton, Walsh, Proudlock, McCaffery, Bennett, Armstrong, Wilkes

- 1992/93 Season -

(Back): Sendall, Gabbiadini, Davey, Barnsley, Thorpe, Potts
(Middle): Holden, Holliday, Hawke, Walsh, Oghani, O'Hanlon, Edmondson, Walsh
(Front): Holmes, Hampton(Physio), Knighton(Chairman), McCreery(Manager), Dalziel, Arnold

SEASON 1992/93

DIVISION 3 (formerly Division 4)

No.	Date	Opposition	Res.	H.T.	Att.	Goalscorers	O'Hanlan	Williams	Thorpe	Holmes	Knight	Barnsley	Gabbiadini	Davey	Oghani	Watson	Proudlock	Walling	Edmondson	Connelly	Sendall	Walsh	Holliday	Dalziel	Gaig	Potts	Hawke	McCreery	Arnold	Holden	Prins	Gallimore	Finley	Burgess	White	Hopper	Delap	Heron
1	15 Aug	WALSALL	3-4	1-1	4199	Oghani, Watson, O.G.	1	2	3	4	5	6	7*	8	9	10	11#	12	14																			
2	29	LINCOLN	2-0	0-0	4023	Oghani, Watson	1	2	3	4		6	7*	8	9	10		5	11	12																		
3	1 Sep	BURY	5-1	2-0	4660	Oghani(2),Gbbiadini,Wlliams,Watsn	1	2	3	4		6#	7*	8	9	10		5	11	12	14																	
4	5	Barnet	0-2	0-0	2733		1	2*	3	4		6	7	8	9	10		5	11	12																		
5	8	Cardiff	2-2	0-1	6859	Watson, Gabbiadini	1	2	3*	4		6	7	8	9#	10		5	11		14	12																
6	12	YORK	2-1	0-1	5355	Sendall	1	2		4		6	7*	8	9	10		5	11		12	3																
7	19	Chesterfield	0-1	0-0	3362		1	2	3	4		6	11*	7	9	10		5	8		12																	
8	26	SCUNTHORPE	0-*2	0-1	4772		1	2	3	4		6	7*	8	9	10			11		12		5#	14														
9	3 Oct	HALIFAX	1-1	1-0	3824	Watson		2*	3	4			7#	8	9	10		6			12	14	5		1	11												
10	10	Rochdale	2-2	2-1	2543	Watson, Barnsley	1	2*	3	4		5			9	10		6			14					11	7	8#	12									
11	17	WREXHAM	0-2	0-1	3520		1		3	4			8	9*	10		2									11#7		14	12	5								
12	24	Torquay	2-0	1-0	1960	Arnold, Babbidini	1	2		6			7	8		10							3				9	5	11	4								
13	31	SCARBOROUGH	2-2	0-1	3150	Arnold, Hawke	1	2		6		8	7		10*					12			3				9	5	11	4								
14	3 Nov	Colchester	1-2	1-1	3263	Barnsley(pen)	1	2		6		8	7		10*					12			3				9	5	11	4								
15	7	GILLINGHAM	1-0	1-0	3213	Watson	1	2	11					10	7			8			12	6	3				9	5*		4								
16	21	Doncaster	2-1	1-0	2159	Proudlock, O.G.	1	2	11				6		10	7		8			5		3				9			4								
17	28	NORTHAMPTON	2-0	1-0	3603	Hawke, Davey	1	2	11				6	12	10*	7		8			5		3				9		14	4#								
18	12 Dec	CREWE	1-3	1-1	3487	Oghani	1	2			8*	10#	6	9		7	12				5		3						11	4	14	14						
19	9	CARDIFF	1-2	1-2	3691	Arnold(pen)	1	2					6	12	10*	7		11			8		3				5	9			4							
20	12	Darlington	1-1	1-1	1596	Oghani	1		2				6	7		4	11				8		3				5	9										
21	16	Scunthorpe	0-0	0-0	2570		1		2	14			6	7	10*		4	11		12	8		3				5#	9										
22	19	York	2-2	1-1	3071	Oghani, Proudlock	1		2	5			6	7	10	12	4	11			8		3*				9											
23	23	CHESTERFIELD	3-1	1-1	3103	Watson, Oghani, Walsh	1		3	5			6	7	10	11	4	2			8						9											
24	26	Lincoln	1-2	0-0	2947	Oghani	1		3	5			6	7	10	11	4	2			8						9											
25	6 Feb	Walsall	1-2	0-1	2817	Oghani	1		3	10*			6	7		2	4	11			8						5	9		12								
26	13	BARNET	0-1	0-1	4020		1		3			4	12	6	7		11	5	2		8					10*		14	9#									
27	20	Bury	0-6	0-6	2723		1		3			2	12	10	7		9	6	11		8						5		4									
28	27	ROCHDALE	3-0	1-0	3021	Oghani(2), Arnold	1		3					8	7		10	4	6								5	9					2	11				
29	6 Mar	Halifax	2-0	1-0	1309	Oghani, Arnold(pen)	1		3				12	8	7		10	4									5*	9	6				2	11				
30	9	SHREWSBURY	1-0	0-0	4022	Davey	1		3			12		8	7		10	4									5	9	6*				2	11				
31	13	Gillingham	0-1	0-0	3307		1		3			6	12	8	7		10	4									5*	9					2	11				
32	20	COLCHESTER	0-2	0-0	3003		1		3				12	8	7		10	4	6								5*	9					2	11				
33	23	Northampton	0-2	0-1	2561		1			6			12	8	7*		14	4	2			11			3			5	9				2	10#				
34	27	DONCASTER	1-1	1-1	2939	Davey	1			12		11	8	7		10	4*	2								5	9	6		3								
35	3 Apr	Shrewsbury	3-2	1-1	3100	Oghani(2), Davey	1			4		11*	8	7		10		2				14				5#	9	6	12	3								
36	6	Crewe	0-4	0-0	3246		1			4		11#	8	7		10		2			5*			14			9	6	12	3								
37	10	DARLINGTON	2-2	2-1	3297	Davey, Gallimore	1			4		11	8	7		10*		2			5						9	6	12	3								
38	12	Hereford	0-1	0-0	2457		1			4			8	7				2			10			11			5*	9	6	12	3							
39	17	HEREFORD	0-0	0-0	2527		1			4			8	7		10		2			5						9	6	11	3								
40	24	Wrexham	1-3	1-2	5912	Holden	1	11*	3#	4			8	7		10		2									14	9	6	12								
41	1 May	TORQUAY	0-1	0-0	2689		1			4		11*	8	7		10		2								12	5	9	6									
42	8	Scarborough	2-2	1-0	2948	Arnold, Proudlock	1			4*			8	7		10		2									9	6		3						5	12	

F.A. CUP

| 1R | 14 Nov | Wigan Ath | 1-3 | 1-3 | 2963 | Arnold | 1 | 2 | 11 | | | | | | 10 | 7 | | 8 | | 9 | | | | 3 | | | 5* | 12 | 4 | | | | | | | | | 6 |

LEAGUE CUP

1R1	18 Aug	BURNLEY	4-1	2-0	4066	Gabb'ni(2),Barnsley(pen),Watson	1	2	3	4		6	7	8	9	10		5*	11																				
1R2	25	Burnley	1-1	0-1	5524	Oghani	1	2	3	4		6	7	8	9	10		5	11																				
2R1	21 Sep	NORWICH	2-2	1-0	10328	Edmondson, Barnsley(pen)	1	2	3	4		6	7	8	9	10		5	11	12																			
2R2	7 Oct	Norwich	0-2	0-0	8489		1	2	3	4		5		8	9	10			6		7							11	12										

Final League Table

		Pl.	Home						Away						F.	A.	Pts
			W	D	L	F	A	W	D	L	F	A					
1	Cardiff City	42	13	7	1	42	10	12	1	8	35	27			77	47	83
2	Wrexham	42	14	3	4	48	26	9	8	4	27	26			75	52	80
3	Barnet	42	16	4	1	45	19	7	6	8	21	29			66	48	79
4	York City	42	13	6	2	41	15	8	6	7	31	30			72	45	75
5	Walsall	42	11	6	4	42	31	11	1	9	34	30			76	61	73
6	Crewe Alexandra	42	13	3	5	47	23	8	4	9	28	33			75	56	70
7	Bury	42	10	7	4	36	19	8	2	11	27	36			63	55	63
8	Lincoln City	42	10	6	5	31	20	8	3	10	26	33			57	53	63
9	Shrewsbury Town	42	11	3	7	36	30	6	8	7	21	22			57	52	62
10	Colchester United	42	13	3	5	38	26	5	2	14	29	50			67	76	59
11	Rochdale	42	10	8	3	38	29	6	7	8	32	41			70	70	58
12	Chesterfield	42	11	3	7	32	28	4	8	9	27	35			59	63	56
13	Scarborough	42	7	7	7	32	30	8	2	11	34	41			66	71	54
14	Scunthorpe United	42	8	7	6	38	25	6	5	10	19	29			57	54	54
15	Darlington	42	8	5	6	10	23	31	7	8	6	25	22		48	53	50
16	Doncaster Rovers	42	6	5	10	22	28	5	9	7	20	29			42	57	47
17	Hereford United	42	7	9	5	31	27	3	6	12	16	33			47	60	45
18	Carlisle United	42	7	5	9	29	27	4	6	11	22	38			51	65	44
19	Torquay United	42	6	4	11	18	26	6	3	12	27	41			45	67	43
20	Northampton Town	42	6	5	10	19	28	5	3	13	29	46			48	74	41
21	Gillingham	42	9	4	8	32	28	0	9	12	16	36			48	64	40
22	Halifax Town	42	3	5	13	20	35	6	4	11	25	33			45	68	36

SEASON 1993/94

DIVISION 3

No.	Date	Opposition	Res.	H.T.	Att.	Goalscorers	Day	Elliott	Caig	Burgess	Joyce	Gallimore	McMahon	Walling	Valentine	Reddish	Curran	Robinson	Thomas	Davey	Conway	Reeves	Edmondson	Fairweather	Flounders	Graham	Holden	Delap	McCreery	Murray	Rouse	Prins	Pearson	O'Ghani	Barnes	Arnold
1	14 Aug	WYCOMBE	2-2	1-1	7752	Curran, Thomas	1			2	3					8	5		7	10			6	11		4									9	12
2	21	Doncaster	0-0	0-0	2575		1			2				4	5	8			7	10			6	11											9	12
3	28	ROCHDALE	0-1	0-1	5438		1			2#	14	3		4	5	8			7	10			6	11										9*		12
4	31	Torquay	1-1	0-1	3331	Gallimore	1			2	14	3		4	5	8			7	10			6	11									12			9*
5	4 Sep	Scarborough	3-0	2-0	2044	Davey(2), Fairweather	1			2	3			4	5	8			7	10			6*	11					12					9		
6	11	CHESTERFIELD	3-0	2-0	5335	Thomas(2), Walling	1			2	3			4	5	8			7	10			6*	11					12					9		
7	18	Scunthorpe	1-2	1-1	3361	Burgess	1			2	3			4	5	8			7	10			6#	11					14					9*		12
8	25	Chester	0-0	0-0	2911		1			2	3			4	5	8*			7	10			6	11					12					9		
9	2 Oct	GILLINGHAM	1-2	0-0	6446	Valentine	1			2	3			4#	5	8*			7	10		9	6	11						14	12					
10	9	Shrewsbury	0-1	0-1	3254		1			2	3			4	5	8			7	10		9	6								12	11*				
11	16	MANSFIELD	1-1	1-0	4480	Davey	1			2	3			4	5				7	10		9	6													
12	23	Northampton	1-1	0-0	2877	Edmondson	1			2	3			4	5				7	10		9	6	12		8*										11
13	30	WALSALL	2-1	1-1	4216	Reeves, Davey	1			2	3			4	5#				7	10	12	9	6	11*	8											12
14	2 Nov	LINCOLN	3-3	2-1	5098	Walling, Edmondson, Arnold(pen)	1			2	3			4	5	11			7	10		9	6		8*											12
15	6	Wigan	2-0	0-0	2411	Flounders, Reeves	1			2	5	3		4		11			7	10		9	6		8											
16	20	PRESTON N.E.	0-1	0-0	10279		1			2	5	3		4		11			7	10		9	6*		8											12
17	27	Colchester	1-2	1-1	2316	Thomas	1			2	5	3		4		11			7	10		9	6		8*						12					
18	11 Dec	DONCASTER	4-2	1-2	4245	Walling, Thomas, Davey, Edmondson	1			2	5	3		4		11			7	10		9	6								12					8*
19	18	Wycombe	0-2	0-2	5044		1			2	5	3		4					7	10		9	6	8*		11								12		
20	27	Darlington	3-1	3-1	4800	Reeves(2), Graham	1			2	5		3	4						10		9		8*		11			12	7						
21	28	CREWE	1-2	1-1	7073	Reeves	1			2	5	3		4		11*	12		7#	10		9	6							14	8					
22	1 Jan	Hereford	0-0	0-0	2204		1			2	5	3		4			6			10	7	9				11							12	8*		
23	3	TORQUAY	1-1	1-1	4872	Davey		1		2	5	3		4		11*				10	8	9	6						14					12	7#		
24	15	Mansfield	1-0	0-0	2378	Reeves		1		2	5	3		4			6			10	7*	9				11								12		
25	25	BURY	1-2	1-2	4430	Reeves		1		2	5	3#		4		11	12		7	10	8*	9	6						14				6			
26	29	Walsall	1-0	0-0	4833	Reeves		1		2	5	3		4			6		7	10	8	9				11										
27	5 Feb	NORTHAMPTON	0-1		4535			1		2	5			4	12		6		7	10	8*	9				11	3									
28	12	Bury	1-2	1-0	2807	Reddish		1		2	5	3		4		11	6		7	10		9		8*									12			
29	19	Rochdale	1-0	1-0	2927	Davey		1		2	5	3		4		11	6		7*	10		9				12					8					
30	26	SCARBOROUGH	2-0	0-0	4270	Walling, Davey		1		2	5	7		4			6	3		10		9		12			11#	14				8*				
31	5 Mar	Chesterfield	0-3	0-0	2475			1		2	5	3		4		11*	6		7	10		9		12								8				
32	12	SCUNTHORPE	3-1	0-0	4076	Conway(2), Valentine		1		2	3			4	5	11	6		7	10	12	9							8*							
33	19	CHESTER	1-0	1-0	4193	Reeves		1		2	3			4	5	11	6		7	10	8	9														
34	26	Gillingham	0-2	0-1	2586			1		2	3			4	5	11*	6		7	10	8	9							12							
35	2 Apr	DARLINGTON	2-0	0-0	4088	Walling, Thomas		1		2	5	3		4		11	6		7	10	8*	9				12										
36	4	Crewe	3-2	2-1	3679	Robinson, Thomas(2)		1		2	5	3		4	12	11	6		7*	10	8	9														
37	9	HEREFORD	1-2	1-0	4065	Conway		1		2	5	3		4		11#	6		7	10	8*	9	12			14										
38	16	Lincoln	0-0	0-0	2738			1		2	5	3		4		11	6		7*	10	8	9							12							
39	23	WIGAN	3-0	3-0	3796	Thomas, Reeves, Arnold		1		2	5	3		4			6		7	10	8*	9				11										11
40	30	Preston N.E.	3-0	1-0	11383	Thomas, Arnold(2)		1		2	5	3		4	12		6		7*	10	8#	9				14										11
41	3 May	SHREWSBURY	2-1	2-0	8007	Davey, Arnold		1	12	2	3			4	5		6		7*	10	8															11
42	7	COLCHESTER	0-2	0-1	9305			1	12	2	3			4	5		6		7*	10	8															11
43	15	WYCOMBE*	0-2	0-2	10684			1	12	2	3			4	5		6		7	10	8*															11
44	18	Wycombe*	1-2	0-1	6262	Davey(pen)		1	12	2	3			4	5		6		7	10	8*	9														11

* Play-off games

F.A. CUP

No.	Date	Opposition	Res.	H.T.	Att.	Goalscorers	Day	Elliott	Caig	Burgess	Joyce	Gallimore	McMahon	Walling	Valentine	Reddish	Curran	Robinson	Thomas	Davey	Conway	Reeves	Edmondson	Fairweather	Flounders	Graham	Holden	Delap	McCreery	Murray	Rouse	Prins	Pearson	O'Ghani	Barnes	Arnold
1R	13 Nov	Knowsley Utd.*	4-1	3-1	4800	Arnold(2), Davey, Reeves	1			2	5	3		4		11			7	10		9	6*	12												8
2R	4 Dec	STALYBRIDGE	3-1	2-0	5546	Arnold, Gallimore, Edmondson		1		2	5	3		4		11			7	10		9	6*											12		8
3R	8 Jan	Sunderland	1-1	0-1	23587	Edmondson		1		2	5	3		4		12			7	10	8*	9	6							11*				14		
3Rr	18	SUNDERLAND	0-1	0-0	12771			1		2	5			4		11			7	10		9	6							8				3		12

* played at Everton

LEAGUE CUP

No.	Date	Opposition	Res.	H.T.	Att.	Goalscorers	Day	Elliott	Caig	Burgess	Joyce	Gallimore	McMahon	Walling	Valentine	Reddish	Curran	Robinson	Thomas	Davey	Conway	Reeves	Edmondson	Fairweather	Flounders	Graham	Holden	Delap	McCreery	Murray	Rouse	Prins	Pearson	O'Ghani	Barnes	Arnold
1R1	17 Aug	Chesterfield	1-3	1-1	2841	Davey	1			2	3				5	8			7	10			6*	11		4									9	12
1R2	24	CHESTERFIELD	1-1	1-0	4410	Thomas	1			2	14	3		4	5	8*			7	10			6	11#											9	12

Final League Table

		Pl.	Home					Away					F.	A.	Pts
			W	D	L	F	A	W	D	L	F	A			
1	Shrewsbury Town	42	10	8	3	28	17	12	5	4	35	22	63	39	79
2	Chester City	42	13	5	3	35	18	8	6	7	34	28	69	46	74
3	Crewe Alexandra	42	12	4	5	45	30	9	6	6	35	31	80	61	73
4	Wycombe Wanderers	42	11	6	4	34	21	8	7	6	33	32	67	53	70
5	Preston North End	42	13	5	3	46	23	5	8	8	33	37	79	60	67
6	Torquay United	42	8	10	3	30	24	9	6	6	34	32	64	56	67
7	Carlisle United	42	10	4	7	35	23	8	6	7	22	19	57	42	64
8	Chesterfield	42	8	8	5	32	22	8	6	7	23	26	55	48	62
9	Rochdale	42	10	5	6	38	22	6	7	8	25	29	63	51	60
10	Walsall	42	7	5	9	28	26	10	4	7	20	27	48	53	60
11	Scunthorpe United	42	9	7	5	40	26	6	7	8	24	30	64	56	59
12	Mansfield Town	42	9	3	9	28	30	6	7	8	25	32	53	62	55
13	Bury	42	9	6	6	33	22	5	5	11	22	34	55	56	53
14	Scarborough	42	8	4	9	29	28	7	4	10	26	33	55	61	53
15	Doncaster Rovers	42	8	6	7	24	26	6	4	11	20	31	44	57	52
16	Gillingham	42	8	5	8	27	23	4	7	10	17	28	44	51	51
17	Colchester United	42	8	4	9	31	33	5	6	10	25	38	56	71	49
18	Lincoln City	42	7	4	10	26	29	5	7	9	26	34	52	63	47
19	Wigan Athletic	42	6	7	8	33	33	5	5	11	18	37	51	70	45
20	Hereford United	42	6	4	11	34	33	6	2	13	26	46	60	79	42
21	Darlington	42	7	5	9	24	28	3	6	12	18	36	42	64	41
22	Northampton Town	42	6	7	8	25	23	3	4	14	19	43	44	66	38

- 1993/94 Season -

(Back): Prinz, Watson, Graham, Curvan, Valantine, Pearson, Edmondson, Helden, Burgess
(Middle): Hopper, Joyce, Robinson, Walling, Caig, Day, Elliott, Oghani, Gallimore, Thorpe, Conway
(Front): Thomas, Davey, Hampton(Physio), MCreery(Coach), Knighton(Chair), Wadsworth(Man),
Wilkes, Reddish, Arnold   (Bottom): Apprentices

- 1994/95 Season -

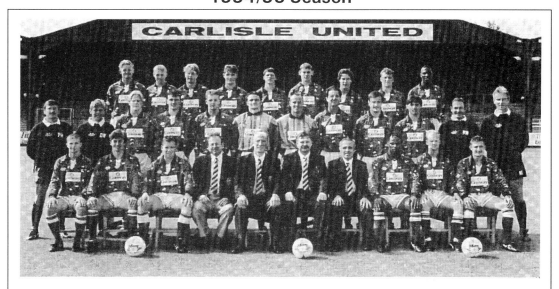

(Back): Reeves, Hopper, Thorpe, Gallimore, Murray, Delap, Prokas, Burgess, Walling
(Middle): Hampton(Physio), Wilkes(Yth coach), Edmondson, Robinson, Conway, Caig, Elliott, Pearson,
Mountfield, Currie, Wadsworth(Man), Day(Coach)   (Front): Dalton, Joyce(Plyr coach), Davey,
(4 Directors), Thomas, Arnold, Reddish

SEASON 1994/95
DIVISION 3

No.	Date	Opposition	Res.	H.T.	Att.	Goalscorers	Caig	Joyce	Gallimore	Walling	Mountfield	Edmondson	Thomas	Currie	Reeves	Davey	Reddish	Thorpe	Pearson	Prokas	Peters	Robinson	Arnold	Elliott	Delap	Hayward	Peacock	Aspinall	Hopper	Murray	Valentine	Conway	Lowe
1	13 Aug	WIGAN	2-1	1-0	6231	Walling, Reeves	1	2	3	4	5	6	7	8#	9	10	11	12	14														
2	20	Torquay	1-1	1-0	3506	Reeves	1	2	3	4	5	6	7	8	9	10*		12	11														
3	27	SCARBOROUGH	2-0	0-0	5720	Reeves, Mountfield	1	2	3	4	5	6*	7#	8	9	10		12	11							14							
4	30	Walsall	2-1	1-1	3610	Reeves(2)	1	2	3	4		6	7	8*	9	10		12	11#	14											5		
5	3 Sep	Scunthorpe	3-2	0-1	3217	Thorpe(2), Edmondson(pen)	1	2	3	4		6*	7	8#	9	10		12	11	14											5		
6	10	EXETER	1-0	0-0	6213	Thomas	1	2	3	4		12	7	8#	9	10		6*	11					14							5		
7	13	MANSFIELD	2-1	1-1	6136	Thomas, Currie	1	2	3	4		6	7	8*	9	10		12	11												5		
8	17	Wigan	2-0	1-0	3003	Reeves, Edmondson	1	2	3	4		6	7	8*	9	10		12	11												5		
9	24	Northampton	1-2	0-1	3508	Reeves	1	2	3	4	6	12	7	8	9	10			14												5#		11
10	1 Oct	DARLINGTON	2-1	1-0	6100	Gallimore, Walling	1	2	3	4		6*	7#	8	9	10		12	11					14							5		
11	8	Lincoln	1-1	1-1	3097	Reeves	1	2	3	4	12	6	7*	8#	9	10		14	11												5		
12	15	COLCHESTER	0-0	0-0	5817		1	2	3	4		6*	7		9	10			11					8#		14					5		12
13	22	BARNET	4-0	2-0	6155	Reeves, Davey, Conway, Thomas	1	2		4	5		7	8*	9	10		12	11											3		6	
14	29	Fulham	3-1	1-0	5563	Mountfield, Reeves, Conway	1		3	4	5	2*	7	8	9	10			11													6	
15	5 Nov	ROCHDALE	4-1	2-1	5984	Edmondson, Davey(2), Reeves	1		3	4	5	2	7	8	9*	10			11			12									14	6#	
16	19	Hereford	1-0	1-0	2531	Conway	1	12	3	4	5	2	7	8*	9	10			11													6	
17	26	DONCASTER	1-1	1-1	7781	Walling	1		3	4	5	2	7	8	9	10			11													6	
18	4 Dec	DARLINGTON	2-0	1-0	8365	Conway, Currie	1		3	4	5	2	7*	8#	9	10		12	11					14								6	
19	10	TORQUAY	1-0	0-0	5141	Thomas	1		3	4	5	2	7	8	9				11		10											6	
20	17	Scarborough	2-1	1-1	1910	Currie, Gallimore(pen)	1*		3	4	5	2	7#	8	9			12	11		10				14							6	
21	26	Hartlepool	5-1	3-1	3854	Gllimore(p),Mntfield,Cnway,Rves(2)	1	12	3	4	5	2		8#	9			7*	11		10				14							6	
22	27	BURY	3-0	2-0	12242	Reeves, Currie, Conway	1		3	4	5	2		8	9	10		7*	11													6	
23	31	Gillingham	1-0	0-0	3682	Walling	1		3	4	5	2		8	9	10		7*	11		12				1							6	
24	14 Jan	PRESTON N.E.	0-0	0-0	10684		1		3	4		2	7*	8	9	10	12		11				5									6	
25	21	Rochdale	1-1	0-1	3289	Walling	1		3	4	5	2	7*	8	9	10	12		11													6	
26	24	Barnet	2-0	1-0	2413	Currie, Davey	1	2*	3	4	5		7	8	9	10			11		12											6	
27	28	FULHAM	1-1	1-0	6891	Thomas	1		3	4	5	2	7	8	9	10		12	11*													6	
28	4 Feb	Doncaster	0-0	0-0	3587		1		3	4	5*	2	7	8	9	10			11		12											6	
29	11	HEREFORD	1-0	0-0	5676	Gallimore(pen)	1		3	4	5	2	7*	8	9	10			11			12										6	
30	18	Preston N.E.	0-1	0-0	11867		1		3	4	5	2	7	8	9	10			14		12									11#		6*	
31	25	Darlington	2-0	1-0	3992	Thomas, Reeves	1		3	4	5	2	7	8	9				11		6*	12											10
32	4 Mar	NORTHAMPTON	2-1	1-1	6755	Walling(2)	1		3	4	5	2*	7	8	9				11		6*	14											10
33	11	Exeter	1-1	1-1	2673	Reeves	1		3	4	5	2	7*	8	9			12	11														10
34	18	WALSALL	2-1	1-0	7769	Reeves(2)	1		3	4	5	2	7	8	9			12	11							7*	6						10
35	25	SCUNTHORPE	2-1	1-0	6704	Aspinall, Hayward	1		3		5	2		8*	9			12	11				4			7	14	6					10#
36	1 Apr	Mansfield	2-1	1-0	5197	Prokas, Thorpe	1	2	3	4	5		7	8	9			12	11#							10	14	6*					
37	4	CHESTERFIELD	1-1	0-1	8478	Robinson	1	11#	3	4	5	2	7					8*								10	6			14	12		
38	8	GILLINGHAM	2-0	2-0	6786	Thorpe, Hayward	1	14		4	5	2	7*		9			8#	11			3				10	6			12			
39	15	Bury	0-2	0-1	5507		1	2	3	4	5			8	9			7*			12				10		6						
40	17	HARTLEPOOL	0-1	0-1	10242		1	2	3	4	5		7			9			11#	14						10		6*		12			
41	29	Colchester	1-0	0-0	3333	Reeves	1	14	3	4		2		7*	8#	9			12		11	5				10						6	
42	2 May	Chesterfield	2-1	1-1	7283	Reeves(2)	1		3	4		2			9				11#		5		1	7		10	12	6*		8	14		
43	6	LINCOLN	1-3	0-2	12746	Conway	1		3	4		2	7	8	9				11*		5					10		12				6	

F.A. CUP

Rd	Date	Opposition	Res.	H.T.	Att.	Goalscorers	Caig	Joyce	Gallimore	Walling	Mountfield	Edmondson	Thomas	Currie	Reeves	Davey	Reddish	Thorpe	Pearson	Prokas	Peters	Robinson	Conway	Lowe
2R	18 Nov	Guiseley	4-1	2-0	6548	Reeves(2), Conway, Mountfield	1	12	3	4	5	2*		8	9	10		14	11				6#	
3R	7 Jan	Sunderland	1-1	0-1	15523	Davey	1		3	4	5	2	7	8	9	10			11				6	
3Rr	17	SUNDERLAND	1-3	0-2	12201	Walling	1		3	4	5	2	7		9	10	8				12	11	6*	

LEAGUE CUP

Rd	Date	Opposition	Res.	H.T.	Att.	Goalscorers	Caig	Joyce	Gallimore	Walling	Mountfield	Edmondson	Thomas	Currie	Reeves	Davey	Reddish	Thorpe	Pearson	Prokas	Delap	Valentine
1R1	16 Aug	Rotherham	0-1	0-1	2055		1	2	3	4	5	6	7	8*	9	10	11	12				
1R2	23	ROTHERHAM	3-1	2-0	5004	Reeves(2), Walling	1	2	3	4	5	6*	7	8	9	10	11	12				
2R1	20 Sep	Q.PARK RANGERS	0-1	0-1	9570		1	2	3	4	12	6	7	8	9	10		14	11#			5*
2R2		Q.Park Rangers	0-2	0-1	6561		1	2#	3	4	8	6	7*	12	9	10			11		14	5

Final League Table

		Pl.	Home					Away					F.	A.	Pts
			W	D	L	F	A	W	D	L	F	A			
1	Carlisle United	42	14	5	2	34	14	13	5	5	33	17	67	31	91
2	Walsall	42	15	3	3	42	18	9	8	4	33	22	75	40	83
3	Chesterfield	42	11	7	3	26	10	12	5	4	36	27	62	37	81
4	Bury	42	13	7	1	39	13	10	4	7	34	23	73	36	80
5	Preston North End	42	13	3	5	37	17	6	7	8	21	24	58	41	67
6	Mansfield Town	42	10	5	6	45	27	8	6	7	39	32	84	59	65
7	Scunthorpe United	42	12	2	7	40	30	6	6	9	28	33	68	63	62
8	Fulham	42	11	5	5	39	22	5	9	7	21	32	60	54	62
9	Doncaster Rovers	42	9	5	7	28	20	8	5	8	30	23	58	43	61
10	Colchester United	42	8	5	8	29	30	8	5	8	27	34	56	64	58
11	Barnet	42	8	7	6	37	27	7	4	10	19	36	56	63	56
12	Lincoln City	42	10	7	4	34	22	5	4	12	20	33	54	55	56
13	Torquay United	42	10	8	3	35	25	4	5	12	19	32	54	57	55
14	Wigan Athletic	42	7	6	8	28	30	7	4	10	25	30	53	60	52
15	Rochdale	42	8	6	7	25	23	4	8	9	19	44	44	67	50
16	Hereford United	42	9	6	6	22	19	3	7	11	23	43	45	62	49
17	Northampton Town	42	8	5	8	25	29	2	9	10	20	38	45	67	44
18	Hartlepool United	42	9	5	7	33	32	2	5	14	10	37	43	69	43
19	Gillingham	42	8	7	6	31	25	2	4	15	15	39	46	64	41
20	Darlington	42	7	5	9	25	24	4	3	14	18	33	43	57	41
21	Scarborough	42	4	7	10	26	31	4	3	14	23	39	49	70	34
22	Exeter City	42	5	5	11	25	36	3	5	13	11	34	36	70	34

256